THE STORY OF HOUSING

THE STORY OF HOUSING

GERTRUDE SIPPERLY FISH
EDITOR

Sponsored by the
Federal National Mortgage Association

MACMILLAN PUBLISHING CO., INC.
New York

COLLIER MACMILLAN PUBLISHERS
London

Dedicated to the
Memory of
Glenn H. Beyer

COPYRIGHT © 1979, FEDERAL NATIONAL MORTGAGE
ASSOCIATION

PRINTED IN THE UNITED STATES OF AMERICA

MACMILLAN PUBLISHING CO., INC.
866 Third Avenue, New York, New York 10022

COLLIER MACMILLAN CANADA, LTD.

Library of Congress Cataloging in Publication Data

Main entry under title:

The story of housing.

"A Fannie Mae book."
Includes bibliographies and index.
1. Housing—United States—History—Addresses,
essays, lectures. 2. Housing policy—United States—
History—Addresses, essays, lectures. I. Fish,
Gertrude S.
HD7293.S749   301.5′4′0973   78–17766
ISBN 0–02–337920–0

Printing: 1 2 3 4 5 6 7 8   Year: 9 0 1 2 3 4

FOREWORD

THE primary purpose of *The Story of Housing* is to serve as a textbook for university students preparing for careers in housing as well as for students in other disciplines that require information on the historical, social, political, and economic nature of housing. The book presents an intricate portrayal of housing's changing nature, suggesting that solutions to complex housing problems involve constructive input from many sectors.

Credit for the initiation of the book goes to Curtis W. Tuck, formerly Director of Public Affairs at the Federal National Mortgage Association. Concept development, writer selection, and editing were the work of Gertrude S. Fish, Ph.D., of the University of Maryland. The American Association of Housing Educators lent its encouragement to the development of the book because there was a dearth of literature about the subject.

In reading the several chapters of the book, it becomes obvious that the writers see housing and its evolution in this country through different filters. Their varying interpretations of events reflect the influences of different academic disciplines, experiences, and political leanings. Thus, one of the strengths of this book is that it encompasses many points of view.

The Federal National Mortgage Association wishes to thank Dr. Fish, all of the chapter writers, and the Macmillan Publishing Co., Inc., for their efforts and accomplishments in producing this needed addition to the literature in the field of housing. We wish to acknowledge, too, the dedicated guidance contributed to this project by Gordon E. Nelson, our former Vice President for Corporate Relations.

OAKLEY HUNTER
Chairman of the Board and President
Federal National Mortgage Association

CONTENTS

Contents

gambrel, roof. The doorway in the center of the long side was flanked by casement windows on either side. This two-room cottage style became popular with later builders, particularly as modified by builders of homes along Cape Cod. There, anchored by the massive central chimney,

Generally facing south to catch the winter sun, and nestled against a hill for protection against the hostile elements, the structures rested on wooden sills without foundations in order to ride the shifting sands the same way that schooners rode the waves. If a site happened to blow away the sturdy house could be trundled across the dunes or even floated to a new location. A recognizable type by the late 1700s, the Cape Cod cottage persisted with minor variations through the first half of the 1800s.[8]

Both styles of houses were added to extensively. The attic in a one-room house could be enlarged into the overhanging second story or another room could be added on the other side of the chimney and another story built above the first. Houses also were frequently enlarged by building a one-story lean-to on the rear. In later houses, the lean-to was made part of the original structure and the roof was built down over it without a break. These houses were called "saltboxes" because their shape resembled the shape of a medieval salt box.

Early houses were topped by thatch roofs. Glass had to be imported and was expensive; oiled paper was used to cover the window openings. Prospective colonists were advised to bring with them thin paper and linseed oil to make windows for their homes.[9] Chimneys were made of wood, lined with clay for fireproofing; although replaced by chimneys of brick or stone in later construction, stick-and-clay chimneys were used on at least some houses in most communities in the 18th century.

Thatch roofs and wattle and daub were not suited to the New England climate. Well before the end of the 17th century, builders began using wooden shingles (or, less frequently, slate or tile) for roof coverings.[10] Exterior walls were covered by weatherboards, overlapping clapboards, or shingles, which also helped to insulate the houses against the cold. Where chimneys were made of brick or stone, a brick topping laid in a decorative pattern might be added.[11] About 1660, a better house might be a clapboarded structure two stories high, with glass panes in the windows and a shingled roof.[12]

Many Puritan colonists in New England came from Eastern English counties with a tradition of building in wood. The House of Seven

---

8 Davidson, *op. cit.*, p. 166.
9 Willison, *op. cit.*, p. 109.
10 Condit, *op. cit.*, p. 12.
11 Pickering, *op. cit.*, p. 43.
12 Willison, *op. cit.*, p. 237.

FIGURE 1–1. The House of Seven Gables in Salem, Mass. [Courtesy of the Historic American Buildings Survey. Photographer, Richard Cheek.]

Gables (c. 1668), Salem, Massachusetts, is more asymmetrical than others built in the same tradition, but it does have the same steep roof-line, massive central chimneys, with glass panes in the windows and a shingled roof (see Figure 1.1).

In the typical New England house, the outside door opened into a small entry hall, from which a steep, narrow staircase led to the second floor or attic. The "hall" with the kitchen was on one side of the entry and the parlor on the other. If a lean-to had been added, it housed the kitchen, storage spaces, and usually a small bedroom. The parlor was reserved for entertaining, though it might be used as the master bedroom as well. Rooms were small and ceilings low, to conserve heat. Smaller houses, of course, had the small entry with its steep staircase and only the "hall" with the kitchen at the rear on one side. Inside walls were usually plastered or, sometimes, paneled.[13] Floors were wide hand-hewn pine boards, smoothed and sanded, and usually bare. The wall paneling eventually was painted, in warm colors, and the color scheme carried out in the chintz curtain hangings and small hooked rugs.

The fireplace furnished heat for the house as well as for cooking. As

13 Pickering, *op. cit.*, pp. 50, 52.

housing improved, openings were made in the central chimney stack for other downstairs rooms. A few houses had stone fireplaces, but in most of the better houses brick was the typical material used. The kettle hung on a hob or on a swinging iron crane fastened to the side of the firebox.[14] The built-in brick oven for baking sometimes was at the rear of the fireplace—a constant threat to the safety of the housewife, since a fire was burning in the fireplace at all times.[15]

Candles, the fireplace, lamps (typically wicks in dishes of oil), and pine knots burning on the fireplace furnished lighting. This last source of light has been enthusiastically described by a contemporary user:

Our pine trees that are the most plentiful of all wood . . . allow us plenty of candles which are very useful in a house, and they are such candles as the Indians commonly use, having no other; and they are nothing else but the wood of the pine tree cloven into two little slices something thin, which are so full of the moisture of turpentine and pitch that they burn as clear as a torch. I have sent you some of them.[16]

Nearly all furniture, like all other goods and supplies, was made at home, even after the colonies moved out of the subsistence stage. Furniture was simple and might be decorated with hand carving—beds, a few chairs and stools, a table, one or more benches, a settle, a few wooden chests, one or more heavy cradles on rockers, and the spinning wheel. The bed might be attached to the wall, with ropes or slats to support the straw sticks. Or it might be a four-poster, sometimes with curtains for privacy and to keep out drafts.[17] As local crafts developed in a community, prosperous families might have a few better pieces of furniture, designed and made locally: serrated cabinets, chests, and cupboards.[18]

With all the work that had to be carried on in these small houses, as well as an increasing family size, furniture that could be put out of the way when not in use and that served more than one purpose was welcome. The settle had space for storage underneath. Chests were used as chairs or tables as well as storage boxes; the trestle table could be taken apart after the meal and set over by the wall. Some chairs were made with arms and a hinged back which could be tilted down to rest on the arms and be used as a table.

[14] Willison, *op. cit.*, p. 237.

[15] Davidson, *op. cit.*, p. 31.

[16] Francis Higginson, "On the Riches of New England." In: Alexander Young (ed.), *Chronicles of the First Planters of the Colony of Massachusetts Bay.* (Boston), 1846, pp. 242–259; and *The Annals of America*, Vol. 1. (Chicago: Encyclopedia Britannica, 1968, p. 99.

[17] Pickering, *op. cit.*, p. 57.

[18] Willison, *op. cit.*, p. 237.

Towns in New England

In New England, the township was the unit of settlement and the importance of the town as a component of American government comes from New England. In each one, the community retained a portion for use as a common pasture, meadow, and woodland, and the remainder was divided into farm lots and house lots for the inhabitants. All individual holdings were first surveyed roughly, numbered, then distributed by lot.[19] The group leaders usually retained control over the distribution of land; poor land was divided as well as good land. Allotments were not made all at one time but in a series of distributions over a period of time as fields were brought under cultivation. Each of the original settlers received a strip of land at each division. Land frequently was given for special purposes—for example, to set up a sawmill—and later settlers received grants of land until all the land was apportioned.[20]

The township included the village, in which the house lots were situated, the farm fields, and the common land. Although linear villages, with house lots along one or both sides of a main street and the farm fields in back, were one kind of village plan, the best known for the New England village is the compact community.[21] In this type, several straight streets lead out in a gridiron pattern from a central open space. The central space, which might be square, oval, or triangular in shape or a wide strip down one side of the street, provided a focus for community life. The meeting house, parsonage, a few shops, and the residences of town officials usually fronted on the central green. More streets were added as the town grew and trees were planted along them.[22]

Houses in the new towns were built fairly close together, but considerable care was used to have a uniform line along the street. Frequently, setbacks were regulated. In Cambridge, in 1631 for instance, the town decreed that "houses shall range even and stand just six feet in their own ground from the street." Even without specific regulations, Reps states, "builders seemed to observe good taste in locating buildings with respect to the street line and adjacent structures."[23]

19 S. E. Morison and H. S. Commager, *The Growth of the American Republic*, Vol. 1, 3rd ed. (New York: Oxford University Press), 1942, p. 56.

20 Wright, *op. cit.*, p. 72.

21 John W. Reps, *Town Planning in Frontier America*. (Princeton, N.J.: Princeton University Press), 1969, p. 157.

22 Christopher Tunnard and H. H. Reed, *American Skyline: The Growth and Form of Our Cities and Towns*. (New York: New American Library of World Literature), 1956, p. 40.

23 Reps, *Town Planning . . . , op. cit.*, pp. 155, 157. In some New England towns, less attention was paid to uniform setbacks as the towns increased in size; street lines became irregular and open space was used for buildings (p. 181).

As new settlers came, they built the same kind of rude booths and huts the early settlers had. Apparently, after a reasonable length of time—considering the problems of housing production—they were expected to replace them with appropriate houses. For example, the Plymouth Colony Records of June 1656 report that one individual who "hath lived long in the woods, in an uncivil way" was to be told to shift "to some neighborhood" by October of that year "or that then his house be pulled down."[24]

The township was a strong unifying force in New England and remained the important unit in colonization. New townships were formed as population expanded, up the river valleys and along the coast, by newcomers, or by groups of settlers who broke away from an established town for religious or economic reasons. Settlers who came to New England from various regions and countries were absorbed into the cultural structure of a township.

Within the general pattern of townships, however, farms situated away from the central village became a regular feature of the New England landscape well before the end of the 17th century—over the protests of the town proprietors. After several divisions of land, some settlers might receive one or more strips in the farming fields which were some distance away from the village. These fields could be cultivated as a separate farm or sold to a recent arrival for a farm.

Boston was established as a town in 1630, with an open market at the center and a main street leading down to the water. The proprietors had a plan for the site, but the narrow winding streets that evolved gave visitors the impression of a town "not built after any regular plan, but . . . enlarged from time to time as the inhabitants increased."[25] As the major seaport for the New England region, Boston grew rapidly. A description in 1663 reports:

The Town is rich and very populous, much frequented by strangers, here in the dwelling of their Governour. On the North-west and North-east two constant Fairs are kept for daily Traffick thereunto. On the South there is a small, but pleasant Common where the Gallants a little before Sun-set walk with their *Marmalet*-Madams, as we do in *Morefields*, etc. till the nine a clock Bell rings them home to their respective habitations, when presently the Constables walk their rounds to see good orders kept, and to take up loose people. Two miles from the town . . . the Inhabitants have Farms, to which belong rich arable grounds and meadows where they keep their Cattle

[24] William Bradford, *Of Plymouth Plantation, 1630–1647*, new ed. (New York: Knopf), 1952, p. 188n.

[25] Joseph Bennett, "The History of New England," Proceedings of the Massachusetts Historical Society, V (January 1861), pp. 108–17, 123–126. In: Wilson Smith (ed.), *Cities of Our Past and Present*. (New York: Wiley), 1964, p. 7.

in the Summer, and bring them to *Boston* in the Winter; the Harbour before the Town is filled with Ships and other Vessels for most part of the year.[26]

Middle Atlantic Colonies

The colonies in the Middle Atlantic region had large enough groups of people from different European nations so that no typical housing style or settlement pattern developed for the entire region as in New England. Rather, each separate colony contributed a distinctive style—sometimes more than one.

New Amsterdam

The plan of settlement for New Amsterdam (1625) was similar to the New England plan, with each settler allotted a house lot in a town and farmlands beyond. Although the Dutch proprietors had a definite plan for the layout of the future New York City, it was not suited to the site and was too complex for the settlers to carry out. Reps states:

It was soon abandoned, and the town developed with little in the way of an overall plan for its growth. New streets were laid out from time to time as they were needed, usually following the lanes that had become established naturally as men and animals followed the most convenient paths between houses, farms, and the fort. This method of growth resulted in streets of irregular alignment and width. As the population increased and land near the fort became more valuable, encroachments on the streets added to the lack of order.[27]

This lack of order bothered the Dutch proprietors; so also did other problems—all of which were common complaints in each colony—such as not building a house, or building an unsuitable one, or building beyond property lines. An ordinance in 1647 appointed three surveyors and gave them authority

. . . to condemn all improper and disorderly buildings, fences, palisades, posts, rails, etc. . . . Likewise we warn all and everybody who may heretofore have been granted lots, that they must erect on their lots good and convenient houses within 9 months . . . or in default thereof such unimproved lots shall fall back to the Patroon, or Landlord. . . .[28]

Later, in 1675, overseers were given power to condemn all lands with abandoned or dilapidated buildings, and in 1683 (under English rule)

---

[26] John Josselyn, "An Account of Two Voyages to New-England, Made During the Years 1638, 1663." (Boston: 1865), pp. 124–126. In: Smith (ed.), *op. cit.*, p. 5.

[27] Reps, *Town Planning* . . . , *op. cit.*, p. 187.

[28] Quoted in Reps, *Town Planning* . . . , *op. cit.*, pp. 187–188.

a lot and block plan was set up in an attempt to have order and uniformity in building along the streets. These early attempts at zoning are interesting as precedents—in actuality, they had very little effect on construction in New Amsterdam.[29]

DUTCH COLONIAL HOUSING

The Dutch West India Company, in its desire for order and uniformity, likewise set up specifications for the houses to be built:

As to the roof-covering, care shall be taken to find out what is the most serviceable material. If no thatch, straw, or anything else can be found, wooden shingles will have to be taken at first. . . . The kitchens in the fort are planned to be 10 feet (deep), which we intend to apply to all lots which are 35 feet deep, but in connection with lots that are 40 or 50 feet deep, while the general construction of the houses must be the same as that of all other houses, the kitchens need not be precisely confined to 10 feet, just as the thickness of the beams need also not be taken so exactly.[30]

These discretionary specifications, too, were ignored—as might be expected under frontier conditions, hasty building, and limited technology.

The settlers in New York used brick and stone as well as wood to build their permanent homes. Unlike New England's, some of the local clay was suited for making bricks. By 1628, brick kilns were operating on Manhattan Island and by 1634 upstate at Rensselaerwyck. However, brick was not used by most settlers for an entire house until around mid-17th century, and stick-and-clay chimneys remained in use on many houses.

The early Dutch town houses built in New Amsterdam and Fort Orange (Albany) had several features which set them apart from the homes of their English neighbors: the stepped-gable end which faced the street and was usually of brick whether or not the rest of the house was of wood; the decorative weather vanes on top of the gable ends; the high "stoep"; and the horizontally divided door, which let in light and air, and kept small children inside and animals outside. The steep roofs were covered at first by thatch, and the small windows frequently were covered by shutters.

The decorated gable ends, the colorful shutters, and the unsymmetrically placed entrance with its high stoop were imported directly with little change from the picturesque streets and squares of the towns of the Low Country.[31]

---

[29] See J. D. McGoldrick, Seymour Graubard, and R. J. Horowitz, *Building Regulation in New York City.* (New York: The Commonwealth Fund), 1944, pp. 26–31.

[30] Quoted in McGoldrick, et al., *op. cit.*, p. 25.

[31] Pickering, *op. cit.*, p. 95.

In both New Amsterdam and Albany, brick houses "after the Dutch modell" continued to be built well into the 18th century, long after the English took over the colony in 1664. A visitor from New England after 1683 described the houses: "The Buildings Brick Generaly, very stately and high, though not altogether like ours in Boston. The Bricks in some of the Houses are of divers Coullers and laid in Checkers, being glazed look very agreeable."[32]

Another type of house was built in and near the Manhattan Island settlements and in nearby regions to which Dutch settlers moved. This style has come to be known as the typical Dutch colonial style, although its prototypes probably were Flemish. These houses, usually 1½ or 2 stories, had chimneys at either end, and their distinctive feature was the low-pitched gambrel roof of unequal degrees of slope on either side which swept down in a curve beyond the front and back walls. This overhang sometimes provided shelter for the entranceway but more often came out far enough beyond the walls to form a porch. These houses were built either entirely of wood and covered by clapboard or shingles or partly of wood with a first story of stone. In the stone houses, white mortar was applied in such a way as to "form areas of interesting texture and color." This style continued to be built under English rule, and the middle class continued to build it after styles changed.[33]

In 1639, the Dutch West India Company made large land grants on Staten Island and in the Hudson River Valley to patroons who were given manorial privileges for bringing over settlers at their own expense.[34] Later, under English rule, similar large grants of land upstate were made to Englishmen. Many of the estates were not cultivated; those that were were worked by tenant farmers. Although life on these manors came to resemble the life styles of wealthy plantation owners in the South, the early manor houses were simple structures "and altogether different from the brick dwellings of urban centers." On large or small estates, the typical manor or farmhouse was a one-and-a-half-story cottage of stone or wood, with a steep-pitched roof and extended eaves, and a window on either side of the front door.

Although they are commonly referred to as "Dutch colonial" houses, they owe nothing in particular to Dutch traditions, or to those of any other single country. Rather they represent straightforward expedients to meet the needs of shelter and protection more or less international in their primitive character.[35]

[32] Quoted in Davidson, *op. cit.*, p. 45.
[33] Pickering, *op. cit.*, pp. 96, 102.
[34] Morison and Commager, *op. cit.*, p. 61.
[35] Davidson, *op. cit.*, p. 50.

Interior of the houses in the Dutch colony, though less symmetrical in layout, were similar to those of New England houses in use and function. Fireplaces were flush with the wall instead of recessed and frequently had a hood and a tile backing. A tile hearth might extend several feet out into the room. Another difference was that a ladder, frequently of a pull-down type, was used instead of stairs to reach the loft or second floor. Interior walls of Dutch homes were whitewashed or painted white or, sometimes, wainscoted. Like the English, Dutch pioneers made their own furnishings—tables, stools, chests, and sleeping benches (and, later, the enclosed bed built into an alcove). The interiors of Dutch houses have long been referred to as being tidy and "neat to admiration."[36]

Homes of the Swedish Colonists

So far as known, log cabins were first built as pioneer homes in permanent settlements in North America in the colony established by Sweden in 1638 at Fort Christina (in present-day Wilmington). The early log cabins were put up hastily, but even with a lack of finish they served the purposes of shelter better than the bark huts and dugouts of the English and Dutch. Peter Kalm, the botanist, describes them:

The whole house consisted of one little room, the door of which was so low that one was obliged to stoop in order to get in. . . .

They found no moss, or at least none which would have been serviceable in stopping up holes or cracks in the walls. They were therefore forced to close them using clay both inside and out. The chimneys were masoned in a corner, either of gray stone (or in places where there were no stones) of mere clay, which they laid very thick in one corner of the house.[37]

The corner chimney seems to have been typical of this Swedish–Finnish construction—the brick chimneys of later cabins also were put in a corner. Roofs were covered with turf, tree limbs, or hand-sawn boards; windows were small openings covered by movable boards.[38]

Later log cabins in the colony were built in a variety of styles, depending on the particular technique used in the areas from which the settlers had come. Built under less time pressure these cabins were usually one-and-a-half stories, of closely fitted round or square logs. In some, the logs were dovetailed and fitted at the corners, the window near the door had glass in it, and the roof was shingled. In others, logs protruded beyond the corners of the wall. Some log cabins later were

[36] *Ibid.*, p. 49.
[37] Peter Kalm's *Travels in North America*, Vol. I. (Trans. by A. B. Benson). (New York: Wilson-Erickson, Inc.) 1937, p. 272. Quoted in Weslager, *op. cit.*, p. 159.
[38] Weslager, *op. cit.*, p. 165.

covered with shingles or clapboards or weatherboards. Some were partitioned into three rooms: an entry, a large combined kitchen and living room, in back of which was a small sleeping room.

The log cabin was intended as a temporary dwelling. It could, however, be enlarged by building another cabin next to it. Some of these additions were flush with the existing cabin. Others were connected to the first cabin by a breezeway—a forerunner of the double-pen cabin used later by pioneers in the lowland South, Kentucky, and Tennessee.[39]

Later Swedish settlers also built log cabins for first homes. After the colony was taken over by the Dutch in 1655 and later by the English in 1664, some Swedish settlers moved to nearby areas and again built log cabins. The influence of the Swedish log cabins on housing in other colonies in the 17th century was, however, relatively slight.

Early Homes in Pennsylvania

Like the New Englanders, William Penn wanted the settlers in his colony to live in communities, with the farming population living in towns for mutual support, education, and social benefits. Agricultural villages with house and building lots around a large open space and farm fields beyond, were part of the plan. Philadelphia (1681) was the focus of the entire complex. Sites for roads to connect the villages with each other and with Philadelphia were selected before the land was distributed.[40]

PHILADELPHIA

Philadelphia was planned at the outset as a large and important city. A public square, in the center of a grid pattern of streets, near or on which were to be the public buildings, provided a focal point for the community. In addition, large squares of open space were reserved for public use in each quarter of the city.[41] As in the New England villages,

[39] For a detailed account of Swedish log cabins, see Weslager, *op. cit.*, Chapter 7.

[40] J. W. Reps, *The Making of Urban America: A History of City Planning in the United States.* (Princeton, N.J.: Princeton University Press), 1965, p. 215.

[41] Reps, *Making of Urban America, op. cit.*, p. 161. By the time the American colonies were established, the grid pattern (uniformly spaced streets parallel or perpendicular to each other) was a standard method of planning colonial towns. It was a simple, easily plotted scheme; more streets could be added without altering the original nucleus. A city with a grid plan was easier to defend than one with curved streets and units of land within the city could be equitably apportioned. The grid scheme was best suited to flat sites such as the one on which Philadelphia was laid out. Later, in the United States, the grid pattern was used for planning many new cities without regard either to its suitability for less uniform topography or to the enhancement or use of natural features of a landscape.

Penn was concerned that the city have a regular street pattern and uniformly spaced buildings well lined up; in contrast to the New England practice, he wanted houses set far apart so that the city would be healthful and, if possible, free of the danger of spreading fires:

Let every house be placed, if the person pleases, in the middle of its plat, as to the breadth of it, that so there may be ground on each side for gardens or orchards, or fields, that it may be a green country town, which will never be burnt, and always be wholesome.[42]

Philadelphia rapidly became an important trading center. By 1684 fisheries, brick kilns, tanneries, and glass works were in operation.[43] As in New England, and in spite of complaints from the proprietors, some settlers moved to the countryside and built freestanding farmhouses away from the compact settlements.

Although brick came to be the popular building material in Philadelphia, frame houses were more common until after the end of the 17th century. Quaker town houses were usually two or three stories, with the narrow end facing the street, as at New Amsterdam. The most characteristic feature of these houses was a roofed-over projection between the windows of the first and second stories called a "pent roof." In the countryside, similar houses with a pent roof were built, usually two stories, and frequently of stone.[44] Before the end of the century, groups of German colonists had settled near Philadelphia and were building stone houses similar to those of the Quakers. These stone houses were usually plain, low buildings with heavy walls, functionally designed like those in the Hudson Valley, to meet immediate needs.

The interior plan of many of the Philadelphia houses was modeled on that of the town house being built in London at about the same time. The front door opened into a hallway, in which were the stairs to the upper floor. Off the hall were two or three rooms in line with each other.

INTERIOR PENNSYLVANIA

Penn, in founding his colony, intended it to be a haven not only for Quakers but for all other groups persecuted for religious reasons or suffering economic hardship. His intensive efforts to advertise the colony made its liberal provisions for religious freedom and economic opportunity well known in Europe. Thus, when the Germans and Scotch-Irish left Europe because of religious and economic upheavals

[42] "Instructions Given by me, William Penn . . . to . . . my Commissioners. . . ." In: Samuel Hazard, *Annals of Pennsylvania*, (Philadelphia: 1850), pp. 527–530. Quoted in Reps, *Making of Urban America, op. cit.*, p. 160.

[43] Morison and Commager, *op. cit.*, p. 77.

[44] Pickering, *op. cit.*, p. 108.

early in the 18th century, they came in large numbers to Pennsylvania. Some came as part of a group with its own leader; others came separately as families or individuals. Many of them, especially the Germans, became indentured servants for seven years to farmers who financed their passage, after which they looked for sites for their own farms.

The Palatinate Germans were familiar with the technique of log cabin construction and built them for their first shelters. Although several styles were used, the typical cabin built by the German craftsmen was of square-hewn logs, carefully notched, with a central chimney and, at first, a thatched roof.[45] Tiles or shingles replaced thatch for roofing relatively soon.

The central-chimney log cabin might have a log or stone floor, and

. . . usually had three rooms on the ground floor, . . . and a deep fireplace measuring from four to sixteen feet long built in the center of the house, and opening into the kitchen. The front door was characteristically off center in a house with a central chimney and usually opened into the kitchen. Some houses of this type consisted of only one story, whereas others had an upstairs.[46]

Bake ovens typically were constructed near the house, usually of stone.

The log cabins were intended for temporary use, but they could be lived in for some time even after the farm was out of the subsistence stage, which usually was within one or two years.[47]

The German settlers had the same kinds of homemade furniture as the New Englanders and the Dutch. For decoration, they used the traditional crafts of their homeland to paint chests and other furniture with unicorns, birds, flowers, fruit, and geometric forms. These motifs later became a part of traditional American folk culture. The blue Conestoga wagon, with its covered top, built to ship produce to Philadelphia and adopted by later pioneers to the West, is another famous contribution of the Germans.

The Scotch-Irish tended more than other groups to immigrate as individuals or as separate families. Usually, they had few resources and went farther out along the frontiers. Unlike the Swedes and Germans, they had had little previous experience with the technique of building log cabins but rather learned it from their neighbors. Chimneys on these log cabins, at least the early ones, were more likely to be on the outside of the cabin rather than worked into the walls as in the cabins built by the more experienced German settlers.[48]

45 R. A. Billington, *Westward Expansion: A History of the American Frontier*, 2nd ed. (with collaboration of J. B. Hedges). (New York: Macmillan), 1960, p. 97.

46 Weslager, *op. cit.*, p. 217.

47 Billington, *op. cit.*, p. 97.

48 Weslager, *op. cit.*, p. 231.

The Palatinate Germans and the Scotch-Irish have been credited with spreading the log cabin into the South and later the West. The immigration from Germany and Northern Ireland continued throughout the 18th century. When the available land in Pennsylvania became filled as far as the Appalachians, or the price became too high, prospective settlers turned southward. Before 1750, Germans from the Palatinate were building log cabins in the valleys of Virginia and the Carolinas, and the Scotch-Irish were building them along the western edge of the Appalachians and into the upper Tennessee Valley.[49]

Regardless of its source, the availability of a technique for building cabins with logs played a vital role in subsequent migrations to western frontiers. Weslager points out:

If the techniques of log cabin construction had remained unknown in America, it is quite possible that the prospective migratory families may have been fewer in number, despite the strong economic incentives to go south or west. . . . There existed from the very beginning, even after means were found to surmount the geographical obstacles, the problem of finding suitable housing at a new location in untamed territory. The pioneer knew that he could not transport sufficient building materials to erect a dwelling house, and even if he could, he lacked skills in carpentry. This obstacle must have been of major concern to a man with a wife and young children who considered abandoning a reasonably comfortable home on the Atlantic seaboard for unsettled and unknown territory. . . . The one-room log cabin which he could build, unaided if necessary, using only an axe, gave him the assurance he needed to guarantee the security of himself and his family.[50]

Colonies in the South

Housing

Jamestown (1607) was intended to become a flourishing city and by 1614 had frame houses along its streets. Their method of construction was English:

The "well-framed houses" and the houses "of framed timber" were constructed along timber-framing styles which consisted of upright posts placed some distance apart, and tenoned into a bottom sill and a wall-plate at top. Brick or plaster was used to fill the space between the timbers, and the entire structure was then covered with plaster, or clapboards.[51]

Soon after Captain John Smith demonstrated in 1612 that tobacco could be cultivated as a cash crop in Virginia, settlers started moving

49 Billington, *op. cit.*, pp. 91–92.
50 Weslager, *op. cit.*, pp. 43–44.
51 *Ibid.*, p. 108.

out of the towns in search of larger tracts of land. In Virginia (and also Maryland), the coastlines offered many excellent sites for harbors, from which planters could ship products directly from warehouses on their own property. In addition to this geographic advantage, the head-rights system of land distribution being used favored the accumulation of large amounts of land. Under this system, persons who emigrated at their own expense were granted 50 acres of land free for each member of their party or for any subsequent immigrants whose passage they paid.[52] Also under this system, the recipient of the grant could select the site. Although there were many small holdings, the typical farm was the large plantation. This system of land distribution, combined with the development of staple products for export, led eventually to the development of a common life style throughout the coastal South.

The southern colonies enjoyed prosperity at an early date. A brick kiln was in operation at Jamestown soon after 1607, and kilns were set up on many plantations, especially in Virginia. Some of the early brick houses were elaborately designed, with clustered chimneys, stepped gable ends, and mullioned windows, or projecting two-story porches.[53] However, most of the plantation houses of the 17th century remained unpretentious and unadorned structures: one-story wooden or brick rectangles, with the doorway in the long side, which opened into the living room (instead of into the small entry as in colder New England). The two chimneys, one at either end of the structure, usually were made of brick and might be tapered in a series of steps.[54] Thatch was the first roofing material but was replaced relatively soon by wooden shingles.

Colonial Cities in the South

In Maryland and Virginia during most of the 17th century, there were only a few provincial towns to serve as county seats. Very few of these towns were social centers, and most of them were deserted when the court or assembly was not in session. The 17th century notion of a city as a "social organism to be carefully nourished and guided in its development for the benefit of the parts that made it up" was nevertheless as strong in the minds of the founders of the southern colonies as elsewhere.[55] The scattered nature of the settlements, away from the influences of church or schools, and the resulting lack of

52 Morison and Commager, *op. cit.*, p. 41.
53 Davidson, *op. cit.*, p. 55.
54 Pickering, *op. cit.*, pp. 121–122.
55 C. N. Glaab and A. R. Brown, *A History of Urban America.* (New York: Macmillan), 1967, p. 7.

community, alarmed the proprietors of both colonies and some church leaders as well. An anonymous appeal was made to London in 1661:

The families . . . being seated after this manner . . . are very remote from the house of God. . . . Many parishes as yet want both churches and glebes; and I think not a fifth part of them are supplied with ministers. . . . Their almost general want of schools . . . is another consequence of their scattered planting. . . . This want of schools, as it renders a very numerous generation of Christians' children born in Virginia . . . unserviceable for any great employments either in church or state, so likewise it obstructs the hopefulest way they have for the conversion of the heathen. . . .[56]

ANNAPOLIS AND WILLIAMSBURG

Although no large number of towns resulted, two state capitals were established, Annapolis in 1695 and Williamsburg in 1698 (after Jamestown burned down). Just as Philadelphia had been planned as a great city, Annapolis and Williamsburg were planned as capitals of important regions, "suitable for the reception of a considerable number and concourse of people" who might be expected to congregate there.[57] Both plans apparently were based on the plan used to rebuild London after the great fire of 1666, which was a modification of the baroque style of city planning. The basic scheme of a baroque plan consisted of a central place on which public buildings fronted and in which monuments might be placed, diagonal avenues spreading out from the center to connect the important parts of the city with the center and with each other, and a grid plan for other streets. Depending upon the amount of activity expected in the city, subordinate centers with radiating avenues might also be set up as focuses. The radiating avenues emphasized the importance of the principal building sites; thus, they terminated at some important public building or monument.[58]

In the most effective baroque schemes, the building of the city was as carefully carried out as the planning.[59] The plans usually specified the kinds of buildings to be sited around the central place or places, their scale and dimensions, and frequently the type of architecture to be used. At Williamsburg, for example, the legislation authorizing the plan specified the form and principal dimensions of the capital building,

[56] "Incentives for Building Towns in Virginia." In: *The Annals of America.* (Chicago: Encyclopaedia Britannica) pp. 227–228. See also: J. C. Rainbolt, "The Absence of Towns in Seventeenth-Century Virginia." In: *Cities in American History*, K. T. Jackson and S. K. Schultz (eds.), (New York: Knopf), 1972, pp. 50–65.

[57] Reps, *Town Planning* . . . , *op. cit.*, p. 140.

[58] *Ibid.*, p. 136.

[59] Lewis Mumford, *The City in History.* (New York: Harcourt Brace Jovanovich), 1961, p. 406.

including the pitch of the roof and size of the windows, and gave detailed instructions for houses. All houses built along the principal street were to be set back six feet, to front alike, and to be larger than the minimum size set for houses along less important streets. The directors of the town were to specify dwelling sizes and setbacks for houses along the other streets, and dwellings on the house lots were to be constructed within two years.[60]

Buildings and plan, of course, complemented each other and "imposed an outward order and uniformity on the city."

The scheme of central place, circles or open squares, dominated by monuments, flanked symmetrically by public buildings, with avenues spreading out from such centers, profoundly altered every dimension of building. Unlike the medieval town . . . one can take in a baroque town almost at a glance. Even what one does not see one can easily extrapolate in one's imagination, once the guiding lines are established. The avenue now became definitely the horizontal frame of the terminal buildings. Though these edifices might be capped by a dome or a towered cupola, the main effect of the plan itself was to increase the importance of the regulating horizontal lines, formed by the lintels, the strong courses, and the cornices: for the first time all these parts were united in a perspective whose effect was intensified by the seemingly infinite length of the avenue.[61]

The regulation of buildings produced some other benefits, as pointed out in a description of Williamsburg in 1724:

The town is laid out regularly in lots or square portions, sufficient each for a house and garden; so that they don't build contiguous, whereby may be prevented the spreading danger of fire; and this also affords a free passage for the air, which is very grateful in violent hot weather.[62]

Appropriately, the "highest and most commanding sites" at Annapolis were set aside for the statehouse and the church. These buildings were placed in huge circles along the main street, the public circle for the statehouse being over 500 feet and the church circle approximately 300 feet in diameter. Several streets radiated outward from the circles; beyond them was a large open area, Market Square.[63]

The design for Williamsburg was a simpler axial plan than that for Annapolis. The principal axis was a broad, long thoroughfare with adjacent streets laid out in a gridiron pattern, a plan used for some later American cities. A square space at one end of the principal street

60 Reps, *Town Planning* . . . , *op. cit.*, p. 139.
61 Mumford, *op. cit.*, p. 390.
62 Hugh Jones, *The Present State of Virginia.* (New York), 1865, pp. 25–32. In: Smith (ed.), *Cities of our Past and Present*, *op. cit.*, p. 22.
63 Reps, *Town Planning* . . . , *op. cit.*, pp. 135–136.

was set aside for the capitol building and one at the other end for the College of William and Mary (founded in 1693). Midway along the street was another square, on or near which were sites for public buildings, including the courthouse and a church. A long green open space, lined with trees, near the middle square provided a view of the governor's mansion and gardens.[64]

These cities, like cities in the North, became centers of social as well as political life in the 18th century:

Even colonial towns of two or three thousand inhabitants afforded more social amenities in the eighteenth century than American cities of many times their population today. There would always be a market house and merchants' exchange, a tavern where the latest English gazettes were taken in and where clubs of gentlemen or tradesmen met for talk, smoke, wine, and singing; a dancing assembly for the social elite; a circulating library; and, in five or six places, a musical society, . . . College commencements, horse-races, and fairs gave entertainment to everyone.[65]

Much of this urbane character has been preserved at Annapolis, which did not develop into a commercial and industrial center, and now also at Williamsburg since its reconstruction after 1926.

CHARLESTON

The coastline of South Carolina had few harbors for private docks; thus, when the colony was founded in 1672, Charleston was laid out as the capital of the province, with a central square for the courthouse and other public buildings and a gridiron pattern of streets. Like other colonial cities, it was oriented to the principal waterway. Here, as at Annapolis and Williamsburg later, setbacks of buildings along the streets were carefully regulated to avoid "undecent and incommodious irregularities."[66] The first houses were of wood, usually one or two rooms, and similar to English designs used elsewhere in the coastal South.

Early Charleston had a mixture of populations—English, Dutch, Barbadians, French Huguenots, and others—and later houses had a variety of features not common elsewhere in the South: stuccoed brick walls, window balconies, Flemish gables, and frequently a piazza across the long side of the house.

In the city, the narrow end of the house faced the street and fronted directly on it. Many homes in the city were the summer homes of plantation owners; others housed a rapidly rising merchant class and a middle class of professionals and skilled workers.

---

64 *Ibid.*, pp. 141–143.
65 Morison and Commager, *op. cit.*, p. 108.
66 Reps, *Town Planning* . . . , *op. cit.*, p. 225.

Plantation houses and the homes of small farmers along the rivers were similar in the 17th century, usually one-and-a-half-story cottages, sometimes with dormer windows on the second floor, with front and rear doors—one facing the water and the other the road. A few plantation houses had two stories and were built of brick.

SAVANNAH

In 1732, James Oglethorpe was given royal permission to found a colony in Georgia made up of settlers from England, most of whom had limited resources and some of whom were from debtors' prisons. Oglethorpe, an experienced town planner, devised a plan for Savannah that, in contrast to baroque city designs, emphasized the neighborhood. The basic unit of the plan was the ward, each ward consisting of 40 house lots, around an open square. Two lots fronting on two sides of each square were set aside for churches, stores, and other public buildings. Reps states:

The Georgia settlements constituted real innovations in urban design. The basic module—ward, open square, and local streets—provided not only an unusually attractive, convenient, and intimate environment but also served as a practical device for allowing urban expansion without formless sprawl. These little neighborhood units, scaled to human size, must also have established a social pattern desirable for a frontier settlement where cooperation and neighborly assistance was essential for survival.[67]

Savannah's later expansion remained under municipal control. Not until after the common land was exhausted in 1856 did the city begin the typical extension of completely built-up streets without open space.

Each increment of growth retained the original concept of the plan. One or more ward units were added in an orderly fashion, and all but one of these squares remains today and gives modern Savannah a distinct character enjoyed by no other American city.[68]

Although houses in the early Georgia communities were the typical one-and-a-half-story cottages built by English settlers in the other colonies, better houses also were built, probably for the proprietors. Such houses were sited some distance apart, as in Philadelphia, and for the same reasons. A visitor in 1745 reported:

Many of the Houses are very large and handsome, built generally of Wood, but some Foundations are brick'd. . . . The Houses are built some Distance from each other, to allow more Air and Garden Room, and prevent the Communication, in Case of any Accident by Fire.[69]

[67] Reps, *Making of Urban America*, op. cit., p. 199.
[68] Reps, *Town Planning* . . . , op. cit., p. 226.
[69] Quoted in Reps, *Making of Urban America*, op. cit., p. 192.

Colonial Building Regulations

So far as the regulation of buildings was concerned, colonial towns had other and more serious problems to contend with than an orderly arrangement of houses along their streets. Wooden houses with thatch or reed roofs (or wooden shingles) and stick-and-clay chimneys caught fire easily. Where these early houses were built close together, as they were in the first colonies—probably for protection—fires spread rapidly. Some towns—Jamestown is one example—were destroyed by fire, at least once.

Early records of the Plymouth Plantation and the Massachusetts Bay colony abound in references to houses that went up in flames because of sparks lighting on thatch roofs. About noon on March 16, 1631, wrote Governor John Winthrop, for instance, "the chimney of Mr. Sharp's house in Boston took fire . . . , and taking the thatch burnt it down, and the wind being N.W., drove the fire to Mr. Colburn's house . . . and burnt that down also. . . ."[70]

Some of the earliest building laws in the colonies have to do with fire control. A Boston ordinance in 1679 ordered that houses should be built of stone or brick and covered with slate or tile roofs.[71] It seems probable that the use of brick or stone as house materials was less from preference than from acceptance of this kind of regulation. This act may not have been enforceable: Charleston also ordained that houses should be of brick but had to rescind the ordinance because bricks were scarce and expensive.[72]

Fire wardens were appointed in most towns and were given authority to inspect the clay-plastered chimneys and require them to be kept clean. The first fire-prevention law in New Amsterdam in 1648 banned the building of such chimneys and gave the wardens power to condemn unsafe chimneys as well as to fine the owners. Further, a property owner could be fined if his house burned down as a result of his negligence. Another ordinance in 1656 ordered that all straw or reed roofs and wooden chimneys be removed.[73]

The laws were strict enough—the problem was to enforce them. The fire inspectors were not popular; frequently, persistent efforts had to be made and the help of higher officials obtained. One example from New Amsterdam may be cited:

[70] Davidson, *op. cit.*, pp. 15–16.

[71] Frank Burton, "Historical Data Concerning Building Legislation." Mimeo, n.d., p. 15.

[72] Pickering, *op. cit.*, p. 140.

[73] McGoldrick, et al., *op. cit.*, p. 27–28.

Jacob Stevenson, who had also gained notoriety in other ways, had been warned by the fire inspectors to repair his house or pull it down. Still it stood and that no attention was given to the warning regarding repairs is indicated by the complaint finally made by a neighbor who said that nothing else was to be expected, not only by himself but by the whole street, but a sudden destruction by fire. An order of the court now included the sheriff, who, together with the fire inspectors, was ordered to forbid, within twenty-four hours, the said Stevenson making any more fire there under such circumstances, or they might pull down the chimney or do anything else they deemed proper.[74]

Continued effort by the Dutch and later the English governors, however, did establish fire zones in New York City before the Revolution where only brick or stone could be used for building materials. Exceptions had to be made for houses built where the ground was too soft to support such heavy materials.[75] Voluntary fire departments also had been organized in most towns and cities in all colonies.

In addition to fire regulations, the colonial towns also made various attempts to control obnoxious uses of property. One Massachusetts ordinance in 1692 required all the towns in the province, including Boston, to designate places where "it would be the least offensive to erect slaughterhouses, still houses, and houses for . . . tallow and currying of leather . . . at which and at no other" those activities were to be carried on. This ordinance was amended in 1710 to permit authorities to forbid the use of any place assigned for these purposes if they became offensive and to require the owner to remove them "or any other nuisance" under penalty of fines.[76] In New Amsterdam, in 1657, colonists were forbidden to throw refuse into the streets and ordered to put all rubbish into designated places. The Ordinance of 1647 in that city considered the "placing of pig pens and privies on the public roads and streets" part of the problem of "disorderly building" which the ordinance was intended to stop. Another ordinance in 1648 specifically forbade the building of privies with outlets level with the ground and opening on the street.[77]

Enforcement of use regulations probably was less easy to accomplish than enforcement of fire regulations, especially in rapidly growing frontier communities. Such regulations, however, did set precedents for later building regulations; also, the efforts to control fire hazards and obnoxious uses indicate some acceptance of the notion that the rights of property owners could and should be restricted for the public good.

[74] *Ibid.*, p. 28.
[75] *Ibid.*, p. 35.
[76] T. W. Mackesey, "History of Zoning in the United States." Mimeo, n.d., pp. 1–2.
[77] McGoldrick, et al., *op. cit.*, p. 30.

Spanish Colonies

Spain established colonies across the southern and southwestern United States from St. Augustine (1565) to San Francisco (1776). Three kinds of settlements were built: missions, for conversions; presidios as military establishments, and pueblos or villas as civil settlements. Frequently, in the more permanent communities, there was little distinction among the different types.[78]

In the missions, the church was the dominant feature, with shops, schools, Indian quarters, hospital, and farm structures around it. Presidios [as at Monterrey (1770) and San Francisco (1776)] were typically within a stockade, with barracks, stores, shops, and a few houses for settlers. The Spanish pueblo towns (such as Los Angeles, established in 1781) followed a standard plan that was closely similar to the New England town plan. The village was in or near the middle of the land tract and the street pattern centered on an open space on which important buildings faced.

St. Augustine, the oldest continuous white settlement in North America, represents almost the only remaining evidence of Spanish colonies in the east. The houses fronted directly on the streets, with gardens and patios in the rear. Typically, the houses were two stories high, with tile roofs and balconies at the upper levels overlooking the entrance and the gardens. Early houses probably were built of wood; later houses of local stone, or a combination of stone for the first floor and wood for the second (like the later Dutch–Flemish houses in the New Amsterdam region).

At the time it was founded Santa Fe (1609) was the capital of the most northerly province of New Spain. The central open space with the governor's palace nearby and other streets centering on the plaza can still be seen. Here the two-story houses were built of adobe, the material most typically used in the Spanish settlements of the Southwest. In these houses, the roof of the house was carried beyond the walls and was supported by heavy wooden beams.[79]

Like other early Spanish settlements (and the later Dutch one at New Amsterdam), Santa Fe suffered somewhat from hasty building and poor execution of plans. A report in 1776 complained that the city consisted "of many small ranchos set at various distances from one another, with no plan as to their location" along one side of the plaza. Similarly, San Antonio, another provincial capital (1730) was reported in 1777 to consist of "59 houses of stone and mud, and 79 of wood, but all poorly built."[80]

---

[78] Reps, *Town Planning* . . . , *op. cit.*, pp. 51–52.
[79] Pickering, *op. cit.*, p. 145.
[80] Reps, *Town Planning* . . . ,*op. cit.*, pp. 54, 58.

Nevertheless, the Spanish left a definite heritage in their later missions (after 1780), presidios, pueblos, and ranchos in the Rio Grande area and southern California. The picturesque houses built by the Franciscans and Indians of adobe and timber or of stone were models for the houses built by later settlers in the 18th and 19th centuries.

Often these structures were built around two or three sides of a courtyard, or patio, which provided the outdoor living quarters of the family. . . . The corridor, or porch, with wooden posts or brick piers supporting a simple shed roof of colorful tiles was a conspicuous feature. . . .[81]

Inside walls were plastered and whitewashed, the plainness relieved by doors painted in bright colors and colorful tile floors. The furniture most commonly consisted of a few chairs, benches, tables, and beds. In the large haciendas, furnishings were more elaborate and resembled those in fine homes in Spain: sofas and chairs upholstered in velvet, decorated chests and tables, and brocaded curtains.[82]

French Colonies

In the 18th century, the French, who controlled the Mississippi Valley until 1763, set up a string of frontier posts and missions, plus a few towns, in the Mississippi River Valley. Many of them later became cities. Detroit (1701) was a fortress town, with narrow streets enclosed within the fort and farm plots outside the town in the typical French pattern of long narrow farmlands running back from the water edge. Since water was the means of transportation, a waterfront or military institution controlling the water was the important feature of most of the French colonial settlements.[83]

Some important French agricultural villages along the upper Mississippi in the 18th century were Cahokia, Prairie du Rocher, Kaskaskia, and St. Genevieve. Although many houses were built of stone, the typical French construction in the Mississippi valley was the hipped-roofed house of vertical posts set in a trench or on a sill, with wall spaces packed with rubble and clay. Only the French settlers seem to have built their houses with logs set vertically. The usual French pioneer house was one-and-a-half stories, containing three or more rooms, with casement windows and a stone chimney (in the center or at the end), and narrow dormer windows in the attic. Typically, an outside staircase led to the upper floor. A house of a prosperous trader might have plastered interior walls, glass windowpanes, and shutters.

[81] Pickering, *op. cit.*, p. 146.
[82] *Ibid.*
[83] Reps, *Town Planning* . . . , *op. cit.*, p. 36.

A distinctive regional French style developed at New Orleans and in the Louisiana bayou country and this style continued in use after the French left. The most typical of these is the Creole house, which was quite unlike the plantation houses in the English South. Its distinguishing features were the wide, columned verandas on all sides of the house, onto which French casement doors opened, the curved hipped roof which came down over the porch without a break, and paired front doors.[84] The chimney was usually in the center, and many of these houses were set on brick piers six or eight feet above the ground. Houses in New Orleans were built close together in this same style. The door opened directly on the sidewalk. Balconies, over which the roof extended, overlooked the courtyard and the gardens in back. Many Creole houses in New Orleans had arched doorways and iron balconies facing the street, onto which French shuttered doors opened.[85]

Interiors of the French-style houses were plain, with wooden floors and plastered or papered walls. As in much of the South, the kitchen usually was in a separate building, frequently across the courtyard from the main house.

As New Orleans expanded, particularly after it became an important American seaport, houses were built in French, Spanish, and a variety of American styles. Nevertheless, New Orleans, like Savannah, retains much of its original character. Its cosmopolitan population, the strength of the early French influence, and relatively slow expansion until after 1800 contributed to this result, but two other conditions also were met. One is that the original plan of the city emphasized the natural attractions of the site along the river in a "street pattern of beauty and interest." The other is that the same emphasis was retained as the city expanded—one important feature is the repetition of the open square at intervals as a major element in the design.[86]

Russian Colonies

Although the Russian style of building did not influence later styles, it is worth noting, since the Russians introduced the log cabin into the Pacific Coast region before American settlers crossed the continent. Beginning about 1808, while the region was still claimed by Spain, Russian traders established a trading port on Bodega Bay, just north of San Francisco, and built a few large ranches in the nearby area. In 1812, the Russian American Company built a fort and settlement at what is now known as Fort Ross.

[84] Henry Glassie, *Pattern in the Material Folk Culture of the Eastern Unied States* (Philadelphia: University of Pennsylvania Press), 1969, p. 117.

[85] Pickering, *op. cit.*, p. 150.

[86] Reps, *Town Planning* . . . , *op. cit.*, p. 104.

The commandant's house constructed in the west corner of the palisaded area, containing six rooms, fireplace, and glass windows, was made of round redwood logs, hewn square at the ends to permit full dovetail notching and flush corners. A total of fifty-nine different structures were erected to accommodate the two hundred to four hundred inhabitants that eventually peopled the settlement. . . . Although the exact number is not known, it is certain that many of the buildings were of notched logs and Fort Ross was described by a contemporary French visitor as resembling a Muscovite village.[87]

The colony was abandoned in 1841 and the property sold.

During the 19th century, prior to the purchase of Alaska by the United States in 1867, at about the same time that Americans were building log cabins in the Mississippi Valley and Great Lakes regions, the Russians were building them in Alaska.

Trading posts, blockhouses, churches and chapels used to Christianize Alaska's Eskimo and Indian population were built by the Russians of both round and hewn logs, and residences ranged from small one-room cabins to multifamily log dwellings. In Sitka in 1865 there were a number of large apartments 150 feet long by fifty to eighty feet wide, three stories high built of dovetailed, hewn spruce logs. They had whipsawed wooden floors tongue and grooved by hand, and the roofs were covered with sheet iron. The logs were painted a lemon-yellow and the roofs red.[88]

Some of the Russian log cabins later were covered with redwood siding from California. In some settlements, the public buildings had architectural features that demonstrated a sophisticated technique of log construction; for example, the wooden spire and onion-shaped dome on the gable roof of the chapel at Kenai (a fishing port near Anchorage).[89]

Late Colonial Housing

Well before 1700, the English colonies had developed products for trade with England, Europe, and the West Indies—tobacco, rice, indigo, and naval stores in the South and furs, grain, provisions, fish, wood, and cattle in the North. In spite of periods of acute depression, the demand for colonial products remained strong, especially after 1700.[90]

[87] Weslager, *op. cit.*, p. 330.
[88] Weslager, *op. cit.*, pp. 323–324. During the gold rushes of the late 19th century, American prospectors added the typical American log cabin, as well as shanties, tents, shacks, and other structures, to the earlier Russian styles. *Ibid.*, p. 327.
[89] *Ibid.*, p. 325.
[90] Morison and Commager, *op. cit.*, pp. 100–101.

TABLE 1–1. Colonial Population in 1701, 1749, and 1775

Colony	1701	1749	1775	Percent Increase, 1701–1749	Percent Increase, 1749–1775
NEW ENGLAND					
Connecticut	30,000	100,000	262,000	233	162
Massachusetts	70,000	220,000	352,000	214	60
New Hampshire	10,000	30,000	102,000	200	240
Rhode Island	10,000	35,000	58,000	250	66
MIDDLE ATLANTIC					
Delaware			37,000		
New Jersey	15,000	60,000	138,000	300	130
New York	30,000	100,000	238,000	233	138
Pennsylvania	20,000	250,000	341,000	1,150	36
SOUTH					
Georgia	—	6,000	27,000	—	350
Maryland	25,000	85,000	174,000	240	105
North Carolina	5,000	45,000	181,000	800	302
South Carolina	7,000	30,000	93,000	329	210
Virginia	40,000	85,000	300,000	112	253
TOTAL	262,000	1,046,000	2,803,000	299	168

SOURCE: U. S. Census. *Statistical View of the United States: A Compendium of the Seventh Census.* (Washington, D.C.: A. O. P. Nicholson), 1854, Table XI, p. 39. All population figures are based on "conjectural estimates, more or less accurate," from colonial records.

The relatively low cost of labor and water transportation gave the colonists trade advantages. Agricultural technology remained more or less at a primitive stage until after 1800. In many settlements, little effort was made to maintain the fertility of the soil or to rotate crops, though sometimes crops were changed and some fields were left to lie fallow. Most of the manufacturing carried on was for local consumption.[91]

Other factors in the prosperity of the 18th century were the increased population in the colonies, from continuous immigration and natural increase and the relatively rapid development of interior regions. Table 1–1 shows the estimated colonial population in 1701, 1749, and 1775 for each of the 13 original states and the percentage increase in population between 1701 and 1749 and between 1749 and 1775. Although all of the population figures are conjectural, the table indicates the general direction of settlement in the 18th century. The fastest-growing regions between 1701 and 1749 were the two newly opened areas of Pennsylvania and North Carolina. Between 1749 and 1775, the rapidity of growth shifted farther south, probably to some extent the result

[91] Wright, *op. cit.*, pp. 77, 83.

of the movement into the back country of Virginia and the Carolinas and into the newly opened territory of Georgia. In the North, New Hampshire was the fastest-growing region between 1749 and 1775. New York had a below-average rate of growth in both periods, probably the result of the restrictive landholding system in that state. The sharp decline in growth rate between the two periods in Massachusetts, Rhode Island, and Pennsylvania, on the other hand, seems to indicate the shift in population to points in the interior as the amount of uncommitted and accessible land in those three areas became scarcer.

The early land policies had stimulated both immigration and interior settlement; in the 18th century, changes in land policies augmented these effects. In New England, in place of grants being made principally to organized groups who desired land for their own use, large tracts were granted to groups of New England merchants, who laid out townships, offered free lots to get settlers, and made their profit from the sale of lots in the remaining townships.[92] In the middle and southern colonies, land was sold outright by the proprietors or the colonial assemblies, and free grants were made to English or colonial land speculators, who were to obtain settlers. The developers used a standard method of colonizing, which consisted of (1) making elementary improvements to attract settlers, (2) bringing in European immigrants, (3) maintaining agents at port cities, and (4) sending out promotional literature.[93]

People with fewer resources could or were forced to move into the interior and "squat." That is, they selected a site, built a house and planted crops, then paid for the land later (or not at all), provided that they had not been forced off by the landowners. In spite of complaints, the right of "squatters" to occupy land in advance of payment eventually came to be recognized before the end of the colonial period.

Interior settlements were all mostly along the river valleys. Various communities built local roads, paid for by a road tax or worked out by local farmers in lieu of taxes. By 1775 the more densely settled areas had a fair system of roads, poorly maintained, supplemented by paths and Indian trails.[94] Boston, New York, Philadelphia, and the Chesapeake Bay region were connected with each other by post roads, and with the interior by local roads of varying quality.

Along the eastern seaboard, an upper class was acquiring wealth and power and being augmented each year by newly rich families. Merchants in seaport towns traveled to England every few years; sons of the rich in the North and South were sent to school in England. English

[92] Reps, *Town Planning* . . . , *op. cit.*, p. 152.
[93] Billington, *op. cit.*, p. 84.
[94] Wright, *op. cit.*, p. 108.

papers and books were read throughout the colonies. Some of the middle class also enjoyed these advantages.[95] Relatively newly settled areas, linked as they were to the seacoast cities, shared in the general prosperity.

One result of increased wealth and contact with England was a change in the design of houses from the simple functional structures of the early colonial styles to the sophisticated Georgian style being used in England. The most fashionable Georgian homes, of course, were built by the wealthy in both the North and South. American builders worked from pattern books available from England. The widespread use of these pattern books had a unifying effect on the large quantity of houses built during the period of its influence. One principal result was a marked homogeneity between homes of the wealthy, wherever built. Within this underlying similarity, the sharpest contrasts tended to be between these homes and the similarly designed but more modest homes of the less wealthy.

Basically the new style emphasized symmetry in proportions and plan and focused on a central feature, usually the entrance. Georgian houses typically had a symmetrical placement of openings along the front of the house: a central doorway balanced by windows on each side and a row of windows placed symmetrically along the second (and third) story above each opening on the first floor. Windows were larger and the lower portion could be raised and lowered. The doorway might be a simple opening with a plain board door or within a small porch with columns. Somewhat more elaborate was the paneled door with molding around the frame. The most ornate and authentic Georgian doorways had pilasters on either side and an entablature or pediment above; frequently, fanlights were placed over the door and a side light on either side. The second-floor window immediately above the doorway also might be accented, and other windows had decorative frames. Roofs were less steep and the ridge was parallel to the facade of the house. If the house had a gambrel roof, dormer windows were placed symmetrically with the lower-floor windows and frequently were accented.[96] A low roof might be surrounded by a balustrade, and frequently a cupola was added—the well-known "Captain's walk" of the New England house.

In the interior, the major change from the earlier colonial styles was the large central hall, with two or more rooms opening from it on each side. Typically, a broad central staircase led from the central hall to another hallway on the second floor, on which all the second-floor rooms opened. Staircases frequently had carved balustrades and

95 Morison and Commager, *op. cit.*, p. 106.
96 Pickering, *op. cit.*, p. 75.

newel posts. Doors were usually paneled and doorways typically accented, but the fireplace mantel and overmantel were the most emphasized features. Paneling was usually painted, as was the woodwork.
Plastered walls also were painted or, sometimes, covered by imported
wallpaper. Ceilings were plastered and decorated, and frequently hung
with chandeliers. Floors were hardwood or parquetry, and more often
covered with imported patterned rugs, and silk brocades and damasks
largely replaced linen and wood for curtains, table covers, and bed
hangings.

Furniture likewise was more elaborate—chests of drawers in place
of storage boxes, chairs instead of stools; upholstered sofas and chairs
as well as decorated tables and sideboards were typical. American
cabinetmakers in northern cities, using the English pattern books of
Chippendale, and later those of Sheraton and Hepplewhite, created
their own distinctive styles for the mansions of the wealthy. In the
South, where local crafts developed more slowly, furniture and furnishings usually were imported. By 1770, mahogany, usually carved
in English designs, had replaced oak and walnut as material for
furniture.

The principal differences between the elaborate Georgian houses in
the various English colonies were in building materials and kind and
extent of decoration. The wealthy in New England cities had their
homes built in wood and local craftsmen "submitted elements of Georgian design to their own imaginative processes and produced an ingen-
uous and engaging regional architecture."[97] The central chimney was
replaced by two chimneys, one at either end of the house, and the
kitchen and storage units might be in a one-story ell in the back.

In Philadelphia, the Georgian houses were usually two-and-a-half or
three stories, built of brick laid in Flemish bond, with a low roof and
a classic balustrade; many had stone trim. Ornamentation on Philadelphia houses tended to be more strictly classical than in New England—
the local Carpenters Company published its own manual in which classical ornamentation was faithfully copied. In the New York area and
upstate, newly rich Dutch and English families built Georgian mansions
in a style closer to the New England version than to the more elaborate
types farther south.[98]

The more elaborate Georgian homes in the South were the plantation
houses: a main house with formal treatment and rich ornament, and
with long low wings on each side, sometimes connected with the house
but frequently freestanding. Four large chimneys added to the impressiveness, and the entrance might be graced by a double portico or two-

97 Davidson, *op. cit.*, p. 81.
98 Pickering, *op. cit.*, p. 112.

story porch. Houses in the southern cities had some resemblance to those in the New England cities, probably as a result of similar spatial restrictions. Town houses at Annapolis tended to be compact brick structures with symmetrical doorways and windows, tall end chimneys, and little ornamentation. At Charleston, houses were built of brick or brick and stucco, with graceful second-floor balconies as in earlier styles, and simple ornamentation. Williamsburg houses resembled those on smaller southern estates and in small communities: frequently simple white clapboard frame structures with regularly spaced dormer windows and large red brick chimneys.[99]

Here, as in other parts, they build with brick, but mostly commonly with timber lined with cieling, and cased with featheredged plank, painted with white lead and oil, covered with shingles of cedar, etc., tarred over at first; with a passage generally through the middle of the house for an air-draught in summer.

Thus their houses are lasting, dry, and warm in winter, and cool in summer; especially if there be windows enough to draw the air.[100]

In the North, the rural houses differed from urban ones principally because of differences in the extent to which local builders adhered to Georgian models. In New England, the saltbox house was built with a symmetrical gable, and enlarged to two stories and four rooms—a style which remains a regular feature of the New England landscape. Some farmhouses in rural Pennsylvania combined features of earlier houses with a Georgian design. Such houses were two rooms deep, with internal gable end chimneys, approximately symmetrical placement of windows and doors, and a low-pitched roof but "they lack most of the stylish trim."[101]

In the interior valleys of the South, the Pennsylvania Germans built some central chimney houses of log or stone on the same plan as the German homes in Pennsylvania. English settlers from small farms in the Tidewater region—forced into the upland South as the large plantation owners increased their holdings—tended to build houses of wood, or more rarely of brick, with limestone chimneys at each end and a two-story porch slightly wider than the central hall across the front. This type of house came to be the predominant style in the interior regions; in the mountain country it was built of logs or stone. In the mountain regions also, the Scotch-Irish log cabin, with its rectangular floor plan and opposed front and rear doors remained practically untouched by the new style.[102]

99 *Ibid.*, p. 134.
100 Jones, *loc. cit.*, p. 22.
101 Glassie, *op. cit.*, pp. 54, 125.
102 Glassie, *op. cit.*, p. 78.

The city and plantation homes of the prosperous continued to be built in the Georgian style until the Revolution and for some time thereafter. In the later homes, ornamentation became more elaborate, especially in the postcolonial period, but there was no change in the basic features of the design. The simpler forms developed in the northern rural areas continued in use well into the 19th century.

Probably a major reason for the popularity of the Georgian style— aside from a lack of strongly entrenched local building traditions—was that it represented a major improvement in interior as well as exterior design. Properly placed doors and rooms opening into the central hall made circulation easier and supplied more privacy. Rooms were larger, their ceilings higher, and their use more specialized: the Georgian design called for parlors, sitting rooms, sometimes a library, a dining room, and several bedrooms.[103]

Various other changes in housing distinguished the late colonial from the early colonial period. By 1770, the majority of the population in rural areas as well as in towns lived in frame houses or in brick or stone houses, where the materials were locally available (and possibly required by local ordinances). The wooden house had the same kind of heavy timber frame as the early houses, clapboard sides, and a sloping shingled roof, but now was more usually one-and-a-half to two-and-a-half stories and had from four to seven rooms and an attic. Most houses had a brick or stone cellar under at least a portion of the house. After 1720, paint was used more freely both inside and outside on wooden houses, although many houses remained unpainted. New houses had double-hung windows; nevertheless, small leaded panes and casement windows were still common. Floors of the majority of houses were broad, heavy planks, usually bare, but plastered walls had become more frequent in all houses. The kitchen typically was under a sloping roof at the rear of the house, or in the basement; in the South it was usually separate from the main building. Frequently a storage shed was adjacent to the kitchen, sometimes with a privy inside; otherwise, outhouses were the rule.[104]

Central chimneys, where in use, by now were most typically made of brick and provided fireplace openings in more than one room. Although the majority of houses were heated by fireplaces, the use of Benjamin Franklin's stove, introduced around 1750, was spreading, except among the poor. This stove was used principally in living rooms —bedroom heat was provided by charcoal warming pans. For lighting, candles were in more general use, usually made at home by most of

103 Pickering, *op. cit.*, p. 73.
104 Wright, *op. cit.*, p. 843.

the families. In some cases these might be supplemented by oil burned in small dishes with lighted wicks.[105]

Cooking was carried on at the open hearth and the bake ovens, water was brought in from the nearest spring or well, or stream, or from the village pump. Clothes were washed in soft water gathered from roof gutters and heated in large iron kettles over a fire.[106]

Bibliography

ADLER, M. J. and CHARLES VAN DOREN (eds.), *The Annals of America.* Chicago, Ill.: Encyclopaedia Britannica, 1968.

BILLINGTON, RAY A., *Westward Expansion: A History of the American Frontier*, 2d ed. (with collaboration of J. B. Hedges). New York: Macmillan, 1960.

BRADFORD, WILLIAM, *Of Plymouth Plantation, 1630–1647*. New ed., with Introduction by S. E. Morison. New York: Knopf, 1952.

BURTON, FRANK, "Historical Data Concerning Building Legislation." Mimeo., n.d.

CONDIT, C. W., *American Building Art: The Nineteenth Century.* New York: Oxford University Press, 1960.

DAVIDSON, M. B., *The American Heritage History of Notable American Houses.* New York: American Heritage Publishing Co., 1971.

FURNAS, J. C., *The Americans: A Social History of the United States, 1587–1914.* New York: Putnam's, 1969.

GLAAB, C. N. and A. T. BROWN, *A History of Urban America.* New York: Macmillan, 1967.

GLASSIE, HENRY, *Pattern in the Material Folk Culture of the Eastern United States.* Philadelphia, Pa.: University of Pennsylvania Press, 1969.

JACKSON, K. T. and S. K. SCHULTZ (eds.), *Cities in American History.* New York: Knopf, 1972.

MACKESEY, T. W. "History of Zoning in the United States." Mimeo., n.d.

McGOLDRICK, J. D., SEYMOUR GRAUBARD, and R. J. HOROWITZ, *Building Regulation in New York City: A Study in Administrative Law and Procedure.* New York: Commonwealth Fund, 1944.

MORISON, S. E. and H. S. COMMAGER, *The Growth of the American Republic.* Vol. I, 3d ed. New York: Oxford University Press, 1942.

MUMFORD, LEWIS, *The City in History: Its Origins, Its Transformations, and Its Prospects.* New York: Harcourt Brace Jovanovich, 1961.

PICKERING, ERNEST, *The Homes of America.* New York: Thomas Y. Crowell, 1951.

[105] *Ibid.*, pp. 843–844. See J. C. Furnas, *The Americans: A Social History of the United States, 1587–1914.* (New York: Putnam's), 1969, pp. 140–142 for a description of sanitation in colonial times.

[106] Wright, *op. cit.*, pp. 843–844.

REPS, J. W., *Town Planning in Frontier America.* Princeton, N.J.: Princeton University Press, 1969.

———. *The Making of Urban America: A History of City Planning in the United States.* Princeton, N.J.: Princeton University Press, 1965.

SMITH, WILSON (ed.), *Cities of Our Past and Present.* New York: Wiley, 1964.

TUNNARD, CHRISTOPHER and H. H. REED, *American Skyline: The Growth and Form of Our Cities and Towns.* New York: New American Library of World Literature, 1956.

U. S. CENSUS OFFICE, *Statistical View of the United States: A Compendium of the Seventh Census.* Washington, D.C.: A. O. P. Nicholson, 1854.

WESLAGER, C. A., *The Log Cabin in America: From Pioneer Days to the Present.* New Brunswick, N.J.: Rutgers University Press, 1969.

WILLISON, G. F., *Saints and Strangers: The Story of the Mayflower and the Plymouth Colony.* 2d ed. London: William Heinemann, 1966.

WRIGHT, C. W., *Economic History of the United States.* 2d ed. New York: McGraw-Hill, 1949.

CHAPTER 2

HOUSING AND CITIES: 1790 TO 1890

MARGARET E. WOODS*

Introduction

BY 1790, the settled areas of the United States were along the coast from Maine to Florida and inland approximately to the Appalachians. Beyond the mountain barriers, small colonies of American pioneers had settled in the river valleys of eastern Tennessee and central Kentucky. Nearly all the total population of 5,300,000 in 1800 lived in the North or South, with less than 1 percent in the trading posts farther west. By 1890, the population was distributed over all the major regions of the contiguous United States. Less than one third lived in the Northeast, one third or more lived in the southern and North Central states, and 5 percent lived in the West (Table 2–1).

Each region had characteristics of soil, climate, vegetation, and water supply that determined the kinds of crops that could be raised, accessibility to pioneers, speed of settlement, and the economically feasible size of farms. The North Central region, for example, included much of the fertile lands of the Mississippi Valley that were suited for comparatively small farms. In contrast, the more mountainous West

---

* See Chapter 1 biographical footnote.

TABLE 2-1. Population of the United States, by Regions, in 1800, 1850, and 1890

	Population, in thousands			Percent of Total Population			Percent Increase	
	1800	1850	1890	1800	1850	1890	1800–1850	1850–1890
Total Population	5,309	23,193	62,979	—	—	—	336	174
Northeast	2,636	8,627	17,407	50	37	28	230	102
South	2,622	8,983	20,028	49	39	32	250	122
North Central	51	5,404	22,410	1	23	35	—	315
West	—	179	3,134	—	1	5	—	1,650

SOURCE: U. S. Bureau of the Census, *Historical Statistics of the United States, Colonial Times to 1970*, Bicentennial Edition, Part 2. (Washington, D.C.: U.S. Government Printing Office), 1975, A 172–183, p. 22.

44

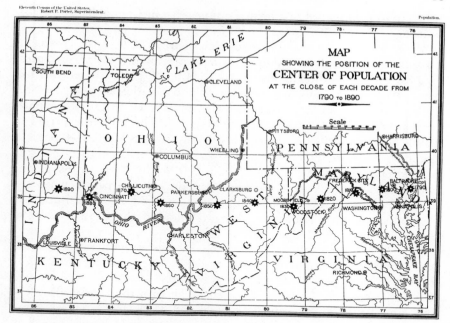

FIGURE 2–1. Map showing the position of the center of population at the close of each decade, from 1790 to 1890.

had large areas of less fertile land that required farming on a larger scale. Nevertheless, although several areas were only sparsely populated, and large numbers of people continued to move into western areas, the extent of settlement over the continent was such that in 1890 the U. S. Bureau of the Census stated:

Up to and including 1880 the country had a frontier of settlement, but at present the unsettled area has been so broken into by isolated bodies of settlement that there can hardly be said to be a frontier line. In the discussion of its extent and its westward movement it cannot, therefore, any longer have a place in the census reports.[1]

The relative rapidity and general direction of the movement of population westward between 1790 and 1890 is shown in Figure 2–1, which traces changes in the center of population. In 1790, the center of population was at a point about 23 miles east of Baltimore; by 1890

[1] U. S. Census Office, *Report on the Population of the United States at the Eleventh Census:* 1890, Part 1 (Washington, D.C.: U. S. Government Printing Office), 1895, p. xxxiv. The census defined a frontier line as an area with a population of at least two but not more than six persons per square mile.

it had moved westward to a point 20 miles east of Columbus, Indiana—a distance of over 500 miles.

By 1890 not only was the population distributed over the continent, but also a comparatively high proportion was living in urban places. In 1790, of a total population of 3,930,000; 95 percent lived in rural areas. There were only five cities with a population of over 10,000, all located along the Eastern seaboard, and only 19 cities with populations between 2,500 and 10,000. Throughout the 100-year period to 1890, the proportion of population living in rural areas—though a declining share of total population—was substantially higher than the proportion living in urban places; in 1890, over three fifths of the nation lived in rural areas. Nevertheless, during this period when the largest proportion of the population was engaged in agriculture, the rate of urban population growth in relation to the growth of total population was spectacular.

The figures in Table 2–2 show the average growth rates of total, rural, and urban population by decades from 1800 to 1890. The growth of rural population kept pace with the growth of total population until about 1860—both increased by about a third every decade—and again between 1870 and 1880 (26 and 31 percent). Urban population, on the other hand, increased at a substantially higher rate than total population in every decade except one (1810–1820). The high rate of urban growth is partly a function of its relatively small share of total population; nevertheless, urban population growth gained substantially after 1840. Of the increase in total population between 1800 and 1840, only 13 percent was in urban population, while of the total increase between 1840 and 1890, 44 percent was in urban population, only 12 percentage points below the rural share. (See Table 2–2.)

This higher urban population by 1890 was living in cities in all parts of the nation. Town building was almost as much a principal activity of the 19th century in the United States as pioneer farming. In 1850 there were 62 cities with populations of over 10,000; by 1890 this number had increased to 354.[2] By 1890, with a few exceptions, nearly every major present-day city of the United States had been established.[3] A network of cities overlaid the continent from coast to coast and from the Gulf of Mexico to the Canadian border.

Both rural and urban development in the continental interior was hastened by improvements in transportation and in agricultural technology, a land policy that encouraged expansion, and markets opened

[2] U. S. Bureau of the Census. *Historical Statistics of the United States, Colonial Times to 1970*, Bicentennial edition, Part 2. (Washington, D.C.: U. S. Government Printing Office), 1975, A 43–56, p. 11.

[3] C. N. Glaab and A. T. Brown, *A History of Urban America*. (New York: Macmillan), 1967, p. 109.

TABLE 2–2. Population of the United States, by Place of Residence, 1800–1890

Year	(in Thousands)			Percent of Total		Percent Increase in Population, 10-year Period			Increase in Total Population in 10-year Period	
	Total	Rural	Urban	Rural	Urban	Total	Rural	Urban	Percent Rural	Percent Urban
1800	5,308	4,986	322	94	6	—	—	—	—	—
1810	7,239	6,714	525	93	7	36	34	52	90	10
1820	9,638	8,945	693	93	7	33	33	32	93	7
1830	12,866	11,739	1,127	91	9	33	31	63	87	13
1840	17,069	15,224	1,845	89	11	33	31	64	83	17
1850	23,192	19,648	3,544	85	15	36	30	94	72	28
1860	31,444	25,227	6,217	80	20	36	28	77	68	32
1870	38,558	28,656	9,902	74	26	22	10	43	48	52
1880	50,156	36,026	14,130	72	28	31	26	42	63	37
1890	62,947	40,841	22,106	65	35	26	13	56	38	62
1800–1840						222	193	473	87	13
1840–1890						268	168	1,098	56	44

SOURCE: U. S. Bureau of the Census, *Historical Statistics of the United States, Colonial Times to 1970,* Bicentennial edition, part 1. (Washington, D.C.: U. S. Government Printing Office), 1975, A 57–72, p. 12.

47

by increased urbanization and industrialization in Europe and the United States.

Federal Land Policy

Among the problems facing the new federal government in 1785 was the establishment of policies that would encourage development of the frontier, protect the pioneers as much as possible from known and unknown dangers in the wilderness, and give them the same protection by law that citizens who remained in the East enjoyed.[4] This last protection was provided by the Ordinance of 1787, which set up the method by which territories would be governed and the conditions for statehood.

The new federal government, weak and in need of money, decided to use the public domain as a source of revenue rather than to disperse it to prospective settlers on easy terms. This viewpoint determined land policy until the Homestead Act of 1862. The policy called for a rectangular survey of lands and division into townships six miles square. Each township was to consist of 36 sections of 640 acres; the minimum unit of sale was one section, which the purchaser could subdivide. Land was to be sold at auction at land offices in each state or territory at a certain minimum price ($1 an acre in 1785). Four sections in each township were reserved by the federal government and one section set aside to maintain schools. No settlements were to be made until the land had been surveyed, and no surveys were to be made until title to the land had been obtained from the Indians. The policy of surveying before selling assured a clear title to the land purchasers.[5] The principal drawback of the land policy to the pioneer farmer was that he did not need and could not afford to buy such a large tract of land. This drawback remained until 1820, when the minimum unit of sale was reduced to 80 acres and the price (which had been raised to $2 an acre in 1796) to $1.25 an acre.

Federal Indian Policy

As Billington has pointed out, no successful policy of dealing with the Indians was ever devised.[6] Conflicts and wars between whites and

4 R. A. Billington, *Westward Expansion: A History of the American Frontier*, 2nd ed. (with collaboration of J. B. Hedges). (New York: Macmillan) 1960, p. 217.

5 S. E. Morison and H. S. Commager, *The Growth of the American Republic*, Vol. 1, 3rd ed. (New York: Oxford University Press), 1942, pp. 261–262. The feedral land policy was based largely on the New England colonial land distribution system.

6 See Billington, *op. cit.*, for detailed discussions and evaluations of the Indian policy at each stage of settlement.

Indians accompanied the march of pioneers across the western frontiers. The general policy was to obtain concessions of land by treaties in exchange for gifts and annuities, then to move the tribes to reservations on land that—at the time—seemed safely remote from settlement. By 1840, nearly all eastern tribes had been moved to reservations set up on lands beyond the Missouri river or to Arkansas, except those allowed to remain on a few reservations in the East.[7] Land opened by treaties with the Indians was relatively quickly filled. In the 1850's, as white settlers moved across the Mississippi, the policy of one large reservation was abandoned, and smaller reservations were set up. In 1871, the government began treating the Indians as dependents rather than as sovereign nations; the Indians were considered wards of the government and were to be trained in agricultural practices and for citizenship. In the 1880's the first appropriation for Indian schools was made, and annual appropriations were made thereafter. In 1887, the Dawes Severalty Act gave authority to the President to divide the reservation lands and grant individual farms to each Indian family or individual; each of those who received a land grant was to be made a citizen of the United States. The remaining reservation lands were to be sold by the government and the profits put into a trust for Indian education.

The Indian policy was unsuccessful for several reasons. Enforcement was lax and the act was not consistently applied to protect the Indians. Across the entire West, squatters moved onto land occupied by the Indians in advance of government treaties and surveys. One of the basic premises of the policy was erroneous—that all Indian tribes would be able to live together peacefully. The tribes from the East were cultivators of the soil and found it difficult to adapt to the hunting culture of the West. In addition, the western tribes looked upon them as intruders. According to Billington, the final outcome—that is, the movement of the Indians to the reservations—was decided less by policy or war than by the destruction of the Indian's food supply, as, for example, the killing off of the buffalo on the plains.[8]

West of the Mississippi, the living conditions of the Indians were much more variable than conditions of those east of the Mississippi, chiefly because of variations in the source of food. As in the East, however, personal possessions were few and land was held in common. In the hunting regions of the Great Plains, the Indians lived in tepees made of buffalo hides, which could be folded quickly, loaded on carrying frames made from the tepee poles, the entire village moved behind fast ponies (horses were introduced by the Spanish).[9] Other tribes in

[7] C. W. Wright, *Economic History of the United States*, 2nd ed. (New York: McGraw-Hill), 1949, pp. 249–250.
[8] See Billington, *op. cit.*, p. 669.
[9] *Ibid.*, p. 420.

the West were both hunters and cultivators and lived in tepees and mud huts or brush shelters. Along the Pacific Coast in Oregon and Washington, better living conditions due to the existence of fishing grounds permitted better housing—plank houses situated in fairly permanent villages. The most advanced Indian culture was found in the mesa regions of Arizona and New Mexico; these tribes used dry-farming methods and irrigation.[10] They lived some distance from the farming fields in communal houses of adobe brick or dressed stone on inaccessible mesas or in cave-like cracks in the cliffs. Their dwellings—each family had two rooms—could be entered only by ladder to the second floor; the only entrance to the first floor was through an opening in the wooden ceiling.[11]

Western Expansion in the South

Figure 2–1 shows that as the center of population moved westward between 1800 and 1830 it also dipped southward. To a large extent, this southward trend was the result of the federal land policy, which held back the western movement of pioneers from the North, and of an improvement in agricultural technology, the invention of the cotton gin in 1793. With this machine, "one man will clean ten times as much cotton as he can in any other ways . . . and one man and a horse will do more than fifty men with the old machines."[12] The cotton gin made it economically feasible to grow cotton whenever climate permitted; and the demand for cotton was high, especially in England, where factories to produce cotton cloth were operating.[13]

Pioneers, nearly all of them from the Tidewater and upland South, journeyed inland over the back country roads to the Gulf Plains and lower Mississippi River Valley until, by 1840,[14] practically all the land suited by climate for cotton-growing was filled. Before moving their families planters usually went into the territory to select the land, which might be purchased from the state or federal government, a speculator, or a squatter who had already settled on it, and who was usually willing to sell out and repeat the process farther inland. The planter frequently

[10] Wright, *op. cit.*, pp. 23–24.

[11] Billington, *op. cit.*, pp. 417–418. In Alaska, the native population used sod or a combination of sod and timber to build their houses.

[12] Letter from Eli Whitney, Sept. 11, 1873, to his father. In: *Annals of America*, Vol. 3. (Chicago: Encyclopaedia Britannica) p. 552.

[13] Billington, *op. cit.*, pp. 311–312.

[14] Billington, *op. cit.*, p. 325. The increase in population in the South was markedly less than in the North Central region later, the principal reason being, of course, the difference in kinds of farms—large plantations as against the large number of relatively small farms farther north.

sent an overseer and slaves to clear the land, plant crops, and build cabins, and then brought the family to the new house.[15]

The most typical house of the planter was a double log cabin with perhaps a lean-to behind one or both cabins, an attic above, and a roofed-over open hall between the cabins. This type of log house, which became known as the dogtrot house, usually was about 40 feet wide and was built in two separate units—logs 40 feet long were difficult to find and to handle. The "trot" had a floor and might be furnished. It was used as a hall, and in the summer, might be used as a kitchen. The two units were typically of equal size and placed symmetrically in relation to each other. The interior plan was similar to that of the central-hall Georgian dwelling of the Tidewater South, on which it was modeled.[16]

This type of log cabin was built throughout the cotton-growing region and also in the Tennessee Valley and in Kentucky. A variant style was two cabins built close together with a chimney between and two fireplaces, but no breezeway.[17]

Planters with fewer resources were more likely to build a one-room log cabin, with the kitchen in a shed on the rear, or a one-story, two-room log cabin without the open hall. Usually these cabins were surrounded by a semicircle of outbuildings.[18]

Slave quarters on the plantations in the western as in the eastern South were separate from the main house, and were built at the most convenient distance from the main house. Throughout the South,

The cabins occupied by the slaves ranged from simple log structures on the small farms, having one room twelve feet square "with no windows—no opening at all except the doorway, with a chimney of sticks and mud," to those described on a large James River, Virginia, farm where the slaves lived in log cabins twenty by thirty feet, with lofts and shingled roofs, "each divided in the middle and having a brick chimney outside the wall at each end (and) intended to be occupied by two families." On the larger, more prosperous farms, . . . the white overseer . . . generally lived in the slave quarters, usually occupying a whitewashed log cabin, larger and better built than those occupied by the black slaves he supervised.[19]

[15] Everett Dick, *The Dixie Frontier: A Social History of the Southern Frontier From the First Transmontane Beginnings to the Civil War.* (New York: Knopf), 1948, pp. 55–56.

[16] Henry Glassie, *Pattern in the Material Folk Culture of the Eastern United States.* (Philadelphia: University of Pennsylvania Press), 1969, p. 96.

[17] C. A. Weslager, *The Log Cabin in America: From Pioneer Days to the Present.* (New Brunswick, N.J.: Rutgers University Press), 1969, p. 72.

[18] Glassie, *op. cit.*, p. 102.

[19] Weslager, *op. cit.*, p. 251.

Living conditions along the borders of the cotton-growing regions repeated early colonial times. Chimneys were likely to be made of wood and clay and were as hazardous as those at Plymouth or Jamestown. Light was provided by the fireplace, pine knots, or homemade lamps. One example is the cob lamp: a wick 15 to 20 feet long was dipped in rosin and beeswax and wound around a corncob from which the pith had been removed and the wick drawn through. A few families had some pewter ware, but most tableware was a set of hand-hewn wooden trenchers of different sizes. Beds were built into a corner of the cabin and covered at first with bear or buffalo skins and homemade ticks. The buffalo, in fact, could provide almost everything needed in the way of food, clothing, and fuel. Hand-hewn wooden troughs at first were set under the eaves to catch rainwater for the household washing, or washing might be done at the nearest stream, where a big iron kettle was kept for this purpose.[20]

The double log cabin tended to be used for several years—since the planters invested profits in more land and more slaves. In the 1850's, reports from visitors to the rural areas of Mississippi, Alabama, Kentucky, Georgia, the Carolinas, and Virginia indicated that even well-to-do planters lived in homes of rough, unhewn logs, with square holes covered by shutters for windows.[21] The lack of chinking between the logs attracted attention; this, according to Weslager, was most probably an adaptation to the heat of summer, since mud and straw were plentiful.[22] Other log cabins might be added to the structure and in time the original two-room house might be expanded into one with four to eight rooms. A spacious veranda might be added across the front, the whole structure covered with weatherboards (after sawmills were established), painted, and turned into the white mansion house.[23]

Some wealthy plantation owners, however, built or remodeled their homes in the building styles that became popular after the Revolution. The first of these was the Federal style, which flourished in the settled areas until about 1820. This style had the same balanced proportions and plan of the Georgian style, but the decorative details were Roman, based on then-current archaeological research, and applied in more delicate designs.[24] It was considered by Thomas Jefferson and many others to be the ideal architectural expression of American republican ideals. Wealthy northern merchants built their homes in this style, in inland as well as in seaport cities (see Figure 2–2). The changes in

20 Dick, *Dixie Frontier*, *op. cit.*, pp. 299–300.

21 Dick, *Dixie Frontier*, *op. cit.*, p. 80.

22 Weslager, *op. cit.*, p. 250.

23 Dick, *Dixie Frontier*, *op. cit.*, p. 81.

24 Ernest Pickering, *The Homes of America*. (New York: Thomas Y. Crowell), 1951, pp. 182–85.

FIGURE 2–2. The Octagon House in Washington, D.C., built in 1799 as the town house of Col. John Tayloe. Its polygonal floor plan and circular and oval rooms illustrate the freedom of expression possible in Federal design. [Photographer: Jack E. Boucher for the Historic American Buildings Survey.]

the interior design continued the trend set by the earlier Georgian toward greater flexibility, specialization, and privacy, although modified somewhat to conform to the classical exterior:

New standards of convenience, comfort, and privacy were introduced, features that had rarely been considered in colonial times. The "modern" house of the Federal period was planned with dressing rooms, butler's pantries, closets, and other areas of specialized purpose—even, as at Monticello, with indoor privies. Rooms that had traditionally been rectangular assumed elliptical and octagonal shapes, the better or more agreeably to serve their separate functions as dining rooms, salons, or whatever. The main staircase that in earlier days had almost universally claimed a prominent place in the entrance hallway, was moved to the side to discourage the casual caller from visiting the upper rooms, thus assuring greater privacy. With a similar objective in mind, a second staircase for service gradually became customary.[25]

[25] M. B. Davidson, *The American Heritage History of Notable American Houses.* (New York: American Heritage Publishing Co.), 1971, p. 121.

The great period of plantation building was later, however, from 1845 to 1860, after the Greek Revival style had replaced the Federal. The principal differences between this style and the earlier Georgian and Federal styles were the simpler decorative details and the use of Greek instead of Roman models for decoration. The Greek Revival style as expressed in the southern mansions had as its most typical feature the wide two-story porch with Greek columns. Sometimes the porch was carried around the sides as well as across the front. Houses in the Greek Revival style were built in a variety of shapes and, particularly in Louisiana, Greek details were combined with earlier regional decorations. The beauty and spaciousness of the plantation houses were enhanced by their surroundings; often they were situated on an elevation, and nearly all of them were set off by landscaped grounds and flower gardens.[26]

The interiors frequently had the central hall plan, with drawing, reception, and other rooms opening from the hall. The interior plan, decorations, and furnishings all expressed the same motif. Rooms, frequently monumental in size, were interconnected so that their entire space could be combined. Doorways, fireplaces, and mantels were the focal points of decoration. The elaborate designs and carvings on furniture gave way to the straight lines of Greek order.[27]

The wealthy cotton growers might own more than one plantation, have winter homes in Montgomery, Mobile, or Natchez, and spend their summers at fashionable watering places.[28] In all these places, housing in the Greek Revival style was built; city homes were likely to be more compact versions of the plantation house. Some had different details according to the city; in New Orleans, for example, iron balconies were retained and Greek columns added.[29]

The most typical house for the middle-class prosperous farmers in the southern states was the full classic Georgian style, one-and-a-half or two stories, with two rooms on each side of a broad central hall (not left open). Typically, there was a pair of internal brick chimneys with small shallow fireplaces for each room, or more rarely, two external chimneys at each end of the house. The exteriors usually were symmetrical, not decorated, and had a gable or hip roof. Interior walls were whitewashed and the woodwork usually was dark.[30]

As the plantation system expanded and the size of plantations increased, many owners with small holdings were forced out. Some of

26 See Pickering, *op. cit.*, p. 204.
27 *Ibid.*, p. 124.
28 Billington, *op. cit.*, p. 326.
29 Pickering, *op. cit.*, p. 210.
30 Glassie, *op. cit.*, pp. 109, 112.

these families, as well as others from the South, went northward up the waterways to the National Road (begun by the federal government in 1811), into southern Indiana and Illinois. Well-established before the influx of Northerners, they left some fairly permanent southern influence on the region.[31] Some of their later houses, for instance, had verandas with two-story columns and spacious rooms opening from a long central hall and were situated in a complex of outbuildings—kitchen, slave quarters, barns, and stables.

Western Expansion in the North

After 1820, large numbers of pioneers from New England and the Middle Atlantic states moved into the Mississippi Valley regions; the movement was especially rapid after 1830. The Erie Canal opened in 1825 and not only made it easier to reach the frontier but also broadened the markets for farm products. Other canals were built, the most successful being those that improved navigation on inland and coastal waterways. Steamboats were replacing flatboats for navigation on the Mississippi by the 1820's; goods could now be transported upstream as well as downstream, thus lowering the cost of imports and making possible a higher profit from the sale of farm products. Improvements in steamboat navigation reduced the length of the journey from Louisville, Kentucky, to New Orleans from 36 days in the 1820's to 12 days by the 1850's. After about 1820, western farmers could ship goods to market down the Ohio and Mississippi Rivers or across the northern water routes to markets in the East and Europe.[32]

In 1830, the federal government modified its land policy with the Preemption Act. Intended to help farmers with little cash to acquire land, the act provided that a squatter who had improved and built a dwelling on a site would have the right to buy the tract at the minimum price before the public auction. Another act in 1841 made this feature an established part of federal land policy until its repeal in 1891. Prior to this, farmers (or professional squatters) who marked out and improved sites before the government was ready to sell the land were liable to lose these holdings to a higher bidder at the land sale. The Graduation Act of 1854 provided that the price of land remaining unsold for 10 years after being offered for sale would be reduced in price to 12½ cents an acre and sold in units of 320 acres. Less valuable plots of land could now be purchased by pioneer farmers at a lower

---

[31] *Ibid.*, pp. 156–157. See also Billington, *op. cit.*, pp. 308–309.

[32] Wright, *op. cit.*, p. 278. Flatboats could not carry goods upstream; before steamboats were in operation, most imports into the West came from the East.

price and the government could dispose of scattered unsold sections of land.[33]

Usually, a group of migrating families traveled together, or joined other families along the way. The migration westward was so large that long lines of covered wagons went over the local and state roads in an almost continuous procession. Most of the pioneer families settled on farms along the roads built during the period, or in the river valleys. From there, they spread inland.

The log cabin was typically the first shelter. It could be built in less than a week, if several men worked on it. One man working alone could build a small cabin in a week or two, but usually log cabins were built at "house raisings," with the work carefully divided so that the various materials were ready as needed. One great advantage was that the log cabin could be built without nails, which were still expensive as well as heavy to transport in crowded wagons.

The first four logs were laid in place horizontally flat on the earth, or if the builder intended to install flooring, he placed the four foundation logs on a base of fieldstones or sections of logs set vertically in the earth at each of the four corners. Then he laid other logs across these members to serve as joists, each notched into place. The sidewalls were heightened by laying successive logs one upon the other to a height of seven or eight feet, or sometimes higher. Each log was held in place by its own weight, reinforced by the weight of the log above and supported by the log below. In actuality, the structural technique, although appearing primitive today, was a unique development representing a notable advance in human technology.[34]

Chimneys most commonly were made of mud and sticks, attached to an end wall, to be replaced later by chimneys of brick or stone.

Interiors might be lined for insulation with animal skins—usually buffalo. The kitchen, bedroom, and pantry were partitioned with quilts and blankets. If a loft had been built in the cabin for children's sleeping quarters, as often was done, that, too, might be divided into bedrooms by means of quilts and blankets. After sawmills began operating, more cabins had floors—usually rough boards until worn smooth; these were scrubbed with wood ashes to keep the original whiteness.[35]

The interior furnishings of the frontier log cabin were simple and practical, and the family's most prized possessions were the articles or utensils brought

33 *Ibid.*, pp. 251–252. Before the Preemption Act, a common practice was to form a claims association, the purpose of which was to keep outsiders from bidding on plots being held by members of the association.

34 Weslager, *op. cit.*, pp. 13–14, 19.

35 Everett Dick, *The Sod-House Frontier, 1854–1890: A Social History of the Northern Plains from the Creation of Kansas and Nebraska to the admission of the Dakotas.* (New York: Appleton-Century-Crofts), 1938, pp. 77–78.

from the East—dishes, wood or pewter spoons and porringers, a clock, spinning wheel, candlesticks, wooden wash tub, a Bible, and the tinder box with its flint and steel. . . . The unpainted benches, stools, tables, and low beds were made of wood, their quality depending on the proficiency of the builder. If there were no candles the cabin was lighted by the knots of the fat pitch pine, sometimes called "candlewood," if it was available, but, if not, the open fireplace provided the only illumination.[36]

The influx of population into these northern regions (which extended into the humid areas across the Mississippi) was so large and the areas so well linked with markets that most of these regions moved out of the frontier stage quickly.[37] By 1840, agriculture in the East was becoming specialized; farmers were raising garden produce, and sheep or cattle to supply nearby urban markets. After the opening of the Erie Canal, agricultural specialization began to spread into the Middle West.[38]

For those who wanted to replace their log cabins with frame houses, pattern books were available from American as well as European sources, and housing styles were communicated through farm journals and other publications almost as quickly to farmers and local carpenter-builders in the West as in the East. The Greek Revival house was as enthusiastically welcomed throughout the newly settled areas of the North as in the plantation areas of the South. One reason for the style's popularity was the ease with which it could be adapted to American houses in town or country. Existing houses could be updated by "the simple addition of a Greek portico"[39] or a two-story front porch supported by columns.

Greek Revival houses in the North were not built on the elaborate scale of the Southern mansions. Some homogeneity was made possible by the widespread use of the pattern books, but, as with earlier styles, builders and clients varied in the extent to which they followed the formal plan number. For new and some old houses, the "temple" house was one popular style. In this type, the narrow side faced the street or road, and the roof ridge projected forward to form the apex of a triangular pediment which was supported by a row of columns across the front of the house.[40] This temple farmhouse became the predominant type throughout the North and out into the Great Lakes area, where it continued to be built long after the Greek Revival had run its course. Midwest and Northeast temple houses were similar: one- or two-story main sections and one or two wings, although the

[36] Weslager, *op. cit.*, p. 19.
[37] Billington, *op. cit.*, p. 304.
[38] Wright, *op. cit.*, pp. 291–298.
[39] Davidson, *op. cit.*, p. 179.
[40] Pickering, *op. cit.*, p. 200.

two-story, single-wing house with the main door in the wing was more prevalent in the western areas.[41]

The Cape Cod cottage, however, continued to be built from New England through central New York and south around the Great Lakes during and after the Greek Revival. The roof pitch was shallower than in the original, and the loft was higher so that small rectangular windows could be placed under the eaves: "Its facade was classically graced, but its traditional floor plan . . . has been left almost intact."[42]

The Greek Revival style emphasized an austere simplicity. Greek Revival houses, North and South, country and city, were painted white and stood out against the landscape. In fact the "templed hills" in the song "America" by Samuel F. Smith (first published in 1832) are said to refer to the numerous templed residences in the American countryside. Within a few years, these white temples were being criticized, and the architect William Downing was recommending that houses be painted in "natural" colors—the colors of stone or grass— that would blend the house with the landscape.[43]

Houses in the Greek Revival style were built in both eastern and western cities, with porticoed entrances or a row of columns across the front, and simple Greek moldings around windows and doors. Its most formal expression was in the city or country homes of the wealthy. In these houses, as on the southern plantations, interior treatment matched the exterior decorations. In less formal houses, the parlor, dining room, and master bedroom typically were on the first floor; the kitchen might be there also or in an ell at the back, or in the basement.

In the frontier areas, log cabins continued to be used by new immigrants and, very often, by the families already established in the areas who possibly preferred the cabins' advantages:

Some families who prospered were able to build houses of frame or stone, often butting the larger house against the original cabin and using it as a kitchen. In areas where planks and clapboards continued to be scarce some families erected new one and one-half or two-story houses of hewn logs, intended as permanent dwellings, and they had advantages over frame houses. They were less flammable, warmer in winter, drier in rainy seasons, needed no paint, and did not fall into disrepair as readily. . . .[44]

The log cabin might also be boarded over and thus have the appearance of the frame house while retaining the advantages of the log cabin.

Log cabins provided a first home for many of the immigrants who came to the Midwest directly from Europe during this period, particu-

41 Glassie, *op. cit.*, p. 132.
42 *Ibid.*, p. 129.
43 Davidson, *op. cit.*, pp. 174, 175.
44 Weslager, *op. cit.*, p. 25.

larly from Germany and Scandinavia. The German settlers some-times replaced their first homes with permanent houses built in the European style: half-timbered, with a filling of whitewashed plaster between the uprights, German double doors at the entrance, steep roofs, heavy walls, and, at first, thatched roofs that were soon replaced by tiles or shingles. These variations, however, produced only "fasci-nating pockets," not an enduring regional style.[45]

Hawaii was one of the regions in which Americans settled in the 1820's. The missionaries, principally from New England, who landed in Hawaii in 1820 after their voyage in sailing ships around Cape Horn, lived at first in steep-roofed huts made of grass, similar to those of the Hawaiians. The native huts typically had one corner of the room raised one or more feet above the ground and covered with mats for sleeping. Cooking was carried on over an open fire in a cavity in the center of the interior.[46] Frame houses were built soon; the oldest remaining frame house in the islands was erected in 1821, using timbers cut and fitted in Boston. Although some lumber was imported from the United States, native timber (usually koa), stone, adobe, and coral were the typical materials used for house building in Hawaii. Early in the 19th century, American whalers began to winter their fleets in the islands; traders and explorers from both Europe and the United States also visited Hawaii. Traders and merchants frequently lived in somewhat more elaborate houses than those of the missionaries—some of the earlier houses had colonial Georgian features, while later ones frequently had some char-acteristics of later 19th century styles. The only royal palace in the United States is in Honolulu. Constructed in 1879, the palace was used by the Hawaiian royal family until the monarchy was overthrown in 1893, then later as a government house after the islands were annexed by the United States in 1898.[47]

By mid-19th century, middle-class homes in the North and Midwest sections of the continental United States had similar characteristics. They were usually one-and-a-half or two-and-a-half stories, had five or six rooms, consisting of a parlor or sitting room, or both, a kitchen, and three or more bedrooms. Either the kitchen or the sitting room was used as a dining room. Interiors of the houses most frequently were white-washed, but some were painted, and others had wallpaper.[48]

[45] Glassie, *op. cit.*, pp. 201, 204.

[46] C. A. Lyman, *Around the Horn to the Sandwich Islands and California, 1845–1850.* Edited by F. J. Taggart. (New Haven, Conn.: Yale University Press), 1925, p. 78.

[47] See *Historic Houses of America* (Edited by Beverley DaCosta.) (New York: American Heritage Publishing Co.), 1971, p. 64.

[48] Glenn H. Beyer, *Housing and Society.* (New York: Macmillan), 1965, p. 28.

Houses West of the Mississippi

By the 1850's, pioneers had moved into the prairie regions west of the Mississippi river to the border of the Great Plains. Earlier groups had skirted the edges of the Great Plains region, when they crossed the continent over the Oregon Trail into the fertile valleys of the Pacific coast. The Mormons, who broke their own trail along the Platte River, had been well established in the Salt Lake region since the 1840's. By the 1880's, cattle raising was a principal productive activity on the grasslands of the Plains. Where there were trees most of the ranchers at first lived in log cabins, then later might build a ranch house.[49] These houses usually began as small frame dwellings of one or two rooms without a basement. Rooms were built onto the existing room as needed; the final ranch house consisted of a line of large rooms, each open to the outside. Sometimes additions were made to the original log cabin; at other times, farmhouses similar to those in the Midwest were built. Wealthy ranchers, of course, might build their ranch houses in a current or favorite building style.

The variety of climates and unfamiliar soil conditions of the Plains, however, held most of the pioneer farmers back from this part of the continent until the 1870's, when machines for farming were available, railroads had been built, and a new land policy was in effect. On the Plains, there was no wood for houses, no trees for shelter, and only sparse rainfall. New farming methods were needed to cultivate the semi-arid regions, since irrigation was feasible only near mountain streams; machines were necessary to cultivate a tract large enough to offset a low yield per acre and to dig wells several hundred feet deep to reach ground water. By the 1870's, well-drilling machinery, wire fencing, and farm machines were available, as well as a technique for dry farming.[50]

Nevertheless, the region would not attract pioneers unless it was linked with markets. Several states had invested in developing railroad transportation, but the heavy burden of state debt for unfinished transportation projects after 1837 led to a demand, particularly in the West, for federal aid to build railroads. Federal land grants for this purpose began in the 1850's and continued until 1872. Typically, each railroad company was given a strip of land 100 feet wide for the roadway, and the railroads received six square miles of land for each mile of track. The alternate sections remained with the government and were to be sold at not less than $2.50 an acre, or double the then-minimum price.[51] The

49 Billington, *op. cit.*, p. 682.

50 See Billington, *op. cit.*, Chapter 34. Wire fences which could be put up much more quickly than wooden fences, such as split rail, were needed to keep cattle out of cultivated fields.

51 Wright, *op. cit.*, p. 254.

railroads also received land from local governments and individuals. In 1869, the first transcontinental railroad line was completed, and by 1883 three more transcontinental lines were in operation.

Another important factor in opening the regions to settlement was a reversal of the federal government's land policy. Since the 1820's, the demand for free land or liberal land laws had been becoming stronger. Although this demand was strongest in the West, it also received intensive support from various groups in the eastern cities. The National Reform Association, an agrarian organization, in the 1840's urged urban workers to "Vote Yourself a Farm" and thus become homeowners, gain respect from others, end poverty, and be freed from an "aristocracy of arrogance."[52] The Homestead Act of 1862 was a commitment by the federal government to hasten the settlement of the continent. However, the Homestead Act was not the answer to the needs of either urban workers or pioneer farmers. Urban unskilled laborers unfamiliar with farming were not attracted in large numbers to the land because they lacked the money to move or to buy the expensive equipment required. So far as the farmers were concerned, many of them were compelled to purchase land from speculators or to settle on isolated farms far from transportation. The unit (160 acres) that could be purchased from the government was either too large or too small for the kind of cultivation suited to the region. In the Mississippi Valley, 80 acres was the typical size of a farm, but in parts of the Great Plains 360 acres or more were required for extensive farming, 2,000 acres or more for ranching, or much less—40 to 60 acres—for an irrigated farm.[53] Other deficiencies in the law, coupled with lax administration, made it possible for speculators to acquire much of the best lands. Under the Homestead Act:

. . . citizens or intended citizens could obtain a tract of 160 acres for a nominal fee after they had improved or resided on it for five years. A commutation clause permitted the exercise of preemption rights after six months residence.[54]

For example, under the commutation clause, by giving proof of residence, after only six months individuals could preempt a 160-acre tract, then resell it at a higher price per acre. Frequently, this claim might be enlarged by purchasing similar claims preempted by squatters or others. The railroad land grants also helped speculators and frequently prevented the purchase of farms near transportation lines.

[52] John R. Commons, et al., (eds.), *A Documentary History of American Industrial Society.* (Cleveland, Ohio: A. H. Clark Co., 1910. Reprinted in *The Annals of America*, Vol. 7, (Chicago: Encyclopaedia Britannica), pp. 338–339.
[53] Wright, *op. cit.*, p. 253.
[54] Billington, *op. cit.*, p. 698.

Usually the whole strip was withdrawn from settlement for several years while the road selected its right-of-way and decided which alternate sections to keep. Frequently even larger tracts were withheld; if lands within the grant were already occupied, the railroad could choose its acreage from nearby territory and the Land Office sometimes set aside strips 60 to 120 miles wide in which corporation officials could make their choice. Until they decided homesteaders were forced to stake their claims from thirty to sixty miles from transportation. Even when that was not done, alternate sections retained by the government near railroads were either sold at $2.50 an acre or limited to homesteads of eighty acres.[55]

Subsequent land acts or amendments to the Homestead Act prior to 1900 were equally ineffectual in helping the pioneer farmer to acquire good land. The Mineral Land Act of 1866, the Timber Culture Act of 1873, the Desert Land Act of 1877, and the Timber and Stone Act of 1878 merely made it possible for private interests to acquire large amounts of the public domain at relatively small cost. Wright suggests that the policy of making public land at first difficult then later fairly easy to obtain should have been reversed:

In the early period when the difficulties and dangers of developing the frontier were great, there was more reason for making access to the land easy. But, as these obstacles decreased and the nation grew in strength while its natural resources diminished, there was need for greater caution in disposing of the public domain. As usual, the country was slow to awake to the changing conditions and legislation fell far behind the needs of the time.[56]

Wright also provides a succinct summary of the benefits and disadvantages that resulted from the federal land policy:

In a listing of the former, it can be said that it hastened the process of settling the country and developing its resources at a period when the nation was none too strong; it facilitated the financing of various undertakings of social importance; it helped to improve the condition of the poorer classes and to attract immigrants; it served to promote a spirit of individualism and a more democratic society.

As disadvantages . . . it may be claimed that it tended to promote what was likely in the long run to prove a wasteful use of natural resources; it scattered the population . . . ; by trying to hasten development it accentuated the business cycles that periodically disturbed the country; and, because of lax-

55 *Ibid.*, pp. 701–702.
56 Wright, *op. cit.*, p. 470. It is interesting to note that the Homestead Act of 1862 remained in effect until the Bicentennial Year, 1976. On October 21, Congress officially closed the West to settlement when it repealed the homesteading provisions of the Act, except as they applied to Alaska, for which the date of repeal will be ten years later. (P.L. 94–579, Laws of the 94th Cong., 2d Sess., Title VII, Sec. 702.)

ness in the formulation and administration of the laws, it often promoted speculation and made possible private gain without any resulting public benefit, though this was not inherent in the general policy. Probably the strengthening of the youthful nation and the promotion of democratic conditions may be considered as outweighing the losses, some of which fell on later generations who could better afford them.[57]

Whatever its failings, the Homestead Act, along with the railroads and improved farm machinery, opened the Great Plains to settlement. According to Billington, the migration into these regions was the "greatest movement of peoples in the history of the United States. Millions of farmers surged westward between 1870 and 1890" into Kansas, Nebraska, the Dakotas, Wyoming, Montana, and Oklahoma.

A larger domain was settled in the last three decades of the century than in all America's past: 407,000,000 acres were occupied and 189,000,000 improved between 1607 and 1870; 430,000,000 acres peopled and 225,000,000 placed under cultivation between 1870 and 1890.[58]

The markets for agricultural products were expanding—cities farther east were growing, England could absorb surpluses, and science and industry were opening new markets. The pioneers who moved into the area were, for the most part, skilled farmers from the Mississippi Valley states (which were becoming overcrowded) and from Europe, mainly from Germany and the Scandinavian countries. Both groups were attracted by "the most effective advertising campaign ever to influence world migrations." Steamship companies, looking for fares, advertised the region in Europe and Western states and railroad lines seeking settlers sent out brochures, maintained immigration bureaus, and set up departments to sell land.[59]

In the regions where wood was available, log cabins were the first homes; in the southwestern areas, adobe and stone dwellings were built as well. Throughout most of the prairies, however, sod was the only material for shelter and fuel. The typical first home on the prairies was the dugout or sod house. Families could stay in the covered wagon or perhaps in a nearby town until a house was built, or in some areas in a railroad passenger car run onto a siding. In some places, the railroad companies built long frame one-room structures for immigrants to live in while waiting for the house to be finished.[60]

The dugout was typically one room excavated in a hillside. Rails or posts were used for door frames and, possibly, windows. The front wall was covered with square-cut blocks of turf (or logs, if available). The

---

[57] *Ibid.*, pp. 254–255.
[58] Billington, *op. cit.*, p. 705.
[59] *Ibid.*, pp. 706–708.
[60] Dick, *Sod-House Frontier*, *op. cit.*, pp. 190–191.

roof sloped back onto the hill and was made of poles or logs covered over with brush, prairie grass, and dirt. (Cattle frequently strayed on top of the house at night.) Furnishings were kept to a minimum—a bed, stove, table, and boxes—and frequently were carried outside in the daytime in order to have room inside to carry on the household work.[61]

The sod house was harder to build than the dugout but lasted longer —an average of six or seven years. Some were small "but a rather pretentious sod house followed a common building plan of sixteen feet wide and twenty feet long."

The sod bricks were made by turning over furrows on about half an acre of ground where sod was thickest and strongest. Care was taken to make the furrows of even width and depth so that the walls of the cabin would rise with regularity and evenness.[62]

Roofs varied from the primitive kind made up of brush, grass, and sod, to a frame roof, for which tar paper was spread over sheeting boards and covered with sod. Doorways and windows were set in the walls and the sod bricks placed around them. The sod house had some serious deficiencies in light, ventilation, and weather resistance:

Few of the sod-covered houses really turned water. A heavy rain came, soaked into the dirt roof, and soon little rivulets of muddy water were running through the sleepers' hair. The sod-house dweller had to learn to migrate when it rained. If the rain came from the north, the north side of the house leaked, and it was necessary to move everything to the south side; if from the south, a move had to be made again. When the roof was saturated it dripped for three days after the sky was bright without.[63]

The sod house, nevertheless, was superior to almost every other kind of first home in one important respect: the sod bricks were fireproof. "There was no . . . danger of destruction by prairie fires."[64]

By the time these Western frontiers were being settled, frame houses could be built more easily, if the money was available. The first frame houses typically might be of rough timber cut at nearby sawmills,[65] but lumber for houses could be shipped in by railroad, as could ornamental trim and possibly other parts of the house—by the 1880's blinds, sashes, doors, and moldings were being made by wood-working machinery in shops.

The notable contribution to easier and speedier construction was a new method of building wooden house frames. Invented in 1833, this

---

61 *Ibid.*, pp. 111–112.
62 *Ibid.*, p. 113.
63 *Ibid.*, pp. 113, 114–115.
64 *Ibid.*, p. 115.
65 *Ibid.*, p. 78.

method of wood framing introduced a wholly new way of construction that was lighter than the heavy timber frame. Its lightness inspired the name "balloon frame"—a derisive prophecy that "a good wind would send such houses flying through the air like balloons."[66] The nail-making machine (introduced around 1777) and the power-driven saw made the use of balloon-frame construction feasible on a large scale. "Its distinguishing characteristic was the use of a large number of light, closely ranked studs and joists which, along with the horizontal sills and plates, were framed together at the edges of the floors and roofs." Construction of the house was reduced to a few basic techniques. Only moderate skill in carpentry "and a saw, hammer, and a bag of nails were needed to build a house or barn in little more than a week." Only a small crew of men were needed to build a whole town.[67]

A type of prefabricated house also could be ordered: the sectional house, which consisted of three sections cut in a size suited for shipment by railroad. For that matter, as the builders pointed out, the farmer could carry the three sections with him in a farm wagon. A sectional house required only two or three people to put up, none of whom needed to be a carpenter. Also, it was not liable to be blown over or damaged by high winds and "was better than a wooden building of ordinary construction." A model with decorative trim could be supplied—at a somewhat higher cost.[68]

The balloon frame, prefabricated parts, and precut decorations made it possible to build houses quickly according to any building plan—or none. No one style dominated new housing built after the Greek Revival era. A Gothic Revival had run concurrently with the other neoclassical styles (Federal and Greek Revival). This style, or styles—there were several—was another import from Europe and became popular around mid-19th century (see Figure 2–3). Its appeal in residential building was to romanticism through picturesque asymmetrical arrangements of towers, turrets, and other additions. Mumford stated:

It was no accident that caused romanticism and industrialism to appear at the same time. They were rather the two faces of the new civilization, one looking toward the past, and the other towards the future; one glorifying the new, the other clinging to the old; industrialism intent on increasing the physical means of subsistence, romanticism living in a sickly fashion on the hollow glamour of the past.[69]

[66] C. C. Calkins (ed.), *The Story of America*. (Pleasantville, N.Y.: The Reader's Digest Assoc.), 1975, p. 238.

[67] Carl F. Condit, *American Building Art: The Nineteenth Century*. (New York: Oxford University Press), 1960, pp. 22–23.

[68] "Prefabs for the Prairies." *Journal of the Society of Architectural Historians*, Vol. 11, No. 1, March 1952, pp. 28–30.

[69] Quoted in Davidson, *op. cit.*, p. 177.

FIGURE 2–3. The barn and carriage house at Springside, Poughkeepsie, New York. Built between 1850 and 1852, destroyed by fire August 1969. Designed by Andrew Jackson Downing. [Photographer: Rollie McKenna for the Historic American Buildings Survey.]

Another popular style was called the Tuscan Revival; houses in this style typically "featured low-pitched, projecting roofs, square towers, and occasional piazzas."[70] A later revival, in the 1880's, looked to the French Renaissance for inspiration. In the post-Civil War period, several styles might be combined in one house—this style is sometimes called "Victorian." Although these houses have been criticized, Davidson points out:

Yet, from the perspective of a century later, we can recognize in the undisciplined exuberance of the so-called Victorian mansion a restless energy that spoke for its times and that sought in all directions to reach some more promising end.[71]

A new type of roof, the mansard, "a roof with a double slope, the lower being longer and steeper than the upper" came into use after the Civil

70 *Ibid.*, p. 219.
71 *Ibid.*, p. 235.

FIGURE 2–4. Chateau-sur-Mer in Newport, Rhode Island illustrates mansard roofs with pavilions and towers. Built 1850–1852. [Photographer: Jack Boucher for the Historic American Buildings Survey.]

War. This roof type gave considerable additional space in attics and was used for every type of building, including some Cape Cod cottages (see Figure 2–4.)[72]

Clearly, the wide range of styles was ideally suited to the rampant individualism of the period. The new generation of wealthy as they built their new homes combined the various elements to suit their own preferences. Frequently these houses were lavishly decorated and the interiors and furnishings contributed to the display; one example is a cast-iron stove available in a Gothic design. Examples of such houses still remain in nearly every sizable city, town, or fashionable resort throughout the United States: solid, imposing, ornate, set in landscaped grounds and adorned with steep mansards, bays, dormers, and towers—all the accoutrements found on millionaires' mansions wherever they were built.[73]

[72] *Ibid.*, pp. 241, 242.
[73] See John Drury, *Historic Midwest Houses.* (Minneapolis: University of Minnesota Press), 1947, for descriptions of such houses in the Midwest.

The style most popular after about 1880, called the "Queen Anne" style (although it reflects English medieval tradition more than styles used during Queen Anne's reign from 1702 to 1714) was used throughout the country.[74] This style, like the Greek Revival, could easily be adopted by builders as well as architects; it was used for houses in the countryside as well as in the cities and for less pretentious as well as more pretentious homes. One adaptation of the style, called the "shingle" or "stick" style, expressed the simplicity and functionalism—on a larger scale—of the early colonial New England homes. Such houses provoked the comment that "the modern American house is built entirely from the inside out."[75]

Although this statement did not describe most of the houses built in the second half of the 19th century, better building technology and less interest in an imposing formal style were beginning to make possible more convenient and usable interiors.

Cities on the Frontier

Towns and cities along the frontier developed about as rapidly as land was opened for settlement. Some of the towns in the Mississippi Valley preceded agricultural settlement: St. Louis, Pittsburgh, and Louisville, for example, had been established as trading posts or forts before American farmers moved across the Appalachians. In some areas, only group settlements were safe, as in Lexington, Kentucky, which began within a fortified palisade.

The new cities that arose as the frontier moved westward seldom were the result of spontaneous growth. Nearly all of them were expected to become centers of thriving regions or, more grandiloquently, "new Philadelphias" or "new Athens." The early federal land policy encouraged town building by the sale of land in large tracts. The method of surveying insured a correct title and also made it a fairly simple matter to plan a town. Later land laws continued to stimulate town building. In 1844, Congress enacted legislation for the reservation of town sites. Three hundred and twenty acres of land could be held for a town site when the area was occupied; this plot did not have to be entered at the land office under the Preemption Act. Owners of town sites could put the plot at the minimum price and dispose of the lots in accordance with the regulations of the state or territory.[76]

Groups of merchants and investors organized into joint stock companies to finance the acquisition and development of western land.

[74] Davidson, *op. cit.*, pp. 237–238.
[75] *Ibid.*, p. 239.
[76] Dick, *Sod-House Frontier, op. cit.*, p. 40.

Towns were planned along transportation routes—most of them at points of exchange from one type of transportation to another. Sometimes the land companies built the roads, but most of the building of highways, canals, and eventually railroads was stimulated by cities in the North and South, and later in the West.

From the time the West was first opened to settlement, it was the scene of not only land speculation, but intense city speculation as well. Men in the East with surplus capital scanned maps looking for likely spots to establish a town, usually at the junction of two rivers, or sometimes at the center of fertile farm districts. Their information often came from a traveler's account, or from personal contact with someone who had been across the mountains. They bought up land, laid it out into lots, gave the place a name, and waited for the development of the region to appreciate its value.[77]

Very few of the pioneer farmers who moved westward were interested in subsistence farming. As in colonial times, their goal was to become less rather than more self-sufficient. Jackson and Schultz state:

For many men less adventuresome than the pioneer farmer of legend, the lure west was the presence of already settled towns and the promise of future growth. Farmers of the Ohio Valley moved principally into agricultural areas that had a local town where they could satisfy their economic needs and barter whatever surplus they might produce. Others moved first to cities like Buffalo, Cincinnati, or Detroit, and only subsequently took up farming.[78]

In addition, many nonfarmers, at least in the northern states, were accustomed to town life and looked upon new towns as fresh opportunities to exercise their talents and skills. "Many settlers came across the mountains in search of promising towns as well as good land. Their inducements were not so much fertile soil as opportunities in infant cities."[79]

Waterway routes not only determined the location of early cities until the railroad era but also provided the means for their economic growth. Commerce was the base, but manufacturing articles that pioneers would need for a period of two or three years also became important. Both commerce and manufacturing attracted population to the cities, and in turn these urban immigrants stimulated further development:

The population growth of these urban centers reflected the magnitude of the human stream that moved across the mountains into the West. . . . These people did more than create an expanding local market; they also brought with them skills to perform new jobs and capital to invest in new enterprises. Choosing cities as carefully as farmers selected land, mechanics and entrepre-

[77] Richard C. Wade, *The Urban Frontier: The Rise of Western Cities, 1790–1830.* (Cambridge, Mass.: Harvard University Press), 1959, p. 30.
[78] K. T. Jackson and S. K. Schultz, *Cities in American History.* (New York: Knopf), 1972, p. 100.
[79] Wade, *op. cit.*, p. 34.

neurs sought the place of maximum opportunity and brightest future. And Western towns competed for these urban migrants, advertising openings for profitable enterprise and specific types of employment.[80]

Some new towns were well-planned developments and represented an effort to make the transition to wilderness as comfortable as possible. For example, before 1820, in New York State, northern Pennsylvania, and the Ohio Western Reserve, land companies (financed by New England or European capitalists) sometimes built sawmills and other mills or provided land for their building. Frequently they built roads or induced the states to build connecting links to waterways or existing roads. Most of the pioneers in these early post-Revolution settlements were from New England and they built small New England villages at, for example, Marietta and Cleveland, Ohio.[81]

In marked contrast to this concern with group welfare rather than profits was the more typical immigration under the aegis of speculators whose principal contributions were "high land prices and conflicting land titles."[82] The city projected as a speculation was relatively easy to lay out as a "grid plan set about a square or on both sides of a main street." The plan of towns along important rivers varied somewhat from this simple scheme by having "a wide street going down to the dock or wharf at the river's edge." Many of these towns are still distinctive, but most of the new towns had few amenities.[83]

The methods used to induce immigrants to settle in the new cities were the same throughout the West and very similar to land speculation propositions before and since.

Newspapers throughout the country ran notices proclaiming the matchless situation of the proposed city. A detailed and sympathetic description of the surrounding country and rivers followed; then settlers were urged to buy quickly before the price of town lots began to skyrocket.[84]

Frequently, someone was hired to write a newspaper article about the new city, copies of which were sent to the East. Either the land company or the community would build a hotel to indicate a confident expectation of business. Free lots might be given to churches, organiza-

[80] *Ibid.*, p. 68.

[81] J. W. Reps, *The Making of Urban America: A History of City Planning in the United States.* (Princeton, N.J.: Princeton University Press), 1965, pp. 212–234, 251.

[82] *Ibid.*, p. 358.

[83] Christopher Tunnard and A. H. Reed, *American Skyline: The Growth and Form of our Cities and Towns.* (New York: New American Library of World Literature) 1956, pp. 69–70. See also Reps, *Making of Urban America, op. cit.*, Chapter II.

[84] Wade, *op. cit.*, p. 32.

tions, businesses, to the first couple married in the town, to the family whose child was the first born in the community, or to an individual who agreed to build a house worth a certain amount.[85]

The scene that greeted the incoming settlers at Columbus, Georgia, in 1828, was probably typical:

The visitor who arrived just before the (land) sale found that an area five miles square had been surveyed. He was conducted down the main street, a long aisle four feet wide that had been cut through the oak forest. On reaching the center of the "city" the guide went into raptures about the future greatness of Columbus: "Here you are in the center of the city." He assured his auditor that this street was to be sixty yards wide and a league in length. Cross streets had been staked off perpendicular to the main street through the forest. Stumps, brush, and even trees stood in the streets.[86]

Squatters moved into new town sites before the land sale.

They had built their houses in clusters. Some were made partly of bark and partly of planks. Since none owned a lot and might not be able to buy the lot on which his house sat, many houses were built on trucks, a sort of low carriage with small log wheels, for the avowed purpose of moving them.[87]

Some enterprising carpenters used prefabrication. "At least sixty frames of houses were lying in piles on the ground . . . made by carpenters to sell to those who bought lots."[88]

A typical frontier city during the land boom of the 1850's in Kansas and Nebraska consisted of one graded street; the rest were footpaths leading down ravines to shabby cabins and huts. Houses usually were one-room affairs until the 1870's, with sleeping accommodations curtained off by blankets. Roads were wide strips of dust in the summer, with stepping stones for crossings. Horseback was almost a universal mode of travel—horseback racing down the main streets provided excitement as also did runaways.[89] In the 1870's and 1880's,

The typical town consisted of a handful of rude one-room shacks made in the cheapest possible manner. . . . Prairie grass grew luxuriantly in the streets. There were not enough buildings around the public square to mark its boundaries. On the west side were three one-story structures. . . . On the north side of the square were two similar buildings. . . . On the east side there was only a store; and the south side was vacant. The south half of the courthouse square was used for a ball ground. . . . The Otoe Indians . . . camped on the public square on their way to their annual buffalo hunts.[90]

[85] Dick, *Sod-House Frontier, op. cit.,* pp. 44—45.
[86] Dick, *Dixie Frontier, op. cit.,* p. 150.
[87] *Ibid.*
[88] *Ibid.*
[89] Dick, *Sod-House Frontier, op. cit.,* pp. 56, 394, 399.
[90] *Ibid.,* p. 391.

The purpose of some of the advertising for cities was merely to sell land:

Many prospective settlers, lured by the promise of city development, would respond to advertisements in Eastern and Western newspapers, buy lots, then move themselves and their families, only to discover that their lots lay under ten feet of swamp water or that the "city" consisted of one muddy street, a saloon, and a newspaper with a distribution of twenty or thirty families . . . in the early 1830's, it was "the era of imaginary villages," a time when great cities and thriving commercial centers existed primarily on lavishly printed maps—and nowhere else.[91]

Town building in the Kansas–Nebraska Territory in the 1850's was so widespread that "certain frontier wits proposed that Congress reserve some of the land for farming before the entire territory was cut up into building lots." Speculators used various devices to acquire more than the 320 acres authorized to be set aside for town sites (at $1.25 an acre). Quoting from a traveler's account, Reps states:

Land preemption regulations permitted the purchase, at nominal cost, of 160 acres of land if it was actually occupied and "improved" by the pre-emptor. A witness was required to swear that the claim had been improved with a habitable dwelling "twelve by fourteen." Richardson tells of such a claim being based on a house "whittled out with a penknife, twelve inches by fourteen." He also mentions the use of a detached window sash without glass hung on a nail in the wall so that a witness might swear that there was a window in the house, a house on wheels that rented for five dollars a day and was moved from claim to claim, and other frauds of the same type.[92]

Another method was to have several settlers preempt adjacent sections of 160 acres, each one to swear at the land office that it was for his own exclusive use and benefit. When the title was obtained, each settler deeded his land to the corporation and received the money for it. "Thus the company secures from five hundred to a thousand acres, cutting it into building lots usually twenty-five by one hundred and twenty-five feet. . . ."[93]

The railroads were a potent force in urbanizing the West. As a railroad line was being constructed, "a chain of ramshackle towns 60 or 70 miles apart was set up at temporary halting places." Billington describes the process:

91 Jackson and Schultz (eds.), *Cities in American History. op. cit.*, p. 105.

92 Reps, *Making of Urban America, op. cit.*, p. 364. Quoted from A. D. Richardson, *Beyond the Mississippi: From the Great River to the Great Ocean.* (Hartford, Conn.: American Publishing Co.), 1867.

93 A. D. Richardson, quoted in Reps, *Making of Urban America, op. cit.*, p. 371.

For a few months, or perhaps a whole winter, the gangs of workers would live in one of the outposts, going out to work each day on the "track trains." Then when the track had nosed out far ahead, the signal to move was given. All fell to work; in a few hours the town was dismantled, piled aboard flatcars, and on its way west, with inhabitants riding atop their dismantled homes. Sixty miles up the road they halted. Willing hands raised the "Big Tent," a floored canvas structure a hundred feet long and forty wide, which held a sumptuous bar, a dance floor, and elaborate gambling paraphernalia. Around it they threw up the ramshackle shacks or tents which held twenty-two more saloons, five dance halls, living quarters for the workers, and homes for the "girls" who were always ready to take away any portion of the workers' wages left by the faro dealers.[94]

Many of the towns in central Kansas, Nebraska, and the Dakota Territory were founded by the railroads.[95] Typically, a real estate corporation made up of railroad officials bought the land where a railroad station was planned, in order to keep out the land speculators. The corporation used the standard methods of attracting settlers—financing the building of a warehouse, offers of free lots, and so forth. Some railroad companies established a new town when an existing town refused a subsidy for the line, using the same techniques.[96]

Housing in the new cities at first was similar to housing in the countryside—log cabins, sod houses, dugouts, tents, or various kinds of temporary structures. Quilts and aprons were used for doors and windows and some houses were papered with newspapers. The sequence of early house types at Lawrence, Kansas, may have been typical of other towns: the first year (1854), a village of tents; sod houses by the next year; and in a few more years, many sod houses replaced by flimsy frame structures. In some of the new towns of the 1850's in Kansas, houses were being built so rapidly for the inrushing population that many of them were shingled by lamplight.[97]

In towns founded after 1833, balloon frame technology made it possible to build frame houses quickly and easily. The balloon frame

. . . made possible the construction of individual houses and smaller buildings with the speed and economy necessary for the quick and orderly development of new cities and of new neighborhoods in established cities. . . . "If it had not been for the knowledge of balloon frames," Solon Robinson, an Indiana agricultural spokesman, told a New York audience in 1855, "Chicago and San Francisco could never have arisen, as they did, from little villages to great cities in a single year."[98]

94 Billington, *op. cit.*, p. 647.
95 Dick, *Sod-House Frontier, op. cit.*, pp. 186–187.
96 Tunnard and Reed, *op. cit.*, p. 127.
97 Dick's *Sod-House Frontier, op. cit.*, pp. 58–59.
98 Glaab and Brown, *op. cit.*, p. 143.

People accustomed to the slow rise of the heavy timber frames marveled at the speed of construction. An account of housebuilding in early Chicago states:

. . . It was not uncommon to see one rise in a single day, and constituting the next day the snug home of a young and enterprising couple, the next with a blanket hanging up for a door with perhaps one or two flaxen-haired bright-eyed urchins lifting one corner and peeping out on the busy world around them.[99]

In San Francisco, houses were built as swiftly as in Chicago. In 1848, at the time of the gold rush, it was a mining town typical of all mining, cattle, or other kinds of towns that held a heterogeneous and rapidly changing population. Such towns typically had an atmosphere created by a combination of hard work, easy money, and few restraints.[100] Housing usually took the form of tents made from flour sacks or old shirts; tarpaper shacks, and perhaps a few houses similar to those in the surrounding countryside. By 1850, a journalist visiting San Francisco was writing:

Of all the marvellous phases of the history of the Present, the growth of San Francisco is the one which will most tax the belief of the Future. Its parallel was never known, and shall never be beheld again. I speak only of what I saw with my own eyes. When I landed there, a little more than four months before, I found a scattering town of tents and canvas houses, and a population of about six thousand. Now, on my last visit, I saw around me an actual metropolis, displaying street after street of well-built edifices, filled with an active and enterprising people and exhibiting every mark of permanent commercial prosperity.[101]

Eventually in the cities the temporary housing was torn (or burnt) down and houses in typical patterns of the period erected. Many of the cities that prospered drew favorable comments on their appearance. A French economist gives a visitor's impression of Cincinnati in 1835:

The architectural appearance of Cincinnati is very nearly the same with that of the new quarters of the English towns. The houses are generally of brick, most commonly three stories high, with the windows shining with cleanliness, calculated each for a single family, and regularly placed along well paved and spacious streets, sixty feet in width. Here and there the prevailing

99 H. E. Pratt (ed.), "John Dean Caton's Reminiscences of Chicago in 1833 and 1834," *Journal of the Illinois State Historical Society*, Vol. 28, April 1935, pp. 10–12. In: Wilson Smith (ed.), *Cities of Our Past and Present.* (New York: Wiley), 1964, p. 52.

100 Billington, *op. cit.*, p. 678.

101 Bayard Taylor, *Eldorado, or, Adventures in the Path of Empire . . . ,* 3rd ed. (New York), 1850. In: Smith (ed.), *op. cit.*, p. 65.

uniformity is interrupted by some more imposing edifice, and there are some houses of hewn stone in very good taste, real palaces in miniature, with neat porticoes, inhabited by the aristocratical portion, and several very pretty mansions surrounded with gardens and terraces.[102]

As soon as they emerged from the log cabin or sod house stage, the new cities found themselves in a continuing competition with other cities. With changes in transportation and the rush of pioneers to successive frontiers, individual cities, to survive, had to be dynamic influences on development and to assume the initiative in creating change. Regardless of natural advantages, a city to achieve and retain dominance over its region had to be innovative and ready to exploit whatever opportunities came or could be persuaded to come its way.[103]

The competition among cities for some particular advantage has been defined by Wade as "urban imperialism"—the competition between fast-growing urban centers, each seeking to attach an undeveloped hinterland. Urban imperialism was necessary sometimes merely for survival as a separate town, but also, and more frequently, to maintain a pace of development or to prevent another city from encroaching on a city's territory.

The struggle for primacy and power—and occasionally survival—was one of the most persistent and striking characteristics of the early urban history of the West. Like imperial states, cities carved out extensive dependencies, extended their influence over the economic and political life of the hinterland, and fought with contending places over strategic trade routes.[104]

For example, for Cincinnati "the object which the Cincinnatians have had in view, almost from the origin of their city, has been nothing less than to make it the capital . . . mart of the West." Manufacturing household furnishings, farm implements, "and a thousand objects of daily use and consumption" was one means selected to accomplish this end. The result was that:

The country trader, who keeps an assortment of everything vendible, is sure to find almost everything he wants in Cincinnati, and, he, therefore, goes thither in preference to any other place in order to lay in his stock of goods.[105]

[102] Michael Chevalier, *Society, Manners and Politics in the United States.* (Trans. by T. G. Bradford). (New York: Anchor Books), 1961. In: Smith, (ed.), *op. cit.*, pp. 44–45.

[103] See C. H. Madden, "The Growth of the Cities in the United States: An Aspect of the Development of an Economic System," for an analysis of the changing ranks of eastern and western cities in the 19th century. Ph.D. dissertation, University of Virginia. (Ann Arbor, Mich.: University Microfilms), 1954.

[104] Wade, *op. cit.*, p. 336.

[105] Chevalier, *loc. cit.*, p. 49.

Towns competed for special advantages that would help them become the focal point of a region. Selection as the state capital was the most valued prize; lesser but distinctively beneficial premiums were to be a county seat or the site of a university or state institution.

The lore of the West is full of the bitter rivalries of enterprising early settlers for a government handout to their community. Contests were none the less bitter because the competing towns were often figments of imagination.[106]

An advantageous location on an important transportation route was the key factor in the growth and development of a city. At such a location, regional as well as local trade was likely to develop.[107] Many cities failed when a trail was changed or a stage coach route shifted. Cities tended to lead in initiating changes in methods of transportation in order to retain or expand their territories.

Another important result of urban imperialism was the leadership that cities provided for the transportation revolution. . . . It was in the cities that road, canal, and railroad projects were instigated and fought for, and in city after city it was local as well as class interest that seemed to determine the direction and scope of transportation innovations. Because cities act somewhat like nations and seek to gain economic control of competing centers, transportation became a weapon in the urban warfare.[108]

Each of the developments fostered in the urban competition "upset established commercial relationships and spurred economic development."[109] Each development in transportation hastened the inflow of people into the back country and, in turn, influenced the growth of cities. The railroad, with its freedom of choice for locations, became the crucial factor in determining the future of many cities—by the 1860's it guided the destiny of cities just as later it controlled the countryside.[110] The future effects of a change in a transportation method had to be recognized early. Chicago provides one example of the results of this kind of foresight:

Through imagination and risk, they [local investors] made Chicago the nation's most important railroad center by 1860 and in the process reoriented the trade of the Middle West. The corn, wheat, and beef that had been flowing south to New Orleans found a new course toward Chicago and the East, from which it was never diverted. By 1890 Chicago had become the nation's

106 D. J. Boorstin, "Competitive Communities on the Western Frontier." In: Jackson and Schultz (eds.), *Cities in American History, op. cit.,* p. 10.
107 Wade, *op. cit.,* pp. 62–63.
108 Jackson and Schultz (eds.), *Cities in American History, op. cit.,* p. 5.
109 *Ibid.,* p. 6.
110 Tunnard and Reed, *op. cit.,* p. 92.

second largest city. . . . In fact, the Windy City, dynamic, powerful and sprawling, became the symbol of the young and ambitious nation. . . .[111]

Every city, of course, could not become a Chicago; nevertheless, successful urban competitors enjoyed substantial rewards in civic pride, increased profits from commerce, and the increased land values that accompanied development in a period of expansion. For example, acquiring a state institution

. . . meant buildings to be built, people to be employed, food, clothing, and services to be bought. It meant clients for the lawyers, patients for the doctors, customers for the shops, guests for the taverns and hotels. Above all, it meant increased population with the increased land values that always came along.[112]

Wade gives an example of the amount of increase that came, at least in the early stages of development, at Lexington, which probably was repeated in other cities. For a series of years, one mercantile wholesale business had sales that "amounted to sixty thousand dollars per month for some length of time." Other similar businesses "grossed $100,000 monthly during the busiest season, though their sustained earnings were less." Just as profits such as these attracted more individuals into merchandising, the increase in land values attracted more investment into land. In 1815, in Lexington, "town lots sell nearly as high as in Boston, New York, Philadelphia, or Baltimore, which shows that this is not a place in the wilderness, as some people suppose it to be."[113]

Land booms were a common occurrence during most of the 19th century; Chicago is only one, although the most frequently cited, example. The English novelist, Harriet Martineau, describing the boom observed during her visit to Chicago in 1836, said ". . . it seemed as if some prevalent mania infected the whole people."[114] Reps cites a report

that . . . some lots changed hands ten times in a single day and . . . the "evening purchaser" paid at least "ten times as much as the price paid by the morning buyer for the same spot!" The school section, which in 1833 had been sold for $38,000, was valued at $1,200,000 in 1836. Land in the present city limits which was worth $168,000 in 1830 had risen in value to more than $10,000,000 at the peak of the boom. Most of this value was fictitious since it was not based on cash sales but on purchases with extremely liberal credit.[115]

The principal hope of profit under the circumstances was in a quick sale. As the new cities developed, they tended to become basically more

[111] Jackson and Schultz (eds.), *Cities in American History, op. cit.,* p. 5.
[112] Boorstin, *loc. cit.,* p. 10.
[113] Wade, *op. cit.,* pp. 50, 53.
[114] Quoted in Reps, *Making of Urban America, op. cit.,* p. 302.
[115] *Ibid.*

alike. "Imitation, not innovation, characterized governmental policies, social class structures, and urban life styles."[116] Perhaps, as Glassie states, "Cities generally are less related to the surrounding rural area than to other, often distant cities and are foreign outposts within folk regions."[117] Cities and towns on the frontier used eastern models in setting up their governments and institutions and in formulating policies. Like the eastern cities, western cities in the 19th century were commercial centers; their class structure as it developed became almost identical with the class structures of cities in the East.

At the apex of a stratifying society stood a merchant or businessman class. Until the 1830's the merchants presided over the affairs and politics of Western towns. There, as in the East and South, economic prowess meant social prestige and political power . . . commercial interests largely continued to govern the cities until the Civil War. . . . While the wealthy of Philadelphia, New York, and Boston rarely numbered more than two to five percent of their respective urban populations, they exercised an inordinate amount of political and social power. In Southern cities businessmen dominated community life and ruled the countryside, especially . . . where the leading cotton capitalists depended upon credit and commercial facilities for carrying on their extensive planting operations. . . .

The professionals, white-collar employees, small businessmen, and skilled workers formed a growing urban middle class that began flexing its political and social muscles in the early 1830's. The working class began to swell in the early 1820's, when foreign immigration joined the native rural migration cityward . . . most wage earners were neither debtors nor paupers. They nonetheless lived close to the level of subsistence. . . . At the bottom of the social structure in the cities were free blacks, working for the most part as common laborers. Urban workingmen and free blacks enjoyed some opportunities for economic and social mobility; class lines were not so rigid that advancement was impossible. Still, such mobility had its limitations, and occurred in small steps up the social ladder. . . .[118]

The supreme contribution of the railroads to urbanization was not in town building so much as in town linking. By 1890, major cities and growing towns, alike in "political institutions, economic organization, and class structure" as well as in objectives and problems, had been interlocked in an urban network across the continent.[119] As the frontier

116 Jackson and Schultz (eds.), *Cities in American History*, op. cit., p. 107.
117 Glassie, op. cit., p. 216.
118 Jackson and Schultz (eds.), *Cities in American History*, op. cit., pp. 107–108. For a discussion of opportunities for social mobility in the 19th century, see Stephan Thernstrom, *The Other Bostonians Poverty and Progress in the American Metropolis, 1880–1970*. (Cambridge, Mass.: Harvard University Press), 1973.
119 Jackson and Schultz (eds.), *Cities in American History*, op. cit., p. 110.

closed, the city was emerging as a major attraction for new generations of migrants.

Like the federal land policy, the rapid urbanization of the continent had positive and negative aspects. On the positive side, it hastened the development of both the West and the nation. The competition between cities brought about rapid improvements in transportation that, in turn, hastened the expansion of agriculture, trade, and manufacturing. "The constant search for new markets furnished an invaluable stimulus to commercial and industrial enterprise."[120]

Unquestionably, rapid urban development contributed to the economic strength of the nation. Further, the very speed of improvements in transportation kept barriers to national unity from becoming operative. Very few areas in the United States between the time of the Revolution and the closing of the frontier were not connected with an urban trading center that itself was linked with other urban centers. The 100-year march into wilderness had not created a series of isolated settlements, each with its own institutions and culture; at each frontier line, urban settlements, with familiar and easily recognized characteristics, served as communication as well as trading centers.

Nevertheless, the same results might have been obtained at a lower cost in both resources and future problems. The promotion schemes of competing cities led to the dispersion of state institutions and transportation lines and, for some, their location at sites with fewer than optimum advantages. When successful, such schemes frequently prevented the centralization of governmental services and contributed to the proliferation of railroads and canals.

In scores of other ways, too numerous to mention, the booster spirit of the upstart West fostered cultural diffuseness. . . . The desire of each town to become the terminus of a canal or a railroad often produced canals and railroads, which became life-promoting arteries all along their way. This competition bred a fantastic transportation network which, by comparison with Western Europe, gave the United States a railroad mileage far out of proportion with her population.[121]

The urban competition undoubtedly smothered promising cities that might have been more strategically situated to function as communication and commercial points than some of the cities that survived. Resources invested by vanquished cities in projects for survival frequently were losses. The concentration on the immediate advantage had consequences for the future; for example, the chaotic nature of town planning, lot selling, and town development laid the groundwork for numerous problems of today's cities. Reps states:

[120] Wade, *op. cit.*, p. 336.
[121] Boorstin, *loc. cit.*, p. 15.

Although land speculation continues to this day, we are not likely to see again such an era of wholesale humbuggery and land butchery. The stamp of the early speculator remains, however, upon most of our cities. At a pace a hundred times slower than the original development, and at enormous expense, modern city planners now are attempting to erase the worse blotches spilled across the country by the boomers, the townsite promoters, and the speculative builders of yesterday. It is an aspect of our urban history in which Americans can take little pride.[122]

Probably one of the most serious results was that, in the speed of urban expansion and the competitive urban race, rural—urban differences were accentuated rather than diminished, and mutually supportive relationships between many dominant cities and their surrounding countrysides failed to develop.

Cities in the East

In 1790, the major cities in the East were commercial centers; each was strategically located with respect to a promising interior and as early as the 17th century had looked to the interior regions as sources of further development. By present-day standards, they were small; the largest, Philadelphia, had a population of 42,500 followed by New York with 33,100. The combined population of the six cities—Philadelphia, New York, Boston, Charleston, Baltimore, and Salem, Mass.—with a population of 8,000 or more inhabitants (the Census definition of a city) was less than 132,000 and represented about 3% of the total population.[123] Morison and Commager describe them:

Their aspect was not unlike that of provincial towns in Great Britain. . . . Brick houses in the Georgian style, often detached and surrounded with gardens and shrubbery; inns with capacious yards and stables; shops and stores with overhanging signs; places of worship with graceful spires after Sir Christopher Wren; market houses or city halls of the same style, often placed in the middle of a broad street or square, with arcades to serve as stalls or merchants's exchange; somewhat ramshackle unpainted wooden houses where the poorer people lived, but hardly one without a bit of garden or yard.[124]

Until about 1850, all urban activities were centered in the downtown area within a radius defined by walking distance:

Most men could not afford a horse or carriage, so the distance between residence and work was limited by their walking speed. The effect was to set the

122 Reps, *Making of Urban America, op. cit.,* p. 380.
    123 U. S. Census Office, *Report on the Population of the United States at the Eleventh Census, op. cit.,* p. lxv.
    124 Morison and Commager, *op. cit.,* p. 303.

radius of a city at about 2 miles, or the distance a man could walk in about 30 minutes. As men went about their tasks on foot, they shared street space with a few men on horseback, some commercial carts and coaches, and the carriages of the wealthy. But congestion in the pretransit city was preeminently the friction of people coming into personal contact with each other as they walked about the city streets.[125]

New cities were laid out in the East as well as in the West, and in more or less the same manner. Reps states:

Typically, the promoters of such towns chose a suitable site, reached some kind of agreement with the land owners if they did not acquire title themselves, had the site surveyed into streets, blocks and lots, and with a handsomely printed map and brochure describing the advantages of the town proceeded to sell lots to anyone with cash for a down payment.[126]

Beginning in the 1820's, specialized towns were established—some state capitals were moved inland to new sites, neatly planned mill towns were set up in New England, and universities became a principal focus of some new small cities. As the interior regions widened, some smaller towns and cities became important; in the canal-building era, for example, canal ports (such as Syracuse, N.Y.) attracted settlers. Somewhat more hastily, towns were constructed in the coal mining region of Pennsylvania, where resources were being developed. Tunnard and Reed describe the building of Pottsville:

Lumber was framed at Philadelphia and transported to the coal town by canal, ready for the joiner. To replace the primeval forest with a thriving town, a city was brought along the canal by boat in sawed-off lengths of wood. . . .[127]

Urban Design

WASHINGTON, D.C.

The preeminent new city was, of course, the national capital. In contrast to many other cities, Washington was carefully planned. Its plan is considered to express the same notion of the urban community as a system and the same desire to consciously shape the urban environment that underlay the meticulous planning of Philadelphia, Savannah, Annapolis, and Williamsburg.[128] Major Pierre Charles L'Enfant, commis-

[125] Glen E. Holt, "The Changing Perception of Urban Pathology: An Essay on the Development of Mass Transit in the United States." In: *Cities in American History, op. cit.*, p. 324.

[126] Reps, *Making of Urban America, op. cit.*, p. 240.

[127] Tunnard and Reed, *op. cit.*, p. 70. See also for descriptions of new types of towns in early 19th century, including the planned utopian communities.

[128] Glaab and Brown, *op. cit.*, p. 251.

sioned to lay out a plan for the new city in 1791, conceived of Washington as the capital of a large nation of 50 states and five million inhabitants—"a city designed as the center of a great enterprise, the eventual scope of which could not be foreseen even by its founders."[129]

The dominant elements in L'Enfant's design, which followed the principles of baroque plans, were the Capitol building, the White House, and the long mall that runs from the Capitol to the present Lincoln Memorial. The Capitol and the White House were situated on the principal avenue and, in accordance with the principles of baroque design, terminated the views from the long and straight streets. Two series of broad avenues radiated out from these two buildings and converged into circular intersections to give order and meaning to the city and to create a series of open spaces. Between the radiating avenues was a gridiron matrix of streets. The Capitol, the White House, and the open spaces (the present circular or square parks) were situated on natural elevations. To the north, the plan ended at a steep bluff, from which an approaching traveler would have an impressive view of the city below.

L'Enfant planned Washington to be a city "which would be both agreeable to the first settlers and capable of being expanded by progressive improvements."[130]

Having determined some principal points to which I wished to make the other subordinate, I made the distribution regular with every street at right angles, North and South, east and west, and afterwards opened some in different directions, as avenues to and from every principal place, wishing thereby not merely to contrast with the general regularity, nor to afford a greater variety of seats with pleasant prospects, which will be obtained from the advantageous ground over which these avenues are chiefly directed, but principally to connect each part of the city . . . by making the real distance less from place to place, by giving to them reciprocity of sight and by making them thus seemingly connected, promote a rapid settlement over the whole extent. . . .[131]

The plan had a few faults, as Reps points out: the distance from the Capitol to the White House was too long for either building to be an effective visual terminal, and there were some awkward intersections between the straight streets and the radial avenues. A more glaring oversight was the failure to provide a site for the third branch of the federal government—the Supreme Court—as dominant as the sites given to the Capitol and White House. Nevertheless,

Certainly in its magnitude, its clever fitting of a generally symmetrical design to irregular topography, and its generous provision of a variety of open

129 Reps, *Making of Urban America, op. cit.*, p. 240.
130 *Ibid.*, p. 243.
131 *Ibid.*, pp. 249–250.

spaces, the plan for Washington must stand as one of the great city planning efforts of all time.[132]

L'Enfant's grand plan was not realized in its entirety; Washington, unlike Annapolis and Williamsburg, did not acquire the symmetrical and unified scheme of buildings and plan that L'Enfant envisioned. Almost from its inception, the plan was changed and modified: L'Enfant, removed as planner after disagreements with the commissioners in charge of raising the public buildings, had no control over the building of the city. Washington developed as a city only very slowly; early in the 19th century, Charles Dickens called it "the city of streets without houses" and the "City of magnificent intentions."[133] Other European visitors made equally scathing remarks about the unfinished capital in the wilderness. As late as 1850, the central portion of the city lacked the uniformity of design and buildings called for by the scheme. A later encroachment on the plan was the building of a railroad station on the mall.[134] Mumford analyzes the problem as follows:

In conceiving the city as a whole, as it would be in its finished form, L'Enfant had dared greatly; and in terms of baroque assumptions and baroque purposes . . . he had planned superbly. But he forgot the strict limits of his assignment. He overlooked the fact that he himself could not build the city he had planned, nor had the political leaders of his generation that power, much though they might recall the classic figures in Plutarch. The country itself would need at least half a century of growth, prosperity, and unification, before it could even begin to fill out such a comprehensive outline; and in the meanwhile, the more modest beginnings which might have been made within a more appropriate frame would be obstructed . . . by the very grandeur of the full-flown scheme.[135]

To most Americans, however, "the Federal City stood as a symbol of what the future promised for the entire country, which, like the capital city, remained unfinished but which boasted of boundless energy, optimism, and natural resources."[136] After the Civil War, when employment for a more consolidated federal government provided an economic base for the city, Washington began to take on its present-day appearance. In 1901, in response to demands for a more attractive city, the Senate Park Commission produced an official plan that led to the eventual realization of much of L'Enfant's early conception.

The plan for the city of Washington influenced the planning of sev-

[132] J. W. Reps, *Town Planning in Frontier America.* (Princeton, N.J.: Princeton University Press), 1969, pp. 322, 323–324.
[133] *Ibid.*, pp. 333–334.
[134] Reps, *Making of Urban America, op. cit.*, p. 262.
[135] Lewis Mumford, *The City in History.* (New York: Harcourt Brace Jovanovich), 1961, p. 407.
[136] Reps, *Making of Urban America, op. cit.*, p. 263.

eral cities that were founded around 1800: one example is Buffalo, N.Y. Some applications of the Washington plan were more the adoption of attractive features than full-scale designs. Many radiating avenues, for example, did not terminate at important buildings; sometimes no sites were provided for such buildings. "A long radial terminating in a park or merely ending at another street," Reps states, "is devoid of interest; while it may arouse the curiosity of the beholder, it never fully satisfies it." In addition, the planners, like L'Enfant, frequently had little or no control over the architecture or kinds of buildings erected.[137]

NEW YORK AND PHILADELPHIA

Two other cities, Philadelphia and New York, had more influence on the urban design of the period than the small city on the Potomac.[138] The use of the gridiron plan for the nation's two largest cities supported its other advantages for frontier town plans, while rejection by New York of elaborate designs for its expansion added another incentive to keep the planning of new cities simple.

Philadelphia and New York City began a faster pace of expansion after the Revolution. Philadelphia extended its original grid plan but reserved less generous amounts of open space. City blocks were divided by narrow streets, some of which eventually were filled with tightly packed row houses and alley dwellings.[139]

The development of the plan of expansion for New York City may illustrate some of the problems encountered by city planners of the period and some of the factors that influenced public policy in city design. In an appeal to the state legislature in 1807, the Common Council of New York City requested that a state commission be appointed "with absolute authority to lay out the undeveloped areas of Manhattan Island." The request acknowledged that the "laying out of streets and roads" and "projecting them in such a manner as to unite regularity and order with the public convenience and benefit and in particular to promote the health of the city" was indeed a municipal function. Attempts to carry out this function, however, had been futile because of "various and complicated difficulties and embarrassments":

The diversity of sentiments and opinions which has heretofore existed and probably will always exist among the members of the Common Council, the incessant remonstrances of proprietors against plans however well devised

138 Reps, *Town Planning . . .* , *op. cit.*, pp. 203, 221. Efforts were made in Philadelphia to preserve the features of the original plan. The squares in the central part of the city were named and city ordinances prohibited their use as burying grounds or dumps, appropriated funds to improve them and set fines for smoking cigars or pipes in any public square. *Ibid.*, p. 220.
139 *Ibid.*, p. 216.

or beneficial wherein their individual interests do not concur and the impossibility of completing those plans thus opposed but by a tedious and expensive course of law are obstacles of a serious and very perplexing nature.[140]

The state commission appointed in response to this appeal was given "the absolute authority" requested with respect to laying out the public streets and parks. It had no authority to map and plan for the privately owned property in the area. "The realization had not yet dawned that regulation of streets and land uses were inextricably intertwined."[141] The commission encountered resistance from the property owners when they attempted to make surveys, and the appointment of the commission stimulated land speculation.[142]

The plan that was laid out for the city provided a dozen north–south avenues of equal width, crossed at right angles every 200 feet by east–west streets. It had several serious deficiencies, in addition to the monotonous pattern imposed on the varied topography of Manhattan: lack of adequate open space or sites for public buildings and a failure to recognize the future importance of avenues running north and south. Whether or not the commission could have evolved a better plan and had it accepted, given the circumstances, is a moot question. Their justification for the simplicity of the design expresses what seems to have been the prevailing view: the conception of a city as merely a physical system of streets and buildings to be arranged for convenience and utility of movement and the development of real estate. They considered carefully what scheme would best meet these objectives:

. . . that is to say, whether they should confine themselves to rectilinear and rectangular streets, or whether they should adopt some of those supposed improvements, by circles, ovals, and stars, which certainly embellish a plan, whatever may be their effects as to convenience and utility. In considering that subject, they could not but bear in mind that a city is to be composed principally of the habitations of men, and that strait sided and right angled houses are the most cheap to build, and the most convenient to live in. The effect of these plain and simple reflections was decisive.[143]

Growth of Urban Population

The growth of the urban population of the United States after 1800 is a local reflection of a worldwide trend toward urbanization, as a result

[140] Quoted in J. D. McGoldrick, Seymour Graubard, and R. J. Horowitz, *Building Regulation in New York City: A Study in Administrative Law and Procedure.* (New York: The Commonwealth Fund), 1944, p. 67.
[141] *Ibid.*, p. 68.
[142] Reps, *Making of Urban America, op. cit.*, p. 297.
[143] *Ibid.*

of industrialization. Industrial development began in England toward the close of the 18th century, then spread to Europe, and later to the United States. During the 19th century, the proportion of world population living in cities of 5,000 or more inhabitants increased from 3 percent in 1800 to 6 percent in 1850 and reached 14 percent in 1900.[144]

In the United States, increased commercial activity and greater access to expanding hinterlands were the principal reasons for urban growth during the first part of the 19th century. The increased commercial activity was the result of "the rapid settlement of the West, the great increase in population, and the phenomenal improvements in transportation."[145] Each development in transportation that broadened the hinterland amplified commercial activity in the terminal cities; in turn, this amplification extended the domestic market for farm products. Less costly and more rapid transportation stimulated the development of manufacturing, made possible a greater specialization, and a rapidly developing division of labor between different sections, between town and country, and between manufacturing and agriculture.[146] Eastern cities between the 1820's and 1860's, especially New York, developed extensive and specialized marketing facilities and became important in financing and as export centers. These specialized activities spread to western cities after 1840.[147]

Prior to the 1840's, mercantile interests tended to invest in land or to enlarge their wholesale selling and financing activities; then, as competition among cities for hinterlands—which was as sharp in the East as in the West—increased, to invest in "a less direct path of commercial promotion, namely, turnpike, canal, and railroad development." For over half of the 19th century, directly or indirectly, the mercantile element

provided jobs for a large portion of the city's working population. As a striking example, as early as 1800 there were nearly 1,000 persons licensed as carters to transfer merchandise to warehouses and to tranship import and export commodities on the streets of New York City, and by 1833 the number of carts operating on the city's thoroughfares was approaching 2,500.[148]

144 Glenn H. Beyer (ed.), *The Urban Explosion in Latin America.* (Ithaca, N.Y.: Cornell University Press), 1967, pp. 30, 118. See also pp. 18–30 for a description of city growth and functions prior to 1800.

145 G. R. Taylor, *The Transportation Revolution, 1815–1860.* (New York: Holt, Rinehart and Winston), 1951, p. 169.

146 Taylor, *op. cit.*, p. 207.

147 Wright, *op. cit.*, pp. 347–348.

148 Allan Pred, "Manufacturing in the American Mercantile City, 1800–1840." In: Jackson and Schultz (eds.), *Cities in American History, op. cit.*, pp. 114, 117–18.

Developments in the 1840's—machine tools, interchangeable parts, and steam power—set the stage for the rise of the factory system after the Civil War. Until mid-19th century, manufacturing for the rapidly broadening market for manufactured products was largely by shop or handicraft production, the domestic or putting-out system (in which raw material provided by the manufacturer was processed at home or sometimes in small shops), and factories near sources of water power. The factory system progressed rapidly after 1840; by 1850 factories were operating in most cities and giving employment to a substantial number of people and accelerating the rate of growth of the urban population.[149]

In most cities, the expanded population lived and worked largely in the downtown area. The first type of urban public transportation, the horse-drawn omnibus, was provided by private companies in the 1820's. The omnibus was the principal means of public transportation until the 1850's, when the horse-drawn streetcar on rails was put into operation in New York City. Before 1880 most large cities had such streetcars in operation, and they remained the principal means of urban transportation until the development of electric railways in the 1880's. The streetcars were privately owned and operated, and, like the horse-drawn omnibus, tended to run only through streets with the densest traffic.[150] Fares were low, but not low enough for most of the population to move very far from the work district:

Although the rural ideal was always influential in American life, only the very wealthy were able to maintain homes away from the heart of cities until the coming of the horse-car lines in the late 1850's, and even then only a few people lived any substantial distance from the sites of work. . . . Horse railroads pushed settlement outward only about another half-mile by 1873 and about another mile and a half by 1887. . . .[151]

The higher population and the increased commercial activity transformed the cities before mid-19th century. One result of the increased congestion—which was augmented rather than relieved by the horse-drawn streetcar—was a relatively rapid deterioration of the urban environment. Few services were municipally provided in the early part of the century; in general, they were either nonexistent or supplied by private companies. As the century progressed this deterioration, in turn, led to stronger demands for public intervention to improve conditions. One notable result of the efforts made to meet these demands was the first direct public intervention in the field of housing, another was the

[149] Taylor, *op. cit.*, pp. 215–217, 389.
[150] Holt, *loc. cit.*, pp. 324–343.
[151] Glaab and Brown, *op. cit.*, p. 155.

higher level of amenity in dwellings that indirectly resulted from governmental actions.

Changes in Urban Housing Patterns

As commercial activities and wholesale trade became more specialized in the cities—with brokers, commission houses, jobbers, and wholesale distribution agencies—the warehouse and commercial districts moved into the bordering residential areas.

The warehouse quarter . . . housed both expanding small-scale workshop industries and a large proportion of the growing commercial activities of the city and, during the middle decades of the 19th Century, made greater claims upon the adjacent residential quarters than all the other segments of the central business district combined.[152]

The expansion of commercial activities and the rising demand for space in the downtown area increased the value of land. For example:

The combination of a steeply declining gradient of land values outward from the urban core and exuberant population growth provided an alluring capital outlet for the seeker of quick gains. And quick gains there were to be made in profusion. By 1823 there were streets in New York which had front-lot values of $1,000 per foot, and from that year onward the total assessed value of Manhattan's real estate spiraled dizzily from $50 million to over $76 million in 1829, to slightly more than $104 million in 1833, to $253,201,191 in 1836. And in the other mercantile cities the maneuvering of property proceeded with equal fervor. In Boston a single $443,883 sale could net close to $100,000, or, on a more ambitious scale, areas as large as East Boston or the South Cove could be manipulated with "cupidity"; and in Baltimore, long before land values peaked, a meager 19 × 63 foot (unoccupied?) lot could bring $27,200.[153]

As population increased, some wealthier families moved outward to surrounding open space along the main turnpikes or urban transportation routes or into nearby small towns, and commuted to work by water or railroad or private carriage.[154] Their houses were designed in the style of the period; until 1820, they were large brick country homes similar to Mt. Vernon or Monticello and after mid-century they were frequently ornate Gothic or Tuscan mansions. Boarding houses provided shelter near the working areas downtown.

152 David Ward, "The Emergence of Central Immigrant Ghettoes in American Cities, 1840–1920." In: Jackson and Schultz (eds.), *Cities in American History,* *op. cit.*, p. 170.
153 Pred, *loc. cit.*, p. 118.
154 Tunnard and Reed, *op. cit.*, p. 62. The movement outward varied among cities; for example, if high prestige sources of employment such as government units or banks were located near the areas, well-to-do families tended to continue to live downtown. See Ward, *loc. cit.*, pp. 165–166.

Another response to increasing congestion was to use the space available more intensively. Around 1800, there were some four-story dwellings, along with the single-family houses; by the 1820's in downtown areas, continuous rows of houses were being built in most large cities for upper-class residents.

The design of the row houses varied among cities and among periods, although the narrow rectangular urban lot, 20 or 25 feet wide, dictated a similar size in most cities. In New Orleans, the town house had the open courtyard, and a more generous spatial arrangement was made possible by the climate and plenty of servants. In Boston, one group of row houses was red brick, four stories, with bow fronts, shutters, and graceful iron railings on the second floor. In New York City, stylish brick row houses along Broadway uniformly had iron railings, marble facing, the Dutch stoop, plate-glass windows, and silver nameplates at the doorway above the basement. In Philadelphia and Baltimore, bricks were soft colored and steps were of marble.[155]

As urban congestion increased, particularly after the Civil War, row houses were built higher, four stories instead of two or three, and in some cities by the 1880's the fronts were covered with brownstone. San Francisco in the 1880's developed "a particularly successful row vernacular, suitable for rich and poor alike"—wooden structures with pitched roofs, bay windows, and exteriors decorated in the Queen Anne style and painted in bright colors.[156]

The interior plan was practically the same in all row houses, regardless of location or building style: an entrance hall opening into three or more rooms placed in line. Frequently, in the North, the kitchen was in the basement with a playroom and pantry nearby. The drawing room, library, and dining room were on the main floor, and bedrooms upstairs.[157]

Row houses were used for business or commerce as well as for residences, and the first floor might have an office opening off the hallway, above which the family, and sometimes employees, lived.[158]

Following the invention of the elevator and its use for transporting passengers apartment houses became, after 1859, the city homes of the growing rich, while others of the same class built elaborate mansions on the outskirts of the city.[159] At first, apartment houses were relatively simple, often converted from the brownstone row houses. Others were lavishly designed, of dark yellow brick trimmed with stone and orna-

---

[155] Tunnard and Reed, *op. cit.*, pp. 58–59, 80–81.

[156] Davidson, *op. cit.*, p. 287.

[157] D. M. Ellis, et al., *A Short History of New York State.* (Ithaca, N.Y.: Cornell University Press), 1957, p. 294.

[158] Tunnard and Reed, *op. cit.*, p. 82.

[159] Wright, *op. cit.*, pp. 867–868.

mented, with special service entrances and stairways. By the 1880's apartment houses were being built in western as well as eastern cities.[160]

The value of land adjacent to the transportation routes increased and building tended to concentrate along the routes. Although service was not provided equally over the entire city, the horse-drawn streetcar gave frequent and regular service at reasonable fares. In turn, this improved transportation stimulated the development of sites in areas within walking distance of the lines, which began to be filled in with residences, largely for a rising middle class.[161]

By mid-century, residential areas in the cities were becoming segregated by income, with the wealthy living in their own distinctive areas, the middle class in less expensive areas, and the poor in the older parts of the city.[162]

More significant in the longer term, perhaps, than the increased territorial coverage was the spatial distance that population dispersal added to traditional social distinctions. In the walking city no significant amount of geographical distance had separated persons of high, middle, and low social status. In the later Nineteenth-Century residential pattern of the emerging metropolis, however, socioeconomic rank could be fairly reliably determined by the distance from the home to the central city; the greater the distance, the higher the rank. The individual now could gauge his relative social position in the directly measurable terms of distance and time from downtown . . . if this were not enough to convince him of his present station, further confirmation was readily found in his neighborhood, for his neighbors were quite apt to be of a status similar to his.[163]

The Urban Environment

For almost half of the 19th century, the older eastern cities continued to use their colonial systems of fire protection, water supply, street cleaning and lighting, and sanitation. Only slowly were improvements made in these facilities and usually not until problems created by the inadequacies of the systems had become acute. Since newer cities tended to model themselves on the older ones, nearly all cities had the same deficiencies. Much of the delay in improving conditions, of course, was caused by limitations in technology; another cause was that the institutional and administrative systems to handle urban problems had not been implemented.

160 Tunnard and Reed, *op. cit.*, pp. 122–124.

161 Holt, *loc. cit.*, p. 328.

162 Oscar Handlin, *Boston's Immigrants: A Study in Acculturation*, rev. ed. (Cambridge, Mass.: Harvard University Press), 1959, p. 15.

163 R. J. Hopkins, "Status, Mobility, and the Dimensions of Change in a Southern City." In: Jackson and Schultz (eds.), *Cities in American History, op. cit.*, p. 217.

Until the 1860's, methods of fighting fires were the same in most of the large eastern cities as in the frontier towns: volunteer fire departments, hook-and-ladder brigades, and a bucket line from the nearest source of water supply—which was seldom adequate. Nearly every city had one or more devastating fires; in fact, a large part of the building regulation of the 19th century was brought about by the extensive concern over the frequent fires.[164] By 1860, at least a few cities had steam fire engines and a paid force of firemen.[165]

Concern over the failure of water supplies in fighting fires led to the development of municipal water supplies. Except for a few cities, including Philadelphia and Baltimore, public water supplies were provided by private companies; householders made arrangements for their own supplies or used wells and springs. Even after public supplies were provided (around the 1840's in New York City), many city residents depended on rainwater and the city pumps.[166] Public supplies were seldom adequate for long. New York City's water-supply system, completed in 1842, had to be enlarged in 1858.

Streets were dimly lighted by moonlight or, on nights when the moon was not shining, by oil lamps until gaslights were introduced, in 1816 in Baltimore and 1827 in New York City; by the 1840's, other cities were using gas lighting, usually provided by private companies. Gaslights were the means of illumination until the coming of electric power in the 1880's.[167]

Until the middle of the century, the police system consisted of a part-time police force often recruited from among the unemployed and usually untrained. They did not wear uniforms and thus could escape without being identified in times of trouble. The Municipal Police Act of 1844 in New York City set up a single body of 800 paid policemen; in 1853, uniforms were made mandatory. This system was adopted in other large cities.[168]

Before 1850, removal of waste in most of the cities, even the large ones, was about the same as in the country. Vaults or cesspools received the waste material from privies or water closets, were only sporadically cleaned, and sometimes overflowed into the ground. Kitchen waste was thrown into the streets or on the ground near the house, to be carried off (sometimes) by open street drains; human waste frequently was carried along in these ditches because of the inadequate waste-disposal system

164 See McGoldrick, et al., *op. cit.*, for the development of fire control regulations in New York City.

165 Wright, *op. cit.*, p. 862.

166 Robert Ernst, *Immigrant Life in New York City, 1825–1863* (New York: Columbia University Press), 1949, p. 22n.

167 Glaab and Brown, *op. cit.*, p. 162.

168 *Ibid.*, p. 96.

in congested areas. Public sewer systems were built only slowly and seldom served an entire city. In 1849 New York City created a municipal department of sewers, but eight years later, three quarters of the city, including most of the slum areas, still were without facilities.[169]

The problems of garbage and rubbish disposal were aggravated by accumulations in backyards, alleys, and on the unpaved streets. Travelers complained consistently about the mud and filth in city streets in all parts of the country. A newspaper criticism of New York City in 1844 merely describes a common urban condition:

That our streets have been horrible enough in times past no one denies, but they are now . . . more abominably filthy than ever; they are too foul to serve as the styes for the hogs which perambulate them. . . . The offal and filth, of which there are loads thrown from the houses in defiance of an ordinance which is never enforced, is scraped up with the usual deposits of mud and manure into big heaps and left for weeks together on the sides of the streets.[170]

Very few cities had any systematic method of cleaning streets until after the Civil War. In New York, in 1866, the Metropolitan Board of Health was given authority to keep the streets clean. Most city streets were not paved at all until around 1860, then with cobblestones or small granite or wooden blocks until 1870, when asphalt or brick began to be used.[171]

The "growth of the cities took place despite bad condition of urban living, not because of appreciable improvements."[172] It might be said that nearly all the growth of population before the Civil War took place while the cities had inadequate water supplies, frequent fires, untrained police, poorly lighted and unpaved streets, and few, if any, miles of public sewers. The recurring plagues and epidemics that struck the seaboard cities focused public attention on the need for measures to improve urban conditions.

The urban death rate rose between 1810 and 1860 in large cities:

In New York City, for example, the crude death rate rose from one death per 46.5 persons in 1810 to one in 27 in 1859; other large cities demonstrated a similar alarming tendency.[173]

From about 1800 on, the larger cities in the East usually had Boards of Health. These Boards frequently had extensive powers to mandate

169 *Ibid.*, p. 87. Boston as part of a disease prevention program had a private system of sewers.

170 *Ibid.*, pp. 86–87.

171 E. C. Kirkland, *Industry Comes of Age: Business, Labor and Public Policy, 1860–1897.* (New York: Holt, Rinehart and Winston), 1961, pp. 241–242.

172 Taylor, *op. cit.*, p. 391.

173 Glaab and Brown, *op. cit.*, pp. 89–90.

the cleaning of streets and premises; they had numerous responsibilities and typically were undermanned for the scope of the task—especially as the increased congestion in relatively small areas made the work never-ending. Some progress was made in preventive health measures after 1850; however, it was not until after the germ theory of disease was expounded in 1883 that "the way opened for intelligent control of com-municable diseases."[174]

One result of interest in public health was the development of com-plete systems of public sewers. Prior to the 1870's, there had been little public knowledge of any particular threat to health from improper waste disposal or impure water supplies.

Although the general relationship between unsatisfactory sewage disposal, water contamination and many diseases, such as typhoid fever and cholera, which decimated urban dwellers, was understood by European scientists in the 1860's and supported by many American public-health leaders, these con-tamination theories and the subsequent germ theory were not accepted widely enough to lead to any public demand for significant changes in methods of waste disposal.[175]

In the 1870's, George E. Waring, later New York Commissioner of Street Cleaning, began a campaign against the defective sanitation in cities.

Waring argued persuasively that not only typhoid fever but most com-municable diseases were the result of filth and decay. Outbreaks of disease, he argued, could often be traced to a foul-smelling house drain or the near-ness of a drainage ditch. . . . To prevent disease-causing bad air, house-hold sanitary fixtures were necessary, and whole communities would have to be systematically cleansed.[176]

The wide publicity this campaign received touched off a general demand for public sewer systems in cities.

While wealthy and many middle-class families could live in less con-gested areas and view the deteriorating effects of congestion and rapid development from carriages, omnibuses, or street cars, the groups who still were tied to points within walking distance of work were less for-tunate. Two such groups, in particular, were largely confined to housing in the most deteriorated areas, Negroes and foreign immigrants.

Housing of Negroes in the City

By 1800, almost every northern state had abolished slavery and by 1830 the practice was virtually eliminated in the North. Abolition came about chiefly because of the conflict between the practice of slavery and

174 Taylor, *op. cit.*, p. 392.
175 Glabb and Brown, *op. cit.*, p. 165.
176 *Ibid.*, p. 164.

the promulgation of the principle of the right to freedom, since the scarcity of labor made owning slaves desirable. At the same time, until after the Civil War, a distinction was made between the rights of former slaves to the protection of life, liberty, and property and the right to political and social equality. The legal position of free Negroes as citizens remained unclear until 1862, when it was decided—a decision confirmed by the Fourteenth Amendment in 1868—that free men of color, if born in the United States, were United States citizens. Prior to this, the status of Negroes varied by states: full citizenship in Massachusetts, political disenfranchisement in Pennsylvania, some freedom in New York, and complete exclusion of rights in several states. Except for some towns, Negroes had little success in breaking down a general pattern of segregation in employment, education, and housing until the 1850's, when some states and cities began to improve educational facilities and bar discrimination in public schools.[177] Abolitionists managed to invalidate the belief (held as strongly in the North as in the South) that underlay discrimination—that the Negro was genetically inferior to the white race—but their efforts until the Civil War were largely spent on behalf of the slaves in the South.[178]

Some proportion of Negroes in the North managed to accumulate property and economic advancement; a few became professionals. These upper classes, who enjoyed distinction principally among other blacks, usually lived in good houses and good neighborhoods. The majority of Negroes, who had much more difficulty than whites in getting out of unskilled labor jobs, tended to live in the poorest sections, in deteriorating houses, in cellars, or in flimsy houses along narrow alleys.[179] The residential pattern in Negro neighborhoods differed sharply from those in white neighborhoods in that all income groups were confined to a particular section of a city. Although the upper and middle classes lived in the better housing areas, only infrequently did they have the choice of living among white families of similar status.

Housing of Immigrants

Throughout the 19th century the largest single source of urban population growth in the United States was the in-migration of people from rural areas and from European countries.

Although the relationship between migration, birth and death rates, and urban growth cannot be examined historically with any precision, it seems

[177] L. F. Litwack, *North of Slavery: The Negro in the Free States, 1790–1860.* (Chicago: University of Chicago Press), 1961, Chapter 3.

[178] Billington, *op. cit.*, pp. 370–372.

[179] Litwack, *op. cit.*, pp. 103, 168–169. Other nonwhite groups also usually were segregated.

reasonably certain that not until well into the Twentieth Century did city dwellers in America reproduce at replacement levels. . . .[180]

The native rural population migrated to the cities throughout the century, as skilled labor sought opportunities in manufacturing and commerce. The native-born in-migrants relatively soon after arrival became dispersed throughout all the housing areas of the city according to their income levels.

Immigrants from Europe began coming in increasing numbers in the 1820's and continued to arrive through the remainder of the century at varying rates. In general, immigration increased in times of prosperity and tended to slow down in times of depression. The causes of this large-scale out-migration from Europe were crop failures, changes in agricultural methods, the spreading factory system that uprooted farmers and artisans, as well as, for many, political and religious dissension. Furthermore, the United States offered some positive attractions: a chance to improve economic and social status, religious and political freedom, and respect for the self-made man. These opportunities had been extensively advertised in Europe by shipping companies, land speculators, labor contractors, and immigrant agents.[181]

Government policy in the United States in the 19th century was to keep newcomers moving in to alleviate the continued labor shortage. The federal and the state governments enacted statutes to facilitate this flow that barred entry only to the permanently disabled. About 5,000,000 people immigrated to the United States between 1820 and 1860 and over 10,000,000 more between 1860 and 1890. During these intervals, the highest proportion of immigrants came from northwestern and central Europe; from the 1870's on, immigrants from eastern and southern Europe made up higher proportions of the total immigration than before 1860.[182]

A large proportion of immigrants did not remain in the port city; for example, some unskilled workers moved on out to construction jobs on roads, canals, and railroads or to work in factories in small villages and cities. Skilled farmers went inland. After 1850, when immigrant societies, municipal employment offices, and a more systematic method of contracting for labor had been established, many immigrants went or were sent directly to a place of employment outside the seaport of entry.

Because the immigrants tended to cluster in certain regions and

[180] Glabb and Brown, *op. cit.*, p. 135.

[181] Ernst, *op. cit.*, Chapter 1.

[182] U. S. Bureau of the Census. *Historical Statistics of the United States, Colonial Times to 1970, op. cit.*, C89–101, p. 106. Total figures of immigration between 1868 and 1890 include also the numbers of native citizens returning from abroad.

cities, the proportion of immigrants who remained was substantial. The early immigrants largely concentrated in the Atlantic seaports, especially New York, Boston, Philadelphia, Baltimore, and New Orleans. Later immigrants concentrated, in addition, at points farther inland— Cleveland, Chicago, Cincinnati, Pittsburgh, and St. Louis.[183] A high proportion of the immigrants were unskilled, poor, and urban rather than farm oriented. Many preferred the city as a source of employment, while others simply did not have the resources to leave.[184]

Since the jobs the unskilled immigrants could hope to get were in the downtown warehouse and commercial districts, where shippers, merchants, and importers were located—and since workdays were 14 or more hours—most of the workers looked for housing as close as possible to such districts. Their first shelters frequently were the boarding houses along the edge of the commercial district, but these were expensive. The next stage, therefore, was likely to be a room in one of the old mansions that were rapidly being converted into tenements. But also, warehouses, breweries, or any structure with four walls and a roof in the older parts of the city were used for housing. Sheds and shanties were put up in backyards, and stables and cellars were converted into dwellings.[185]

As the flow of immigrants continued, the specific housing response varied among cities. Tenement houses were built in some large cities but not in all of them. In Philadelphia, for instance, more row houses were built but made smaller—two stories and 16-feet wide. Each of these structures housed half a dozen families.[186] In Boston, where prior to the 1850's land was cheap in undesirable areas, the poor lived in small one-story houses, frequently without sanitary provisions.[187] Though not overcrowded at first, they became so later—each had an average of 37 persons per house.[188] In Boston, however, immigrants who were able to get out from the most congested portions of the center could find adequate lodgings in the outlying villages where farmlands were being converted into metropolitan areas. Those who were unable to pay transportation clustered in lodgings around the commercial center of Boston.[189]

In the 1850's, Boston builders devised the three-decker building, so called from the three wooden galleries, one above the other. These build-

183 Oscar Handlin, *The Uprooted*. (Boston, Mass.: Little, Brown), 1951, p. 145.
    184 See Handlin, *Boston's Immigrants, op. cit.*, Chapter 2.
    185 Tunnard and Reed, *op. cit.*, pp. 98–99.
    186 *Ibid.*, p. 100.
    187 Handlin, *Boston's Immigrants, op. cit.*, p. 16.
    188 Tunnard and Reed, *op. cit.*, p. 100.
    189 Handlin, *Boston's Immigrants, op. cit.*, pp. 89–100.

ings were constructed back to back; each apartment had a front room entered from the gallery and two small rooms without windows in the rear.[190]

In cities in the interior and in the factory towns, there was more space and low-cost housing was less isolated from the rest of the residential areas. The first house of the immigrant was typically a converted building that housed several families; from these they could move to small cottages or to dilapidated shanties or jerry-built boxlike structures at low rent. As more immigrants came, three- or four-story wooden buildings, frequently without water or sewerage, were built. Conditions in practically all of this housing became as bad as those in the tenements in the larger cities.[191]

Tenements and Public Policy

New York City, which by 1830 had become the major commercial and financial center of the United States and a principal port of entry, probably had the greatest housing problem and some of the worst housing conditions. The first attempts to regulate the construction of tenement housing were made in New York City; thus, a brief overview of some of the highlights in the New York experience can be used to illustrate the conditions under which the idea of public intervention in the field of housing slowly emerged.[192]

The development of housing and other social welfare legislation in the 19th century was for the most part the result of actions by states, under the general police power. The concept of the police power of state came from English common law; the term "police power" was first used in the United States in 1827. In 1851, the police power was defined as:

. . . the power of the legislature to enact "all manner of wholesome and reasonable laws . . . not repugnant to the constitution, as they shall judge to be for the good and welfare of the commonwealth, and of the subjects of the same."[193]

By the end of the century, several states had some kind of regulation with respect to tenements and other buildings. These kinds of regulations developed slowly and in conjunction with strong resistance, even though some types of public regulation of private property had been accepted before the end of the 18th century. Mackesey states:

---

[190] Tunnard and Reed, *op. cit.*, pp. 100–101.

[191] Handlin, *The Uprooted, op. cit.*, pp. 150, 168–169.

[192] For the most complete account, see R. W. DeForest and Lawrence Veiller (eds.), *The Tenement House Problem*, Vols. 1 and 2. (New York: Arno Press and the *New York Times*), 1970. (Reprint ed.).

[193] Sidney Fine, *Laissez Faire and the General-Welfare State*. (Ann Arbor: University of Michigan Press), 1956, p. 151.

It must not be supposed that each of these developments followed in orderly and chronological fashion. They were all more or less simultaneous, some parts of the country finding it necessary, because (of) special local considerations, to experiment with height limitations and others, because of the peculiar prevalence of other sets of conditions, concentrated on the segregation of certain undesirable uses or on a tenement house law or on a building code or fire zone. Nor must it be imagined that the extension of public control to effect these regulations was easily accomplished. Each suggestion of extension of application of the police power was fought bitterly. Every attempt to control the development of private property for the common good was denounced and decried by some interests as "unconstitutional."[194]

The approach to housing reform was through the two major urban concerns of serious epidemics and devastating fires. As more immigrants crowded into New York and other cities and settled in already crowded houses and tenements, living conditions deteriorated rapidly. Public attention was drawn to the overcrowded slums as places from which diseases and plagues could spread to the rest of the city. In New York City, the Board of Health from 1801 to 1892 was the agency charged with responsibility for housing conditions related to health. In 1834, the Board called attention to "the crowded and filthy state in which a great portion of our population live" and suggested that these conditions were responsible for the high death rate. A more comprehensive picture of slum conditions and their relation to health was given in the 1842 Annual Report of the Board: lack of ventilation, several families living in one room, and the large proportion of the population living "in cellars and basements and in courts and alleys." This report contains the first recommendation for city legislation to prevent the use of cellars as dwellings and to regulate the interiors of dwellings when conditions hazardous to health were found.[195] Apparently, no official action was taken; in a later recommendation in 1844, for a municipal program of sanitation and education in public health, the chief inspector mentioned this same plan, saying "not only was it untouched but the seeds which I had planted were neglected and suffered to rot in the ground."[196]

The profits made from the conversion of old residences into tenements and the market provided by the continued flow of immigrants stimulated the building of new tenements. Annual returns of from 7 to 10 percent for rental property (in New York City) and a possible higher return

194 T. W. Mackesey, "History of Zoning in the United States." Mimeo, n.d., p. 14.

195 Deforest and Veiller (eds.), *op. cit.*, pp. 71, 72–73, 75.

196 J. H. Griscom, "The Sanitary Condition of the Laboring Population of New York, A Discourse Delivered On the 30th of December, 1844, at the Repository of the American Institute," New York, 1845. Reprinted in: *The Annals of America*, Vol. 7. (Chicago: Encyclopaedia Britannica), 1968, p. 213.

encouraged property owners to make the maximum use of the site.[197] Experimentation in housing consisted largely of finding methods to use available space to its limits.

One result was that, in the 1850's, the old residences were torn down and compact tenements constructed over the entire lot. These new tenements impressed observers as a great improvement over the previous cellars, attics, and shacks. Each unit had two rooms and a hall, was about 18 feet wide and 20 feet long; there were 24 residences on each floor. Within a few years, these flimsily constructed three- and four-story "railroad" tenements spread throughout the lower part of the city. One, Gotham Court, without heat or plumbing, was five stories, built between two alleys.

Twelve doors opened onto the wider of the two alleys, and each door provided entry for the ten families living in each section of the building—two families to a floor in identical two-room apartments, with a main room about 15 by 9½ and a bedroom about 15 by 8½. The structure housed around 500 people without provision for plumbing or heat. Ten years later a row of privies had been placed in the basement, but by then more than 800 people had crowded into the structure.[198]

A model workingmen's home built in 1855 by a philanthropist consisted of six stories of three-room apartments, all small and over half without windows, with gaslights in the hall and privies in a shed in the alley.[199] In a few years, this model tenement had "degenerated into one of the worst in the city." This experience was frequently cited as a reason for not building model tenements.[200]

The Association for Improving the Conditions of the Poor, organized in 1843, investigated the slums of New York City over a seven-year period, beginning in 1846. In 1853, they issued the first report on tenement housing conditions in the United States, described them, and called for legislative action to remedy them.[201] In 1857, a committee appointed by the New York State Assembly to examine the conditions of "tenant housing" again stressed that public action was long overdue:

The tenant house is the offspring of municipal neglect, as well as of its primary causes, over-population and distribution. As a city grows in commerce and manufacture, the store and workshop encroach upon the dwelling house and dispossess its occupants. This was the time when lawful regulation should have entered but did not. . . . The tenant house is built upon speculative capital and its construction is economical of convenience. . . .

[197] Tunnard and Reed, *op. cit.*, p. 100.
[198] Glaab and Brown, *op. cit.*, p. 161.
[199] Handlin, *The Uprooted, op. cit.*, p. 148.
[200] DeForest and Veiller (eds.), *op. cit.*, p. 86.
[201] *Ibid.*, pp. 76–77.

The tenant house, I conclude and asseverate, is the legitimate point at which to commence the positive work of social reform.[202]

The Superintendent of the Department for the Survey and Inspection of Buildings, in a report in 1862 to the Board of Aldermen of New York City stated that the "tenement house system . . . was one requiring the most stringent laws and their most rigorous enforcement." Many were firetraps—over shops full of highly inflammable materials. Rear houses were frequently not separate dwellings but had to be reached through the hallways of structures in front and were dangerous in case of fire. The relationship between such hazards and outbreak of fires apparently was clear—a law in 1862 required some alterations of present tenements with respect to fire hazards.[203]

Structural hazards received particular attention in 1867 when the state legislature gave the Superintendent of Buildings power over construction and alterations of tenement houses with respect to "the method of constructing halls and stairways and the height of ceilings." Also, he had power to decide on any alterations needed in existing tenements to provide safe escape in case of fire. The act required that all new tenements be fireproof.[204]

In 1867, the state legislature passed the first tenement housing law in the United States. This act regulated the construction of new tenements: It established minimum requirements for the size of rooms, ventilation, and sanitation; required permits for occupancy of cellars not previously used as residences; and prescribed minimum spaces to be allowed between main and rear buildings on a lot.

It was a really drastic piece of legislation for its time and is actually the basis upon which our present law is predicated.[205]

The legislation, at the least, prevented the building of more barracks. Now the dimension of legality was added to the problem of maximum use of sites. A competition sponsored among architects in 1878 to provide a suitable design for this kind of housing produced the "dumbbell" tenement (see Chapter 3 for details).

The selection of this design for an award, as well as the motivations for such a design were criticized sharply on March 16, 1879, by the

---

202 Quoted in J. P. Comer, *New York City Building Control, 1800–1941.* (New York: Columbia University Press), 1942, pp. 12–13.

203 *Ibid.*, p. 12.

204 McGoldrick, et al., *op. cit.*, p. 64.

205 L. W. Post, *The Challenge of Housing.* (New York: Farrar, Straus and Giroux), 1938, p. 106. The law regulated construction of tenements only in New York City and Brooklyn.

New York Times, which predicted—accurately—a tenfold increase in the evils of tenement housing if the design was used:

The limitations of the designs by the architects were the shape of the lots, and cheapness of construction; they were required to plan a cheap house or houses with air and light in the rooms, on a lot 25 feet broad, enclosed between other houses, and 100 feet deep. If the prize plans are the best offered, which we hardly believe, they merely demonstrate that the problem is insoluble.[206]

The dumbbell tenement (sometimes called the "old law" tenement to distinguish it from the "new law" tenements built after 1901) acquired the distinction of being the worst in the world. They were built by the thousands:

By 1888 there were over thirty-two thousand such buildings, containing a human population of more than one million, not to mention rats, vermin, and other parasites.[207]

In 1879, another state law corrected one deficiency of the 1867 law by requiring that future tenement houses should have a 10-foot open space in the rear of the lot and not cover more than 65 percent of the site. Other legislation followed: an act in 1882 that assembled previous regulations into one act and another in 1887 that limited the number of families who could occupy a dwelling. This act also required that all previously erected tenement houses were to be furnished with water when the Board of Health so ordered "at one or more places on each floor occupied or intended to be occupied by one or more families."[208]

Once legislation was undertaken, the State of New York seems to have adopted the recommendations of the various reports, although very slowly and in a piecemeal fashion. The real problem was that the laws were not and perhaps could not be enforced. One primary reason was the change in the general attitude toward what Morison and Commager define as the question "To what extent shall the federal and state governments regulate the affairs of men, in order to save, and possibly to improve, society?"[209] Two distinct views toward this question were held after the Revolution by government officials and political parties. One was that all economic activities, including agriculture, would flourish without government assistance, particularly without direct aid from the federal government. The other was that the federal govern-

---

206 Quoted in DeForest and Veiller, (eds.), *op. cit.*, pp. 101–102.

207 Davidson, *op. cit.*, p. 283.

208 McGoldrick, et al., *op. cit.*, p. 43n. This legislation was challenged in the celebrated Trinity Church case; it was declared unconstitutional in 1892 but finally upheld in 1895. See Beyer, *Housing and Society, op. cit.*, p. 451

209 Morison and Commager, *op. cit.*, p. 129.

ment should actively promote national economic self-sufficiency. Various sections of the general public, however, not only sanctioned intervention by some level of government in economic affairs but also expected it:

Americans . . . were not much interested in elaborate theories as to the proper role of government in economic affairs. They believed that economic conditions should constantly improve and that the government had a simple and direct obligation to take any practicable measure to forward such progress.[210]

In practice, states, and to a lesser extent, the federal government, accepted this obligation and interfered in economic affairs through promotional as well as regulatory activities such as the federal tariff, state premiums and bounties, and federal and state promotion (as well as regulating and sometimes financing) of banks and such public works as turnpikes, bridges, canals, and railroads.[211]

In 1837, a Supreme Court decision, upholding the power of a state to provide a free bridge for public use in competition with a private toll bridge, stated "for perhaps the first time in the Supreme Court, the modern doctrine of social responsibilities of private property":

While the rights of private property are sacredly guarded, we must not forget that the community also have rights, and that the happiness and well-being of every citizen depends on their faithful preservation.[212]

Against this background, states and, to some extent, the federal government might have been expected to extend their intervention in "the affairs of men" to include regulatory action in the field of social as well as economic welfare under the police power. Instead, the progress of industrialization in the second half of the 19th century—the period when urban problems were becoming acute—was accompanied by the development of a strong attitude against government restrictions that would adversely affect specific private interests.[213]

A strong belief evolved, and was actively promoted, that economic progress would solve all social problems and that government interference on behalf of any special groups would upset the harmonious workings of economic law. Economists in particular, as a result of their strong beliefs in "the immutability of the laws of economics, the efficacy of self-interest, the merits of competition, and the inefficiency of government," promoted the doctrine

210 Taylor, *op. cit.*, pp. 352–353.
211 *Ibid.*, p. 383.
212 Morison and Commager, *op. cit.*, pp. 559–560.
213 Fine, *op. cit.*, p. 23.

. . . that the state must pursue a policy of laissez faire, or noninterference with the economic interests of society. It could best promote the general welfare by making itself as inconspicuous as possible and by relying on individual initiative both to augment the national wealth and to cope with the social problems of the age.[214]

Throughout the latter part of the 19th century, the courts upheld the doctrine of nonintervention and seriously limited the scope of state social and economic legislation by means of narrow interpretations "on the admitted right of the states to promote the general welfare through the exercise of the police power." The courts had considerable scope for determining public policy after the ratification of the Fourteenth Amendment to the constitution in 1868. This Amendment provided, among other things, that "no State . . . shall . . . deprive . . . any person of life, liberty, or property, without due process of law."[215]

Writing in 1893, William Guthrie correctly observed that American constitutional history during the previous thirty years had been "little more than a commentary on the Fourteenth Amendment." Guthrie might well have added that the net result of this "commentary" had been to establish that amendment as the bulwark of property rights and of the doctrine of laissez faire.[215]

Since a legislative restriction on the use of real property

. . . limits the rights of an owner to use his property as he pleases (excepting always the common law concept of nuisance), it is in derogation of his common law rights and hence a "deprivation of property without compensation." To the extent to which it imposes additional expense—and admittedly the added expense is very great—it constitutes a further "deprivation of property." Accordingly the statutes and the administrative action taken pursuant thereto are subject to challenge under the Fourteenth Amendment unless the courts find them to be a proper exercise of the police power.[216]

In general, New York State courts upheld the exercise of the police power so far as legislation for fire protection or health was concerned.[217] The relationship between housing and health was difficult to demonstrate conclusively and became subject to close scrutiny. One example is a New York State Act of 1884 that prohibited the manufacture of

214 *Ibid.*, pp. 52, 56.
215 *Ibid.* p. 141. These rights were protected against federal action by the Fifth Amendment. The Fourteenth Amendment protects them against state action under the national constitution. Previously, each state constitution specified the rights that were protected against the action of a particular state.
216 McGoldrick, et al., *op. cit.*, p. 17.
217 *Ibid.*, pp. 46, 63.

cigars in the living quarters of tenement houses as harmful to health. The court declared the Act unconstitutional. Fine reports:

If the legislature passes an act ostensibly for the public health and in so doing deprives a citizen of his property or interferes with his liberty, the courts must examine the act and "see whether it really relates to and is convenient and appropriate to promote the public health." "A law enacted in the exercise of the police power must in fact be a police law." And looking at the act in question, the court decided that it was not intended to protect the health of cigar makers. "It cannot be perceived . . . how the cigarmaker is to be improved in his health or his morals by forcing him from his home and its hallowed associations and beneficent influences, to ply his trade elsewhere."[218]

The general effect of the support given to laissez-faire was to retard social legislation rather than to halt it altogether. Concurrently with the rise of that attitude, an opposed attitude also developed: "that the state could best promote the general welfare by positive exertion of its powers." Proponents of this point of view

. . . regarded the democratic state not as an evil force but as an instrument that the people could and should use to further their common interests, to ameliorate the conditions under which they lived and worked, and to provide for their health and safety and, to some extent, for their social and economic security.[219]

As the problems of economic development became more apparent and as various groups gained in political strength, this viewpoint gained greater recognition. In spite of the doctrine of laissez-faire, state legislatures passed a large amount of social legislation in the last two decades of the century.[220] The intervention doctrine, however, did not become an effective one for action until after 1900.

Another factor related to the problems of enforcing housing legislation was that social welfare legislation was an innovation in the 19th century. Fine points out:

Although public authorities had hardly played a passive role with respect to the economy in the era before the Civil War, governmental responsibility in the postwar years had to be recognized in areas where there had been little or no awareness of such responsibility previously, and new techniques of regulation and control had to be devised.[221]

It is not possible to determine whether inexperience in writing social legislation, the general weakness of administration at all levels of

218 Fine, *op. cit.*, p. 157.
219 *Ibid.*, pp. 167–168.
220 *Ibid.*, pp. 352–369.
221 *Ibid.*, p. 369.

government during much of the 19th century, or the efforts of pressure groups was responsible for the lack of results from legislative efforts to regulate tenement building. One particular problem of housing regulation is that a large number of people own real estate under widely varying conditions; some flexibility is needed in administering the laws. The New York legislature provided for this in various ways, as, for example, allowing for appeals by property owners or giving the enforcing agencies discretionary powers in applying the provisions. These modifications appear to have been fully taken advantage of. For example, the Board of Health had the power to modify the provisions of the act of 1879 in special cases. Veiller has pointed out that, although the 1879 law required that the building not cover more than 65 percent of the site

. . . in a few years, the Board of Health was found to be permitting new tenements to occupy as much as 85 and even 90, per cent of the lot.[222]

An investigation of building agencies in New York City in regard to the application of discretionary powers stated, among other criticisms

that the discretionary power vested in the building commissioner has been applied to so many sections of the law that it practically meant that there were no fixed or determined building laws, but that all buildings might be erected, altered, or repaired at the discretion of the head of the building department.[223]

On the other hand, the enforcing agencies complained that they were effectively prevented from enforcing the laws. In 1873, for example, the Board of Health requested a New York State Senate investigating committee to amend the building laws to permit the Board to demand that its specifications as to drainage, plumbing, ventilation, light, and obstructions be followed.

Under the existing law . . . orders to make changes in tenement houses were too often delayed in the interest of money-saving; and "all sorts of influences" were brought to bear upon the officers of the department to delay enforcement."[224]

The Board stated that the existing law "was so unpopular with real estate owners that the 200 or more provisions of the sanitary code were in reality a dead letter."[225]

An 1868 report of the Superintendent of Buildings states:

---

[222] De Forest and Veiller (eds.), *op. cit.*, p. 100.
[223] Comer, *op. cit.*, p. 26.
[224] *Ibid.*, p. 23.
[225] *Ibid.*

. . . laws and orders from this department are willfully defied and treated with contempt by all parties who are well acquainted with the law's delays and who generally succeed in their unlawful undertakings in a manner which renders this department powerless to act.[226]

One advantage of legal delays to the tenement builder was that the building could be sold before the law could be applied; the new owner, presumably unaware of the violations, could not be prosecuted and neither could the builder, since he no longer owned the building.

Frequently, responsibility for building regulation was shifted from one agency to another, or authority for it was divided among agencies. Veiller, in his recommendation in 1900 for the establishment of one department to be charged with responsibility for tenement housing, states:

A study of the movement for tenement house reform in this city during the past sixty years points to the conclusion that a large part of the failure to accomplish this reform has been due to the lack of some one special body charged with the care and oversight of the tenement houses. At present the enforcement of the different laws in relation to these buildings is divided among four different city departments . . . each one of which is charged with many other duties. . . . It is apparent that the enforcement of the tenement house laws, being only a small part of the work of these four different departments, must receive a comparatively small amount of attention. . . . Responsibility being divided, it is difficult to hold any particular person or department accountable for the enforcement of the law.[227]

Perhaps an important part of the ineffectiveness of the legislation in the 19th century was that once a law was passed, efforts relaxed. There was no follow-through to see whether the provisions of the law were carried out, whether they needed modification, or how best they might be applied. Veiller comments:

The mistake that is too often made by many people is in losing their interest and in feeling that their work is accomplished when some legislative reform has been achieved. So far from being the termination of their efforts such a period should really mark the beginning of their main work. Any important change in the laws will at first bring opposition from those interests which are affected by it. Unless its friends are alert, it frequently happens that important legislative reforms are within a year or two nullified by the interests adversely affected.[228]

[226] *Ibid.*, p. 20. See also for outline of proceedings that brought about delays in court actions.

[227] DeForest and Veiller (eds.), *op. cit.*, pp. 28–29.

[228] Lawrence Veiller, *Housing Reform: A Hand-Book for Practical Use in American Cities.* (New York: Charities Publication Committee), 1910, p. 172.

Restrictive legislation, as Beyer points out,[229] was not of itself a means to provide good housing for the increasingly large numbers of people who needed low-cost dwellings. Some positive action in this respect was made in New York City and elsewhere after mid-19th century by limited dividend corporations. Although better tenements were not built on the scale needed, the model buildings demonstrated that higher standards could be used and could be reasonably profitable. The model tenement may have improved the situation only for a relatively small proportion of the immigrants, since they typically were intended to attract the skilled laborers, "the company preferring to cater to the best element among the workingmen."[230]

Any ideas of providing publicly financed housing were rejected. It was questionable whether the city—or, for that matter, the state—could have financed building a sufficient number of dwellings to house the rapidly increasing population who needed low-cost housing. The major argument against public housing was that, since housing was not a "natural monopoly," responsibility for providing it did not seem to be within the scope of public responsibility and would be unwarranted competition with private enterprise.[231]

Regulatory action by itself, of course, with or without model tenements would not improve the housing situation of immigrants in the absence of jobs, adequate wages, and access to areas beyond the congested inner city. But, ineffectual as the attempts at public regulation of housing were in the 19th century, they did provide the basis for later and more effective government intervention to improve housing conditions.

Federal Action in Housing

The federal government did not take any direct action in the housing field until 1892, when it authorized an investigation of conditions in the slums of several cities. This small-scale project collected a large amount of data on slum conditions; its principal interest is that it marks the first time the federal government took direct action in the housing field.

The federal government did set some precedents for the future, with respect to housing in general, in the income tax laws. The first federal income tax law for the United States was passed in 1862 to help finance the Civil War; a similar tax had been proposed in 1815 to help finance the War of 1812, but the war ended before a tax was imposed. The Civil War income tax was allowed to lapse in 1872; a later attempt

---

229 Beyer, *Housing and Society, op. cit.*, p. 454.
230 DeForest and Veiller, *op. cit.*, pp. 99, 108–109.
231 Kirkland, *op. cit.*, p. 260.

to revive it in 1894 was stricken down by the Supreme Court as unconstitutional.

The first income tax laws, though short-lived, are important in housing, since they served as models for the income tax laws of the 20th century. The provisions of the income tax laws of the 1860's of relevance to housing were the deductions permitted for payments of state and local taxes and for interest on personal indebtedness. These exclusions applied to taxes on real estate and interest on home mortgages as well as to other kinds of taxes and interest payments. Deductions were not allowed for special tax assessments by municipal or state governments.

Considered in the light of income tax theory, the basis for such allowances to individuals is not clear, since such expenses may or may not be related to the production of income, especially income from wages and salaries. However, when the law was passed, farmers, nearly all of whom were owners, represented a high proportion of the population. The principal source of revenue for states and localities was the general property tax levied on real property. Amounts of personal property, then as ever, were difficult to ascertain, even though it was known that such property represented an increasingly large proportion of wealth. Thus, the tax on real estate assumed a larger proportion of the general property tax during the course of the century. One reason for adopting an income tax to help finance the Civil War rather than a tax on real estate was that a tax on land would fall "with very heavy, if not ruinous, effect upon the great agricultural states of the West and Southwest." One member of Congress stated:

I cannot go home and tell my constituents that I voted for a bill that would allow a man, a millionaire, who has put his entire property into stock, to be exempt from taxation, while a farmer who lives by his side must pay a tax.[232]

At any rate, the exemptions were continued in subsequent tax laws, presumably on the basis of the belief that different amounts of tax and interest payments by people of the same income does make for differences in true income.

Another provision in the early income tax laws was an allowance for a deduction from income of amounts paid for the rent of a dwelling by renters. In 1864, a similar deduction was extended to owner-occupants of residences. Several annual reports of commissioners of internal revenue suggested that a definite amount for rent be set, in view of some excessively large amounts being deducted. The commissioners

---

[232] E. R. A. Seligman, *The Income Tax. A Study of the History, Theory, and Practice of Income Taxation at Home and Abroad*, 2nd ed. (New York: Macmillan), 1921, p. 431. See also pp. 494–495.

also recommended that the rental value of the owner-occupied residence be added to other income and taxed. No action was taken on these suggestions in the 1860's. The whole subject was dropped in the 1894 tax law—no deduction was allowed for rent and the rental value of owner-occupied houses was not specifically mentioned as a part of income.[233]

Another precedent for contemporary legislation comes from attempts by the federal government to guarantee the civil rights of Negroes after the Civil War. On April 9, 1866, Congress passed an Act stipulating that all citizens of the United States, regardless of race or color, had equal rights to purchase, lease, or sell real property (Public Acts of the 39th Congress, Session 1, Ch. 31, Sec. 1). This Act barred the states from overt discriminatory actions in housing but did not prevent such actions by individuals. Consequently, it is of interest principally as the historical antecedent of the fair housing legislation enacted a hundred years later.

Housing in 1890

The chief improvements in housing between 1790 and 1890 came from technological developments and the improved municipal services that led to major changes in the mechanical equipment of the house and—to a much lesser extent—in sanitation. Indirectly, because both the federal and state governments encouraged the manufacture of consumer products during the century as well as the development of municipal services, these changes in housing might be credited to public actions of the period. Eventually, standards of housing quality evolved that were applicable to all housing.

The general pattern of distribution of technological improvements during the century was frequently from a public building (hotels, etc.) to homes of the wealthy, then, later, to middle-class homes, and finally to homes of the poor. In other words, the availability of a technical improvement did not necessarily mean that the product was in general use throughout the century by a majority of families. Also, improvements in mechanical equipment were largely in urban homes—many houses in rural areas did not have such amenities as running water, indoor plumbing, or central heating until almost mid-20th century.

The wood- or coal-burning stove began to replace the fireplace for heating in the 1820's, and its use for this purpose continued in most urban and rural homes for the remainder of the century. The second-floor rooms were heated by pipes from the stove or by warm air rising

[233] Seligman, *op. cit.*, pp. 438ff., 511–512.

up from the first floor.[234] A central heating hot-air furnace was invented in 1815, but not until 1860 had this kind of equipment been installed in most homes of the well-to-do. This slow development seems to have been the result of the expense of installation and the cost of operation.

Oil lamps with glass shades and wicks were developed around 1800. Various kinds of oil products were used in them until 1860 when, after the production of oil began in 1859, kerosene came to be used almost exclusively. The kerosene lamp remained the principal means of lighting most homes, urban and rural, for the rest of the century. Gaslights were used to some extent in homes of the well-to-do after 1840, and candles continued to be used as well.[235] The availability of electricity and transmission stations in urban areas in the late 1880's made electric power available in homes for lighting, cooking, and heating, but the use of electrically operated equipment at home is largely a 20th-century development. Even as late as 1930, "the electrical network was sporadic, current too expensive, the apparatus too highly priced and too delicate for the household."[236]

Cast-iron stoves burning wood or coal came into use for cooking before 1820. Improved designs in the 1840's "drew the same interest in its time as the streamline-kitchen a century later."[237] The use of the cast-iron range spread fairly rapidly, and open fires became a luxury for the rich or a necessity for the poor.[238] After gas was available and being manufactured, a gas range was developed, but it was adopted in homes only very slowly. "Readily as they took to cookstoves, the possibility of firing them with gas was little exploited until after the Civil War. And in any case this derivative of coal could develop only in step with the gradual, though steady, growth of coal mining . . . from the local specialty of a few states to a chief pillar of the national economy."[239]

Refrigeration was one of the necessities of life in the hot, humid summers of the eastern United States, from colonial days on. Through the 19th century, the principal means of refrigeration was to store food in cellars or near wells, or, in the countryside, to build ice houses. The invention of the ice cutter in the 1820's and various later supportive inventions during the 19th century finally led to the commercial production of ice for use in homes; insulated home iceboxes, supplied

234 Wright, *op. cit.*, p. 854.

235 *Ibid.*, p. 855.

236 Siegfried Giedion, *Mechanization Takes Command: A Contribution to Anonymous History.* (New York: Oxford University Press), 1948, p. 542.

237 *Ibid.*, p. 536.

238 Wright, *op. cit.*, p. 854.

239 Furnas, *op. cit.*, p. 429–430.

with ice by local dealers, came into general use until (and after) mechanical refrigerators were manufactured, around 1916 or 1917.[240]

So far as water supply, plumbing, and sanitation were concerned, a general backwardness prevailed through most of the century. One reason, of course, was the lack of central water supplies, or, if available, their inadequacy. Small towns might not have public supplies (beyond wells and pumps), and farms usually did not. After houses were connected to city water supplies, running water became available first in basements (where the kitchen was likely to be), then on the first floor, and finally on upper floors. Water was heated in a boiler attached to the kitchen stove, then carried to places of use; some houses were equipped with wash basins to which water was pumped by hand.[241] Upper classes in cities had hot and cold running water in their homes by the 1860's.[242]

An American patent for an improved water closet was issued in 1833 but water closets were not in general use until after 1860. They were installed in houses more frequently after 1840, as concern over city health conditions became more general; usually water was pumped by hand and sewage carried off to the underground vault or cesspool. Indoor toilets, of course, became more general in urban areas after the campaign in the 1880's to have residences connected with public sewer systems. Another type of facility was the earth closet which at the time was expected to be almost as useful.[243]

The bathroom as a separate room in the house and provided with facilities for bathing was largely a 20th-century development. By 1900, some of the well-to-do had complete bathrooms in their homes, but in general the essential elements of a dependable supply of hot water and a bathtub were lacking.[244] Early built-in bathtubs were made of wood and lined with metal.[245] Through most of the 19th century, bathing at home was mostly by use of a sponge and a portable container for the water.[246] A portable bathtub was developed in the 1870's; the use of this appurtenance, sometimes with a unit for heating the water, continued into the 20th century—possibly a reflection of the slowness with which existing houses were remodeled to include a full bathroom.[247]

Appliances to lighten household work were not available in any quantity until after the small electric motor was marketed in 1889.

240 Giedion, *op. cit.*, pp. 598, 602.
241 *Ibid.*, pp. 684–685.
242 Wright, *op. cit.*, p. 854.
243 Davidson, *op. cit.*, p. 262.
244 Giedion, *op. cit.*, p. 682.
245 Wright, *op. cit.*, p. 854.
246 Giedion, *op. cit.*, p. 659.
247 *Ibid.*, pp. 666, 684.

Some hand-operated appliances, however, had been invented—a vacuum cleaner (1859), dishwasher (1865), and washing machine (1869).[248] Although not adopted to any extent, they are interesting as examples of the early recognition of both the need for and profitable opportunities in the mechanization of household work.

After 1850, most furniture was machine-made and more likely to be purchased from a retail store than commissioned from a cabinet-maker. Furniture designs through much of the century in both Europe and the United States tended to imitate classical, medieval, or other motifs, but various technological improvements made articles of furniture more comfortable; one example is the use of metal springs in upholstered sofas, chairs, and beds. Frequently furniture was sold in "suites" (to have all furniture in a room match), and upholstered furniture was elaborately decorated. Power looms made carpeting less expensive, and the living and dining rooms of the middle as well as the upper class were carpeted. Wallpaper also became less expensive and more widely used.[249]

The use of stoves and furnaces for heating and improved lighting made it possible to use more of the central space in rooms. Beginning in the 1870's,

. . . the interior of a house, even in regions where the winters were cold, could be opened up to provide a new sense of space. Indeed, one of the significant developments . . . was the expansion of the hall into a large and informal main living area. With this new freedom of interior planning the traditional parlors . . . those "ceremonial deserts," as one critic called them, began to seem useless and out of place in modern life. The best room in the house became the "living room," where general domestic activities could be enjoyed by all members of a household.[250]

Since homes were designed mostly for well-to-do families with servants, arrangement of kitchens and other work space did not receive the attention they were given later. Still, "household engineering was in a stage of rapid development, and the confusing mixture of styles and nonstyles overlaid progressive advances in the basic standards of living, even in houses of modest pretention."[251] In 1869, Catherine E. Beecher and her sister Harriet Beecher Stowe (of *Uncle Tom's Cabin* fame) published *The American Woman's Home*, "a guide to the formation and maintenance of economical, healthful, beautiful, and Christian homes." The Beechers recognized that many women were doing their own housework and that many were living in houses of considerably

248 *Ibid.*, pp. 548–553, 558.
249 Wright, *op. cit.*, p. 855.
250 Davidson, *op. cit.*, p. 265.
251 *Ibid.*, p. 235.

fewer than 15 rooms. Their principles of design were intended to apply to all kinds of houses, regardless of style, purchase price, or size.

. . . what concerned them principally was that a house should function efficiently, agreeably, and economically—in the disposition of rooms and stairs to avoid unnecessary steps and climbing, the utilization of facilities to avoid waste of time and movement, the design of space-saving furniture, and such essential matters as heating, lighting, and ventilation. Kitchens were arranged with scrupulous regard for convenience and utility. New urban services were exploited, sanitary facilities, gas for lighting, and the like, and absorbed into the fabric of the house.[252]

Several decades passed before all these concepts were even partially accepted, but the pattern for the contemporary functional house had been conceived by 1890.

According to the national census, there were 11,483,318 occupied dwellings in the United States in 1890, including

. . . any building or place of abode in which any person was living at the time the census was taken, whether a room above a warehouse or factory, a loft above a stable, a wigwam on the outskirts of a settlement, a hotel, a boarding or lodging house, a large tenement house, or a dwelling house as ordinarily considered.[253]

This figure represented an increase of 28 percent in the total number of dwellings in the country since 1880. The distribution of dwellings by regions for each 10-year period from 1850 to 1890 is shown in Table 2–3. This distribution, as would be expected, parallels the distribution of population shown in Table 2–2. During the 40-year period, the proportion of dwellings in relation to the total number of dwellings declined fairly steadily in the North Atlantic region, increased steadily in the North Central and Western regions, and remained practically unchanged in the South.

The average number of persons to a dwelling was 5.9 in 1850, and 5.4 in 1890. The highest proportion of dwellings housed only one family, except in some of the large cities (those having populations of 100,000 or more). The census definition of family in the 19th century included all persons living alone and inmates of institutions and hotels as well as a family as usually understood. In 1890, there were 12,690,152 families according to this definition, or 11 percent more families than dwelling units. This higher proportion of families to dwellings was largely in the industrialized cities of New York and New England.

252 *Ibid.*
253 United States Census Office, *Report on the Population of the United States at the Eleventh Census, op. cit.*, p. clxxxviii.

TABLE 2-3. Distribution of Dwellings in the Contiguous United States, 1850–1890

	1890	1880	1870	1860	1850	Percent Increase in Number of Dwellings, 1850–1890
United States Total number of dwellings	11,483,000	8,956,000	7,048,000	4,970,000	3,362,000	241
	Percent of All Dwellings					
North Atlantic Region	26	27	30	36	41	113
South Atlantic Region	15	15	16	13	16	207
South Central Region	17	18	17	14	15	310
North Central Region	37	36	34	34	27	370
Western Region	5	4	3	3	1	1,329

SOURCE: U. S. Census Office, *Report on the Population of the United States at the Eleventh Census: 1890*, Part 1. (Washington, D.C.: U. S. Government Printing Office), 1895, Table 86, p. 913. The total number of dwellings for each census has been rounded to the nearest thousand. Figures for 1850, 1880, and 1890 are for occupied dwellings only; those for 1860 and 1870 are for both occupied and unoccupied dwellings. Figures for 1850 and 1860 do not include dwellings of the slave population.

114

The proportion of dwellings with three or more families (which typically were apartments and tenements) varied among the large cities, as also did the extent to which families were crowded into them. In New York City, 43 percent of dwellings housed three or more families and 82 percent of the city's families lived in them. The corresponding figures for Chicago were 17 and 39 percent, respectively, for Boston, 17 and 37 percent, and for Cincinnati, 21 and 48 percent. In contrast, less than 2 percent of dwellings in Philadelphia, San Francisco, Washington, Detroit, Omaha, Denver, and Indianapolis had three or more families and only 6 percent or less of the families in each of these cities lived in them.[254]

The data in Table 2–4 show the results in 1890 of the major population migrations that took place in the United States during the 19th century. As indicated in Tables 2–2 and 2–4, the increase in rural population during the decade from 1880 to 1890 (13 percent) was well below the increase in national population (26 percent) in the same period. The census of 1890 reported that 16 percent of areas in the United States suffered a decline in rural population and that these areas were located in all five regions. The steepest drop during the decade was in the North Atlantic states, where the net decline in rural population took place. The other regions had net gains in rural population but slower rates of rural growth. Most of the growth in rural population was in the western region (an increase of 43 percent in 1890 over 1880) and, to a lesser extent, in the South Central states, (an increase of 16 percent), but in both those areas rural population grew substantially less than the total regional populations (71 percent and 23 percent, respectively).

On the other hand, all the regions had substantial increases in urban population between 1880 and 1890. Under the census definition of urban place as one having a population of at least 8,000 (changed in 1900 to 2,500 or more), over half the population of the North Atlantic states was living in an urban area by 1890, as also was almost a third of the population of the western region, and over one quarter of that of the North Central area. The most rural regions were in the South, but even there, urban population had increased by over 50 percent in one decade. Urbanization in 1890, however, was highly concentrated. Of the total number of cities with populations of 8,000 or more (448) and the total proportion of national population living in them (29 percent), a little less than half were in the North Atlantic region, another third in the North Central states; the remainder were fairly evenly

254 U. S. Census Office, *Report on the Population of the United States at the Eleventh Census, op. cit.*, p. cxcvi.

TABLE 2–4. Distribution of Rural, Urban, and Foreign-born Populations of the Contiguous United States in 1890, by Regions

Region	Percent Increase in Total Population, 1880–1890	Percent Increase in Rural Population, 1880–1890	Urban Population			Percent of Total Foreign-born Population	
			Number of Cities with 8,000 or More	Percent of Total Regional Population	Percent Increase, 1880–1890	1890	1850
United States	26	13	448	—	62	—	—
North Atlantic	20	−1	199	52	42	42	59
South Atlantic	17	1	36	16	51	2	5
South Central	23	16	37	10	79	4	6
North Central	29	11	152	26	91	44	29
Western	71	43	24	30	114	8	1

SOURCE: U. S. Census Office, *Report on the Population of the United States at the Eleventh Census: 1890*, Part 1. (Washington, D.C.: U. S. Government Printing Office), 1895, pp. lxviii, lxx, lxxxiv.

divided among the other three regions (8, 8, and 5 percent for the South Atlantic, South Central, and West, respectively).

The proportion of the national population born in a foreign country represented 15 percent of the total population of the United States in 1890, an increase from 10 percent in 1850. This population was somewhat more diffused in 1890 than in 1850, when almost three fifths of the foreign-born were concentrated in the North Atlantic states and less than a third in any other single region. The diffusion, however, was more a redistribution between the North Atlantic and North Central regions than a general diffusion over the nation; in 1890 these two regions accounted for 86 percent of the total foreign-born population, with the next highest proportion (8 percent) in the western states.

Glossary for Chapters 1 and 2*

ACCOUTREMENT: Trappings; equipment, specifically, a soldier's outfit other than clothes and weapons

ADZE: A hand cutting tool having its blade at right angles to its handle and usually curved: used with a sweeping blow for dressing timber

AEGIS: Protection

ALCOVE: Recessed portion of a room

ARTISAN: One trained to do a certain job or skill

BALUSTRADE: A short post or pillar in a series supporting a rail

BROCADED: Rich cloth woven with a raised design, as in silk, velvet, gold, or silver

CASEMENT WINDOW: A metal or timber window with the sash hung vertically and opening outward or inward

CHINTZ: A cotton cloth with a printed flower pattern in a number of colors and usually glazed

CLAPBOARD: A lapping weatherboard, usually thicker at the lower edge than at the upper, for the walls of a building

CONESTOGA WAGON: A style of wagon for freight with broad wheels for deep soil and prairie traveling

CONTIGUOUS: Meeting or joining at the surface or border; example: contiguous houses or counties

CUPIDITY: Very great desire for wealth

CUPOLA: A dome, especially a small dome on a circular or polygonal base crowning a roof or turret

DAMASK: A silk fabric, having some parts raised in the form of flowers and other figures

DORMER WINDOW: A window placed vertically in a sloping roof and with a roof of its own

DOUBLE HUNG WINDOW: Windows moving up or down with equal ease; two sashes of a window hung with cords and weights

DUGOUT: Large square pits dug in the ground or along a river bank or hillside that might house several families

EARTH CLOSET: A privy in which

---

* Contributed by Guido LaMonaca, Celia Kobitz, and Arlene Lawson, students in Dr. Fish's course on the Development of Housing Policy at the University of Maryland, Fall semester, 1976.

earth is used as a covering, or as an absorbing agent

EAVES: The projecting lower edges of a roof, overhanging walls of a building

ELL: An addition to a building usually at right angles

ENCROACHMENTS: An inroad made by advancing beyond the proper, original, or customary limits

ENTABLATURE: The upper part on top of a column order

ENTREPRENEUR: An organizer of business, trade, or entertainment

FACADE: An elevation or exterior front view of a building

FANLIGHT: A semicircular window with radiating sash bars, like the ribs of a fan placed over a door or window

FLEMISH BOND: Stretcher–header–stretcher

FLEMISH WALLOONS: People living in southern Belgium and nearby parts of France

FRENCH HUGUENOTS: French protestants in the 16th and 17th centuries

FURROW: A trench in the earth made by or as by a plow

GABLE: The triangular upper part of a wall under the end of a ridged roof, or a wall rising above the end of a ridged roof

GAMBREL ROOF: A roof with two slopes of different pitch on either side of the ridge

GLEBES (HOUSE): Rectory or vicarage

HAND-HEWN: A hand cut or chopped job done with a sharp instrument; may be done for decorative use

HEARTH: The pavement on which a fire is made, usually in a chimney; the floor of the fireplace; also a corresponding part of the stove

HEATHER: A low growing plant with scalelike, overlapping leaves and stalks of small, bell-shaped, purplish-pink flowers

HINTERLAND: The district inland from the coast or river

HIP ROOF: Has sloped instead of vertical ends

HOMOGENEITY: The character or quality of being the same family or kind

INDIGO: A deep violet-blue dye, obtained from certain plants

JERRY-BUILT: Built cheaply and unsubstantially out of insufficient materials

LAISSEZ-FAIRE: Motto of 18th century French economists who protested excessive government regulation of industry

MULLION WINDOW: Window with a vertical post or other upright dividing it into two or more lights

NEWEL: The upright post or the upright formed by the inner or smaller ends of steps about which steps of a circular staircase wind; in a straight flight staircase, the principal post at the foot or the secondary post at a landing

PALISADE: A fence or fortification consisting of a row of stakes or posts set firmly into the ground, then sharpened on top

PARQUETRY: An inlay of geometric or other patterns in wood used especially for floors

PEDIMENT: The low triangle mass at the ends of a building surrounded with a cornice

PENT ROOF: A roof sloping one way only; same as shed roof

PIAZZA: The term used for veranda generally in the colonial period, and in the south; an open space, usually oblong, surrounded by buildings; a long covered walk supported by columns

PILASTER: A shallow pier or rectangular column projecting only slightly from a wall, offset on wall can also be a corner support

PORTICO: An open space covered by a roof supported by columns; a kind of modern day porch

POST ROAD: Road on which couriers made trips; posthouses were along road

PRESIDIO: A garrisoned place; a military post; also a Spanish penal settlement

PROMULGATION: The making known of a public or official announcement

SERRATED CABINETS: A cabinet with sharp notches along the edges

SETTLE: A long seat or bench, generally of wood with a high back, accommodating several persons at once

SHINGLE STYLE: Walls of upper stories and often ground story have uniform covering of shingles; even post of verandas and porches may be shingled

SPAR: A timber of smaller diameter than a mast

SQUATTER: Settler on land without proper title to it

STEPPED GABLE: The triangle upper portion of a wall at the end of a pitched roof; has a stepped look

STILL HOUSE: A distillery

STOEP: A very small covered platform at the door of a house

STRING COURSE: A projecting course of bricks (sometimes two or three) forming a narrow horizontal strip across the wall of a building

STUCCO: Coating for walls; a fine plaster mode of lime and gypsum with sand and pounded marble

TENON: A projecting part cut on a piece of wood for insertion into a corresponding hole in another piece to make a joint

TURF: The upper stratum of earth and vegetable mold filled with roots of grass and other small plants so as to form a kind of mat; sward; sod; also a piece or slab of this

VERANDA: An open gallery or portico usually roofed, attached to the exterior of a building; in the United States often called a porch or piazza

VERMIN: Disgusting animals of small size (fly, lice, bedbugs, fleas, etc.)

VERNACULAR: The use of a dialect native to a region or country rather than a literary, cultured, or foreign language. Also, relating to a period place, or group, esp. relating to being the common building style of a period or place

WAINSCOT: A wooden facing for an interior wall, usually paneled

WATTLE: A mixture of branches and leaves held together by clay

YEOMAN FARMER: A gentleman farmer owning a small estate of land

Bibliography

ADLER, M. J. and CHARLES VAN DOREN (eds.), *The Annals of America.* Chicago, Ill.: Encyclopaedia Britannica, 1968.

BEYER, G. H., *The Urban Explosion in Latin America.* Ithaca, N.Y.: Cornell University Press, 1967.

———, *Housing and Society.* New York: Macmillan, 1965.

BILLINGTON, RAY A., *Westward Expansion: A History of the American*

Frontier. 2d ed. (with collaboration of J. B. Hedges). New York: Macmillan, 1960.

CALKINS, C. C. (ed.), *The Story of America*. Pleasantville, N.Y.: Reader's Digest Assoc., 1975.

COMER, J. P., *New York City Building Control, 1800–1941*, New York: Columbia University Press, 1942.

CONDIT, C. W., *American Building Art: The Nineteenth Century*. New York: Oxford University Press, 1960.

DAVIDSON, M. B., *The American Heritage History of Notable American Houses*. New York: American Heritage Publishing Co., 1971.

DEFOREST, R. W. and LAWRENCE VEILLER (eds.), *The Tenement House Problem*. Vols. 1 and 2. New York: Arno Press and The New York Times, 1970. Reprint edition.

DICK, EVERETT, *The Dixie Frontier: A Social History of the Southern Frontier From the First Transmontane Beginnings to the Civil War*. New York: Knopf, 1948.

———, *The Sod-House Frontier, 1854–1890. A Social History of the Northern Plains From the Creation of Kansas and Nebraska to the Admission of the Dakotas*. New York. Appleton-Century, Crofts, 1938.

DRURY, JOHN, *Historic Midwest Houses*. Minneapolis, Minn.: University of Minnesota Press, 1947.

ELLIS, D. M., *et al. A Short History of New York State*. Ithaca, N.Y.: Cornell University Press, 1957.

ERNST, ROBERT, *Immigrant Life in New York City, 1825–1863*. New York: Columbia University Press, 1949.

FINE, SIDNEY, *Laissez Faire and the General-Welfare State*. Ann Arbor, Mich.: University of Michigan Press, 1956.

FURNAS, J. C., *The Americans: A Social History of the United States, 1587–1914*. New York: G. P. Putnam's Sons, 1969.

GIEDION, SIEGFRIED, *Space, Time, and Architecture*. Cambridge, Mass.: Harvard University Press, 1949.

———, *Mechanization Takes Command: A Contribution to Anonymous History*. New York: Oxford University Press, 1948.

GLAAB, C. N. and A. T. BROWN, *A History of Urban America*. New York: Macmillan, 1967.

GLASSIE, HENRY, *Pattern in the Material Folk Culture of the Eastern United States*. Philadelphia, Pa.: University of Pennsylvania Press, 1969.

HANDLIN, OSCAR, *Boston's Immigrants: A Study in Acculturation*, Rev. ed. Cambridge, Mass.: Belknap Press of Harvard University Press, 1959.

———, *The Uprooted*. Boston, Mass.: Little, Brown, 1951.

HAVIGHURST, WALTER, *Wilderness for Sale: The Story of the First Western Land Rush*. New York: Hastings House, 1956.

HAYS, S. P., *The Response to Industrialism, 1885–1914*. Chicago, Ill.: University of Chicago Press, 1957.

HINES, GUSTAVUS, *Oregon: Its History, Condition, and Prospects*. New York: C. M. Saxton, 1859.

Historic Houses of America, New York: American Heritage Publishing Co., 1971.

JACKSON, K. T. and S. K. SCHULTZ (eds.), *Cities in American History.* New York: Knopf, 1972.

KIRKLAND, E. C., *Industry Comes of Age: Business, Labor, and Public Policy, 1860–1897.* Vol. VI. *The Economic History of the United States.* New York: Holt, Rinehart & Winston, 1961.

LITWACK, L. F., *North of Slavery: The Negro in the Free States, 1790–1860.* Chicago, Ill.: University of Chicago Press, 1961.

LYMAN, C. S., *Around the Horn to the Sandwich Islands and California, 1845–1850. A Personal Record.* (Edited by F. J. Taggart.) New Haven, Conn.: Yale University Press, 1925.

MCGOLDRICK, J. D., SEYMOUR GRAUBARD, and R. J. HOROWITZ, *Building Regulation in New York City: A Study in Administrative Law and Procedure.* New York: Commonwealth Fund, 1944.

MACKESEY, T. W., "History of Zoning in the United States." Mimeo., n.d.

MADDEN, C. H., *The Growth of the Cities in the United States: An Aspect of the Development of an Economic System.* Ph.D. dissertation, University of Virginia, 1954. Ann Arbor, Mich.: University Microfilms.

MORISON, S. E. and H. S. COMMAGER, *The Growth of the American Republic.* Vol. I. 3d ed. New York: Oxford University Press, 1942.

MUMFORD, LEWIS, *The City in History: Its Origins, Its Transformations, and Its Prospects.* New York: Harcourt Brace, Jovanovich, 1961.

PICKERING, ERNEST, *The Homes of America.* New York: T. Y. Crowell Co., 1951.

POST, L. W., *The Challenge of Housing.* New York: Farrar & Rinehart, 1938.

"Prefabs for the Prairies." *Journal of the Society of Architectural Historians,* Vol. 11, No. 1, March 1952, pp. 28–30.

REPS, J. W., *Town Planning in Frontier America.* Princeton, N.J.: Princeton University Press, 1969.

———, *The Making of Urban America: A History of City Planning in the United States.* Princeton, N.J.: Princeton University Press, 1965.

RICHARDSON, A. D., *Beyond the Mississippi: From the Great River to the Great Ocean.* Hartford, Conn.: American Publishing Co., 1869.

SELIGMAN, E. R. A., *The Income Tax. A Study of the History, Theory, and Practice of Income Taxation at Home and Abroad.* 2d ed. New York: Macmillan, 1921.

SMITH, WILSON (ed.), *Cities of Our Past and Present.* New York: Wiley, 1964.

TAYLOR, G. R., *The Transportation Revolution, 1815–1860.* Vol. IV, *The Economic History of the United States,* edited by Henry David *et al.* New York: Holt, Rinehart & Winston, 1951.

THERNSTROM, STEPHAN, *The Other Bostonians: Poverty and Progress in the American Metropolis, 1880–1970.* Cambridge, Mass.: Harvard University Press, 1973.

TUNNARD, CHRISTOPHER and H. H. REED, *American Skyline: The Growth and Form of Our Cities and Towns.* New York: New American Library of World Literature, 1956.

U. S. Bureau of the Census, *Historical Statistics of the United States, Colo-*

nial Times to 1970. Bicentennial ed., Parts 1 and 2. Washington, D.C.: Government Printing Office, 1975.

U. S. Bureau of the Census, *A Century of Population Growth. From the First Census of the United States to the Twelfth, 1790–1900.* Washington, D.C.: Government Printing Office, 1909.

————, *Report on the Population of the United States at the Eleventh Census, 1890.* Part 1. Washington, D.C.: Government Printing Office, 1895.

————, *Center of Population, 1890.* Census Bulletin No. 34. Washington, D.C.: Bureau of the Census, 1891.

————, *Population of the United States by States and Territories, 1890.* Census Bulletin No. 16. Washington, D.C.: Bureau of the Census, 1890.

VEILLER, LAWRENCE, *Housing Reform: A Hand-Book for Practical Use in American Cities.* New York: Charities Publication Committee, 1910 (copyright, 1910, Russell Sage Foundation).

WADE, R. C., *The Urban Frontier: The Rise of Western Cities, 1790–1830.* Cambridge, Mass.: Harvard University Press, 1959.

WESLAGER, C. A., *The Log Cabin in America: From Pioneer Days to the Present.* New Brunswick, N.J.: Rutgers University Press, 1969.

WRIGHT, C. W., *Economic History of the United States*, 2d ed. New York: McGraw-Hill, 1949.

CHAPTER 3

HOUSING IN THE UNITED STATES: 1890–1929

STEVEN E. ANDRACHEK[*]

Introduction

THE UNITED STATES is a nation torn between egalitarian ideals and discriminatory practices, and its history would tend to indicate that such has always been the case.[1] The Europeans who settled in America were frequently fleeing tyranny and discrimination, and they sought places where they could practice their own ideas. Although these ideas were sometimes as oppressive as those they had fled, a certain egalitarianism often resulted from the bitter experience of injustice and the desire to control it. But the liberal, the conservative, the adventurer, the mercenary, the outcast, all formed rapidly a new society which became as exploitive of the natural and human resources of the "new continent" as their counterparts in the Old World![2]

This new society, although more pluralistic than the first, was dominated by the Protestant Ethic and more specifically by the all-encompassing Puritanism. Max Lerner refers to Puritanism as "the fullest amalgam of religion, economics, and politics within a single mold that Americans ever achieved."[3] Puritanism was characterized

[1] Jackson Toby, *Contemporary Society: Social Process and Social Structure in Urban Industrial Societies.* (New York: Wiley), 1964, p. 548.

[2] This is the author's own interpretation of the history of the United States and is, naturally, subject to debate.

[3] Floyd Mansfield Martinson, *Family in Society.* (New York: Dodd, Mead), 1970, p. 15.

[*] STEVEN E. ANDRACHEK (Ph.D. candidate, Cornell University) is State Housing Specialist with the Missouri Cooperative Extension Service, University of Missouri–Columbia. The author wishes to thank Mrs. Marilyn Hagan and Sharon Laux, graduate students, for assisting in gathering some of the source material and Mrs. Evelyn Bennett for typing the manuscript.

by a devotion to activity and work, to achievement and success, to a strong moral orientation which tended to be rigid and uncompromising, and to interpersonal relations which were, at least outwardly, devoid of strong affection. Individual aspirations were suppressed, even within the family, to the principles of industry, frugality, parsimony, and obedience to God, which manifested itself in this world by a devotion to work.[4] Martinson says: "The Puritan's work was never done for it was labor itself, not any of its products, that God commanded."[5]

Thus social legislation in the United States insured "workmen" against sickness and accident, provided "workmen" with retirement plans, and sought means of providing "workmen" with adequate housing.[6]

The failure of the United States to pursue social welfare benefits for the general population as opposed to the working population was an error that has yet to be solved. Current housing programs still require that families have sufficient funds and employment prospects before loans for homeownership are made and even those housing efforts aimed at low-income groups carry requirements that focus on good character, income potential, sound family money management practices, and the ability to pay rental or mortgage demands on a monthly basis. The inadequate efforts in general social welfare programs (i.e., public welfare or relief) are, therefore, intentionally inadequate, since they serve a clientele that remains outside of the work force and the directives of achievement and success as imposed on the law by private morality.[7]

Although Puritanism appears to have failed as a totalistic social system, its influence on American life has been tremendous, and its partial continuity into the modern period is unquestionable. Martinson says:

From its start in 1630, the Massachusetts Bay settlement, unlike many of the colonies, was a family settlement. The Puritans and their descendents became the primary leaders of the emerging American society during the colonial period—and the colonial period occupies nearly half of the entire course of American history from the founding of the first colony in 1607, to the present time. Thus these early settlers established Puritanism—for better or worse—as one of the continuous factors in American life and thought.[8]

4 *Ibid.*, p. 16.
5 *Ibid.*
6 Edward McNall Burns and Phillip Lee Ralph, *World Civilizations: From Ancient to Contemporary*, Vol. 2. (New York: Norton), 1958, p. 255.
7 The author suggests that the lack of a comprehensive social welfare program is by intent, or possibly incompetence. Neither reflects well on the nature of our social system.
8 Martinson, *op. cit.*, p. 15.

The demands of the frontier required that great effort be directed against such natural barriers as the forests and prairies and against the human barriers as represented by the Indian Nations and the several European powers obstructing the manifest destiny of the United States. The struggle against nature and the protracted wars with the Indians, Great Britain, and Mexico required much of the energy of the republic. Coupled with the turmoil of Jacksonian Democracy and the sectional conflicts that were resolved in the Civil War, the United States had little opportunity to concern itself with social welfare. It is perhaps of some surprise that the United States managed, as a still rural nation, to engage in as many actions and conflicts as occupied its population and government.[9]

The second half of the 1800's, especially that period following the Civil War, marked the end of the free land frontier in the sense of its original conception. The best land was already occupied, the virgin forests reduced to stumps, the battle with nature won, the Indian Nations destroyed, the threat of foreign intervention significantly reduced, the national railroad network completed, and the urban-industrial base established—all in the 1800's.

Between the Panic of 1873 and the Panic of 1893, more than 100,000 miles of new railroads had been laid, bringing the total mileage of track to 170,000. By the turn of the century, another 23,000 miles of track was added to the system largely to fill out the already existing network.

Advancements in science and technology, as well as the ruinous results of uncontrolled growth and overspeculation in industry, resulted in the formation of huge corporate mergers, pools, and trusts to bring order and discipline to manufacturing as well as place American industry in a competitive position with foreign cartels.

The 19th century also marked the end of the "old" European immigrations to the United States. The movement of population from northern Europe to America was largely associated with the free land frontier and the need for skilled artisans, while the "new" European immigrations from southern and eastern Europe, consisting mostly of unskilled and illiterate peasantry, seemed well suited for the demands of America's reorganized but labor-hungry industry.[10]

---

[9] Contrary to popular opinion, the author submits that most of American History is a history of violence and injustice with little concern for human rights and social welfare.

[10] This account is based on the author's interpretation of United States History as presented in: Oscar Handlin, *America: A History.* (New York: Holt, Rinehart and Winston), 1968, passim; and Richard Hofstadter, William Miller, and Daniel Arron, *The United States: The History of a Republic.* (Englewood Cliffs, N.J., Prentice-Hall), 1957, passim.

In a general summary of the period from 1850 to 1890, Handlin states:

While the Civil War and Reconstruction absorbed the outward attention of the people of the United States, other forces profoundly transformed the country. Even when the newspaper headlines still dealt with battles and debates over the fate of the freemen, the interior pages carried news of industrial and commercial developments that were fully as significant.

In the forty years after 1850, the United States ceased to be primarily an agricultural nation producing raw materials for the more advanced economies of Europe; it became one of the world's great manufacturing powers. That change and the associated increase in population, wealth, and productivity altered the country's social and political order and in time drew it into a new role in world affairs.[11]

As Americans "reexamined" the social order they had built in the light of "progressive" and "liberal" ideals, the traces of Puritanism that had early been ingrained in the social system became evident and were not incompatible with the rise of Social Darwinism and other repressive philosophical systems which justified the suppression of the great mass of people now moving toward the urban-industrial centers. The motivational forces which had served early rural America were well established and the "cry of the aggrieved," though given some attention by social reformers, had yet to wait for a later period in history to be heard. The dualism in America's legalistic tradition was recognized by a few, but the poor and illiterate industrial and agricultural serfs, black and white, native born and immigrant, still had duties to perform in the service of the nation.[12]

The years from 1890 to 1929 were critical to the development of the United States as a powerful nation-state. The imperatives of imperialism relegated the cause of social injustice to a lesser role than a reexamination of values might have indicated. Reorganized industry and the political leaders of the 1890's faced the effects of the agricultural slump of 1887 and the economic depression of 1893. In the face of these internal disruptions the Homestead Strike of 1892 created by a cut in wages was put down by Pinkerton detectives and the Pennsylvania State Militia and the Pullman Strike of 1894 created by the layoff of one third of the work force and a wage cut of 40 percent (while the rent and purchase price of company houses remained the same, as well as the food and clothing prices at the company stores) was broken by federal troops ostensibly assigned to protect the mails.

[11] Handlin, *op. cit.*, pp. 515–516.
[12] It is the author's contention that the "Progressive Movement" is much overrated.

In addition, the federal courts used the Sherman Antitrust Act as a strikebreaking legalism declaring strikes to be conspiracies in restraint of interstate commerce. The depression of 1893–1898, while only a pause in the greater destiny of the republic, assisted industry and government in the defeat of labor, the disbanding of large gangs of roaming unemployed (i.e., the dispersion of Coxey's Army and the arrest of General Coxey in Washington, D.C.) and the end of the free-silver movement.

It should not be forgotten that it was as late as 1896—the dawn of the Progressive movement—that the Supreme Court of the United States established the "separate but equal" doctrine (*Plessy* v. *Ferguson*), declaring "If one race be inferior to the other socially, the Constitution of the United States cannot put them on the same plane."[13] In a similar vein President Wilson established the Committee of Public Information and pushed through Congress the Espionage Act of 1917 and the Sedition Act of 1918. All were intended to curtail free speech and constitutional liberties during World War I.

Reform and social welfare are determined by the perceived social problems of a society. If the problems are not perceived by the social classes with the power to institute reforms no attempt will be made to solve the problems. Even perceived problems are placed on a hierarchy of needs in terms of corrective action. While these observations seem apparent they are frequently overlooked. Many social problems were selectively perceived by the power structure of the 1890's and the early 20th century, but the screening process placed first emphasis on the integrity of the industrial system and territorial expansion and secondarily on the demands of the new middle class and the traditional ideals of the American aristocracy. While some consideration was given to the great masses, reforms were superficial and generally not enforced.

When peace came to the United States after World War I the conservation reaction set in as the means of dealing with the problems, internal and external, of the new superpower the nation had become. Of the deeply entrenched social problems facing the republic, Handlin says:

The politicians of the 1920's rarely faced these issues head on. Yet the return to normalcy that Warren G. Harding advocated in 1920 did not materialize. The changes of three decades could not be undone. Behind the familiar cycle of recurring elections, a transformation in the structure of government was taking place. Whether this transformation, which emphasized individualism rather than community needs, was capable of dealing

[13] Charles E. Silberman, *Crisis in Black and White.* (New York: Vintage Books), 1964, p. 107.

with the post war social and economic problems was a question that the depression of 1929 would soon answer.[14]

In summary, the social milieu of the period from 1890 to 1929 was not conducive to housing reform either by private groups or the national government. Leading churchmen, urban reformers, humanitarians, and philanthropists did begin to study the housing conditions and general social problems of the immigrants, blacks, and native-born poor during this period, but surveys, settlement houses, campaigns against saloons and vice, movements encouraging garden cities and urban parks, the spread of the Social Gospel, and the rise of boys' clubs barely touched the people. They could not counterbalance the great processes at work which were creating the very problems some few reformers were becoming aware of. A few municipal and state governments developed housing and other social reform programs in the critical years of America's emergence as a consolidated nation-state, but the weight of the central government was applied only on a situational basis to assure the expansion of the capital base and the victory of the nation in its military adventures.

Although the history of housing from 1890 to 1929 is a history of half-hearted reform and very few in-depth programs, it is also a history of the foundation of housing reforms to come later as well as the story of some unusual and interesting experiments and proposals. While attention tends to focus on private and governmental reforms, frequently through legislation, it must be kept in mind that housing construction and the shelter needs of all income and class levels were being met, however inadequately, by the people themselves. Meeting shelter needs is a prerequisite of survival, but the methods of meeting shelter needs during the turn of the century was also the problem.[15]

The Census and Housing

There are only a few great trends in terms of population that relate to housing conditions from 1890 to 1929. The population, in total numbers, grew steadily from 1890 to 1930. In 1890, the United States had a population of 62,947,714 people or 21.2 persons per square mile. By 1930, the population had increased to 122,775,046 or 35.6 persons per square mile. In a 40-year period the nation's population had almost doubled. Perhaps the more important factor is that in gross numbers about 60,000,000 people were added to our population between 1890

14 Handlin, *op. cit.*, p. 823.

15 The vernacular architecture tended to take the form of folk architecture in rural areas and organized capital-investment architecture (i.e., tenements) in highly urbanized areas.

TABLE 3–1. Population of the United States in Census Years[1]

Year	Population	Pop. per sq. mi.	Year	Population	Pop. per sq. mi.
1790	3,929,214	4.5	1890	62,947,714	21.2
1800	5,308,483	6.1	1900	75,994,575	25.6
1810	7,239,881	4.3	1910	91,972,266	31.0
1820	9,638,453	5.5	1920	105,710,620	35.6
1830	12,866,020	7.4	1930	122,775,046	41.2
1840	17,069,453	9.8	1940	131,669,275	44.2
1850	23,191,876	7.9	1950	150,697,361	50.7
1860	31,443,321	10.6	1960	178,464,236	60.1
1870	39,818,449	13.4	1960[2]	179,323,175	50.5
1880	50,155,783	16.9			

[1] Unless otherwise indicated, figures are for conterminous United States; that is, Alaska and Hawaii are excluded.

[2] Figures are for 50-state area. *Note:* Estimated population of the 50-state area for May 1, 1967 was 197,566,000.

SOURCE: U. S. Bureau of the Census.

and 1930. (See Table 3–1.)[16] Significantly, immigrants accounted for a large portion of the population increase. For example, from 1880 to 1890 the United States population increased from more than 50,000,000 to almost 63,000,000, but from 1880 to 1889 a total of 4,640,000 foreign born arrived in the United States. In the peak year of 1882, almost 640,000 foreigners arrived (of those 250,600 were German, 105,300 were Scandinavians, and 103,000 were from Great Britan).[17]

A comparison of the population increase from 1880 to 1930 with the total number of immigrants admitted from all countries for the same period indicates that the period from 1880 to 1930 saw the largest numbers of foreign-born people entering the United States in its history. (See Tables 3–1 and 3–2.)[18] Specifically, the United States population increased by 59,827,332 (from 62,827,332 in 1890 to 122,775,046 in 1930) from 1890 to 1930, but of that number 22,325,970 were immigrants (total for the period from 1891 to 1930). Therefore, approximately 37 percent of the population increase from 1890 to the Great Depression was the result of immigration.[19]

Because immigration played such an important role in the population growth of the United States from 1890 to 1930, it is important to recognize its characteristics. The benchmark year 1882 (see Table

[16] Source: U. S. Bureau of the Census.

[17] Hofstadter, et al., *op. cit.*, pp. 451–452.

[18] Source: Immigration and Naturalization Service, U. S. Department of Justice.

[19] *Ibid.*

TABLE 3–2. Immigrants Admitted from
All Countries

Period	Numbers
1881–1890	5,246,613
1891–1900	3,687,564
1901–1910	8,795,386
1911–1920	5,735,811
1921–1930	4,107,209

SOURCE: Immigration and Naturalization Service,
U. S. Department of Justice. Taken from the *World Al-
manac and Book of Facts*, 1974 Edition, New York: Newspaper Enterprise Association, Inc., p. 145.

3–3 for the fluctuations of immigrants by numbers and years) was
more than a peak year for the influx of the foreign born. It marked a
shift from peoples of the Anglo-Saxon and northwestern areas of
Europe to southern and eastern Europe, as the primary ethnic groups
moving to America.[20] As previously indicated the early settlers of
America were in search of prime farm land and business opportunities.
Many were educated, skilled craftsmen, and experienced workers (although they were not always prepared for the rough frontier and harsh
environment of North America) and after some adjustment large
numbers found the "good life" they sought.

The waves of immigrants that followed the early settlers also
dreamed of good farmland and business wealth and were encouraged
to do so by agents of American railroads, steamships, and industry.
But they were generally peasants, unskilled and illiterate, and the
United States was already occupied by English, German, and Scandinavian Protestants who controlled the land and the industry as well as
the government. Opportunity awaited the peasants of Italy, Hungary,
and Slavic East Europe, but it was in the form of common labor in the
rising urban-industrial centers. So the "new wave" remained in the port
cities of their landing or gravitated to the established and growing
factory and mining towns (see Figure 3–1).[21] In these centers of industry where factories operated 24 hours a day and a meal or clothing
could be had at "double or nothing," depending on the flip of a coin, a
symbiotic relationship was developed with the urban political bosses.
The new-wave immigrant, feeling isolated and betrayed by the "American Dream," sought to preserve his language, religion, and ethnic
identity by following the dictates of the political machines in voting

20 Hofstadter, et al., *op. cit.*, p. 478.
21 *Ibid.*, p. 479.

TABLE 3–3. Number of Immigrants by Years: 1820–1924

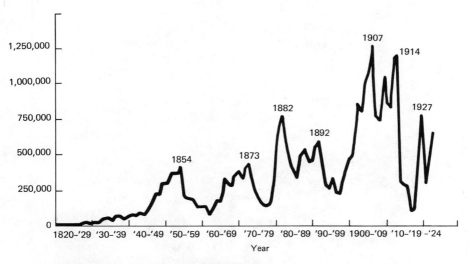

Source: Harry Jerome, *Migration and Business Cycles*
(New York: National Bureau of Economic Research, 1926), p. 34.

matters in exchange for questionable naturalization papers, gifts, and donations in times of personal trouble, protection from alien laws, patronage jobs for the young, and sympathetic, if self-serving, reverence for ethnic identity and values. Reformers were unwelcome to both the new immigrants and the political bosses, since they represented the pious side of the Puritan Ethnic.

"By 1910, such immigrants, along with Negroes migrating from the South, made up two-thirds of all the workers in 21 major branches of American industry"[22] and "by 1912, some 60 percent of the miners and some 58 percent of the iron and steel workers were foreign born, and an additional 15 to 20 percent were their native-born children."[22a] Thus, it was the characteristics of immigration and not immigration itself that contributed to many of the social problems of the 1890's and the 20th century.

Efforts to stop the great influx of people were largely unsuccessful until the Great Depression. Only during World War II and the early phase of the "Cold War" did the refugee problem temporarily increase immigration again. But even during those troubled times the peak years of the "new migration" could not be challenged.[23]

[22] *Ibid.*
[22a] Handlin, *op. cit.*, p. 696.
[23] Source: Immigration and Naturalization Service, U. S. Department of Justice.

FIGURE 3–1. New York City: View of Hester Street showing overcrowding—"The most densely populated spot in the world." ca. 1900. [Courtesy of the National Archives and Records Service, General Services Administration.]

The second great trend in terms of population was the movement of people to urban areas. This involved three major subtrends: the migration of native-born Americans from the farm to city; the migration of native-born blacks from the rural south to the urban-industrialized north; and the direct influx of immigrants into urban areas. In 1890, 35.1 percent of the U.S. population lived in urban places, in 1900, 39.1 percent, in 1910, 45.7 percent, in 1920, 51.2 percent, and in 1930, 56.2 percent. While urbanism had long been affecting the nature and organization of American society, the 1920 Census confirmed the obvious—more than half of the nation's population lived in urban areas.

By census definition, rural America came to an end in the 1890–

TABLE 3–4. Urban and Rural Population

Census Years	Urban		Rural	
	Number (in thousands)	Percent of Total	Number (in thousands)	Percent of Total
1790	201	5.4	3,727	94.6
1800	322	6.1	4,986	93.9
1810	525	7.3	6,714	92.7
1820	693	7.1	8,945	92.9
1830	1,127	8.7	11,738	91.3
1840	1,845	10.8	15,224	89.2
1850	3,543	15.3	19,648	84.7
1860	6,216	19.8	25,226	80.2
1870	9,902	25.7	28,656	74.3
1880	14,129	28.2	36,026	71.8
1890	22,106	35.1	40,841	64.9
1900	30,159	39.7	45,834	60.3
1910	41,998	45.7	49,973	54.3
1920	54,157	51.2	51,552	48.8
1930	68,954	56.2	53,820	43.8
1940	74,423	56.5	57,245	43.5
1950	96,467	59.0	54,229	41.0
1960	125,268	69.9*	54,054	30.1

* New definition of urban; including urban-fringe areas and unincorporated places of 2,500 or more population.

SOURCE: U. S. Bureau of the Census.

1929 period (see Table 3–4).[24] This period was a time of trial and reorganization for the agricultural sector. There had long existed the myth of the virtues of rural life and the almost spiritual value of agriculture, and under such illusions independent small farmers pushed headlong into marginal lands with little consideration for climate, soil, the distribution of produce, or the proper mix of crop to place.

It was not until the bitter and somewhat desperate process of liquidation took place that the large, wealthy, consolidated family farm could adopt specialization, mechanization, efficient capital use, and technology to support the vast urban populations with relatively few farm workers. The growth of industry, the spread of the railroads, and the advancement of science drew the interest of farmers and eventually complemented the urban trends. Although farm tenancy actually continued to rise from 1890 through 1910, the increase came largely from the old South where the effects of the Civil War and unique regional problems prolonged the agony of ruralism.[25]

24 Source: U.S. Bureau of the Census.
25 Handlin, *op. cit.*, p. 663.

The change in agricultural patterns produced a stream of rural migrants to cities. The percentage of Americans born outside of their state of residence remained high in the early 1900's and represented not a shift from birthplace to the farm frontier, but a reverse pattern from rural to urban. The rural areas of Pennsylvania, New York, Illinois, Indiana, Wisconsin, Kentucky, Tennessee, Missouri, and the New England states showed a marked decline in population in the early 20th century.[26] In addition, the special conditions in the American South and the manpower needs of northern industry, especially during the two World Wars, created a flow of rural blacks to northern cities. The nature of the urbanizing process, resting as it did on the new immigration and the rural dispossessed, set the tone for America's unfortunate urban experience. The laissez-faire policies of the local (with some notable exceptions) and federal governments toward the rapidly growing cities created a new frontier of hardship which was, in its own way, as bitter and cruel as the old land frontier of the nation's westward expansion.

The census provides a picture of the number of dwelling units and tenure in relation to the total population from 1890 on as well as the number of permanent housing starts in nonfarm areas (see Tables 3–5 and 3–6). Due to the demographic factors at work, housing production in the cities generally lagged behind the housing needs. Housing starts in the periods between 1890 to 1904; and 1917 to 1930; and in 1930, fell short of the 1889 figure of 342,000 starts. The number of persons per household remained fairly high throughout the period from 1890 to 1930 (1890, 5.0; 1900, 4.8; 1910, 4.5; 1920, 4.3; 1930, 4.10; as compared to the 1970 figure of 3.1 persons per dwelling unit). The housing boom from 1905 to World War I began to meet housing demand, but the war years dealt a severe blow to housing construction. The mid-1920's restored production, but the Great Depression and World War II again created housing shortages.[27] Writing in 1931 Edith Wood described the gains and losses in housing production from 1905 on as follows:

The housing shortage at the end of the War [World War I] came as a surprise to most of the people in the United States. Before the war there had been in our country an average annual urban production of about 400,000 new dwellings, which took care of replacements and increase of population. In 1917 and 1918 almost no building was done except by the Federal Government. Private building was expected to resume briskly as soon as the War was over. It started to do so, but halted. The cost of a home—labor and

26 *Ibid.*, p. 668.
27 Edith Elmer Wood, *Recent Trends in American Housing.* (New York: Macmillan), 1931, pp. 83–85.

TABLE 3–5. Occupied Dwelling Units and Tenure of Homes: 1890–1930

Year[1]	Total Occupied Dwelling Units	Total Population		Occupied Units Reporting Tenure	Tenure of Homes			
		Number of Persons	Per Occupied Dwelling Unit		Owner-occupied		Renter-occupied	
					Number	Percent	Number	Percent
	139	140	141	142	143	144	145	146
TOTAL								
1930	29,904,663	122,775,046	4.1	29,321,891	14,002,074	47.8	15,319,817	52.2
1920	24,351,676	105,710,620	4.3	23,810,558	10,866,960	45.6	12,943,598	54.4
1910	20,255,555	91,972,266	4.5	19,781,606	9,083,711	45.9	10,697,895	54.1
1900	15,963,965	75,994,575	4.8	15,428,987	7,205,212	46.7	8,223,775	53.3
1890	12,690,152	62,947,714	5.0	12,690,152	6,066,417	47.8	6,623,735	52.2
NONFARM								
1930	23,300,026	92,617,533	4.0	22,917,072	10,549,972	46.0	12,367,100	54.0
1920	17,600,472	74,096,351	4.2	17,229,394	7,041,283	40.9	10,188,111	59.1
1910	14,131,945	59,895,306[4]	4.2[4]	13,672,044	5,245,380	38.4	8,426,664	61.6
1900	10,274,127	(2)	(2)	9,779,979	3,566,809	36.5	6,213,170	63.5
1890	7,922,973	(2)	(2)	7,922,973	2,923,671	36.9	4,999,302	63.1
FARM								
1930	6,604,637	30,157,513	4.6	6,404,819	3,452,102	53.9	2,952,717	46.1
1920	6,751,204	31,614,269	4.7	6,581,164	3,825,677	58.1	2,755,487	41.9
1910	6,123,610	32,076,960[4]	5.2[4]	6,109,562	3,838,331	62.8	2,271,231	37.2
1900	5,689,838	(2)	(2)	5,649,008	3,638,403	64.4	2,010,605	35.6
1890	4,767,179	(2)	(2)	4,767,179	3,142,746	65.9	1,624,433	34.1

[1] These figures are not exactly comparable with other years since they are based on sample surveys.
[2] Not available.
[3] Estimated.
SOURCE: U. S. Bureau of the Census, *Historical Statistics of the United States, Colonial Times to 1957.* Washington, D.C., 1960, p. 395, Series N139–146.

135

TABLE 3–6. Permanent Dwelling Units Started in Nonfarm Areas, Number and Expenditures: 1889–1930

Year	Total	1-Family	2-Family[1]	Multi-Family	Total[2]
		Dwelling Units Started (1,000)			Expenditures for New Units ($1,000,000)
			By Type of Dwelling		
	106	109	110	111	115
1930........	330.0	227.0	29.0	74.0	1,570
1929........	509.0	316.0	51.0	142.0	3,040
1928........	753.0	436.0	78.0	239.0	4,195
1927........	810.0	454.0	99.0	257.0	4,540
1926........	849.0	491.0	117.0	241.0	4,920
1925........	937.0	572.0	157.0	208.0	4,910
1924........	893.0	534.0	173.0	186.0	4,575
1923........	871.0	513.0	175.0	183.0	3,960
1922........	716.0	437.0	146.0	133.0	2,955
1921........	449.0	316.0	70.0	63.0	1,795
1920........	247.0	202.0	24.0	21.0	1,710
1919........	315.0	239.0	36.0	40.0	1,258
1918........	118.0	91.0	13.0	15.0	391
1917........	240.0	166.0	32.0	43.0	769
1916........	437.0	267.0	69.0	101.0	1,255
1915........	433.0	262.0	73.0	97.0	1,192
1914........	421.0	263.0	72.0	87.0	1,081
1913........	421.0	263.0	72.0	85.0	1,108
1912........	426.0	259.0	71.0	97.0	1,113
1911........	395.0	249.0	62.0	84.0	1,000
1910........	387.0	251.0	58.0	79.0	1,028
1909........	491.0	328.0	73.0	91.0	1,272
1908........	416.0	286.0	65.0	65.0	1,034
1907........	432.0	291.0	59.0	82.0	1,037
1906........	487.0	316.0	69.0	103.0	1,170
1905........	507.0	336.0	64.0	107.0	1,154
1904........	315.0	207.0	45.0	63.0	690
1903........	253.0	174.0	30.0	48.0	607
1902........	240.0	171.0	32.0	37.0	572
1901........	275.0	177.0	32.0	66.0	610
1900........	189.0	123.0	31.0	35.0	433
1899........	282.0	....	....	....	608
1898........	262.0	....	....	....	574

136

T A B L E 3 – 6 . *Continued*

Year	Dwelling Units Started (1,000)				Expenditures for New Units $1,000,000
		By Type of Dwelling			
	Total	1-Family	2-Family[1]	Multi-Family	Total[2]
	106	109	110	111	115
1897........	292.0	.....	.....	.....	643
1896........	257.0	.....	.....	.....	606
1895........	309.0	.....	.....	.....	679
1894........	265.0	.....	.....	.....	594
1893........	267.0	.....	.....	.....	583
1892........	381.0	.....	.....	.....	763
1891........	298.0	.....	.....	.....	612
1890........	328.0	.....	.....	.....	790
1889........	342.0	.....	.....	.....	806

[1] Includes 1- and 2-family dwellings with stores.
[2] Includes nonhousekeeping public construction but excludes nonhousekeeping private construction for all years.
S O U R C E : U. S. Bureau of the Census, *Historical Statistics of the United States, Colonial Times to 1957*. Washington, D.C., 1960, p. 393, Series N106–115.

materials had doubled. Would people pay the increased price? Few cared to do so, even if they could, as sudden deflation in prices might wipe out half their investment.

The volume of home-building in 1919, instead of reducing the shortage, was only 58% of normal. That of 1920 reached only 37% of normal. There was by that time a numerical shortage of over a million homes. The maximum shortage was at the end of 1921, when it reached at least one and a quarter million. Some responsible estimates placed it higher. Then the tide turned. Nineteen twenty-two held its own. Each year thereafter showed substantial gains. By 1926 the end of the shortage was in sight. By 1928 it had been reached. In a nation-wide numerical sense, there was no longer a housing shortage. We were back where we were before the War, with qualitative rather than quantitative needs. So far as net progress was concerned, ten years had been lost.[28]

During the period of shortages, Wood reports, housing standards were lowered and rents increased sharply. Structures fell into disrepair, single-family units were turned into apartments, existing apartments were divided into smaller rental units, unsound vacant housing was occupied, the "doubling-up" of families was common. Overcrowding was

[28] *Ibid.*, pp. 84–85.

reported everywhere. Therefore, the quantitative rebound made during
the late 1920's left the nation still saddled with a serious qualitative
housing problem.[29]

Homeownership has long been considered part of the "American
Dream" and social critics have placed an emphasis on this form of investment that borders on morality. But census figures indicate that the
1890–1930 period was an age of renters, due largely to high immigration and migration into urban areas and the low wages paid by
industry. In addition, home mortgages were considered high-risk investments, while rental property was considered favorably. Between
1890 and 1920 homeownership actually decreased in the United States
due to the urban trend. Although Wood's figures differ slightly from
present historical census data, her observations, circa 1931, were
correct:

There has been a slow, but steady decrease in home ownership in the United
States for some decades, and a slow, but steady increase in the proportion of
mortgaged homes.

	Percent of Total Homes		Percent of Owned Homes	
	Rented	Owned	Free	Encumbered
1890	52.2	47.8	72.	28.
1900	53.9	46.1	68.7	31.3
1910	54.2	45.8	67.2	32.8
1920	54.4	45.6	61.7	38.3

The percentage of owned homes varied from 37.2 in the Middle Atlantic
states to 56.4 in the West North Central, and from 30.7 in the State of
New York (30.9 in Georgia) to 65.3 in North Dakota. Among the cities,
New York has the lowest percentage of ownership (12.7), while in the
borough of Manhattan it is only 2.1. These are 1920 figures.

The ten cities with populations over 100,000 having the highest percentages
of home ownership are:

Des Moines	51.1
Grand Rapids	50.2
Toledo	49.4
Omaha	48.4
Youngstown	47.8
Kansas City	47.6
Reading	46.6
Baltimore	46.3
Seattle	46.3
St. Paul	46.1

29 *Ibid.*, p. 85.

It will be observed that 50% of home ownership has been attained in only two of our large towns.[30]

Census information related to housing indicates the period from 1890 to 1930 was an era of great population growth and high rates of immigration and migration to urban areas. Housing construction was cyclical in nature and renting was more significant, in numerical terms, than homeownership. Persons per dwelling unit was high but slowly lowered over the period. The social conditions that actually prevailed are more vividly the topic of descriptive reports, as we shall see below.

The Social Milieu and Housing Conditions

Observers and reformers of housing conditions at the turn of the century began to realize the nature of industrialization, urbanization, imperialism, immigration, and migration, and the social milieu that had developed from these forces. The social order was successful if one thought in terms of spreading across a continent and wiping out the native population, or in terms of defeating other nations in war, or in terms of railroads and steel production. But all of these things were accomplished at a fearful price. The price was a human one, and the social problems of an entire nation would begin to take their toll by adding one upon the other until internal conditions would begin to sap the strength of the republic.

Those who saw the social problems of 1890 and the 40 years following began from a Puritan view. They mixed morality and humanism in odd ways, but they did begin the social reform movement. The early reformers did not necessarily oppose the system; they simply wanted to clean it up a bit. One early "humanitarian" observed that the poor conditions of the cities were the result of the "typical immigrant . . . a European peasant, whose horizon has been narrow, whose moral and religious training has been meager and false, and whose ideas of life are low."[31]

It is difficult to separate the character of the reformers from their observations of urban life and housing conditions and a mistake to do so, since they set the tone for many of the social welfare programs that still exist. That great American reformer, Lawrence Veiller, often showed more concern for the American system than the "evil" social conditions he observed in the city life of immigrants. While expressing concern for the condition of the masses, he worried about how "American institutions" could be "maintained" and observed, "It is useless to expect a conservative point of view in the workingman, if his home is

30 *Ibid.*, pp. 37–38.
31 Hofstadter, *op. cit.*, p. 512.

but three or four rooms in some high building in which dwell from twenty to thirty other families."[32] Veiller was very much concerned with Puritan values, and he went on to say, "Where a man has a home of his own he has every incentive to be economical and thrifty, to take his part in the duties of citizenship, to be a real sharer in government. Democracy was not predicated upon a country made up of tenement dwellers nor can it survive."[33] In 1910 Veiller found room overcrowding a serious social problem in the tenements and room overcrowding was "bound up with another social problem; namely, the lodger evil."[34] The "lodger evil," which adds to overcrowding, was the practice of poor immigrant families taking in "boarders or lodgers" to "supplement the family income." The obvious answer to "lodger evil" was to pass laws limiting the number of people by room "with reference to the amount of cubic air space in it."[35] But the problem was one of enforcement. Veiller states:

In order to enforce, inspections must be made at night. It is only then that the lodgers and boarders, the chief causes of over-crowding, are to be found. To question the tenement dwellers in the daytime with regard to their practice of taking in boarders or lodgers is to ask them to convict themselves, and such investigations are of little value. To adequately carry on night inspections of the homes of the poor would require an army of inspectors. It would involve, moreover, an invasion of the privacy of the home, which is repugnant to American institutions. The routing out of workingmen's families after midnight in order to determine whether they have boarders or lodgers living with them would be intolerable.

To cope with the problem of overcrowding and the lodger evil effectively the law should place upon the landlord the responsibility for an undue number of people in his house, as it has already placed upon him in the case of women of ill-repute responsibility for their character. In certain classes of tenements the taking in of lodgers or boarders, except with the written consent of the landlord, must be prohibited and the landlord must be held responsible for any departure from this rule. This principle has not as yet been recognized by any american city, but it is one that must be established if this evil is to be overcome.[36]

Veiller was interested in the type of people who might be responsible for "lodger evil" warning that other cities should not make the mistake of New York City, and he urged communities not yet affected to guard

32 Lawrence Veiller, *Housing Reform: A Handbook for Practical Use in American Cities.* (New York: Charities Publication Committee and Russell Sage Foundation), 1910, p. 6.

33 *Ibid.*, pp. 6–7.

34 *Ibid.*, p. 33.

35 *Ibid.*, p. 34.

36 *Ibid.*, pp. 34–35.

against the problems he described. Commenting on "lodger evil," he said:

This prevails chiefly among the foreign elements of the population, more especially among the Italians and Poles, and in some cities, the Hungarians and other Slavic races. It also prevails among the Jews in the larger cities. It is fraught with great danger to the social fabric of the country. It means the breaking down of domestic standards. It frequently leads to the breaking up of homes and families, to the downfall and subsequent degraded career of young women, to grave immoralities—in a word, to the profanation of the home.[37]

Allen, writing for the Extension Service of the U. S. Department of Agriculture as a home economist, saw as late as 1930 the "true" intentions of immigrants and in these intentions the reason for poor housing conditions.

The new immigration, with its varying standards of living, conflicting ideals, and strong race hatreds came very fast and many of our older national ideals suffered as a result of it. A large number of people who came here during this period cared nothing for the existing ideals of the Americans. Their old-world ways suited each national group well enough, and they came faster than they could be re-educated and assimilated or brought into harmony with one another. Many of them were willing to herd together in any fashion because they had no intention of remaining here after they had secured the means to return to and live in ease in their native lands. This attitude on their part explains one of the reasons for the size of households in New York City, where some of the forerunners of this group had already arrived in 1870.

The large numbers among these immigrants who came here without means and with no intention of remaining after having amassed a modest fortune, account in part for the large number of wage earners in industrial communities who do not own their own homes. In 1911 no wage earners in Manhattan owned their own homes, and probably as high as 99 percent of the wage earners in several other cities did not own them either. Approximately 90 percent of the wage earners in all industrial cities and communities in the United States did not own their homes at this time.[38]

Although the moral code of the Puritan Ethic appears to have reduced the objectivity of some of the early reformers, Veiller called on 16 years of experience in tenement house work to write the following description of housing conditions in the New York of 1910:

. . . we have today the tenement house system prevalent throughout New York as the chief means of housing the greater part of the city's population,

[37] *Ibid.*, p. 33.
[38] Edith Louise Allen, *American Housing: As Affected by Social and Economic Conditions.* (Peoria, Illinois: The Manual Arts Press), 1930, pp. 131–132.

FIGURE 3–2. Typical old style air shaft (five stories high), ca. 1900. [Courtesy of the National Archives and Records Service, General Services Administration.]

over two-thirds of the people living in multiple dwellings; we have today over 100,000 separate tenement houses; we have a city build-up of four and five story buildings, instead of two-story and three-story ones; we have over 10,000 tenement houses of the hopeless and discredited "dumb-bell" type with narrow "air-shafts" furnishing neither sunlight nor fresh air to the thousands of people living in the rooms opening on them; we have over 200,000 tenement houses of the older type in which most of the rooms are without air or ventilation; we have over 100,000 dark unventilated rooms without even a window to an adjoining room; we have 80,000 buildings, housing nearly 3,000,000 people, so constructed as to be a standing menace to the community in the event of fire, most of them, built with wooden stairs, wooden halls and wooden floors, and thousands built entirely of wood.

Over a million people have no bathing facilities in their homes; while even a greater number are limited to the use of sanitary conveniences in common with other families, without proper privacy; over a quarter of a million people had in the year 1900, no other sanitary convenience than antiquated yard privies; and even today 2,000 of these privy sinks still remain, many of them located in densely populated districts, a source of danger to all in the neighborhood, facilitating the spread of contagious disease through the medium of the common house-fly."[39]

Jacob Riis was more descriptive than most of the social reformers, since he was inclined to accompany the Sanitary Police as they made their rounds through the maze of New York tenements. Riis maintained what was in effect a diary of his experiences, although his publications were considered the objective work of a housing investigator. Because of his descriptive powers, mixed as they were with his Dickensian style, Riis' works gained some popularity and a great deal of concern, if little action, for tenement dwellers of New York (see Figure 3–2).[40]

The housing conditions of the immigrants, migrants, and other poor as described by Veiller and Riis were rooted in the housing forms of old New York. A frequently used reference point is 1901 because of the passage of the New York Tenement House Act of 1901 which was considered a progressive legislative milestone. More will be said of this later. Although referring to a number of architectual forms, tenements constructed before 1901 were identified as "old law tenements" and those constructed after 1901 as "new law tenements." (See Figure 3–3.)[41] Typical "old law tenements" were two-story "cottages" originally intended to house one, or at most, two families and three-story or four-story row house-type structures intended to house one upper-income family. These structures were often converted into tenements or apartments that housed an entire family in each room. Barracks-type structures of a military or dormitory nature were also hastily thrown up to provide for the early influx of immigrants.

Gray tells us that "in 1833 there was built what appears to be the first 'tenement house'—a house, for the occupation of several tenant families.[42] According to Gray, tenement houses began to emerge as the dominant house form in New York City around the period of the Civil War, and, by 1860, there were several hundred housing an

39 Veiller, *op. cit.*, pp. 9–10.

40 Jacob A. Riis, *The Battle With the Slum.* New York: Macmillan, 1902.

41 James Ford, *Slums and Housing: With Special Reference to New York City —History—Conditions—Policy*, Vol. 1. (Cambridge, Mass.: Harvard University Press), 1963, p. 210.

42 George Herbert Gray, *Housing and Citizenship: A Study of Low-Cost Housing.* (New York: Reinhold), 1946, p. 8.

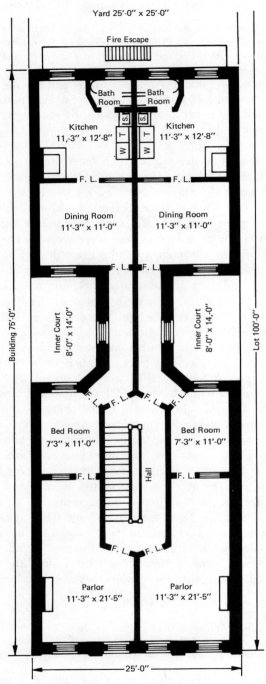

Yard 25'-0" x 25'-0"

Fire Escape

Bath Room — Bath Room

Kitchen 11,-3" x 12'-8" — Kitchen 11'-3" x 12'-8"

S. — S.
W — T — W — T

F. L. — F. L.

Dining Room 11'-3" x 11'-0" — Dining Room 11'-3" x 11'-0"

F. L. — F. L.

Inner Court 8'-0" x 14'-0" — Inner Court 8'-0" x 14'-0"

F. L. — F. L. — F. L. — F. L.

Bed Room 7'3" x 11'-0" — Bed Room 7'-3" x 11'-0"

Hall

F. L. — F. L.

F. L. — F. L.

Parlor 11'-3" x 21'-5" — Parlor 11'-3" x 21'-5"

Building 75'-0"

Lot 100'-0"

25'-0"

FIGURE 3–3. "New Law" tenement plan (25-foot lot; two-family floor plan), ca. 1901. [Courtesy of the National Archives and Records Service, General Services Administration.]

"average of sixty-five people per house."[43] It was at this time that the standard lot of 25 feet in width and 100 feet in depth began to experience total coverage by structures. This began by the addition of rooms to existing tenements and later new tenements were constructed with the intent of covering the entire lot. Gray says:

Tenement houses were still being converted from old private houses, occupying the entire width of the lot so that the only windows were in the front and rear walls—converted into tenement houses with two to four apartments to the floor. To accomplish this, the extra bedrooms were located back in the interior and had their only light and ventilation through the front and rear rooms. From the original houses two rooms deep they were subdivided or extended first to four, then to six and eight rooms deep—respectively eight, twelve, and sixteen rooms on each floor, only four of which had any outside light or ventilation. These became known as "railroad tenements."[44]

If a lot was completely covered by the tenement structure, and the lots on each side experienced the same degree of coverage, side walls met with no space between structures and the only light that could enter a tenement was through the front windows and doors (and sometimes from rear windows provided the rear wall of another structure was not flush with it). In addition problems of adequate water supply, sewage facilities, artificial lighting, and general maintenance and upkeep plagued the tenements. Overcrowding was compounded when poor families sublet their rooms and apartments as sleeping facilities for those without housing in order to obtain a small extra income to help pay the rent. As an example of just one of the additional problems of the tenements, we can refer to the water closet which was defined as an "inside water-flushed sewer-connected fixture (a substitute for a privy)."[45] The problem was some tenements did not have any sanitary facilities whatsoever, and those with water closets often had indoor privies located directly over cesspools—landlords had either intentionally or unintentionally used the term water closet.

The later part of the 1800's saw an increasing tenement problem despite the settlement-house movement, model tenements, employers' industrial housing, limited dividend housing companies, philanthropic housing trust funds, and tenement-house legislation. Gray describes a model tenement house plan developed from a competition in 1879 as follows:

The prize winning drawings so crowded the land with rentable rooms that adequate air, light and a decent degree of privacy was impossible; yet in

43 *Ibid.*
44 *Ibid.*
45 *Ibid.*, p. 8.

the following year 399 buildings were built from this design, and for decades after, thousands more. They became known as "dumbbell apartments" and "double deckers." They were a major contribution to New York's worst housing. There were better plans presented in the competition but they did not "bring in the most revenue." That is the traditional attitude of private capital toward housing for families of low income; it is not good housing which has been the *sine qua non*, but good returns. Good low-rent housing of decent standards were not produced in any appreciable quantity by private capital.[46]

A typical dumbbell tenement was six stories, consisting of 14 rooms to each floor of which only 4 rooms on each floor had direct access to natural light. (There were variations of this plan, but they were not improvements.) A small recessed inner court at the entrance, on each side, gave the structure the appearance of a dumbbell in some of the variations.[47]

An examination of two representative city blocks in New York might assist us in drawing a picture of housing conditions under the "old law tenement" situation. One square city block might consist of a variety of buildings such as converted two-story cottages and three- or four-story row houses along with a barracks building and a number of railroad tenements. A number of tenements might be five or six stories in height standing next to several two- and three-story converted structures that had additional rooms built onto the rear. The entire city block would probably be covered with structures with a few small courts, alleys, and yard spaces. Street-level spaces, facing onto the streets, would be mixed commercial and apartment types. In viewing such a city block perhaps the most striking image would be the apparent diversity of structures in age, facade, height, and so on. Yet such a city block would, in essence, be representation of some of the worst and older slum conditions of "old law tenements."[48]

A second city block (i.e., square block) might consist of an endless series of slightly newer six-story dumbbell tenements, built wall to wall, covering all of the square block except for a few air shafts and perhaps three narrow courts separating four great clusters of tenement houses. The striking view of such a city block would probably be the impression of sameness and cramped quarters.[49]

Both such city blocks would be typical of the New York City of 1900 and considering that both would lack adequate facilities of every kind (i.e., open spaces, sunlight, sewage facilities, water closets, artificial lighting), it would be difficult to find favor with one as opposed

46 *Ibid.*, p. 9.
47 Ford, *op. cit.*, p. 206.
48 *Ibid.*
49 *Ibid.*

to the other. Such conditions led to the "Tenement House Act of 1901" which required, among numerous provisions, that no new tenement could occupy more than 70 percent of a given lot (except for corner lots where coverage by a structure could go as high as 90 percent of the lot) and that the size of lots should be at least 50 feet in width and 100 feet in depth. Such restricted lot coverage and increased lot size, along with other requirements (the requirements of the 1901 Act are discussed in more detail later in this chapter), would allow for relatively large inner courts on both sides of the center section of new tenements so that all rooms could have access to the open air.

After 1901 the construction of "new law tenements" and the repair and maintenance of "old law tenements" was considered a practical, if not total, answer to the housing conditions of the poor by the leading housing reformers of the day. Those social reformers writing before 1901 were describing the transformed tenement buildings, the railroad tenements, and the dumbbell or double-decker tenement houses which constituted "old law tenements." Those social reformers writing after 1901 described not only the "new law tenements," but also the vast inventory of "old law tenements" that clung to life far beyond the 1890 to 1929 period. In fact, Nathan Straus, in *The Seven Myths of Housing*, reported that as late as 1944 approximately two million people in New York City still lived in tenements condemned by the Tenement House Committee of 1885.[50]

The social milieu interacted with the housing conditions of 1890–1929 intertwining cause and effect in a maze of relationships. The social reformers, housing investigators, and humanitarians of that age were as much the product of the forces at work as were the poor and the rejected. While there were outstanding examples of great deeds and farsighted planning, it is perhaps the tragedy of that period that most people of high and low station failed to rise above their times. Some historians and social philosophers have suggested it is a myth to label any period of the past as a "Golden Age." That is at least one debate from which turn-of-the-century America is safe.

Housing Investigations

The late sociologist Pitirim Sorokin reflected near the end of his long and productive career on the "amnesia" and "discoverer's complex" characteristic of so many of his fellow scholars.[51] Sorokin found

[50] Nathan Straus, *The Seven Myths of Housing*. (New York: Knopf), 1944, p. 79.

[51] Pitirim A. Sorokin, *Fads and Foibles in Modern Sociology and Related Sciences*. (Chicago: Henry Regnery Co.), 1956, pp. 3–4.

among his colleagues a disregard for the past that bordered on "amnesia" and a tendency to plunge into contemporary research without benefit of didactic history, which tended to result in the "rediscovery" of the principles of social norms and human interaction as well as the structure and nature of group formation and organization. He pointed out that the Greek, Roman, and Oriental civilizations not only carried out extensive surveys and studies, but codified their findings into "unambiguous and clear" laws for the orderly operation of the family, city, and state.[52]

While some of the early American social reformers and housing investigators conducted outstanding comparative, cross-cultural, and historical studies of housing conditions, many others appeared to suffer from the amnesia and discoverer's complex Sorokin discussed. Often, housing and social reformers seemed at a loss to deal with the complexities of the social phenomena confronting them and, therefore, their means of investigation were simplistic and almost naive. City reformers and housing investigators were not alone in this naivete, but they regrettably provided some outstanding examples. The contemporary observer has the uneasy feeling that the insight, objectivity, experimental orientation, and sheer dynamic curiosity for the nature of things found in the collected works of Benjamin Franklin were characteristics not studied, emulated, and built upon but were, rather, consigned to the fate of dusty bookshelves.[53]

Lawrence Veiller's advice to the people of 1910 emphasized the need for housing reform movements based on the essentials of housing investigation, but his methods left much to be desired. Veiller lamented the many problems facing the housing investigator, especially the lack of objective standards. As a means of attacking this problem he and his associates devised a schedule card to be used in the evaluation of individual dwelling units. A "percentage" system was developed so that key factors could be assigned a numerical value. As an example of the use of the evaluation system Veiller suggested:

Thus, in reporting as to cleanliness it is suggested that the following scheme be adopted: That the investigators be allowed to answer only in the following terms: "Very Clean," "Clean," "Dirty," "Somewhat Dirty," "Filthy," and in addition be required to indicate these facts on a percentage basis, thus —"Very Clean" shall be deemed 100%, "Clean" 80%, "Somewhat Dirty" 60%, "Dirty" 40%, "Filthy" 0%. Similarly with regard to repair: The investigator should be permitted to answer in only three terms as to the condition of repair; viz., "Good," "Fair," "Bad," and these should be numerically

52 *Ibid.*, pp. 230–231.
53 We refer here not to imaginative creativity alone, but to the implementation of collective knowledge and new findings.

expressed by 100, 50, 0. The observance of these principles will be found to be of great help.[54]

Of this "objective" method of investigation Veiller explains his purpose in these words, ". . . its main end should be the formulation of measures by which the adverse conditions discovered may be remedied."[55]

Part of the "formulation of measures" included schedules that were on a card of "five inches wide by eight inches long," the use of "different colors" for "different purposes," and the use of "ink" in all evaluations. Orderly procedures were essential, as Veiller pointed out, lest the housing investigator becomes confused and so jumps "from one portion of the building to another."[56] To forestall this potential confusion, Veiller elaborates:

The properly prepared schedule arranges the classes of facts to be noted, in the same order on the card as will be actually followed by the investigator in his progress through the building beginning either at the cellar and ascending through the building to the roof, or beginning at the roof and descending to the cellar and out-premises. Where there are many apartments or families in a building and it is desired to learn many facts with regard to each apartment or family, it will be found essential to prepare separate schedules for each apartment or family, separating the facts thus ascertained from the general points of information with regard to the building itself.[57]

While such social reformers as Lawrence Veiller and Jacob A. Riis enlisted the support of individual and organized volunteers to carry out housing investigations, early municipal legislative housing investigation committees long before the Civil War, focusing on safety, sanitation, and health, swept through tenement areas as teams frequently consisting of sanitation inspectors, reporters, and police. (See Tenement House Department of the City of New York violations form.)

Although the humanitarian volunteers often accompanied a sanitation inspector or police officer to complete their investigative schedules, legislative committees and commissions openly identified tenement areas as dangerous due to rampant crime and immorality and did not disguise the quasi-military nature of their fact-finding operations, justifying the heavy police guard and sudden invasions of slum areas on the grounds they constituted "hazardous duty" among foreign populations.[58]

54 Veiller, *op. cit.*, pp. 59–60.
55 *Ibid.*, p. 55.
56 *Ibid.*, p. 58.
57 *Ibid.*
58 Edith Elmer Wood, *The Housing of the Unskilled Wage Earner: America's Next Problem.* (New York: Macmillan), 1919, p. 30.

TENEMENT HOUSE DEPARTMENT OF THE CITY OF NEW YORK

Borough of MANHATTAN

Viol. _____ 1903.

To the Tenement House Commissioner
of The City of New York.
    Sir:— I respectfully report that on _____ 17 _____ 1903, I examined the premises and tenement house,

Compl. _____

NEW YORK, _____ June 17 _____

No. _____ 117 Av. C

DIPHTHERI

The said tenement house is a _____ building, _____ 7 _____ stories and _____ 0 _____ in height, _____ feet front, _____ feet deep,
and is arranged to accommodate _____ 0 0 3 5 5 5 5 5 5 _____ families on a floor, and _____ 33 _____ families in the whole building.

The Owner is _____ recorded _____ Address _____

the Agent is _____ Address _____

I found the facts to be as follows:

403 CL.   Accumulation garbage, rubbish, dirt, papers, etc. in yard, front areaway, N. & S. shafts, interior court.

400 CL.   Painted walls & whitewashed ceilings 3 W.C. compts. halls 1 ... stories dirty.

82 R   Plaster on walls of above W.C. compts. broken & defective.

R   Seats of middle W.C. compts. 3 story broken & defective.

450 M   Two ash cans, not adequate to 33 families.

Report Reviewed _____

_____ A. Kamholtz _____ Inspector _____ 116 _____ Dist.

Approved _____ Charles R. Bell _____ Chief Inspector.

CHIEF INSPECTOR
Per _____ R.B.

Street _____ Ave. C _____ No. _____ 117 _____ Dist. _____ 116 _____ Borough of _____ Manhattan
                                                   ECM

To the Tenement House Commissioner. Sir:—
    I recommend that the following orders be issued in this case:

403—   Remove the accumulations of rubbish from the yard, front
        areaway, N. & S. shafts, interior court, etc.

400—   Thoroughly cleanse the walls and ceilings of the three
        w.c. compartments in the halls on the 1,2,3,4,5,6,7 stories, etc.

82—   Remove from the walls all broken, loose and defective plaster
        plasxxxx in the said w.c., etc.

251—   Repair the seat of the middle w. c. in the hall on the 3rd
        story.

450—   Provide proper and separate receptacles for ashes.

FIGURE 3–4. New York: Violations form, Tenement House Department, June 1903. [Courtesy of the National Archives and Records Service, General Services Administration.]

The humanitarian social reformers, buttressed by their Puritanical background, did not look with favor on tenement dwellers, but they did manage a certain sympathy. The Municipal legislative committees and commissions seemed driven by the same Puritanical motivation, but lacked the sympathetic saving grace of the humanitarians. The New York and Brooklyn government committee on tenant houses of 1857 stated their inspection teams "penetrated to localities and witnessed scenes which in frightful novelty, far exceeded the limit of . . . previously conceived ideas of human degradation and suffering."[59] The New York Council of Hygiene of the Citizens Association showed a similar elitism in 1865 when it stated in its housing investigation report that the danger of immigrant tenements was "the entire absorption of the artisan and middle classes into the common herd of the utterly dependent and tenant-house class."[60]

When the federal government entered the field of housing investigation in 1892, there was some hope that the attitude of housing researchers might improve, but the resulting 1894 report titled "The Slums of Baltimore, Chicago, New York and Philadelphia" began by defining slums as "dirty back streets, especially such streets as are inhabited by a squalid and criminal population," and emphasis was placed on the large number of saloons per block and the high crime rate.[61] The federal housing investigators were not well received by the immigrant peoples described as "squalid and criminal." The lack of real intent to deal with housing problems is reflected in the summary of the 1894 federal report on slums, in which slums were defined in terms of crime and squalid populations and emphasis was placed on high rates of crime and the saloon culture. The summary concluded:

The extraordinary freedom from sickness in the slums of New York reflected great credit on the health board of that city. In 311 tenements visited not a single adult sick in bed was seen, except where the sickness was due to an increase in the population, and very few children. Of what village of the same population can the same statement be made?[62]

The report continues:

Without any exception it was found that the air in the tenement houses was as pure as in any residence visited.[63]

The 1894 federal report on slum conditions in cities of 200,000 or more in population ignored the 1894 report of the New York City

59 *Ibid.*
60 *Ibid.*
61 *Ibid.*, p. 29.
62 *Ibid.*, p. 41.
63 *Ibid.*

Board of Health. Wood reviews the findings of the New York City
Board of Health as follows:

The Board of Health estimated at this time that there were 39,000 tenement
houses in New York. Of these it had listed 2,425 containing 15,726 families,
as having bad structural or sanitary conditions. The agents of the committee
visited these first. Eventually they visited 8,441 houses. Most of their statistics refer to 3,984 houses with 33,485 apartments with 16,756 dark
rooms, affecting 71,015 persons. They found 37,469 persons depending on
toilets listed as "bad" and 38,157 depending on toilets listed as "very bad."
Only 306 out of 255,033 persons investigated had access to bath-tubs. In
hundreds of cases from 90 to 100 percent of the lot was covered by buildings. More than five-sixths of the houses had their toilet arrangement in the
yard, and nearly half of the remainder in the cellar. Only fifty-one were supplied with toilets in their apartments. A trifle over half the houses had their
water supply in the hall. Five hundred and twenty-seven houses (over one-
eighth) were dependent on a yard supply. The remainder had water in the
apartment. More than one-fourth of the houses had no fire escapes, and more
than another fourth had improper or insufficient ones. Bad conditions of halls
and cellars, and various manifestations of dirt and dilapidation are also tabu-
lated.[64]

The different conclusions reached by federal housing investigators
and the New York Board of Health are striking. Far too much evidence has been gathered to give any credence to the conclusions of the
federal report of 1894. While condemning the slums and the immigrant population of large cities, the federal report found reason to
be satisfied with the housing conditions studied. The federal report
was a sham serving the Puritan morality by condemning the immigrant
population, but supporting the integrity of the social order by focusing
on crime and the saloon culture and avoiding the housing needs and
social welfare concerns of the people. Poor research methods were
combined with the values and vested interests of the ruling classes.

The irony is that the federal report contradicted the findings of the
New York City Board of Health by rejecting that body's statistics,
which painted a less than happy picture, in favor of praising the
Board of Health and the municipal government for the fine job accomplished in providing adequate housing.

The legal morality of the 1890's and early 1900's could only attack
the evils of the outsiders; it could not attack the system which ignored
the call for justice and social reform because it could not and would
not attack the class structure it served. Contrary to prevailing opinion
the first major incursion of the federal government into the field of
housing was a step backward.

[64] *Ibid.*, pp. 40–41.

Housing investigations in New York City near the turn of the century are most often given as examples simply because New York was the port of entry for so many immigrants and the center of attraction for large numbers of rural migrants as well. The rapid industrialization of the city and the concentration of wealth in so small a geographic area provided the city with the means to support a great population of low-paid common laborers. However, other cities faced housing problems similar to New York, if not on so grand a scale, and housing investigations and research were conducted on a sizable scale in Washington, D.C., Boston, San Francisco, Baltimore, Richmond, Chicago, St. Louis, Philadelphia, Cincinnati, Providence, Columbus, Grand Rapids, and Minneapolis.

Generally housing surveys in cities other than New York emulated Veiller's lackluster and unimaginative approach, and the outcome was seldom different. They highlighted immorality, crime, saloons, overcrowding, inadequate water supplies and waste disposal systems, dark rooms, filth, and high rates of disease and infant mortality. Fire hazards and tenement coverage of 90 to 100 percent of the total space of lots were also frequently mentioned in surveys.

A few of the large cities did not have a significant tenement problem, but, lacking that problem, most faced an appalling inadequacy of community services, such as inadequate sewage systems.[65]

In 1931 Edith Wood wrote of the several years after World War I and the 1920's:

The post-war period has not been rich in housing surveys of the older type. So much information showing bad conditions had been gathered and so little had been done to remedy them that there was small incentive to go on. Why survey again?[66]

Nevertheless the postwar years saw the development of a number of housing surveys by municipal and state governments, and some federal agencies not directly associated with housing began to report on housing conditions as part of their overall analysis of social problems. Private clubs and organizations also continued their efforts to improve housing conditions, using surveys and housing investigations as the basis of their lobbying for local, state, and federal housing legislation and the enforcement of existing codes.[67]

Some postwar surveys developed more sophisticated "census-like" procedures for housing investigations, and the rise of Human Ecology as a distinct discipline along with emergence of the "Chicago School"

[65] Wood, *Housing of . . . Wage Earner, op. cit.*, pp. 46–59.
[66] Wood, *Recent Trends . . . , op. cit.*, p. 19.
[67] *Ibid., passim.*

of sociologists and ecologists began to move housing investigation into a conceptual framework worthy of the name of scientific research (Park and Burgess published *The City* in 1925).[68]

While a few social reformers such as Jacob A. Riis (*How the Other Half Lives; A Ten Year's War; The Battle with the Slum*) had escaped the dull schedule card approach toward housing investigations of the 1890's and early 1900's, their means of so doing depended on what can only be characterized as sad stories and bleeding hearts. Riis' touching accounts of "Pietro and the Jew," "Jim," and "The Unnecessary Story of Mrs. Ben Wah and Her Parrot" were sympathetic, but also patronizing.[69] With the ecological theories of the "Chicago School" came not only scientific concepts but such well-written social commentaries as Louis Wirth's "Some Jewish Types of Personality" (1926) and "*The Ghetto*" (1928), which did not suffer from Sorokin's historical "amnesia" or the "discoverer's complex," but they expressed deep-rooted insight and an urbanity and charm of style and understanding unrivaled by the old housing investigators.[70]

In addition, the need for adequate statistics, while not achieved during the 1920's, became an issue the federal government would eventually be forced to face. Wood wrote in *Recent Trends in American Housing* in 1931:

Virtually every civilized country in the world except the United States has national census figures to show what proportion of its population is living in crowded or overcrowded conditions. The number of persons in the family divided by the number of rooms which the family occupy gives the coefficient of room density. Any density over one is found to exert an unfavorable influence on health, increasing with the density. Anything over two is grossly bad. . . .

Some countries, as Norway and Holland, collect through their census much other housing information in addition to room density. Home ownership is the only subject connected with housing on which our American census has given us information, except the items about farm homes . . . and increasingly meaningless figures on families and dwellings.

A strong effort was made by the American Association of University Women, aided by thirty-odd other organizations, to get the number of rooms per family on the population schedule of the 1930 census. The only result was a promise to make the inquiry experimentally in a couple of cities, and even

[68] For an excellent review of the growth and development of Human Ecology, see George A. Theodorson (ed.), *Studies in Human Ecology.* (Evanston, Illinois: Row Peterson and Co.), 1961, *passim.*

[69] Riis, *op. cit.,* Chapters 7, 10, and 17.

[70] For a review of the selected works of Louis Wirth, see Albert J. Reiss, Jr. (ed.), *Louis Wirth: On Cities and Social Life.* (Chicago: The University of Chicago Press), 1964, *passim.*

this got crowded out at the last minute. The inclusion of such an obviously trade-inspired item as the possession of a radio instead of one so packed with social significance as the number of rooms per family, was particularly disheartening.[71]

Just as investigations of urban housing conditions focused on the tenements of New York City, even though housing surveys had been conducted in a number of other population centers throughout the nation, little attention was given to rural housing conditions. The social reformers tended to look toward urban America for problems and solutions. As the influence of the U. S. Department of Agriculture's Experiment Stations, Extension Agriculture Agents, County Home Demonstration Agents, and Farm Bureaus grew, more surveys were conducted of rural housing conditions (frequently rural voluntary groups and farm organizations assisted in the collection of information). The postwar period witnessed a rise in the number of rural housing studies.[72]

Plumbing statistics dominated postwar rural housing surveys, but the lack of modern conveniences, despite Elmer Forbes' concern for the growth of rural "slum spots," were difficult to translate into meaningful evaluations of the conditions of rural life and shelter needs. Most of the problem of evaluation was the result of poor sampling procedures which selected white middle-class farm households as sources of information and there seemed to be a concentrated effort to collect information related to the rise of the new technology (i.e., automobiles, telephones, kitchen equipment, sewing machines, etc.).

In reference to this second tendency, Wood observed that the "Selected Farm Expenses" section of the 1920 Census contained "certain rather curiously selected items."[73] Thus the 1920 Census reported that of all United States farms 7 percent had gas or electric lighting, 10 percent had water piped into the dwelling unit, 30 percent had automobiles, and 38.7 percent had telephones.[74]

The problem of sampling is evident in the U. S. Department of Agriculture study "The Farm Women's Problem" (1920), which based its findings on the results of 10,044 questionnaires distributed to farm women in 33 states by county Home Economics agents. The questionnaires were long and relatively complex, requiring time, cooperation, and a degree of education for successful completion. As a result, the findings indicated 32 percent of the households had piped water, 65 percent had water in the kitchen (piped or indoor pumps), 21 percent

[71] Wood, *Recent Trends*. . . , *op. cit.*, pp. 27–28.
[72] *Ibid.*, pp. 29–35.
[73] Wood, *Recent Trends*. . . , *op. cit.*, p. 30.
[74] *Ibid.*

had bathtubs, 15 percent had indoor toilets, 96 percent had door and window screens, and 95 percent had sewing machines.[75] Although these figures represented a class of farm families with above-average socio-economic status, an unexpected group of characteristics emerged which called attention to the contributions of housewives to the national work force and reinforced the drive to improve work centers, especially the kitchen, in the farm home. It was found that 87 percent of the house-wives never took a vacation, 96 percent did their own washing, 92 percent did their own sewing, and 94 percent did their own baking, while only 15 percent had electric power machinery to assist in these tasks (actual farm work employed electric power machinery in 42 per-cent of the total tasks). In addition, the housewife averaged 11.3 hours of work per day.[76]

Such investigations as "The Farm Women's Problem" led to a series of studies culminating in Hildegarde Kneeland's 1929 address to the 10th National Conference on Housing, which dealt with the need for the "scientific kitchen":

At such a Conference as this, concerned with the lofty problems of the Mon-ster City, it takes considerable courage to introduce that most humble of topics—the domestic kitchen. But I find my support in so doing in the most potent of modern arguments—that of numerical magnitude. I am asking you to consider, not the kitchen, but twenty-six million (26,000,000) kitchens. I am claiming your attention for the workshops of the largest occupational group in the nation—a group so large that if it were listed in the Census of Occupations it would form one-third of our entire working population.[77]

Kneeland reported that the Bureau of Home Economics found home-makers spent an average of 51 hours a week (a week being 7 full days) at work in the home, and, more specifically, 50 percent worked be-tween 42 and 56 hours a week, and 33⅓ percent worked 56 hours or more a week. Since these figures accounted only for work time by the homemaker herself, the additional homemaking tasks conducted by children, husbands, and hired labor brought the average hours per week devoted to homemaking to more than 60 hours. Since this average refers to seven-day weeks for fifty-two weeks a year, "we are dealing here with an industry that seldom allows vacations or holi-days."[78]

[75] *Ibid.*, p. 31.

[76] *Ibid.*

[77] Hildegarde Kneeland, "Abolishing the Domestic Lock-Step—The Scientific Kitchen." In: *Housing Problems in America. Proceedings of the Tenth National Conference on Housing, New York City, 1929.* (New York: National Housing Association), 1929, p. 15.

[78] *Ibid.*, p. 18.

While admitting data were gathered from small samples, Kneeland stated:

But sufficient evidence is at hand to suggest that for the 12,000,000 *rural housewives* these records are quite representative, *at least for the middle class homes.* For the town and city women the number of records is too small to warrant generalization. But even if a more extensive study of urban families would considerably lower these averages, the provision of meals alone would still rank as our largest single industry, employing the equivalent of as many full-time workers as all of the manufacturing industries together.[79] [Emphasis added.]

Kneeland advocated "the methods of management developed by industry be applied to "housekeeping" by making "motion studies" and "time schedules" common to the housewives' education. Such managerial efficiency would result in the "scientific kitchen" characterized by separate working surfaces for each type of work, the arrangement of equipment in step-saving sequence, compact working areas, the placement of major equipment at convenient heights, and the grouping of equipment around work centers where it is most frequently used.[80] The implementation of these management techniques through the development of the "scientific kitchen" was thought to eventually lead to the easing of the work burden of the rural housewife, although even the "100% efficient" kitchen would require great amounts of time and labor because of the nature of the housekeeping and food preparation industry lacking, as it does, mass production, division of labor, and advanced machinery.[81] The failure to free the rural housewife from the burdens of labor even with the "100% efficient" kitchen was no tragedy, however:

There is little reason why this should greatly concern us. If in the future we continue to prefer private housekeeping to its large-scale substitute, we shall be fully willing to pay the price, because it makes possible a way of living which seems to us more important than productive efficiency.[82]

The discovery of the burdens of the great labor force identified as housewives, the evolution of the Home Economics education effort (which appears in many cases to deal with exactly the same issues today as it did in the 1920's—household management and kitchen efficiency seemingly constituting one of the great unsolvable problems

---

79 *Ibid.*
80 *Ibid.*, pp. 19–25.
81 *Ibid.*, p. 25.
82 *Ibid.*

of human beings), as well as the lack of adequate facilities (i.e., plumbing statistics) in rural areas constituted a lost opportunity to characterize homemakers as productive workers.

The rural housing investigations thus far described added to perceived differences between the "Monster City" and rural areas, established a tradition of very poor survey techniques of rural housing conditions (therefore tying government Agriculture and Home Economics agencies to the service of the upper and middle classes), and missed entirely the social welfare implications suggested by Kneeland's statement, "I am claiming your attention for the largest occupational group in the nation. . . ."[83]

The Puritan Ethic, having intruded into rural housing investigations, denied the reality of the house as a workplace and morally rejected the labor force operating within the house. Kneeland's surrender of the rights of labor for women (i.e., homemakers)—"we shall be fully willing to pay the price"—left the American female out of the recognized work force, and since the United States only provides social welfare benefits of a respectable nature to the workingman, the American homemaker is indeed paying the price of nonrecognition and exclusion. We do not suggest that rural housing investigators "caused" the second-class citizenship status of American women, but they did reinforce it.[84]

It must be kept in mind that the housing reformers and humanitarians of the turn of the century were not social revolutionaries, nor were they adherents of the political theories of the Social Democratic left that had emerged in Europe. They were, instead, moralists rooted in the Puritan Ethic, and, as such, they supported the elimination of "evil." They were activists only in the sense that they did not ignore social problems (i.e., evils) as most did but sought out to destroy them and restore America to its original "purity." In the final analysis they supported the system and attempted to work through established institutions. This approach, combined with moralistic motivation and weak investigative techniques, doomed them to failure.

83 One would assume "the largest occupational group in the nation" would command more than "respect." Women in general, and homemakers in particular, get little more than society's "respect," missing out on such trivia as power, wealth, and social welfare benefits. Having been well socialized into their roles women present the greatest minority (or is it majority?) problem facing the modern world.

84 "Traditional family life" and "sound American values" have long been defended by Colleges of Home Economics and their Extension Services. While not going into a long discussion of the matter, this means they have supported middle-class values and conformity. In that sense they are a reactionary force in American society.

Legislation

The assumption was that where private enterprise failed legislation and government action could provide the means for a united and ultimately successful attack on poor housing conditions.

Seldom did the social reformers attempt to organize the immigrants, migrants, and other rural and urban poor in the cause of social justice for they were not, in the Puritan view, worthy or capable of achieving the best the nation could offer, and further, such an act bordered on social revolution. Social reformers acted on behalf of the poor and ill-housed, not with them. Organization for housing legislation, therefore, occurred with the humanitarian groups of the upper and middle classes, thus ensuring the stability of the social system.

This does not mean the housing reformers (and other social reformers) were not instrumental in acting as change-agents, but it does mean they served the system by providing a communications link to the establishment which acted as a bellwether clarifying for the power elite the minimum actions necessary to pacify the emerging new classes and the poor. By defusing the issue of class conflict the social reformers rendered a disservice to the great mass of poor in the ultimate sense but obtained limited goals on behalf of the poor in the specific sense.

Because the period from 1890 to 1929 marked a time of industrial and agricultural reorganization and the emergence of the United States as a world power in the political and military sectors, very little legislation was passed during this time for the improvement of housing conditions. However, the limited legislation passed and the suggested framework for future housing legislation set the stage for the type of action government would take for the improvement of housing during the rest of the century.

Housing reformers centered their analysis of how to achieve adequate housing for the people through legislation on two principal concepts. The first dealt with restrictive housing legislation, which sought to prevent the maintenance of existing inadequate housing and housing services by upgrading and then enforcing minimum standards. Restrictive legislation also sought to prevent the construction of new housing units that did not meet minimum standards.

The second approach dealt with constructive housing legislation (as opposed to restrictive), which sought to provide adequate housing through established programs in communities (i.e., local and state legislation) directed toward the provision of "good" or suitable new housing. For those groups with limited incomes, constructive housing legislation would provide adequate and suitable new housing at or below cost. The concepts of restrictive versus constructive housing legislation do not appear mutually exclusive, and considering that some foreign governments employed both approaches during the 1890–1929 period, a debate over which approach was correct appears to be a false issue.[85] Yet that was exactly the debate that developed among housing reformers in the United States. In addition to debating a false issue, the problem of progressively moving from one to the other developed.

Veiller muddied the waters in his book, *A Model Housing Law*, by suggesting stages of action in housing, beginning with first solving the "kindergarten" housing problems and then moving to solve the "postgraduate" problems. He stated:

That legislation alone will solve the housing problem is of course absurd. But the point that we wish to lay emphasis upon is that in most cases the largest results have come from legislative action and that until certain fundamental Evils have been remedied it is futile, or worse, to adopt the methods of housing reform which may be said to belong to the post-graduate period rather than to the kindergarten stage of a community's development. In other words, we must get rid of our slums before we establish garden cities; we must stop people living in cellars before we concern ourselves with changes in methods of taxation; we must make it impossible for builders to build dark rooms in new houses before we urge the government to subsidize building; we must abolish privy vaults before we build model tenements. When these things have been done there is no question that effort can be profitably expended in the other directions mentioned.[86]

Veiller's argument is similar to the common complaint heard concerning the space programs of the 1960's and 1970's which called for a solution to social and political problems on Earth before engaging in adventures on the Moon and Mars. That would be a long wait indeed. Veiller's influence was so great by 1914, when he published *A Model Housing Law*, that his emphasis on restrictive housing legislation and stage-by-stage development of housing problem solutions dominated the thinking of housing reformers. This approach doomed significant legislation for housing reform to the merry-go-round of false issues and endless delays. In 1919, Edith Wood commented on the fruits of such a flawed policy:

In the United States, if we except the interesting experiment embodied in the Massachusetts Homestead Commission, a housing loan statute in Oklahoma and the very recent war housing activities of the Federal Government, we

85 Wood, *Housing of . . . Wage Earner*, pp. 19–20 and 60–61.
86 Lawrence Veiller, *A Model Housing Law*. (New York: Survey Associates, Inc.), 1914, p. 7.

have confined ourselves to restrictive legislation. For this policy, the report of the New York Tenement Housing Commission of 1900, the success of the New York tenement house law, and the activity of Lawrence Veiller and his associates of the National Housing Association are largely responsible. That the New York tenement house law has been productive of great good, or that Mr. Veiller's experience and services entitle all that he says on the subject to careful consideration, no sensible person would deny. It may, however, be questioned whether in a matter vitally affecting the welfare of something like thirty millions of our people, the opinion of any one man, however eminent, ought to be accepted as final, especially when the weight of foreign authority is decidedly on the other side.[87]

As might be expected, early housing legislation was at the municipal level and, because New York City was the port of entry of so many immigrants and the focus of housing investigations, that city became the leader of housing legislation of the restrictive type. By 1890, New York City had an established tradition of housing legislation, including "The Tenement Housing Act of 1879," "The Consolidation Act of 1882," and "The Tenement House Act of 1887."

These housing laws addressed themselves to such matters as cellars, water supplies, water closets, garbage collection, windows, air space by apartment, and janitor ratios to numbers of families per tenement. In addition to incorporating housing into the matrix of total community services, health and sanitation, safety features, maintenance and repairs, and ratio factors of people per apartment to adequate facilities were the subjects of early housing laws.

"The Tenement House Act of 1895," based on the recommendations of the Tenement House Committee of 1894, continued the tradition of housing legislation, although only a few of the Committee's extensive recommendations were incorporated into the 1895 Act. While the 1895 Act simply continued a tradition the informational source of the Act—the Tenement House Committee of 1894—was probably of greater significance, since it covered a wide range of topics and provided the basis for the more progressive legislation to follow.

For example, the 1894 Committee recommended that

1. The Board of Health be empowered to condemn and destroy unsanitary buildings with "reasonable compensation to the owners."
2. "No tenement or lodging-house subsequently constructed shall occupy more than 70 percentum of an interior city lot; nor more than 90 percentum of a corner lot; and that, in computing the amount of the lot covered by the building, all shafts or courts of less than 25 square feet in the area shall be considered as part of the solid building and not as part of the free-air space."

[87] Wood, *Housing of . . . Wage Earner, op. cit.,* 61–62.

3. Buildings, and especially staircases, should be fireproof.
4. Each room in all tenements should have a separate window "opening into the outer air."
5. Water closets should have windows "opening into the outer air," and the floor of water closets should be waterproof to allow for flushing and washing without leakage.
6. The ceilings of basement apartments must be at least two feet above ground level.
7. No wallpaper should be used in future construction, and all existing wallpaper in tenements must be removed.
8. Halls without natural light must be artificially lighted, and each hall on each floor "shall be lighted until 10:00 o'clock at night."
9. The Board of Health shall be required to prevent overcrowding, and in the case of "insufficient ventilation at least 400 cubic feet of air shall be afforded to each adult and 200 to each child under 12 occupying a room."
10. A tenement may not be used as a lodging-house, stable, or for the storage of rags.
11. The laws requiring the filing of the tenement owner's name, address, and a description of the property owned shall be enforced.
12. Small parks and playgrounds should be constructed "in the district east of the Bowery and Catharine Street and South of Fourth Street, and that the city be authorized to issue bonds to the amount of $3,-000,000 for such purposes."
13. New schools should have sufficient open-air playgrounds and an adequate "number of scholars," and existing schools should have playgrounds attached.
14. Rapid transit facilities should be constructed "as one of the principal means of prevention of over-crowding of houses and districts."
15. Fully equipped bathing establishments, "on the European models," shall be constructed with low entrance fees.
16. Public drinking fountains and lavatories shall be constructed in "tenement-house districts."
17. Electric street lights should be "extended as rapidly as possible throughout all parts of the tenement-house district."
18. The number of kindergartens should be increased within the framework of the public school system.
19. "A law be passed making the offences of soliciting and the maintenance of houses of prostitution in tenement-houses punishable with greater severity than when they are committed elsewhere."
20. Additional sanitary inspectors be added to the Board of Health and additional sanitary police "be detailed from the police department to the health department," provided said police pass a civil service examination under the supervision of the New York Municipal Civil Service.[88]

88 This account is based on Ford, *op. cit.*, pp. 193–197.

With reference to the 1894 Committee Report and the 1895 Act James Ford commented:

Only a few of the Committee's recommendations became law in the Tenement House Act of 1895. Perhaps its greatest immediate contribution was the securing of two small parks for the Lower East Side and the provision of school playgrounds and recreation piers. The report itself is, however, a classic among housing studies, and its appearance presumably influenced profoundly the thought and arguments of specialists and civic leaders in housing. It is questionable whether the radical improvements achieved in the Tenement House Act of 1901—passed only six years later—would have been possible except for the studies made for the Committee of 1894 and the infiltration of their findings in the writings of the intervening years and in the minds of citizens.[89]

"The Tenement House Act of 1901" was based on the work completed by the Tenement House Committee of 1894 and the Tenement House Commission of 1900, which was appointed by Governor Theodore Roosevelt for the purpose of investigating housing conditions in both New York City and Buffalo. Robert W. de Forest was elected Chairman of the Commission and Lawrence Veiller acted as Secretary. Ford observes:

In the fields of law-making and civic action, the Commission's contributions were of unique value. Recommendations, based upon detailed and well-judged study, were incorporated in the Tenement House Act of 1901, which has served, directly or indirectly, as the chief working model for most of the tenement-house legislation of America since that date.

Though more recent legislation has been based upon Veiller, *Model Tenement House Law*, published in 1910, and Veiller, *Model Housing Law*, first published in 1914 and revised in 1920, these were modeled upon the Tenement House Law of 1901, which had been framed chiefly by Lawrence Veiller and, in so far at least as architectural and structural requirements were concerned, by I. N. Phelps Stokes; they departed from it in the increasing strictness of provisions but little in fundamental structure.[90]

"The Tenement House Act of 1901" provided for many of the reforms suggested by the 1894 Committee (but not written into law in the 1895 Act) as well as the 1900 Commission.

Provisions of the 1901 Act included:

1. An extensive definition of terms and procedural steps for compliance with, and enforcement of, the law itself (this was especially important because previous housing laws had been difficult to enforce due to the use of vague terms).

89 *Ibid.*, p. 197.
90 *Ibid.*, p. 217 and n. p. 217.

2. Fireproofing of the first tier of beams in the cellar of tenements and for the installation of fire retarding insulation in all openings from the cellar, such as stair halls, light wells, dumbwaiter shafts, and hollow walls.

3. At least two means of escape from fire located at "remote" distances from each other and usually consisting of one fireproof stair hall and one stair-type (as opposed to ladder-type) exterior fire escape (see Figure 3–5).

4. Running water and water closets in each apartment in tenements and exposed plumbing pipes (in existing structures at least one water closet had to be provided for every two families and they were to be connected to sewer lines whenever possible).

5. All cellars, court walls, and shafts had to be whitewashed or painted white or constructed of light-colored stone or brick.

6. All basements had to be damp-proofed, all old wallpaper had to be removed, most animals were restricted from tenements, and "suitable" garbage receptacles had to be provided for each tenement.

FIGURE 3–5. Air shaft. Dumbbell-type tenement. Bridge fire escapes at ends. ca. 1900. [Courtesy of the National Archives and Records Service, General Services Administration.]

7. Permits had to be obtained by landlords for the use of cellars or basements as rental units.

8. To prevent overcrowding at least 400 cubic feet of air space had to be provided for each adult and 200 cubic feet for each child.

9. Any tenement landlord who was informed his property was a house of prostitution or that "any part" of his property was being used for purposes of prostitution had to begin proceedings for the removal of these tenants within five days or the "permission of the owner was assumed" regarding prostitution, and the owner was subject to a fine of $1,000.

10. Permits for new construction, alteration, or conversion of buildings would be issued only after all plans and specifications had been reviewed by the Tenement House Department and occupation could not take place until a Certificate of Compliance was issued after a full inspection of the structure.

11. Landlords were subject to fines and imprisonment should the permit or certificate requirements be bypassed.

12. All landlords were required to register by name with a description of their tenement property and were informed on registration of the procedures to be followed for permits, certificates, notices, summons, and court orders.

13. The Tenement House Department was created and placed under the direction of a Commissioner who directed the department's Bureau of Records, New Building Bureau, and Bureau of Inspection.

14. The Bureau of Inspection was empowered to make monthly inspections of all tenement houses and reinspections of all buildings found in violation of housing laws, and the Bureau was legally required to employ not less than 190 inspectors for these purposes.

15. The Tenement House Department and its three Bureaus, in cooperation with the Department of Health, were granted widespread jurisdiction and powers over tenement houses and could refer violations of the law to the Corporation Counsel for court action.[91]

The much praised "Tenement House Act of 1901" and the work of the 1900 Commission as well as the activities of the Tenement House Department (as created by the 1901 Act) were landmarks and reference points for housing reformers of the period. Since de Forest and Veiller headed the 1900 Commission and acted as Commissioner and Deputy Commissioner of the Tenement House Department, their model for housing reform legislation was much in demand. Veiller published, in book form, several versions and revisions of New York's legislation which was, in any case, founded on Veiller's earlier models. "The Tenement House Act of 1901" was copied by a number of other municipal governments and housing reformers pushed for its adoption (or some version of Veiller's published models) at state and local levels throughout the nation.

[91] This account is based on *Ibid.*, pp. 217–225.

The point should be made that the 1901 Act was not only a land-mark of idealized housing reform legislated into action, but also the beginning of a move toward housing legislation at the state level. Municipal governments continued to pass housing legislation, but a number of state governments entered the field, even though the state housing legislation that finally won approval may have applied to only one or two cities within a given state. (For example, a state housing law referring to first-class cities may have, in practical terms, been aimed at the one or two cities in that state that were classified as first class—thus state housing legislation, while significant in moving housing legislation from local to state levels, was somewhat mislead-ing, since most urban areas and virtually all rural areas were not touched by the legislation.) What follows is a partial list of major state housing legislation growing out of the progressive period (most laws passed after 1901 are based on Veiller's model and/or the 1901 Act in New York):[92]

State	Legislation
Pennsylvania	1. Tenement house law for first-class cities (Philadelphia) passed in 1895.
	2. An expanded housing law passed and also repealed in 1913.
	3. Tenement house law for second-class cities (Pittsburgh and Scranton) passed in 1903.
New York	1. Tenement house law for first-class cities (New York and Buffalo) passed in 1901.
	2. Housing law for second-class cities passed in 1913 and repealed in 1915.
New Jersey	1. Tenement house law for all cities and towns passed in 1904.
Connecticut	1. Tenement house laws for all cities, boroughs, and towns passed in 1905, 1911, and 1913.
Wisconsin	1. The statewide tenement house law passed in 1907, but was declared unconstitutional in 1909.

[92] List based on combining information from Wood, *Housing of . . . Wage Earner, op. cit.,* pp. 80–82; and Wood, *Recent Trends. . . , op. cit.,* pp. 113–114.

State	Legislation
	2. Tenement house law for first-class cities (Milwaukee) passed in 1909.
Indiana	1. The tenement house law, which had features of a comprehensive housing law, passed in 1909 and applied to all cities over 59,000 in population by 1913. 2. The housing law was extended to all incorporated cities by 1917.
California	1. Tenement housing laws for all cities, towns, and counties passed in 1909, 1911, 1913, and 1915. The 1919 revision of the California statutes repealed or blocked many of the earlier provisions.
Kentucky	1. Tenement house law for first-class cities (Louisville) passed in 1910. 2. Tenement house law for first-class cities repealed in 1922.
Massachusetts	1. Tenement house law for all towns, subject to local approval, passed in 1912. By 1919 the law was adopted by 23 towns. 2. Tenement house law for all cities, subject to local approval, passed in 1913. By 1919 the law was adopted by one city.
Michigan	1. A statewide housing law for all cities and organized villages of 10,000 in population or more was passed in 1917.
Minnesota	1. Housing law for first-class cities (Minneapolis) passed in 1917. Adopted by the City of St. Paul in 1918.
Iowa	1. A statewide housing law was passed in 1919.
Oregon	1. Housing code for Portland passed in 1919. Revised to block many of the 1919 provisions in 1920 and revised again in 1930.

In 1919, Wood observed that, while a great deal of progress had been made to that date in municipal and state legislation, most emphasis, except for the limited cases of company housing, philanthropic limited-dividend housing ventures, housing trust companies, and model tenement housing ventures, was on restrictive housing legislation to the exclusion of constructive housing legislation. She concluded that a beginning had been made in "only one-half of the task."[93] Although Edith Wood was one of the more enlightened housing experts of the early 20th century, she restricted her arguments for constructive housing legislation by imposing her "respect" for the U. S. Constitution on the only feasible method of achieving constructive legislation, that is, through the federal government. Wood found some hope in "ingenious" methods of obeying the Constitution and yet providing the means for federal intervention in housing, such as the use of interstate commerce court decisions and expansion of federal lending programs for housing construction, but she set the bottom line regrettably low:

We admit at once that a national housing act similar to the British Housing of the Working Class Act, or the Belgian, Italian or Dutch housing laws would be impossible in the United States. So far as these contain restrictive or mandatory features, Congress has no power to legislate along such lines for the several states. The state is the largest unit which may impose restrictive standards, the largest unit which may lay definite obligations on local authorities in respect to *such a purely local matter as housing.*[94] [Emphasis added.]

Since it is our point to belabor the influence of the Puritan Ethic on the early housing reformers and the lack of restraint on the part of the corporate state in the pursuit of its goals, Wood's statement suits our theme.

Having documented the horrors of tenement housing and other social problems, the housing reformers moved to seek restrictive housing legislation and stage-by-stage housing improvement. Having fought the good fight and achieved limited results, they surrendered to the interests of the power elite on constitutional grounds.

The heyday of social reform and housing legislation of a progressive nature ended with World War I. During the reactionary governments of the 1920's "not a single restrictive housing law, state or local" was "enacted in the United States."[95] Success did not even come with the much sought after municipal and state legislation of the reform period. Iowa, Illinois, Pennsylvania, and Massachusetts all attempted

93 Wood, *Housing of . . . Wage Earner*, p. 90.
94 *Ibid.*, p. 240.
95 Wood, *Recent Trends. . .* , *op. cit.*, p. 115.

additional legislation following the war, and only the Iowa legislature was in the mood for new housing reform acts.[96]

A number of earlier housing laws were repealed or "watered-down" during and after the war and, unfortunately, not even the model laws worked very well. In 1909 the New York Bureau of Municipal Research conducted a "friendly investigation" of the New York Tenement House Department (as established in the 1901 Act) and found more than 66,000 violations of the housing law pending. A large number of the pending violations had been classified as "pending" by the Tenement House Department year after year.

Due to these circumstances more than 58 percent of the time of the inspection force was used for reinspection of violations, and therefore the monthly inspection of all tenement buildings was impossible. Many landlords still had not registered by name and description of property, and those that did frequently refused to answer inquiries regarding violations and timetables for improvement of conditions. Most violations had not been forwarded to the Corporation Counsel for prosecution, and those that were forwarded were generally not acted on. Both the Tenement House Department and the Corporation Council often suffered from the unexplainable problem of lost records. Surveys later found that school sinks and privy vaults had "entirely disappeared" where "sewer connections were possible" and that 35 percent of "dark rooms" had been lighted. "By 1920 all windowless rooms had openings to the outer air" or "to neighboring rooms by the cutting through of windows." By 1930 a large number of new apartment buildings conforming to the provisions of the 1901 Act, had been constructed but were occupied largely by upper- and middle-income groups, and few new tenements or apartments had been constructed in areas designated as slums.[97] Such was the fate of the early housing reform movement in the United States.

The role of the federal government in housing reform between 1890 and 1929 was almost nonexistent. In 1892, after much debate over the constitutionality of federal intervention in the local and private area of housing, Congress passed a resolution (Public Resolution 22—52nd Congress) for the investigation of slums in cities of 200,000 or more in population. This investigation of Baltimore, Boston, Brooklyn, Buffalo, Chicago, Cincinnati, Cleveland, Detroit, Milwaukee, New Orleans, New York, Philadelphia, Pittsburgh, St. Louis, San Francisco, and Washington, D.C. was to be carried out by the U. S. Department of Labor. However, only $20,000 was appropriated for the investigation, and the Commissioner of Labor was forced to limit

96 *Ibid.*, p. 114.
97 This account is based on Ford, *op. cit.*, pp. 223–225.

the study of slum conditions to parts of Baltimore, Chicago, New York, and Philadelphia.[98]

No significant findings were made, and, as we have seen in our discussion of housing investigations, a disservice was done to the tenement poor, since some parts of the federal report "whitewashed" housing conditions. The only significance of the 1892 resolution was the precedent set for federal intervention in housing affairs, although that would have come anyway, precedent or no, with the advent of World War I.

Three federal housing laws were passed in 1918 to provide housing for laborers in the war-related industries. In March 1918 Congress authorized the Emergency Fleet Corporation of the U. S. Shipping Board to provide housing facilities for workers in the shipyards (Public Law 102—65th Congress). In May 1918, (Public Law 149—65th Congress) and June 1918 (Public Law 164—65th Congress) Congress authorized the Bureau of Industrial Housing in the Department of Labor and the U. S. Housing Corporation to provide housing for "war workers."[99] In addition, the Ordnance Department was ordered to provide housing, largely in isolated areas, for workers engaged in the manufacture of explosives.

For these projects Congress appropriated over $175 million. The Ordnance Department depended heavily on "ready-cut housing" and "dormitories," since it assumed its housing facilities were for the duration of the war only, although provisions were made for "schools, churches, social and health centers," and "shopping facilities."[100] Some 45,000 people were housed by the Ordnance Department and the largest single project was in Old History, Tennessee, where more than 10,000 people were housed. After the war the housing functions of the Ordnance Department were passed to the Department of Labor.[101]

The Housing Division of the Emergency Fleet Corporation (U. S. Shipping Board) was granted authority by Congress to lend money to subsidiary holding companies, that is, federal funds were loaned to realty companies incorporated by the shipbuilding companies to build housing. "The shipbuilding companies or their subsidiaries owned the land and managed the houses."[102] The government provided the money

[98] Glenn H. Beyer, *Housing and Society.* (New York: Macmillan), 1965, pp. 453–454.

[99] Housing and Home Finance Agency, *Chronology of Major Federal Actions Affecting Housing and Community Development, July, 1892 through 1963.* (Washington, D.C.: U. S. Government Printing Office), 1964, p. 1.

[100] Wood, *Recent Trends. . . , op. cit.,* p. 71.

[101] *Ibid.*

[102] *Ibid.,* p. 78.

for the houses, held mortgages to the houses, and supervised the planning and architecture of the structures. About 55,000 people were housed by the Emergency Fleet Corporation, and in addition to the construction of apartments, dormitories, and hotels more than 5,000 single-family units were built.[103]

The Bureau of Industrial Housing (Department of Labor) worked through the U. S. Housing Corporation, although the Bureau was in operation providing wartime housing before the U. S. Housing Corporation because it received its appropriations first. In March 1918, the Bureau of Industrial Housing published a 15-page pamphlet, "Standards Recommended for Permanent Industrial Housing Developments," under the guidance of Lawrence Veiller and other town planners and architects. Specifications for materials, space, and construction were fairly liberal except for the section "Rooms, Number, and Use of" which tied space provisions to income instead of family size stating: "For higher-paid workers, 5-room type referred, with parlor, large kitchen, 3 bedrooms and bathroom . . . . For lower paid workers, 4-room type desirable, with parlor, kitchen, two bedrooms and bathroom."[104] The relatively high standards of this publication were adopted by the Bureau of Industrial Housing and eventually by the Housing Corporation and, although the Emergency Fleet Corporation did not formally adopt the standards, it used them as guidelines.

The U. S. Housing Corporation, frequently mentioned in housing literature, got off to a late start and actually existed for only 109 days between the time it began full operation and the Armistice. (The Corporation lingered for some time afterward for purposes of managing property and disposing of the housing inventory it had accumulated.)

Housing activities of the Bureau of Industrial Housing (Department of Labor) were under the final authority of the Housing Corporation, which also carried out independent projects. To facilitate cooperation between the Bureau and the Corporation, Otto M. Eidlitz acted as both Director of the Bureau and President of the Corporation. The U. S. Housing Corporation is given special recognition in the history of federal housing intervention because its mission was to directly build, own, and manage the housing it planned. Some 38,000 people were housed through Corporation projects. Since the fate of the Corporation was tied to the war, its major efforts ended before they could have any lasting effect.

During the war, "plans were gotten under way for 128 sites in 71 communities. For 83 of these projects, specifications were completed,

103 *Ibid.*, p. 71.
104 *Ibid.*, p. 70.

for 60, contracts were let and in 40, construction was already started."[105] Wood noted, however, "The Armistice did away with the reason for all this. Where contracts had not been made, plans were at once dropped. Where work had not started, contracts were cancelled. Projects not well advanced or not likely to be useful in peace times were abandoned. Others were curtailed."[106]

The story of the U. S. Housing Corporation in the postwar years is a dismal one. The Ordnance Department had little difficulty selling, dismantling, or transferring to other government units its housing stock. The Emergency Fleet Corporation had operated on what was basically a subsidy program, and therefore its housing stock was already in the hands of private corporations. But the U. S. Housing Corporation owned outright much of the housing it had built and managed.

While the Corporation acted quickly to stop production at the war's end, forces both within and without the Corporation sought authorization to complete worthwhile projects. Some housing reform groups lobbied to continue the Corporation as a permanent federal housing agency. Long battles over the peacetime function of the Corporation continued for many years with charges of extravagance in construction techniques brought against the Corporation. When, following the intent of Congress, the Corporation attempted to divest itself of its holdings, it was attacked by Conservative leaders for attempting to offer first opportunity of purchase to the residents. And when it did sell off its holdings, whether to individual families or private corporations, it was accused of not receiving adequate compensation. The Corporation finally managed to complete several projects, sell its holdings to individual families or, if necessary, to speculators, and transfer what was left to government agencies for various uses. Thus it was that Congress satisfied itself as defender of the constitution and the private enterprise system.[107]

The only other significant federal housing legislation of the postwar period (and before the Great Depression) was Public Law 18— 67th Congress passed in June 1921. This law appropriated funds for the new Division of Building and Housing within the National Bureau of Standards.[108] It should also be mentioned, as a footnote to the history of the progressive movement, that President Theodore Roosevelt created the President's Housing Commission during his term of office, which recommended government housing loans and government purchase of slum property for improvement purposes.

105 *Ibid.*, pp. 73–74.
106 *Ibid.*, p. 74.
107 *Ibid.*, pp. 74–82.
108 Housing and Home Finance Agency, *op. cit.*, p. 1.

Housing legislation at the municipal, state, and federal levels in the 1890–1929 period was supported by the widespread development of zoning ordinances. Once again New York City led the way, adopting the first modern zoning ordinance in 1916. The typical zoning ordinance at that time divided land use into three categories—single-family units, commercial, and industrial—and if a city was relatively large the fourth category of "apartment district" was added.

Zoning ordinances were usually not adopted by local governments without the support of enabling legislation at the state level. The remarkable spread of zoning during the 1920's was the result of several factors. First, the zoning movement had a broad base of support which included many prominent officials not associated directly with housing reform. The concept of zoning was so popular a number of propagandistic tracts were written and widely circulated, including "A Zoning Primer," which was a seven-page pamphlet released in 1922 (and was revised in 1926) and "A Standard State Enabling Act" released in 1923.[109] By 1931 about 35 states had passed enabling legislation and most were copies of the 1923 publication.[110] The second reason for the rapid spread of zoning was related to the first, that is, local and national leaders having little interest in tenement housing reform or housing legislation joined the housing reformers in support of zoning. While housing reformers struggled for every foot of ground in the battle for restrictive housing legislation, zoning sailed through state legislatures in the form of enabling acts and was enacted by countless communities.

Zoning had, in fact, become one of the fads of the 1920's. Since it cost little to obtain in human energy and effort, it replaced rather than complemented housing reform. Something could be done after all—a community obtained a map, superimposed three or four "districts" on the map by drawing lines, and progress had been achieved. The concept spread so rapidly zoning progress reports were mimeographed and distributed throughout the nation, and especially to newspapers eager to report on the movement.[111] Wood reported:

The last progress bulletin issued, bringing the story to January 1, 1931, showed 981 zoned communities in the United States of all sizes from tiny hamlets to the largest cities. Their aggregate population exceeded 46 million, nearly two-fifths of the urban population. The State of New York had the largest number of zoned communities with 159 and New Jersey next with 120. Then followed California, Illinois, Massachusetts, Pennsylvania, Ohio, Michigan, Wisconsin, and Kansas in the order named.[112]

109 Wood, *Recent Trends. . .* , *op. cit.*, p. 129.
110 *Ibid.*
111 *Ibid.*
112 *Ibid.*, pp. 33–34.

Even the United States Supreme Court upheld zoning in the 1926 case of the *Village of Euclid* v. *Ambler Realty Company* on the grounds that the intrusion of one form of land use into an area designated for another purpose was a form of public nuisance.[113] The Ambler Realty Company had proposed selling land it owned in a residential area for industrial use. Therein lies the explanation of the widespread support of zoning by the public and the leadership and the support of state legislatures, local governments, and the U. S. Supreme Court.

Zoning was at an elementary level during the 1920's. Its principal purpose was to stabilize land values and protect single-family residential districts. As long as industry was zoned to established areas, which frequently included tenement areas and "wrong-side-of-the-track" housing, the property value and integrity of single-family residential areas were protected. Since this protection was for the upper and middle classes, it received support.

Should it become necessary for financial reasons to accommodate huge development companies or new industries there was always a local Board of Appeals to grant "variances" on the grounds of "hardships." While zoning was perceived by many to be a product of progressive ideals, its faddish application during the 1920's was superficial and gave little hint of the complex zoning and housing issues that would arise in the second half of the century.[114]

Housing legislation and zoning during the period from 1890 to 1929 broke new ground and established some precedents for future action, but, in truth, housing as an essential aspect of national life was ignored by most of the nation's leaders, who remained spellbound with industrialization, the new technology, and the call of imperialism.

Conclusion

In 1919, Edith Wood wrote:

Roughly stated, one-third of the people of the United States are living under subnormal housing conditions . . . and about a tenth are living under conditions which are an acute menace to health, morals and family life, conditions which tend to produce degenerative changes in those subject to them.[115]

In 1931, Edith Wood wrote:

[113] *Ibid.*, pp. 132–133.
[114] Richard F. Babcock, *The Zoning Game: Municipal Practices and Policies.* (Madison, Wisconsin: The University of Wisconsin Press), 1966, pp. 3–18.
[115] Wood, *Housing of . . . Wage Earner, op. cit.*, p. 7.

The situation may be summed up in briefest form by saying that, in 1917, one-third of American families were living in good homes, one-third in fair homes, more or less lacking in conveniences, but not wholesome, while the last third occupied the oldest and worst castoff houses which no one else wanted. The housing of this last third was definitely sub-normal by any decent standard, and was having a deleterious influence on health, morals, and family life. The housing shortage after the war made this situation appreciably worse, enlarging the boundaries of the group which suffered. The subsequent period of intensive building brought it back to so-called normal. We are now approximately where we were fourteen years ago.[116]

In 1972, Richard Parker wrote:

. . . 50% of American families cannot afford mortgages on even $20,000 homes, let alone homes costing $34,000. Moreover, the 1960 census found over a quarter of all housing in the United States either deteriorating, dilapidated, or lacking in such elemental facilities as hot running water or indoor plumbing. (In states like Alabama and Mississippi, the percentage was almost half; only 44% of Mississippi's housing was considered sound by Federal standards.)[117]

The social system that existed in the United States between 1890 and 1929 did not end with the Great Depression, or World War II, or the Korean War, or the Southeast Asian Wars. Its basic structure survived those events because the system thrives under such conditions. National housing conditions, subservient to the social system, were unsatisfactory between 1890 and 1929, and they remain unsatisfactory to the present.

Bibliography

ALLEN, EDITH LOUISE, *American Housing: As Affected by Social and Economic Conditions*. Peoria, Illinois: The Manual Arts Press, 1930.

ARONOVICI, CAROL, *Housing and the Housing Problem*. Chicago: A. C. McClurg and Co., 1920.

BABCOCK, RICHARD F., *The Zoning Game: Municipal Practices and Policies*. Madison: The University of Chicago Press, 1966.

BEYER, GLENN H., *Housing and Society*. New York: Macmillan, 1965.

BURNS, WILLIAM MCNALL and RICHARD LEE RALPH, *World Civilizations: From Ancient to Contemporary*, Vol. 2. New York: Norton, 1958.

FORBES, ELMER S., "Rural and Suburban Housing." In: *Housing Problems in America: Proceedings of the Second National Conference on Housing, Philadelphia, 1912*.

———, "Housing Conditions in Small Towns." In: *Housing Problems in*

116 Wood, *Recent Trends. . .* , *op. cit.*, pp. 8–9.
117 Richard Parker, *The Myth of the Middle Class: Notes on Affluence and Equality*. (New York: Harper and Row), 1972, p. 156.

America: Proceedings of the First National Conference on Housing, New York, 1911.

FORD, JAMES, *Slums and Housing: With Special Reference to New York City, History, Conditions, Policy,* Vol. 1. Cambridge, Mass.: Harvard University Press, 1936.

GOSSETT, THOMAS F., *Race: The History of an Idea in America.* New York: Schocken Books, 1965.

GRAY, GEORGE HERBERT, *Housing and Citizenship: A Study of Low-Cost Housing.* New York: Reinhold, 1946.

HANDLIN, OSCAR, *America: A History.* New York: Holt, Rinehart and Winston, 1968.

HOFSTADTER, RICHARD, WILLIAM MILLER, and DANIEL ARRON, *The United States: The History of a Republic.* Englewood Cliffs, N.J.: Prentice-Hall, 1957.

Housing and Home Finance Agency, *Chronology of Major Federal Actions Affecting Housing and Community Development, July, 1892 through 1963.* Washington, D.C.: U. S. Government Printing Office, 1964.

KNEELAND, HILDEGARDE, "Abolishing the Domestic Lock-Step—The Scientific Kitchen." In: *Housing Problems in America: Proceedings of the Tenth National Conference on Housing, New York, 1929.* New York: National Housing Association, 1929.

MARTINSON, FLOYD MANSFIELD, *Family in Society.* New York: Dodd, Mead, 1970.

PARKER, RICHARD, *The Myth of the Middle Class: Notes on Affluence and Equality.* New York: Harper and Row, 1972.

RIIS, ALBERT J., JR. (ed.), *Louis Wirth: On Cities and Social Life.* Chicago: The University of Chicago Press, 1964.

RIIS, JACOB A., *The Battle with the Slum.* New York: Macmillan, 1902.

SILBERMAN, CHARLES E., *Crisis in Black and White.* New York: Vintage Books, 1964.

SOROKIN, PITIRIM A., *Fads and Foibles in Modern Sociology and Related Sciences.* Chicago: Henry Regnery Co., 1956.

STRAUS, NATHAN, *The Seven Myths of Housing,* New York: Knopf, 1944.

THEODORSON, GEORGE A. (ed.), *Studies in Human Ecology.* Evanston, Illinois: Row, Peterson and Co., 1961.

TOBY, JACKSON, *Contemporary Society: Social Process and Social Structures in Urban Industrial Societies.* New York: Wiley, 1964.

VEILLER, LAWRENCE, *A Model Housing Law,* New York: Survey Associates, 1914.

———, *Housing Reform: A Handbook for Practical Use in American Cities.* New York: Charities Publication Committee and Russell Sage Foundation, 1910.

WOOD, EDITH ELMER, *Recent Trends in American Housing.* New York: Macmillan, 1931.

———, *The Housing of the Unskilled Wage Earner: America's Next Problem.* New York: Macmillan, 1919.

CHAPTER 4

HOUSING POLICY DURING
THE GREAT DEPRESSION

GERTRUDE S. FISH*

The President's Conference on Home Building and Homeownership

HERBERT HOOVER'S policy in the face of the worsening economic situation was that

the federal government must help the people, but the people must bear the burden and not expect miracles.[1]

[1] Harris Gaylord Warren, *Herbert Hoover and the Great Depression.* (New York: Oxford University Press), 1959, p. 114.

---

* GERTRUDE S. FISH received a doctoral degree in the fields of Housing and City Planning from Cornell University in 1973. She is engaged in teaching and research at the University of Maryland, College Park.

† This chapter includes a section on the Home Owners Loan Corporation (HOLC) by Carey Winston. Carey Winston was, from 1942 to 1975, Chairman and Treasurer of the Carey Winston Company, a mortgage banking and realtor firm in Washington, D.C. He is a past President of the Mortgage Bankers Association of America, the Metropolitan Washington Mortgage Bankers Association and the Washington Board of Realtors and has been Vice President of the National Association of Real Estate Boards. He has also served as Assistant General Manager of the Home Owners Loan Corporation and as Deputy Member of the Federal Home Loan Bank Board.

He provided leadership to stabilize wages and prices and promote industrial peace. He urged the state governors, who at that time controlled a greater share of the national resources than the federal government did, to initiate public works and other state and local programs. In 1930 Hoover seemed confident that the economic downturn would reverse itself. By early 1931 he sounded more defensive and blamed it on worldwide conditions. By late spring of that year, when Austria's largest bank collapsed, his confidence was weakening.[2]

In August 1931, President Hoover charged a planning committee of 34 leaders in the housing sector to investigate

. . . the problems presented in home ownership and home building, with the view to the development of a better understanding of the questions involved and the hope of inspiring better organization and removal of influences which seriously limit the spread of home ownership, both town and country.[3]

The Secretaries of the Departments of Commerce and Interior were the joint chairmen of the Planning Committee. The Planning Committee appointed 25 study committees, each to report on a specific topic at a conference in Washington, D.C., from December 2nd to 5th that same year. Six correlation committees were also appointed to deal with "questions of aim and method common to the 25 fact-finding committees."

President Hoover, in his charge to the Planning Committee said,

Adequate housing goes to the very roots of the well-being of the family, and the family is the social unit of the nation. It is more than comfort that is involved, it has important aspects of health and morals and education and the provision of a fair chance for growing childhood. Nothing contributes more to happiness or sound social stability than the surroundings of their homes.[4]

The President also suggested to the Conference the idea of a system of banks to buy and sell mortgages as investments. The conference pooled and sifted the best information available at that time and aroused public interest in the subject.

One of the most active members of the Conference was Lawrence Veiller, for he was a member of two of the correlating committees and the chairman of a third. Lawrence Veiller had drafted New York City's Tenement House Act of 1901, and at the time of the Conference (30

---

[2] Martin Fausold (ed.), *The Hoover Presidency: A Reappraisal.* (Albany: State University of New York Press), 1974.

[3] John M. Gries and James Ford (eds.), *Housing Objectives and Programs.* (Report of the general sessions of The President's Conference on Home Building and Home Ownership). (Washington, D.C.: National Capital Press), 1932, p. xv.

[4] *Ibid.*

years later) was Director and Secretary of the National Housing Association in New York City. As Chairman of the Standards and Objectives Correlating Committee his report included the observation that

In the too small kitchen a woman is baked when the roast is done, and stewed when the soup is finished. She would not be fit to nurse a baby after that, neither would it be safe to allow a teething baby to sit at the table, while the mother works.[5]

The Committee on Legislation and Administration cited four works by Veiller, even though he was not on their committee. Their report suggested that

Employers of labor, especially where the plant is large and is located away from centers of population, should undertake the housing of their employees. . . .[6]

As models of housing for workers, the Committee on Industrial Decentralization cited Radburn, N.J., Sunnyside Gardens on Long Island, and the planned suburbs of London (Welwyn and Letchworth).

Edward Filene of Boston wrote a paper calling for a "General Housing Corporation, which will operate throughout the country to build, equip, and own homes of the types most in demand by persons of the average income."[7] Dr. Ray Lyman Wilbur, Secretary of Commerce and cochairman of the Conference, cited the need for enabling legislation providing for slum clearance and capital for limited dividend corporations to build decent housing.[8] And Veiller, as a member of the Committee on Blighted Areas and Slums, called attention to the fact that the definition of public use was still restricted to

. . . one in which *all* of the public may participate, as, for instance, in the use of a street, park or a public place.[9]

Dr. Coleman Woodbury, a member of the study Committee on Business and Housing made a strong statement about the need for information from surveys to provide a ". . . record of population movement and changes in land values."[10]

The report of the Committee on Technological Developments gave an account of rammed earth as a building material. Earth is pounded

5 *Ibid.*, p. 173.
6 *Ibid.*, p. 167.
7 John M. Gries and James Ford (eds.), *Slums, Large-Scale Housing and Decentralization.* Report of the President's Conference on Home Building and Home Ownership. (Washington, D.C.: National Capitol Press), 1932, p. 171.
8 *Ibid.*, pp. xi, xii.
9 *Ibid.*, p. 50.
10 *Ibid.*, p. 163.

in forms to make square blocks. As a building material, rammed earth has many of the qualities of stone, that is, great strength and excellent insulating properties. There is a group of buildings and a church near Sumter, South Carolina, and a residence in Cabin John, Maryland made of the material, and the Committee recommended that an investigation be made of the possibilities for its expanded use.

The Committee on Housing Research defined its major task to be finding out "First, what blocks or impedes good housing, and second, what promotes or facilitates good housing."[11] The report called for the establishment of a Housing Research Foundation and observed that

Inspecting the committees' fields more closely from the standpoint of research they appear to fall naturally into several groups, according as their emphasis is placed upon problems of environment; structural considerations; financial, business and income problems; appearance and function; and education.[12]

The Committee on Finance was chaired by Frederick Ecker, President of the Metropolitan Life Insurance Company. Most of the 20 members were officers of lending institutions. They recommended fairer and more accurate assessments and reduced dependence on real estate taxes coupled with more dependence on income tax, and they urged that limited dividend properties and their dividends not be exempt from taxation. Their report also stated that

In principle, the individual should pay for his housing as he pays for his bread, his clothes, or any other necessity of life, without special help or assistance from the state.[13]

There was a dissenting statement at the end of the report which said

The members of the committee seem to have considered the entire home financing problem not from the point of view of the home buyer, but from the point of view of the investor who is anxious about his security.[14]

The Committee on Legislation and Administration recommended the creation of Federal regional mortgage discount banks and other aids to mortgage investment [see Editor's note below]. At the conclusion of the Conference, a resolution was passed by the body as a whole endorsing

[11] Gries and Ford (eds.), *Housing Objectives* . . . , *op. cit.*
[12] *Ibid.*, p. 257.
[13] John M. Gries and James Ford (eds.), *Home Finance and Taxation: Loans, Assessment and Taxes on Residential Property.* (Report of the President's Conference on Home Building and Home Ownership). (Washington, D.C.: National Capitol Press, Inc.), 1932.
[14] *Ibid.*, p. 51, from the dissenting statement of Harry Kissell, President of the National Association of Real Estate Boards, Springfield, Ohio.

President Hoover's proposal to establish a system of home loan discount banks. The resolution noted that such a system would

. . . relieve the present financial strain upon sound savings banks, trust companies and building and loan associations, but will also have a permanent value to the nation as a whole as a means of promoting home ownership in the future.[15]

The reports of the Conference, published in eleven volumes, made detailed recommendations on planning for residential districts; home finance and taxation; slums; house design, construction, and equipment; home repair and remodeling; household management and kitchens; homemaking and information services. The roster of participants included outstanding people in all fields, such as Charles F. Kettering of General Motors, Edith Elmer Wood, Lawrence Veiller, sociologist William F. Ogburn, and several home economists from universities across the country, including Martha Van Rensselaer· of Cornell, Kate North of Oklahoma, Abby Marlatt of Wisconsin, Mary Matthews of Purdue, Agnes E. Harris of the University of Alabama, Effie Raitt of the University of Washington, and Helen Atwater, editor of the *Journal of Home Economics.*

The interest that the conference generated in housing, the communication that it facilitated, and the resulting recommendations for actions needed to promote "home ownership and home building" had a strong influence on the steps taken during the Depression years. The people who knew most about housing had had an opportunity to study the problems, communicate with each other, and publish their considered recommendations. Many of their recommendations became official policy during the decade of the 1930's. The Federal Home Loan Bank System was created under the Hoover Administration, and under the Roosevelt Administration came the Home Owners Loan

Editor's Note: If a home buyer borrows $10,000 to buy a house, the face value of the mortgage is $10,000. If the mortgage lender sells the mortgage note to an investor for less than the face value then the mortgage is being sold at a discount, the amount of the discount being measured as a percent of the face value. For example, a mortgage note for $10,000 sold at a 3% discount would be sold for $9,700. Since the home buyer still is obligated to pay back all of the $10,000 that he borrowed, the investor, in effect, will get a higher rate of interest than the rate at which the loan was made. The larger the discount the higher the effective rate of interest received by the investor even though the home buyer's mortgage remains unchanged. Since the bank which originated the mortgage usually continues to collect the payments the home buyer often is not aware that he owes the money to some other investor. Regional discount banks would buy and sell mortgages as investments.

[15] Gries and Ford (eds.), *Housing Objectives* . . . , *op. cit.*

Percent able-bodied
unemployed

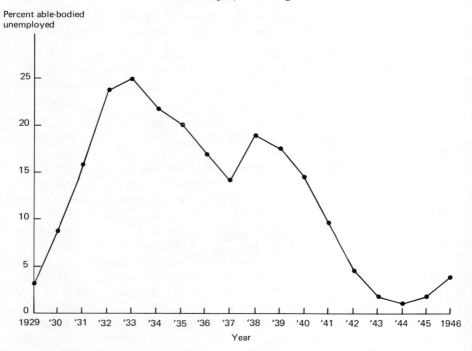

FIGURE 4–1. Rate of unemployment, 1929–1946. [Source: *Employment and Earnings: January 1976,* Vol. 22, No. 7, Bureau of Labor Statistics, Government Printing Office, Washington, D.C., p. 24.]

Corporation (HOLC), the Federal Housing Authority (FHA), the Federal National Mortgage Association (FNMA), public housing, and the census of housing. Economic recovery during the 1930's as illustrated by the unemployment rate, was a long, slow process (see Figure 4–1), and housing policy was shaped in large part to combat unemployment.

Housing policy also was designed to contribute to "sound social stability" as noted by President Hoover in his charge to the Conference Planning Committee. The assumption was that a person who owns a house has an interest in upholding the economic and social systems in which he lives in order to protect his claim to his property.

Federal Home Loan Bank System

During 1931 and 1932 the banking crises and the suspension of the gold standard in several European countries deepened the depression. Fear and panic in the major financial centers caused them to withdraw their investment funds from the United States. A large part of those funds were withdrawn in the form of gold, and the gold outflow increased in May 1932 when the collapse of the credit of Austria's largest private bank caused banking difficulties in Germany. England suspended gold payments in September. International trade declined.

In this country the prices of stocks moved fitfully downward. In July 1931, the market value of all stocks listed on the New York Stock Exchange had been $47.4 billion. By the same time the next year their value had fallen to about $15.6 billion.[16] As people's confidence in the economic and banking systems evaporated they began to withdraw their bank deposits. Banks with long-term investments could not raise cash to cover the withdrawals, since they could not demand their money until the due dates of the loans. The banks were in what is known as an illiquid position; that is, they could not turn their investments into cash. During the last half of 1932, bank failures occurred in unprecedented numbers. Many of those in difficulty had a large proportion of their investments in mortgages.

The rate of mortgage foreclosures rose (see the graph of National Real Estate Cycles in Figure 4–2), for when individuals went to the banks to try to renew their mortgage loans the banks had no money to lend and asked for payment of the debt. The number of mortgage notes coming due was high because it was common practice to make short-term mortgage loans, many being for three to five years. The borrower did not make periodic payments to reduce the amount of the loan (called the principal) but only paid the interest on the loan once a year. Usually at the end of the term of the mortgage the borrower could have the note extended for another short term, but when all banks were in need of cash they could not renew the loans. When borrowers could not pay the banks the principal amounts due, the banks foreclosed and took possession of the properties, usually selling them at public auction for less than they were worth in order to recover cash from the investment.

One other weakness in the mortgage system stemmed from the small amounts that borrowers were able to obtain as first mortgages. Lending institutions would risk around 40 percent of the value of a piece of real estate on a first mortgage. The buyer then either had to have the cash to complete the transaction or find someone willing to lend him the balance on a second, or junior, mortgage, so called because that lender's claim on the property was subordinate to that of the holder of the first mortgage. The second mortgage holder also could institute foreclosure proceedings. This system resulted in the necessity

[16] *Twentieth Annual Report of the Secretary of Commerce, 1932.* (Washington, D.C.: United States Government Printing Office), p. xiv.

The Real Estate ANALYST

OCTOBER 26
1938

Roy Wenzlick
Editor

A concise easily digested monthly analysis based upon scientific research in real estate
fundamentals and trends...Constantly measuring and reporting the basic economic factors
responsible for changes in trends and values...Current Studies...Surveys...Forecasts

Copyright 1938 by REAL ESTATE ANALYSTS, Inc. — Saint Louis

VOLUME VII · Real Estate Economists, Appraisers and Counselors

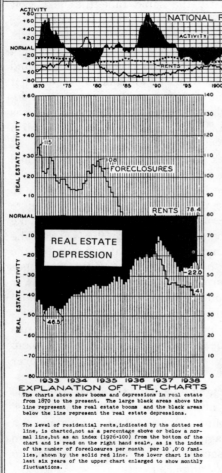

EXPLANATION OF THE CHARTS

The charts above show booms and depressions in real estate
from 1870 to the present. The large black areas above the
line represent the real estate booms and the black areas
below the line represent the real estate depressions.

The level of residential rents, indicated by the dotted red
line, is charted, not as a percentage above or below a normal line, but as an index (1926-100) from the bottom of the
chart and is read on the right hand scale, as is the index
of the number of foreclosures per month per 10,000 families, shown by the solid red line. The lower chart is the
last six years of the upper chart enlarged to show monthly
fluctuations.

REAL estate sales, after correction for seasonal influences, increased considerably in the United States in September in spite of the war scare in Europe, bringing them to within 22% of normal. At the bottom of the depression they were 46.5% below normal, and at the top of the boom they were 41% above normal.

Foreclosures dropped again, reaching a new low for the recovery.

New building showed the largest gain in comparison with a year ago experienced in a number of years.

Rents showed practically no change, dropping by one-tenth of a per cent.

The general business outlook, at least for the next six months, is splendid. The rapid increases in the values of stocks during the past month indicate that informed investors are extremely optimistic. We believe that the real estate and building field, which advanced during the last few months in the face of the obstacles that proved powerful depressants to general business, will advance still more rapidly when the general trend is upward.

FIGURE 4–2. Page from *The Real Estate Analyst*, October 26, 1938.

of renewing or refinancing the debt on a property many times before most borrowers were able to retire the debt completely. This left them vulnerable to foreclosure.

If the banks had been able to borrow money themselves to carry them through the crisis they probably would not have foreclosed the mortgage loans. When so many properties were offered at auctions and so few people had funds with which to bid on them the prices that the properties brought sometimes did not pay off the principal amounts due. Junior mortgage holders often lost their entire investments.

It was to supply a source of credit for lending institutions that the Federal Home Loan Bank System was created. Charles Haar reminds us that

As far back as 1919, Senator Calder had introduced a "Bill to Create a Federal Home Loan Board and Home Loan Banks for the Purpose of Aiding and Financing the Construction of Homes" but it never became law.[17]

In accordance with the suggestions of President Hoover and the resolution passed by the Conference on Home Building and Home Ownership, Congress passed the Federal Home Loan Bank Act which created the Federal Home Loan Bank Board in 1932.[18] The agency was to have purchased mortgages from lending institutions throughout the country in order to stimulate them to make new loans. The theory was that with the Bank Board as a purchaser and source of liquidity, lender banks would be more confident in lending on homes. The increased construction activity would spur employment and facilitate homeownership.

In effect, the Federal Home Loan Bank Act created a system of district home loan banks organized to achieve a nationwide pool of mortgage credit. The savings and loan associations, savings banks, and insurance companies that became members of the system were subject to regulation by the Federal Home Loan Bank Board, had a source of credit in the district bank, and were part of a network that could move money from one region to another as it was needed. (See Figure 4–3.)

Each savings and loan association, savings bank, or insurance company joining the system brought shares of stock equal to 1 percent of the value of its mortgage loans. Further, the Reconstruction Finance Corporation (RFC), which was created by legislation under the Hoover administration in 1932, was authorized by the legislation to issue debt obligations (such as debentures and bonds) so that each

---

[17] Charles M. Haar, "Background of Federal Housing Credit." In: William L. C. Wheaton, Grace Milgram, and Margy Ellin Meyerson (eds.), *Urban Housing.* (New York: The Free Press), 1966, p. 347.

[18] Public Law No. 304, 72nd Congress, approved July 22, 1932.

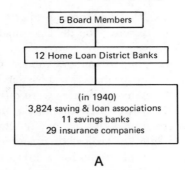

A

FIGURE 4–3. A. Diagram of the Home Loan Bank System. B. Federal Home Loan Bank Districts.

district bank had funding of $5 million. The district banks were to loan money to the institutions within their districts on the security of home mortgages up to 12 times the amount of stock the institution had bought. For example, if a member in District 2 (the New York district) had had $1 million in outstanding mortgage loans at the time it joined the system, it would have been required to buy shares of stock equal to 1 percent of $1,000,000 or $10,000. The District Bank could then lend up to 12 times $10,000 ($120,000) to the lending institution to meet withdrawals from savings accounts or requests for mortgage credit. Thus, none of the costs of the system were a charge against the federal budget. However, the impact of the Home Loan Bank System on the faltering mortgage market was not strong enough.

In 1933, 49% of the $20 billion home mortgage debt was in default. The monthly rate of foreclosures was approximately 26,000—an average of 1,000 per day.[19]

Mortgage lenders faced heavy losses, local jurisdictions could not collect property taxes, and the construction industry was virtually idle. If the American system was to recover or even survive, it was imperative that the government should invade the mortgage market.

The result was two government funds, each of $2.3 billion, and administered, respectively, by the Farm Credit Administration under William I. Meyers and the Home Owners Loan Corporation under John H. Fahey to offer the substitution of government-backed bonds for the alternative of foreclosure or default.[20]

[19] Cecilia M. Gerloff (ed.), *The Federal Home Loan Bank System*. Office of International Home Finance, The Federal Home Loan Bank Board, 1971. Library of Congress #72–187328.

[20] John Franklin Carter, *The New Dealers*. (New York: Da Capo Press), 1975, p. 159.

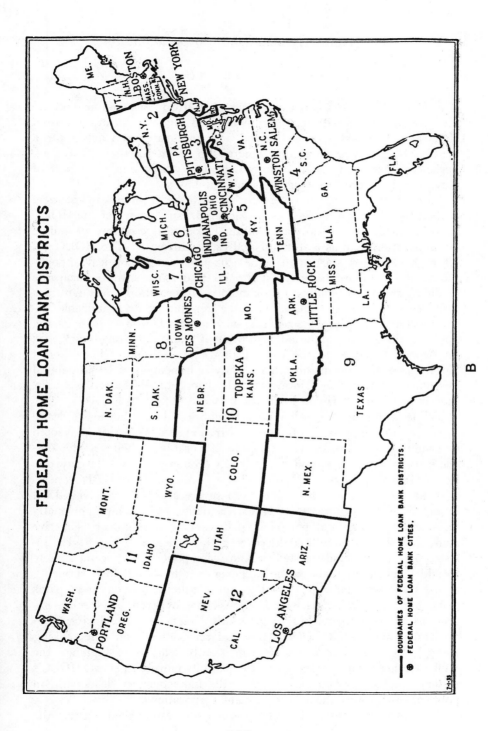

FEDERAL HOME LOAN BANK DISTRICTS

—— BOUNDARIES OF FEDERAL HOME LOAN BANK DISTRICTS.
⊛ FEDERAL HOME LOAN BANK CITIES.

B

187

Home Owners Loan Corporation

CAREY WINSTON

The Home Owners' Loan Corporation (HOLC) was unique and we all hope that there will never again be need for such an organization. Yet, even if our hopes are realized and no future need arises for a broad salvage operation of this general type, some of the HOLC's experiences have been useful in improving one vitally important part of American life—the financing of home purchases.

Part of the story, however—the HOLC as a study in political economy—seems appropriate as background. The history of the HOLC may be no less significant as a study in political economy or public administration than as a study of real estate financing. The HOLC got off to a very bad start with some extremely inept political appointments and with organization, staff, and leadership entirely incapable of doing or comprehending its mammoth job creditably. Yet within a few years, it had gained an enviable reputation for admirable accomplishment as a humane relief agency and for honesty and economy. And it gained this reputation just when it was foreclosing mortgages on American homes at the rate of thousands a month. The biggest single cause of the transformation, in my judgment—and I find general agreement—was the appointment of the late John H. Fahey as Chairman of the Federal Home Loan Bank Board.

While avoiding discussion of personalities, I do, however, desire to convey my impression of the role Mr. Fahey's leadership played in determining to a considerable degree—favorably, I believe—the outcome of this unique episode in political economy. It was largely due to Mr. Fahey's efforts that "politics" were removed from HOLC operations so that within a short time even severe critics of the New Deal found little to disparage in HOLC actions. Mr. Fahey personally initiated recruiting and personnel policies that built a very effective staff, and then gradually reduced it without demoralizing it. He insisted on economy and resisted pressures for policies that seemed likely to add to eventual costs to the taxpayer, yet he keyed loan servicing to the basic original objective of granting relief. He took great pains to keep on good relations with Congress, not by granting special concessions to constituents but by presenting facts and convincing Congressmen that the HOLC was fair and reasonable even when taking away homes by foreclosure. He consistently worked to liquidate the HOLC rather than to perpetuate or expand its power. In short, HOLC's history emphasizes and demonstrates the importance of leadership in political institutions and in government corporations.

As previously stated, the corporation was established during the summer of 1933 to help families prevent loss of their homes through mortgage foreclosure or tax sale. The program provided for the following:

1. The exchange of HOLC bonds (with federal guarantee first of interest only but, later, beginning in the spring of 1934, with guarantee of both interest and principal) for home mortgages in default.

2. Cash loans for payment of taxes and property reconditioning. HOLC loans were restricted to mortgages in default (or mortgages held by financial insitutions in distress) and secured by nonfarm properties with dwelling space for not more than four families and appraised by the HOLC at not more than $20,000. No loan could exceed 80 percent of HOLC appraisal, nor could any loan exceed $14,000. Loans were to bear 5 percent interest and were to be amortized by monthly payments during their 15-year life. This amortization plan was new to the home financing business—it being the practice generally to grant three-year term loans. In good times these notes were easily renewed, but in the depression years the holders demanded payment, thus precipitating foreclosure action and dramatically focusing on the need for government action to save the homes of the people so threatened—hence the HOLC.

Serious troubles arose in the beginning in building an adequate organization on short notice and in initiating the actual lending operations, but by the autumn of 1934 over 400 HOLC offices were accepting applications. During the initial lending period—from June 1933 to 1935—the HOLC received 1,886,491 applications for $6.2 billion of home mortgage refinancing, an average of $3,272 per application. According to estimates, HOLC refinancing was requested for about 40 percent of all mortgaged properties of qualifying size, value and location, and for about one fifth of all the nation's nonfarm, owner-occupied dwellings. Nearly half the applications, however, were withdrawn or rejected. Roughly, one million refinancing loans totaling $3.1 billion and averaging $3,039 per loan were made. Seventy percent of these were made during the 12-month period beginning in March 1934. For the country as a whole, owners of about 1 out of 10 nonfarm, owner-occupied dwellings (one- to four-family structures) and 1 out of 5 mortgaged dwellings received HOLC refinancing aid. Seventy-five percent of the loans were for less than $4,000 and amounted, on the average, to 69 percent of the HOLC appraised value of the property. The average loan cost $39 to close.

Appraising of the homes presented a critical and difficult problem. In an effort to obtain the quality of appraisals desired, the HOLC trained and supervised appraisers, most of whom it employed on a part-time basis. HOLC training of personnel in, and systematizing of, appraisal methods are credited with having helped raise the general level of American real estate appraisal methods. The HOLC standard was based on three factors weighted equally: (1) the estimated current market price, (2) the cost of a similar lot at the time of appraisal plus the cost of reproducing the building, less depreciation, and (3) the capitalization of the monthly reasonable rental value of the property for the last 10 years. This formula generally yielded appraisals above the then prevailing market prices. In addition to its appraisal, the HOLC obtained a credit report on all applicants.

Little detailed information is available about the properties on which the HOLC made loans, the borrowers, or the loans refinanced. Nevertheless, there is clear evidence that their circumstances were bad, though they were not the very worst distress cases of the early depression. A special study of a sample of cases in Connecticut, New Jersey, and New York revealed the following: Over half the families applying for loans had monthly incomes of from $5 to $150; 6 percent of the applicants, most of whom had more than one dependent, were from 35 to 55 years old, 7 out of 10 applicants had purchased the property in the 1920's; most properties were less than 15 years old when the loan application was filed; one third of the properties were used to some extent for business purposes, but 43 percent were single-family dwellings having no business use; 87 percent had central heating; and 84 percent had the same number of baths as families.

One third of the sample loans in these three states were on houses in New York City and slightly more were in communities of less than 25,000 population. One fourth were appraised at less than $5,000 and 40 percent from $5,000 to $8,000; two thirds were in districts classified as "residential" and "stable." The properties were in moderately good physical condition, inasmuch as in 70 percent of the cases the appraiser had estimated depreciation at less than 25 percent. Over half the loans in these three states were for less than $5,000; three fourths were for from 60 percent to somewhat over 80 percent of the appraisal; even on the basis of estimated current market values, 54 percent of the borrowers had an estimated equity in the property of one fourth or more above their obligations on the property.

At first, servicing of loans consisted of little more than the mailing of monthly statements of payments due. Gradually, however, the HOLC developed much more elaborate and effective loan servicing methods. Each account delinquent for more than two or three months received individual attention; and in more difficult cases an HOLC representative tried to help the borrower plan and adjust his affairs. Amounts of mortgage payments in arrears were frequently added to the remaining balance. Varied, extensive, and time-consuming efforts were made to help prevent foreclosure; borrowers—especially those who showed good faith —were treated very leniently.

Yet the HOLC acquired almost 200,000 houses—82 percent by formal foreclosure and the remainder by voluntary transfer—half of these by the end of 1937. In New York and Massachusetts, more than 40 percent of all loans were foreclosed, the average for the Mountain and Pacific coast states was slightly over 11 percent. At the time of foreclosure most loans had been many months delinquent—56 percent for 18 months or more. The HOLC attributed foreclosure to the following reasons: noncooperation of the borrower, 45 percent; obstinate refusal to pay, 22 percent; total inability to pay, 18 percent; abandonment of property, 11 percent; and death of borrower and legal complications, combined, 5 percent. In only a small minority of cases did the HOLC conclude that economic conditions made impossible the successful carrying of the loan; much more significant was the borrower's lack of determination to make the necessary effort—not his economic inability to meet his financial obligations.

The special study of cases in Connecticut, New Jersey, and New York throws some light on factors associated with differences in foreclosure rates. "Overhousing," as suggested by loan amounts and average rental values high in relation to income, seemed commonly associated with foreclosures. Above-average foreclosure rates also were associated with the younger and the older borrowers; with properties having some business use; with properties of higher value, more rooms, and high ratios of land to total value; with loans for larger amounts and with higher loan-to-value ratios. The total amount due at time of foreclosure averaged 11 percent more than the original loan.

The management and sale of properties acquired by the HOLC were for many years a major problem. Each house was treated as an individual problem. Local real estate brokers were relied upon, for the most part, to handle details with general policies, major decisions, and overall supervision coming from the HOLC. An average of $451 per property was spent on reconditioning and $135 on maintenance during HOLC ownership. Most houses were rented until sale after foreclosure could be arranged on satisfactory terms. Special and successful efforts were made to reduce fire losses, and, for some time, HOLC acted as a self-insurer on the properties it owned. The HOLC ordinarily announced a price at which each property would be sold and made the necessary listing with brokers. The HOLC made no effort to protect the market to sell at what were considered sacrifice prices. The HOLC did, however, offer prospective buyers financing terms which at the time were more favorable than those obtainable elsewhere.

On the basis of its own accounting, the HOLC computed its total net loss on properties acquired—all of which were later sold—at $310 million. The average loss per property (after deducting income earned while the property was owned) was $1,568. Losses were especially heavy in Massachusetts, New Jersey, and New York. Two thirds of all properties had been sold by December 1940. In the final accounting, total sales prices equaled 93 percent of the original HOLC loan payment.

HOME OWNERS' LOAN CORPORATION
STATISTICAL ACCOMPLISHMENTS

1. LIFE SPAN

Created by Act of Congress, June 13, 1933
Stopped accepting loan applications, June 25, 1935.
Stopped closing loans, June 13, 1936.
Corporation liquidated at a profit, April, 1951.

2. ORGANIZATION

The Federal Home Loan Bank Board consisting of five members had general jurisdiction. This was accomplished through the office of a General Manager, three Deputy General Managers and six Assistant General Managers with appropriate Department and Division Heads.

Legal Division was headed by one General Counsel, four Associate General Counsels, 764 salaried Attorneys and 8,360 fee Attorneys.

Personnel at its greatest point number 19,000 headquartered in Washington and 491 offices throughout the Country.

3. ACTIVITY

Applications received: 1,886,491.
Loans Closed: 1,018,390.
Dollar Volume of Loans: $3,092,870,784 for an average of $3,039.00 per loan.
Foreclosure experience totalled $200,000,000 with 92 percent recovery.

HOLC lending was not confined to refinancing distress mortgages. By June 30, 1937, 444,226 reconditioning loans for $83 million had been completed an average of $190 a case. In other words, more than 4 out of each 10 original borrowers received supplemental loans for reconditioning.

To prevent tax defaults and to insure continuation of insurance coverage, the HOLC by 1934 found it desirable to make additional loans for taxes and insurance, and within a few years an extensive program had been developed for the collection of accruing taxes and insurance premiums with regular monthly payments. Formal or informal extensions of time for payments of amounts in default constituted, in effect, a large amount of lending. Though the HOLC believed that it was using its authority to grant extensions wherever conditions justified its so doing, pressure to increase its authority and to liberalize payment terms led Congress to pass in 1939 the Mead–Barry Act, permitting the HOLC to add as much as 10 years to the original 15 years of loan life. Monthly payments for amortization of the loans were thereby reduced. The interest rate for all borrowers was cut one tenth—from 5 to 4½ percent—in October 1939. By the end of 1942, however, only 30 percent of outstanding loans—generally, the larger loans—had received Mead–Barry extensions. Most borrowers simply failed to request liberalization of the loan terms. Purchasers of properties from the HOLC received loans and advances of $604 million through March 31, 1951; the record of these loans has been good.

In carrying out its functions, the HOLC faced unique and difficult administrative problems. Some of the original HOLC personnel appointments were unfortunate, the result of political maneuvering in some areas and unwise decisions in the face of pressing need for immediate action. But, before the end of 1933, better standards had become effective. In its first 15 months, the HOLC built to its peak an organization of 19,000 employees; thereafter, staff reductions were made more or less regularly. Enough local offices were maintained into the 1940's to permit easy personal contact with most borrowers. Local staffs were supervised by regional offices, which, in turn, were subject to general policies formulated at the national level. In addition to its staff of salaried personnel, the HOLC maintained personnel on a fee and commission basis for appraisals, legal work, and property management and sale. The HOLC made deliberate efforts to develop and maintain good personnel policies. Morale was good, especially in the early years, and large amounts of uncompensated overtime were worked voluntarily.

Except at the start of its operations, HOLC financing was subject to general and increasing direction of the U. S. Treasury. By 1941 Treasury control dominated. Fortunately for its financial record, the HOLC was able to take advantage of large declines in the rates of interest at which the government could borrow funds. For the period 1933 through 1949, the average rate paid by the HOLC was 2.243 percent; the net spread between what it paid for and what it received on loans made was about 2.5 percent. The HOLC met its operating costs out of its own income, subject, however, to limits specified by Congress in the original appropriation process for salaries, personnel, office space, equipment, and supplies. The HOLC never spent for operations the full sum authorized by Congress.

Most observers and supporters originally expected the HOLC to lose money—perhaps a great deal. Yet by the spring of 1951, the HOLC was finally liquidated—at a slight profit. Borrowers had paid off their loan balances, for the most part, and the remaining loans outstanding were sold to private institutions. Many things explain this surprisingly good outcome. In a broad sense, perhaps, the desire of homeowners to keep their homes was most important; good management by the HOLC and a large decline in the rate of interest it had to pay for borrowed funds were also important.

To my knowledge, it was the first and only government agency or corporation to liquidate and go out of business at a profit to the U. S. Treasury.

Relief and the Expansion of Government Powers

Gertrude S. Fish

Care of the poor in the United States was largely a local matter until 1929. Families "took care of their own" as the first line of defense, and the community was responsible for caring for those not cared for by their families. Some counties ran "poor farms," where poor people could live and help grow their own food. The amount of relief extended by the community was fashioned to inspire families to take up their rightful burden, and the opprobrium attached to accepting relief did nothing to encourage idleness.

In introducing the topic of work relief programs in the 1930's Burns contrasted the relief problem before the crash in 1929 with the relief problem after it and found that there was a new factor to contend with— "*large-scale, continuing unemployment.*"[21] (See Figure 4–1.) The Hoover Administration passed the Emergency Relief and Construction Act in July 1932 to set up the Reconstruction Finance Corporation (RFC) with a loan fund of $300 million that states and localities could borrow from at 3 percent interest. Knickerbocker Village in New York City was one of the few housing projects built under the RFC program. Most of the money was borrowed by banks and railroads.[22] By the time the Democratic Administration of Franklin Delano Roosevelt took office in 1933 that money was gone and a desperate need for large-scale, long-term relief was politically recognized and accepted. By 1933, 14 million people were out of work (see Table 4–1), and many others had been reduced to working only part-time. The government admitted a rate of unemployment of 25 percent, foreclosures on homes were taking place at a rate of 1,000 a day, and families doubled up in homes with relatives in their efforts to cope with the crisis. A "Bank Holiday" was declared by the President in 1933 when banks could no longer pay their depositors the money in their accounts. The country was bankrupt, and the threat of revolution was immediate and growing.

Facing in 1933 a desperate national crisis, the administration employed its great powers to accomplish three ends; relief, recovery and reform.[23]

The immediate and overriding concern was to put people to work. The Federal Emergency Relief Act (FERA) parceled out $500 million

21 Arthur Burns and Edward A. Williams, *Federal Work, and Relief Programs.* (Washington, D.C.: U. S. Government Printing Office), 1941.

22 Charles A. Beard and George H. E. Smith, *The Future Study of The New Deal.* (New York: Macmillan), 1934, p. 13.

23 Arthur Meier Schlesinger, *The New Deal in Action: 1933–1938.* (New York: Macmillan), 1939.

T ABLE 4–1. Employment Status of the Noninstitutional Population, 1929 to Date

(Numbers in thousands)

Year and Month	Total Noninsti- tutional Popula- tion	Total Labor Force		Civilian Labor Force							
		Number	Percent of Popula- tion	Total	Employed			Unemployed			Not in Labor Force
					Total	Agri- culture	Nonagri- cultural Indus- tries	Number	Percent of Labor Force		
									Not Season- ally Adjusted	Season- ally Adjusted	
1929	(1)	49,440	(1)	49,180	47,630	10,450	37,180	1,550	3.2	—	(1)
1930	(1)	50,080	(1)	49,820	45,480	10,340	35,140	4,340	8.7	—	(1)
1931	(1)	50,680	(1)	50,420	42,400	10,290	32,110	8,020	15.9	—	(1)
1932	(1)	51,250	(1)	51,000	38,940	10,170	28,770	12,060	23.6	—	(1)
1933	(1)	51,840	(1)	51,590	38,760	10,090	28,670	12,830	24.9	—	(1)
1934	(1)	52,490	(1)	52,230	40,890	9,900	30,990	11,340	21.7	—	(1)
1935	(1)	53,140	(1)	52,870	42,260	10,110	32,150	10,610	20.1	—	(1)
1936	(1)	53,740	(1)	53,440	44,410	10,000	34,410	9,030	16.9	—	(1)
1937	(1)	54,320	(1)	54,000	46,300	9,820	36,480	7,700	14.3	—	(1)
1938	(1)	54,950	(1)	54,610	44,220	9,690	34,530	10,390	19.0	—	(1)
1939	(1)	55,600	(1)	55,230	45,750	9,610	36,140	9,480	17.2	—	(1)
1940	100,380	56,180	56.0	55,640	47,520	9,540	37,980	8,120	14.6	—	44,200
1941	101,520	57,530	56.7	55,910	50,350	9,100	42,250	5,560	9.9	—	43,990
1942	102,610	60,380	58.8	56,410	53,750	9,250	44,500	2,660	4.7	—	42,230
1943	103,660	64,560	62.3	55,540	54,470	9,080	45,390	1,070	1.9	—	39,100
1944	104,630	66,040	63.1	54,630	53,960	8,950	45,010	670	1.2	—	38,590
1945	105,530	65,300	61.9	53,860	52,820	8,580	44,240	1,040	1.9	—	40,230
1946	106,520	60,970	57.2	57,520	55,250	8,320	46,930	2,270	3.9	—	45,550
1947	107,608	61,758	57.4	60,168	57,812	8,256	49,557	2,356	3.9	—	45,850

(1) Not available.

SOURCE: *Employment and Earnings*, January 1976, Vol. 22, No. 7, Library of Congress Number 70–11379. (Washington, D.C.: U. S. Government Printing Office), p. 24.

to the states between 1933 and 1935 to develop work programs for the employable. The Rural Rehabilitation Division of FERA extended credit to farmers and gave them direct assistance in the form of food, clothing, and other necessities. The Federal Surplus Relief Corporation distributed the huge price-depressing surpluses in agricultural products through the relief programs. Women took part in canning projects and made clothing, towels, and bedding from surplus cotton. Also under FERA, there was an Emergency Education Program to give work to unemployed teachers, a college student aid program, and a Transient Division of FERA to set up camps and work-relief for the growing number of "tramps." The Civilian Conservation Corps (CCC) gave work to young men improving and constructing recreational areas, planting forests, and other conservation projects. A program in the Department of Interior to build communities of subsistence homesteads sought to place families where they could grow some of their own food. (The lot sizes ranged up to five acres.)

While FERA programs had operated by giving grants to the states and by trying hard to encourage equitable and effective programs through cooperation with state officials, there was a stubborn reluctance in many rural localities to giving relief to the urban poor. Also, some dishonesty was inevitable in the administration of the programs under crisis conditions. In 1935, the Social Security Act offered financial assistance to states willing to undertake aid programs for unemployables, and an executive order by the President created the Works Projects Administration (WPA) to give jobs to the ablebodied. The WPA program sought to remedy some of the difficulties of the grant method by establishing federal control at all levels of the operation. Personnel were all federal employees, projects needed federal approval, and pay to the workers was disbursed from the Treasury.

Under the administration of Harry L. Hopkins the WPA employed almost four million people in building public structures such as schools, sewer systems, playgrounds, parks, libraries, hospitals, bridges, airports, irrigation systems, and roads. While the business sector grumbled about the costs of the programs, saying that the dole would be cheaper, no one denied that the program improved morale and provided long-term benefits for the country.

Recovery: Court Contests of Government Powers

The legality of federal housing programs has hinged on the interpretation by the courts of the phrases "public use" and "general welfare," and the allocation of the power of eminent domain (the taking of property by a government from a citizen for a public use). Lawrence Veiller, in the President's Conference on Home Building and Home Ownership, reminded his committee that the phrase "public use" could be (and had been) interpreted to mean

. . . one in which *all* the public may participate, as, for instance, in the use of a street, a park, or a public place.[24]

In 1933, the National Industrial Recovery Act (NIRA) authorized funds for slum clearance and low-income housing as recommended by the President's Conference on Home Building and Home Ownership. Under NIRA, the Public Works Administration built low-rent housing by direct federal construction programs in 37 cities. The legal question of whether the federal government had the right to exercise the power of eminent domain (taking private property for public use) was tested in federal courts in several cases. There was an adverse decision in the case *United States* v. *Certain Lands in the City of Louisville.* The court ruled that the federal government did not have the right to exercise the power of eminent domain for the purposes of slum clearance and low-cost housing.[25]

After the drought in 1934, the work started under the Rural Rehabilitation Division was continued under the Resettlement Administration, and many families were moved from their farms in the Dust Bowl sections of the midwestern states to farms carved out of federal lands. The Resettlement Administration projects included the three greenbelt towns (Greenbelt, Maryland; Green Hills, Ohio; and Greendale, Wisconsin) which were experiments in suburban town planning built near Washington, D.C., Cincinnati, and Milwaukee. These new town projects included about 15,000 units for working-class people as recommended by the President's Conference on Home Ownership and Home Building, but the programs created a strong protest from representatives of private enterprise who did not want the federal government meddling in their markets.

Suit was brought to prevent the purchase of land for a Resettlement Administration project in the case *Township of Franklin* v. *Tugwell.*[26] The court ruled that Congress lacked the power to authorize such projects.[27] In September 1937, the Resettlement Administration was transferred to the Department of Agriculture and became the Farm Security

24 Gries and Ford (eds.), *Slums* . . . , *op. cit.*, p. 50.
25 *United States* v. *Certain Lands in Louisville*, 9 F. Supp. 137 (1935). In: William Ebenstein, *The Law of Public Housing.* (Madison: The University of Wisconsin Press), 1940, p. 39.
26 *Township of Franklin* v. *Tugwell*, 66 D.C. App. 42, 85 F. (2d) 208 (1936).
27 Leon Keyserling, "Legal Aspects of Public Housing." In: *Housing Monograph Series*, No. 1: *Residential Building.* U. S. Natural Resources Committee, 1939, p. 32.

Administration, the forerunner of the Farmers Home Administration of today.

Supreme Court decisions interpreted the connection between "the general welfare" and "public use." Article I of the Constitution states:

The Congress shall have the power to lay and collect Taxes, Duties, Imports and Excises, to pay the debts and provide for the common defense and general welfare of the United States. . . .[28]

The question was: did the law mean that Congress had the power to collect monies for the powers already stipulated, or did it mean that Congress was thereby given a broad power that encompasses whatever need arises? The decision in the case *United States* v. *Butler*[29] upheld the right of Congress to spend for the general welfare not limited by the other enumerated powers of Congress in the Constitution.

The Supreme Court upheld the power of the state of North Dakota to provide housing for its residents in the case *Green* v. *Frazier*.[30] In this case, public purpose within the meaning of the taxing power was the main issue and the right of the state to exercise the power of taxation for public housing was sustained. Keyserling noted that:

While this decision merely held that housing was a public purpose the only additional feature necessary to bring housing under the general welfare-clause would be to regard it as a public purpose national in scope.[31]

According to the interpretation of the clause "general welfare" in *United States* v. *Butler*, federal action on behalf of the "general welfare" is limited to appropriating money; that is, Congress has the right to tax and spend money to provide for the general welfare of the citizens. The federal government was denied the power of eminent domain and, therefore, could appropriate the money but not the land for public use. However, states could exercise the right of eminent domain, and a court decision in New York State in April 1935, upheld low-cost housing and slum clearance as public use.[32]

By upholding the constitutionality of the Municipal Housing Authorities Law the court established the following propositions: (1) that slum-clearance and low-cost housing is a public purpose; (2) that the power of eminent domain may be employed for acquiring property for such purpose; (3) that public moneys may be used; (4) that the housing authority may own, operate, and control the projects; (5) that housing authorities serve

28 U. S. Const. Art. I, sec. 8.
29 297 U.S.1, 56 Sup. Ct. 312, 80 L. Ed. 102 A.L.R. 914 (1936).
30 *Green* v. *Frazier*, 253 U.S. 233, 40 Sup. Ct. 499, 64 L. Ed. 878 (1920).
31 Keyserling, *loc. cit.*, p. 34.
32 *New York City Housing Authority* v. *Muller*, 279 N.T.S. 299 (1935).

the protection, safety, and general welfare of the people; (6) that bonds of housing authorities are legal obligations; and (7) that they are exempt from taxation.[33]

By working through state housing authorities the NIRA (National Industrial Recovery Act) Housing Division and PWA authorized 51 projects with 21,769 units.

The legal framework for the enactment of a long-term public housing program was being forged during these years.

Reform: The National Housing Act of 1934

While the HOLC was successful in stemming the flood of foreclosures, the effect of the program on the total mortgage market was limited. The legislation applied only to mortgages that were in default. The mortgage market was still in a state of collapse, and unemployment was at an all-time high of 24 percent. There was a need for jobs and a need to entice more money into circulation. Eccles notes:

The significance of a new housing program that could revive the economy was not lost on President Roosevelt. He knew that almost a third of the unemployed were to be found in the building trades, and housing was by far the most important part of that trade. A program of new home construction, launched on an adequate scale, not only would gradually help put these men back to work but would act as the wheel within the wheel to move the whole economic engine. It would affect everyone, from the manufacturer of lace curtains to the manufacturer of lumber, bricks, furniture, cement, and electrical appliances. The mere shipment of these supplies would affect the railroads, which in turn would need the produce of steel mills for rails, freight cars, and so on.[34]

The President, however, did not want a housing program which would require large capital expenditures from the current budget. During a meeting of the National Emergency Council late in 1933 John Fahey requested an additional $2 billion in funding for the HOLC, and this request for a large amount of money that would appear as a budget expenditure for the coming year precipitated an urgent request by President Roosevelt for ideas to get the government out of the lending business—some way to set in motion the complex of economic forces that could liquidate the relief program. It was suggested that a new housing program might be a partial remedy, so the President appointed Frank Walker chairman of the President's Emergency Committee on Housing to investigate possible programs and determine what would be

---

33 Ebenstein, *op cit.*, p. 65.

34 Marriner Stoddard Eccles, *Beckoning Frontiers: Public and Personal Recollections.* Edited by Sidney Hyman. (New York: Knopf), 1951, p. 145. The following account relies heavily on the Eccles book.

needed to get one under way. Frank Walker appointed Winfield Riefler of the Federal Reserve Board as the economic adviser and secretary of the committee. Members were John Fahey, Harry Hopkins, Frances Perkins, Averell Harriman, Rexford Tugwell, Henry Wallace, and Marriner Eccles (pronounced Eh'-culls). Walker thought that whatever was done should be assigned to an already existing agency to preclude expansion of the government bureaucracy; Eccles felt that "the proper role of government should be that of generating a maximum degree of private spending through a minimum amount of public spending."[35]

Eccles suggested that he and Riefler draft some legislation for discussion by the committee. They secured a staff consisting of a lawyer from the Reconstruction Finance Corporation (RFC), an expert on consumer credit, and a housing expert. These five men shaped what was to be the Federal Housing Administration (FHA).

Walker suggested that the legislation be drafted as an amendment to the act that set up the Home Loan Bank Board. John Fahey would then have been the administrator for the whole of the government's housing-mortgage program. However, as the drafting of the bill progressed, Fahey took the position that the program to insure mortgages under the bill would put the building and loan leagues at a disadvantage in the mortgage market, since theirs were not insured loans. His resistance to the program caused a change in the provisions of the legislation to create a new agency to administer it, even though he was successful in adding a provision for the Federal Saving and Loan Insurance Corporation (FSLIC) to insure the deposits in building and loan associations.

The overall thrust of the legislation, the National Housing Act of 1934, was to encourage the investment of idle funds in housing construction and to provide employment for the building trades. Title I insured financial institutions against losses on modernization and improvement loans up to 20 percent of their aggregate loan volume in this area. Title II, written mostly by Winfield Riefler, spelled out a mortgage insurance program that insured lending institutions against losses on mortgage loans, a program that included the following provisions:

1. The mortgages were to be on 1- to 4-family units.
2. The amount of the mortgage was not to exceed $16,000.
3. The loans were not to exceed 80 percent of the appraised value of the property.
4. The term of the mortgages was not to exceed 20 years.
5. The interest rate was not to exceed 5 percent.
6. In case of default, payment of insurance would be in the form of

35 *Ibid.*, p. 148.

three-year FHA debentures (IOU's) bearing an interest rate of not more than 3 percent.

7. The FHA Administrator was authorized to set a premium charge for the insurance.

8. A Mutual Mortgage Insurance Fund which would serve as a pool of funds to pay off defaulted mortgages was established and funded with $10 million made available by the Treasury.

Title III authorized the Federal Housing Administrator to establish national mortgage associations to buy up mortgages. The associations could raise funds to buy the mortgages by issuing notes, bonds, debentures, or other obligations.

Because insured deposits were more secure, the interest rate offered on them could be lower. In order to lend mortgage money at the lower FHA rates, Fahey argued that savings and loan associations needed the same kind of insurance that the banking system enjoyed under the Federal Deposit Insurance Corporation (FDIC). Title IV created the Federal Savings and Loan Insurance Corporation (FSLIC) to insure the accounts of building and loan, savings and loan, and homestead associations and cooperative banks, and the accounts of all federally chartered savings and loan associations. It also included the Federal Home Loan Banks in the activities in Title I and Title II. Furthermore, Federal Home Loan Banks were empowered to issue debentures and bonds as obligations of all the Federal Home Loan Banks.[36]

When the bill was submitted to Congress it was assigned to the Banking and Currency committees in both houses. John Fahey and the Savings and Loan League lobbyist, Morton Bodfish, lobbied vigorously against the part of the bill that was to stimulate new housing. Eccles comments:

They got the insurance plan they wanted, but, as things developed, it seemed that they would have preferred to kill the whole housing bill even though they lost the insurance benefits contained in Title IV.[37]

The building and loan associations had enjoyed a position in the mortgage market that gave them few competitors; they saw the provisions of Title II as taking away that preferred position and opening up the mortgage market to the commercial banks. Mutual Savings Banks and some insurance companies were also opposed to having commercial banks enter the mortgage market for the same reasons.

[36] *Evolution of the Federal Government in Housing and Community Development: A Chronology of Legislative and Executive Actions, 1892–1974.* (Report prepared for the Subcommittee on Housing and Community Development of the Committee on Banking, Currency and Housing of the House of Representatives, October, 1975.) (Washington, D.C.: U. S. Government Printing Office), pp. 4–5.

[37] Eccles, *op. cit.*, p. 154.

TABLE 4–2. FHA Loans Made

(*In millions*)

1934	$ 30
1935	427
1936	615
1937	526
1938	798
1939	954
1940	1026

SOURCE: Table I-1, p. 6 in *Federal Credit Agencies, A Report for the Commission on Money and Banking.* (Englewood Cliffs, N.J.: Prentice-Hall), 1963.

Senators Robert F. Wagner of New York and Alben Barkley of Kentucky helped get a favorable vote in the Senate Banking and Currency Committee. The House committee was influenced by Bodfish to diminish the provisions of the bill, but amendments during the debate in the whole House and the work of the conference committee that composed the differences between the House and Senate versions restored the original provisions. The bill was passed June 30, 1934.

Albert Dean, one of the drafters of the legislation and an expert on consumer credit, was put in charge of the modernization and improvement program. This part of the program was given wide publicity, and an advertising campaign was launched to encourage the citizenry to use the loans (see Figure 4–4A,B). Title I loans, as they were called, generated $1 billion worth of activity with losses of only 5 percent on the loans. Its success was partly due to the able and enthusiastic administration of Albert Dean.

The administrator chosen for the insurance part of the program, Title II, was unfamiliar with the mortgage business and unenthusiastic about the program. The large banks and insurance companies were reluctant to participate in the program—Eccles said that the reform of the mortgage market that FHA represented threatened their previous high interest rates and large profits. Therefore, they wanted the FHA program to fail so that they might go back to doing business as usual.

Procedures for appraising properties were made exceedingly strict, and the FHA insurance program languished (see Table 4–2).

The effects of the National Housing Act of 1934 were many and lasting. Some of the specific effects were to enable borrowers to obtain a high percentage of the appraised value of a house in a single mortgage, thus lessening the need for second and third mortgages. Lower interest rates made homeownership more affordable and available to a larger

FIGURE 4–4. Advertisements for Title I (Home Improvement) Loans.

segment of the population. Monthly amortization of principal and interest over a longer length of time regulated the handling of loans and provided more security to both the lender and the borrower. Insurance of the loans made more money available for mortgage lending because the risk involved was diminished for the lending institutions. Smith

Certainly....
We'll lend you money
to fix your Home!

You have a good job, Mr. Doe . . . you have a steady income and a good credit reputation. That's security enough! We're glad to make you a loan to put your home in good repair."

Typical of conversations at our bank these days . . . as more and more *(name of town)* residents hear about Modernization Credit. This new plan makes it easy to protect and improve home property. Loans up to $2,000 . . . with monthly repayments scaled to suit individual incomes . . . over convenient periods up to 3 or even 5 years. Inquiries are welcomed.

BUILD, BUY OR REFINANCE THE NEW WAY!

Now you can really OWN your own home! Finance with ONE FIRST MORTGAGE . . . covering up to 80 percent of the appraised property value. No second mortgage . . . no refinancing. It's as easy to *own* your own home under the Federal Housing Administration's plan as it is to pay rent! Ask any of our staff.

THE BLANK TRUST CO.

FHA 410

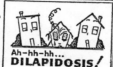

Ah–hh–hh...
DILAPIDOSIS!

Does your home show the symptoms? Does the roof leak, do steps sag, faucets trickle?

Dilapidosis can be prevented—can be *cured*—with a dose of Modernization!

Under the terms of the National Housing Act we are lending responsible borrowers up to $2,000 for permanent home improvements. Repayable monthly, out of income, over a 2-, 3-, or even 5-year period. Come in and let us explain the details.

• • •

We will also be glad to tell you about building, buying, or refinancing a home with one Insured Mortgage—the new plan that leads *to real* home ownership.

BLANK TRUST CO.

FHA 403

But
I don't *want*
to go Home!

Do your children prefer to play at the neighbors'?

Children are sensitive to surroundings . . . even though they can't explain, in so many words, *why* rooms are uncomfortable and uninviting!

There's a new way of paying for home repairs and improvements—monthly, out of income, over a convenient 2-, 3-, or even 5-year period.

We are lending responsible borrowers up to $2,000 for modernizing homes.

★

Insured First Mortgage loans are also available here. The new way to build, buy, or refinance a home out of your income.

Come in and let us tell you about the Federal Housing Administration's plan for owning a better home.

BLANK TRUST CO.

THE TEXT
of these ads may
be changed to
conform to your
local conditions

noted that the educational and competitive effect of FHA practices on the mortgage-lending industry pressured lenders of conventional mortgages to offer terms and conditions approximating those of FHA loans, thus restraining mortgage lending in general from excesses.[38]

---

[38] Wallace F. Smith, *Housing: The Social and Economic Elements.* (Berkeley, Calif.: The University of California Press), 1971, p. 476.

The market for mortgages as investments, which had been largely local before the standardized appraisal methods instituted by the HOLC and FHA, gradually became national in scope, because institutions with large amounts of money to invest (such as insurance companies) no longer had to be able to inspect the properties themselves to judge the quality of the structures. The reliance on the FHA appraisal and the reduction in the risk involved afforded by the FHA insurance of the loan made mortgages a more attractive investment.

One of the lasting and important effects was that the federal government had forged a flexible way of influencing the mortgage market and, secondarily, the amount of activity in the construction industry. By making federal insurance of loans a factor in the supply of mortgage credit available, the construction industry became responsive to a government policy, one that could be adjusted to create a desired effect in the national economy. When the court decided in *United States* v. *City of Louisville*[39] that the Federal government had no power to take land by eminent domain for its own low-rent housing projects, further emphasis was focused on the power that the government *did* have, namely, that of influencing credit. Hear notes that

. . . the home builder has relatively little equity investment—in fact in his dependence upon credit he resembles more closely the retailer than the ordinary producer. Hence even modest shifts in central monetary and fiscal policies evoke sharp reactions in the housing industry.[40]

Colean commented that when credit is made available to special groups by government policy it is made available in accordance with a measure of need rather than a measure of risk.[41] The series of modifications in the extension of credit for homeownership during the 1930's resulted in a structural change in the system from a pure market determination to one based in some instances on need as determined by government policy.

Writers cite different reasons for the failure of the private sector of the economy to form the mortgage associations authorized by the National Housing Act of 1934. The number of housing units started had fallen from over 900,000 annually in 1924 to 93,000 in 1933, so that there was not a great demand for new mortgages. Then, too, investing in mortgages ties up money for long periods of time, and even with the FHA insurance there was much uncertainty in the business community about the future of private enterprise while President Roosevelt, with

39 *United States* v. *City of Louisville*, p. 352, p. 338.
40 Haar, *loc. cit.*, p. 352.
41 Miles L. Colean, "The Environment of Real Estate Finance." In: Wheaton, et al., *op. cit.*

the approval of the Congress, was leading the country through what amounted to social revolution. What would be the position of private property? Was there to be inflation and higher interest rates? Also, bankers were not giving strong support to the FHA mortgage insurance program, partly out of resistance to having the government become active in a domain that had been exclusively theirs.

Jesse Jones, the Administrator of the Reconstruction Finance Company (RFC) (see Figure 4–5), was not known for letting opportunities slip by. He explained the reluctance of the financial community to form mortgage associations, saying,

Times were so pessimistic that no one would put up money for common stock in such an enterprise. We wanted private investors to own the business, to do the work and make a fair profit. But we couldn't induce anyone to try it.[42]

Jones proceeded to form the RFC Mortgage Company in the spring of 1935. The RFC Mortgage Company bought and sold FHA mortgages on houses constructed after April 1, 1935, and made loans to finance or refinance income-producing properties such as apartment houses, hotels, and office buildings.

The opportunity to establish national mortgage associations was ignored by the private financial sector, and in 1938 President Roosevelt requested the FHA administrator to establish the Federal National Mortgage Association as a subsidiary of the Reconstruction Finance Corporation (RFC). It is possible that if the banks and insurance companies had instead formed their own national mortgage association there would have been no need to form the Federal National Mortgage Association (FNMA). However, when the recovery faltered in 1937 and there was a renewed urgency to stimulate the construction industry Jesse Jones acted to form a secondary mortgage market.

We then formed the Federal National Mortgage Association. In the jargon of the government's alphabetical agencies, it quickly came to be called Fannie Mae. Before she was a year old, Fannie Mae had authorized and purchased 26,276 mortgages aggregating more than $100,000,000, and had found it necessary to start foreclosures on only twenty-five of them. While Fannie Mae bought insured mortgages on new homes, including large-scale housing projects, the RFC Mortgage Company continued to buy insured mortgages on old homes.[43]

Fannie Mae was formed as a subsidiary of the Reconstruction Finance Corporation, and later, when there was a move to start another such

[42] Jesse H. Jones, with Edward Angly, *Fifty Billion Dollars: My Thirteen Years With the RFC.* (New York: Macmillan), 1951, p. 749.
[43] *Ibid.*, p. 151.

FIGURE 4–5. First Board of Directors of Reconstruction Finance
Corporation, sworn in on February 2, 1932 by James L. Dougherty. *From left to right:* James L. Dougherty; Ogden L. Mills,
member ex officio (Under Secretary of Treasury); Paul Bestor,
member ex officio (Federal Farm Loan Board); Harvey Couch;
Charles ("Helen-Maria") Dawes; Jesse H. Jones; Eugene Meyer.
Wilson McCarthy was not sworn in until February 4th.

association, Jesse Jones blocked it, saying, "We have one. We don't
need any more."[44]

The volume of Fannie Mae's activity did not become a major factor
in the secondary mortgage market until after World War II, however,
when it was authorized to purchase VA-guaranteed loans.[45] During
World War II, the Association did little else but sell off its portfolio,
and it remained in a quiescent state until late 1948 (see Table 4–3).[46]
The possibility of using FNMA as a deliberate tool of countercyclical

44 Conversation with Miles Colean, April, 1976.
45 For a detailed discussion of how the secondary market works, see Chapter
11 by Curtis W. Tuck in this volume.
46 Jack M. Guttentag, "The Federal National Mortgage Association." In:
*Federal Credit Agencies, A Series of Research Studies Prepared for the Commis-
sion on Money and Credit.* Englewood Cliffs, N.J.: (Prentice-Hall), 1963, p. 69.

TABLE 4–3. FNMA Mortgage Activity All Programs by Fiscal Year
(Dollars in thousands)

Fiscal Year	Purchases	Sales	Repayments	Other Credits	Year-end Portfolio Number of Mortgages	Year-end Portfolio Amount
1938	37,952	—	69	—	9,765	37,883
1939	92,006	345	4,318	—	31,419	125,226
1940	49,293	7	10,474	1,005	41,876	163,033
1941	45,935	8	13,719	1,128	52,026	194,113
1942	38,813		16,891	520	58,820	215,515
1943	7,081	126,694	23,473	212	18,603	72,217
1944	338	(41)	13,011	47	15,995	59,538
1945	113	38,416	11,201	3	2,895	10,031
1946	23	213	3,469	—	2,246	6,372
1947	63	11	1,457	5	1,835	4,962
1948	47,390	—	1,262	—	8,283	51,090
1949	423,546	—	10,027	114	70,512	464,495
1950	946,397	311,292	35,778	8,190	156,083	1,055,632
1951	855,692	272,405	48,994	11,046	223,561	1,578,879
1952	604,973	39,866	67,421	8,518	291,066	2,068,047
1953	585,709	60,000	86,541	9,516	346,851	2,497,699
1954	480,783	575,067	92,021	10,255	318,530	2,301,139

SOURCE: *Background and History, 1975*, (Washington, D.C.: Federal National Mortgage Association), p. 54.

economic policy was hardly conceived of in 1938 when the association was created. The emphasis at that time was on expansion alone, rather than on a flexible policy that would be expansionary at some times and contractionary at other times.[47]

Reform: The Housing Act of 1937

Howard Becker, in the 1960's, wrote that ". . . social problems are what interested parties think they are . . ." and they emerge through identifiable stages. The first stage occurs when an objective condition (housing that is crowded, unventilated, and without natural light, for instance) is identified by some one or group of people as undesirable, dangerous, or potentially so. The second stage in the development of a social problem requires that the concern of the few who identified the problem become the concern of many. Widespread concern must be aroused and public action to solve the problem must be demanded. The third stage finds an institution or agency being created to take the responsibility for dealing with the problem.

In summary, every social problem has a history and develops through a series of stages, each stage a change in who defines the problem, the kind of definition it is given, and the resulting actions taken in an attempt to solve the problem.[48]

Stage I

The identification of poor housing as a social problem was first noted at a port of entry on the East Coast where the housing shortage was most severe. A sanitary inspector in New York City called attention to the crowded and unhealthy housing conditions that immigrants were renting in 1834. The efforts of that inspector, Gerritt Forbes, constituted the first stage in a sequence of events that culminated in the New York Tenement House Law of 1901.

Stage II

In the intervening 67 years a constant and disproportionate effort developed the "widespread concern" that was necessary before public action was possible.

A whole generation of surveys, reports, and agitation by public-spirited citizens was necessary before the first feeble tenement house law was enacted by the New York legislature in 1867. Another generation spent its efforts in procuring a series of amendments gradually raising the standards of that

---

[47] *Ibid.*, p. 83.
[48] Howard S. Becker (ed.), *Social Problems: A Modern Approach.* (New York: Wiley), 1966, p. 13.

law, until the most important revision produced the New York Tenement House law of 1901 and provided a Tenement House Department in the city government to administer it.[49]

The social problem defined by that sequence of events was that society placed no restraints upon exploiters of the poor in their need for housing. The Tenement House Department set up minimum standards for rental housing in the City of New York, and this law represented a significant step in the acceptance by society of a responsibility to ensure a minimum level of shelter for families who could not afford to pay for it themselves.

Some housing legislation forbids a bad house, other legislation attempts to provide a good house.

Robert F. Wagner was an associate justice of the Supreme Court of New York State in 1921 when the court upheld a state law limiting rents and setting conditions for evicting tenants. His opinion stated: "The very reason for the existence of a representative government such as ours is in the protection of the welfare of the people. . . ."[50] He was to play a key role in the next drama in the history of housing as a social problem.

In 1933, Mary Simkovitch, director of Greenwich House of New York City, approached Wagner, by then a United States Senator, when Democratic Party leaders were writing the National Industrial Recovery Act (NIRA). She proposed that housing be included in the public works program. NIRA became law June 16, 1933. Under the law, the Federal Emergency Administration of Public Works was authorized to make loans to limited-dividend corporations, whose profits were limited by law. This program resulted in 3,123 dwelling units from seven projects. The limited-dividend corporations were required to put up 30 percent of the funds for a project, and their lack of equity funds curtailed the program. This short-lived limited-dividend program under NIRA in 1933 resulted in enthusiastic participation of labor organizations in Pennsylvania in building housing for workers, however, and their continued involvement in the cause of housing for low-income families led to the organization of the Labor Housing Conference (LHC). Catherine Bauer, who had just published her book *Modern Housing*, accepted the position of director of the Labor Housing Conference in the summer of

[49] Edith Elmer Wood, "The Development of Legislation." In: *Public Housing in America*, compiled by M. B. Schnapper. (New York: H. H. Wilson Co.), 1939, p. 71.

[50] Timothy McDonnell, *The Wagner Housing Act*, (Chicago: Loyola University Press), 1957, p. 19. Quoted by Wagner in a speech at Yorkville, July 16, 1937; in Collected Papers of Senator Robert F. Wagner (unpublished), Vol. 3, Section 3, No. 52, preserved at Georgetown University, Washington, D.C. The following account relies heavily on McDonnell's book.

1934. She immediately began organizing a campaign for the passage of a public housing bill, a campaign that brought the American Federation of Labor (AFL) with its considerable political influence to the support of public housing.

Mary Simkovitch was also a leader in organizing the National Public Housing Conference (NPHC), a pressure group with the purpose of generating support for public housing. The National Public Housing Conference, known today as the National Housing Conference, gathered influential and energetic people to its cause. The group received valuable support from Harold L. Ickes, the Secretary of Interior, and the group advocated placing the public housing agency within the Department of Interior. Catherine Bauer, however, as Director of the Labor Housing Conference (LHC), advocated an autonomous housing agency.

Ernest Bohn, a member of the City Council of Cleveland, was instrumental in the organization of the National Association of Housing Officials (NAHO), a group formed in Chicago in November 1933 with the purpose of facilitating the exchange of ideas and information among housing officials and other interested persons. Miles Colean served on NAHO's Executive Committee; Coleman Woodbury was appointed Executive Director.

Catherine Bauer and John Edelman (of the American Federation of Hosiery Workers) set about getting the support of the American Federation of Labor, which included the building trades, for the public housing program.

All three groups cooperated to generate public demand for a public housing program. The NPHC members wrote articles to educate groups such as public health officials, teachers, and social workers and made speeches throughout the country. The NAHO people wrote articles directed toward municipal administrators, and Ernest Bohn arranged for three European housing experts, Sir Raymond Unwin and Miss Alice Samuel of England and Mr. Ernst Kahn of Frankfurt, to tour 14 cities in the United States to survey conditions in housing and suggest possible solutions. A group including Sir Raymond Unwin and Lady Unwin and Ernest Bohn were invited to the White House to give an oral report of the six-weeks study made throughout the United States, arrangements having been made through Mrs. Eleanor Roosevelt.

A summary report was written and a national convention of 75 important people in housing was held in Baltimore the following October. The problem had been well documented by the tour group. Leaders from all over the country, including the three public housing groups (NPHC, NAHO, and LHC), met and discussed these facts for four days and published their recommendations in a report, *A Housing Program for the United States.* Ideas were clarified, support for the public housing program was consolidated, and much publicity was generated.

The second stage of the process of evolution of a social problem was being accomplished by these three groups, the NPHC, NAHO, and LHC. By January 1935, there was considerable public interest in the need for a program to provide housing for low-income families.

Also, as a result of the report to President Roosevelt, the President's attention had been drawn to the need for coordinating the government programs that had direct effects on housing. He created the Central Housing Committee under the chairmanship of his uncle Frederick Delano to attempt to form a national housing policy. The committee was made up of the heads of several agencies concerned with housing plus one other member from each agency, and included as secretary a Mr. Peasley, a nephew of Frederick Delano. Peasley and Loomis, a committee member from the Home Loan Bank Board, "could spin more red tape than you could wind on a bobbin," and Stewart MacDonald and Miles Colean of the FHA dubbed the Central Housing Committee "the two-hours-of-lost-motion club."[51] However, the Central Housing Committee represented the first recognition of the need for an agency to unify and coordinate housing policies.

While support for public housing was growing, so was opposition. The National Association of Real Estate Boards (today the National Association of Realtors) viewed with alarm any incursion by the government into the domain of private enterprise, and declared that normal building for middle-income families would result in vacancies in older buildings and thus provide units suitable for housing poorer families. A report to the NAREB Board of Directors included the following statement:

Very serious repercussions to our national life will follow if government continues its policy of direct action in becoming landlord to masses of its people, and the same can be said if its becoming the holder of mortgages on the homes of its citizens. The ultimate result will be that we will find government supporting the citizen instead of the citizen supporting government. . . .[52]

The National Retail Lumber Dealers Association opposed the public housing program because the buildings were not to be made of wood. They advocated the development of a low-cost single-family home. Lee F. Johnson, an active proponent of public housing throughout his long career in government, assessed the lobby against it saying:

[51] Conversation with Miles Colean, August 9, 1976.
[52] Walter S. Schmidt, "Report Concerning Certain Federal and Private Activities in the Field of Real Estate and Housing," made to the Board of Directors of NAREB, Detroit, May 30, 1935. NAREB files, Chicago.

The National Association of Home Builders is only one part of the lobby. Its principal partners in the local battle are the National Association of Real Estate Boards and the United States Savings and Loan League. Behind this junta stand the even more powerful Mortgage Bankers Association of America, United States Chamber of Commerce, and Producers Council.[53]

Stage III

President Roosevelt was becoming convinced that something should be done about the housing problem. Shortly after the delegation headed by Ernest Bohn and Sir Raymond Unwin had reported to him on conditions in the 14 cities which they had inspected, he wrote a letter to one of his friends who was objecting to the fact that land used for public housing and slum clearance was taken from the tax rolls. The letter demonstrated that he was no longer debating whether something should be done but was looking for an acceptable method of solving the problem. In the letter he said:

Here, however, is one phase of urban housing that I should like to have your slant on. Let us suppose for the sake of example that there are ten thousand families in a given city whose earning power is so low that they can afford to spend say ten dollars a month for the item of rent in their budget. What are we going to do with them? Are we going to compel them to live under slum conditions, let us say in one room, for which they pay ten dollars a month? Has society as a whole no obligation to these people? Or is society as a whole going to say we are licked by that problem? Private capital cannot afford to do anything about it and, therefore, these ten thousand families must continue to live in one room for each family.

You quote one President. Another President said "We are faced with a condition and not a theory. I wish you would give me a solution."[54]

In January 1935 the New York people in the National Public Housing Conference (NPHC) drafted a housing bill that put the administration of the public housing program in the Department of Interior under Ickes. Mary Simkovitch and Helen Alfred asked Senator Robert Wagner of New York to sponsor the legislation. Wagner had grown up in the slums of New York City and had been active in New York State Senate in promoting legislation to better the conditions of the people in the tenements. One of the people who had worked with him during those years was a young lawyer named Franklin Delano Roosevelt, and they were good friends. Before the end of that session of Congress, Wagner had introduced the bill and managed to have it assigned to the Committee on Education and Labor, a committee whose members were apt to give it a sympathetic hearing.

53 Lee F. Johnson, "The Housing Act of 1949." In: Nathan Straus, *Two Thirds of a Nation: A Housing Program.* (New York: Knopf), 1952, p. 209.
54 McDonnell, *op. cit.*, p. 100.

In the meantime the Labor Housing Conference group in Philadelphia had approached Representative Henry Ellenbogen from Pittsburgh to sponsor a bill that put more emphasis on employment and the necessity of stimulating the building trades and which called for a new and independent agency to administer the program. Ellenbogen had written the Home Owners Loan Corporation legislation, and he wrote a bill that clearly defined the financial provisions for a public housing program. When he introduced it in the House, however, it was assigned to the conservative Committee on Banking and Currency. McDonnell, in his account of the progress of the bill, noted that

The referral of the bill to this particular committee and the attitude of the chairman of the committee killed the bill in 1935 and 1936 and almost killed it in 1937.[55]

Representative Henry Steagall of Alabama was Chairman of the Banking and Currency Committee, and he killed the bill by never taking any action on it. When Congress adjourned in August 1935, both bills died.

1936 was an election year. Wagner's legislative assistant, Leon Keyserling, was given the task of drafting a new bill. Ellenbogen worked with Keyserling, and Catherine Bauer and others gave technical assistance. Wagner set about selling the idea to the voters, and he managed to get a favorable vote in the Senate on the new bill. However, Ellenbogen again failed to get the bill out of the Committee on Banking and Currency in the House, and President Roosevelt found it impolitic to support the bill in an election year. And so the effort in 1936 failed.

When the next session of congress convened there was general acknowledgement that some housing bill would be passed in that session. Many of the groups who had simply opposed the bill before, changed their tactics to trying to modify the bill to support their own interests. Some of these suggestions were incorporated in order to minimize opposition. The contention began to center on the provisions of the bill, specifically whether the administering agency would be in the Department of Interior or an independent agency. Secretary Ickes had strong support of the New York group in the NPHC, and he thought he could get the cooperation of both the President and Henry Steagall in placing the agency under his administration.

It was at this point that the legal division of the Public Works Administration (PWA) in the Department of Interior strongly advised Senator Wagner that recent court decisions made a change in emphasis from the provision of decent housing to the relief of unemployment

[55] *Ibid.*

necessary. The PWA division expected at that point that the housing agency created by the bill would become part of the Department of Interior (their department) so they reviewed the bill very carefully and made some suggestions.

The first draft of the 1937 bill was ready by February 5, 1937. Hearings were held in the Senate in April and May for all interested groups to give their views on the bill. Little opposition was voiced, and there was speculation that the opposition had decided to focus their efforts on the hearings of Steagall's House Committee on Banking and Currency. The Senate Committee on Education and Labor reported the bill out in July, and debate in the Senate began August 2. Rural and southern senators felt that the benefits of the bill would go only to cities; others believed that New York would benefit disproportionately. Senator Byrd of Virginia succeeded in placing a limitation on the amount of money to construct the dwelling units built under the bill; Senator King amended the bill to forbid any "demonstration projects"; Senator Walsh of Massachusetts added an amendment that required slum clearance as a part of the program, and Senator Logan of Kentucky was successful in amending the bill to place the United States Housing Authority in the Department of Interior. Finally, on the afternoon of August 16, the Senate voted on the bill. It passed by a vote of 64 yeas, 16 nays, and 15 not voting. Senator Wagner had won a victory for the public housing supporters.

Chairman Steagall, meanwhile, had left Washington during the third week in July to go home to Alabama, and no date had been set for his committee to hold the necessary hearings on the bill. Wagner had gone to the President to ask for his support. The President convinced Representative Steagall that he "wanted the bill reported out of his committee favorably and within a short time,"[56] and the House Committee on Banking and Currency began holding hearings August 2. Those testifying included Miles Colean, Everett Dirksen, Henry Ellenbogen, Harold Ickes, Ernest Bohn, and Mayor Fiorello La Guardia of New York City. Heavy pressure was brought to bear on the committee members by the American Federation of Labor (AFL) to support the bill.

Secretary Ickes had captured the support of William Green, President of the American Federation of Labor by telling him that President Roosevelt wanted the housing agency to be placed in the Department of Interior. With the backing of both the AFL and Chairman Steagall, he was able to amend the bill in the committee, thus winning the placement of the agency within his department. However, Ickes was

[56] *Ibid.*, p. 345.

not successful in convincing the President that he should appoint the man he wanted to be Administrator.

After much strife among the leaders of the various public-housing groups, it was decided that Senator Wagner should propose the name of Nathan Straus to the President to be appointed the first Administrator of the United States Public Housing Authority. Roosevelt sided with Wagner on this appointment. Straus and Ickes could not get along with each other, so it worked out that Straus administered the Authority almost as if it were an independent agency. Ickes would have nothing to do with it after Strauss took over as Administrator.[57]

The committee approved the bill August 16. The same afternoon that the Senate passed the bill, the hearings before the House committee were concluded.

Steagall arranged for the bill to be debated in the House August 18 under a special rule that would require a vote on the bill before adjournment that same night. After long and contentious debate the final vote in the House was taken at nine o'clock August 18 with a count of 275 yeas, 86 nays, and 70 abstentions.

Since the bill passed by the House was different than the one passed by the Senate, it was necessary for a committee made up of members of both houses to meet to iron out the differences. The conference committee met for 11½ hours August 20 to make the necessary compromises, and while neither house expressed confidence in the negotiators or approval of their compromises, both houses voted in favor of their results. On September 1, 1937, the bill was signed by the President and became the law of the land. One of the ironies of fate (and legislative procedure) decreed that the official name of the bill, when it finally passed, was the Wagner–Steagall Housing Act.

The third stage in the evolution of housing as a social problem had been brought to a successful conclusion—an agency had been created to deal with it. In its final form the bill provided for the United States Housing Authority, a permanent agency, to be set up in the Department of Interior, its purpose being

. . . to provide financial assistance to the States and political subdivisions thereof for the elimination of unsafe and insanitary housing conditions, for the development of decent, safe, and sanitary dwellings for families of low income, and for the reduction of unemployment and the stimulation of business activity, to create a United States Housing Authority, and for other purposes.[58]

[57] *Ibid.*, p. 306, from statements of Ernest Bohn and Warren Vinton (personal interviews).

[58] Public Law No. 412, 75th Congress, First Session, Chapter 896.

Control of whether or not to have public housing was placed at the local level. The local housing authority had to apply to participate in the program, thus avoiding the resentment engendered by the Resettlement Administration. Senator Byrd's amendment restricted the amount spent for units in cities of less than 500,000 population to $4,000 per unit and $1,000 per room. In larger cities, the limits were $5,000 per unit and $1,250 per room. Senator Walsh's amendment required that for each unit built, one slum unit had to be either eliminated or repaired, a practice called equivalent elimination. No more than 10 percent of the total funds were to be spent in any one state in response to those who thought that New York might benefit disproportionately, and no loans made by the Housing Authority were to be for more than 90 percent of the cost of project. The Act provided $500,000 for such loans to be made at the rate of interest ½ percent above the current Federal borrowing cost and paid back in 60 years. The federal government was committed to make "annual contributions" to the local housing authorities to cover the principal and interest of the loans, a bookkeeping device that spread the budgetary expenditures over the 60-year

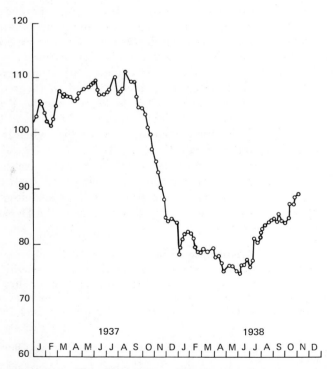

FIGURE 4–6. *New York Times* Weekly Business Index, 1937–1938. [Courtesy of the *New York Times*.]

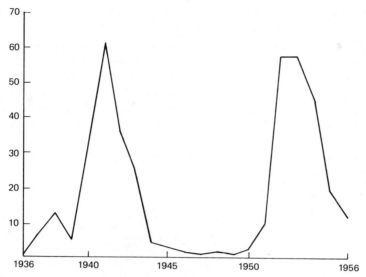

FIGURE 4–7. Units of low-rent public housing completed, 1936–1956 (in thousands). [Source: Ray Ginger, *People on the Move: A United States History*, Allyn and Bacon, Boston, 1975, p. 635.]

term. In lieu of paying taxes the local authority made an annual payment to the local government equal to 10 percent of the shelter rent of the projects (shelter rent means rent without the cost of utilities). The shelter rent of a project, then, had to cover only the cost of utilities, maintenance and repairs, administration by the local housing authority, and the payment in lieu of taxes.

Beginning in August 1937, there was a new downtrend in business that threatened to undo all the recovery made by the country since 1933 (see Figure 4–6). Government had begun to cut back on relief and recovery spending in response to pressure from the business community for a balanced budget, but the business and financial classes lacked the confidence necessary for them to commit capital expenditures and provide employment to take the place of the government programs. Therefore, the trend toward recovery suffered a sharp setback.

Under the shock of the recession, Congress early in 1938 increased the sum at the USHA's disposal from $500,000,000 to $800,000,000 and also provided easier conditions for the insuring of private loans under the FHA. The progress of the USHA program was held up for a time by the dearth of local housing agencies, but, once this hurdle was surmounted, results began to appear. By November 1, commitments of $576,000,000 had been made in 142 cities. Meanwhile, the more liberal terms offered by the FHA led to a marked speeding up of private construction.[59]

From Figure 4–7 we can see that production of public housing rose to over 60,000 units in the early 1940's, but to keep the size of the program in perspective, it is suggested that the reader look at Figure 4–8 and note the relative percent of private versus public housing throughout United States history. Total production of federally assisted housing up to the year 1975 had resulted in only 2.12 percent of the total housing stock.

Abner Silverman characterized the tenants using public housing as follows:

In the late thirties and early forties, the Local Housing Authorities housed working class families of low income. They were poor, but most of them were employed and accustomed to urban living. In those days, indeed, Local Housing Authorities carefully screened out, or imposed quotas on, applicant families receiving relief, those who had unpleasant social histories or living habits, or those who were not normal families. The ideal was to rehouse a cross-section of the low-income families of the community, in terms of income, of family size, and of source income.[60]

What groups of people gain and what groups lose from a policy which gives housing to low-income families at a reduced cost?

Some slum landlords lose income as a result of public housing for their business has been taken over by the government. All taxpayers must contribute more to cover the costs of annual contributions. Construction workers gain from the allocation of resources into the construction of public housing. And low-income families gain better housing.[61]

The Census of Housing

The Constitutional Convention of 1787 provided for a decennial census of the population in Article I, Section 2. The census, begun in 1790, was taken in order to assess the states for the costs of the War of In-

---

[59] Schlesinger, *op. cit.*, p. 54.

[60] Abner D. Silverman, *User Needs and Social Services*. A report prepared for The House of Representatives, Subcommittee on Housing, Committee on Banking and Currency, February 1971, mimeo.

[61] Hugh O. Nourse, *The Effect of Public Policy on Housing Markets*. (Lexington, Mass.: Lexington Books), 1973, pp. 41–42.

FIGURE 4–8 [OPPOSITE]. Public and private housing starts, 1900–1975. [Data source: Bureau of the Census, U.S. Department of Commerce: (1) *Housing Construction Statistics* 1889 to 1964; (2) *Construction Reports, Housing Statistics*, series C20; data compilation, analysis, and estimate by NAHB Economics Department.]

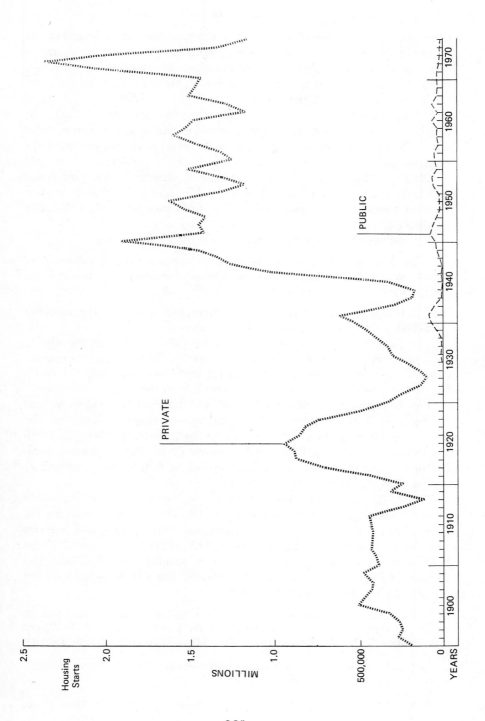

dependence and to apportion each state's representation to Congress. As a matter of self-interest, states were motivated to count everyone in order to be allotted as many representatives as possible; on the other hand, a state was constrained to be accurate, since its share of the costs of the war depended on the count also.

Colonists resisted being counted, however, because they thought the number in the household would determine the tax the householder would be required to pay, and when the results of the census were published the citizenry was disappointed that the total count was only 3,929,214. However, subsequent censuses indicated that the count had been fairly accurate and that the public had exaggerated impressions of the size of the population. The total population in 1800 was 5,308,483.

The census of 1810 called, in addition, for a statement of

. . . the kind, quantity, and value of goods manufactured, the number of establishments, in some cases, and the number of machines of various kinds used in certain classes of manufactures . . ."[62]

The censuses of 1820 and 1840 also attempted to include the statistics of industry, but these efforts were not successful.

The field work for the first census in 1790 took nine months to complete; the one in 1840 took 18 months. The first six censuses counted only population, and the federal staff only added up the count by state or territory, not by cities, towns, counties, etc.

The censuses of 1850, 1860, and 1870 asked the value of real estate in each area enumerated (counties, townships, or cities). The number of slave houses was counted in the census of 1860; in 1890 the information obtained included "number of families in house; number of persons in house; number of persons in family; home owned or rented, and if owned, whether mortgaged. . . ."[63]

The 1900 and 1910 questions included home owned or rented, if owned whether mortgaged; and the one for 1920 added questions for market value, original amount of mortgage, balance due, and interest rate for nonfarm mortgages homes.[64] The 1930 census asked if the home was owned or rented and value or monthly rental. The 1930 Census of Population also asked whether or not the household owned a radio (40.3 percent did).[65]

62 *The History and Growth of the United States Census, 1790–1890.* A report prepared for the Senate Committee on the Census by Carroll D. Wright and William C. Hunt, 1900. (Washington, D.C.: U. S. Government Printing Office), p. 22.

63 *Population and Housing Census Questions 1790–1970.* Form 70–82–1 (4/18/64), Bureau of the Census.

64 *Ibid.*

65 Virgil D. Reed, "From Tube to Radios," *Printers Ink*, April 5, 1940, p. 40.

During the President's Conference on Home Building and Home Ownership, Coleman Woodbury cited the need for information from surveys. The Works Progress Administration, employing personnel from the work-relief rolls, completely covered 203 urban areas with eight million dwelling units or 45 percent of the total number of urban families, and published the results.[66] (New York City was considered such a special case that it was not included in the computations.) The data showed that an average of 40 percent of the units were owner-occupied; over half the owner-occupied units were mortgaged. The quality of the housing varied by region, but overall quality was measured by some of the same criteria used by the U. S. Census Bureau today, i.e.,

Since substandard housing may result from a variety of objective and subjective conditions, it is not possible to set up a precise and rigid definition of the concept. However, absence of sanitary facilities, unsafe condition of the physical structure of the dwelling, overcrowding, and the presence of extra families are all factors which render a dwelling unit substandard.[67]

The surveys listed 15 percent of the dwelling units as having no private indoor flush toilet, 20 percent without private bathtubs or showers, 40 percent lacking central heating, and 17 percent with more than one person per room.

The bill (S.2240) that provided for a national census of housing in 1940 was introduced by Senator Wagner on April 25, 1939. His contention was that the census was needed for the formulation of a national housing program (but the bill was amended to strike out that phrase—see Appendix at the end of this section). The bill asked for an appropriation of $8 million for one and only one census of housing in 1940. The Senate passed the bill June 24 and sent it to the House of Representatives where it was referred to the Committee on the Census. The report to the House of Representatives by the Committee on the Census referred to the WPA surveys, saying that they "had been of great use to private business and to Government . . ." and "have demonstrated the great value and immediate usefulness of housing data."[68]

The report also listed the organizations approving the bill as

Department of Commerce
Department of Agriculture

[66] *Urban Housing: A Summary of Real Property Inventories Conducted as Work Projects, 1934–1936.* (Washington, D.C.: U. S. Government Printing Office), 1938.

[67] *Ibid.,* p. 4.

[68] Report No. 1319, House of Representatives, 76th Congress, submitted by Matthew A. Dunn, Chairman of the Committee on the Census; July 26, 1939.

Federal Home Loan Bank Board
Federal Housing Administration
United States Housing Authority
National Association of Real Estate Boards
American Federation of Labor
United States Conference of Mayors
Producers Council
American Institute of Architects
Construction League of America
American Institute of Architects
Construction League of America
Associated General Contractors of America
National Retail Lumber Dealers Association
National Lumber Manufacturers Association
Portland Cement Association
National Lime Association
National Sand and Gravel Association
Structural Clay Products Institute
Metal Window Institute
National Association of Master Plumbers
National Paint, Varnish and Lacquer Association
American Federation of Labor (AFL)[69]

The character of the list implies that people expected more than just an enumeration of housing. *The United States News* of April 19, 1940 reported that the 1940 census would be the basis of a far-reaching reform program, one that would concern itself with redistribution of income, and more planning in business, housing, and education. One of the summary captions said, "Census figures to be used as a basis for a housing program."[70] The article stated

By tying together the results of the income and housing questions, officials will prepare a factual basis for arguments that the government could spend millions wisely and well on a large-scale housing program.[71]

It was the inclusion of questions about income that stirred much of the opposition of the 1940 census. Senator Tobey of New Hampshire introduced a resolution in February 1940 to omit questions 32 and 33 from the census questionnaire, questions which asked for household income information.[72] (Enumerators were required to ask only for wages or salary, including commissions, up to $5,000. Recipients of incomes in excess of $5,000 were to be recorded as $5,000 plus.) Senator Tobey submitted that no authorization to require such in-

69 *Ibid.*, p. 2.
70 *The United States News*, April 19, 1940, p. 28.
71 *Ibid.*, p. 28.
72 U. S. 76th Congress, 3rd Session, Senate Hearing February 28–March 1, 1940 on S. res. 231.

formation was enacted in any law and that local political appointees would not keep income information confidential. The inference was that census takers were temporary workers who could not be restrained from gossiping by fear of losing their jobs, and that a person's income was a very private matter, one which the government has no right to pry into. The investigation into a WPA scandal had found that secret official files had been turned over by WPA workers to political party bosses who had used the information to coerce relief workers to vote against their own convictions or lose their relief jobs. The specter of centralized planning and concurrent loss of individual freedoms was taken very seriously indeed.

The 1940 census found 37,438,714 dwelling units (see Table 4–4), 45 percent of which lacked some or all plumbing facilities; 50 percent of the dwelling units cost less than $3,000, 50 percent cost more (median value); 45.7 percent of whites owned their homes, while only 23.7 percent of nonwhites owned theirs. Notice the relationship between median value of a unit and median gross rent for both whites and non-

TABLE 4–4. Selected Housing Characteristics for the United States: 1940 to 1970

	1940	1950	1960	1970
TOTAL INVENTORY..........	37,438,714[1]	46,137,076[1]	58,326,357[2]	68,679,030[3]
Total vacant................	2,474,913	3,186,176	5,302,482	5,229,283
Gross vacancy rate..........	6.9	6.9	9.1	7.6
Total owner occupied........	15,230,950	23,613,528	32,796,720	39,885,180
Percent of all occupied......	43.6	55.0	61.9	62.9
Unit in structure.............	37,325,470	45,983,398	58,314,784	67,699,084
1 unit....................	27,507,946	32,229,548	44,525,121	48,863,438
Percent.................	73.7	70.1	76.4	72.2
2–4 units..................	5,889,226	8,676,183	7,551,865	9,006,950
Percent.................	15.8	18.9	13.0	13.3
5 or more units............	3,928,298	5,077,667	6,237,798	9,828,696
Percent.................	10.5	11.0	10.7	14.5
Percent 1.01 or more persons per room..................	20.2	15.8	11.5	8.2
Structure built in last 10 yrs...	15.9	20.8	27.5	25.0
Median age................	25.3	28.2	27.2	23.0
Median value...............	$3,000	$7,400	$11,900	$17,100
Median gross rent............	$27	$42	$71	$108
Median income of families or primary individuals........	NA	NA	$4,800	$7,700
Percent of total units lacking some or all plumbing facilities:				
United States............	45.3	35.4	15.9	6.9
In SMSA's................	21.3	20.6	9.3	3.5
In central cities...........	19.9	18.7	9.5	3.5
Not in central cities........	24.6	23.5	9.2	3.5
Outside SMSA's............	67.4	54.2	29.3	14.1
Urban.....................	23.3	20.4	8.8	3.4
Rural......................	74.7	62.8	33.7	16.9

TABLE 4–4. *Continued*

	1940	1950	1960	1970
White and other races:				
Percent lacking plumbing....	42.6	30.6	7.5	4.8
Percent 1.01 or more persons per room...............				
	29.0	13.3	9.7	6.7
Percent owner............	45.7	57.0	64.4	65.4
Median value............	$3,100	$7,700	$12,200	$17,600
Median gross rent..........	$28	$44	$73	$112
Median income of families and primary individuals.......	NA	$2,600	$5,100	$8,100
Nonwhite:[4]				
Percent lacking plumbing....	79.5	61.6	41.9	16.9
Percent 1.01 or more persons per room...............				
	43.6	32.1	28.3	19.4
Percent owner............	23.7	34.9	38.4	41.6
Median value............	$800	$3,000	$6,700	$12,300
Median gross rent..........	$14	$27	$58	$89
Median income of families and primary individuals....	NA	NA	$2,500	$4,700

SOURCE: Sixteenth Census of the United States: 1940 Housing Vol. II *General Character-istics;* 1950 Census of Housing, Vol. I *General Characteristics*, Part I United States Summary; United States Census of Housing, 1960 United States Summary, *States and Small Areas; General Housing Characteristics*, United States Summary, 1970 HC(1) A-1; *General Social and Economic Characteristics of the Population*, United States Summary, 1960 and 1970 Census of Population.

[1] Total inventory includes Alaska and Hawaii. Characteristics for these areas are not available for 1940.

[2] Total inventory is based on complete count data, characteristics are based on sample data.

[3] Total includes vacant, seasonal, and migratory. Characteristics are presented for year round units only.

[4] 1970 data are for Black.

whites. Nonwhite median rents were half that of whites, but the median value of the units rented by nonwhites was roughly only a quarter of the median value of units rented by whites.

While the median value of all units increased from $3,000 in 1940 to $17,100 in 1970, rent levels increased from $27 to only $108. While we can attribute part of the rise in cost of units to better housing (the number with more than one person per room decreased from 20.2 to 8.2 percent of the total and the number lacking some or all plumbing facilities decreased from 45.3 percent in 1940 to 6.9 percent in 1970), some of the rise is due only to the effect of inflation. A dollar with buying power of 100¢ in 1950 would buy only 81¢ worth of goods in 1960, 62¢ worth in 1970, and about 42¢ in 1976.

Housing costs as a percentage of income, however, dropped for whites from 20 percent in 1950 to 17.2 percent in 1960 to 16.6 percent in 1970. Table 4–4 also shows that in 1960 a median rent was 27.8 percent of a median income for nonwhites; in 1970 a median rent was 22.7 percent of median income for blacks.

Appendix

Union Calendar No. 521

76th CONGRESS
1st SESSION

S. 2240

[Report No. 1319]

IN THE HOUSE OF REPRESENTATIVES

JUNE 26, 1939
Referred to the Committee on the Census

JULY 26, 1939

Reported with amendments, committed to the Committee of the Whole House on the state of the Union, and ordered to be printed

[Omit the part struck through and insert the part printed in italic]

AN ACT

To provide for a national census of housing.

1   *Be it enacted by the Senate and House of Representa-*

2 *tives of the United States of America in Congress assembled,*

3 That to provide information concerning the number, ~~charac-~~

4 ~~ter~~ *characteristics (including utilities and equipment),* and

5 geographical distribution of dwelling structures and dwelling

6 units in the United States ~~and concerning the social and~~

7 ~~economic characteristics of their ownership and use, neces-~~

8 ~~sary to aid in the formulation of a national housing program~~

9 ~~and in the administration of housing legislation,~~ the Director

10 of the Census shall take a census of housing in each State,

11 the District of Columbia, Hawaii, Puerto Rico, the Virgin

12 Islands, and Alaska, in the year 1940 in conjunction with,

(sidebar) AN ACT   S. 2240   To provide for a national census of housing.

2

1   *at the same time, and as a part of* the population inquiry

2   of the sixteenth decennial census. ~~Such census of housing~~

3   ~~shall relate as closely as possible to the day and month~~

4   ~~provided by law for the population census.~~ The Director

5   of the Census shall be authorized to ~~make~~ *collect* such sup-

6   plementary ~~studies~~ *statistics* (either in advance of or after

7   the taking of such census) as are necessary to the com-

8   pletion thereof.

9   SEC. 2. All of the provisions, including penalties, of

10 the Act providing for the fifteenth and subsequent decennial

11 censuses, approved June 18, 1929 (46 Stat. 21; U. S. C.,

12 Supp. VII, title 13, ch. 4), shall apply to the taking of the

13 census provided for in section 1 of this Act.

14   SEC. 3. For the purpose of carrying out the provisions

15 of this Act, there is authorized to be appropriated, out of any

16 money in the Treasury not otherwise appropriated, not to

17 exceed ~~$8,500,000~~ *$8,000,000* to cover the estimated cost

18 of such census.

Passed the Senate June 23 (legislative day, June 22),
1939.

Attest: EDWIN A. HALSEY,
                                        Secretary.

Calendar No. 698

76th Congress	SENATE	Report
1st Session		No. 647

NATIONAL HOUSING CENSUS

June 21 (legislative day, June 15), 1939.—Ordered to be printed

Mr. Wagner, from the Committee on Banking and Currency, submitted the following

REPORT

[To accompany S. 2240]

The Committee on Banking and Currency, to whom was referred the bill (S. 2240) to provide for a national census of housing, having considered the same, report favorably thereon with amendments and recommend that the bill do pass.

The bill as amended by the committee authorizes the Director of the Census to conduct a census of housing in 1940 in conjunction with the sixteenth decennial census, "to provide information concerning the number, character, and geographical distribution of dwelling structures and dwelling units in the United States and concerning the social and economic characteristics of their ownership and use, necessary to aid in the formulation of a national housing program and in the administration of housing legislation." In accordance with the suggestions of the Bureau of the Budget that if the bill were to provide for a single census (in the year 1940) and to authorize an appropriation not to exceed $8,500,000, it would not conflict with the program of the President, the committee has amended the bill as introduced to embody these suggestions.

The bill is strongly approved by the Department of Commerce, and by the various Government agencies concerned with housing including the Federal Housing Administration and the United States Housing Authority. The proposal for a housing census has been urged by the National Association of Real Estate Boards, the American Federation of Labor, the National Association of Housing Officials, the United States Conference of Mayors, and many business groups.

The committee believe that a housing census is essential to insure the most economical and intelligent development of residential construction, with its great potentialities for the investment of idle capital, stimulation of durable-goods industries, and the relief of unemployment. The information to be obtained is desired and needed by

★

Government and business alike.   Such censuses have been the basis of
housing programs in the principal European countries for many years.

Investment in housing represents one-fourth our national wealth;
and in the form of either loans, commitments, or guaranties, the
Federal Government has an interest of approximately $10,000,000,000
in housing.   Yet this is the one branch of our national economy where
reliable statistical information is sorely lacking.   The local housing
surveys conducted with emergency relief funds in the past 6 years
have, where available, been of great use to private business and to the
Government, but have not sufficed to provide a national picture on a
unified basis.   They have been conducted only in certain communities,
under widely different conditions, and with definitions and tabulations
which are not entirely comparable.   They have been taken at different
periods and many are already out of date.   These local surveys, however, have demonstrated the great value and immediate usefulness of
housing data, and served to develop and test necessary techniques.
National needs can be met only by a country-wide census taken in
connection with population, covering all classes of structures and
dwelling units and offering a basis for the comparison of various localities and income groups.

The authorization of not more than $8,500,000 represents a cost
estimate by the Bureau of the Census for obtaining, compiling, and
analyzing the information, amounting to about 25 cents per individual
schedule for each of the approximately 35,000,000 housing units to
be covered in the census.   This contrasts very favorably with the
cost of between 60 and 80 cents per individual schedule in the local
housing surveys referred to above.

The committee believe that the survey is both desirable and necessary and that the amount authorized represents an economical
expenditure for the work to be performed.   They, therefore, recommend that the bill be enacted.

O

MINORITY REPORT ON S. 2240

A minority group of the Committee on the Census make the following report with reference to S. 2240 for the consideration of the House.

We feel that the consideration of the said bill by the Committee on the Census did not allow proper time for consideration and suggest the following in support of our position:

1. This bill was by a majority vote of the committee tabled when it was first brought up for consideration. The committee were of the opinion at that time that this attempt to take a census of housing was for the purpose of assembling propaganda and agitation for further Government housing projects. The minority feel that this objection has not been overcome by the committee amendments to this bill.

2. The Director of the Bureau of the Census never appeared before the committee to explain the scope of this bill as amended. The minority contend that this bill was reported out without the benefit and counsel of the Bureau of the Census.

3. We contend that the authorization for an appropiration of $8,000,000 to carry out the purpose of this act is entirely without foundation. There is no justification for this amount; in fact, the Committee on the Census made no study whatsoever of the practical cost of this census of housing.

4. We question the wisdom of imposing upon the Bureau of the Census, whose duty is to take a population census, the task of taking a housing census if the demand for the same comes solely from those Government boards and bureaus who are desirous of furthering Government and Government-subsidized housing projects.

Respectfully submitted.

J. Roland Kinzer.
Carl T. Curtis.
Robert A. Grant.
Charles Hawks, Jr.
W. H. Wheat.
Frederick C. Smith.

O

Summary

When we speak of "the population of the United States" we are apt to envision an aggregate of individuals counted up one by one by the census takers to produce the grand total. No sense of interdependence or "groupness" emanates from the addition of numbers. However, the people who lived through the decade of the 1930's were reminded daily by their deprivation that the society in which they lived had become highly interdependent. Urban families depended on farmers for food; factory workers no longer made their own soap and shoes but bought them from others who specialized in making only soap or shoes; transportation networks speeded the exchange of goods, and money as a medium of exchange became more important as the universal measure of worth. During the Great Depression, money as a medium of exchange failed, the flow of goods and services was choked off, the web of interdependence fell apart, and survival required that people retrench into a more unspecialized way of life. People survived the crisis partly by making their own soap and shoes and growing their own food; partly by doing without many of the amenities of life that they had been enjoying; and partly by the aid organized by the government.

The graphs of such things as the marriage rate (Figure 4–9), fertility ratio (Figure 4–10), birth and death rates (Figure 4–11), immigration rate (Figure 4–12), and population growth rate (Figure 4–13), give a visual outline of the effect of the decade on the human group within the boundaries of the United States. In the terms of human ecology, the adaptation of the group to its environment had been disrupted; the normal supply channels for food and shelter were not working, and the group responded by contracting its numbers. The shape of the population pyramids for decades to come would demonstrate the effect of the 1930's on the size of the population (see Figure 4–14).

The turbulent years of the 1930's represented a social revolution in the sense that the old economic "rules of the game" had to be modified. Because unemployment was a major problem during the depression and because the construction and furnishing of homes has such a strong impact on the employment rate, housing became a central issue and part of the relief, recovery, and reform effort.

Money for mortgage loans was made more available to borrowers and lenders by the creation of the Home Owners' Loan Corporation (HOLC), by the Federal Housing Administration (FHA), and by the Federal National Mortgage Association (FNMA). The tax money in the Treasury stood behind the promises and programs of each agency.

According to Wendt, the basic framework for the Federal housing

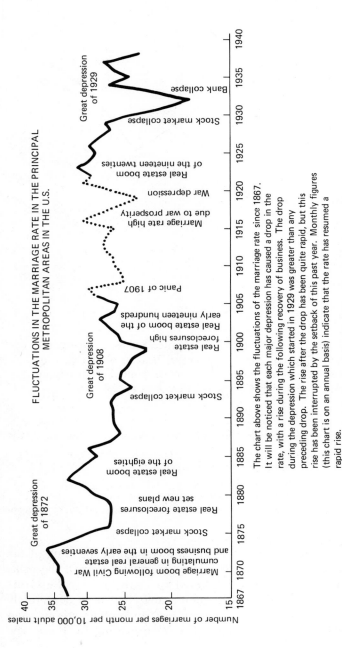

FLUCTUATIONS IN THE MARRIAGE RATE IN THE PRINCIPAL METROPOLITAN AREAS IN THE U.S.

The chart above shows the fluctuations of the marriage rate since 1867. It will be noticed that each major depression has caused a drop in the rate, with a rise during the following recovery of business. The drop during the depression which started in 1929 was greater than any preceding drop. The rise after the drop has been quite rapid, but this rise has been interrupted by the setback of this past year. Monthly figures (this chart is on an annual basis) indicate that the rate has resumed a rapid rise.

An increase in the marriage rate increases the demand for homes, for furniture, and for all types of household appliances. A marriage boom has generally preceded a real estate boom.

FIGURE 4–9. Fluctuations in the marriage rate in the principal metropolitan areas. [Source: *The Real Estate Analyst*, October 26, 1938, p. 1074.]

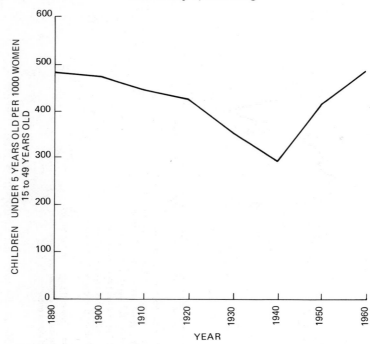

FIGURE 4–10. Fertility ratio for the United States: 1890–1960.
[Source: U. S. Department of Commerce, Bureau of the Census,
United States Census of Population, 1960: United States Sum-
mary. General Population Characteristics, PC(1) 1B U.S.]

policy was established during the depression years. It included the
following five concepts;
1. Housing is a problem of the federal government.
2. The goal is individual homeownership.
3. Federal manipulation of credit as the means to the goal.
4. Slum clearance as a cooperative venture of federal and local governments.
5. Public housing for the purposes of slum clearance.[73]

What was represented was not so much a change in spending of tax
monies as a shift in the attitudes of society in general toward the poor.
Because the economic system had faltered so badly during the Great
Depression, a large proportion of the total society had been desperately
poor through no fault of its own. Poverty lost some of its stigma, and
government shouldered some responsibility for providing for those who

[73] Paul Wendt, *Housing Policy—The Search for Solutions*. (Berkeley, Calif.:
University of California Press), 1963, pp. 151–152.

Per 1,000 population

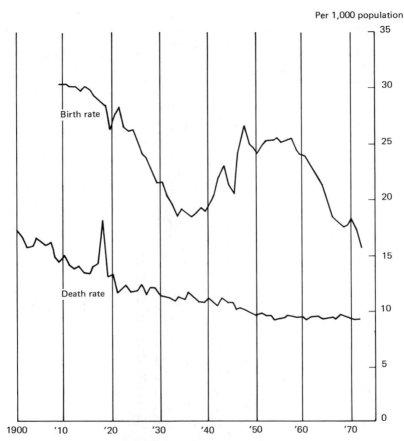

FIGURE 4–11. Birth and death rates: 1900–1972. [Source: *Social Indicators*, Office of Management and Budget. U. S. Government Printing Office, Washington, D.C., 1973, Chapter 8.]

were in need. Those who were not poor came to expect government to do so as well as those who were poor.

President Roosevelt had cast the federal government in the role of promoter of society's welfare.[74] The New Deal established links between municipal governments and Washington, D.C. that illuminated the needs of the cities. The 1920 Census had demonstrated that over half the population lived in urban areas of more than 2,500 people, yet state governments drew their support and attitudes from the rural Jeffersonian traditions. The crisis of the Great Depression, whose

[74] Mark I. Gelfand, *A Nation of Cities: The Federal Government and Urban America, 1933–1965*. (New York: Oxford University Press), 1975.

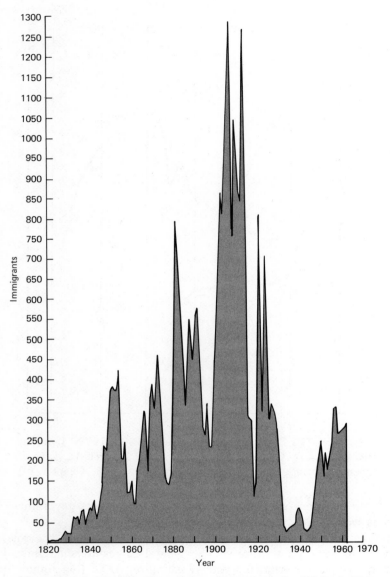

FIGURE 4–12. Number of immigrants to the United States: 1820–1962. [Source: U. S. Bureau of Census, *Historical Statistics of the United States*, Washington, D.C., 1960, Table C88–114; *Statistical Abstract of the United States, 1963*, Table 123.]

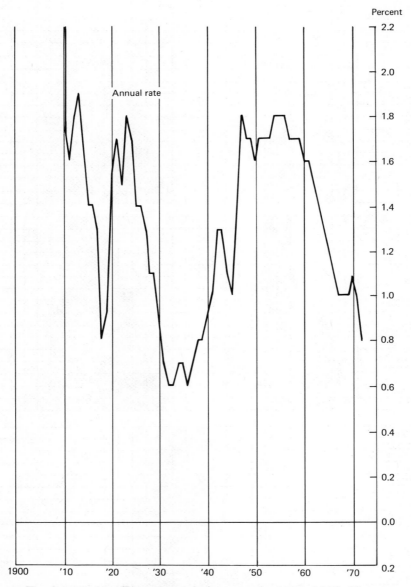

Percent

Annual rate

FIGURE 4–13.   Rate of population growth: 1910–1972. [Source: *Social Indicators*, Office of Management and Budget. U. S. Government Printing Office, Washington, D.C., 1973, p. 232.]

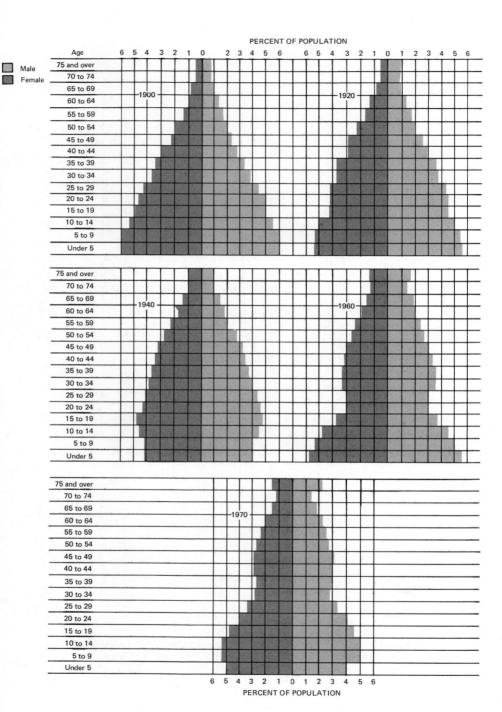

PERCENT OF POPULATION

miseries fell heaviest on urban populations, brought urban concerns into focus. It was the federal government that responded to their needs rather than the state governments. In a society that had always thought of itself as rural, attention had been focused on urbanity and urban problems.

Bibliography

The Beginning Of The Decade

ARNOLD, JOSEPH L., *The New Deal in the Suburbs: A History of the Greenbelt Town Program, 1935–1954.* Columbus, Ohio: Ohio State University Press, 1971. This scholarly study contains an excellent bibliography on the subject.

BURNS, ARTHUR E. and EDWARD A. WILLIAMS, *Federal Work, and Relief Programs.* Washington, D.C.: United States Printing Office, 1941.

EBENSTEIN, WILLIAM, *The Law of Public Housing.* Madison: University of Wisconsin Press, 1940.

Evolution of Role of the Federal Government in Housing and Community Development: A Chronology of Legislative and Selected Executive Actions, 1892–1974. A Report for the Subcommittee on Housing and Community Development of the Committee on Banking, Currency and Housing, House of Representatives, 94th Congress, First Session, October, 1975. Washington, D.C.: U. S. Government Printing Office.

GERLOFF, CECELIA M. (ed.), *The Federal Home Loan Bank System of the United States,* Library of Congress #72–187328, 1971.

GRIES, JOHN M. and JAMES FORD (eds.), *Home Finance and Taxation: Loans, Assessment, and Taxes on Residential Property.* Report of the President's Conference on Home Building and Home Ownership. Washington, D.C.: National Capitol Press, 1932.

———, *Housing Objectives and Programs.* A Report on the general sessions of The President's Conference on Home Building and Home Ownership. Washington, D.C.: National Capitol Press, 1932.

———, *Slums, Large-Scale Housing and Decentralization.* Report of The President's Conference on Home Building and Home Ownership. Washington, D.C.: National Capitol Press, 1932.

HAAR, CHARLES M., "Background of Federal Housing Credit." In: William L. C. Wheaton, Grace Milgram, and Margy Ellin Meyerson, *Urban Housing.* New York: Free Press, 1966.

The Real Estate Analyst, October 26, 1938. Roy Wenzlick, editor.

Twentieth Annual Report of the Secretary of Commerce, 1932. Washington, D.C.: United States Government Printing Office.

FIGURE 4–14 [OPPOSITE]. Population by age and sex: 1900–1970. [Source: *Social Indicators,* 1973, Office of Management and Budget, U. S. Government Printing Office, Washington, D.C., 1973. Stock #0324–00256, p. 238.]

Home Owners' Loan Corporation

BURNS, ARTHUR E. and EDWARD A. WILLIAMS, *Federal Work, Security, and Relief Programs*. Washington, D.C.: U. S. Government Printing Office, 1941.

COLEAN, MILES L., *American Housing—Problems and Projects*. For Twentieth Century Fund, 1944.

GERLOFF, CECELIA M., *Federal Home Loan Bank System*. Federal Home Loan Bank Board, Library of Congress Catalog #72187528.

HARRIS, C. LOWELL, *History and Policy of the Home Owners' Loan Corporation*. National Bureau of Economic Research, 1951.

HOAGLAND, HENRY E. and LEO D. STONE, *Real Estate Finance*, Homewood, Ill.: Richard D. Irwin, Inc., 1973, pp. 466–474.

The Home Owners' Loan Corporation, Its Problems and Accomplishments June 13, 1933–June 13, 1936. Federal Home Loan Bank Board Library.

Public Law #304 of the 72nd Congress, approved July 22, 1932. Washington, D.C.: The Public Printer.

RUSSELL, HORACE (General Counsel), *The Blue Book; The Home Owners' Loan Corporation Legal Department*. Federal Home Loan Bank Board Library.

The National Housing Act of 1934

BEYER, GLENN H., *Housing and Society*. New York: Macmillan, 1965.

Building the American City, Report of the National Commission on Urban Problems to the Congress and to the President of the United States, Paul H. Douglas, Chairman, Government Printing Office, Washington, D.C., 1968.

COLEAN, MILES L., *The Environment of Real Estate Finance in Urban Housing*. New York: Free Press, 1966.

———, *A National Policy on Federal Intervention in Mortgage Finance and Community Development*, paper delivered to President Eisenhower, May, 1952. Unpublished.

———, *The Impact of Government on Real Estate Finance in the United States*, National Bureau of Economic Research, 1950.

ECCLES, MARRINER S., *Beckoning Frontiers: Public and Personal Recollections*, edited by Sidney Hyman. Alfred A. Knopf: New York, 1951.

Evolution of Role of Federal Government in Housing and Community Development: A Chronology of Legislative and Selected Executive Actions, 1892–1974. Washington, D.C.: U. S. Government Printing Office, #54–725, October 1975. ($2.50).

GREBLER, DAVID, M. BLAND, and LOUIS WINNICK, "The Growth of the Residential Mortgage Debt." In: *Capital Formation in Residential Real Estate*. Princeton, N.J.: Princeton University Press, 1956.

HAAR, CHARLES M. "Background of Federal Housing Credit", *Urban Housing* edited by William L. C. Wheaton, Grace Milgram, Margy Ellin Meyerson. The Free Press: New York, 1966.

JONES, JESSE, H. with EDWARD ANGLY, *Fifty Billion Dollars: My Thirteen Years with the RFC.* New York: Macmillan, 1951.

SEMER, MILTON and JULIAN ZIMMERMAN, *The Changing Role of FHA Mortgage Insurance in the Mortgage Market and the Secondary Market.* A report prepared for the Office of the Assistant Secretary for policy Development and Research, U. S. Department of Housing and Urban Development, Washington, D.C., January 1975. Unpublished.

The Housing Act of 1937

BECKER, HOWARD S. (ed.), *Social Problems: A Modern Approach.* New York: Wiley, 1966.

JOHNSON, LEE F., "The Housing Act of 1949." In *Two Thirds of a Nation: A Housing Program,* Nathan Strauss (ed.). New York: Knopf, 1952.

McDONNELL, TIMOTHY, *The Wagner Housing Act.* Chicago: Loyola University Press, 1957.

NOURSE, HUGH O., *The Effect of Public Policy on Housing Markets.* Lexington, Mass.: Lexington Books, 1973.

Public Law No. 412, 75th Congress, First Session, Chapter 896.

SCHLESINGER, ARTHUR MEYER, *The New Deal in Action: 1933–1938.* New York: Macmillan, 1939.

SCHMIDT, WALTER S., *Report Concerning Certain Federal and Private Activities in the Field of Real Estate and Housing.* NAREB files, Chicago, May 30, 1935.

SILVERMAN, ABNER D., *User Needs and Social Services.* Report prepared for the House of Representatives, Sub-committee on Housing, Committee on Banking and Currency. February, 1971.

WOOD, EDITH ELMER, "The Development of Legislation." In *Public Housing in America,* compiled by M. B. Schnapper. New York: H. H. Wilson Co., 1939.

The Census of Housing

Historical Statistics of the United States: Colonial Times to 1970, Part I, Bureau of the Census, 1975.

Population and Housing Census Questions 1790–1970, Bureau of the Census, Form 70–82–1; April 18, 1969.

Report of the Committee on the Census, Report No. 1319, House of Representatives, 76th Congress, 1st Session, submitted by Matthew A. Dunn, July 26, 1939.

The United States News, April 19, 1940, p. 28.

Urban Housing: A Summary of Real Property Inventories Conducted as Work Projects, 1934–1936, Government Printing Office: Washington, D.C., 1938. A report by the Works Progress Administration, Division of Social Research.

WRIGHT, CARROLL D. and WILLIAM C. HUNT, *The History and Growth of the United States Committee on the Census.* Washington, D.C.: U. S. Government Printing Office, 1900.

Chapter 5

HOUSING IN THE DECADE OF THE 1940'S— THE WAR AND POSTWAR PERIODS LEAVE THEIR MARKS

Mary K. Nenno*

Introduction

ON APRIL 1, 1940, a Census of Housing was taken in the United States. For the first time in the history of the country, a complete count of dwellings was made, together with detailed findings on these dwellings by type, size, price range, condition, occupancy or vacancy, facilities, and equipment.[1]

In brief, the 1940 enumeration showed a national population of al-

[1] Facts in this section are summarized from the 1940 Census of Housing. U. S. Bureau of the Census, *1940 Reports on Housing*, Vol. II, Part 1, United States Summary.

* MARY K. NENNO is Associate Director for Policy Development of the National Association of Housing and Redevelopment Officials in Washington, D.C., responsible for coordination of legislative and administrative policy. She is the author of two books both published by NAHRO in 1974 (*Required: A Local Housing Assistance Plan* and *Housing in Metropolitan Areas*), and numerous articles on national housing legislation and policy.

Ms. Nenno received her B.A. degree from Elmira College, Elmira, New York and did graduate work at the University of Pennsylvania and the University of Buffalo, receiving an M.A. in Public Administration from the latter institution. She recently completed an assignment as Visiting Professor of Housing Research and Development at the University of Illinois, Urbana-Champaign.

most 133 million persons occupying 37.5 million dwelling units, with more than 56 percent classified as renters. The median or typical housing unit was 25 years old; 40 percent of the units were more than 30 years old. In urban areas, more than 23 percent of all dwelling units had no private bath, and more than 10 percent were in need of major repairs.

In rural communities, the percentage of deteriorated units was considerably higher, and on farms higher still. In 1940, one of every five families was crowded into housing which afforded less than one room per person.

The 1940 Census of Housing facts can be summarized as follows:

	Total	Urban (In Millions)	Rural Non-farm	Farm
Total Dwelling Units	37.3	21.6	8.1	7.6
Needing Major Repairs or Without Private Bath	18.2	6.2	5.2	6.9
No Gas or Electricity	8.2	1.3	1.7	5.2
No Refrigeration Equipment	10.9	2.7	3.1	5.1
No Central Heating or Stoves	4.3	1.4	0.9	1.9

The facts of the 1940 Census documented the impact of the decade of the 1930's and the depression. Population had increased by only 7 percent, but the ratio of new nonfarm dwelling construction to net additions in the number of families was only 3 to 5. About half the unprovided families in 1940 were living doubled-up or in makeshift shelters. Thus, the decade of the 1940's began with a backlog of housing demand and a residue of poor housing conditions. President Franklin D. Roosevelt stated in the mid-1930's that "one third of the nation was ill-housed."

Also carried over into the decade, beginning in 1940, was the beginning of a new federal government intervention into housing—publicly assisted housing efforts generated by the 1930 conditions of unemployment and slums. This was principally by the Federal Housing Administration (FHA), whose mortgage insurance program had been created in 1934 to address the problems affecting homeowners and the residential construction industry, and the public housing program for low-income families, which originally was launched under the Public Works Administration in 1933 but achieved a new, permanent status under the United States Housing Act of 1937.

By the time the decade of the 1940's ended, all these housing conditions would be altered—impacted first by the demands and shifts of World War II, and then by those of the postwar period. The economic and social life of the nation, including its housing, would bear the marks of this tumultuous decade.

Trends in Housing Construction and Inventory

The pattern of new housing starts in the 1940's mirrors the impact of World War II and its postwar period. Housing starts totaled 603,000 units in 1940, declined almost 50 percent by 1942, reached a low point of 142,000 units in 1944, then spurted back to a total of almost 1.5 million units in 1949. As the postwar construction gained momentum in 1946, the number of annual housing starts reached the highest point since the previous record year of 1926—1 million units (contrasted with 937,000 units in 1926).

The pattern of ownership also shifted over the 10-year period. In 1940, 88 percent of new housing starts were under private ownership. This proportion dropped to 84 percent in 1942, as publicly owned war housing reached an annual peak production of 87,000 units. It quickly recovered and surpassed 96 percent in 1943, and escalated to almost 100 percent for the balance of the decade.

A more impressive public sector picture is shown if units *financed* by public funds (not all publicly *owned*) are analyzed. In the 1940 through 1945 period, 579,000 permanent nonfarm dwelling units were financed with public monies, amounting to 22 percent of all units. In addition, as will be discussed below in the section The World War II Impact on Housing, if *temporary* housing is also counted, the public-financed starts in this period would be 44 percent of all war housing units. The national debate between the proponents of private housing dominance and public housing participation, which characterized both the war and postwar housing efforts, was reflected only minimally in the annual construction starts figures. However, this 1940's decade debate had widespread impact on the national housing legislation of 1949, the decade of the 1950's, and beyond.

The decade of the 1940's also substantially altered the construction costs of housing, and the tenure of dwelling units. In the 10-year period, the construction cost of average housing unit almost doubled—from $3,825 to $7,525. In addition, the proportion of one-family, sales-type housing continued to dominate private new construction at a level ranging from 80 to 89 percent. This fact, coupled with shifts in the existing inventory, resulted in a growth from 44 to 55 percent in owner-occupied dwellings for the 10 years. This sudden shift in tenure was directly attributable to the wartime restrictions on building and the shortage of wartime housing. The 15 percent rise in the proportion of owner-occupied units over the 4½-year period from April 1940 to October 1944 was greater than for any comparable period for which data are available.[2] (See Table 5–1.)

The private construction industry organization also was affected by the demands of building in the 1940's. In 1938, the Bureau of Labor Statistics found that the average builder of single-family homes in 72 cities constructed only 3.5 houses per year.[3] A study by the Department

TABLE 5–1. Nonfarm Housing Unit Starts, 1940–1949
(In thousands of units)

	Total Starts	Ownership		Average Construction Cost per Unit	Private Sales Structures
		Private	Public		
1940	602.6	529.6	73.0	$3,825	85%
1941	706.1	619.5	86.6	4,000	86%
1942	356.0	301.2	54.8	3,775	84%
1943	191.0	183.7	7.3	3,600	74%
1944	141.8	138.7	3.1	3,500	83%
1945	326.0	325.0	1.0	4,625	89%
1946	1,023.0	1,015.0	8.0	5,625	89%
1947	1,268.0	1,265.0	3.0	6,650	88%
1948	1,362.0	1,344.0	18.0	7,725	84%
1949	1,466.0	1,430.0	36.0	7,525	80%

SOURCES: U. S. Bureau of the Census, Department of Commerce, *Housing Construction Statistics, 1889 to 1964*, Washington, D.C., 1966, Table A-1; and Glenn H. Beyer, *Housing; A Factual Analysis*. (New York: Macmillan), 1958, Table A-1, p. 18 and Table A-4, p. 307.

of Labor found that in 1949, a total of 109,800 builders constructed 698,200 houses for an average of 6.36 houses per builder in that year.[4] While this was a significant increase, it reflected a gradual rather than a decisive movement toward volume construction. The decade ended still dominated by small-scale, handicraft building.

In 1949 only 900 builders, (less than 1 percent of all private builders) constructed 100 or more housing units annually. While not impacting significantly on total housing construction starts or total builder organization, the large rental housing developments financed beginning

[2] "Trends in Housing During the War and Post-War." *Monthly Labor Review*, U. S. Department of Labor, January, 1947, pp. 12–13.

[3] Glenn H. Beyer, *Housing: A Factual Analysis*. (New York: Macmillan), 1958, p. 84.

[4] *Ibid.*

in 1935 with FHA-insured mortgages and public housing contracts, and those constructed during the war period by public agencies for war housing, were to be forerunners providing strategic background experience for the larger-scale rental housing developments of the 1950's and the 1960's.

Still another area where the decade of the 1940's was to alter the housing future was in the area of technological development seen dramatically in house equipment—lighting, heating, plumbing—to some extent in construction methods, and in the production of housing.[5] To meet the needs of wartime housing, many new large organizations entered the housing field, utilizing both prefabrication and site assembly-line fabrication methods. New possibilities for the automatic control of heating, lighting, and mechanical equipment were made possible by wartime advances in the field of electronics. Thick plastic sections and laminated structural members were made possible as a result of high-frequency electric heating for molding processes. Plastic pipe and tubing, first used in wartime housing, was developed for use also for drainage lines, downspouts, bathtubs, shower stalls, lavatories, and kitchen cabinets.

Among other developments, gluing methods developed for the wartime aircraft industry provided quicker drying time, stabilizing the moisture content of wood, making possible precision manufacture of interchangeable wooden parts. Many types of subassemblies, ranging from complete window units to prefabricated closet and storage units, led to new preassembled housing components. Resin-bonded plywood, laminated structural members, or lightweight metallic girders or trusses, all experimented with by wartime industry, made long-span structural members economical to use. This led directly to the possibility of housing construction utilizing continuous spans between exterior bearing walls, making it possible to omit interior bearing walls and fixed partitions.

Government contracts for housing in war production areas permitted several of the struggling house manufacturers to get better established. Factory-made prefabricated panels were used not only for housing (much of it being temporary in character) but also for dormitories, school buildings, and other war construction. Many a GI had his first experience with prefabricated housing during this period.[6]

The Veterans Emergency Housing Program of 1946 sought to stimulate the prefabricated housing industry by assistance through the Reconstruction Finance Corporation, but only six companies went into

5 Howard P. Vermilya, "Potential Technical Development of Post-War Houses." *Insured Mortgage Portfolio*, Federal Housing Administration, September, 1943, p. 24.

6 Beyer, *Housing: A Factual Analysis, op. cit.*, p. 106.

actual production. Attempts to make prefabricated houses out of both steel and aluminum failed, the most dramatic example being the well-publicized "Lustron House," launched in 1946.[7]

While not all wartime experimentation had successful applicability in postwar housing construction, it opened up a new period of experimentation in use of materials, equipment, and construction methods which was to change dramatically the appearance and fabric of American housing.

The World War II Impact on Housing

The United States had experienced a brief period of intervention in housing during World War I, when an extreme shortage of housing for war workers stimulated federal government support of the U. S. Shipping Board and the U. S. Housing Corporation to construct housing for workers in munitions factories and related industries. The total federal investment amounted to $175 million. These funds were not entirely used because not all the housing was built before the Armistice. The U. S. Shipping Board constructed a total of 9,000 houses, 1,100 apartments, 19 dormitories, and 8 hotels in 24 localities. The U. S. Housing Corporation built and managed 25 community projects that included 5,000 single-family homes, as well as apartments, dormitories, and hotels.[8]

This experience spawned the first major confrontation between those who believed that the federal government should engage in housing activities that private enterprise could not perform, and those who believed that the government should not engage in any aspect of the housing business. The 1918 solution was a clear victory for the private enterprise advocates, as the federal government sold all the housing properties of the two corporations that were not turned over to other government agencies. The issue was dormant until the Depression of the 1930's.[9]

Because the nation concentrated its resources in its defense industries in 1940, housing did not have a high priority. Not until two million migrant defense workers had trouble finding shelter, and labor turnover exceeded 500 percent in some areas, were emergency housing actions initiated. There was a scramble of the agencies to build war housing, resulting in overlapping jurisdictions and lack of coordination. The series of shifts in Federal housing policy and FHA Adminis-

[7] Glenn H. Beyer, *Housing and Society.* (New York: Macmillan), 1965, Footnote, p. 477.

[8] *Congress and American Housing, 1892–1967.* (Washington, D.C.: U. S. Government Printing Office), February 1968, pp. 1–2.

[9] Beyer, *Housing and Society, op. cit.*, p. 455.

trators is one of the important housing stories of the 1940's, not to be clarified until the creation of the Housing and Home Finance Agency in 1947 and the passage of the 1949 Housing Act.[10]

Depending on what components are included, the government-supported housing program produced between 1.6 million and 1.9 million housing units for defense purposes. If new construction alone is considered, the program produced totals 1.6 million units, of which 780,000 housing units (48 percent) were publicly financed. An additional 255,000 housing units were made available through conversions of existing housing, of which 48,000 (19 percent) were publicly financed. The summary figures are as follows:[11]

Federally Supported War Housing, 1940–1944

Type of Housing	Housing Units
Privately financed new construction	836,000
Publicly financed conversions	48,000
Publicly financed temporary new construction including demountables, dormitories and trailers	583,000
Publicly financed permanent new construction	197,000
Privately financed conversions	207,000
Total	1,871,000
Total New Construction	
Privately financed	836,000
Publicly financed	780,000
Total	1,616,000
Total Conversions	
Privately financed	207,000
Publicly financed	48,000
Total	255,000
Grand Total (all units)	1,871,000

In terms of the confrontation between the advocates of a totally private housing construction effort and a public agency housing role, the total war production effort ended, if not in a close race, in a decided contest—with 56 percent of the total units produced by privately financed industry and 44 percent with direct public financing.

The issues involved in the public–private sector debate on develop-

10 Charles Abrams, *The Future of Housing*. (New York: Harper and Row), 1946, p. 298.
11 Abrams, *op. cit.*, p. 305.

ment of war housing were quickly drawn. The setting for the debate resulted from the initiatives of public housing agencies during the decade of the 1930's in stimulating construction employment by developing housing for low-income families. This activity had originally started as a program of the Public Works Administration in 1933. It was given permanent status under the United States Housing Agency (USHA) in the United States Housing Act of 1937.

The case for public agency involvement in the housing field was summarized in a speech by Senator Robert F. Wagner in 1935:

The object of public housing, in a nutshell, is not to invade the field of home building for the middle class or the well-to-do which has been the only profitable area for private enterprise in the past. Nor is it even to exclude private enterprise from major participation in a low-cost housing program. It is merely to supplement what private industry will do, by subsidies which will make up the difference between what the poor can afford to pay and what is necessary to assure decent living quarters.[12]

The private enterprise viewpoint was summarized by the President of the National Association of Real Estate Boards:

Housing should remain a matter of private enterprise and private ownership. It is contrary to the genius of the American people and the ideals they have established that government become landlord to its citizens. . . . There is sound logic in the continuance of the practice under which those who have initiative and the will to save acquire better living facilities and yield their former quarters at modest rents to the group below. . . .[13]

The passage of the 1937 Housing Act brought new opportunities for publicly assisted housing. On the eve of the decade of the 1940's, the federally assisted housing inventory consisted of 32 Public Works Administration projects that had been transferred to local housing authorities, two transferred to the Puerto Rico Reconstruction Administration, and 17 projects operated temporarily by the United States Housing Authority (USHA). USHA had entered into loan contracts with 171 local housing authorities for the construction of 413 publicly owned projects containing 145,646 housing units; 30 projects were actually in occupancy.

Including the funds authorized by the Congress for the fiscal year beginning on July 1, 1940, the total public housing program was expected to provide housing for 160,000 families in 435 projects in 208 communities in 35 states, the District of Columbia, Hawaii, and Puerto Rico. Local Housing Authorities had been created in 450 locali-

[12] Nathaniel S. Keith, *Politics and The Housing Crisis Since 1930.* (New York: Universe Books), 1973, pp. 32–33.
[13] *Ibid.*, p. 33.

ties in 37 states. There was also a publicly assisted inventory under the Farm Security Administration (formerly the Rural Resettlement Administration) that had been generated in 1935—164 rural projects of 20,000 dwelling units, including three greenbelt "new towns."[14] All this activity was exclusive of the mortgage insurance programs of the Federal Housing Administration (FHA), which provided federal guarantees for privately owned housing. By 1940, the FHA was providing mortgage insurance for 40 percent of all private housing starts.

After September 1939, the shadow of World War II began to affect all federal domestic programs, first under the rubric of "defense." On June 28, 1940, the Housing Act of 1937 was amended to authorize the use of its loan and subsidy provisions for housing defense workers during the emergency. From this point on, there was a rapid and continuing succession of federal war housing legislation and federal housing administrative reorganization.[15] These include the following:

1. July 21, 1940: An office of Defense Housing Coordinator was established in the Council of National Defense to plan and carry out defense housing programs, in cooperation with private enterprise.
2. September 9, 1940: $100 million was appropriated by the Congress for the erection of defense housing by the War and Navy Departments.
3. October 14, 1940: The basic defense housing law, the so-called Lanham Act, was passed providing direct federal financing and construction by public agencies.
4. January 11, 1941: The President established the Division of Defense Housing Coordination to try to coordinate defense housing activities of 16 federal offices involved.
5. March 22, 1941: Congress passed the Second War Powers Act, providing for priorities and allocation powers to the President to be used in war housing priorities systems.
6. March 28, 1941: The Congress amended the National Housing Act to provide more liberal mortgage insurance to builders constructing housing in critical defense areas.
7. March–December, 1941: The Congress passed a series of temporary shelter acts and appropriated funds for emergency housing for defense and war workers.
8. February 24, 1942: President Roosevelt, using his war powers, consolidated all federal housing functions into a new National

14 M. H. Schoenfeld, "Progress of Public Housing in the United States." *Monthly Labor Review*, U. S. Department of Labor, August 1940, pp. 267–82.

15 *Congress and American Housing, op. cit.*, pp. 48–49; and Keith, *op. cit.*, pp. 40–44, 73.

Housing Agency (NHA) under a single administrator with broad powers. All publicly financed housing functions were consolidated into a Federal Public Housing Authority (FPHA) built around the nucleus of the United States Housing Authority.

In all of these legislative and administrative activities was a continuing confrontation between private and public housing interests. A special committee of the Twentieth Century Fund advocated the containment of the public housing effort to its original program of ". . . providing housing for families whose incomes place them clearly beyond the reach of other methods."[16]

Ultimately, the Administrator of the National Housing Agency, John B. Blandford, Jr., was able to steer a course between private and public housing interests. His decision was to authorize private construction wherever there was reasonable expectation of continued economic need for housing after the war and wherever private builders would meet the wartime restriction on size, location, and occupancy. Otherwise, he authorized publicly financed housing.[17]

In summing up the difficulties and complexities of the war housing program in March 1943, Administrator Blandford stated:

There have been and probably always will be, conflicting views on the need for housing during this war period. Many communities opposed any war housing; many still oppose it, with the very real fear that over-building will end in a collapse of all real estate values after the war. Many groups in many communities felt war workers should be housed in barracks, opposed all family accommodations on the theory that men should be willing to leave their families as if they were going into the armed services.

Other groups wanted to build as usual, even after the war began. They opposed the limitations on costs and the use of materials. Still other groups, knowing that thousands of people were living under unsatisfactory conditions, wanted at least part of the peace-time housing program to be continued to provide better living standards for those people. Still others, opposed to the expenditure of public funds for any type of housing, advocate private financing regardless of the danger of over-building in many communities. . . .

Too much emphasis cannot be placed on the fact that the decisions controlling war housing—nationally or locally—must be based on the needs of the war program and cannot be predicated on a peace-time program of improving community housing conditions or on supplying a continued volume of business during wartime. Even when the market, the need, and the building capacity are available when judged by peace-time standards, new construc-

---

[16] Housing Committee, Twentieth Century Fund, "Defense Housing Program," *Monthly Labor Review*, Department of Labor, December, 1940, pp. 1412–1416.
[17] Keith, *op. cit.*, p. 43.

tion cannot be authorized unless necessitated by imperative war requirements. That hard fact is not unique to the housing industry but is common
throughout our war economy. It is not the product of anyone's arbitrary will
but is part of the price we have to pay to win the war.[18]

An additional permanent impact resulting from World War II and
the war housing effort was the geographic shifting of population and
housing to the south and far western states.[19] Most of the military
installations were located in these areas, and these were the only areas
to show population increases during the war years. Defense workers,
many of them from farms, migrated to the leading Pacific Coast cities
to work in airplane factories, shipyards, and other war industries.

In addition to the influx of war workers requiring housing facilities,
increased employment of the local population resulted in more people
who could afford their own homes or apartment. From 1940 to 1945,
the population of the Pacific Coast states increased by more than a
fourth, followed by the South Atlantic States.[20] The migration of war
workers amounted to a population shift of 8 to 10 million people. There
undoubtedly was an accompanying additional migration not directly
related to war production jobs as such.[21] All of these shifts had a
permanent impact on housing demand.

The Postwar Housing Emergency

Discussion about postwar housing policies did not wait for the cessation
of the war. As early as 1943, the National Housing Agency began to
develop staff recommendations for federal housing directions in postwar
America—both the immediate transitional problems, including disposition of the war housing stock, and broader questions of long-range
housing policy. A critical question was the rehousing of the millions of
veterans who soon would be returning to civilian life.

In terms of the conveyance and disposition of war housing, a series
of congressional actions between 1945 and 1950:

1. Authorized the use of public war housing to house veterans and families of distressed servicemen.
2. Provided for special pricing of permanent war housing for veterans.
3. Provided for the disposition of all war and veterans housing.[22]

Nearly all the permanent public war housing was built before Pearl
Harbor. Temporary housing (not suited for long-term use) was built

18 *Ibid.*, p. 44.
19 M. F. Jessup, "Trends in Housing During The War and Post-War Period,"
Monthly Labor Review, U. S. Department of Labor, January 1947, pp. 21–22.
20 *Ibid.*, p. 21.
21 Keith, *op. cit.*, p. 43.
22 *Congress and American Housing, 1892–1967*, *op. cit.*, pp. 46–47.

near military installations and war industries; and was put up quickly
and at minimum cost. The law required that temporary war housing be
removed as quickly as possible, but the extreme housing shortage
caused local communities to move more slowly in disposition. Permanent multifamily public war housing projects were conveyed to local
housing authorities for use by low-income families. Individual and two-
family houses were sold to homeowners, particularly returning veterans.[23] Some of the housing remains to this day, much of it at or near
university campuses.

In 1944, the Congress passed the Serviceman's Readjustment Act,
better known as the "GI Bill of Rights." Title III of this Act authorized,
among other things, the guarantee by the Veterans Administration of
loans to veterans in order to purchase, build, or improve homes.[24] This
action inaugurated a highly successful and popular program for veterans of World War II, which ultimately was extended to Korean War
veterans and to members of the Armed Forces with two or more years
of continuous active duty. By amendment in 1945, veterans were
authorized to use their VA loan guarantee for 10 years; after termination of World War II this was subsequently increased to 11 years and
13 years. About 40 percent of World War II veterans obtained their
houses under VA guaranteed or loans (see Table 5–2).

The VA-loan guarantee program was designed to encourage private
lending to veterans with the federal government guaranteeing part of
such loans so that in case of default and foreclosure the loss to the
lender would be minimized.

As originally enacted, the amount of the guarantee was not to exceed
$2,000, and the loan was limited to a maximum of 20 years. These
terms did not attract lenders. In 1945, the maximum amount of the
guarantee was raised to $4,000 and the maturity of the loan to 25
years. While there was an immediate spurt of VA loan activity following enactment in 1944, it was not until 1950—when Congress increased
the amount of the guarantee to 60 percent, or $7,500, whichever was
less, and the maximum maturity was increased to 30 years—that the
program became really attractive to private lenders. After this time, the
number of annual VA housing starts consistently topped 100,000 units,
reaching a peak in 1955, of 393,000 or 24 percent of all private nonfarm housing starts in that year.

The unique feature of the VA loan program was that it did not
limit the amount of the guaranteed mortgage to some percentage of the
total value of the home. Rather, it allowed mortgage lenders to make
loans up to 100 percent of the purchase price, with VA insurance

23 Beyer, *Housing and Society*, *op. cit.*, pp. 474–475.
24 *Congress and American Housing, 1892–1967, op. cit.*, p. 30–31.

TABLE 5–2. VA-Guaranteed Housing Starts Related to
Total Private Nonfarm Housing Starts,
1946–1950
(Units in thousands)

	Total Private Nonfarm Units*	VA-Guaranteed Housing Units	Percent of Total
1946	1,015.2	91.8	9.0%
1947	1,265.1	160.3	12.7
1948	1,344.0	71.7	5.3
1949	1,429.8	90.8	6.3
1950	1,908.1	191.2	10.1

* Does not include mobile homes.
SOURCE: National Commission on Urban Problems, *Building the American City*, Washington, D.C., 1968, Table 14, p. 107.

against any losses up to 60 percent of the amount of the loan, subject to a maximum cost to VA of $7,500.[25]

It was rare for any such loan to lose more than 60 percent of its value, so the $7,500 limit in most cases provided full protection for a loan up to $12,500. This price level was well within the purchase price of housing through the early 1950's, particularly for resales of existing houses. The VA guarantee made it possible to virtually eliminate down payments. Up until 1950, about two thirds of all VA loans were used for existing housing. The maximum allowable interest rate on VA-guaranteed home loans was 4 percent during the first nine years of the program, and 4½ percent during the next five years. From 1944 until 1950, the Act permitted combination Veteran Administration–Federal Housing Administration loans, with the FHA insuring the first 80 percent and the VA the remaining 20 percent. (In 1977, the VA guaranty was 60 percent of value of the home or $17,500, whichever was less; in 1978, the amount was raised to $25,000.)

While the major reliance of the VA loans was on private financial institutions, the VA was also authorized in 1950 to make direct federal loans where private financing was not available. This proved to be a small but useful program in some small towns and rural areas.

After the removal of wartime restrictions on residential construction in the fall of 1945, the Civilian Production Administration announced its Reconversion Housing Program to be effective in January 1946. Preference ratings were set up for building materials in short supply

[25] National Commission on Urban Problems, *Building American City*, Washington, D.C., December 1968, pp. 103–104.

giving preference to veterans in the construction of moderate-priced houses and apartments.

On January 26, 1945, President Truman issued an executive order establishing the Office of Housing Expediter and charged it with preparing plans and programs and recommending legislation for veterans' housing. He named Wilson W. Wyatt as its chief administrator.

In a report to the President on February 7, 1946, the Housing Expediter reported the following: In October, 1945, 1.2 million families were living doubled-up with other families; an additional 2.9 million married veterans would need homes by December 1945; more than half a million nonveterans who would marry during the course of the year would be looking for homes. In total, 3.5 million families would be looking for homes in 1946, and about 1.1 million new families would need homes in 1947. To accommodate this need, only 945,000 vacant units would be available in 1946, and 430,000 vacant units in 1947. Thus, by the end of 1946, more than 2.5 million families would need homes.[26]

On February 8, 1946, the President announced "The Veterans' Emergency Housing Program," calling for a total of 2.7 million new nonfarm homes by the end of 1947. Most of the proposals in this new program required legislation. After a difficult battle in the Congress, the new legislation was passed substantially intact, on May 22, 1946. It included provisions to (1) continue and strengthen price controls on building materials; (2) set up allocations and priorities for residential builders in purchasing equipment; and (3) provide subsidy payments to stimulate the production of building materials and equipment. A proposal to set price ceilings on the sale of existing houses and building lots was defeated. The Housing Expediter indicated his intent to stimulate expansion of factory fabrication of houses through allocation of surplus war plants and materials, and through guaranteeing the market for the product. As it progressed, the Veterans Emergency Housing Program made a substantial contribution to the increase in construction starts of new dwellings, pushing the figure to more than 1 million units in 1946. This number is contrasted with only 300,000 in 1945. But opposition to price controls and to factory fabrication of housing production, combined with the Republican gains in the 1946 election, brought an end to the program. Wyatt resigned in December, and President Truman signed an Executive Order terminating the program on January 11, 1947.[27]

After the removal of wartime restrictions on residential construction

[26] *Veterans' Emergency Housing Program: Report to the President from Wilson W. Wyatt,* Housing Expediter, February 7, 1946.

[27] Keith, *op. cit.,* pp. 60–67.

in late 1945, and emergency measures to stimulate production of building materials and equipment, the home-building industry moved quickly
to respond. The number of new permanent nonfarm dwellings during
the first six months of 1946 increased more rapidly than ever. Housing
starts for this period were greater than for all of 1945.[28] Private housing construction was on its way back and to record levels, surpassing
in 1946 the previous high year of 1925 and reaching almost 1.5 million
units annually by the end of the decade.

Significant factors in this residential construction revival were FHA-
insured and VA-guaranteed mortgage programs. The FHA, founded
in 1934, provided a permanent system of government insurance for
residential mortgages. In the period 1946–1950, FHA and VA programs assisted in financing 30 percent of all new nonfarm housing
starts. Of particular significance, the FHA assisted in financing 80
percent of all "multifamily" housing starts. A critical backstage factor
in this effort was the Federal National Mortgage Association (FNMA),
which, in its secondary mortgage market function, purchased FHA
and VA mortgages.[29]

A significant action also took place in 1946, when the Farmers
Home Administration was created in the Department of Agriculture.
While both the United States Housing Act of 1937 and the National
Housing Act of 1934 (as amended in 1938) carried provisions for
rural housing, they were relatively inactive. Establishment of a home
for rural housing in the Department of Agriculture prepared the way
for new activity when the Housing Act of 1949 expanded rural housing
beyond farms, and provided new support for expanded farm housing
support.

New activity in developing direct publicly financed and publicly
owned housing fell to the low level of 1,000 units in 1945. While it
rose slightly to 18,000 units in 1948, it remained for the Housing Act
of 1949 to help reassert activity in this area to make rural housing
programs an important part of national policy.

The Housing Act of 1949—The Unfinished Agenda

Beyond the immediate postwar housing emergencies, larger long-term
housing issues increasingly provided a topic for public dialogue beginning in 1943. World War II had diverted activities of both private
and public housing interests to more immediate concerns, but the
latent confrontations were always present. Also increasingly present
as the war crisis receded was the "Unfinished Agenda" of housing

[28] Jessup, *loc. cit.*, p. 15.
[29] Beyer, *Housing: A Factual Analysis, op. cit.*, Table 5, p. 129.

needs identified in the 1940 Census. The pressures of wartime housing activity did not encompass the needs of low-income families, nor the increasing evidences of community blight.

A variety of efforts were concerned with these needs. While the United States Housing Act of 1937, which created the public housing program, had incorporated a provision requiring the elimination of one slum dwelling for every new public housing unit built, this was a minimal effort. As the number of new public housing units declined during and after the war, that provision became almost inoperative. In 1947, the American Public Health Association (APHA) released its three-volume study setting forth a new technique for measuring the structural quality of housing. The association was responding to the 1940 Census findings that more than 18 million dwelling units needed major repairs or were without private bath.[30] But, in addition to the focus on the structural quality of individual housing units, there was an increasing focus on the quality of the residential neighborhood and on the declining physical status of communities.

Again, the American Public Health Association released in 1948 a pioneering report on "Planning The Neighborhood."[31] The concept of the neighborhood as a basic planning unit did not have universal acceptance, and the APHA report stirred critics to raise questions about its validity. A common attack suggested that "neighborhood planning" could lead to racial, ethnic, religious, or economic segregation.[32]

But, whatever the resolution of the question about the neighborhood as the appropriate planning unit, there was no question about the slum condition—many of the nation's cities had developed large blighted areas and many families were living in a poor environment. In addition, there was a recognition that the word "slum" also encompassed rural concentrations of bad dwellings. These growing conditions of blight, documented in the 1940 Census and exacerbated by the chaotic condition resulting from wartime material shortages, were increasingly recognized as a growing drain on the physical, economic, and social health of the nation. A new breed of books about redevelopment of declining cities began to appear in the 1940's and mushroomed in the 1950's.[33]

An additional major public issue jarring the American conscience in the 1940's was that of housing discrimination and segregation.

[30] American Public Health Association, *An Appraisal Method for Measuring the Quality of Housing*, 3 vols., 1947.

[31] American Public Health Association, *Planning the Neighborhood*, Public Administration Service, Chicago, 1948.

[32] Beyer, *Housing and Society, op. cit.*, p. 318.

[33] For example, see Louis Justement, *New Cities for Old.* (New York: McGraw-Hill), 1946, p. 232.

Leaders such as Robert C. Weaver (later to be the Housing and Home Finance Agency (HHFA) Administrator and first Secretary of the U. S. Department of Housing and Urban Development) contributed to this dialogue by documenting the conditions in 1940 publications.[34]

Administrator Blandford of the National Housing Agency began to move public and Congressional thinking toward postwar housing needs in 1943. In September of that year, in an interview in *Architectual Forum*, he went beyond immediate responses to wartime housing questions and talked about the future:

On the Desirability of Continuing a Consolidated Housing Agency

In my judgment, the advantages secured in war-time from a unified approach to housing apply with equal force to the post-war period, if we are to achieve a really adequate post-war housing program. There is increasing realization that housing is one, broad, interrelated problem, rather than a series of unrelated problems which can be neatly segregated into separate compartments. This realization is a reflection partly of the experience we have all gained through a unified attack on war housing; it also reflects broader recognition by all groups of the realities of the housing program. I therefore believe that teamwork and unified approach to housing should be preserved in the post-war period.

On Whether Federal Assistance for New Low-Rent Housing Should be Continued After the War

Our broad longterm objective for postwar housing must be a maximum program to provide housing for all American families. Within that framework, the challenge to private enterprise is to do as much of the job as possible. The area for privately financed operations will be limited only to the extent that private capital does not meet adequately the needs of the low-income groups. To determine the extent to which direct federal financial assistance will be required for acquisition of land and construction in post-war housing, we must have first some early indication of what part of the total need for housing can be met by private enterprise, either unaided or with only indirect assistance of insurance and secondary credit. This determination must be made by the communities themselves, operating through local housing authorities, local planning commissions, the building industry, and lending institution.[35]

Following up on this early initiative, Administrator Blandford, on March 9, 1944, set forth some of the basic principles for a peacetime housing program:

[34] Robert C. Weaver, *The Negro Ghetto.* (New York: Harcourt Brace Jovanovich), 1948.

[35] Keith, *op. cit.*, p. 46.

Housing serves human needs. The family centers around the home. The Nation centers around the family. Decent housing cannot create utopia. But decent housing is vital to the health, safety and welfare of the families of the nation.

All American families should get decent housing. This includes millions of veterans who will need homes. It includes families in rural shacks and urban slums. It includes all minority groups. We have the manpower, resources, industry, and brains to do the whole job.

The slums must go. Their economic and social cost is intolerably high. They must be replaced gradually through a rounded program which includes decent housing within the means of slum dwellers.

Housing should conserve when it can. Investments in present housing have value. Fundamentally sound housing that has commenced to run down should be rehabilitated and repaired before it is too late. Neighborhoods should be maintained, rather than discarded or allowed to decay.

The Federal Government's role in housing should be supplementary. It should do what cannot be done otherwise. It should help private enterprise to serve the largest possible portion of the nation's housing needs. Public agencies must be ready to withdraw from any area when better incomes or lower costs enable individuals, cooperatives, labor groups or business organizations to pick up the responsibility and carry it forward. But the government's role, while supplementary, involves bedrock responsibility for making sure that decent housing for all the people is gradually achieved.[36]

Also, in the Spring of 1944, the Senate Committee on Postwar Economic Policy and Planning established a subcommittee on housing and urban development, naming Senator Robert A. Taft, Republican of Ohio, as its chairman. When the subcommittee opened its hearings on June 1, 1944, with National Housing Agency (NHA) Administrator Blandford as its first witness, the five-year legislative process that was to culminate in the passage of the Housing Act of 1949 was under way.

Despite the admonition in January 1944 by Mrs. Dorothy Rosenman, chairman of the privately convened National Housing Conference, that "neither the public housing cause, nor the interests of private housing can be furthered without a united front," the series of Congressional Committee hearings and actions beginning in 1944 were the focal point for the two camps of private and public housing interests to do battle.[37]

A barrage of public statements, publications, and testimony emanated from both sources.[38] On the one side, private housing interests

[36] *Ibid.*

[37] Dorothy Rosenman, "A Truce Upon Your Housing," *Survey Graphic*, January 1944, pp. 20–22.

[38] For publications, see the bibliography at the end of this chapter.

led by the National Association of Home Builders and the National Association of Real Estate Boards (now National Association of Realtors) opposed the continuation of the National Housing Agency that was consolidated after the war, and with one exception, opposed the low-rent public housing program. On the other side, a coalition of labor, the National Public Housing Conference, the National Association of Housing Officials, the National Committee on Housing, and other "public interest" groups supported the permanent continuation of the National Housing Agency, the extension of the public housing program, the establishment of an urban redevelopment program, and a total housing effort in support of postwar housing needs projected by the NHA.[39]

The unanimous report of the Senate Subcommittee on Housing and Urban Development on August 1, 1945, under Senator Taft, later to be known as "Mr. Republican," was a major setback for the private housing interests. It recommended the continuation of the NHA, generally accepted NHA estimates of housing needs and supported the resumption of the public housing program.[40] But this was only the beginning of the struggle. In July 1947, both houses of the Congress authorized a Joint Committee to study all phases of housing. The committee conducted hearings in Washington and 32 other cities. When it reported on March 15, 1948, the majority supported and extended the recommendations of the earlier Senate Subcommittee.[41] The final passage of the bill on July 15, 1949, as the Housing Act of 1949 had many heroes, but the leadership role taken by Senator Taft was certainly the critical one.[42] The decision in the House of Representatives to sustain the public housing program as a part of the bill was a close one, 209 to 204.

As finally passed, the Housing Act of 1949 began with a new "Declaration of Purpose" that was to become the rallying cry for progressive housing forces for three decades—"a decent home and a suitable living environment for every American family." The declaration in full is:

The general welfare and security of the Nation and the health and living standards of its people require housing production and related community development sufficient to remedy the serious housing shortage, the elimination of substandard and other inadequate housing through the clearance of slums and blighted areas, and the realization as soon as feasible of the goal of a decent home and a suitable living environment for every American

39 Keith, *op. cit.*, pp. 56–57.
40 *Congress and American Housing*, *op. cit.*, pp. 37–38.
41 *Ibid.*, p. 38.
42 Keith, *op. cit.*, pp. 72–73.

family, this contributing to the development and redevelopment of communities and to the advancement of the growth, wealth, and security of the nation.

In describing the new act, the Housing and Home Finance Agency summarized as follows:

The act provides that private housing enterprise shall be encouraged to serve as large a part of the total need as it can; that local public bodies shall be encouraged to undertake positive programs to assist the development of well-planned residential neighborhoods, the development and redevelopment of communities, and the production of lower costs of housing of sound standards of design, construction, livability, and size for adequate family life; and that governmental assistance shall be given to eliminate substandard and other inadequate housing through the clearance of slums and blighted areas, to provide adequate housing needed for urban and rural non-farm families of low incomes where such need is not being met through reliance solely upon private enterprise and to provide decent, safe, and sanitary farm dwellings and related facilities where the farm owner demonstrates that he lacks sufficient resources and credit to provide such housing.[43]

The 1949 Act had six basic titles:

TITLE I—SLUM CLEARANCE AND COMMUNITY DEVELOPMENT AND REDEVELOPMENT

This title authorizes the Housing and Home Finance Administrator to make loans and grants to localities to assist locally initiated, locally planned, and locally managed slum-clearance and urban redevelopment undertakings. A local public agency would, after public hearing acquire (through purchase or condemnation) a slum or blighted or deteriorating area selected in accordance with a general city plan for the development of the locality as a whole. The local public agency would then clear the land and make it available, by sale, or lease, for private or public redevelopment or development in accordance, with a predetermined local redevelopment plan for the area.

The act authorizes $1,000,000,000 in loans over a 5-year period. Advances of funds would be available to finance the planning of local projects, and temporary loans for the acquisition and clearance of land repayable when the land is sold or leased for redevelopment. Long-term Federal loans would be available to refinance the portions of the sites which are leased and would be secured by the rentals from the leased land.

The act also authorizes $500,000,000 in federal capital grants over a 5-year period, in order to help meet the loss involved in connection with slum clearance operations. This loss would be shared on a 2 to 1 basis—the

[43] Housing and Home Finance Agency, *A Handbook of Information on the Housing Act of 1949*. Washington, D.C., July, 1948, p. 30.

federal government making up two-thirds of the loss and the local government making up one-third.

Title II—Amendments to National Housing Act

This title provides for temporary extensions (through August 31, 1949) of FHA's Title I and Section 608 mortgage insurance operations; also for a $500,000,000 increase in its Title II insurance authorization. The extensions under Title I relate to small loans for alteration and improvement and new construction and under Section 608 to rental housing. The increase in insurance authorization applies to all types of housing under Title II, owner-occupied, small and large scale rental and sale housing, including cooperative housing.

Title III—Low-Rent Public Housing

This title amends the United States Housing Act of 1937 by authorizing federal contributions and loans for local programs involving not to exceed 810,000 additional units of low-rent public housing over a 6-year period. The Public Housing Administration may authorize local authorities to commence construction of 135,000 units each year. The President, however, is authorized to accelerate the program to not more than 200,000 units per year or to retard the program to not less than 50,000 units per year, subject to the total authorization of 810,000 units, if he determines, after advice from the Council of Economic Advisers, that such action is in the public interest.

Title IV—Housing Research

This title authorizes the Housing and Home Finance Administrator to undertake and conduct technical research and studies which will promote reduction in housing construction and maintenance costs and stimulate the increased production of housing.

The research may also be concerned with improved building codes; standardized dimensions and methods for the assembly of home-building materials and equipment; improved residential design and construction; new types of materials, equipment and construction; and may relate to appraisal, credit, housing needs, demand and supply, land costs, use and improvement, and related technical and economic research. The Administrator shall also prepare estimates of national housing needs and encourage and assist localities to make studies of their own housing needs and markets and plans for housing and community development.

Title V—Farm Housing

The Secretary of Agriculture is authorized to extend financial assistance to farm owners to enable them to construct, improve, or repair farm housing or other farm buildings. This title authorizes loans aggregating $250,000,-000, contributions for a period of 5 years not exceeding $5,000,000 per year, and loans and grants for a period of 4 years totaling $25,000,000 for minor improvements and land purchases or development.

TITLE VI—MISCELLANEOUS PROVISIONS, HOUSING CENSUS

Among the miscellaneous provisions in the bill, the Director of the Census is directed to take a census of housing in 1950 and decennially thereafter.

This title amends and supercedes existing provisions for the conversion of eligible state-aided low-rent or veterans' housing projects to low-rent housing assisted under the United States Housing Act of 1937.

The National Banking Act is liberalized with respect to the authority of national banks and State member banks of the Federal Reserve System to purchase or underwrite certain obligations of local public housing and slum-clearance agencies.

Passage of this comprehensive Act in July 1949 made it possible for the decade to end on an "upbeat" as far as housing was concerned. The long-delayed actions for better housing and communities were about to begin.

Housing Status as the Decade Closed

The 1950 Census of Housing documented the trauma of the war and postwar years. It showed a total population of 151 million living in 43 million dwelling units. There was a net gain in dwelling units over 1940 of about 23 percent.[44] The largest increases came in the South Atlantic states (23 percent) and the Pacific states (49 percent) as forecast because of shifts in housing to meet defense housing needs.

The definition of housing quality was slightly altered between the two census periods. The 1940 Census enumerated housing units "needing major repairs," while the 1950 Census described "dilapidated" units. Both censuses counted lack of plumbing facilities.

The 1950 Census showed marginal improvement over 1940 in housing quality. In 1940, 38 percent of all dwelling units in the United States needed major repairs, lacked running water, or lacked private bath. This compared with 37 percent in 1950 (equating units "needing major repairs" in 1940 with "dilapidated" units in 1950). However, there was some shifting of conditions within this overall category. The proportion of housing units with a flush toilet increased from 60 percent in 1940 to 71 percent in 1950, and the number of units with a private bathtub or shower increased from 56 percent to 69 percent.

The 1950 census results revealed, however, serious conditions that required attention:

- 46 percent of dwelling units were 30 years of age or older (compared to 41 percent in 1940).

[44] Statistics for the following section are taken from the 1950 Census. U. S. Bureau of the Census, Department of Commerce, *1950 Census of Housing, Volume I, General Characteristics, United States Summary.*

- 15 percent of dwelling units were "overcrowded," with 1.01 or more persons per room (compared to 20 percent in 1940).
- 37 percent of dwelling units were dilapidated, or lacked plumbing and hot water (compared to 38 percent in 1940).

The 1950 condition can be summarized as follows:

	Total	Urban	Rural
		(In millions)	
Total Dwelling Units (occupied and vacant)	46.1	29.7	16.4
Age of Structure (30 years, 4 months or more)	20.3	13.3	7.0
Sound or Deteriorating Units (lacking plumbing or hot water)	12.1	4.5	7.6
Dilapidated Units	4.3	1.9	2.4
Units with 1.01 or More Persons in Room (overcrowded)	6.6	3.7	2.9

One of the most dramatic shifts of the decade was the increased proportion of home ownership. It rose 11 percent from 44 percent in 1946 to 55 percent in 1950 and reflected directly wartime restriction in production of housing units (see Table 4–4, Chapter 4).

The median number of persons per unit declined from 3.3 to 3.1, showing a slight trend to smaller households. The average value of a nonfarm housing unit had risen almost 150 percent, from $3,000 in 1940 to $7,400 in 1950, and the median gross rent by 56 percent, from $27 per month to $42.

As the decade of the 1940's closed, there was room for some optimism about housing progress generally, and in particular about federal government initiatives. In 1947 a degree of unity had come to the constantly reorganized federal housing agencies with the creation of the Housing and Home Finance Agency. It was headed by an administrator with "Coordinating powers" over its constituent agencies, which included the Federal Housing Administration, the Public Housing Administration, the Home Loan Bank Board, and the Federal National Mortgage Association.[45] The passage of the 1949 Housing Act created new initiatives and resources.

Moving ahead to the 1950's it was not possible to foresee that the Korean War would restrict long-term housing progress, as World War II had done in the 1940's. Nor could it be foreseen that the 1949 Act victory would provide only temporary respite from the

[45] *Congress and American Housing, op. cit.,* p. 35.

private–public housing confrontation. In reporting on the passage of the act in October 1949, Lee F. Johnson warned: "The attack on slum clearance and public housing has shifted from Washington to every city, town, and rural area in the country."[46] This fact was confirmed in an article in *Savings and Loan News of August,* 1950, subtitled ". . . Why Political Housing, Even Though a Law is on the Statute Books, Needn't be a Reality in Your Community."[47] The high promise of the 1949 Act, in particular that for the public housing program, was subject to future disappointments. But these are stories for the 1950's.

Bibliography

Books

ABRAMS, CHARLES, *The Future of Housing.* New York: Harper and Row, 1946, 428 pp.

American Public Health Association, *An Appraisal Method for Measuring the Quality of Housing,* 3 vols. 1947.

BEYER, GLENN H., *Housing and Society.* New York: Macmillan, 1965, 595 pp.

———, *Housing a Factual Analysis,* New York: Macmillan, 1958, 355 pp.

COLEAN, M. L., *American Housing Problems and Prospects: The Factual Analysis,* Twentieth Century Fund, New York, 1944, 466 pp.

Congress and American Housing, 1892–1967, Washington, D.C.: United States Government Printing Office, 1968, 50 pp.

Housing and Home Finance Agency, a Handbook of Information on The Housing Act of 1949, Washington, D.C., July 1949, 30 pp.

KEITH, NATHANIEL S., *Politics and The Housing Crisis Since 1930.* New York: Universe Books, 1973, 232 pp.

JUSTEMENT, LOUIS, *New Cities For Old.* New York: McGraw-Hill 1946, 232 pp.

LASCH, ROBERT, *Breaking the Building Blockade.* Chicago: University of Chicago Press, 1946, 316 pp.

National Association of Housing Officials, *Housing for the United States After the War,* May 1944, 65 pp.

ROSENMAN, DOROTHY, *A Million Homes A Year.* New York: Harcourt Brace Jovanovich, 1945, 333 pp.

STRAUSS, NATHAN, *The Seven Myths of Housing.* New York: Knopf, 1944, 314 pp.

WEAVER, ROBERT C., *The Negro Ghetto.* New York: Harcourt Brace Jovanovich, 1948, 404 pp.

---

[46] L. F. Johnson, "Victory at Last for Housing," *Survey,* October 1949, pp. 438–442.

[47] "Government Housing Set-Backs," *Savings and Loan News,* August, 1950, pp. 14–17.

Periodicals

Architectural Forum
  "Public Housing and The United States Housing Agency—Arguments of
  Public Housing's Proponents and Opponents," January 1940, p. 2–12.
Duns Review
  S. J. Dennis, "The Housing Shortage-Causes and Effects," June 1946, p.
  11–16.
Federal Home Loan Bank Board Review
  "The Houses We Live In: New Results of the 1940 Census," May 1942,
  pp. 259–263.
  "Defense Housing: A Proving Ground for New Ideas in Construction,"
  September 1941, pp. 402–406.
Fortune Magazine
  "The Industry Capitalism Forgot," August 1947, pp. 61–67, 167–170.
  Special Issues on "Housing," January 1947 and August 1947.
Insured Mortgage Portfolio
  "Potential Technical Development of Post-War Houses," September 1943,
  pp. 24–25ff.
  P. H. Cormick, "FHA and Urban Decentralization," December 1941, pp.
  32–35ff.
  "FHA Experience with Rental Housing," April 1940, pp. 11–12.
  "New National Census of Housing," September 1939 and January 1940,
  page 15ff.
Law and Contemporary Problems
  Special Issue on "Housing," January 1947.
Monthly Labor Review
  M. H. Schoenfeld, "Progress of Public Housing in the United States,"
  August 1949, pp. 267–282.
  M. F. Jessup, "Trends in Housing During the War and Post-War Period,"
  January 1947.
  "Defense Housing Program," Housing Committee, Twentieth Century
  Fund, December, 1940, pp. 1412–1416.
Municipal Yearbook
  "Housing Developments," American Municipal Association.
National Association of Housing Officials (NAHO)
  B. M. Pettit, "The Housing Honeymoon Is Over; Slum Clearance Has
  Begun," September 1943, p. 3.
NAHO News
  H. G. Brunsman, "The Housing Census of 1940," August–September
  1941, p. 46–47, 66–67.
Journal of Housing
  L. N. Bloomberg, "What Has Happened to The Quality of The Hous-
  ing Supply Since 1940," July 1946, pp. 137–138.
  "D-Day in Housing: Taft Subcommittee Report," August 1945, pp.
  127–129ff.
  "Realtors, Home Builders, U. S. Chamber of Commerce Challenge Ad-

ministrator John B. Blandford, Jr., on Public Housing," November 1944, pp. 19–21.

National Real Estate Journal

"Hobert Brady answers Nathan Strauss," April 1944, pp. 16–19.

J. B. Blandford, Jr., "Our Post-War Housing Job," June 1943, pp. 10–15.

Pre-Fabricated Housing

"Survey and Recommendations on Post-War Housing," Twentieth Century Fund, April 1944, pp. 10–11.

Public Housing (Superintendent of Documents)

"Public Housing Goes to War," April 1942, pp. 1–4.

Savings and Loans News

"Government Housing Set-Backs: These Instances of an Impressive Number of Private Enterprise Victories Indicate Why Political Housing, Even Though a Law Is on the Statute Books, Needn't Be a Reality in Your Community," August 1950, pp. 14–17.

M. L. Colean, "Building A Post-War Housing Policy," March 1943, pp. 4–6.

Survey

L. F. Johnson, "Victory at Last for Housing: How the 1949 Act Got Through the Congress with But Five Votes to Spare, and the New Possibilities It Brings to the Unhoused Public," October 1949, pp. 538–542.

Survey Graphic

Dorothy Rosenman, "A Truce Upon Your Housing," January 1944, pp. 20–22.

Special Issue on "Homes," February 1940.

CHAPTER 6

A NATIONAL POLICY ON FEDERAL INTERVENTION IN MORTGAGE FINANCE AND COMMUNITY DEVELOPMENT

MILES L. COLEAN*

Vastness, Complexity, and Inconsistency of Federal Intervention

DURING twenty years of Democratic Administration, the federal government has intervened at almost every point in residential mortgage financing as well as in numerous ways that affect the de-

* MILES COLEAN earned a degree in architecture from Columbia University but became known as an economic consultant to firms and trade associations, among them notably the Mortgage Banker's Association of America, and mortgage financing institutions. He has written books and articles in the field.
Early in 1952, when General Eisenhower was contemplating running for the Presidency on the Republican ticket, he asked Aksel Nielsen of Denver, who for many years had been his close friend and financial advisor, to inform him of

velopment of cities. Activities and agencies have been added from year to year as new issues have developed or new pressures were exerted. More than twenty federal agencies and subagencies are concerned with these activities; and successive administrative reorganizations have only increased the number.

The federal program has been improvised in a progression of crises —the mortgage crisis and the depression of construction in the 1930's; the growth of slums during depression and war; the defense housing crisis of the early 1940's; the postwar housing shortage; the inflation crisis of 1950; the defense housing crisis of 1951 and 1952.

The federal influence, though pervasive, is without a recognizable settled policy. No principle for intervention has been established; and, under the circumstances, no limit to the expansion of the Federal jurisdiction is discernible. Conflicts and inconsistencies are manifold. For example: (1) two mortgage insurance and guarantee systems compete for private investment funds; (2) at the height of the postwar inflation, the mortgage policy was at odds with any idea of credit restraint; (3) public housing policies have at many points—from standards and costs to location of projects—been in conflict with the mortgage insurance systems and with local plans, opinion, and custom; and (4) public housing tax-free financing has been in conflict with the Treasury policy of reducing the volume of tax-free issues and in competition with private financing in the tight money market of 1951 and 1952. These are only a few of the many such instances that might be cited.

Although this area of national policy may appear to be of a specialized character, its political implications are so deep and its range of influence on the whole private economy so broad that it should stand in the forefront of the issues with which a new Administration must deal.

Questions Demanding Policy Determination

The federal government is now too deeply involved to withdraw. It can either move forward as it has in the past, allowing interventionary measures to accumulate through a succession of emergencies, or undertake to establish a consistent policy by which its future activity may be guided and limited.

A consistent federal policy cannot be accomplished by an effort to gloss over the deep inner conflicts—such as the clumsy and half-hearted

---

government policies related to housing and to make recommendation for changes. Aksel Nielsen then asked Miles Colean to help prepare a memorandum that would serve the General's purposes in this respect. This chapter is the memorandum that was prepared and sent to Aksel Nielsen in May of 1952.

attempt at coordination by the Housing and Home Finance Agency. It can be achieved only by a careful review of the present extent and methods of Federal intervention and a reconsideration of principles by which the federal function should be determined, followed by appropriate legislation.

Such review and reconsideration are long overdue. A change in Administration provides not only an ideal but also probably the only opportunity for a major readjustment of program.

The following are the areas where new policy determinations are most needed.

Federal Aid to States and Municipalities for Public Housing, Urban Redevelopment, Schools, Hospitals, and Other Community Facilities

Federal aid has so far been made in the form of capital grants, loans, and, in the case of public housing, annual "contributions to make up for operating deficits." Aid is granted by agreements with the states except for public housing, urban redevelopment, and airport construction, *where agreements are made directly with local bodies.* Involved are such agencies as the Public Housing Administration, the Housing and Home Finance Agency, the Federal Security Agency, the Bureau of Public Roads, and the Civil Aeronautics Administration.

The main policy questions are: To what extent should such aid be given? In what manner should the aid be provided? Should all such aid be handled by federal–state agreements or should federal–local agreements be permitted? How much control should the federal government exercise over the details of the use of the money it has donated or loaned?

Federal Influence on the Supply of Mortgage Funds for Private Home Purchase and Rental Housing

This area concerns the chartering and supervisory functions of the *Home Loan Bank Board*, the loan functions of the *Home Loan Banks*, the mortgage insurance functions of the *Federal Housing Administration*, the guarantee, insurance, and lending functions of the *Veterans' Administration*, the loan purchase function of the *Federal National Mortgage Association*, and the credit control functions of the *Federal Reserve Board and the Housing and Home Finance Agency*.

Here there are a number of profound questions to be considered (aside from the important question of coordination to be discussed later): Is it desirable to continue these functions in their present form, or at all? Should the federal government, through these various means, attempt directly to influence the volume of new building and the types of houses erected? Should it use the FNMA and the provision of direct loans as a means of maintaining a submarket interest rate on certain classes of loans? Should the federal government provide a secondary mortgage facility as a means of assuring greater stability to the flow of private mortgage funds?

Federal Control Over Private Construction and Real Estate Investment

Most directly concerned here are the emergency powers over the use of materials, prices, rent, and mortgage credit. There is general agreement that the present emergency controls on materials will be removed as rapidly as increased supplies become available. The continuance of price control, however, though only a standby basis, is resolutely sought by the present Administration, while rent control has become so involved in political pressure that its future removal can be accomplished only by greater courage than has so far been manifested. Selective credit controls on consumer financing and real estate loans also are devices of great appeal to economic planners. The decision on the continuance of authority to impose these controls will have to be made early in the next Administration.

Federal Advisory and Consultive Services

Federal advisory and consultive services, backed by technological and economic research, are offered by *Public Roads*, *Civil Aeronautics*, *Housing and Home Finance*, *FHA*, *National Bureau of Standards*, *Bureau of the Census*, *Bureau of Foreign and Domestic Commerce*, and the *Bureau of Labor Statistics*. Without interfering with private decisions, such services can aid in advancing building techniques and in alerting builders and lenders to the characteristics of their markets. The extent, nature, and reliability of these services, due to the lack of policy, has varied widely from year to year. Serious consideration of this area is badly needed.

The Appropriate Organization for Administering the Continuing Functions of the Federal Government

It is obvious that not all the diverse agencies dealing in one way or another with mortgage credit and community facilities should be combined in one superagency; and it is the considered judgment that the combination of incongruous elements has already gone too far, particularly in HHFA with its mixture of credit functions, welfare functions, and public works functions within policymaking, coordinating, and operating activities. The present organization has proven cumbersome, costly, and confusing and has as frequently provided a means for avoiding decisions as for making them. The problem of what to do in this situation should be resolved before a new set of officials develop a new interest in its preservation. Other questions of organization will arise, particularly as regards research and advisory facilities.

Recommendations

General Policy

Every effort should be made, by reconsideration of the tax system and otherwise, to lessen the dependence of the states and localities upon the federal government for financial aid.

Where financial aid for community development is provided, it should, wherever possible, be granted through the states according to a set formula (as is done with the highway program); and the widest possible leeway should be given to states and localities in determining the details of expenditures.

In respect to mortgage credit, the federal policy should be one of aiding to stabilize the flow and equalize the distribution of private funds. It should not be one of exercising direct and detailed influence on the building market, or of entering the lending market directly or indirectly with government funds, or of attempting to regulate the rate of interest by arbitrary devices.

Direct control of building and lending by regulating the use of materials or the terms of loan transactions should be avoided, reliance being placed rather on general monetary controls. Rent control should be ended.

Greater attention should be given to strengthening the private building and financing systems by providing technological and market information.

Separation of Credit and Welfare Functions

The mere fact that both public subsidy and private credit deal with housing is an unwise basis for their combination in a single agency. The welfare function and the credit function are as different as it is possible to be. The first depends for its operation on an individual, official judgment of need. It is entirely apart from the market economy. The second depends on the operation of market forces and is itself an important element in the market economy.

Mortgage credit is a part of the general credit and monetary system of the country. It is activated in the same way as other credit operations are activated—by an evaluation of risk and a payment of interest, with the interest rate fluctuating according to the market economy— the only way that an adequate supply of mortgage money can be assured is to permit mortgage borrowers to compete freely for funds with other borrowers.

As originally conceived, FHA mortgage insurance was simply a device which, by spreading risk and insuring risk (through a payment of the borrower), improved the competitive position of mortgage borrowers. FHA insurance in no way altered or interfered with market forces. While its government auspices permitted it to start full grown with national coverage, its function was entirely compatible with a private credit system, and it involved nothing that could not ultimately have been accomplished by private means.

The Home Loan Bank system was also entirely private both in its conception and in the methods of its operation. Its member institutions are all private institutions financed with private savings. The regional banks are now entirely owned by the member institutions. The only distinctive governmental function involved is to see that the flow of credit from the regional banks to member institutions is regulated in a manner compatible with the government's general credit and monetary policies.

Despite these characteristics, neither FHA nor the Bank System, as presently organized, have any direct relationship with the general credit and monetary authorities. Instead they are combined with a distinctly welfare function—public housing—and they are operated mainly from a welfare point of view rather than a credit point of view. That is to say, a measurement of risk tends to be replaced by an official judgment of need; an effort is made to determine interest rate and other mortgage terms not by what is necessary to attract private investment but by an official judgment of what an interest rate ought to be, irrespective of market conditions.

The only way that a credit system can be operated on a welfare basis is to substitute government support for market appeal. The result, as is now rapidly becoming evident, is a public credit system, operated independently of the financial market, in which funds are not bid for but are distributed according to official decisions as to who ought to get the money. Followed to the end, this kind of credit system becomes a political instrument of the powerful and dangerous sort.

So long as the FHA and the Home Loan Bank system are subjected to a welfare point of view—which is inevitable so long as the present administrative organization prevails—the trend toward a political credit system is unavoidable.

It is equally true that the public housing function cannot be subjected to the principles of private credit. Its whole basis—the selection of special groups for special public benefits—is entirely inconsistent with those principles. As a thing apart from the private market system, it is better to keep it apart in administrative organization so that it can be clearly recognized for what it is and operated accordingly, and so that present confusion in the underlying disparity of functions can be eliminated.

On these considerations, it is recommended that the HHFA be eliminated, and, the operating agencies be regrouped as suggested below.

Aid for Community Development

Federal aid to cities should have the main objective of eliminating existing slums and assuring the continuous renewal of the urban structure in order that our cities may be efficient centers of business and culture and healthful, convenient, and attractive places in which to live.

The present rigid formulas for aid for public housing and urban redevelopment should be modified so as to provide for greater state and local responsibility and to permit greater scope to state and local initiative.

All aid should be in the form of loans or capital grants, subject annually to the control of the Appropriations Committees of the Congress.

Aid should be granted through the states on a prorata basis according to nonfarm population and should be administered by a Bureau of Community Development under the jurisdiction of the Secretary of Commerce. The Department of Commerce is recommended as the proper place for such an agency because it now has jurisdiction over related functions of highway and airport development and because it contains important research and informational bureaus relating to community development.

Status of Mortgage Credit Agencies

The Home Loan Bank Board and the Federal Housing Administration should be returned to independent operating status. The Veterans' Loan Guarantee Service should remain in the Veterans' Administration but should be given divisional status in that agency.

There is no savings or administrative advantage to be gained from a "coordinating" agency involving these instrumentalities. They have different functions, and they largely deal with different types of lending institutions. There is nothing to "coordinate" between them. Between the FHA and VA systems more similarity exists, and a greater coordination of appraisal and inspection practices of the two would be desirable. This, however, can be accomplished without administrative union. Because the VA system is temporary and because it deals with a special group of borrowers, it is recommended that it remain separate from the program of FHA, which is designed to be available to all, over an indefinite period of time.

The FHA system should be greatly simplified. By almost annual accretions of new formulas designed to meet special ideas and passing fancies, the fundamental concept of a mutual insurance system based upon an appraisal of risks has been badly obscured. This basic concept should be restored.

The Federal National Mortgage Association

It is recommended that the Federal National Mortgage Association be established as a federally chartered institution for the purpose of stabilizing the mortgage market by the purchase and sale of FHA and VA loans. Its capital would be subscribed by lending institutions using the FHA and VA systems, and it would have authority to issue debentures to provide additional funds for the purchase of FHA and VA mortgages.

The Association should have a board of directors selected by the President, each of whom should be experienced in mortgage lending, but none of whom is an official of another federal agency.

Open Market Committee of the Federal Reserve System

In order fully to coordinate the policies of the federal mortgage credit agencies with those of the central monetary and credit authorities, it should be required that the heads of the mortgage credit agencies consult with and follow the policies of the Open Market Committee of the Federal Reserve System on the following matters:

1. Interest rates on FHA and VA insured and guaranteed mortgages.
2. Interest rates on debentures issued by FHA foreclosed properties.
3. Interest rates charged by the Home Loan Banks.
4. Interest rates on debentures issued by the Home Loan Banks and the Federal National Mortgage Association and the volume of debentures issued.
5. Prices offered by the FNMA for purchase and sale of FHA and VA mortgages.

Research and Information

The Federal government should, as a means of assuring sound public policy and of giving adequate guidance for private decisions, maintain appropriate statistics on the building and mortgage lending situations. It should also provide information on and evaluations of research in building technology, recommend programs of further research, and, in the absence of private facilities for the purpose, conduct such research.

No research activity should be under the jurisdiction of, or be financed by funds provided by, an operating agency. The Research Division of HHFA should be abolished.

Statistical research should be conducted by the Bureau of the Census and the Bureau of Labor Statistics, based on recommendations of a committee to be established in the Bureau of the Budget, composed of representatives of the operating agencies and of interested private groups.

Technological research information should be based on programs approved by the Building Research Advisory Board (a privately financed subsidiary of the National Academy of Sciences, composed of representatives of government and industry) and the Bureau of Standards and the Forest Products Laboratory.

CHAPTER 7
FEDERAL HOUSING PROGRAMS: 1950–1960

ALBERT M. COLE*

Introduction

THE HISTORY of the federal government housing program in the 1950 decade is one of transition—how the new administration met its responsibility, how it succeeded sometimes and how it failed sometimes, how it encouraged reliance on private enterprise and local initiative and less federal intrusion into housing and urban affairs. Many years earlier the Great Depression with its attendant suffering,

* ALBERT M. COLE is a lawyer, former Congressman, Administrator of the Housing and Home Finance Agency (1953–1959), and President, Reynolds Metals Development Corporation.

The author acknowledges the interest with which Dr. Gertrude S. Fish reviewed and edited the manuscript.

277

apprehension, and tension had set the stage for government intervention. When General Eisenhower became President in 1953, major
shifts of policy were expected, as the Republican party had made an
issue of deficit spending and federal intervention in housing.

In 1950 President Truman had curtailed housing credit and public
housing construction to conserve materials for the Korean War and to
reduce inflationary tendencies. The first three years of the decade were
a period of waiting, an interlude between the high promise of a decent
home made by the 1949 Housing Act and the end of the war.

During those years Congress, however, had enacted several significant laws: appropriation of funds for the purchasing of mortgages
by the Federal National Mortgage Association (FNMA), for defense
housing, and for cooperative housing; an incentive to homeownership
(1951) by amending Section 1034 of the Internal Revenue Code allowing the taxpayer deferment of capital gains realized through the
sale of the principal residence; transfer of FNMA from the Reconstruction Finance Corporation (RFC) to the Housing and Home Finance
Agency (HHFA); and termination of the Home Owners Loan Corporation (HOLC).

President Eisenhower had promised in his political campaign to
initiate policies that would be liberal in their benefits to people. When
the time came to appoint an Administrator of the Housing and Home
Finance Agency, he selected Albert M. Cole, a rather conservative
member of Congress serving on the House Banking Committee, who
had energetically opposed the public housing section and had voted
against the Housing Act of 1949.

Strong opposition to the confirmation arose in the Senate, and Senator Humphrey called the appointment "like putting a fox in the chicken
coop." The hearing in the Senate Banking and Currency Committee
and debate on the floor of the Senate crackled with deep concern. In
many quarters he was deemed too conservative, and his opposition to
public housing became the focal point in the debate. However, the
nomination was confirmed, a pivotal factor being the support of Senator
Robert Taft, a major public housing advocate. He had elicited a promise
from Cole that the public housing law would be administered fully
in fact and in spirit.

On March 11, 1952 the new Administrator of the Housing and
Home Finance Agency was sworn in by President Eisenhower. The
President told me in a private chat: "As you know, we don't have a
housing program. But more and better housing is a very important
part of the plans this Administration wants to develop, so . . . I want
you to look over the agency carefully and come back and recommend
what types of program you think we should present to Congress."

After 20 Democratic years, this was a Republican's first view from the "inside." It was not, however, the horror scene the opposition had predicted, for the operations were quite efficient and the staff excellent.

Program Development

The HHFA organization, policies, regulations, programs, and results were scrutinized and evaluated through, among other activities, one-to-one staff discussions, conferences with the Bureau of the Budget, and meetings with constituent Commissioners. A study was designed by the Agency which encompassed a four-pronged approach—government, industry, the public interest, and nongovernmental expertise.[1]

After obtaining some perspective from this study, the Agency then, in a second stage, proceeded to elicit ideas, opinions, and suggestions from a wide spectrum of people and organizations. As spring faded into the Washington summer, this materialized in a series of conferences in Washington with the representatives of most of the major interest groups in housing. The Washington conferences had been unofficially dubbed "shirt-sleeve conferences." The Agency was a magnet —and often a repellent—for a wide range of political, social, and economic segments of our national life. The result was an interesting, provocative, but affirmative effort to assist the new Administration.

Meetings were also held in cities around the country "to get the view of those who own and rent homes as well as those who provide them," seeking discussions of long-range problems in housing. "The purpose of the community meeting," our announcement said, "is to enable me to hear directly from a good many people of all walks of life, what they think of the housing situation in terms of the homes and neighborhoods where they live. . . ."

Conferences were held in Chicago, Omaha, San Francisco, Albuquerque, and continued in Dallas, Memphis, Miami, New York City, and New Orleans. In short, from the West Coast to the East Coast countless numbers of persons had an opportunity to be heard. The reactions from the participants—taxicab drivers, civic leaders, real estate men, bankers, union and religious leaders, minority groups—were varied. The agency heard complaints about lack of mortgage funds. Suggestions were made to permit the Federal Housing Administration (FHA) and the Veterans Administration (VA) mortgage note rates to seek the "market level" in order to compete with other investments, while others demanded that government control interest rates. A contention was made that FHA rehabilitation loans were too restrictive.

[1] See Chapter 4 by Fish: President Hoover's Conference on Home Building and Home Ownership in 1932.

The National Association for the Advancement of Colored People (NAACP) proposed federal regulations to prevent discrimination by lending institutions against Negroes.

The audience in Dallas, composed of approximately 200 people was remarkable because those in attendance applauded each speaker, regardless of his view. That conference, according to the *Dallas Morning News* (August 12, 1953), "appeared to be split along two lines— namely, those in favor of, and those opposed to federal housing." The statements ranged from a flat demand that "the government get out of the housing field" to impassioned pleas that Uncle Sam "pitch in and build thousands more low-cost housing units."

The President's Advisory Committee on Government Housing Policies and Programs

In September 1953, President Eisenhower established an Advisory Committee to advise the Administrator of the Housing and Home Finance Agency and the President on government housing policies and programs. The research and studies undertaken within the Agency as well as the findings of the "shirt-sleeve conferences" were the guidelines used for the agenda. The topics dealt with by the Advisory Committee included FHA and VA housing programs, urban development, rehabilitation and conservation, housing credit facilities, and the organization of federal housing activities in the federal government.

The Administrator was designated as chairman, and 22 people, recognized as authorities in housing, were selected as members. The committee was divided into six groups. The Executive Committee was chaired by the Administrator; subcommittees on FHA and VA Housing Programs by Rodney M. Lockwood; on Urban Redevelopment, Rehabilitation and Conservation by James W. Rouse; on Housing for Low-Income Families by Ernest J. Bohn; on Housing Credit Facilities by George L. Bliss; on Organization of Federal Housing Activities in the Federal Government by Aksel Nielson. The other members of the committees were executives with background in mortgage banking,

FIGURE 7–1. The President's Advisory Committee on Government Housing Policies and Programs. ALBERT M. COLE, *Chairman.*
1, George L. Bliss; 2, Ernest. J. Bohn; 3, Ehnes A. Camp, Jr.; 4, Miles L. Colean (not shown); 5, A. R. Gardner; 6, Richard J. Gray; 7, Richard G. Hughes; 8, Rodney M. Lockwood; 9, William A. Marcus; 10, Norman P. Mason; 11, Robert M. Morgan; 12, Thomas W. Moses; 13, Aksel Nielsen; 14, Robert B. Patrick; 15, James W. Rouse; 16, Bruce C. Savage; 17, John J. Scully; 18, Alexander Summer; 19, James G. Thiromes; 20, Ralph T. Walker; 21, Paul R. Williams (not shown); 22, Ben H. Wooten; 23, W. Herbert Welch, *Executive Director.*

real estate, labor, banks, savings and loan associations, home building, lumber, architecture, and financing.

Throughout the work of the Advisory Committee the debates often were vigorous and, at times, acrimonious. This, coupled with some hyperorthodoxy tendencies among the committee members, permitted no naps during the discussions. However, in the debate over public housing, Ernest Bohn, a long-time fighter for public housing, convinced Bruce Savage—a real estate broker and anti-public housing—so completely that Bruce became a "born again" evangelist, and was later appointed Commissioner of Public Housing. James Rouse—later developer of Columbia—had a hand in persuading Aksel Neilson—businessman and friend of the President—to approve billions of dollars of federal funds for cities. The members of the committee had all studied the massive and seemingly unyielding problems and had arrived at an amazing consensus.

Three months later the committee presented a report[2] to the President recommending action in five main areas:
  • Reorganization of the Housing and Home Finance Agency.
  • Special assistance for families of low income.
  • A vigorous attack on slums.
  • The effective maintenance and utilization of existing housing.
  • A steady increase in the volume of building of new homes.

The outstanding characteristic of the change evidenced by the committee on housing policy was, perhaps, the insistence upon the comprehensive thrust of programs to alleviate urban problems. "No single recommendation of the Committee could be considered an adequate solution in itself," the report stated. "A piecemeal attack on slums simply will not work—occasional thrusts at slum pockets in one section of the city will only push slums to other sections unless an effective program exists for attacking the entire problem of urban decay." "It must be reemphasized that these recommendations are a part of a comprehensive program and that no one, nor even an exclusive grouping of these recommendations can serve to accomplish the aims of the Committee."

The report was published and widely distributed to Congress, the Executive branch of the government and to national and local organizations with great fanfare. It became the basis for the Agency's recommendation to the President for the Administration's housing program.

While all of the planning and policy formation was going on, the

2 The President's Advisory Committee on Government Housing Policies and Program—A Report to the President—Superintendent of Documents, U. S. Government Printing Office. December 1953.

regular bureaucratic activities of government agencies ground inexorably forward. The Bureau of the Budget was making decisions about money for public housing, decisions that would restrict the ability of the HHFA Administrator to carry out the new plans. The Bureau of the Budget was the arm of the President in the decision process. All of the agencies and departments had to submit their recommendations to the Bureau of the Budget which made the final decision, subject to the President's approval. That is, the Bureau made the decision, and the Agency was bound by it unless appealed to and overturned by the President. By the latter part of December 1953 all recommendations of all agencies and departments had been considered, all controversies had been negotiated and settled, billions of dollars allocated and justified, and the huge document (the size of the Washington, D.C. telephone Yellow Page book) with thousands of entries completed. The document was ready to be sent to the Government Printing Office—it was "locked-up" in the term of the Bureau. The Bureau of the Budget had decided in the transition period and in the absence of policy guidelines, that funds for 20,000 public housing units be allocated. This conflicted with the figure of 35,000 that had been recommended by the Agency in order to show active support of public housing by the Administration. Thus, the burden was put upon the Administrator of HHFA if a change was to be made in this figure. I asked for an appointment with the President to appeal for a modification in the decision to limit public housing units to 20,000 per year.

The Oval Office of the White House is a special place, with a special environment. The atmosphere seemed particularly dramatic late that December evening as the President stood ready to switch on the lights of the traditional Christmas tree in the Ellipse. Five minutes before the last official act of the day, three men entered the office: Roland Hughes, Deputy Director of the Bureau of the Budget; Sherman Adams, Chief of Staff of the White House, and myself.

I pointed out that the Administration had announced its approval of 35,000 units each year, and that, while the 15,000-unit difference might not be too significant, it demonstrated good faith toward offering more hope to the low-income people for the goal of decent housing. The President was also reminded that he had said to Treasury Secretary, George Humphrey, at a Cabinet meeting: "Now, George, we are going to be liberal toward people and conservative toward economics."

The Deputy Director of the Budget urged that the 20,000 figure be retained—that to "unlock" the budget at this late moment would cause tremendous mechanical as well as fiscal maladjustments. The President was reminded of the need to restrict spending which had heretofore been too expansive. I countered that this decision would be the key to the Administration's policy. After a few moments of silent contemplation, the President turned to Mr. Hughes and asked that the budget be unlocked to add the increased number of units—turned again, pressed a button, and the Christmas tree glowed in the Ellipse.

Housing Act of 1954

The President's special message on housing delivered to Congress in January 1954 was the first public announcement of what the Administration intended to do in the housing program. The message followed the major recommendations of the Advisory Committee. It emphasized the need for broader programs to assist the conservation and rehabilitation of salvageable areas of our cities, together with liberalization of FHA mortgage insurance programs for low-income families displaced by slum clearance and other activities; reorganization of FNMA with private funding and, finally, authority to the President to adjust the terms of insured and guaranteed mortgages.

In synchronization with the President's message, the Agency had been busily drafting the new legislation, consulting with and securing the approval of leaders in Congress and the involved agencies of the Executive Branch and, also, the President. The legislation was introduced in the House by Rep. Jesse Wolcott (R) at the 83rd Congress, and a companion bill by Senator Homer Capehart (R) in the Senate. The legislation moved through Congress with unusual speed for such a major program, and the debate disclosed an unexpectedly narrow gap of disagreement.

But once more the continuing "contest of unit numbers" took the stage during the consideration of the bill. Despite the President's urging that the Congress authorize 35,000 units of public housing during each of the next four years, there was widespread talk of defeat of the housing program and of the personal setback the President might suffer. This resulted from reports that Congress would approve only 20,000 units. The possibility of defeat was reinforced by the fact that the Senate and the House bills, while containing provisions to carry out the other housing programs of the President, had no authorization for public housing. The Administration's position was that a request for a new authorization for the 35,000 units was unnecessary because the Act of 1949 had approved 135,000, a sufficient umbrella to cover the full 35,000. It should be noted that while "authorizations" grant permission to build, "appropriations" grant the funds to build.

Although it was leaked that the Bureau of the Budget was secretly hoping for the Appropriations Committee to keep the level at 20,000, the Administrator of HHFA was steadfastly trying to justify the Administration's position for support of public housing at 35,000 units yearly. Through careful negotiations with Congress the Agency was able to obtain an appropriation for 35,000 units with the proviso that this limit would not be exceeded in ensuing years. "By the skin of our teeth," one agency official—with deference to Thornton Wilder—described the successful negotiations between the leaders of Congress, the White House staff and the Agency. The 35,000 level continued through the entire decade, though the battle had to be refought each year (Figure 7–2).

Although there was no strong opposition to the passage of the bill, nevertheless the minority members of the House Banking Committee filed a "Minority Report" to H.R. 7839 (83rd Congress, 2nd Session, Report 1429, March 29, 1954). It detailed "fundamental disagreement" with the majority, including: (1) failure to maintain traditional veterans housing preferences; (2) failure to provide a realistic workable secondary market (FNMA requirement of a 3 percent contribution by the lender); (3) delegation to the President of control of real estate credit (to set maximum interest rates on FHA and VA mortgages); (4) failure to authorize any units of public housing; (5) failure to establish safeguards against mortgaging out; and (6) failure to require builders to provide home buyers a warranty.

The bill was passed and became law in August 1954.

The legislation was enacted with the purpose of placing greater reliance on private rather than governmental action. The Act included several liberalizing amendments to the FHA mortgage insurance programs designed to attract private investment in urban areas. The Federal National Mortgage Association was rechartered to be funded by private rather than federal capital with the intent that, in time, the Association would become a private corporation. A new urban renewal program was designed to place the major responsibility for development upon the private sector. A voluntary home mortgage credit program under which private financing institutions undertook to make mortgages available where needed, particularly in remote areas, was added.

To carry out the policy of substantial increase in local responsibility, the Act provided that a community was required to have a workable program for eliminating and preventing slums and blight before new contracts for public housing, slum clearance, and urban renewal programs would be approved. New public housing contracts were to be made available only for communities where a slum clearance and urban redevelopment or urban renewal project was being carried out with federal assistance, and only if the local governing body certified that the housing project was needed to assist in meeting the relocation requirements of those displaced by the project.

The Advisory Committee had suggested the possibility that it might take 200 years to accomplish slum clearance if the 1953 rate were maintained. Faced with that grim prognosis, the 1954 Act contained

HOUSING AND HOME FINANCE AGENCY

OFFICE OF THE ADMINISTRATOR • *Washington 25, D. C.*

MAR 23 1954

MEMORANDUM TO: Sherman Adams
                 The Assistant to the President
                 The White House

SUBJECT   : Public Housing Program for the Next Fiscal Year

       You will recall, of course, that the President strongly urged
that the Congress authorize the construction of 35,000 public housing
units during each of the next four fiscal years. Because the present
limitations in law on the public housing program are the result of
riders to the appropriations act, it has been decided that action should
properly be taken to implement the President's recommendation by the
House Appropriations Committee. Both Mr. Slusser and I urged
Congressman Phillips and his subcommittee to adopt the President's
recommendations.

       I am now advised that the committee will probably recommend
only 20,000 units for the 1955 fiscal year and 13,000 units for the 1956
fiscal year. The appropriations bill carrying out these recommendations
will probably be reported on Friday, March 26.

       The President's program for public housing is a matter of
great importance to all of the public interest groups interested in the
provision of housing for low income families. Failure on the part of
the Congress to accept his recommendations is bound, in my judgment, to
raise serious criticism in these quarters.

       I am advising you of the present situation because I am
confident that the expected action on the part of the House Appropriations
Committee will cause considerable questioning of the President himself at
his next press conference. You may therefore want to consider supplying
the President with a carefully prepared written statement which he can
use to answer inquiries from the press. If you decide that such a
statement should be prepared we will be glad to furnish a draft for your
consideration.

       I am sending a copy of this memorandum directly to Mr. Hagerty
since I am sure he will want to discuss the matter with you.

Albert M. Cole
Administrator

FIGURE 7–2. Memo to Sherman Adams, March 23, 1954.

sections designed to accelerate programs of conservation and rehabilitation, new and more liberal FHA mortgage insurance programs,
as well as expanded financial assistance to help the communities stem
the tide of blight.

Notable among these programs were two new ideas authorizing

FHA mortgage insurance to assist in the rehabilitation of existing dwellings as well as construction of new dwellings in slum clearance and urban renewal areas.

As authorized by the Housing Act of 1954, the recommendations for the Agency reorganization, assistance to low-income families, an all-out attack on slums, maintenance of existing housing, and development of new construction made by the President's Advisory Committee, were implemented by HHFA.

Five Areas for Action

Reorganization of the Housing and Home Finance Agency

The Housing and Home Finance Agency reorganization was the result of a long effort to bring about a workable relationship of seemingly disparate policies and programs. To cap the idea of a comprehensive approach, the Administration decided to strengthen the powers of HHFA to coordinate and supervise its constituent agencies. The agencies and programs required coordination to meet effectively the needs of the urban areas.

It is a fact of life that reorganization of the Executive Branch is the accepted practice of each incoming Administration, and the Eisenhower White House was no exception. A number of studies was undertaken to recommend improved management techniques as well as to establish lines of responsibility and authority to carry out presidential policies.

The Federal Housing Administration (FHA), the Public Housing Administration (PHA), and the Federal Home Loan Bank Board (FHLBB) received their powers directly from Congress and the Commissioners and Board members were appointees of the President. The President's Advisory Committee had recommended that HHFA be reorganized, and the Hoover Commission (which had been charged to examine the management of departments and agencies) also filed a report advising on HHFA reorganization. Early in 1953 Nelson Rockefeller, Milton Eisenhower, and Arthur Fleming were selected as a team to advise the Administration on reorganization of the Executive Branch. From time to time they also met with the Administrator to discuss HHFA management.

The studies undertaken for the reports revealed that, although the Administrator had great responsibility in coordinating and supervising the constituent agencies, he had little authority in carrying out the presidential programs. Though this may have been pleasing to some of the mortgage bankers, the situation tended to frustrate effective coordination and supervision of the functions necessary to implement urban renewal and other housing programs.

To overcome this deficiency, the Bureau of the Budget, which had firm ideas about how the reorganization was to be conducted, developed a plan. In order to avoid encroachment and controversy from parties with vested interests, the plan was prepared under tight security measures and, after approval by the White House, it was then delivered to the Commissioners. The FHA Commissioner was disturbed by the wrestling away of a portion of the Agency's independence and protested vigorously. The opposition by FHA and its supporters caused the Bureau of the Budget to put a freeze on the reorganization plan and, much later in the year, instead of being submitted to Congress as a piece of substantive legislation, it suffered the ignominy of being presented as a condensed rider to an appropriation bill. The rider, enacted in June 1954, authorized the Administrator "to assign and reassign functions, to reorganize and to make whatever changes, including the reallocation and transfer of administrative expense funds, and authority when applicable, necessary to promote economy, efficiency and fidelity in the operations of HHFA."

At the end of 1954 the Administrator issued Reorganization Order No. 1 which created the Community Facilities Administration and the Urban Renewal Administration. Upon enactment of the Order the new Housing and Home Finance Agency (HHFA) consisted of the following constituent agencies:

The Federal Home Loan Bank Board (FHLBB)
• To regulate and provide credit to federally chartered savings and loans.

The Federal National Mortgage Association (FNMA)
• To buy and sell mortgages, providing liquidity to lenders and stability to the mortgage market.

The Public Housing Administration (PHA)
• To administer the public housing program.

The Federal Housing Administration (FHA)
• To offer insurance against loss to mortgage lenders in order to improve the competitive position of mortgage borrowers.

The Urban Renewal Administration (URA)
• To provide loans and grants to communities for slum clearance and redevelopment projects.

The Community Facilities Administration (CFA)
• To offer planning grants and loans, college and university dormitory loans, and loans for city services.

The Agency administered other programs such as the Voluntary Home Mortgage Program, the Minority Group Division, and International Housing.

FEDERAL HOME LOAN BANK BOARD (FHLBB)

The Federal Home Loan Bank Board was created in 1932 to help provide a source of housing credit for the savings and loan industry. Its purpose was to provide, through its 12 Federal Home Loan District Banks, a central credit facility to supplement the financial resources of its member institutions. The functions of the Federal Home Loan Bank Board were to be accomplished through the Federal Home Loan Bank System. Building and loan associations, mutual savings banks, and insurance companies could be members of the System. In 1934, Title IV of the National Housing Act created the Federal Savings and Loan Insurance Corporation to insure the savings accounts of savings and loan associations and related types of thrift institutions.

Supervision of Federal Savings and Loan Associations, of other insured savings associations and, to a lesser degree authorized by statute, of other members of the Federal Home Loan Bank System was conducted by the officers of the regional banks as agents of the Federal Home Loan Bank Board. Thus, the major functions of the Board in the 1950's included the promotion of savings and economical home financing through the federal savings and loan system and the Federal Savings and Loan Insurance Corporation, and the provision of reserve funds to their members through the Federal Home Loan Banks.

From 1932 until 1942 the Federal Home Loan Bank Board consisted of five members, one of them the chairman. From 1942 until 1947 the powers of the Board were placed in a single person, the Federal Home Loan Bank Commissioner. In 1947, by Reorganization Plan No. 3, a three-member Home Loan Bank Board was created to be part of the National Housing Agency, and later was transferred to the Housing and Home Finance Agency. The Board's relations with Congress, which had deteriorated badly in the immediate postwar years, were restored in the early 1950's, and remained good for many years.

The President's Advisory Committee in 1953 recommended that the Home Loan Bank Board be included as one of the constituent agencies of the Housing and Home Finance Agency. This decision, that the Home Loan Bank Board continue as a constituent agency of the HHFA, reflected an intent that the Board's finance and credit operations recognize home ownership and other social goals, as indeed the Federal Home Loan Act and the Home Owners' Loan Act of 1933 had mandated from the beginning. Furthermore, President Eisenhower's appointee as Chairman, Walter McAllister, was the only chairman in the history of the Board from Hoover to Carter who was at the time of his appointment a managing officer of an insured savings and loan association.

The Internal Revenue Service in 1952 subjected savings and loan associations to a normal corporate income tax for the first time. As a practical matter, however, the provisions permitting allocations to reserves before taxes until the reserve fund equaled 12 percent of net worth meant the associations would not, for the most part, be subjected to corporate income taxes. Accordingly, the new tax provisions did not erode the ability of the savings and loans to continue to provide necessary mortgage financing. This tax situation was to continue until the 1962 and 1969 changes in the Internal Revenue Code.

All federal savings and loan associations in the 1950's, and indeed until 1976, were mutual institutions, as were the vast majority of state-chartered associations. A mutual savings and loan was considered to be owned by its shareholders. Some states chartered savings and loan associations which had permanent transferrable equities often called permanent or guaranteed stock. Section 5(i) of the Home Owner's Loan Act of 1933, as amended in 1948, explicitly recognized conversions of federal associations to state stock associations under plans found to be equitable by the Board and the Insurance Corporation. Some such conversations had actually taken place before 1948. This was a reversal of the trend in the 1930's, which saw many conversions from stock form to mutual, both federal and state chartered.

Federal savings and loan associations in the late 1940's and early 1950's sometimes still referred to the savings accounts as "shares" and the savings accounts holders as "shareholders." As noted, it was generally assumed that these "shareholders" were the actual owners of mutual associations. However, conversions from federal mutual to state stock form in the late 1940's and early 1950's took place on an accelerating basis. It appeared on close scrutiny by the HHFA, that upon the consummation of such conversions the shareholders of the federal associations had very little or no further ownership interest in the institution, and that the conversion process itself had been extremely profitable to a few individuals. As a result of this study, I wrote a letter to Senator John J. Sparkman taking the position that the Board's policies and practices as to conversions did not adequately protect the public. I argued that the Board should continue to withhold approvals for all applications for conversion to the stock form of organization until Congress acted to deal with the problems outlined in the letter. The moratorium on such conversions dating from that time continued in effect, with sporadic exceptions, until it was reduced to temporary statutory form in 1974 and expired on June 30, 1976. Statutory and regulatory changes have aimed in substantial part toward eliminating the private profit opportunities from the conversion process. Regulations now in effect for such conversions differ dramatically from the conversion policies of the late 1940's and early 1950's, but such conversions are still the subject of much controversy.

The combination of skilled management, freedom from income taxes, relatively low inflation after the close of the Korean War, and a viable real estate and home-construction market resulted in a decade of success and prosperity for the institutions under the control of the Board. However, some strong voices were heard from 1953 on to urge at least partial change from portfolios dominated by fixed rate long-term mortgage instruments. Thus, a number of insured institutions started writing variable interest rate loans which were to be extremely helpful to those particular institutions when the credit crunches began in 1966. Supervisory authorities, however, found it difficult to shed their memories of unhappy experiences with deflation in the early 1930's, and to give leadership to this industry-led move to protect against future inflation.

I had increasing difficulty in coordinating and supervising an agency which had regulatory functions as part of its reponsibilities. This, coupled with Congressional and industry pressures, provided the right "mix" for legislative action, resulting in its separation from HHFA. In 1955 the Home Loan Bank Board was renamed the Federal Home Loan Bank Board and given independent status.

FEDERAL NATIONAL MORTGAGE ASSOCIATION (FNMA)

The Federal National Mortgage Association by 1954 had experienced a successful and long period of service to the home mortgage industry. The 1954 Act provided a new charter for FNMA, and the HHFA Administrator was designated Chairman of the Board with authority to name the officers and directors. Contrary to the accepted custom of new administrations in asking for resignations from holders of political appointments, I retained the officers of FNMA.

The Charter Act specifically authorized the Federal National Mortgage Association to conduct and to maintain separate accountability for the three principal activities or operations described below:

- *Secondary Market Operations.* These operations to be privately financed, were designed to provide supplementary assistance to the private secondary market for residential mortgages by providing more liquidity for mortgage investments, i.e., FNMA would raise money from private investors to buy mortgages from lenders.
- *Special Assistance Functions.* These functions were to be operated exclusively for the account of the government and almost entirely with funds borrowed from the United States Treasury. They were designed to provide special assistance for certain residential mort-

gages when either the President of the United States should deem
it in the public interest or Congress should specifically designate
special programs.

• *Management and Liquidating Functions.* These functions, to be
operated exclusively for the account of the government, were designed for management of mortgages acquired before 1954.

The Charter Act charged FNMA with the responsibility under its
secondary market operations ". . . to provide supplementary assistance
to the secondary market for home mortgages by providing a degree of
liquidity for mortgage investments, thereby improving the distribution
of investment capital available for home mortgage financing. . . ."

In order to accomplish this supplementary function in the market,
FNMA was directed that: "In the interest of sound operation, the prices
to be paid by the corporation for mortgages purchased in its secondary
market operations under this section should be established . . . within
the range of market prices for the particular class of mortgages involved, as determined by the corporation."

Further, "the volume of the corporation's purchase prices, sales prices,
and the charges or fees, in its secondary market operations . . . should
be effected only at such prices and on such terms as will reasonably prevent excessive use of the corporation's facilities. . . ."

Finally, FNMA was to accomplish this supplementary function and
meet the requirements and yet be self-supporting. This self-supporting
provision further evidenced the Congressional intent that the Secondary
Market Operations were to be managed, to the maximum extent practicable, as the operations of a wholly private corporation would be managed.

FNMA had a sensitive position in the Executive Branch as its activities played an important part in the monetary and fiscal policy as viewed
by the Congress, the Treasury, and the Federal Reserve System. The
Association was charged with maintaining "a degree of liquidity" in the
FHA and VA mortgage market with the intention of improving the
distribution and availability of mortgage funds. By buying mortgages
from mortgage bankers and other lenders, FNMA put cash into their
hands to make new mortgages. By selling mortgages FNMA took cash
out of circulation. Thus, through purchases or sales of mortgages the
Association could impact the economy via the housing market by coun-
teracting or accelerating a boom. Therefore, the Administration, by exercising its judgment through HHFA, had an important stake in
FNMA's marketing policy.

For example, in 1957 FNMA purchased $1 billion in mortgages and,
in 1958, the Administration, recognizing that the nation was in an economic slump, undertook to expedite certain measures aimed at stimulating residential construction. The Emergency Housing Act of 1958 in-

TABLE 7–1. Summary of Corporation Mortgage Activities by Calendar Years*
(Dollars in thousands)

Year	Purchases	Sales	Repayments	Other Credits	Year-End Portfolio Number Mortgages	Year-End Portfolio Amount
Total	$11,388,441	$2,348,354	$1,245,138	$627,732	586,634	$7,167,217
1954	24	—	—	—	2	24
1955	86,049	—	393	—	9,483	85,680
1956	574,538	5,014	6,154	335	62,114	648,715
1957	1,021,044	2,887	28,721	2,310	146,860	1,635,841
1958	259,535	465,568	39,156	9,962	128,337	1,330,690
1959	734,569	3,474	47,472	14,525	187,144	2,049,788
1960	980,495	42,093	65,116	21,083	259,138	2,902,991
1961	624,390	521,999	79,016	54,433	254,976	2,871,933
1962	547,427	390,667	104,029	78,085	253,151	2,846,579
1963	181,290	779,824	109,723	76,531	191,712	2,061,791
1964	197,548	78,091	120,044	64,295	190,787	1,996,909
1965	756,933	46,562	125,612	62,193	239,978	2,519,475
1966	2,080,617	73	133,047	70,690	388,409	4,396,282
1967	1,399,602	11,744	169,912	92,224	469,930	5,522,004
1968	1,944,380	358	217,743	81,066	586,634	7,167,217

* Also the Corporation's fiscal year.

creased by $500 million the special assistance fund for purchase of home mortgages which were not otherwise marketable, and for the purchase of mortgages generally as a means of aiding and maintaining the stability of high-level economic activity and created a new FNMA special assistance revolving fund of $1 billion for the purchase of FHA and VA mortgages on new homes. The easy credit conditions in 1958 marked the first year of significant sales of mortgages, but with the credit crunch beginning in 1959, FNMA entered the market again and purchased $850 million of mortgages.

It is not the purpose here to judge the debate over whether the federal government should use housing programs as economic countercyclical instruments, but to establish the role of HHFA as a supervisor. Table 7–1 provides a summary of mortgage activity and a comparison of FNMA activity with FHA and VA starts from 1954 to 1968.

FEDERAL HOUSING ADMINISTRATION (FHA)

In 1952 Miles Colean identified the intermingling of "effective demand" and "social need" in the extension of mortgage credit as an area requiring the new President's concern. Colean recommended that the two be separated completely with all social need or welfare functions administered by an agency created for that specific purpose. His intent was to preserve the soundness of the FHA and the Home Loan Bank

System which extended mortgage credit upon considerations of risk (effective demand). His recommendation was not acted upon.

The complexity of the situation was underscored by a recommendation of the Hoover Commission that FHA be reorganized in such a manner that it would provide its own financing without having federal credit behind the debentures, and that the agency be revamped into a private corporation. In response to this, I pointed out that FHA did pay its own way, but eliminating its public purpose would hit particularly hard at urban renewal programs. "Special 'welfare' FHA mortgage insurance is needed for this purpose," I said.

FHA's record had been one of extraordinary success, with a minimum of government involvement and with major private contribution. The loss ratio was small, indeed, and the mutual reserve funds were substantial. This record, in large part, was due to sound and conservative underwriting policies which were designed to insure practically nonrisk ventures. The Agency, using these practices, assisted millions of Americans in the purchase of their homes (Table 7–2).

That part of the population roughly described as "the industry"—mortgage bankers, investors, etc.—found the FHA method completely acceptable, designating it as a "credit function" as distinguished from a "welfare function." Suggestions to liberalize the underwriting practices were referred to as allowing "barnacles" to accumulate on FHA. Mortgage bankers and generally other mortgage lenders, strenuously opposed the "barnacles" on the hull of the Agency ship.

"Credit" functions in this context could be defined broadly as those in which the home buyer or renter pays for the cost of the housing. "Welfare" functions are those where the government either pays part of the cost through a subsidy, or accepts part of the unusual risk, e.g., housing located in blighted neighborhoods.

It is ironic that the recommendations of the President's Advisory Committee which were adopted in the Administration Housing Program and in the Act of 1954 and which affixed "barnacles" to the FHA structure encountered very little opposition. New FHA Sections 220 and 221 were included in the family of insured mortgages. These amendments provided for liberalized mortgage insurance to assist in the rehabilitation of existing dwellings, in the construction of new dwellings in slum clearance and urban renewal areas, and in the relocation of families displaced by urban renewal.

Section 220 provided that instead of the usual requirement of "economic soundness" in evaluating the mortgage, the Administrator could certify that the urban renewal plan conformed to the general plan of the locality and that, therefore, the mortgage was deemed insurable. The program was further liberalized by providing an allowance of up to 10 percent for profit and risk to the developer. Section 221 was liberalized

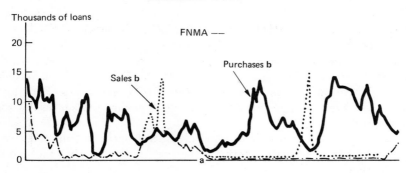

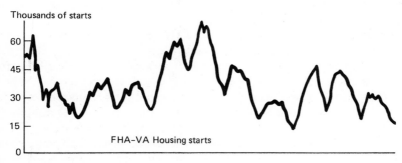

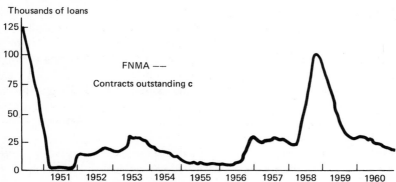

a Negligible volume, generally from none to 100 loans.
b Excludes loans purchased from RFC, Defense Homes Corporation, and PHA. Excluded mortgage-bond exchanges from 1960 sales (57,558 loans).
c Includes advance and stand-by commitments and purchases authorized but not completed as well as undisbursed funds.
SOURCE: Federal National Mortgage Association and U. S., Housing and Home Finance Agency, *Housing Statistics*, various issues.

by extending the amortization and other terms and, in 1959, it permitted the substitution of "replacement costs" for "value" in determining the amount of the insurable mortgage for multifamily structures.

The new urban renewal programs, containing the latest underwriting features, caused some internal conflict in HHFA. Traditional FHA standards sometimes clashed with urban renewal objectives when, for example, FHA appraisals of projects needing mortgage credit were so low that developers could not get enough money on credit to build a specific project. This conflict required action in order to coordinate both programs, and I imposed procedures designed to ensure the success of the urban renewal program.

Some opposition to this joining of credit and welfare functions continued. It was thought that perhaps the profitability of that high-powered "barnacle"—FHA Section 608—might have softened some of the objections. However, the issue of welfare versus credit did not fade; instead, it returned in another cloak.

Few in the housing field equated FHA Section 608 with welfare functions. This liberal program, which began in 1946, was designed to create almost instant housing to meet a serious need for dwellings for defense plant workers and their families and for returning World War II veterans. It produced during a four-year span thousands of units in short order and met a large part of the housing needs, but in spite of its worthiness, the program was seriously beset by problems.

Section 608 contained regulations which permitted builders, sponsors, and developers to obtain FHA insurance for mortgages. Among the most significant were a larger loan in relation to the value of the building, a longer amortization period (with smaller monthly payments), a softening of constraints on property location as a criterion in evaluating the risk, and minimum supervision of the builder's estimate of cost construction.

As a consequence of the flexibility and potential for high profits that the Section 608 program carried, more than 7,000 apartment builders had taken advantage of the federal benefit during 1946–1950, the most active period of this program.

Windfall profits were derived from the operations and fortunes were made (often in less than a year) with little or no cash investment. Some of the windfall profits were due to construction efficiently managed below estimated costs, but the greater proportion of windfalls produced by the projects occurred through wilful contractual violations such as spurious contract specifications, fraudulent cost estimates, illegal withdrawal of cash reserves, and fixed land appraisals.

Based upon complaints, a probe was initiated in 1954 into the Section 608 program which disclosed that in 1410 cases of the 1547 investigated, windfalls to builders amounted to $113 million—a return of 472 percent on cash investment. In a typical case, a corporation organized by a man and his wife with a capital of $1,000 submitted an application for mortgage insurance on a building estimated at a cost of $5.5 million. FHA insured it for $5 million which, on paper, appeared to be sound underwriting. On that basis, the couple secured a loan for $5 million. The actual cost of the building was $4 million. The net result was their pocketing $1 million in addition to profits anticipated from rentals of the building.

In another case, three individuals secured FHA Section 608 insurance on 11 projects for an estimated cost of $12 million. Obviously the costs were padded for the projects were built for $7.368 million and the FHA insured mortgage permitted the sponsors to obtain a cash windfall of $3.5 million.[3]

While Section 608 was a large-scale building operation that dealt in millions of dollars, FHA Title I was a modest but multifold home-improvement program that benefited largely the middle- and low-income homeowners. It provided insured loans that were discounted by contractors at qualified banks, which in those instances acquired a status of bona fide holders.

Despite the fact that this program had been effectively carried out since the 1930's there were strong suspicions of a nationwide pattern of abuse. Many complaints had been filtering in over a period of time telling of the unsavory techniques. These fraudulent activities were brought to my attention and I uncovered them to the FHA Commissioner.

As an example, crews of 100 to 500 "suede shoe" boys would move into neighborhoods of small homeowners, fleece them, and quickly move on. The "salesman" would talk a gullible homeowner into an improvement protected by FHA insurance. The improvement or addition might never be made or installed or be a hasty, shoddy piece of work, but the homeowner had signed a note, now in the hands of a bank. It was reported that thousands of people across the country had been defrauded by this illegal method.

In the past, FHA had taken a lackadaisical attitude in investigating the complaints. In response to 163 complaints concerning Title I activities between 1949 and 1952, FHA had investigated only nine. As of late 1953, despite the seriousness of the situation and the urgency to bring about corrective action, no efforts by FHA to accelerate the investigation of either Title I or Section 608 had been made.

Therefore, a committee composed of the Counsel to the President, Director of the Bureau of the Budget, Director of the FBI, Deputy At-

3 *U. S. News & World Report*, October 22, 1954.

torney General, White House Chief of Staff, and the Administrator of HHFA, was organized. After a thorough examination, the Committee reported that a large number of citizens had been victimized; that the Department of Justice received countless complaints placing blame on FHA for the widespread swindles; and that repeated requests to the FHA Commissioner by HHFA and the Departments of Justice over the course of a year for decisive action against Title I frauds and Section 608 misfeasance had been unheeded.

The President ordered that HHFA undertake a full-fledged investigation and that the officials responsible for the situation be dismissed. I selected a Los Angeles lawyer and experienced investigator, William F. McKenna, to organize an extramural team of expert professionals to undertake an all-inclusive inquiry into the Section 608 and Title I complaints. The short and intensive investigation which ended in the fall of 1954 produced a series of dramatic results.

A number of key FHA officials resigned, were suspended, or were removed. Among them were the commissioner, two assistant commissioners, general counsel, and some of the regional officers including the chief underwriter, the chief of construction, an examiner, a director, an assistant director and a supervisory appraiser. By the end of 1956 about 750 indictments were returned and about 350 convictions obtained.

In another move, loopholes allowing use of padded costs in 608 projects were successfully closed by adoption of a cost certification process requiring builders to submit itemized sworn statements of the actual construction cost. Moreover, through the ensuing lawsuits filed by the Department of Justice and lengthy negotiations with builders, millions of dollars of windfall profits were recovered for the Treasury coffers.

The Senate Banking and Currency Committee had started an inquiry at the same time the HHFA investigation was being conducted. After long hearings and abundant testimony, Chairman Homer Capehart estimated the total windfall profit figure at $1 billion. Paul E. Healy of the *Saturday Evening Post* (February 26, 1955) called it "one of the biggest scandals in the history of the United States, both in numbers of individuals participating and amount of money involved." He added, "Perhaps more important was the fact that the investigation has proven that the Executive Branch can investigate itself, if so minded."

Special Assistance for Low-Income Families

Notable among the special assistance programs were two new ideas authorizing FHA mortgage insurance to assist in the rehabilitation of existing dwellings as well as construction of new dwellings in slum clearance and urban renewal areas.

The legislative history of many of the earlier housing acts pointed to the conclusion that all efforts to solve urban problems should be coordinated in a total and comprehensive attack. In 1951, Catherine Bauer,[4] the dynamic and multifaceted advocate of public housing, said that there should be a comprehensive approach to all the urban problems, that a piecemeal approach was wrong, that we needed to bring out all the tools that were available in the locality to help revitalize the city. The consensus was that no single program or subset of programs would suffice to solve urban problems.

This idea of lifting the sights of the city beyond a project-by-project approach was an important feature of the 1954 Act, following strong recommendations of the President's Advisory Committee. The Act provided that before public housing, slum clearance or FHA mortgage insurance—Sections 220 and 221, would be assisted by the federal government, the community had to develop a plan for dealing with the causes of slums and urban decay. This plan was called the Workable Program.

The Workable Program required a community to show in its plan that it was providing for seven specific needs:

- Establishment of adequate standards of health and safety for housing.
- Undertaking of a comprehensive plan for the community's future development.
- Analysis of the neighborhoods in the community to identify those where something should be done about blight.
- Administrative organization capable of coordinating and carrying out a community program.
- Financial resources to support the locality's share of an urban renewal program.
- Housing resources to meet the needs of those displaced by urban renewal.
- Assurance that the community as a whole would be fully informed and have an opportunity to take part in developing and executing an urban renewal program.

The Workable Program which was submitted by the community to HHFA for approval, had to be renewed each year in order to continue with the federally assisted project. "If you want public housing" the city was told, "you must face up to your total problems." One thousand cities were involved in Workable Programs by the end of 1959. The cities encompassed 54 percent of the urban population in 45 states, where local officials and citizens' groups were busily planning for community development. The carrot of federal assistance offered incentives to eliminate piecemeal efforts.

4 Catherine Bauer Wurster, leading advocate of public housing; first Research Director of the U. S. Housing Authority.

The idea of a comprehensive approach was sound—urban scholars had pointed out the need for unified economic, social, and political solutions—and this program offered one practical method of achievement. But there was grumbling, complaining, and opposition. It was charged that the Workable Program unnecessarily delayed public housing as well as other projects, that bureaucratic processing of applications delayed planning and that the plans became "unworkable."

In response to criticism from some mayors and the National Association of Housing and Redevelopment Officials (NAHRO), among others, Congress in 1955 repealed the Workable Program as a precondition for public housing project approvals. However, through a strong Agency effort the Workable Program's essential requisites were reinstated in the Act of 1956. To some, impatient with time schedules of approvals and the difficulties in complying with the seven requirements, the program was a burden. However, it could be said that it was the precursor of programs such as Demonstration Cities, Model Cities, and some aspects of Revenue Sharing—which contained the elements of the Workable Program—later adopted by other Administrations in the 1960's and the 1970's that required a measure of comprehensive approach. The Eisenhower Administration placed the Workable Program in the forefront of its achievements in housing. True, the goal was not easy to achieve, but the effort was deemed essential.

TABLE 7–3. Private and Public Housing Starts

Period	Private Units		Public Units		Total Units	
	Number of Units	Percentage of Total	Number of Units	Percentage of Total	Number of Units	Percentage of Total
Nonfarm						
1945	324,900	99.6	1,200	0.4	326,100	100.0
1946	1,015,200	99.2	8,000	0.8	1,023,200	100.0
1947	1,265,100	99.7	3,400	0.3	1,268,500	100.0
1948	1,344,000	98.7	18,100	1.3	1,362,100	100.0
1949	1,429,800	97.5	36,300	2.5	1,466,100	100.0
1950	1,908,100	97.8	43,800	2.2	1,951,900	100.0
1951	1,419,800	95.2	71,200	4.8	1,491,000	100.0
1952	1,445,400	96.1	58,500	3.9	1,503,900	100.0
1953	1,402,100	97.5	35,500	2.5	1,437,600	100.0
1954	1,531,800	98.8	18,700	1.2	1,550,500	100.0
1955	1,626,600	98.8	19,400	1.2	1,646,000	100.0
1956	1,324,900	98.2	24,200	1.8	1,349,100	100.0
1957	1,174,800	96.0	49,100	4.0	1,223,900	100.0
1958	1,314,200	95.1	67,800	4.9	1,382,000	100.0
1959	1,494,600	97.6	36,700	2.4	1,531,300	100.0

1974 Fact Book, U. S. League of Savings & Loan Association, p. 19.
SOURCE: Bureau of the Census.

The public housing program was often considered the bellwether of federal government programs. However, the program continued through the 1950's and beyond as a small segment of total annual starts (Table 7–3). In 1950 public housing starts were 43,800 or 2.2 percent of the total private and public starts. In 1959 the starts were 36,700 or 2.4 percent of the total; two peak years were 1951 with 71,200 starts, or 4.8 percent of the total, and 1958 with 36,700 starts or 4.9 percent of total. The 4.9 percent of total private and public starts achieved in 1958 was the highest proportion, not only of the decade, but for the period 1945 to 1973.

A second measure of the program was the amount of money appropriated each year for annual federal contributions, the money that pays the mortgages on the projects. Table 7–4 includes the range not only for the decade, but for the total program prior to 1971. Appropriations are a telling indication of Congressional and Administration concern and demonstrate the depth of commitment to shelter low-income people. At the end of 1959 there were slightly over 585,000 dwelling units owned or supervised by the Public Housing Administration.

During the decade there occurred a mass migration of southern rural blacks to the big city ghettos. At the same time Puerto Rican poverty-stricken families discovered the city of gold—New York. Most of these migrants were unaccustomed to city apartment life, and when they became public housing tenants the population heterogeneity increased.

Robert Weaver discussed this problem saying:

Slums in American cities today house families which hold a wide range of value and evidence a variety of behavioral patterns. Some are households with female heads and are stable nonetheless; others may be ungrammatical but adhere to high moral standards; still other evidence all the other attributes of middle class behavior and are dedicated to its values, if not recipient to its rewards. All three groups have ambition and talent, but fight an uphill battle in maintaining respectability and achievement for themselves and their children. It was from these families that public housing made its earlier election and its initial successes, it is these families which if they have access to decent shelter in good neighborhoods will immediately respond to the new environment. . . . In contrast, certain elements now concentrated in the slums, however, present clear and well-defined problems. They include the confirmed middle-age winos, the established prostitutes, . . . the hardened criminals and the like, who either resist rehabilitation or require long-term assistance of the most intensive type. They are multiethnic and constitute the real hard core. In addition, the classical problems of families which usually evidence some form of antisocial behavior are well represented among slum residents.[5]

5 Robert C. Weaver, *The Urban Complex.* (New York: Doubleday), 1960, p. 28.

TABLE 7–4. Low-Rent Public Housing Appropriations for Annual Contributions[1]

Fiscal year	Public Law No.	Date	Dollars in thousands In year	Dollars in thousands Cumulative
1941–49			$ 69,402	$ 69,402
1950	81–266	Aug. 24, 1949	5,000	74,402
1951	81–759	Sept. 6, 1950	7,500	81,902
1952	82–137	Aug. 31, 1951	10,000	———
	82–375	June 5, 1952	3,600	95,502
1953	82–455	July 5, 1952	29,880	125,382
1954	83–176	July 31, 1953	32,500	———
	83–357	May 11, 1954	10,800	168,682
1955	83–428	June 24, 1954	63,950	———
	84–219	Aug. 4, 1955	4,100	236,732
1956	84–112	June 30, 1955	81,750	———
	84–814	July 27, 1956	450	318,932
1957	84–623	June 27, 1956	93,000	411,932
1958	85–69	June 29, 1957	95,000	———
	85–766	July 27, 1958	3,900	510,832
1959	85–844	Aug. 28, 1958	107,500	———
	86–213	Sept. 1, 1959	8,000	626,332
1960	86–255	Sept. 14, 1959	120,000	———
	86–651	July 14, 1960	12,000	758,332
1961	86–626	July 12, 1960	140,000	———
	87–332	Sept. 30, 1961	5,322	903,654
1962	87–141	Aug. 17, 1961	165,000	1,068,654
1963	87–741	Oct. 3, 1962	180,000	1,248,654
1964	88–215	Dec. 19, 1963	197,000	1,445,654
1965	88–507	Aug. 30, 1964	200,000	———
	89–16	Apr. 30, 1965	8,320	1,653,974
1966	89–128	Aug. 16, 1966	220,000	———
	90–21	May 29, 1967	21,597	1,895,571
1967	89–555	Sept. 6, 1966	250,000	———
	90–21	May 29, 1967	5,000	———
	90–392	July 9, 1968	6,042	2,156,713
1968	90–121	Nov. 3, 1967	275,000	———
	90–392	July 9, 1968	20,000	———
	91–47	July 22, 1969	7,168	2,458,781
1969	90–550	Oct. 4, 1968	350,000	———
	91–47	July 22, 1969	16,000	———
	91–305	July 6, 1970	13,616	2,838,397
1970	91–126	Nov. 26, 1969	473,500	3,311,897
1971	91–556	Dec. 17, 1970	654,500	[1]3,966,397

[1] A new appropriation in 1972, "Housing payments" covers payments for all of the following: Annual contributions; college housing; rent supplements; home ownership assistance; and rental housing assistance.

SOURCE: *Evolution of Role of the Federal Government in Housing and Community Development: A Chronology of Legislative and Selected Executive Actions, 1892–1974.* A Report for the Subcommittee on Housing and Community Development of the Committee on Banking, Currency and Housing, House of Representatives, 94th Congress, First Session, October, 1975. Washington, D.C.: U. S. Government Printing Office, p. 234.

But there were hundreds of public housing projects and thousands of low-income people living in very good environments. The occupants of these projects contributed to stable communities, and many were upwardly mobile. Not all, however, were as upwardly mobile as the young Navy Lieutenant, James Earl Carter, Jr. who, upon returning from the Navy with his wife Rosalynn, moved into a public housing project in Plains, Georgia.

In his book, Jimmy Carter, having mentioned that he had resigned from the Navy, said:

We went back home . . . in 1953 we had saved a few thousand dollars from our regular savings bonds program since my Annapolis days. Though we felt young and confident, we had no idea what our life would be like when we returned home. Not having an assured income, we applied for and were assigned an apartment in the new public housing project in Plains. I remember on the way home from Schenectady, we stopped in Washington to visit our Congressman. He was an extremely small man, physically cocky and constantly preoccupied. He showed us around the Capitol building and in one of his apparently standard speeches, described to us the problem of living near people who occupied public housing quarters. Rosalynn and I glanced at one another but did not comment.[6]

Jimmy Carter was not your typical public housing occupant, but many others with very humble beginnings were able to improve their lot.

Public housing design has always been troublesome and controversial. Prior to and during the 1950 decade the design of public housing was of concern to the federal and local agencies, as well as some architects and social scientists. Generally, both Congress and the various Executive Branches looked upon the projects as structures to be built with concern for saving "unnecessary" costs. The usual project was a sound commercially designed and constructed building with as few "frills" as possible.

Design received the attention of the President's Advisory Committee, which cautioned against boxlike shelter and recommended that projects should be built at lower densities and conform more closely to local dwelling patterns and construction practices to avoid an institutionalized character and to facilitate the sale of public housing when no longer needed for low-income families. Local authorities often deviated from such broad, cautionary policies. A famous deviation became a nightmarish example by which to frighten planners, architects, and officials and offered much fuel to public housing opponents.

Pruitt and Igoe, a black man and a white man from St. Louis, Missouri, became heroes in World War II. A new public housing project

6 Jimmy Carter, *Why Not The Best?* (Nashville: Broadman Press), 1975, pp. 64–65.

designed by an internationally famous architect was named for these two heroes and construction started in 1955. The project was hailed as an architectural model of design. Superlative plans for the project included a beautiful park, with the latest playground equipment and lavish landscaping around the high-rise buildings. The project contained 2,800 housing units with blacks and whites segregated in separate but adjacent buildings. The original cost rose from $14,000 per unit to $18,500 and up, thus forcing many reductions in construction specifications, which in turn reduced the human environment. The park never took form, density was computed to be 100 persons per acre, and services badly deteriorated during the first year and a half. Then, in the words of one official "All hell broke loose." This mass of humanity— white, black, poor, frightened, crushed, disadvantaged, and disheartened—generated vandalism and crime, and caused property damage to a degree rendering the project uninhabitable. The Pruitt-Igoe project was dynamited after the city condemned it. A product of Pruitt-Igoe and the Darst-Webbe apartments where he was raised is the erstwhile world heavyweight boxing champion, Leon Spinks, who said, "When you're raised in a place like this, all you can think of is to get out."[7]

The problems of public housing continued to absorb the federal and local agencies. Recognition of the bad conditions brought about some new ideas to cope with the situation. One such plan was to provide single-family homes rather than high-rise apartments, in order to create a more human atmosphere—more conducive to family life—and in an effort to reduce the institutional character of the projects. Overcrowding and the high density of the multifamily and multistory apartments in cities other than St. Louis appeared to contribute to vandalism and unhealthful living conditions.

The choice of scattered sites was strongly advocated by the Agency in 1958, on the theory that in solving some of these issues, the housing could blend into local neighborhoods, and also because sizeable and reasonably priced vacant or slum land for large projects was becoming increasingly difficult to find in all but the smallest towns.

The program of scattered sites was received in many areas with enthusiasm. Shortly, however, the proposal became highly controversial with the established residents saying, "I don't want those folks and those houses in my neighborhood, destroying the value of my property, bringing poverty, vandalism, and trash to the doorstep of my home, my family, and my children." This angry cry was quite effective in slowing progress to a snail's pace.

In many instances problem families destroyed their public housing;

7 *The Washington Post*, February 19, 1978. Leon Spinks defeated Muhammad Ali on February 15, 1978.

in too many instances did local communities reject scattered sites; in too few instances was the upward mobility of the tenants successful; in too few instances were disease and crime statistics lowered; and the total housing needed for low-income families was not solved.

A Vigorous Attack on Slums

URBAN RENEWAL

The Act of 1954 created a new program, Urban Renewal, and a new agency. The Urban Renewal Administration was organized as a constituent of HHFA, and its mission called for a vigorous attack on slums by two methods: (1) a comprehensive program, and (2) a project-by-project approach under Title I Slum Clearance and Redevelopment.

The comprehensive program envisioned that the community would undertake a complete revitalization of not only the slums, but other affected areas as well. This would require, among other actions, new street and recreational layouts, changes in zoning regulations, and new efforts to improve transportation, education, and employment opportunities in order to alleviate crime and disease. In order to accomplish these goals, huge amounts of federal, state, and local money, as well as the cooperation of the private sector would be required.

The reorganization of HHFA was designed to assist in the total attack. The Workable Program, coupled with efforts for conservation and rehabilitation, and citizens' action, represented the comprehensive planning envisioned by the Act. One important aspect of the Act was Section 701 which provide loans and grants to state, metropolitan, or regional planning agencies.

The Workable Program was a mechanism to achieve a major part of the comprehensive approach to urban problems. Charles A. Horsky, President of the Washington Housing Authority and one-time White House coordinator for the District of Columbia wrote in late 1959:

. . . Housing, per se, is not the entire problem; it is one vital aspect of the total economic and social fabric of the country. The housing problem of low-income families cannot, therefore, be solved by housing measures alone.

The response of the Administration to this need for a total program was to place not only public housing but slum clearance and redevelopment as well as the new "urban renewal" FHA Sections 220 and 221 within the orbit of the Workable Program. The Title I slum clearance and redevelopment segment of urban renewal provided that the local public agency, through grants-in-aid and loans from the federal government, would acquire property in an urban renewal area. The agency would then demolish and remove buildings to eliminate or prevent the spread of blight, and thus provide land for public facilities, streets,

parks, utilities, and other services, or dispose of the land at its fair value
for use in accordance with the urban renewal plan. Under the 1949 Act
the land was to be reused for predominantly residential uses, but the
new Act merely provided that it should "achieve community objectives
for the establishment and preservation of well-planned residential neighborhoods."

"Urban Renewal," a term which is used indiscriminately, should be
understood as encompassing the comprehensive program formulated to
alleviate deterioration of the inner city, while Title I, on the other hand,
is a project-by-project approach, permitting the acquisition of blighted
property for renewal by developers.

A redevelopment program involves a maze of complex decisions and
activities on the part of literally hundreds of people, spanning a wide
spectrum of economic, political, and human issues. The decisions are
made by federal agencies, local government officials, regulatory agencies, private, professional, business, and social organizations. Some of
the activities include selection of a site, tentative planning for the reuse
of the site; securing approval of gevernmental agencies; appraisal for
acquisition; acquisition of the site by negotiation or condemnation; relocation of occupants; market, soil, and topography studies; demolishing
structures and preparing the land for sale. Final site and reuse plan is
then prepared, which involves the proposed structure; offering for sale;
selection of private developers; approval by HHFA, FHA, lenders;
market analysis; architectural and engineering studies; execution of
federal and city approved contracts between the agency and developer;
approval of the city Fine Arts Council when applicable, architectural
and construction contracts and supervision of contruction; renting or
selling property; and management.

With multifold decisions required of many agencies and often with
conflicting policies, it was almost a miracle that the completion of a program was successful. The results were mixed—there were some extraordinary accomplishments and some dismal failures. In many cities excellent and vital areas would not have been developed without this program.

Some of the early programs of the 1950 decade were begun in New
Haven, Pittsburgh, Washington, D.C., Philadelphia, New York, Boston, Chicago, Little Rock, Huntsville, Mobile, Portland, Norfolk, and
San Francisco. Construction of projects involved multi- and single-family housing, large and small commercial buildings for retail, office, and
other uses. All of these were undertaken by private developers. Some of
these projects were financed through conventional lenders, some using
FHA insurance, and some FNMA special assistance funds.

The Gateway Center in Pittsburgh, a 50-million dollar project with three office towers, was opened and occupied by 1953. It was followed by other commercial developments, and pointed toward the need for relocation and other housing. A new civic organization was organized—Action Housing, Inc.—which became a model for other cities to follow. The program began slowly in the 1950's, and through concerted efforts blossomed into a substantial housing program for many middle-income city dwellers.

It is often believed that residential redevelopment may be an operation of mammoth developers making windwall profits. The government "write-down" of the price of the land seemed a great boon to the private builder, a subsidy which he could add to his profit. Other benefits appeared to be equally attractive, although experience has offered another picture.

Many cities began their programs with high expectations. In New Haven, Mayor Richard Lee had embarked on a large and imaginative redevelopment plan for the city which included practically all of the elements of the urban renewal program—excellent planning; a well-rounded offering of commercial and residential development with financial studies depicting success; profit to the developers; increased taxes to the city; and enthusiastic citizens' support.

For a few years the program prospered but then came to a slow, grinding halt. The officials, professionals, and businessmen were confronted with the realities and complexities of the process of real estate development. The time schedule and costs exceeded estimates, the real demand did not coincide with the studies, and there were difficulties with businesses' relocation. All these problems, and many more, rather effectively punctured the dream.

In Washington, D.C., the federal government approved a plan for redevelopment of a 550-acre triangle of land in the southwest section of the city, behind the Capitol and extending to the Washington Channel of the Potomac River. This area was probably one of the worst slums in the country. The National Capital Planning Commission drew up plans for redevelopment in 1951, and a comprehensive plan was designed by architect Chloethiel Smith. The plan immediately became controversial, with lenders saying no one would live in the southwest. Builders saw the area as suitable only for cheap walk-ups, others wanted the area as a self-contained Negro establishment rather than allowing them to disperse throughout the city.

However, the developer of the first apartment building in the southwest, James M. Scheuer of New York, saw a large tract of land of centrally located city acreage, unobtainable in a private market, and offering incentives to the builder. Yet, with all the assistance—including FHA Section 220—by the end of the 1950's he had constructed only one building. The investment became three times the original estimate, and the developer was putting up $15,000 per month to keep the building going. The vacancy rate was 25 percent, and Scheuer decided that he had been naive. But later he and other developers continued to build. Jeanne R. Lowe, who described these situations in her book *Cities in a Race With Time*, said that the southwest site later emerged as an attractive, racially integrated community, counting among its residents Congressmen and Senators, including Hubert Humphrey, living in highrise apartments and town houses with modern shops, churches, schools, a legitimate theater, and many excellent restaurants, as well as hundreds of public housing units.

Another city that undertook many and varied projects, was Philadelphia. These included a redevelopment in Eastwick, the largest project in the country, where homes for 10 to 12 thousand middle-income families were planned: the Northwest Temple area, Southwest Temple, East Poplar, and Society Hill, a food distribution center in Whitman, slum clearance for public housing in the University and West Mill Creek projects; and the scheduling of four conservation programs within the year.

These sketchy case histories are illustrative of many cities and provide a sampling of the problems, successes, and failures of the slum clearance and redevelopment programs.

By 1959, studies of slum clearance and redevelopment were showing that "the process set up by the Housing Act of 1949 is now a demonstrable success."

There are now over 500 urban renewal projects under one form or another of federal aid contract in more than 300 cities. For the first time, the number of projects in execution exceeds those in planning. Close to a billion, two hundred million dollars of capital grant money has been reserved for specific projects. While it is true that only ten projects have had their contracts completely fulfilled, the following 1957 year-end figures give a very real indication of the progress that has been made:

	Total	Under Way	Completed (12–31–57)
Land Acquisition	155	82	73
Relocation	152	80	72
Site Clearance	136	81	55
Site Improvements	63	37	26
Supporting Facilities	56	33	23
Land Disposition	57	35	22

During the federal fiscal year just starting (July 1, 1958), it is expected that there will be available for disposition four times as much land as was disposed of in the fiscal year just ended, and it is further anticipated that the amount disposed of in the current fiscal year will be 50 percent greater than that for the past year. There are some 124 redevelopers, both large-scale and small-scale concerns, who have already bought land or agreed to buy land.[8]

By the end of the decade the urban renewal activity was national in scope with only a few states where there were no localities participating (Figure 7–3). The long lead time required from enacting of the law to execution of the projects accounted for a slow beginning, but there was marked acceleration in the last half of the decade and the years 1960–1963 (Figure 7–4).

Although the urban renewal projects were widely distributed throughout the nation, economist Martin Anderson in his book *The Federal Bulldozer* pointed out that they were mainly concentrated in big cities where big money was spent. Despite the fact that this statement was true, smaller cities were recipients of proportionate funds, but the very nature of the program would seem to dictate some concentration on slums which were located in the largest cities.

Anderson also gave a comprehensive account of most of the criticisms of the slum clearance and redevelopment program under the heading "Beliefs and Facts." Among other criticisms, he stated that much of the Title I program would eventually have been constructed by private enterprise without any government intervention, that the constitutionality of the program was questionable, and private lending institutions were not as active as was claimed. Anderson also contended that the claim of increased local real estate taxes received by cities through redevelopment was a myth and, therefore, their coffers did not benefit from the program.

On the other hand, William L. Slayton, Commissioner of Urban Renewal Administration, in a paper delivered to the Chartered Surveyor's Annual Conference at Cambridge University, in 1965, stated: "As a tax generator, we find from experience to date that the real estate tax return from the areas redeveloped or to be redeveloped will be about four-and-a-half times the tax return prior to redevelopment."

The story of urban renewal is not complete without some understanding of the actors on the urban scene, as hundreds of people provided unique and dedicated contributions. Most were fascinating personalities with absorbing histories. One of the many—atypical—could be selected as a case study.

Robert Moses, crowned "The Power Broker" by Caro,[9] was said to have shaped New York City. Any map of the city proves it, (said Caro) for, with one exception, Moses built every major road leading into the

[8] Marshall J. Miller, et al., *New Life for Cities Around the World, International Handbook for Urban Renewal.* (New York: N.Y. Books, Inc.), 1959.
[9] Robert C. Caro, *Annals of Politics* (condensed in *The New Yorker*, July/August, 1974.)

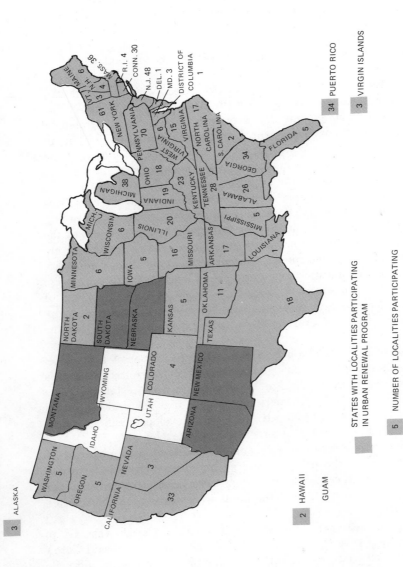

FIGURE 7–3. Map showing participation in Urban Renewal Program, June 30, 1963.

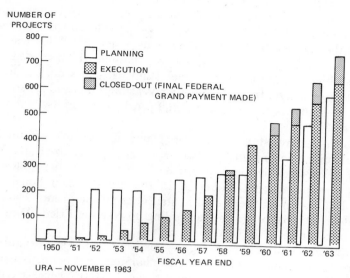

NUMBER OF
PROJECTS

□ PLANNING

▨ EXECUTION

▨ CLOSED-OUT (FINAL FEDERAL
GRAND PAYMENT MADE)

URA — NOVEMBER 1963

FISCAL YEAR END

FIGURE 7–4. Urban renewal project by status, 1950–1963.

city. He built seven bridges including the Triborough and Verazzano. His spectacular achievements included the creation of several parks, adding 22,000 acres to the existing inventory. When Moses finished with housing in New York it was said that a total of 709,000 people were living in buildings in which he had been the moving force. Although Moses was not on the public housing authority, Caro states that "no site was selected, no brick was laid without his approval."

In redevelopment projects, Robert Moses decided what should be torn down, what should be built, by whom, and on what terms. He had been the "dominant force" in the creation of two private developments, Stuyvesant Town and Peter Cooper Village.

Despite his wheeling and dealing and the huge amount of housing built, no one charged Moses with pocketing any ill-gotten money. Caro discussed the close association of politicians to projects; the favored developers, real estate and appraisal firms, and architects, most of whom secured contracts by negotiation. Robert Moses often said how proud he was of this expert team who got things done. However, a United States Senate study (cited by Caro) showed that a group of developers headed by a former slum furniture dealer and a Tammany politician— alleged to have been selected by Moses—made millions by milking tenants in the Manhattan Town project.

It is no mere euphemism when people say that Robert Moses "built" all those gigantic projects. His ability to press the correct power levers was not matched in America. He performed many of the functions of the planners, the architects, the financiers, even the legislators and administrators. He did it. His technique was simple and direct, and he said, "If the end does not justify the means, what does?" He was impatient, often ignoring laws, rules, and regulations which tended to impede his objective. He once told me: "I am used to securing approval for millions of federal funds by phoning Washington," and asked, "Why are you so stuffy as to insist upon staff work, procedures, and written documents?"

Criticism and resistance to the programs of the Moses Slum Clearance Committee was mounting. Mayor Wagner's response to the Workable Program's requirement of citizens' participation listed dozens of citizens' groups actively interested in the renewal and housing programs. But his report "neglected to state that all the groups listed were opposed to the city program," according to Walter Fried, Director of the regional office of HHFA.

Moses had no interest in the "goo-goos," "do gooders"—organizations concerned with good government, city planning, and better housing for New York. The federal government, through HHFA, was paying for two thirds of the public cost, and James Follin, the Urban Renewal Commissioner tried to make Moses follow the rules—and failed. Believing the cavalier attitude of Moses toward regulations of the programs was causing havoc, it was finally decided to curb the troublesome Mr. Moses.

Our conference on the subject with Moses became a one-sided "sunshine" process. *The New York Times*, in big headlines, implied that we were attempting to stifle New York City's progress with bureaucratic red tape. About the same time, we discussed the problem with some of the influential New York citizens. Bob Moses, we said, was not only ruining the program in New York City, but stood an excellent chance of causing great harm to the national effort. A request for assistance in putting a halter on Moses was met with sympathy and good wishes, but no help, because Moses held extraordinary economic and political power which exerted a great degree of control over the business community.

After all, "he did get things done" as people said, and perhaps a majority of New Yorkers looked upon Robert Moses as the Master Builder, who obtained magnificent results. Also many people believed that the beneficial results justified the means. I did not agree. The Agency applied a persistent pressure, insisting upon compliance with the government policies and regulations, and ended much of the abuse. Moses resigned at the end of the decade.

Among the problems of the urban renewal program was the relocation of displaced families. Therefore, it should be of little surprise that

Mr. Moses generally ignored the relocation regulations, since the operation was extremely difficult and complex, with intense emotional overtones. There were almost insurmountable barriers to relocating residents displaced by the slum clearance program in decent, safe, and sanitary dwellings, as provided by the Act of 1949. While the Act contained no statutory requirement for paying moving expenses, the Agency was allowed to pay these out of project funds, of which the federal government paid two thirds. In 1956 Congress authorized moving expenses as part of project costs and set a ceiling of $100 per family, increased to $200 in 1959. Allowances were also authorized for business relocation. The observance of this provision by the local authorities left much to be desired. The unfamiliar social objectives coupled with the practical difficulties of finding the decent homes caused much confusion, and local officials often rendered poor service.

During the decade, nearly two million blacks had migrated from the rural south to the cities of the north, and most of them settled in the central cities. Slum clearance, almost by definition, had a disproportionate impact on these citizens, and a good number were dispossessed of their homes, both rented and owned, and some of them never found a decent home replacement.

In Boston, studies[10] were undertaken which described the removal of the residents from their slum homes. But in general, it was the poor rather than blacks who were specifically displaced. These studies revealed tragic stories of the uprooting and attendant misery of helpless families faced with eviction orders from the government. Poor people did not have the political strength necessary to save their neighborhoods from the planners.

On the other hand, statistics pointed to the fact that in some cities displaced families were relocated in decent housing. Jeanne R. Lowe described the valiant efforts of Assistant Supervisor for Tenant Relations, James Banks (National Capital Housing Authority), relocating blacks in the Washington area projects. Although Lowe cited some distressing individual situations, she showed that of the 1,049 families living in Area B (when the Agency acquired the properties and assumed responsibility for the residents) only 39 families moved to another slum. Most of the others moved to better homes, 411 to low-rent housing, 515 to decent private shelter. Not one person had been evicted for unwillingness to move. Furthermore, the families moved to all parts of the city. After the entire southwest area had been cleared, the Washington Housing Association, a citizens' group, studied the whereabouts

---

10 Herbert Gans. *The Urban Villagers.* (New York: Free Press), 1962. Marc Fried, "Grieving for a Last Home", in Leonard Duhl (ed.) *The Urban Condition.* (New York: Basic Books), 1963.

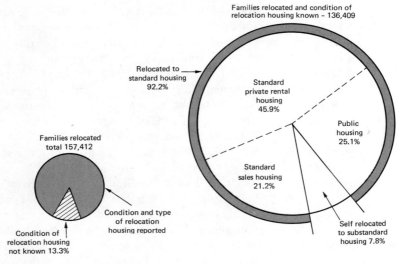

Families relocated and condition of
relocation housing known – 136,409

Relocated to
standard housing
92.2%

Standard
private rental
housing
45.9%

Public
housing
25.1%

Families relocated
total 157,412

Standard
sales housing
21.2%

Condition and type
of relocation
housing reported

Self relocated
to substandard
housing 7.8%

Condition of
relocation housing
not known 13.3%

USA – November 1963

FIGURE 7–5. Relocation of families from urban renewal projects, June 30, 1963.

of the displacees. They reported that an overwhelming number of the 23,900 former southwest residents who had accepted the redevelopment Agency's assistance had improved their housing conditions.[11]

William L. Slayton, Commissioner of the Urban Renewal Administration reported in 1963 on the national relocation problem. Through June 1963, he said, more than 152,000 families had been relocated from urban renewal (slum clearance) areas. Reports were available on the housing conditions of nearly 87 percent of all relocated families. "Over 92 percent of those whose rehousing conditions have been reported moved into decent, safe and sanitary housing, meeting the requirements of the approved relocation plans." (See Figures 7–5 and 7–6.)

Wolf Von Eckardt, a nationally famous architectural critic for *The Washington Post*, wrote that urban renewal had displaced fewer people than the freeway and other public activities, let alone private building. Furthermore it was the only program offering compensation to the displaced. A critique of urban renewal comes from Von Eckardt:

Urban renewal has made many mistakes. But most of its critics—a strange alliance of liberals, sociology professors, and ultra conservatives—tend to blame the rash for the measles. For urban renewal has forced a reluctant na-

11 Jeanne R. Lowe, *Cities in a Race with Time*. (New York: Random House), 1967.

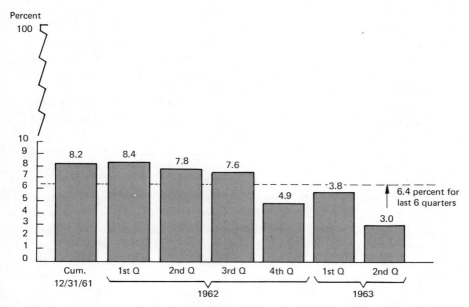

FIGURE 7–6. Percent of families self-relocated into substandard housing cumulative through December 31, 1961 and quarterly through June 1963.

tion to come to terms with the problems of its cities. It opened a Pandora's box of unexpected evils and everyone is shocked to find that the urban disease is worse and its cure more complex than we had so naively expected.[12]

CITIZENS' GROUPS

Supplementing the government programs, the Administration sponsored and encouraged participation by citizens' groups. One such activity was the American Council to Improve our Neighborhoods (ACTION), founded on a recommendation of President Eisenhower's Advisory Committee on Housing. At the launching of this organization, the President called the home improvement, slum redevelopment program "a job that must be done." He stressed that

. . . in such works there must be a reliance on the people in the local communities, although the Federal Government was ready to lend aid. "There is no question as to the need," he suggested, recalling that about a million houses are becoming blighted each year. He said it was very wonderful to find local groups trying to stop housing blight because slum conditions caused "the erosion of the decency and the dignity" of homeowners.[13]

12 Wolf Von Eckardt, *A Place to Live.* (New York: Delacorte Press), 1967.
13 *The Washington Star*, November 16, 1954.

ACTION embraced three basic elements of the city—places to live, places to work, and transportation from one to the other. ACTION's first task was a multimillion dollar public service advertising and information program conducted by the Advertising Council. Through ACTION efforts, scores of effective, adequately financed, and professionally directed local citizens' groups were organized.

ACTION carried out continuous programs of research, worked with citizens, private enterprise interests, and public agencies, conducted hundreds of conferences and seminars for an interchange of ideas and experiences. It also provided a flow of technical services and information to companies, nonprofit organizations, public agencies, and others and responded to thousands of inquiries.

ACTION was a private, nonprofit organization, with no governmental ties except the original "push" given by the President. It was financed by grants from foundations, grants and loans from businesses, and membership fees. The board of directors was drawn from the private sector and included officials of some of the largest industries in the country, educators, union labor officials, and presidents of women's organizations. Two of the moving forces of the group were Andrew Heiskell, Chairman of the Board of Time, Inc., and Richard King Mellon, head of the Mellon family enterprises in Pittsburgh.

While ACTION was not a neighborhood group, its nationwide influence was such that industry leaders and citizens of many places were stimulated and became active in lending assistance to solutions of urban problems. To many, ACTION provided the initial exposure to the need and the critical nature of the problem, and increased awareness on the part of the community leaders, business and industry executives, social workers, and local officials in various cities throughout the nation. ACTION took its promotional program to many cities, holding workshops, instructional sessions, and gatherings attended by leaders of the communities. In many cases, organizations were then formed by the local citizens to advise people in their locality about redevelopment and urban renewal programs for their city. Some specific associations were organized as a direct result of ACTION's efforts, for example, the successful ACTION Housing Inc. in Pittsburgh, and the Metropolitan Development Corporation of Syracuse.

For their part, HHFA sponsored other citizens' groups; among them, the following activities illustrate the range of the Agency's efforts to supplement governmental programs:

The Women's Congress on Housing. The government, through its mortgage insurance programs, had a big stake in the $100 billion Americans would spend for homes in the next decade. "Why not check the real experts—the women who know what a house should be, because they work in them all day." The idea was proposed and directed by

FIGURE 7–7. Cartoon from *Life*, June 4, 1956. Raising the roof of the American home. Housing Chief Albert Cole is assailed by a tornado of talk from housewives. House shows some of their complaints: it is too small, lacks individuality, has useless picture windows.

Annabelle Heath, Assistant Administrator of HHFA, later Vice President of FNMA. In 1956 HHFA invited 103 housewives from around the United States to come to Washington and to speak out "on a subject near their hearts—houses."

From the ladies, Cole hoped to learn what kind of houses will be good loan-risks, e.g., what kind of houses they want and will keep on wanting until the mortgage is paid off.[14] (Figure 7–7.)

It probably was the first housing conference for women to share their expertise with the federal government. What the housewives wanted were houses with better planned work areas, better defined zones of quiet and noise. They were willing to give up gadgets for space. They admitted many builders were turning out good products, but the ladies had come to let their hair down. And they did. "Many mass-produced houses," said one, "are a disgrace to the American standard of living,

14 *Life Magazine*, June 4, 1956, p. 66.

ugly outside and inefficient inside." There were bitter complaints about stupid landscaping and about picture windows that had no view.[15] Wide publicity was given the findings of the meeting, both in the media and throughout the industry, and some of the later changes in housing design should be directly attributed to the Women's Congress on Housing.

Conference of Advisory Committees on Cooperative and Elderly Housing. Advisory committees composed of experts in cooperative and elderly housing were held from time to time by HHFA and FHA. The needs of elderly for low-income houses was also researched by the Public Housing Administration.

As a result of the cooperative studies, a number of amendments were passed by Congress liberalizing and expanding the program. In 1955 the FHA Commissioner was directed to appoint a special Commissioner for Cooperative Housing, upgrading the activity. In the housing legislation at the end of the decade (P.L. 372, 86th Congress, 1959), the limits on the amounts of FHA mortgages for cooperative housing were increased, and mortgages could include community facilities adequate to serve the residents and others in the area. Similarly, in response to reporting by various committees, the 1959 Act authorized the Administrator to make direct loans to projects—new and existing—for elderly persons. Additional amendments further liberalized FHA's mortgage insurance programs for housing for the elderly.

Industry Executives' Advisory Committee. In 1958 HHFA invited to Washington board chairmen, presidents, and chief executives of some of the largest corporations and industries in the country. The purpose of the meeting was to inform these corporate executives of the tremendous activities of the Housing and Home Finance Agency, its impact on the federal budget, and its effect on the financial and economic structure of the country, the consumers and users in the nation, as well as producers and industry. It was determined at this meeting that the large corporations were rather unfamiliar with the activities of the Agency and were surprised at its size and reach. It was determined that this ad hoc Committee would continue providing the Agency with suggestions, ideas, and advice for the improvement of programs, policies, and procedures.

Housing for Minority Families Group. Federal agencies are intermittently harrassed, praised, unappreciated, and needed, and often faced with impossible work loads and pressures from many sources. Under such conditions it could be expected that the early stages of sweeping cultural and social changes might go unnoticed. This is not always the case, however, and it is less apt to be true if an agency is charged with policy guidance.

[15] *Ibid.*

With a few exceptions, there were no substantial federal government policies or programs directed toward separate but equal housing. However, some local public housing programs, of course, were designed for blacks, and were segregated housing. FHA insuring of mortgages excluded housing in "minority" neighborhoods. Other than minority housing advisors, there were no blacks in official positions in HHFA or its constituent agencies.

In 1950, in Washington, a black would not be served in a restaurant with white customers. A black could not attend a performance at the National Theatre, nor could a black even enter Garfinkel's department store. In 1950 a black could not purchase or rent a house in a white neighborhood.

A change begun to take place in 1953 when the Supreme Court handed down a decision which opened up the restaurants of Washington to blacks. Following this, blacks were admitted to all the department stores and theatres. These actions provoked an awakening of the difficulties blacks were experiencing in obtaining housing.

During the confirmation hearings in 1953, I had testified that I believed in integrated housing and, in what was considered an unprecedented public statement by a high federal official, I told the Detroit Economics Club that the most critical problem of housing was the racial exclusion from the greater and better part of the housing supply. Conforming to that spirit HHFA took a number of steps which laid the foundation of what later would become an active civil rights housing program.

In the "shirtsleeve conferences" much evidence was presented of the poor quality and overcrowding in housing and of the discrimination in lending practices experienced by blacks in most cities. Numerous proposals were presented at these conferences to alleviate overcrowding, discrimination, and segregation in housing.

In 1953 the President's Advisory Committee on Housing reported deep concern with the housing problems of minority groups, noting some expanded efforts on the part of FHA to study and seek possible solutions. The report also stated:

Too often the opportunities of minority groups to obtain adequate housing are extremely limited or nonexistent. Too often the working of our free economy does not provide solutions that benefit minorities. The recommendations contained herein, if supplanted by changes in the attitude of private investors and bolstered by a vigorous administrative practice, offer a basis for substantial improvement in the housing conditions of minority groups.[16]

[16] The President's Advisory Committee on Government Housing Policies and Programs. Report to the President, December 1953, U. S. Government Printing Office, p. 2.

In 1954 HHFA organized a conference on Housing for Minority
Families to develop practical methods for accelerating the achievement
of goals in housing for minorities. The meetings were held for two days
in the "Old Treaty Room" of the Executive Office Building. The people
attending the conference not only represented widely differing views,
but were acknowledged leaders of social, financial, political, religious,
as well as building and labor groups. The 25 participants included
officials of the American Council on Human Rights, the National Association for the Advancement of Colored People, a Savings Bank,
American Jewish Conference, National Lumber Dealers and Home
Builders, National Council of Negro Women, and the American
Federation of Labor.

It was not surprising that the views expressed were as widely divided
as the representation. For example, one of the first proposals by the
NAACP was that FHA should not insure housing, particularly large
developments, in which there was discrimination against minorities.
Catherine Bauer said there was place for positive federal responsibility
whether through regulations or voluntary action, although she felt she
could not espouse the NAACP position. One of the other members
contended that such an action would limit rather than facilitate the
flow of mortgage funds to minority housing. Another said that a number of mortgage lenders indicated that ample financing was available
for Negro housing occupancy if so "labeled," and that the problem
was not financial but unavailability of land for minorities. A savings
and loan official made a statement that their associations were opposed
to many governmental activities in the housing field, that they opposed
government interference in any form, and considered such activities as
socialism.

The president of a large savings bank in New York spoke of their
successful experience with mortgages for minorities, inasmuch as the
bank followed a nondiscriminatory policy and accepted FHA and VA
mortgages in all parts of the country. The president of the National
Association of Home Builders stressed that their members had agreed
that "Negroes are entitled to houses as good in every respect as those
produced for white buyers." The Home Builders were willing to build
all the housing they could market and for which they could secure
financing, and intended to build in those places in the community where
society would permit them to build. An official for the American
Federation of Labor said that the labor groups were deeply concerned
with the minority housing problem and read their last convention's
approved resolution stating their firm stand on equal opportunity in
housing regardless of creed, color, or national origin. "While we
recognize that traditional patterns of community life cannot be changed
overnight, we insist it is the positive responsibility of the federal govern-

ment to help eliminate segregation and discrimination in housing," he added.

Positions were stated, but compromise or affirmative cooperative action were difficult to reach and, although there was a general determination to continue the effort, when the Agency attempted to organize it again, there were few people interested and the program was abandoned.

However, dramatic changes were occurring in the nation. In 1954 the Supreme Court handed down the case of *Brown* vs. *Board of Education*, striking down segregation in public schools. Blacks successfully asserted their right to sit anywhere on a bus in Selma, Alabama, a massive civil rights march took place in Mississippi, and black-voter-registration drives in the south were vigorously pursued. President Eisenhower called out federal troops in Little Rock, Arkansas to enforce school integration, and later, in December 1957, New York became the first city to legislate against racial discrimination in the housing market, followed by many cities and states which began to enact legislation requiring open occupancy for housing.

In 1959, HHFA Administrator Norman Mason initiated discussions with various groups involved in minority housing problems, and created a special position to serve minorities. In the same year the Agency embraced the concept that the federal government has an inherent and basic responsibility to administer the housing programs equally for all of its citizens. Further, Administrator Mason selected a community-relations committee to encourage and strengthen activities of community groups and civic groups to accomplish a federal minority housing policy. A Public Interest Advisory Committee with 28 representatives from welfare, labor, minorities, veterans, religious, and women's housing and educational organizations was formed and met with the Administrator and staff to consult and advise the Agency.

A growing awareness on the part of local and federal governments coupled with the strong impact of social activists created the atmosphere in which President Eisenhower signed the Civil Rights Act of 1960. The law opened the doors for the improvement of the well-being of minorities.

The Effective Maintenance and Utilization of Existing Housing

The Eisenhower Administration emphasized conservation and rehabilitation of houses as an important element in the program of revitalization of the nation's cities. The idea of preserving good but declining areas was so logical that it became an integral part of urban renewal. The President's Advisory Committee had estimated that, at the rate provided in the 1953 budget, it would have taken no less than

200 years to clear the slums, and also noted that through demolition and new construction it would have been impossible to eliminate slums. Therefore, additional and supplemental action was deemed essential.

Tools had to be furnished by the federal government. Six more amendments to the law were enacted during the decade as devices to assist in the program of conservation and rehabilitation. In the 1954 Act, a new program in mortgage insurance (FHA Section 220) was authorized for use of rehabilitating existing dwellings in urban renewal areas, and another program—FHA Section 221—was created to permit rehabilitation of dwellings for persons dislocated by urban renewal activities. FHA Section 225 authorized insurance of advances to a mortgagor made pursuant to provisions of an open-end mortgage. Open-end mortgages provide that the outstanding balance of an existing mortgage can be increased in order to advance additional loan funds without the necessity of executing a new mortgage.

FHA Section 203, the regular sales housing program, liberalized the amounts of mortgages permitted on existing houses which might be rehabilitated. Also, loans were made available for rehabilitation of existing multifamily structures in blighted areas.

The FHA Home Improvement Program (Title I) was liberalized during the decade, the last time being 1956, when the loan limit was raised from $2,500 to $3,500 on single-family and nonresidential structures, and the maturity was increased from 3 to 5 years "if in the public interest." Multifamily structure loan limits were raised from $10,000 to $15,000. Authority was given to FNMA in its special assistance function to purchase mortgages issued on the urban renewal rehabilitation programs. This support was the cause of a marked increase in activity.

Not content to rely solely on government programs, the Administration encouraged and unofficially sponsored a number of efforts by citizens and civic and business organizations to join in local programs of conservation and rehabilitation of their neighborhoods. The American Council to Improve our Neighborhoods (ACTION) adopted conservation as one of its primary concerns. Through advertising, research studies, workshops, seminars, and other conferences with local people, ACTION encouraged and suggested incentives and methods to bring about community programs. Stimulated by ACTION and encouraged by HHFA, building product manufacturers joined together to sponsor a nationwide neighborhood conservation program. Under the sponsorship of the United States Chamber of Commerce, 27 trade associations interested in housing joined 40 manufacturers of building products and set as a goal the improvement and repair of 20 million homes at an expenditure of over $50 million. The National Associations of Real Estate Boards, under the energetic leadership of Fritz Burns (the only man ever to serve as both president of the National Association of Home Builders and of the Real Estate Boards) organized a nationwide program. Under the motto "Build America Better," teams of experts were sent to communities to give advice upon request of the local real estate boards and city officials. Accompanied by extensive advertising, the Build America Better concept stimulated many communities to undertake the mission of conservation. Although the organization stressed a private enterprise approach, their policy permitted any government assistance which would be considered appropriate by the community.

Among other national movements to stimulate rehabilitation, an association of the manufacturers of building products created Operation Home Improvement. Although this was a fix-up concept, HHFA encouraged the effort by participating in meetings and discussions.

Much of the support for the privately sponsored programs of conservation and rehabilitation was looked upon as an effort to restrict government programs of public housing and slum clearance and redevelopment. But, as it can well be understood, the enormous task confronting the cities could not be solved by government action alone, and HHFA deemed it highly desirable to let the supplemental tools of private resources be employed.

The programs that evolved showed a marked progress but fell short of solving urban blight. There are no complete data to measure the accomplishments in this field, and a brief review discloses some varying interpretations of the progress made. Commissioner Slayton reviewed the situation on rehabilitation in urban renewal areas for the decade, and his report published in 1963 showed that over 45,000 structures and 107,000 dwelling units were identified as current work load; rehabilitation had been completed or in process on 57 percent of the structures and nearly 44 percent of dwelling units. Slayton found it especially gratifying that the number of dwelling units on which rehabilitation had been completed rose nearly 37 percent during the 1963 fiscal year. These data relate only to urban renewal and not projects like Build America Better.

On the other hand, Martin Anderson, a critic of urban renewal, wrote that the federal program, as distinguished from private activity, might require "eighteen hundred years" to rehabilitate the existing inventory of substandard homes.

This, of course, is an extreme comparison, and does not account for the fact that the program can grow and become more effective, and that the inventory of substandard homes will be reduced substantially by private efforts.

As of December 31, 1959, 157 urban renewal projects involved some federally assisted rehabilitation. Within these projects there were 111,314 homes that the officials of local renewal agencies had decided to rehabilitate rather than demolish. . . . Of these only 6.6 percent have actually been rehabilitated.[17]

By 1956 NAHRO *Journal of Housing* was headlining possible failure of "Homebuilders Slum-Curers" in New Orleans and Miami, two cities where efforts had run high; and in 1959, the Journal pointed to an "Operation Fix-Up" in Philadelphia to call rehabilitation treatment for slums unsuccessful.

In other cities many of the efforts were more successful. Los Angeles attempted the enforcement of health standards and housing codes through the Building Department; Baltimore had a "Fight Blight" campaign to enforce codes; Chicago appropriated $55,000 to administer the first year of its conservation program; New York City proposed a block-by-block mortgage for rehabilitation; Cleveland planned to establish a new municipal bureau to deal exclusively with housing rehabilitation; Philadelphia undertook rehabilitation of 114 residential and 13 commercial structures in the Washington Square project; New Haven, in Worster Square and elsewhere, upgraded 1,000 dwelling units; Little Rock, Arkansas, successfully mixed new construction with rehabilitation; big, middle-size, and even some small cities across the country had some conservation, rehabilitation, or even paint-up, fix-up programs in their neighborhoods.

During the decade the groups of citizens and industry organizations provided substantial rehabilitation and conservation progress. Was this effort a success, was it worthwhile, or was it of little value? The Administration considered the effort—if short of success—very worthwhile.

Whether the programs in the decade made an "effective dent" or not, or whether they provided test cases, or were "transitional" movements to the future, the Administration was convinced that they were important tools in the struggle to revitalize the city. As with the 95-year-old senior citizen, commenting on the present state of his life, "It is great, considering the alternative."

Increased Volume of New Construction: The Quest for Programs to Supplement Federal Support

In 1957 the President suggested that the Governor's Conference join the Federal Administration in creating a Joint Federal State Action Committee charged with: (1) designating functions which the states are ready and willing to assume and finance wholly or in part by the Federal government; (2) recommending the federal and state revenue adjustments required to enable the states to assume such functions; and (3) identifying functions and responsibilities likely to re-

17 Martin J. Anderson, *The Federal Bulldozer.* (Cambridge, Mass.: M.I.T. Press), 1964, p. 149.

quire state or federal action in the future and recommending the level of state or federal effort, or both, that will be needed to assure effective action. The Governor's Conference adopted a resolution establishing the Joint Federal State Action Committee on June 24, 1957.

The Joint Federal State Action Committee reported in December 1957 (Progress Report # 1) and recommended: (1) that financial and administrative participation by the states in meeting problems of slum clearance and urban renewal be increased; (2) that each state create an agency with special responsibility for the handling of problems of urban development, housing, and metropolitan planning; and (3) that federal grants to stimulate programs in the states should be adopted in cases of only clear-cut national interest, and that the grant programs have built-in terminal mechanisms and state control over their administration. Following this, in January 1958, the President's budget message contained a recommendation that each state should establish an agency for housing, urban development, and metropolitan planning; that states and localities should be required to provide an increased share of the net cost of urban renewal.

As a result of this joint Federal–State Action Committee some states increased their financial and administrative participation; a number of states and cities created special agencies for urban development, housing, and metropolitan planning. The adoption by the states of programs for federal grants rather easily could be designated to be in the national interest. The control of states over grant programs was met with some lack of success.

The effort to attract private incentives to supplement federal programs was the basis for the adoption, in the 1954 Act of the Voluntary Home Mortgage Credit Program, operated out of the office of the Administrator. This was a home mortgage credit program under which private financing institutions undertook to make mortgage credit available when needed, particularly in remote, small communities. As the program continued under the policy of providing funds "where needed," the Agency assisted minority families in securing home mortgages.

From the beginning of the program to December 31, 1959, the Division had received 128,859 applications and had made 40,657 loans for approximately $400 million dollars. These loans were confined to areas with a population with less than 25,000 (small communities) and, particularly, for minority groups in all areas. For example, the VHMCP made 8,500 loans for $85 million for individual minority mortgagors in metropolitan areas.

THE 1959 HOUSING ACT

At the January 1958 Convention of the National Association of Home Builders, Senator John Sparkman termed President Eisenhower's budget proposals on housing "inadequate." He said that a retrenchment and retreat ran all through the President's Housing message, saying, "where existing programs depend on government mortgage support by direct loans, the Administration would chalk them off by raising the interest rates." Further, "where a program such as urban renewal provides assistance through grants, the proposal is cut back."

The Administration pointed out that the measures proposed in the Emergency Housing Act would help home building in 1958 to a production rate 10 percent higher than in 1957. Through speeches and other news releases, officials of the Administration stated that housing programs could be seen as leading the United States out of a slump, and that in 1958 there would be an increase of 100,000 new housing private starts which would have "a beneficial snowballing effect on the entire economy."

An Emergency Housing Act was passed in April 1958 aimed at stimulating residential construction. It provided for: reduced down payment on FHA Sections 203 and 220—sales housing; increase by $50 million for FNMA special assistance to FHA military housing; increase from 4 to 4½ percent interest rate ceiling on FHA Section 803 —military housing; extension of veterans home loans guaranteed and direct loan program for two years; increase of the maximum amount of VA direct loans from $10,000 to $13,000; increase of the interest rate ceilings on VA homes from 2½ to 4¾; limit of the interest rates on VA direct loans to the interest rates on guaranteed loans; repeal of the requirement that FHA and VA control discount on FHA and VA home loan mortgages; and strengthening of the voluntary home mortgage credit program.

Also, in April 1958, in a surprise move, the President removed the two percent down payment requirement on GI loans. "This extra no down payment push will probably provide the power needed to get the stalled VA programs rolling again," he said. A real estate editor for the *New York Journal American* put it this way, "President Eisenhower pulled an Easter rabbit out of his hat on Friday which should start builders and mortgage brokers pouring back into the VA mortgage market."

In 1959 the climate as viewed by the Administration had changed. Congress passed on omnibus housing bill which would have increased authorizations for FHA, urban renewal, FNMA Special Assistance, public housing and college housing, as well as authorized new direct loans for housing for the elderly. Citing, among other reasons, the extravagant inflationary impact and substitution of federal spending for private credit, the President vetoed the bill. Congress then passed another version of the bill deleting some of the provisions—in the hope that this would become law—but leaving most of the section substantially similar to the first legislation. But the President again vetoed the bill, because he ultimately judged that it was not much different from the previous one.

The contest of public housing unit authorization had continued during the debate. In July 1959 the Administrator, Norman Mason, testified on the President's veto message in a Senate Committee and stated that, without any new statutory authority, there were presently under annual contributions contract 101,600 units of public housing which were not yet under construction. He stated further that recent experience indicated an annual rate of public housing construction starts of approximately 20,000 units. At that rate there was approximately a five-year supply of unused public housing authority under annual contributions contract. The President's veto message stated that: "even though we have over 100,000 previously authorized public housing units as yet unbuilt, the bill will authorize 190,000 more."

Representatives of NAHRO stated that it was unfortunate that the veto message contained language the effect of which conveyed the erroneous impression that no more units are needed, since so many are already unbuilt. They pointed out the long lead time from the execution of the annual contributions contract to the completion of construction. Discussing the 100,000 unused units, it was suggested that the sizable figure had been caused by unnecessary roadblocks and restrictions.

Apparently, the basic public housing program was not under serious attack. The Mortgage Bankers Association filed a statement suggesting a review of all spending programs, investigating their productivity and effectiveness. They called attention to the fact that such a review had not been undertaken since the enactment of the major legislation of 1954 until the Chairman of the Subcommittee initiated studies of mortgage credit and related questions in the spring of 1959.

A third effort by the Congress finally resulted in the Housing Act of 1959. The President signed the bill, since some of the objectionable provisions had been eliminated, and, in balance, he felt that the Act was adequate.

Commenting on the legislation, *The Journal of Housing* (October 1959) said:

The President's signature marked the end of another dramatic year in the colorful up-and-down history of housing legislation. It was a year in which the veto power was used to cut down, not one, but two good housing measures —measures not too unlike the one that finally was enacted.

It was a year of sparkling oratory on behalf of housing on Capitol Hill. It was a year in which housing and urban renewal racked up impressive bipartisan support. And it was a year climaxed with enactment of a kind of law that, for the most part, should encourage every housing, redevelopment, and urban renewal official.

One impressive result of the Act of 1959 was FHA Section 203 mortgage insurance, which received a boost that—with the exception of 1950—produced more single-family FHA mortgages than in any prior year of its existence.

Some of the major provisions of the Housing Act of 1959 were additional grant authorizations for urban renewal; federal assistance in urban renewal areas without regard to the "predominantly residential" requirement; increase of relocation payments for families and businesses in urban renewal areas as well as payment for other governmental action; authorization of 37,000 public housing units with provisions to encompass larger families and the elderly; acquisition of land in urban renewal areas by the Public Housing Authority at a fair market value; increase of mortgage amounts that could be insured (Section 203— Sales), and decrease of down-payment schedules; two new programs for the elderly by means of direct loans and FHA insured mortgages, and additional authorizations for college and military housing, and for farm housing research.

The Housing Act of 1959 also authorized HHFA to make loans to private nonprofit corporations to build housing for the elderly (Section 202). These were long-term loans (up to 50 years) with a low interest rate. This action provided, in turn, rental housing ranging from $62.00 for an efficiency to $78.00 for one-bedroom unit monthly, for persons 62 years of age and older.

A measure of the importance of the 1959 Act is that it provided that the mortgage insurance authorization of PHA (outstanding at any one time) be increased to $8 billion as contrasted to $3 billion in the 1956 Act.

The Administration throughout the decade had been deeply concerned with the control of the budget. As the decade drew to a close it became more difficult to balance the idea of being liberal toward people and yet conservative in economics. A conservative spending policy seemed to have priority in the thinking of the Executive Branch.

SPECIAL NEEDS—SPECIFIC PROGRAMS

The needs of special groups were served by the Veterans Administration and the Farmers Home Administration (FmHA). The guaranteed home loan activity of the VA has, throughout the years, offered liberal home loans for veterans of our armed services. The 1950 decade was a busy one for the VA (Table 7–5) and shows a government agency filling a great need.

The FmHA was established with the purpose of serving a variety of needs in rural areas. The 1949 Act gave the FmHA authority to make housing loans to farmers as a part of the national housing programs. (For a time it was debated whether to administer the loans through HHFA or the United States Department of Agriculture [USDA], but the program was placed in USDA.) The number of loans obligated by FmHA during the decade represented a significant contribution to the rural families of America (Table 7–6). The high volume of activity in 1959 reflects the impact of the Government's monetary and fiscal policy and an upsurge in the economy.

The Community Facilities Administration (CFA) supervised a special purpose housing program by granting direct loans at low interest rates to colleges and universities for student and faculty dormitories, dining halls, and student union building. In 1950 Congress initially authorized $300 million for this program, and by the end of 1959 a total of $1.175 billion had been spent on 890 projects completed or under construction, serving about 60,000 students and faculty in public and private institutions throughout the nation.

Many special housing needs are unique and do not respond to broad national government programs. To help meet these requirements, Congress authorized HHFA and its constituent agencies to undertake housing aid for Alaska, Hawaii, and Guam, and for families in the armed services and workers in national defense areas. These special needs were met by a combination of FHA insurance and FNMA purchase of mortgages. Some of the standards were relaxed to overcome reluctance on the part of private lenders to invest in mortgages in these areas. The standard FHA mortgage ceiling for insurance of loans was removed. FNMA was directed, so far as practicable, to purchase these mortgages if their quality met the purchase standards imposed by

TABLE 7–6. Rural Housing Section 502 Loans
Obligated Fiscal Year 1950 through 1959

Fiscal Year	RH-502		Housing Starts (Initial)[1]
	Number	Amount	
1950	3,923	18,005,422	2070
1951	5,181	23,876,810	2455
1952	4,225	20,991,427	1810
1953	3,442	19,265,857	1702
1954	2,818	16,067,934	1375
1955	N/A		N/A
1956	561	3,720,904	386
1957	3,358	21,290,884	1792
1958	4,944	33,065,871	2394
1959	8,186	60,674,466	4723

[1] Represents new construction.

SOURCE: Obligations Report, Management Information Staff, Farmers Home Administration, USDA, March 29, 1977.

TABLE 7–5. VA Guaranteed Primary Home Loans Closed by New and Existing Homes[1]

Period	Total			New Homes			Existing Homes		
	Number of Loans	Pur. Price (In Thous.)	Amt. of Loans (In Thous.)	Number of Loans	Pur. Price (In Thous.)	Amt. of Loans (In Thous.)	Number of Loans	Pur. Price (In Thous.)	Amt. of Loans (In Thous.)
1944–1945	41,064	$ 210,506	$ 197,868	2,656	$ 15,777	$ 15,046	38,408	$ 194,729	$ 182,822
1946	403,561	2,435,551	2,365,070	64,973	454,811	421,675	338,588	1,980,740	1,943,395
1947	487,667	3,571,561	3,204,649	198,446	1,619,319	1,463,539	289,221	1,952,242	1,741,110
1948	248,540	2,052,563	1,726,753	107,573	989,672	835,842	140,967	1,062,891	890,911
1949	173,419	1,480,478	1,266,842	83,777	774,099	669,378	89,642	706,379	597,464
1950	369,069	3,203,025	2,868,303	208,893	1,855,196	1,704,019	160,176	1,347,829	1,164,284
1951	409,329	4,169,122	3,632,523	286,475	3,010,410	2,697,855	122,854	1,158,712	934,668
1952	301,698	3,183,370	2,692,685	192,202	2,080,778	1,807,232	109,496	1,102,592	885,453
1953	318,118	3,511,152	3,034,135	202,897	2,283,135	2,026,574	115,221	1,228,017	1,007,561
1954	407,340	4,672,605	4,222,799	243,191	2,878,929	2,665,503	164,149	1,793,676	1,557,296
1955	643,226	7,682,459	7,092,459	387,646	4,792,877	4,537,748	255,580	2,889,582	2,554,711
1956	502,007	6,454,174	5,857,973	313,486	4,197,578	3,909,797	188,521	2,256,596	1,948,176
1957	302,047	4,144,048	3,752,651	218,800	3,137,592	2,889,946	83,247	1,006,456	862,705
1958	143,519	2,013,959	1,859,826	94,049	1,388,163	1,310,987	49,470	625,796	548,839
1959	210,511	2,942,463	2,781,695	145,414	2,121,590	2,051,281	65,097	820,873	730,414
1960	143,287	2,077,017	1,981,691	104,760	1,605,447	1,554,132	38,527	471,570	427,559
1961	132,889	1,909,281	1,828,313	78,483	1,197,651	1,170,237	54,406	711,630	658,076
1962	187,077	2,749,100	2,648,977	87,936	1,388,627	1,357,255	99,141	1,360,473	1,291,722
1963	187,889	2,897,672	2,798,223	75,305	1,243,380	1,214,053	112,584	1,654,292	1,584,170
1964	177,594	2,858,784	2,764,388	60,348	1,041,291	1,015,322	117,246	1,817,493	1,749,066
1965	159,582	2,708,779	2,615,262	48,935	897,389	872,562	110,647	1,811,390	1,742,700
1966	156,918	2,677,957	2,597,584	53,101	1,007,359	980,438	103,817	1,670,598	1,617,146
1967	200,018	3,478,564	3,395,346	60,435	1,171,970	1,143,070	139,583	2,306,594	2,252,276
1968	210,946	3,863,383	3,771,674	71,423	1,463,435	1,430,229	139,523	2,399,948	2,341,445

[1] Excludes refinancing loans and alterations and repair loans, and mobile home loans.
[2] Excludes direct loans sold and guaranteed since January 1963.

private institutional investors. FNMA paid more than the market rate (often as high as par or 100 percent), and this opened up housing opportunities not otherwise available.

Summary

The innovative housing philosophy during the 1950 decade had a great impact on the expansion of the programs, and the total inventory of dwelling units increased by more than 12 million. The advent of the new Administration brought forth forecasts of a decrease in federal intervention, lowering of deficit spending, and reorganization of the Housing and Home Finance Agency. Many of the programs, nonetheless, followed the policy established during the 1930's which became the basic structure in federal housing programs for years to come.

During the decade the nation made startling progress in catching up on the housing deficit built up during the Depression and World War II. In 1940 there were 132 million people in 37.5 million units, or 0.28 houses per person; in 1960, 180 million people lived in 58 million units, or 0.32 units per person, even though the population had grown rapidly. The decade was characterized by the suburbanization of the cities. While urban renewal programs cleared away decayed housing in some of the central city areas, the mortgage credit programs—Federal Housing Administration and Veterans Administration—and the proliferation of roads and automobiles encouraged suburban placement of the 12 million new houses built between 1950 and 1960. The suburbs were white, but central cities became increasingly black and poor.

The pent-up demand for housing contributed to a postwar rate of change in the size and shape and scale of cities. In 1960 76 percent of the total were single-family units as opposed to only 70 percent in 1950, reflecting the postwar stampede to the suburbs. During the decade there had been a dramatic decrease in units lacking plumbing, from 35.4 percent to 15.9 percent of the total.

Through many ways and means and abundant legislation, the housing policy set out during the decade was effectively carried out. As recommended by the President's Advisory Committee, HHFA was reorganized, given greater powers of coordination and supervision, and acquired two new constituents: the Urban Renewal Administration and the Community Facilities Administration.

A new comprehensive approach to revitalize the cities was taken, through the Workable Program, to assure local support. Private investors and builders, local community and neighborhood groups, and local state agencies gained expanded involvement. A new program of low- and moderate-income housing with FHA insurance and FNMA purchase of mortgages was established. Expansion of Title I—clearance and redevelopment programs—joined with rehabilitation and conservation of blighted but sound residential, commercial, and industrial structures.

As the decade drew to an end, however, tighter controls were enforced over budget and spending in a pervasive conservative mood. An economic slowdown occurred in the latter part of 1957, and the President's response to attacks for what was labeled as inadequate budget proposals was to recommend increased aid. The resulting growth of the housing production was followed almost immediately in 1959 by inflationary spiraling.

Congress passed the liberal Housing Act of 1959 which was vetoed by the President as too inflationary. His reluctant approval of the final Act of 1959 nonetheless, set the stage for an upward swing in production despite the Administration's conservative posture toward economic considerations.

While other factors bear upon the production rate of dwellings, government programs are undoubtedly a major influence.

Bibliography

ADDE, LEO, *Nine Cities, The Anatomy of Downtown Renewal*. Washington, D.C.: Urban Land Institute, 1969.

American Academy of Political and Social Science, Vol. 314, Philadelphia, 1957.

ANDERSON, MARTIN, *The Federal Bulldozer*. Cambridge, Mass.: M.I.T. Press, 1964.

BANFIELD, EDWARD C., *Government and Housing in Metropolitan Areas*. New York: McGraw-Hill, 1958.

CARO, ROBERT C., *The Power Broker. The New Yorker*, July and August, 1974.

CARTER, JIMMY, *Why Not the Best*. New York: Bantam Books, 1975.

Cities Around the World, International Handbook for Urban Renewal. New York: Books International, 1959.

COLE, ALBERT M., *What the Aged Need in Homes. New York Times Magazine*, August 4, 1959.

COLEAN, MILES, *Renewing Our Cities*. New York: The Twentieth Century Fund, 1953.

ESKEW, GARNETT L., *Of Land and Men*. Washington, D.C.: Urban Land Institute, 1959.

Federal National Mortgage Association, *Charter Act as Amended through December 31, 1971, Office of General Counsel, FNMA*, Washington, D.C., 1971.

———, *Background and History*, 1938–1969.

FISHER, ROBERT MOORE, *Twenty Years of Public Housing*. New York: Harper and Row, 1959.

Fortune Editors, *The Exploding Metropolis*. New York: Doubleday, 1958.

GANS, HERBERT J., *The Urban Villagers*. New York: Free Press, 1962.

GLAAB, CHARLES N. and THEODORE BROWN, *A History of Urban America*. New York: Macmillan, 1976.

GRIER, EUNICE and GEORGE GRIER, *Privately Developed International Housing*. Berkeley, Calif.: University of California Press, 1960.

HEALEY, PAUL F., *The Truth About the Housing Scandals. Saturday Evening Post*, February 26, 1955.

HOWARD, EBENEZER, *Garden Cities of Tomorrow*. London: Faber & Faber, 1961.

JACOBS, JANE, *The Death and Life of Great American Cities*, New York: Random House, 1961.

Journal of Housing, National Association of Housing and Redevelopment Officials, Annual volumes 7–16, 1950–1959.

Life Magazine Editors, *Angry House - Wife Speaks on Housing. Life*, June 4, 1956.

LOWE, JEANNE RE., *Cities In a Race With Time*. New York: Random House, 1967.

McFARLAND, CARTER, *Challenge of Urban Renewal*, Technical Bulletin #37, Washington, D.C.: Urban Land Institute, 1958–1962.

MAISEL, SHERMAN J., *Housebuilding in Transition*. Berkeley, Calif.: University of California Press, 1955.

MILLSPAUGH, MARTIN and GURNEY BRECKENFELD, *The Human Side of Urban Renewal*. Baltimore, Md.: Fight Blight, Inc., 1958.

MOSES, ROBERT, *Working for the People: Promises and Performances in Public Service*. New York: Harper and Row, 1956.

MUMFORD, LEWIS, *The Culture of Cities*. New York: Harcourt Brace Jovonovich, 1938.

MYERSON, MARTIN and EDWARD C. BANFIELD, *Politics, Planning and Public Interest, The Case for Public Housing in Chicago*. New York: Free Press, 1955.

NASH, WILLIAM, *Residential Rehabilitation; Private Profits and Public Purposes*. New York: McGraw-Hill, 1959.

National Housing Conference, *Year Book*, 1954.

NEUTRA, RICHARD, *Survival Through Design*. New York and London: Oxford Union Press, 1954.

New York Journal American, April 11, 1958.

The President's Advisory Committee on Government Housing Policies and Program: A Report to the President of the United States, December, 1953. Washington, D.C.: U. S. Government Printing Office.

RAPKIN, CHESTER and WILLIMA G. GRIGSBY, *Residential Renewal in the Urban Core*. Philadelphia: University of Pennsylvania Press, 1963.

ROBINSON, GERALD, *Federal Income Taxation of Real Estate*. Boston: Warren, Gorham & Lamont, 1973–75.

SEMER and ZIMMERMAN, *Evolution of Federal Legislative Policy in Housing*, Report to H.U.D., 1973 (unpublished).

SLAYTON, WILLIMA, *Development and Redevelopment in the United States*, Surveyors Annual Conference, Cambridge University, Cambridge, 1965; *Report on Urban Renewal*, Subcommittee on Housing, Committee of Banking and Currency, House of Representatives, November 21, 1963. Washington, D.C.: Government Printing Office.

Statistical Abstract of the U.S., Department of Commerce, 1961, p. 747.

TUNNARD, CHRISTOPHER and HENRY R. REED, *American Skyline*. Boston: Houghton Mifflin, 1955.

U. S. Congress, *Hearings on Housing Act of 1959*, Veto, S. 57, July 23–31, 1959, S. 57, 65, 612, Committee on Banking and Currency U. S. Senate, 86th Congress, Senate Library, 1345.

————, *Hearings on Housing Act of 1969*, Committee on Banking and Currency, House of Representatives, January 28–February 3, 1959. 87th Congress, Senate Library, H. 1709,2.

————, *Hearings, FHA Investigations*, Committee of Banking and Currency, U.S. Senate, 83rd Congress, 2nd Session, 1954, p. 1303.

————, *Hearings on Housing Act of 1954*, Committee of Banking and Currency, U.S. Senate, March 9–15, 1954, 83rd Congress, Senate Library, Vol. S.1072,6.

————, *Hearings on Housing Act of 1954*, Committee on Banking and Currency, House of Representatives, March 2–18, 1954, 83rd Congress, Senate Library, Vol. 1442,7.

————, *Hearings on Nomination of Albert M. Cole to be Administrator of the Housing and Home Finance Administration*, Committee on Banking and Currency, U. S. Senate, March 2 and 6, 1953, 83rd Congress, Senate library, Vol. 1036,2.

U. S. Federal Home Loan Bank Board, *Report of Operations, 1955–1960*, Government Printing Office, Washington.

U. S. Housing and Home Finance Agency, *Annual Reports 1950–1959*, Government Printing Office, Washington.

U. S. News & World Report Editors, *Quick Million in Housing*. Washington, D.C., October 22, 1954.

United States Savings & Loan Association, *1974 Savings & Loan Fact Book*, Chicago, 1974.

WEAVER, ROBERT J., *The Urban Complex*. New York: Doubleday, 1964

CHAPTER 8
HOUSING IN THE 1960'S

ROBERT R. RICE*

Introduction

THE DECADE of the 1960's saw many significant events which had great impact on housing in the United States. It was a time of rapid social and demographic change, potent but varied political pressures, new legislation, new technology, and numerous other developments which influenced the quality of living for every citizen. The quantity and quality of housing in existence at the beginning of the 1960's was the result of many years of accumulated construction and normal destruction of houses through aging and decay, obsolescence, age, fire, flood, or demolition.

Before the 1960's, the United States relied primarily on high residential construction rates and the "filtering process" to improve the general living environment. It was increasingly evident, however, that simply erecting more housing for the middle- and upper-income groups, who then released older homes for the less prosperous (the filtering process), was not effective in meeting the needs of an increasing number of minority and low-income families. It was also becoming clear that better housing alone would not improve the quality of life for the poorer segment of society.

Housing legislation in the 1960's took an evolutionary approach toward meeting the nation's housing needs, as new emphasis was placed on providing housing to particular groups such as the poor and elderly.

* ROBERT R. RICE, Associate Dean, College of Agriculture and Director, School of Home Economics, University of Arizona, Tucson, Arizona. Ph.D. from Cornell University, 1967. Glenn H. Beyer, major professor. Past president, American Association of Housing Educators.

Instead of emphasizing the home financing program as it did in the 1950's, the government embarked on direct and indirect subsidies. It also reemphasized the goal spelled out in the 1949 Housing Act of providing a "decent home and a suitable living environment" for all Americans.

Between 1960 and 1970, the number of people in the United States increased by almost 24 million, or 14 percent,[1] but this growth was not evenly distributed across the land. There were several important changes in population characteristics which had great impact on housing. The 1960 census confirmed what many people already knew from first-hand observation: this historically predominantly rural nation had become urbanized! In the growing national awareness that the United States was emerging as a metropolitan nation, "no single event accounted for this recognition; indeed, the big 'happenings' of the period —Sputnik, integration at Little Rock High School, the downing of the U-2 inside Russia—all served to hinder the development of a national urban consciousness." Instead, that was to be ". . . the product of the sheer weight of numbers and the activities of businessmen, academicians, and practical politicians."[2]

In 1960, of the nearly 53 million households, only 4 million were farm households. By 1970 the number of households had increased to nearly 63 million and more than 60 million of these were nonfarm, as compared to fewer than 3 million farm households.[3] The shifts in population during the decade that made this a nation of cities showed suburban areas surrounding cities growing by more than 33 percent.[4]

A growing population and a sustained trend toward urbanization were key variables in housing in the 1960's, but other factors had deep impact as well. The death rate in 1970 was about the same as in 1960, but the birth rate dropped from 23.3 per 1,000 people in 1960 to 18.4 in 1970; marriages increased from 8.5 per 1,000 in 1960 to 10.6 in 1970; and divorces increased from 2.2 to 3.5.[5] The change in birth rate was significant, helping drop household size from 3.4 persons to

[1] United States Bureau of the Census, *Census of Housing: 1960. States and Small Areas*, Vol. I. United States Summary, Part 1. (Washington, D.C.: Government Printing Office), 1963, p. S5.

[2] Mark I. Gelfand, *A Nation of Cities*. (New York: Oxford University Press), 1975, p. 276.

[3] United States Bureau of the Census, *Historical Statistics of the United States, Colonial Times to 1970*. Bicentennial Edition, Part 1. (Washington, D.C.: U. S. Government Printing Office), 1975, p. 43.

[4] James F. Blumstein and Eddie J. Martin (eds.), *The Urban Scene in the Seventies*. (Nashville, Tenn.: Vanderbilt University Press), 1974.

[5] United States Department of Health, Education and Welfare, *Vital Statistics of the United States, 1970*. (Rockville, Maryland: Public Health Service, Health Resources Administration, National Center for Health Statistics), 1974.

3.1 over the 10-year period.[6] The increase in marriages and divorces, however, had more immediate impact on the demand for housing. Both added to the number of household formations and the need for additional dwelling units.

Out of the 1950's and into the 1960's, the nation's interests focused mainly on meeting housing demands of the middle- and upper-income families. The economy was expanding, the federal government was facilitating home financing for middle-income housing, and many families had both the desire and the resources to buy new homes. This demand, coupled with assembly-line mass production construction techniques of the times, produced many large-scale monotonous housing developments. These subdivisions, with row after row of nearly identical units, became so prevalent across the nation that many people began to wonder if a country that had been noted for its cultural variety and individualism would not end up housing its people in identical "little boxes." A song reflecting these events reached a degree of national popularity.

> Little boxes on the hillside,
> Little boxes made of ticky tacky
> Little boxes on the hillside,
> Little boxes all the same;
>
> There's a green one and a pink one
> And a blue one and a yellow one
> And they're all made out of ticky tacky
> And they all look just the same.[7]

But while some people were viewing with concern the monotony of the ticky tacky suburban homes, others turned their attention to crises in central cities. Some observers of housing problems in the United States have sharpened the focus on the more serious issues by calling them "the Black problem," and a brief look at the figures gives some support to this emphasis. In 1960, the proportion of black population was 10 percent, increasing to 11 percent by 1970. During this period, the number of blacks living within the suburban rings of all metropolitan areas of the country remained at a relatively static 4 percent, while the percentage of blacks inhabiting the central cities increased from 16 to 20 percent.[8] "Nationwide, 25 percent of all nonwhites living in central cities occupied substandard units in 1960, compared to 8

[6] United States Bureau of the Census, *Census of Housing Characteristics for States, Cities and Counties*, Vol. 1. United States Summary, Part 1. (Washington, D.C.: U. S. Government Printing Office), 1972, p. 36.

[7] Melvin Reynolds, *Little Boxes and Other Handmade Songs*. (New York: Oak Publishing Co.), 1964, p. 28.

[8] Blumstein and Martin, *op. cit.*, p. 179.

percent of all whites."⁹ As we shall see, the majority of housing problems in the 1960's were centered in the cities and especially concentrated in the cities' ghettos. The term "ghetto" originally referred to
the Jewish quarters in 16th century Venice and later to the Jewish
sector of any city. In the course of time, the term has undergone
changes, and one of the current meanings is "low-income neighborhood
with abominable housing."¹⁰

Following World War II, mechanization of farming in the South
forced more and more blacks to migrate to the North seeking better
jobs and living conditions. What they most often found were higher
rent, poor and overcrowded housing, inadequate sanitation and bad
health conditions, and higher priced merchandise in their shopping
areas. They also found many of the same discrimination practices in
the job market they had left behind in the South.

Education in these areas was also a concern. Experts agreed that
the quality of schools was inferior within lower-income neighborhoods.
Many teachers simply did not want to cope, or were afraid to cope,
with the discipline problems, lack of equipment and materials, and
poorer facilities in schools in these areas. All these factors greatly influenced and still do influence the quality of education, thus tending to
perpetuate the existing problems. Inferior education leads to inferior
jobs which lead to inferior salaries, which lead to inferior housing in
low-income neighborhoods. So the circle is complete.

Jacob Riis described New York in the mid-1800's as viewed by a
legislative committee when they came to see

. . . how crime and drunkeness came to be the natural crop of a population
'housed in crazy old buildings, crowded, filthy tenements in rear yards, dark,
damp basements, leaking garrets, shops, outhouses, and stables converted
into dwellings, though scarcely fit to shelter brutes," or in towering tenements, 'often carried up to a great height without regard to strength of the
foundation walls.' What matter? They were not intended to last. The rent
was high enough to make up for the risk to the property. The tenant was not
considered. Nothing was expected of him and he came up to the expectation,
as men have a trick of doing. Reckless slovenliness, discontent, privation, and
ignorance were left to work out their inevitable results, until the entire
premises reached the level of tenant-house dilapidation, containing, but
sheltering not, the miserable hordes that crowded beneath smouldering,
water-rotted roofs, or burrowed among the rats of clammy cellars.¹¹

9 *The Report of the National Advisory Commission on Civil Disorders*
(Washington, D.C.: U. S. Government Printing Office), March 1, 1968, p. 257.
   10 Harlem Youth Opportunities Unlimited, Inc., *Youth in the Ghetto.* (New
York: Orans Press), 1964, p. 135.
   11 Jacob A. Riis, *The Battle with the Slum.* (New York: Macmillan), 1902,
pp. 12–13.

That was an 1857 slum. The Harlem ghetto of 1964 as described by some of its tenants:

A 28-year-old woman: They need to get rid of these slummy buildings. The children can't live in these buildings—not to be brought up right. There's filth! They need better schools, they need better playgrounds, more community centers. They need a whole lot! It is not a small thing they have to do, and they are taking too much time in doing them.

And from a 15-year-old girl: Now, they had been complaining to the Department of Health about conditions in the building, about all the violations; no lights in the hall, the rats and roaches literally moving the tenants out of the building, and about six months ago the plumbing in the basement got jammed up somehow or other and there has been standing water in the basement, and the flies and maggots and everything else has been breeding there. Now, yesterday I understand something happened in one apartment; rats forced the woman out of her apartment. She couldn't at all control the rats; they were running all over the kitchen and all throughout the house and everything.[12]

It is clear that in the cities of the 1960's, even as in the cities more than a century before, there were poor houses, poor and minority families, and inadequate support services to provide health, security, and education. By the mid-1960's, an estimated 56 percent of all Negroes in the United States were concentrated in relatively small sections of most central cities and in large areas of a few.[13]

Often the aggregate size of a city's housing needs were less of a problem than the degree of concentration of problems in small areas of the city. Substandard housing in these areas was correlated with poverty families and poverty in turn was highly correlated with race. Actually, Negro outmigration from the South had dropped significantly in the early 1960's, but the movement of whites from the central cities picked up. By 1966, nonwhites accounted for about 23 percent of the population of cities of more than 250,000, nearly double the figure for 1950.[14]

In the years following World War II and leading up to the 1960's, the primary public interest and the major Federal Government efforts had been directed toward increasing the quantity rather than the quality of housing. With the new decade, professionals in housing began to place increasing emphasis on the social and psychological aspects of housing. Housing was seen not only as a backdrop for activities, but

[12] Harlem Youth Opportunities Unlimited, Inc., *op. cit.*, p. 315.

[13] Frank S. Kristof, *Urban Housing Needs Through the 1980's: An Analysis and Projection* (Research Report No. 10. (Washington, D.C.: Government Printing Office), 1968, p. xii.

[14] Gelfand, *op. cit.*, p. 353.

also as a part of the ecological environment which could shape family and community behavior. "Though the evidence is scattered, taken as a whole it is substantial. The type of housing occupied influences health, behavior, and attitude, particularly if the housing is desperately inadequate."[15] The effects which may result from poor housing include "a perception of one's self that leads to pessimism and passivity, stress to which the individual cannot adapt, poor health, and a state of dissatisfaction; pleasure in company but not in solitude, cynicism about people and organizations, a high degree of sexual stimulation without legitimate outlet, and difficulty in household management and child rearing; and relationships that tend to spread out in the neighborhood rather than deeply into the family."[16]

Housing tended to become viewed as an instrument of social policy and public housing projects, not just as shelter, but as a means to improve the physical, social, and psychological well-being of the citizens. As this perspective of public housing was gaining wider acceptance, the results of a comprehensive and classic study in the field of housing were published. *The Housing Environment and Family Life*[17] attempted to determine the measurable effects of housing on physical and mental health.

The findings of the longitudinal study indicated that families from better housing (a large public housing project in Baltimore) were only slightly better off on variables of morbidity and episodes of illness than were families in substandard housing. Wives in public housing were more satisfied with their living environment, and families tended to become more neighborly than those in substandard housing; but few differences appeared in families' perception of their social standing. There appeared to be a little difference between the two groups of families in adult behavior patterns in such matters as cleanliness, orderliness, and repair of furnishings. Hypotheses anticipating improved school performance by children were in general not borne out. While the results of this excellent study were not conclusive, they did raise some serious questions about just how much social and physical improvement could be expected from better housing alone.

Traditionally, the construction of public housing at the national level was opposed by two groups: the rural conservatives who were against federal spending, particularly in the cities; and urban businessmen, such as real estate brokers and contractors, who objected to housing projects for lower-income groups because they felt these

15 Alvin L. Schorr, *Slums and Social Insecurity*. (Washington, D.C.: United States Department of Health, Education and Welfare), 1963, p. 31.

16 *Ibid.*, pp. 31–32.

17 Daniel M. Wilner, et al., *The Housing Environment and Family Life*. (Baltimore, Md.: Johns Hopkins Press), 1962.

projects raised property and income taxes and cut into profits. Rural congressmen had been effective in Washington, and businessmen were often successful at the local level in blocking federal housing projects.

The New Frontier

As the decade of the 1960's got under way, the country was experiencing a business recession, and there was not widespread public interest in urban problems or in supporting major efforts to improve housing. Those who were more aware of the seriousness and complexity of these problems were not optimistic about prospects for solving them. It was apparent that if there was any hope for significant progress on a national level, the federal government would have to provide the direction and leadership.

The Housing Act of 1959 authorized a new program which would have impact on subsequent legislation and represented a change in direction for federal programs in housing. The new Federal Housing Administration (FHA) program was designed to provide direct federal loans to private nonprofit corporations for rental housing for the elderly. This was the forerunner of later subsidy programs. While the machinery was established to get some of these projects under way, other government activity in housing was limited in 1960.

The political scene was not so uneventful, since 1960 was an election year. John F. Kennedy had won the election by a narrow margin and, even before his inauguration, he provided some clues to the direction of his Administration through the announcement of some presidential appointments. One was Robert C. Weaver as chief administrator of the Housing and Home Finance Agency (HHFA). Weaver was well qualified for the job. He had been graduated from Harvard as an economist and had published in his field. Most of his experience had been in government positions, and he had promoted public housing as a means of helping the poor. An additional factor, viewed in many quarters as an asset for Kennedy was the fact that Weaver was to occupy the highest post in the Executive Branch ever held by a Negro up to that time.

Shortly after Kennedy took office he made known his concerns for improvements in housing and communities. In his State of the Union Message on January 31, 1961, less than two weeks after taking the oath of office, he called for a new housing program under a new Department of Housing and Urban Affairs. Two days later he sent a special message to the Congress reporting that he had taken action to stimulate residential construction and public works through expanding long-term credit, reducing interest rates on Government-backed loans, and expanding the public facility loan program.

Within a month, the President delivered another special housing message in which, in addition to the recommendation to broaden existing programs, he listed three basic national objectives: (1) to renew cities and assure sound growth of metropolitan areas, (2) to provide decent housing for all Americans, and (3) to encourage improvement in the construction industry. The President also noted that government attention and resources were needed in the closely related fields of transportation and open space. In this message, Kennedy again recommended establishment of a new Department of Housing and Urban Affairs. Six weeks later he transmitted a draft bill to Congress which would have established a Cabinet level Department of Urban Affairs and Housing.[18]

With this flurry of activity, the Administration hoped to give momentum to proposals and programs designed to fill the gaps or areas of housing and community development which were in need of special help and attention. Families in the upper-middle-and-above income categories appeared to be faring well. The lower-middle and low-income families needed assistance.

The 1961 Housing Act was an omnibus bill dealing with many programs, but its general intent was to "assist in the provision of housing for moderate- and low-income families, to promote orderly urban development, to extend and amend laws relating to housing, urban renewal, and community facilities, and for other purposes."[19] The bill repealed the previous requirement that a community must have a "workable program" for the prevention and elimination of slums as a prerequisite for Section 221 housing.[20] This requirement had been a stumbling block for many communities in obtaining federal assistance. This easing of federal requirements, plus a speed-up in processing of applications from cities and the authorization of substantially more funds than in the past, helped urban renewal spur one of the biggest construction booms in metropolitan history. The program refinements and increased federal funding also encouraged greater private investment in urban renewal projects. This cooperative spirit and demonstrated faith in the future of cities helped create a new feeling of optimism.

The 1961 bill included two new features, a program interest subsidy and a direct loan program. The interest subsidy took the form of below-

18 Subcommittee on Housing and Community Development of the Committee on Banking, Currency and Housing, *Evolution of Role of the Federal Government in Housing and Community Development* (House of Representatives, 94th Congress, First Session. (Washington, D.C.: U. S. Government Printing Office), October 1975, p. 75.

19 *United States Statutes at Large.* 87th Congress, 1st Session, Vol. 75. (Washington, D.C.: U. S. Government Printing Office), 1961, p. 149.

20 See Chapter 7 by Albert M. Cole in this volume.

market interest rates for rental housing mortgages to assist low- and moderate-income families and displaced families. The direct loans were authorized to permit the Federal National Mortgage Association (FNMA) to purchase original mortgages and service them at below market rates. The chief beneficiaries were the families who had incomes too high to qualify them for public housing but not high enough for them to rent decent private housing without government subsidy. The subsidy concept was further expanded by the 1961 Act through authorization of payments up to $120 per year on units occupied by the elderly in public housing projects. This subsidy was the first ever given to finance not only capital costs but also the operating costs of housing projects.

Kennedy's attempts to establish a Cabinet level department for cities to help the country achieve the goals of the "New Frontier" were unsuccessful. While the Administration did commit some tactical errors in pushing the proposal, the major problem was simply the lack of votes on Capitol Hill. Rural interests and influence in Congress had not changed significantly. The 1960 Census had confirmed major shifts in population from rural to urban areas, but more time was needed for these shifts to be reflected in the representatives sent to Congress.

In the year following the passage of the 1961 Housing Act, major efforts were undertaken to implement provisions of the Act. The Administration also made efforts to coordinate and integrate various government activities and functions in the broad field of housing and urban development.

An additional piece of legislation, the "Senior Citizen's Housing Act of 1962" authorized more funds for existing programs to provide low- and moderate-cost housing, both urban and rural, for the elderly. As a group, the elderly experience many of the same housing problems as other segments of the society, but some are more intense and stressful. The low income of the elderly is a major factor in the quality of their housing. While incomes of the elderly did rise relative to the rest of the population between 1960 and 1970, they started from a very low level.

By 1970, 9.1 percent of all elderly households still had homes with incomplete plumbing, compared with 5.9 percent for the population as a whole.[21] The elderly spend a larger portion of their income for generally poorer housing. Low fixed incomes with high fixed costs make them more susceptible to the effects of inflation, tax increases,

---

21 United States Department of Housing and Urban Development, *Housing in the Seventies.* A Report of the National Housing Policy Review. HUD Publication No. HUD-PDR-64. (Washington, D.C.: U. S. Government Printing Office), 1974, p. 169.

and serious illness. Research has indicated the elderly will entertain visitors in their dwelling only if they have an area they can keep "presentable."[22] Further, generally low retirement income dictates small and compact dwellings, which complicate design and room arrangement. The one problem not faced by elderly households is overcrowding measured by the one person per room standard. Only 1 percent were overcrowded in 1970, compared to 8 percent of all households in the United States.[23]

A Significant Event

A significant event for the nation and especially for minority families was the Executive Order issued by President Kennedy on "Equal Opportunity in Housing." This order directed federal departments and agencies "to prevent discrimination in the sale, lease or occupancy of residential property owned or operated by the Federal Government."[24] After two years in office, the Presidential edict made good a campaign pledge to bar discrimination in the sale or rental of federally assisted housing.

As it turned out, the 1961 Housing Act was the only important piece of urban legislation added to the statute books during Kennedy's tenure in the White House. Authorizations were expected to last for three to four years, and a new bill was planned for the Presidential election year of 1964, but an assassin's bullet removed Kennedy from the scene before the HHFA proposals were ready.[25]

Political scientist Richard Leach noted that Kennedy may be "best remembered as the first President to understand the implications of the metropolitan revolution in the United States and as the first to try to do something about it."[26]

The Great Society

When Lyndon Johnson inherited the leadership of the country, he brought to it quite a different orientation from his predecessor. Kennedy had been a city man who understood the problems but still saw promise in the cities, if they could be made better places in which to

[22] William C. Loring, "Design for a New Housing Market: The Old," *Architectural Forum*, Vol. 114, No. 3, March 1961, p. 119.

[23] United States Department of Housing and Urban Development, *Housing in the Seventies, op. cit.*

[24] Subcommittee on Housing and Community Development of the Committee on Banking, Currency and Housing, *op. cit.*, p. 84.

[25] Gelfand, *op. cit.*, p. 321.

[26] *Ibid.*, p. 347.

live. Johnson, coming from a small community in Texas, apparently did not feel comfortable in the city, even though he had spent most of his adult life in Washington, D.C. He did, however, feel a deep sympathy for the city's poor, as he had grown up seeing at first-hand the effects of poverty.

To help educate himself on the problems of the cities, and other issues as well, Johnson sought out some of the "best minds" in the country for counsel and advice. Many of the ideas and insights he obtained were expressed in the commencement address delivered at the University of Michigan in May 1964. It was this speech in which Johnson described the crisis of American cities and his vision of a future "Great Society."

Even before his "Great Society" address, Johnson had sent to the Congress a message on housing and essentially recommended a continuance of Kennedy programs. He urged authorization of more housing units, extension of the low interest direct Federal loan program for housing for the elderly, passage of urban mass transportation legislation, and a $1.4 billion for urban renewal over a two-year period.[27] Among other things, he recommended that Congress establish a Department of Housing and Community Development.

The Administration also declared an unconditional "War on Poverty" that had significant implications for housing. "While there are many facets to the attack on poverty, housing has a major role to play. It has long been recognized that poverty and bad housing are closely related. Each can be both cause and effect."[28] The administration was demonstrating a greater concern for the human element of housing than had ever been shown before.

With considerable political maneuvering, Johnson was successful in getting through Congress urban mass transportation legislation which authorized grants or loans by HHFA to assist states and local public agencies in financing the acquisition, construction, and improvement of mass transportation facilities and equipment.[29] The time was still not right for a new Cabinet level department for housing, so Johnson did not push it. He had not really had time to establish a program of his own and the Congress was in a period of limbo.

Under these conditions, the Housing Act of 1964, offering little that was new or innovative, was essentially a continuation—with some reshaping and refinement—of existing federal housing and urban programs. Housing programs for the elderly were increased and extended

[27] Subcommittee on Housing and Community Development of the Committee on Banking, Currency and Housing, *op. cit.*, p. 87.

[28] Housing and Home Finance Agency, *18th Annual Report*. (Washington, D.C.: U. S. Government Printing Office), 1964, p. 2.

[29] Subcommittee on Housing and Community Development of the Committee on Banking, Currency and Housing, *op. cit.*, p. 88.

to cover the handicapped as well. There were also substantial authorizations in several other areas, including demonstration projects in urban renewal and low-income housing.

In the summer of 1964, Congress enacted the Civil Rights Act of 1964, the most far-reaching civil rights legislation in the nation's history. The Act covered a wide range of civil rights, including voting, antidiscrimination in public accommodations, and under any program or activity receiving federal assistance.[30]

The 1964 Presidential election saw Johnson win by a landslide, with solid backing from the metropolitan areas. Winning office on Johnson's coattails were two more Democratic senators and 37 new Democratic representatives. With a two-to-one majority in Congress, the Democrats were solidly seated and Johnson's "Great Society" was on its way!

Johnson immediately formed 13 task forces to deal with the nation's many and varied problems. The 1964 Task Force on Metropolitan and Urban Problems did an in-depth study of the problems of the cities. The major emphasis was to make the cities better places in which to live and work, and to spend one's leisure time. The task force recommendations to the President stressed the human element in urban renewal and included extending the Executive Order barring discrimination in all of the following areas: housing, the construction of community centers, block grants to municipalities for social services, and federal assistance for upgrading law enforcement personnel.[31]

In a number of messages to Congress, Johnson emphasized the urgent need for attention and action on the problems of cities. In his March 1965 message to Congress specifically on "The Problems of the Central City and Its Suburbs," he said:

The modern city can be the most ruthless enemy of the good life, or it can be its servant. The choice is up to this generation of Americans. In our time, two giant dangerous forces are converging on our cities; the forces of growth and decay.

Let us be clear about the core of this problem. The problem is people and the quality of the lives they lead. We want to build not just housing units, but neighborhoods; not just to construct schools, but to educate children; not just to raise income, but to create beauty and end the poisoning of our environment.[32]

Johnson offered Congress a broad range of proposals, including a study of building codes and zoning laws, expanded urban renewal and public housing, an open space program, rent supplements and the

[30] *Ibid.*

[31] Gelfand, *op. cit.*, p. 368.

[32] United States Department of Housing and Urban Development, *Annual Report 1965.* (Washington, D.C.: U. S. Government Printing Office), 1965, p. 3.

establishment of a Department of Housing and Urban Development (HUD). Considerable controversy developed over the rent supplements program, and the Administration had a tough fight over some of the other housing proposals, but the time had finally come for a Cabinet level department to represent the interests of the cities.

Johnson's request for a Department of Housing and Urban Development met little serious opposition. The Act creating HUD passed September 9, 1965, but the department was not actually organized until February 1966. As early as 1941 there had been a proposal offered to consolidate federal government activity in housing and urban affairs into one Cabinet level department, but it took more than a decade from the first formal attempt to create a "Department of Urbiculture" in 1954 to finally establish HUD.

Johnson made some politically expedient alterations in Kennedy's earlier proposal, notably substituting the name Housing and Urban Development for Urban Affairs and Housing. "By placing housing first, the administration hoped to ease the anxiety of those in the construction industry, especially the home-builders and bankers who feared that their interests would be submerged in an urban department."[33] The term urban affairs was misunderstood and opposed in some quarters and "the Administration chose the term 'development' to indicate HUD's primary mission extended only to the quality of the physical environment of urban areas."[34]

By the creation of HUD and the elevation to cabinet level status the function and administration of what had been the Housing and Home Finance Agency were greatly simplified. A Secretary, assisted by five Assistant Secretaries, a General Counsel, and a Director of Urban Program Coordination were designated to administer the Department. "The Act transferred to the Secretary all the functions, powers, and duties of the Housing and Home Finance Agency, the Federal Housing Administration, and the functions, powers, and duties of the heads and other officials of those agencies."[35] The Federal National Mortgage Association was also transferred to the Department.

By February 1966, HUD was finally organized. Johnson moved quickly to announce the appointment of Robert Weaver, administrator of HHFA, as the new HUD Secretary. Following senatorial approval, Weaver became the first Negro Cabinet officer in the nation's history.

The Housing and Urban Development Act of 1965, viewed as a significant piece of legislation, was placed high on the list of triumphs

[33] Gelfand, *op. cit.*, p. 375.
[34] *Ibid.*, p. 376.
[35] Subcommittee on Housing and Community Development of the Committee on Banking, Currency and Housing, *op. cit.*, p. 107.

for the Administration. President Johnson was pleased with the bill because it included most of his recommendations. Two new subsidy programs were authorized in the Act: a rent supplement program, under which federal payments could be made to meet a portion of the rent of qualified low-income families, and a new subsidy program which permitted local public housing authorities to lease privately owned units and make them available to low-income families eligible for regular public housing. In part, these programs were designed to counter the stigma often attached to public housing projects.

The 1965 Housing Act also contained special provisions for disadvantaged persons, which were intended to increase the volume of good housing for low-income families, the handicapped, the elderly, and those displaced by natural disaster. Section 115 provided for small grants to low-income homeowners in urban renewal areas to bring their homes up to code or urban renewal plan requirements. The wide ranging bill covered many other programs, including such diverse issues as providing funds for local housing code enforcement, covering the cost of relocating historic structures that were within urban renewal project areas, and providing relocation payments for families and businesses displaced by government activities.

The introduction to HUD's Second Annual Report (1966) included the theme: "Man in a changing environment." The introduction went on, "Now we are mounting a far greater, more comprehensive attack on the urban problem than any we have previously conceived. We can no longer deal with the physical rebuilding of urban areas without regard to the human problems and the measures needed for human betterment."[36]

It was becoming increasingly clear that more housing units alone would not solve the nation's problems. It would take the combined efforts of many to find solutions. Realizing this, President Johnson issued Executive Order 11297, which designated the HUD Secretary as convening authority to bring about closer cooperation and coordination between government agencies such as the Office of Economic Opportunity (OEO), Health Education and Welfare (HEW), Department of Interior, and others concerned with cities and the people who live within cities.

The year 1966 saw more recommendations made for legislation to aid the troubled urban areas. One of these, the Demonstration Cities Program, was highlighted by Vice President Hubert Humphrey in remarks to the U.S. Conference of Mayors in Dallas on June 13, 1966:

[36] United States Department of Housing and Urban Development, *HUD Second Annual Report.* (Washington, D.C.: U. S. Government Printing Office), 1966, p. 6.

The Demonstration Cities Program will be an increment of new money for your city. You will not lose a single program you have got. In addition to these regular, on-going programs, special grants would be extended to demonstration cities. These grants would not be siphoned away from other Federal programs.

I want to emphasize also that the benefits of this program would be available to those cities—on a first come first serve basis—who have plans to show that they are ready to mount a full-scale attack on the slum problem. Get yourself organized; get your plans; and have a program that really makes your city a demonstration city.

Critics of this proposal do not attack it as a bad bill, but rather out of the fear, it seems, that it isn't big enough and that everybody can't participate immediately, or that only the big cities have a chance. Big cities need this program and can use it. But the greatest beneficiaries will possibly be the smaller cities, because they are getting organized and this program would enable some of them virtually to eliminate slums and blight.

The ultimate size of the Demonstration Cities Program will be determined not by any figures or numbers game resulting from academic or even congressional debate but by the cities themselves and their ability to put to work all these aids in a concentrated way. This will not be instant slum clearance. It will be a continuing program that begins with large-scale planning, continuous action and social as well as economic rehabilitation. So my plea to you is: let's get the program started. Then we can measure our rate of expansion by our readiness to put these demonstrations into large-scale operations.[37]

On November 4, 1966, the Demonstration Cities and Metropolitan Development Act was passed, and from it came the much publicized Model Cities Program (with the increase in confirmation politics in the 1960's, "demonstration" cities was a phrase which Congress found less acceptable than "model" cities). As Humphrey had said it would, the Act authorized grants and technical assistance to help communities of all sizes participate in demonstration programs rebuilding or restoring entire sections and neighborhoods of slum and blighted areas through concentrated and coordinated use of federal aid together with local, private, and governmental resources. Particular emphasis was placed on new and innovative approaches to deal with urban problems and coordinate all the resources available to implement the proposals.

After a city was designated as a Model City project, it received a one-year planning grant. During this period particular problems of its model neighborhood area were analyzed and strategies for achieving the goals were established. A final comprehensive plan developed by

[37] Hubert H. Humphrey, *Better Cities for Tomorrow.* (Washington, D.C.: U. S. Government Printing Office), 1966, p. 7.

the city had to include a five-year forecast of how the neighborhood would be improved and had to detail action programs.

More than 1,000 cities sent in proposals to be considered as Model Cities projects. HUD was to choose which would be funded. Among the first few chosen were the proposals from Detroit, which focused on rehabilitation of a crime-ridden neighborhood in a heavily populated slum area; Philadelphia, where they wanted to train the unemployed in a Negro slum area to take over new shops and small industries when the slum was redeveloped into a new business center; and St. Louis, where the plan called for integration of two adjoining neighborhoods, one white and one black.[38]

In a 1967 review of highlights, HUD noted, among other things, that Model Cities programs were under way in 63 communities, the 100,000th dwelling unit on urban renewal land was completed, some 28,000 units were provided for senior citizens, and an experiment with "instant rehabilitation" had been tried in the renovation of a New York apartment in 48 hours. In this operation the building was gutted, and complete kitchen and bathroom packages were lowered through the roof for installation.[39]

Another federal program which was designed to encourage production of low-rent housing had its beginnings in the 1966 Act. It became known as "turnkey." In the dedication of the first turnkey project to be completed, Claridge Towers, a high-rise for the elderly in Washington, D.C., HUD Secretary Weaver explained how the program worked: "A builder or developer comes to the housing authority with a proposal to build. If the local authority likes the idea, it contracts to buy the finished project at a fixed price. Federal funds are still used in the purchase of the building, but the contractor is able to obtain normal commercial financing for construction."[40] Claridge Towers was finished 10 months after its inception—in quite a contrast to other projects which often took three to four years. Turnkey saved both time and money and made better use of local production processes and financing. In addition to reducing development costs, turnkey increased activity under the regular public housing program. The 1967 HUD Annual Report described turnkey as one of the most important breakthroughs in low-income housing in 30 years.[41] By the end of

38 Clay Coss, *We Can Save Our Cities*. (Washington, D.C.: Civic Education Service), 1967, pp. 122–123.

39 United States Department of Housing and Urban Development, *HUD 3rd Annual Report*. (Washington, D.C.: U. S. Government Printing Office), 1967, p. 12.

40 "First 'Turnkey' Project Completed for HUD," *Architectural Record*, Vol. 141, No. 3, March 1967, p. 35.

41 United States Department of Housing and Urban Development, *HUD 3rd Annual Report, op. cit.*, p. 8.

1972, more than 200,000 units were under turnkey contracts indicating that the program did indeed help produce houses.[42]

These and other accomplishments were fighting the battles but not winning the war on poverty. Nor was the nation on the brink of achieving the "Great Society." More was needed. And housing alone was not enough.

What was needed was a coordinated effort that involved not only the building and rebuilding of physical facilities, but a simultaneous attack on the human problems—of poverty, of unemployment, of education, of health deficiencies. There were scores of federal, state and local programs designed to meet these needs in their use of all the effective programs in individual slum neighborhoods where there was a concentration of problems.[43]

A series of events which underlined the fact that housing was not enough and that there was not enough housing, at least good housing, were the civil disorders which erupted in cities across the nation between 1965 and 1968. A great deal has been written about the riots of the 1960's—some accurate and some not. Some sources blame the news media, e.g., the publicity and television coverage given to the disturbances, for adding fuel to the already burning fire. Some accounts describe police handling of the disturbances as brutal, unfair, even hostile. Figures on the numbers of people who actually participated in the riots vary according to the source.

The significance of it all was that there were civil disturbances in the United States. Property was destroyed, many persons were hurt and some killed. These riots were not the first in the nation's history. There were civil disturbances in 1917, 1935, and 1943. But those of the 1960's, as never before, caused the nation to look for causes—and more important to search for solutions. Public attention was focused on ghetto problems which led directly to new government programs designed to ameliorate the conditions which had led to the riots.

On July 28, 1968 President Johnson appointed a group of influential persons to a Commission on Civil Disorders. The Chairman of the Commission was Governor of Illinois Otto Kerner, and its Vice-Chairman was New York City Mayor John Lindsay. Other members included United States Senators Fred Harris of Oklahoma and Edward Brooke of Massachusetts; United States Representatives John Corman, California; William M. McCulloch, Ohio; Katherine Peden, Commissioner of Commerce from Kentucky; Herbert Jenkins, Atlanta Chief of Police;

[42] United States Department of Housing and Urban Development, *Housing in the Seventies, op. cit.,* p. 17.

[43] Robert C. Weaver, "Rebuilding American Cities: An Overview," *Current History*, Vol. 55, No. 328, December 1968, p. 321.

Roy Wilkins, Director of the NAACP; Charles Thornton, Chairman of the Board of Litton Industries; and I. W. Able, President of United Steel Workers of America (AFL–CIO).

The Commission was to study the disorders and to answer three basic questions:

What happened?
Why did it happen?
What can be done to prevent it from happening again?[44]

The Commission responded, after much investigation and study, with the following basic conclusions:

Our Nation is moving toward two societies, one black, one white—separate and unequal.

Reaction to last summer's disorders has quickened the movement and deepened the division. Discrimination and segregation have long permeated much of American life; they now threaten the future of every American.

This deepening racial division is not inevitable. The movement apart can be reversed. Choice is still possible. Our principal task is to define that choice and to press for a national resolution.

To pursue our present course will involve the continuing polarization of the American Community and ultimately, the destruction of basic democratic values.

The alternative is not blind repression or capitulation to lawlessness. It is the realization of common opportunities for all within a single society.[45]

The urban disturbances of the 1960's were responsible for the creation of two commissions which greatly influenced federal housing policies. The first of these appointed by President Johnson January 12, 1967 was the Douglas Commission, named for Senator Paul H. Douglas, its Chairman. The Commission was charged to recommend solutions, particularly ways in which the federal government, industry, and the local communities could best increase the supply of decent low-cost housing. The major recommendation of the Commission was to direct the nation's housing assistance toward the poor.

The second committee, also appointed by Johnson in 1967, was the Kaiser Committee, whose Chairman was industrialist Edgar Kaiser. The responsibility given to this Committee was to "find a way to harness the productive power of America . . . to the most pressing unfulfilled need of our society—that need is to provide the basic necessities of a

44 *The Report on the National Advisory Commission on Civil Disorders.* (Washington, D.C.: U. S. Government Printing Office), March 1, 1968, p. 1.
45 *Ibid.*

decent home and healthy surroundings for every American family now imprisoned in the squalor of the slums." Recommendations of the Kaiser Commission included establishing a 10-year goal of 26 million new and rehabilitated housing units, 6 million of these for lower-income families. This recommendation had significant impact on future congressional actions and governmental policies.[46]

Programs intended to rehabilitate central cities had begun with the passage of the 1949 Housing Act, and these programs became known as "urban renewal" in 1954. Continuing through the 1960's, the programs were broadened and extended to include federal loans and grants for many related projects, in addition to slum clearance and redevelopment. By the end of 1968, there were 962 communities participating in 2,038 urban renewal projects and a total of 16,074 dwelling units on urban renewal project land had been completed.[47]

Urban renewal received considerable criticism directed primarily at the forcible eviction and dislocation of families in slum areas. Many critics equated urban renewal with Negro removal and with some justification, for often black ghettos with "abominable housing" were the targets of renewal projects.

The 1968 Housing Act attempted to counter some of the problems experienced in urban renewal projects and also to deal with the crisis issues spotlighted by the central city riots. The Act stated that thereafter, new residential units in urban renewal projects were to be for low- and moderate-income families, with at least 20 percent for low-income families. Relocation subsidies were expanded and new subsidy programs were authorized to reduce mortgage interest rates for housing for lower-income families. In addition, it provided a special high-risk insurance fund to encourage approval of applications from buyers who could not meet normal mortgage credit standards. Riot insurance, through a program of federal reinsurance against loss from riots and civil disorders, was authorized to encourage private companies to insure property in areas threatened by such disorders.

Despite the shift in emphasis in early urban renewal projects from clearance to rehabilitation and conservation projects, and despite the removal of some of the nation's worst slums and the providing of solid brick and mortar as well as psychological uplift for many central cities, it was still the consensus of some critics that "urban renewal programs succeeded only in perpetuating the ghetto by relocating it.

[46] United States Department of Housing and Urban Development, *Housing in the Seventies, op. cit.,* pp. 17–18.

[47] United States Department of Housing and Urban Development, *Nineteen Sixty-Eight Annual Report.* (Washington, D.C.: U. S. Government Printing Office), 1968, p. 30.

They have certainly not helped to rebuild the ghetto and transform it into a viable social sector of the metropolis."[48]

President Johnson's message to the Congress February 26, 1968 on "The Crisis of the Cities," recommended extension of several existing programs, revising and improving others, and additional funding for virtually all the existing housing and community development programs, including urban renewal, model cities, assistance to urban transportation systems and to comprehensive planning, and research and development. In addition, Johnson formalized a 10-year goal proposing that during the period the nation produce 26 million housing units, including 6 million units for replacement of substandard housing.

The Housing and Urban Development Act of 1968 placed into legislative form the President's recommendations and was the first domestic legislation to provide the goal of a specified number of housing units for people in a specific length of time.

It was appropriate that the 1968 bill be signed in front of the new HUD building. Late in 1963, Marcel Breuer had been commissioned to design a new building for the Housing and Home Finance Agency, which later became the new home of the Department of Housing and Urban Development. In the early part of the summer of 1968, the building was nearing completion and the various offices and divisions of HUD scattered throughout Washington, D.C. were ready to move under one roof for the first time. The new HUD home, functional and attractive, had been built for one of the lowest square foot costs of any contemporary government building.[49] By August the move was complete and the building was ready to serve as a fitting backdrop for Johnson's signing of the Housing and Urban Development Act of 1968.

The brief signing ceremony that sunny August day had been well planned but not well publicized—for the safety of the President. The President was obviously pleased with the bill but was fully aware of the challenge ahead for the American people as he spoke briefly to the crowd, mostly Federal employees. The crowd strained to hear and to see and broke into applause as the housing bill was signed. They had witnessed an interesting vignette of history.

In addition to establishing the 10-year national target goals for housing production, the 1968 Act contained two notable sections which climaxed the proliferation of subsidy programs during the 1960's. Section 235 provided assistance to lower-income families in becoming homeowners and Section 236 provided subsidies. Later evaluation of

48 Bennett Harrison, *Urban Economic Development.* (Washington, D.C.: The Urban Institute), 1974, p. 146.

49 United States Department of Housing and Urban Development, *Nineteen Sixty-Eight Annual Report, op. cit.,* p. 64.

FIGURE 8–1. President Johnson signing the 1968 Housing Act
August 1, 1968 at 11:52 A.M. *From left to right:* William A.
Barrett, (D) Pa.; William B. Widnall, (R) N.J.; Edmund
Muskie, (D) Me.; John Sparkman, (D) Ala.; Wright Patman,
(D) Tex.; Hubert H. Humphrey, (D) Minn.; Michael Feighan,
(D) O.; Robert Weaver, Secretary of HUD; Samuel H. Friedell,
(D) Md.

these programs by the Nixon administration[50] indicated they were inefficient, i.e., they cost the federal government more than recipients
realized in benefits and, in general, did not achieve the anticipated
results. In some respects, the results were even counterproductive, producing, for example, higher instead of lower construction costs, higher
default and foreclosure rates, and community opposition rather than
support.

The actual number of housing units constructed as results of subsidy
programs is not an accurate reflection of tangible results either. "The
exact addition is difficult to estimate, but various analyses suggest
that for every 100,000 units subsidized during the 1960's and early
1970's, perhaps as few as 14,000 represent net additions to the
housing stock."[51] The reason for this is that many builders dropped

[50] United States Department of Housing and Urban Development, *Housing
in the Seventies, op. cit.,* p. 64.
[51] *Ibid.,* p. 135.

plans to construct nonsubsidized units when more profitable opportunities to build subsidized units became available. On another level, a critic of housing subsidies had pointed out that "when provided on a large scale, the subsidies increase the demand for land, labor, and materials and therefore help to inflate construction costs and rents. This penalizes every home buyer and tenant in the nation who lacks a pipeline to subsidy."[52]

The year 1968 ended on a political note as the people went to the polls in November and elected Richard M. Nixon to the Presidency. The first Republican President in eight years, he lost no time in appointing as Secretary of HUD former Michigan Governor George Romney who was described as a "first-rank executive with a strong personal orientation to the needs of the people."[53]

Secretary Romney did not view the situation into which he stepped as a particularly bright picture. The problems of housing a growing nation continued to be many and complex. Even the normally optimistic and positive HUD reports acknowledged that "1969 was a crisis time in housing and urban development. Inflation, tight money, high interest rates, and scarce mortgage credit slowed housing construction and dampened the homeownership plans of many citizens. Businessmen became increasingly aware of the plight of the cities as tensions rose in blighted areas. . . ."[54]

One source described the situation: "A housing crisis is building up in the United States. The shortage of acceptable shelter that has long been afflicting the poor and the black is spreading to the white middle-class and even to quite affluent families. It may be that conditions are at their worst right now. . . . The unmet needs that piled up gradually in recent years have suddenly gone critical."[55]

Inflation was a gigantic obstacle preventing the nation from staying on track in achieving national goals established the year before. In fact, the 1.5 million units built in 1969 were not a very auspicious start on the catch-up plan of 2.6 million per year targeted in the 10-year national goal. In Secretary Romney's words, "We're losing ground every year. We're not even building enough to stand still."[56]

    [52] Gurney Breckenfeld, "Housing Subsidies are a Grand Delusion," *Fortune*, Vol. LXXXV, No. 2, February 1972, p. 137.
    [53] Walter F. Wagner, Jr., "An Innovator, Some Administrators, Some Homework and Some Hopes," *Architectural Record*, Vol. 145, No. 1, January 1969, p. 9.
    [54] United States Department of Housing and Urban Development, *Annual Report*. (Washington, D.C.: U. S. Government Printing Office), 1969, p. 5.
    [55] Lawrence A. Mayer, "The Housing Shortage Goes Critical," *Fortune*, Vol. LXXX, No. 7, December 1969, p. 99.
    [56] Walter McQuade, "An Assembly-Line Answer to the Housing Crisis," *Fortune*, LXXIX, No. 5, May 1969, p. 99.

Industrial Technology

Romney, being a Michigan product, was well familiar with the assembly-line techniques of the automobile industry and could not understand why many of these same methods of technology and production could not be applied to the housing industry.

Previously, application of advanced industrial technology in the production of houses had been painfully slow, evolutionary if you wish to be more kind, but there had been definite and obvious constraints. The traditional home building industry was extremely fragmented, comprising more than 110,000 builders—the majority of whom annually produced less than 25 units each and most of these were single-family houses rather than multifamily units. With such fragmentation and localism in the "housing industry" there were few incentives, and fewer resources, for individual entrepreneurs to experiment with risky new products and techniques.

Another of the more serious and difficult problems which tended to discourage innovation and experimentation in housing was the multitude of divergent and restrictive state and local building codes. At the beginning of the 1960's, it was estimated that there were 2,500 local building codes.[57] These codes and the provincialism and isolationism of local interest have been credited with preventing the use of a major portion of the available technology.

Codes have a direct impact on housing costs. Most of the country's local building codes were established half a century or more ago, and many have managed to resist change. The construction industry, perhaps more than any other major industry, depends upon the skill of the individual workman, and this has had a profound effect on building codes. The codes were originally written based on experience with traditional, on-site construction. At that time the idea of a factory-built house, or even factory production of housing components, had not been considered. To protect against inferior workmanship, the codes required wide margins of safety which frequently demanded more materials and work than could currently be justified by good engineering practice. Once codes were established, local craftsmen and material suppliers tended to oppose changes which would reduce labor or materials in home construction. One estimate placed the resultant excess cost at $1,000 per house.[58]

Clearly, local building codes were one of the barriers that restricted general development and adoption of technological innovations. "It

[57] Norbert Brown, "Local Building Codes: A National Problem," *Architectural Forum*, Vol. 115, No. 6, December 1961, p. 24.

[58] "Round Table Ponders $1-billion-a-year Cost of Too Many Codes:" *House and Home*, Vol. XIV, No. 1, July 1958, p. 118.

is difficult for any organization to design and offer for sale a competitively priced, well-designed and well-engineered group of houses which could be built in a wide range of localities when the code requirements vary so greatly from place to place. Housing is thus denied the full advantages of mass production which have contributed so significantly to other sectors of the economy."[59]

During the decade, some progress was made in improving the building code situation. Most cities adopted one of four model codes which had gained recognition and acceptance on a national or regional level. There are actually few significant or major differences in these model codes, and if it were possible to get countrywide adoption of any of the four, without local change, most code problems would become insignificant. Unfortunately, local variations—ostensibly to meet local problems but actually not needed in most cases—have clouded the picture.

Some states have passed legislation which overrides the restrictions of local codes. California passed a uniform code for housing produced in a factory, provided for certification by a state agency of in-factory quality control, and then permitted that product to be placed on sites throughout the state, regardless of conflicting local restrictions. A similar development was the chartering of quasi-public development corporations such as the Urban Development Corporation of New York which, through its state charter, can produce housing and place it anywhere in the state, regardless of overly restrictive local codes.

In a U. S. Government publication of the early 1960's[60] it was noted that United States industries spent, on the average, roughly 1½ percent of sales income for research and development. On this basis, the housing industry should have spent as much as $360 million per year, a figure 6 to 10 times greater than the amount actually spent. Matching this unfortunate record was government research activity. Less than 1 percent was concerned with housing and city problems in 1968. Research in these areas was first authorized in the Housing Acts of 1948 and 1956 and further provided for in 1965 and 1966, but total research activity in housing was grossly inadequate. In May 1967, HUD established an Office of Urban Technology and Research, and, in the legislation of 1968 and 1969, the federal government further demonstrated that more significance was being placed on the role of research and technology as essential components of a systematic approach to achieving housing goals.

The cyclical nature of economic forces in the housing market and the

59 Executive Office of the President. Office of Science and Technology, *Better Housing for the Future* (Washington, D.C.: U. S. Government Printing Office), 1963, p. 10.
60 *Ibid.*, p. 7.

seasonal pattern of construction in many regions also inhibited incorporation of new technology and advanced managerial approaches into the
industry. The struggle against economic forces beyond its control has
been one of the more frustrating problems of the housing industry. The
supply of mortgage credit is very sensitive to fluctuations in the national
economy. In an overheated economy, most anti-inflation legislation and
governmental controls tighten the supply of money. This has an immediate impact on the sale of houses. Tight money in 1966, for example, dealt the mortgage market a crushing blow and home building
plunged to a 20-year low. Conversely, when the economy is in a slump
and the government attempts to stimulate business, it takes a considerable length of time for the housing industry to "gear-up" and respond.

Despite all the housing industry's problems, handicaps, and foot-
dragging, one segment was not standing still. The mobile home industry had been around for over 40 years, but between 1960 and 1970 the
number of mobile homes had grown from 767,000 units to 1,847,000
units, a 141 percent increase.[61] This rapid increase in factory production was due, in part, to refinements in assembly-line techniques and, in
part, to the fact that mobile homes, as personal property, were not
subject to local building codes. The industry was putting on an aggres-
sive drive to produce low-income housing and, in less than a generation,
mobile homes had emerged as a major source of such housing. These
units were made available as detached single-family homes, attached
row housing, stacked as "town houses," and in multiples of "modules"
for apartment buildings. The 12-foot-wide units, which began mass
production in 1962, accounted for well over three fourths of unit sales
by 1967.[62] It should be noted that mobile homes are not very mobile
once they are placed on their first site; an estimated 60 percent of all
mobile homeowners have never moved their units.[63]

While mobile homes most nearly fit the theoretical model of industrialized housing, nearly all houses today use some factory-built components, a considerable increase from 1969 when about half the homes
used prefabricated components.[64] Factory-manufactured components include trusses and panels for floors, ceilings and walls, prehung doors and
windows, and cabinets of all types. An evolutionary step gaining popu-

[61] "Lines and Numbers: Housing Trends, 1960–1970," *HUD Challenge*,
Vol. III, No. 4, April 1972, p. 31.

[62] Elsie Eaves, *How the Many Costs of Housing Fit Together*. (Washington,
D.C.: U. S. Government Printing Office), 1969, p. 101.

[63] Report of the National Commission on Urban Problems to the Congress and
the President of the United States, *Building the American City*. (Washington,
D.C.: U. S. Government Printing Office), 1972, p. 439.

[64] United States Department of Housing and Urban Development, *Housing
in the Seventies, op. cit.*, p. 199.

larity is the use of mechanical cores, containing an entire kitchen or bathroom, or a combination of a kitchen and one or more bathrooms. They are set in at the site as a complete unit containing all fixtures, plumbing, and electrical wiring.

A number of housing manufacturers market more or less conventional houses with varying degrees of factory components. Some fabricate complete or nearly complete housing packages to be assembled on site. Others ship packages which vary from "precut" houses, which have all the lumber cut to size, to others that ship packages with modules or panels or sections completed in a factory and ready for quick on-site erection.

There were relatively few attempts to produce complete dwelling construction systems. The aerospace concept of "systems" implies total control from project initiation, to design, to production, all usually under one roof. If housing manufacturers would adopt this approach, they could increase their ability to control costs and extend their responsibility to include the entire operation, even to management of completed housing developments.

There was an interesting development in the 1960's which saw involvement in housing production by large organizations previously uninvolved with the shelter industry. General Electric, Westinghouse, and ITT are examples. Generally, these entrances into the housing market took the form of a merger or acquisition of a successful shelter-producing firm with proven ability to function within the market.

Mergers of this kind were marriages of convenience. The outside firm acquired additional return of revenue from a source diversified from their main stream of activity while the housing producer acquired the backing of large capital required to buy and hold large acreages of land necessary for that expansion. In these cases, neither management personnel nor procedures were significantly changed on the part of the shelter-producing firm; therefore, industrialization of the production of housing was not, at least, a direct goal.[65]

In addition to the generally modest improvements in the processes of home construction, the industry also made some advances with new materials, such as plastics, fiberglass, and epoxy. Plastic came into its own with the development of plastic pipe for plumbing systems. The material also was used experimentally for exterior walls and shingles, and many other construction products. Fiberglass was used for exteriors and complete plastic–fiberglass bathroom assemblies were developed. Resin epoxy adhesives developed in space technology found increasing application in housing construction.

[65] Auburn University Engineering Systems Design Summer Faculty Fellows, *Starsite*. (Washington, D.C.: U. S. Government Printing Office), 1972.

By comparison with other industries, however, advances in design, materials, or methods of house construction had been very modest and a 20th century Rip Van Winkle, awakening at the close of the 1960's after a 20-year sleep and looking at the housing industry, would hardly have known he overslept.

Operation Breakthrough

A major program announced in May 1969 was dubbed "Operation Breakthrough." The project was designed for two major purposes: first, to develop ways to produce housing in large volume using better technology, materials, construction techniques, and management and marketing programs; and second, to deal with the problem of assuring the availability of markets to absorb the increased volume of housing once it was produced. It was clear that large initial investments in plant, equipment, and management were required for volume housing production, and it would be worthwhile only if assured continuing markets were available.[66] HUD's role in Operation Breakthrough was threefold: (1) locating construction sites and markets large enough to encourage and sustain volume housing production; (2) funding; and (3) facilitating cooperation from consumer groups and state and local authorities in support of the Breakthrough effort.[67]

By June, 1969, thousands of requests for proposals had been issued to interested firms or individuals across the nation. Two types of proposals were to be submitted by September. The first was for a complete housing system that could be produced in volume and the second was for innovative components which could contribute to a complete housing system.[68]

Though Breakthrough was announced in May, funding was not authorized until December 24 when the federal government responded to the nation's bleak housing picture with yet another bill—The Housing and Urban Development Act of 1969. This extended and expanded existing programs as usual, but also broke new ground in several areas. To counter the criticism that urban renewal was removing more low-rent housing than it was replacing, the requirement was established that any housing demolished for an urban renewal project must be replaced on a unit-by-unit basis for low- and moderate-income families.

---

[66] United States Department of Housing and Urban Development, *Operation Breakthrough Questions and Answers.* (Washington, D.C.: U. S. Government Printing Office), March 1971, p. 1.

[67] Harold B. Finger, "Operation Breakthrough: A Nationwide Effort to Produce Millions of Homes," *HUD Challenge*, Vol. 1, No. 1, November–December 1969, p. 7.

[68] *Ibid.*, p. 8.

The Act also contained a section known as the Brooke Amendment, which limited rents charged by local housing authorities to 25 percent of the tenant's income. Another interesting development was an amendment which for the first time permitted FHA to insure loans up to $10,000 for the purchase of mobile homes.

The portion of the bill which received the most publicity was the authority given to the HUD Secretary to override local building codes and zoning restrictions where they interfered with HUD tests of new building techniques. With this roadblock removed, Operation Breakthrough was under way.

It was hoped that the Breakthrough project could make a significant contribution to the achievement of the 10-year national goal, not only by using the most advanced technology, but by coordinating the efforts of many elements: governments at every level, business, industry, labor, financial institutions, voluntary organizations, and community individuals, all working together to meet the challenge of providing a "decent home and suitable living environment" for every family.

The public attitude toward industrialized housing has traditionally been skeptical, if not downright negative, perhaps in part because of memories of post-World War II "prefab" structures. The degree to which Operation Breakthrough dispelled the public's negative feelings toward industrialized housing could be significant. Only in retrospect from a vantage point in the 1970's, would it be possible to judge the success of the program.

Land Use

Any overview of housing must take into account land and land use. Although recent technology has made it possible for man to exist in outer space, at least for relatively short periods of time, real estate brokers have not yet been able to list any "space for sale." Also, few people in this country "live" on water. Therefore, careful use of terra firma in building new homes is essential. Of course, more than houses are involved in decisions about land use. Agriculture, transportation systems and facilities, parks and recreation space are all essential and also compete for priority and expansion. For example, "between 1960 and 1970, state expenditures for park land acquisition increased more than fourfold."[69]

When houses, businesses, and cities were first being located over the countryside, land was plentiful, people were few, and there was little

69 William K. Reilly, *The Use of Land.* (New York: Thomas Y. Crowell), 1973, p. 111.

formal effort to control their placement. It was well into the 20th century, 1916 to be more precise, before New York City passed a zoning resolution which became the basis for subsequent comprehensive land use regulations in this country. Zoning ordinances are the most common form of local land use control. They generally prescribe how parcels of land in communities may be used for residential areas, commerce, or industry. In addition, zoning attempts to control population density by establishing minimum lot sizes for each dwelling or by limiting the number of families per acre. Sometimes there are requirements governing building bulk by specifying maximum height or proportion of lot which may be occupied.

In the past, local governments exercised zoning power delegated to them by the states. More recently, however, as land use problems have become more complex and community interests overlap or conflict, some states have reasserted their authority over land within their borders and have accepted the responsibility to control and preserve the environment. Some states, especially those with smaller land areas, now have plans which regulate land on a statewide basis. Hawaii enacted such a law in 1961. California, particularly pressed by extremely rapid population growth, proposed a plan whereby private development corporations chartered by the state would use federal loans for land acquisition. The land purchased would fit within a master plan and would be sold to private builders and developers to provide recreational facilities, residential housing, commercial or industrial complexes according to the plan. In this way, more rational and organized land development and urbanization could take place.[70]

Subdivision controls or regulations are another mechanism to control land use. Whereas zoning codes refer to the kind of building development on individual lots, subdivision controls regulate the way large undeveloped areas are divided and made available for buildings. Obviously, subdivision and zoning ordinances can be mutually dependent, and both are necessary for orderly growth. Sometimes, however, the codes are too restrictive and discourage growth, intentionally or unintentionally.

Low-income families, for example, have been effectively excluded from some areas through zoning or subdivision controls which require large lots, high minimum floor space, extensive off-site improvements, or substantial amounts of land for public use. These requirements increase the price of housing beyond the reach of lower- or middle-income

[70] Governor's Advisory Commission on Housing Problems, *Report on Housing in California.* (Sacramento: California State Printing Office), January 1963, p. 53.

families. Some communities defend their zoning ordinances, saying that only through them are they able to achieve orderly development and to control population densities. Critics agree that zoning does serve legitimate purposes in facilitating land planning and guarding against incompatible development, but they argue that it is wrong when it covers up racial, ethnic, or economic exclusivity.

At the federal and state levels, there has been significant activity in the development of programs and regulations to plan and control land use. Comprehensive statewide plans to regulate land use have already been mentioned. At the national level, the Housing Act of 1961, for the first time, provided financial assistance to local public bodies to help acquire permanent open-space land, as long as it played an important part in an overall area plan. In the following year, the President urged that Congress provide a program of matching grants to states for open spaces and outdoor recreation.[71] Again in 1964, the President recommended assistance for open space programs but also suggested programs for helping states acquire land in advance for public improvements and to assist private developers in acquiring and improving land for planned subdivisions.[72] The Housing and Urban Development Act of 1965 provided more money and enlarged open space land programs to include grants for urban beautification and improvement.[73]

The following year, as a part of the Demonstration Cities and Metropolitan Development Act, the Secretary of HUD was directed to carry out a comprehensive program of studies, research, and analyses to document and define urban environmental factors and share this information with states and communities.

Grants were authorized as a part of the New Communities Act of 1968 for open land urban renewal projects, where land was to be used for low- and moderate-income houses.

An important piece of legislation affecting land use at the close of the decade was the National Environmental Policy Act of 1969. In this Act, Federal agencies were directed to include, for every action significantly affecting the quality of the environment, a detailed statement on the environmental impact of the proposed action.[74] This requirement was difficult to accomplish, but it did force more careful and thorough analysis of project benefits and liabilities, which the public could then evaluate. The effect of this law (and state and local laws patterned after it) on land use, housing projects, expanded recreation and transportation facilities would become more evident in the 1970's.

[71] Subcommittee on Housing and Community Development of the Committee on Banking, Currency and Housing, *op. cit.*, p. 82.

[72] *Ibid.*, p. 88.

[73] *Ibid.*, p. 100.

[74] *Ibid.*, p. 154.

Summary

Even though the United States enjoyed an expanding economy, significant scientific advancements and tremendous technological achievements in other fields, equal progress in meeting the basic housing needs for many families did not materialize in the 1960's. Housing statistics in terms of the number of units, vacancy rates, and substandard units did tend to show improvements. At the end of the decade there were fewer substandard houses and housing production had exceeded household formations. Yet there was still a major lack of knowledge about the relationship between people and housing, and there did not appear to be any meaningful measurement of housing quality or satisfaction with it. The size and scale of federal urban assistance had been too small and too widely dispersed. Building practices were still archaic and wasteful, and many of the anticipated benefits of regional and metropolitan planning were still unrealized.[75]

Several years of experience with housing subsidies and federal programs of various sorts had taught the lesson that there was no such thing as inexpensive housing. It was also apparent that, even when better housing was provided, it did not always produce better people. At the turn of the decade some critics sensed a feeling of disillusionment. One said, "Today, the public housing program goes without its traditional liberal and intellectual support; it goes without union support; and it goes without any broad demand among the electorate. And as for the poor, they go without decent housing."[76]

If the decade of the 1960's did not solve the nation's housing ills, it did accomplish one major and vital task. It created a growing awareness of the extent and seriousness of housing and environmental problems and sincere and innovative schemes were developed to try to solve the problems—both housing and people problems. The experimental programs which failed and those which achieved limited success were overshadowed by the problems which yet remained.

Bibliography

Books

Auburn University Engineering Systems Design Summer Faculty Fellows, *Starsite* (*Search to Assess Resources, Social, Institutional, Technical, and Environmental*). Washington, D.C.: U. S. Government Printing Office, 1972.

[75] Robert A. Goldwin (ed.), *A Nation of Cities: Essays on America's Urban Problems.* (Chicago: Rand McNally), 1966, p. 4.

[76] Michael A. Stegman, "The New Mythology of Housing," *Trans-action*, Vol. 7, No. 3, January 1970, p. 55.

BLUMSTEIN, JAMES F. and EDDIE J. MARTIN, *The Urban Scene in the Seventies.* Nashville, Tennessee: Vanderbilt University Press, 1974.

COSS, CLAY (ed.), *We Can Save Our Cities.* Washington, D.C.: Civic Education Service, 1967.

EAVES, ELSIE, *How the Many Costs of Housing Fit Together.* Research Report No. 16 Prepared for the Consideration of the National Commission on Urban Problems. Washington, D.C.: U. S. Government Printing Office, 1969.

Executive Office of the President, Office of Science and Technology. *Better Housing for the Future.* Washington, D.C.: U. S. Government Printing Office, 1963.

GELFAND, MARK I. *A Nation of Cities,* New York: Oxford University Press, 1975.

GOLDWIN, ROBERT A. (ed.), *A Nation of Cities: Essays on America's Urban Problem.* Chicago: Rand McNally, 1966.

Governor's Advisory Commission on Housing Problems. *Report on Housing in California.* Sacramento, California State Printing Office, January 1963.

Harlem Youth Opportunities Unlimited, Inc., *Youth in the Ghetto.* New York: Orans Press, 1974.

HARRISON, BENNETT, *Urban Economic Development: Suburbanization, Minority Opportunity, and the Condition of the Central City.* Washington, D.C.: The Urban Institute, 1974.

Housing and Home Finance Agency, *18th Annual Report.* Washington, D.C.: U. S. Government Printing Office, 1964.

HUMPHREY, HUBERT H., *Better Cities for Tomorrow.* United States Department of Housing and Urban Development. Washington, D.C.: U. S. Government Printing Office, 1966.

KRISTOF, FRANK S., *Urban Housing Needs Through the 1980's: An Analysis and Projection.* Research Report No. 10. Washington, D.C.: U. S. Government Printing Office, 1968.

REILLY, WILLIAM K. (ed.), *The Use of Land.* A Task Force Report Sponsored by the Rockefeller Brothers Fund. New York: Thomas Y. Crowell, 1973.

The Report of the National Advisory Commission on Civil Disorders. Washington, D.C.: U. S. Government Printing Office, March 1, 1968.

Report of the National Commission on Urban Problems to the Congress and to the President of the United States, *Building the American City.* Washington, D.C.: U. S. Government Printing Office, 1972.

REYNOLDS, MELVINA, *Little Boxes and Other Handmade Songs.* New York: Oak Publishing Co., 1964.

RIIS, JACOB A., *The Battle with the Slum.* New York: Macmillan, 1902.

SCHORR, ALVIN L., *Slums and Social Insecurity.* Washington, D.C.: U. S. Department of Health, Education and Welfare, 1963.

Subcommittee on Housing and Community Development of the Committee on Banking, Currency and Housing, *Evolution of Role of the Federal Government in Housing and Community Development.* House of Representatives, 94th Congress, First Session. Washington, D.C.: U. S. Government Printing Office, October 1975.

United States Bureau of the Census, *Historical Statistics of the United States. Colonial Times to 1970*. Bicentennial Edition, Part 1. Washington, D.C.: U. S. Government Printing Office, 1975.

————, *Census for Housing: 1970. Housing Characteristics for States, Cities, and Counties*, Vol. I. United States Summary, Part 1. Washington, D.C.: U. S. Government Printing Office, 1972.

————, *Census of Housing: 1960. States and Small Areas*, Vol. I. United States Summary, Part 1. Washington, D.C.: U. S. Government Printing Office, 1963.

United States Department of Health, Education and Welfare, *Vital Statistics of the United States*, 1970. Rockville, Maryland: Public Health Service, Health Resources Administration, National Center for Health Statistics, 1974.

United States Department of Housing and Urban Development, *Housing in the Seventies*. A Report of the National Housing Policy Review. HUD Publication No. HUD-PDR-64. Washington, D.C.: U. S. Government Printing Office, 1974.

————, *Operation Breakthrough Questions and Answers*. Washington, D.C.: U. S. Government Printing Office, 1971.

————, *Annual Report*. Washington, D.C.: U. S. Government Printing Office, 1969.

————, *Nineteen Sixty-eight Annual Report*. Washington, D.C.: U. S. Government Printing Office, 1968.

————, *HUD 3rd Annual Report*. Washington, D.C.: U. S. Government Printing Office, 1967.

————, *HUD Second Annual Report*. Washington, D.C.: U. S. Government Printing Office, 1966.

————, *Annual Report 1965*. Washington, D. C.: U. S. Government Printing Office, 1965.

United States Statutes At Large. 87th Congress; 1st Session. Vol. 75. Washington, D.C.: U. S. Government Printing Office, March 1971.

WILNER, DANIEL M., et al., *The Housing Environment and Family Life*. Baltimore, Md.: Johns Hopkins Press, 1962.

Periodicals

BRECKENFELD, GURNEY, "Housing Subsidies are a Grand Delusion," *Fortune*, Vol. LXXXV, No. 2, February 1972, pp. 136–139ff.

BROWN, NORBERT, "Local Building Codes: A National Problem," *Architectural Forum*, Vol. 115, No. 6, December 1961, pp. 124–125.

Finger, Harold B., "Operation Breakthrough: a Nationwide Effort to Produce Millions of Homes," *HUD Challenge*, Vol. 1, No. 1, November–December 1969, pp. 6–9.

"First 'Turnkey' Project Completed for HUD," *Architectural Record*, Vol. 141, No. 3, March 1967, p. 35.

"Lines and Numbers: Housing Trends, 1960–1970," *HUD Challenge*, Vol. III, No. 4, April 1972, p. 31.

LORING, WILLIAM C., "Design for a New Housing Market: The Old," *Architectural Forum*, Vol. 114, No. 3, March 1961, pp. 119–121ff.

McQUADE, WALTER, "An Assembly-Line Answer to the Housing Crisis," *Fortune*, Vol. LXXIX, No. 5, May 1, 1969, pp. 99–103ff.

MAYER, LAWRENCE A., "The Housing Shortage Goes Critical," *Fortune*, Vol. LXXX, No. 7, December 1969, pp. 86–86ff.

"Round Table Ponders $1-billion-a-year Cost of Too Many Codes, Proposes a Simple 6-point Program to Speed Reform," *House and Home*, Vol. XIV, No. 1, July 1958, pp. 112–119.

STEGMAN, MICHAEL A., "The New Mythology of Housing," *Trans-action*, Vol. 7, No. 3, January 1970, pp. 55–62.

WAGNER, WALTER F., JR., "An Innovator, Some Administrators, Some Homework and Some Hopes," *Architectural Record*, Vol. 145, No. 1, January 1969, p. 9.

WEAVER, ROBERT C., "Rebuilding American Cities: An Overview," *Current History*, Vol. 55, No. 328, December 1968, pp. 321–326, 364.

CHAPTER 9

RACE AND HOUSING

JACK E. WOOD, JR.*

The Identification of the Problem

THROUGHOUT the nation's entire history almost every important aspect of American life has been influenced by the consideration of race, and the subordination of people of color has contributed to the psychological and economic security of white society. For black Americans, such subjugation, often brutally enforced, had been a condition of life since 1619 and, except for a brief interlude after the Civil War, was effectively sustained until the 1950's.

Because of the relationship of housing to all phases of life and because of the special and pervasive nature of the residential process, no area of activity provided a more effective means of achieving and sustaining such subjugation than racial discrimination and segregation in

* JACK E. WOOD, JR. is an urban consultant with an extensive background in the housing/civil rights field. During the decade of the 1960's he served as National Director of Housing for the NAACP and, later, as Executive Co-Director of NCDH. Mr. Wood has served as an advisor to numerous federal and state agencies, and has served as consultant to the Committee for Economic Development (CED), The Academy of Science and various other private and public interests. As a senior official of The New York State Urban Development Corporation, he also directed The Harlem Redevelopment program.

housing. And no institution functioned more effectively to foster and support that system than the federal government.

Since the civil rights demands for fair housing in the 1960's were triggered in part by the damaging effect of past policies, it may be instructive to review the role of government over the last century.

Early Legislation

Shortly after the Civil War, in an effort designed to insure the effectiveness of the Thirteenth Amendment, the Congress of the United States passed the Civil Rights Act of 1866 (Title 42 U. S. Code):

All citizens of the United States shall have the same right in every State and Territory, as is enjoyed by white citizens thereof to inherit, purchase, lease, sell, hold and convey real and personal property.

With the passage of that law, the Congress thus affirmed the right to own land as an inherent and natural right to be enjoyed by all American citizens without racial restriction. The statute became a basic law of the federal government with regard to the equality of all persons in the ownership and occupancy of real property and it was upheld in principle repeatedly in court decisions dating back to 1917.

In 1917, in the case of *Buchanan* v. *Warley*, 245 U. S. 60, the Supreme Court held that an ordinance adopted by the City of Louisville, Kentucky, which sought to restrict the areas in which Negroes and whites might live, violated the Fourteenth Amendment. The special significance of that case was that while the Court acknowledged that in *Plessy* v. *Ferguson*, 163 U. S. 537 (1896) it had sanctioned the doctrine of separate-but-equal in the areas of schools and transportation, that doctrine had limitations and could not be extended to the area of property rights.

In so ruling, the Court based its decision on two grounds which consistently prevailed in subsequent state and federal decisions involving cases of housing discrimination. The first was that the Fourteenth Amendment specifically mentioned property. The second was the recognition of the applicability and intent of the aforementioned Title 42.

Judicial invalidation of racial zoning ordinances spurred the use of racially restrictive covenants, imposed either by subdividers or through neighborhood agreements. These "gentlemen's agreements," which prohibited ownership or occupancy by nonwhites, by clauses in deeds to property, gained widespread acceptance, and from 1917 to 1948 they were effectively enforced by state courts throughout the nation and in the District of Columbia. Even the United States Supreme Court, by indirection, approved the outrageous doctrine of the times, that an

American citizen could be enjoined from owning a home, or even residing in a home he owned, because of his race.

Finally in 1948, in *Shelley v. Kraemer*, 334 U. S. 1, the Supreme Court ruled that enforcement of restrictive covenants by state courts was a violation of the 14th Amendment. Three decades of court approval for such segregatory agreements had put the stamp of governmental approval on residential segregation and had delineated the areas of nonwhite occupancy in the cities and towns.

Effects of Housing Acts of 1934, 1937, 1949

The federal government had begun to subsidize housing by insuring mortgages for lenders and by constructing public housing for low-income families. In 1934, it established the Federal Housing Administration (FHA) to insure loans for private builders and lending institutions in order to encourage construction of middle-class housing. In 1937, it created the Public Housing Administration (PHA) in order to lend direct assistance to local municipalities for the construction of low-rent housing for low-income families.

In 1949, in a Housing Act otherwise noted for its comprehensiveness and expanding view of federal responsibility, a new concept of slum clearance and redevelopment emerged. Urban Renewal, as it later would be titled, began with the potential of becoming the most significant housing effort ever engaged in by the federal government. Designed to eradicate slums and halt the spread of urban deterioration, it was ideally positioned to identify and chart new and desirable directions in urban growth.

As with other federal programs, however, Urban Renewal was predicated on prevailing perceptions of race in housing. Since blacks, as a consequence of both racial prejudice, economic disadvantage, and the impact of earlier federal programs, had been forced to reside in older, more dilapidated central city areas, they were disproportionately affected by Urban Renewal. The program caused the mass upheaval of black families living in ghettos across the nation and forced their relocation into a similar but more congested pattern of segregation. Capitalizating on the absence of firm, federal policy of nondiscrimination many municipalities seized upon Urban Renewal as an effective means to recapture desirable areas for predominantly white developments.

The problem was that when the federal government entered the housing field, judicial enforcement of racial covenants was in full flower; city planners were firmly committed to the belief that the homogeneous neighborhood was the ideal in urban living, and the myth that non-white occupancy lowered property values was a cardinal article of faith among realtors, home builders, and lending institutions. Federal housing officials, drawn from those same ranks, threw the full weight of government acceptance behind residential segregation. FHA began its career by making clear the undesirability of mixing different social and racial groups. Racially restrictive covenants were required for every property on which FHA extended loan insurance. Its *Underwriting Manual*, which set a national standard for residential design and construction, furnished builders and lenders with a model race-restrictive covenant for their guidance and use.

In 1950, after the Supreme Court had interdicted judicial enforcement of racial covenants, FHA changed its policy to a neutral course and ceased the official advocacy of racial segregation. Private builders and massive suburban developers alike, however, continued to obtain FHA-insured loans to construct racially restricted housing.

By December 31, 1959, FHA-insured mortgages and loans amounting to more than $61,000,000,000 had been advanced to private lending institutions and builders in the United States. Of this amount, $41.4 billion was involved in the financing of 5,272,000 home mortgages; $7.3 billion in multifamily projects, and $12.4 billion in 23,357,000 property improvement loans. It was estimated that less than 2 percent of the new construction made possible by these funds was available for occupancy by Negro American citizens.

Low-cost, low-rent public housing was built under a separate-but-equal concept and federal officials announced a policy of leaving racial occupancy patterns to local housing authorities. The result was the establishment of a pattern of public housing projects in the nation's cities segregated by race, income, and geographic location. By 1960 more than 2000 projects had been constructed in 1000 cities across the nation, housing nearly 2 million people. While the effort represented a capital investment of over $3 billion, the social and economic cost to America would prove to be considerably greater.

In summary, the federal government in the first quarter of a century of its housing effort was able, by means of an extensive array of cash and credit devices, including loans, grants, and mortgage insurance, to subsidize the construction of more than 11,500,000 housing units through its FHA and Veterans Administration system, nearly 600,000 project apartments through its PHA system, and to encourage hundreds of cities to undertake the clearance and renewal of slums and blighted neighborhoods. In addition, federally insured banks and lending institutions supplemented the entire effort by underwriting the racially restrictive policies of private industry in mortgage financing.

The pattern of residential segregation in our central city areas thus became firmly entrenched with the development of racially separate housing projects and, more often than not, the relocation by race of urban renewal displacees into these ghettos. Outside the central city areas, the rapid growth and expansion of suburbia was taking place on a metropolitan scale. New towns and cities began to emerge, occupied almost exclusively by white families.

Spreading the Concern

In the latter part of the 1950's, as the federal government moved slowly toward a policy of nondiscrimination in housing, many states and cities helped pave the way by passing resolutions, ordinances, or statutes prohibiting discrimination or segregation in a portion of the housing supply.

The New York State Committee Against Discrimination in Housing

As early as 1944 the New York City Council passed an ordinance prohibiting discrimination in all future housing which received total or partial tax exemption or any other direct or indirect aid from the city. In 1950 a statewide law was passed with similar coverage, barring discrimination in all future publicly aided projects. The 1944 law, though limited in scope, had been induced by a narrow court decision which literally suggested the enactment of legislation as an effective means of redress. In *Dorsey v. Stuyvesant Town Corporation*, 229 NY 512, the court upheld the right of the publicly aided developer to deny admission to blacks. The court ruled that tax abatement and other forms of aid provided under the New York State Redevelopment Companies Law did not constitute state action within the meaning of the 14th Amendment.

The ruling spawned the establishment of the New York State Committee Against Discrimination in Housing (NYCDH). That Committee, representing local civil rights groups, labor, religious and civic organizations, was the forerunner of numerous other state committees which quickly began to emerge across the nation. This spontaneous movement had the effect of creating a national network of volunteer state agencies all similar in structure, social philosophy, and purpose. By the end of 1950 the movement had led to the establishment of the National Committee against Discrimination in Housing (NCDH), and the beginning of a highly organized effort to accelerate the enactment of fair housing legislation.

As an organization formed by 37 major national civil rights, civic, religious, and labor organizations, NCDH was able on a national level to achieve a degree of coordination which enhanced the effectiveness of fair housing legislative campaigns and gained added stature and legitimacy for the movement. Inspired by leadership at the state and national levels and moved by deep social and moral concerns, local fair housing committees began to spring up in cities and towns across the entire nation. Their membership generally was comprised of local members of the NAACP, the American Jewish Congress or Committee, the AFL–CIO, the Urban League, or any of several other major organizations whose national officials were either officers or directors of NCDH. This unusual degree of intraorganizational relationship in a volunteer operation had immediate benefits, and more fair housing laws were enacted within a shorter period of time than was the case with legislation covering other areas of civil rights, such as employment and public accommodations.

Since the early laws of 1944 and 1950 were fairly limited in scope, the definition of "publicly assisted" housing was soon expanded to include developments financed with government-insured mortgages. By the end of 1957, six states had passed laws prohibiting discrimination in such publicly assisted housing.

The first law barring discrimination in the private housing market was passed by New York City in 1957. One year later, the City of Pittsburgh, Pennsylvania passed a similar ordinance. By 1959 four other states (Colorado, Connecticut, Massachusetts, and Oregon) had enacted fair housing laws broadly inclusive of the private housing market.

United States Commission on Civil Rights

In 1957 Congress passed Civil Rights legislation which established a Commission to study the problem. In formulating its recommendations on housing, the Commission drew upon an exhaustive study of the problem accomplished by means of research and hearings conducted in several major cities. Adding to the weight of evidence in support of its recommendations were supplementary studies undertaken by duly appointed state advisory bodies in 48 of the 50 states. The findings and recommendations of these states' bodies to the Commission served largely to supplement and confirm the Commission's own conclusions, independently reached.

In 1959 the United States Commission on Civil Rights submitted its report to the President of the United States. In its findings and recommendations pertaining to the problem of discrimination in housing, the Commission stated that "The Constitution prohibits any governmental discrimination by reason of race, color, or national origin. The operation of federal housing agencies and programs is subject to this principle."

The Commission also recognized the applicability and effect of Title 42 U. S. Code 1982 and stated:

Because of the paramount national importance of this problem, the Commission finds that direct action by the President in the form of an Executive Order on equality of opportunity in housing is needed. The Order should apply to all federally assisted housing, including housing constructed with the assistance of federal mortgage insurance or loan guarantee as well as federally aided public housing and urban renewal projects.

The significance of the report on housing by the Civil Rights Commission, therefore, goes beyond its disclosure of discrimination in federally assisted programs and its strong recommendation for Executive action; of even greater importance was the fact that a broad cross section of the nation's leadership in private and public life had arrived at the same conclusion and submitted the same recommendation.

The Commission on Race and Housing

Another major group representing the private sector had previously issued a similar report. The Commission on Race and Housing conducted a comprehensive study over a three-year period with the financial support of a private foundation. In its report to the American public, the Commission acknowledged that a decent home and a suitable living environment for every American family had become the goal of national policy in housing. It stated that:

Studies carried out by this Commission demonstrate that realization of these goals of national policy is seriously hampered by racial segregation and discrimination in the distribution of housing facilities and benefits provided under federal laws. Moreover, the policies of the federal housing agencies which encourage or permit racial distinction in the distribution of federal housing benefits are inconsistent with the Constitution of the United States and the spirit of the housing acts of Congress.

The Commission on Race and Housing offered an extensive list of recommendations affecting federal, state, and local government, the housing industry and voluntary citizens' associations. The Commission recognized the role of federal involvement in discrimination in housing and recommended Executive action to aid in the resolution of the problem.

Those two major reports gave new impetus to an embryonic fair housing movement which, with little organization and even less funding, had begun working in various ways to end racial discrimination in housing and to advance a pattern of open occupancy.

Over the years several private groups, representing various interests, had sponsored the construction of small clusters of nondiscriminatory housing. Some of the new, open-occupancy communities were sponsored by religious groups and social service organizations long identified with programs fostering racial equality. Others were sponsored by private builders who found such efforts profitable. All of them, generally, encountered strong opposition from government and the construction and finance industry. Nonetheless, by the end of the 1950's, a survey revealed that more than 50 new interracial residential communities had been successfully developed, and the report of the national studies on race and housing was expected to have an encouraging effect on the trend. While this type of "grass roots" fair housing activity was characteristically local and received limited public recognition, it nonetheless was a vital part of the fair housing movement. In America, nothing succeeds like success. And the example of numerous, socially viable, interracial developments operating at a profit was frequently cited by scholars and civil rights technicians alike.

Thus, as the 1960's got under way, a nationwide grass roots effort had already achieved a proliferation of fair housing legislation and, through NCDH, had begun to make its presence felt. Forty-four million of the nation's population resided in states and cities covered by fair housing legislation, and the number of volunteer groups involved in the effort had risen above 200.

President Kennedy's Executive Order

President Kennedy's 1960 campaign promise to issue an executive order prohibiting discrimination in all federally assisted housing, aside from being morally right, was also politically strategic. Finally, after a two-year delay, the President responded to nationwide demands, and on November 20, 1962 Executive Order #11063 was issued. The order, while far from being the comprehensive document many had hoped to receive, was, nonetheless, historic in its significance. It put the moral force of the federal government squarely behind the principle of equal opportunity in housing. The proliferation of fair housing laws, of course, continued unabated, propelled in part by the limitations of the executive order. By 1965 an NCDH survey revealed that 16 states had passed laws banning discrimination in substantially all the private housing market, and 56 cities had passed laws of varying degrees of coverage. In addition, the number of active fair housing committees and related groups had increased from 300 in 1963 to more than 1,000 by the end of 1965.

There was no question that the movement was continuing to grow in size and force. There was, however, serious question regarding the extent to which the movement, under existing program limitations, could materially affect the role and progress of blacks in American society.

The year 1963 witnessed the beginning of a black revolution which had a profound effect on the focus and substance of governmental policy and character of its leadership. Militant leaders began, with dramatic effectiveness, to demand and obtain major changes in the way American government and society dealt with injustices in the area of civil and political rights. By the middle 1960's, the social and physical transformation that had occurred in the nation's cities and suburbs was widely described as an urban crisis, and the tragic effect on peoples' lives increasingly was exposed.

The continuing large-scale migration of blacks from rural areas to central cities in search of new opportunities had proceeded apace with the massive shift of whites from cities to suburbia. As a result the racial ghettos had grown larger and more congested, and the isolation of blacks from better jobs, decent housing, and good education had reached explosive proportions. The tragic division and alienation in America was so extensive that society seemed bent on self-destruction, and the summers of the 1960's were marked by large-scale riots and racial disorders of such tragic proportions that the whole social and political climate of the nation was changed.

The national picture on race and housing could scarcely have been more disturbing. Nearly 20 years had elapsed since the government of the United States, in 1949, had committed itself to the provision of "a decent home and a suitable living environment for every American family." Yet in 1968, six million American families were living in substandard housing and the number included a very substantial proportion of the nation's black population.

In the 10-year period 1958 to 1968, laws advancing fair housing had been enacted by 23 states and 155 localities. But the laws varied widely in coverage and many were inadequately administered. The nation, which still lacked a uniform national open housing policy, was in difficulty.

During the period, four new Presidential Commissions were appointed to analyze the various public and private actions which had brought the nation to a state of crisis. The National Commission on Violence, The President's Committee on Urban Housing, and The National Commission on Urban Problems all reached conclusions bordering on a central theme; the federal government, which had exhorted racial separation in the past, was now in trouble.

National Advisory Commission on Civil Disorders

It was the report of the National Advisory Commission on Civil Disorders which had the most sobering and profound effect on the nation's fair housing movement. In an extraordinary document, the Commission probed and examined the entire fabric of American social and economic life revealing the pervasive penetration of racism in black and white relationships.

In its report to the President and the nation in March 1968, The Commission indicated, "Our nation is moving toward two societies, one black, one white—separate and unequal." The report served to confirm the conclusion of the nation's fair housing leadership. Past policies had brought about cleavages and divisions in American societal life that neither the nation nor its people could endure. A massive effort would be required, particularly in jobs, housing, and schools, to provide new opportunities and to improve the quality of life. The Executive arm of the government had laid the record bare.

Between April and August of 1968, the Legislative and Judicial branches of the federal government took three unprecedented and far-reaching actions which had the potential for turning the nation around.

The nation's fair housing movement, its members and its allies, played a major role in creating the climate and providing the information and technical assistance which led to these major breakthroughs.

Designating an Agency to Solve the Problem

The Civil Rights Act of 1968—Title VIII

On April 11 the Congress enacted federal legislation establishing equal opportunity in housing as the official policy of the United States. The successful passage of the law was victory for President Lyndon B. Johnson over a Congress which previously had rejected a similar proposal.

The earlier apprehensiveness of the Congress about legislating full residential freedom for black Americans, however, found its way into the provisions of Title III. The law was drawn to embrace the housing market progressively and its sanctions became effective in three stages. During 1968, its prohibitions covered only federally owned or assisted housing. In 1969, coverage was expanded to include almost all conventionally financed apartment units. Finally, in 1970 it expanded to cover the sales of most single-family houses. The ultimate coverage of the law embraced approximately 80 percent of the nation's housing.

Discounting the significance of this phased approach, the major implication of Title VIII for the fair housing movement was that a key impediment to the goal of open housing had been removed; people were disabused of the right to discriminate on the basis of race, color, creed, or national origin. The nation's fair housing movement, which had relied so long on voluntarism, could now lean on the law.

On June 17 the U. S. Supreme Court, in one of its most important decisions, *Jones* v. *Mayer* 392 U. S. 409 (1968), held that the Civil Rights Law of 1866, enacted under authority of the 13th Amendment, barred all racial discrimination in all housing, private as well as public.

The historic case had been carried to the Supreme Court by NCDH and three of its affiliates in the civil rights/fair housing movement.

After concluding that the Black Codes following the Civil War were substitutes for the slave system, the Court said:

. . . when racial discrimination herds men into ghettos and makes their ability to buy property turn on the color of their skin, then it too is a relic of slavery.

The Court's decision reinforced the constitutionality and propriety of Title VIII, and automatically accelerated the phased effect of the law.

The Housing Act of 1968

On August 1, the 1968 Housing and Community Development Act was signed into law, providing the nation with the most comprehensive housing legislation ever enacted by the Congress. The Act charged the Department of Housing and Urban Development with the responsibility to generate the construction of 26 million dwelling units over a ten-year period with particular emphasis on meeting the needs of low- and moderate-income families.

Thus in the brief span of four months in 1968, stated national housing policy underwent a complete change. The framework was created, for the first time in the nation's history, to wipe out slums and ghettos and to provide black Americans and other minorities the same options in housing choice that white homeseekers enjoyed as a matter of course.

Devices of Resistance

The enactment of such historic fair housing laws and subsidized housing programs did not, of course, automatically eliminate all barriers and obstacles to equal housing opportunity. Over the years, several other devices had been woven into the law of suburban jurisdictions and a whole new pattern of institutionalized systems had emerged with the growth and development of suburbia. Foremost among such systems were various exclusionary land use controls and administrative procedures which, when subtly employed, could be just as effective in barring minority residents as the more flagrant policies of the past.

The rapid growth and expansion of suburbia in the 1950's and 1960's had accelerated the exodus of large corporate and industrial complexes from the city. These industries had carried with them the very same jobs at nonskilled, and semiskilled levels which minorities, trapped in the inner-city ghettos, needed for their survival. The logical solution—opening new opportunities and building new units available to low- and moderate-income families—was not acceptable to suburbia before or after the passage of Title VIII. The use of such exclusionary devices as restrictive building and construction codes and large-lot zoning requirements thus increasingly were employed by suburbia to prevent the development of housing which might attract minority occupants. Another procedural device which was used with increasing effectiveness was a local administrative prerogative provided with the cooperation of the federal government—the power to veto subsidized programs unacceptable to the community.

The issues confronting the fair housing movement toward the close of the 1960's thus remained substantive, notwithstanding dramatic changes and improvements which had occurred in federal policies, procedures, and programs. Indeed, it may be said that the civil rights progress of the 1960's resulted in heightening the complexity of the open housing effort. The rationale for change had shifted almost overnight from morality and brotherhood to compliance with federal law. Fair housing volunteers who had cut their teeth on moral suasion, functioning as social generalists, increasingly were required to demonstrate highly technical skills and professional expertise in analyzing and coping with the zoning, planning, financing, development, and marketing of housing. The bankers and builders and brokers of housing had not been particularly impressed with the seriousness of the new laws, and their tendency to do business as usual would have to be reversed.

The interrelationships between housing, jobs, training, education, transportation, and other aspects of community life, affected by complex economic as well as social considerations, began to assume a new level of significance in the hierarchy of fair housing program strategies.

Summary

In summary, by the end of the decade it had become increasingly clear to fair housing and civil rights leadership that a new and frightening array of institutionalized systems had emerged to thwart the federal goal of equal opportunity in housing.

The challenge to the fair housing and civil rights leadership was to mount new programs of research and litigation and to insure that every public and private action translated the law into reality.

Bibliography

ABRAMS, CHARLES, *The City is The Frontier*. New York: Harper and Row, 1965.
————, *Forbidden Neighbors*. New York: Harper and Row, 1955.

CARTER, R. L., D. KENYON, P. MARCUSE, and L. MILLER, *Equality*. New York: Pantheon Books, 1965.

CLARK, KENNETH B., *Dark Ghetto*. New York: Harper and Row, 1965.

KAPLAN, MARSHALL, *Urban Planning in the 1960s*. Cambridge, Mass.: The MIT Press

MILLER, LOREN, "Government's Responsibility for Residential Segregation." In: J. Denton (ed.), *Race and Property*. Berkeley, Calif.: Diablo Press, 1964.

National Committee Against Discrimination in Housing (NCDH) *Jobs and Housing*. New York, 1970.

————, *How The Federal Government Builds Ghettos*. New York, 1968.

SCHUSSHEIM, M. J., *Toward A New Housing Policy, The Legacy of the Sixties*. New York, CED Paper #29.

WEAVER, ROBERT C., *Dilemmas of Urban America*. Cambridge, Mass.: Harvard University Press, 1965.

————, *The Negro Ghetto*. New York, Harcourt Brace Jovanovich, 1948.

WILLIAM, NORMAN, *Planning Law and Democratic Living*, Vol. 20, *Law and Contemporary Problems*. Durham, N.C.: Duke University School of Law, 1955.

CHAPTER 10

HOUSING IN THE 1970'S

DONALD SULLIVAN*

Overview

HALFWAY through the 1970's housing observers were asking when the "seventies" would begin! Not since the depression of the 1930's had there been such a set of convulsions, booms, and ultimately confusion in the provision of shelter. America was undergoing widespread changes in its political, economic, and social fabric. Few aspects of the society escaped the upheavals in values and attitudes that first emerged in the 1960's.

This chapter will examine the ramifications of societal change as it affected housing policy during the early years of the 1970's. Our aim is to understand the forces that influenced the tremendous variations in housing production over the period from 1970 to 1975 and the trends that will probably influence housing policy for the coming decade. The major influences on housing policy and production during the 1970's can be summarized as follows:

    1. *Inflation*—Rapid yearly increases in all component parts of housing, especially interest rates, material, and land costs.

    2. *Energy Crisis*—Americans faced the realities of resource scarcity.

* DONALD SULLIVAN, Ph.D. Cornell University 1969, is now Director of the Graduate Program in Urban Planning at Hunter College of the City University of New York.

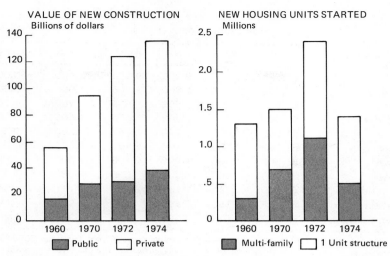

FIGURE 10-1. New construction—value and units started: 1960-1974. [Source: U. S. Bureau of the Census.]

It implications began to affect the design, location, and basic approach to housing.

3. *Watergate*—Led to the collapse of public confidence in government institutions.
4. *Consumerism*—Growing awareness on the part of Americans of their rights regarding the quality of housing began to influence governmental agencies and the housing industry.
5. *Environmental Planning*—The ecology movement began to stimulate legal controls over the use of land as well as the consideration of limits to population growth, both affecting the provision of housing and movements to integrate the suburbs.
6. *Abandonment of the Central City*—Vast areas of older urban areas in the northeast and central section of the country witnessed the destruction of thousands of housing units, leading to rubble-strewn areas adjacent to the downtown districts.

The People and Their Housing Conditions

The 1970 United States Census of Housing showed that the American people had experienced major improvements in the quality of their housing since 1960. In terms of deterioration, inadequate plumbing, and overcrowding, the data indicate that less than 10 percent of American households were living in substantard housing compared with 19 percent of the start of the 1960's. However, while general conditions had improved with regard to shelter, significant changes in the demo-

TABLE 10–1. Bergen County, New Jersey
Construction Home Costs, 1959–1976

Cost Components	1959	1962	1963	1965	1966	1976
Land	$4,600	9,000	9,200	9,500	13,400	$30,000
Carpentry	$1,550	1,800	1,800	1,800	1,900	3,000
Electrical	$ 425	600	606	695	760	1,700
Plumbing	$ 945	1,500	1,500	1,575	1,605	3,600
Heating	$ 700	1,000	1,150	1,150	1,200	2,500
Lumber	$1,800	2,100	2,100	2,422	2,575	6,500
Millwork	$1,600	1,900	1,900	2,200	1,800	2,600
Driveway	$ 250	300	300	250	425	1,250
Garage doors	$ 160	155	155	140	143	250
Insulation	$ 188	193	193	250	250	600
Kitchen cabinets	$ 310	543	543	565	574	1,800

These are rough estimates of home building costs for various years between 1959 and 1976. The figures, culled from long-time Bergen builders, are only estimates. They may vary according to the home built, the materials used during construction, and building specifications.
SOURCE: John Banaslewzki, "Price of Homes up 328% in 17 Years," *The Sunday Record*, June 13, 1976, Bergen County, New Jersey p. C-18.

graphic characteristics of the population, which influenced housing, began to emerge.

Spiraling inflation coupled with a chaotic money market greatly restricted the participation of households in the home-buying market. By the end of 1971, the demand for the traditional single-family, free-standing American home began to constrict severely. The home buyer in the 1970's experienced a double dose of inflation. Not only did he or she pay a constantly inflating price for housing, but had to finance it at higher interest rates.[1] In 1973, for example, the price of single-family houses rose 10 percent from that of 1972. Thus, in a year's period, excluding land, $2,500 was added to the price of a $25,000 house due to extraordinary price hikes in lumber, plywood, and labor. Costs rose sharply in petroleum-based products such as roofing, plastics, plumbing pipes, and electrical wiring. Between April 1970 and October 1973, the percentage increase in a single-family home price was more than twice that of the percentage increase in the income of homeowners. During this 30-month period, the median value of a single-family home jumped 41 percent from $17,000 to $24,100. The median income for homeowners during this period rose less than 19 percent from $9,700 to $11,500. Analysis of the price hikes in building materials for a metropolitan housing market illustrate the reality of inflation translated into the housing dollar. (See Table 10–1.)

[1] "Housing in '74: Nosedive Recovery and 1.8 Million Starts," *House and Home*, Vol. 44, No. 5, November 1973, pp. 79–80.

The energy crisis and inflation were not the only factors affecting the participation of Americans in the housing market of the 1970's. A major recession in the national economy compounded the difficulties faced by the home buyer from 1972 onward. Millions of Americans found themselves in unemployment lines and the reaction to what history might call a depression further slowed the construction of housing. Like all markets, the housing market operates according to a delicately balanced set of weights in terms of supply and demand. Once the psychology of fear enters the marketplace the demand for a commodity begins to diminish. Housing starts peaked at 2.4 million in 1972 and fell to 1.3 million in 1974. The years 1974 and 1975 evidenced a sharp decline in the production of housing, while the percentage of workers unable to find work reached nearly 9 percent across the nation. Unofficial estimates of unemployment during this period were doubled for women and minorities. Unemployment reduced the number of Americans who were able to improve their housing.

Consumer Response

The consumer found that adaptation was necessary with regard to the definition of housing in terms of size, location, tenure, and financing. The demand for multifamily housing grew significantly during the 1970's with apartment construction reaching nearly 50 percent of all new units. Changes in life styles and cultural acceptance of the apartment certainly influenced the movement away from the single-family home. However, the inflated cost of single-family home was the main incentive behind the shift in consumer behavior, especially for the increasing number of elderly, single, and divorced persons. Often limited in terms of income, these segments of the population were left with choices among apartments, mobile homes, and alternative life styles such as communal living, institutional care, and inner-city restorations. Another major development in consumer behavior was the increasing acceptance of the condominium as an alternative. Combining the advantages of single-family financing and taxation benefits with cooperative sharing of maintenance expenses, condominiums evolved into a major housing choice during the 1970's. For example, the Florida coastlines attracted tens of thousands of northern retirees who found that condominium ownership offered a financially beneficial means of transferring the money made on house sales into this form of housing.

Mobile Homes

The Housing Act of 1969 authorized FHA insurance for mobile home loans up to $10,000 over a 12 year repayment period. By 1970,

TABLE 10–2. U. S. General Housing Characteristics: 1970 to 1974

Characteristics		1970	1971	1972	1973	1974*
U. S. housing inventory, total units	mil.	66.6	64.3	66.6	68.2	69.8
Total occupancy	mil.	62.6	58.7	60.8	62.2	63.5
New construction, value	$bil.	95	110	124	135.5	134.4
Construction, other than housing	$bil.	67	80	94	102.9	96.1
Residential, including farm	$bil.	32	43	54	57.6	49.1
New housing units						
Started	thous.	1,469	2,084	2,379	2,057	1,352
Single-family units	thous.	815	1,153	1,311	1,133	889
Two or more units	thous.	654	932	1,068	924	463
Mortgage debt, residential outstanding	$bil.	339.2	274.7	422.5	471.9	506.1
Residential loans underwritten by FHA and VA:						
FHA	$bil.	11.9	14.6	12.3	7.5	6.5
VA	$bil.	3.4	5.9	8.2	7.4	7.2
Average new home sales price:						
FHA-insured	$thous.	N/A	N/A	N/A	22.1	29.7
VA-guaranteed	$thous.	N/A	N/A	N/A	27.3	31.2
Conventional	$thous.	N/A	N/A	N/A	35.2	37.9
First mortgage interest rates on single-family homes (averages, all lenders):						
New homes	%	N/A	7.60	7.45	7.78	8.71
Existing homes	%	N/A	7.54	7.38	7.86	8.84
Mobile home units shipped to dealers in the U.S.	thous.	401.2	496.6	575.9	566.9	329.3

* Estimates

SOURCE: U. S. Department of Housing and Urban Development, U. S. and Foreign Statistical Profile; Housing and Other Characteristics, 1976.

the Federal Home Loan Bank Board had authorized savings and loan associations to finance mobile home purchases. Prior to this legislation the financing and insuring of the mobile home was subject to wide-scale variation throughout the nation.[2] Acceptance of the mobile home increased rapidly during the 1970's (see Table 10–2). In 1972, 575 thousand mobile home units were shipped to dealers in the United States. By 1973 mobile homes accounted for 20 percent of all housing starts. The importance of the mobile home in the housing market becomes particularly clear when the data are broken down to reflect that:

1. By 1972, mobile home sales were 45 percent of all new single family homes.
2. Eighty percent of all homes under $20,000 and 97 percent of those under $15,000 were mobile homes.

The impact of inflation and rising housing costs (see Table 10–3) brought increasing numbers of households to mobile home living. By

TABLE 10–3. U. S. Consumer Price Index and Selected Housing Costs (1967 = 100)

	1971	1972	1973	1974
All items	121.3	125.3	133.1	147.7
Housing (total)	124.3	129.2	135.0	150.6
Shelter*	128.8	134.5	140.7	154.3
Rent	115.2	119.2	124.3	130.2
Homeownership†	133.7	140.1	146.7	163.2
Fuel and utilities	115.0	120.1	126.9	150.2
Household furnishings and operation	118.1	121.0	124.9	140.5

* Includes hotel and motel rates not shown separately.
† Includes home purchase, mortgage interest, taxes, insurance, and maintenance and repairs.
SOURCE: U. S. Department of Housing and Urban Development, *U. S. and Foreign Statistical Profile: Housing and Other Characteristics*, 1976.

the mid-1970's over 8 million people lived in 3.4 million mobile homes in the U.S.A.[3]

The adjective "mobile" is a misnomer as most homes are stationary on privately owned lots or in one of the 15,000 mobile home parks located throughout the nation. At a time when most households earning under $20,000 annually were excluded from the new home market, the mobile home provided an opportunity for moderate-income households to achieve the dream of a new home. It would appear that the

[2] For a detailed analysis of the evolution of the mobile home, see Margaret J. Drury, *Mobile Homes*. (New York: Praeger), 1972.
[3] Robert Cassidy, "The Needed Revolution in Mobile Homes," *Planning*, Vol. 39, No. 11, December 1973, pp. 12–15.

future of the lower-cost segment of the housing market will be in the area of industrialized, factory-produced units. With growing concern for quality control and industry regulation at all levels of government, it is also possible that design breakthroughs might improve the physical quality of the typical mobile home. The combination of demand and need for this form of housing brought about greater quality control in the production of industrialized housing. The mobile home industry was slowly building support for national building codes rather than overly stringent local codes. Equally important were breakthroughs with labor unions so as to allow the utilization of low-skill workers in factory assemblage rather than paying costly building-trades rates for production costs.

The Role of Government

Overview

Not since the 1930's has the federal role in the provision of housing undergone such a metamorphosis. In tracing the evolution of national policy through the first six years of the 1970's, one notes a dramatic shift not only in the philosophy of governmental involvement, but also in the very nature of federal–local relationships. In what might be called the "decade of localism," the nation attempted to deal with macro issues without the degree of centralized control necessary to finely tune the economy. The development of federal policy can be divided into three relatively distinct periods:

1. 1970–1972: Continuance of Great Society efforts
2. 1973–1974: Government collapse and moratorium
3. 1975–1976: Localism

The evolution of national housing legislation provides a convenient means for examining the experience of the 1970's. The Housing Acts and their key provisions will be summarized in order to better explain the changes that have emerged in the American housing system.

The 1970 Housing and Urban Development Act

The bill passed by the Congress in 1970 continued most of the programs initiated under Lyndon Johnson's administration. It provided for increased spending for rent supplements, model cities, public housing, and subsidies for both homeownership and rental housing. These subsidies were a continuation of Sections 235 and 236 of the 1968 legislation. One of the most promising provisions of the 1970 Act was the enactment of the Urban Growth and New Communities Development Act of 1970 designed to encourage the building of "new towns."

The 1970 Act also called for the creation of a Community Development Corporation to oversee a $500 million program of federal guarantees of obligations issued by private and public developers of new communities. The maximum outstanding obligation could not exceed $50 million for a single project. Clearly by 1970 the government was willing to articulate the need for some form of a new community–new town program for the United States. Although minimal, the allocation as well as the Act of 1970 lent some credence to the possibility of a genuine new town policy. Otherwise, the 1970 Act extended the promises of the 1960's to provide all Americans with a "decent" home with a strong federal influence in the operating programs.

Revenue Sharing

The beginnings of a national policy oriented toward decentralization of federal power were given impetus by the revenue sharing program enacted in 1972.[4] Its implications for housing policy would be seen in later housing acts, but the ground rules were being developed in 1972. Basically, the localities and states were pressuring the federal government for more flexibility in the utilization of tax dollars. States and cities wanted wide discretion in local projects without federal "strings" attached to grants. The formula developed for revenue sharing called for a division of funds, allocating one third to the state and two thirds to the local government. Approximately $6 billion per year was allocated for the initial year of revenue sharing. Congress also provided that all general local governments were eligible recipients of revenue sharing funds. In addition, Congress provided that county areas, townships, and municipal governments were entitled to a revenue sharing allocation of no less than 20% nor more than 145% of the statewide average per capita entitlement. Simply stated, the Revenue Sharing movement had begun and elaborate equations had to be developed to allocate federal monies equitably. The quiet revolution toward what would be called the "new federalism" had begun. Its true impact will not be known for years to come, but revenue sharing represents at least a shift away from federal specificity to local options.

Housing Moratorium of 1973

In January 1973, the nation learned that its hopes for the 1968 Housing Act had been crushed. The low- and moderate-income subsidy programs for home ownership (Section 235) and rental housing (Sec-

[4] For a detailed analysis, see *General Revenue Sharing: An A.C.I.R. Reevaluation Advisory Commission on Intergovernmental Relations*, October 1974, Washington, D.C.

tion 236) had erupted into major public scandals.[5] The 1968 Act called for the building of 24 million housing units for low- and moderate-income households. By 1972 the Nixon administration decided that it would not spend the $500 million allocated for these programs and relied on a HUD study to order a moratorium on spending.[6] In 1973 all funds were cut off to builders when scandals surfaced in every part of the American housing system, ranging from corrupt FHA officials to real estate agents and bankers.

The poor were sold homes that were overappraised and overfinanced. Most were in need of vast repairs that low-income families could not afford. The heart of the scandals revolved around good will as much as criminal behavior. In designing programs to allow low- and moderate-income Americans to participate in the dream of homeownership, few realized that a tighter control or performance system would be necessary for monitoring purposes. Federal money suddenly became available in neighborhoods which had been denied private capital as well as FHA insurance for years. Many structures had been abandoned, and many more suffered from years of poor maintenance. Real estate speculators acquired parcels that were given cosmetic repairs, in the case of the scandals, and poor families were then encouraged to acquire them. With federal subsidies available to bring the interest rates down to as low as 1 percent, the lenders or mortgagees were delighted to accept the difference between 20 percent of the mortgagors' income and the total monthly housing cost. This monthly cost included the payments for principal, interest, taxes, insurance, and the mortgage insurance premium. Unfortunately, abuses arose when profit maximization by private developers and realtors was allowed to take place at the expense of consumers with little or no experience in owning or purchasing a house. The abuses were not reserved to existing or rehabilitated housing. Many new houses built under the 235 program were poorly constructed, utilizing the cheapest kind of building materials. The failure of the Federal Housing Administration to control the worst forms of real estate speculation was the major single abuse. The granting of FHA insurance to homes of such poor quality that they clearly would not survive the life of the mortgage, was basically fraud. The end result of these scandals led to the wholesale abandonment of tens of thousands of units throughout the nation, making the federal government one of the largest slum owners in history as it repossessed houses financed under the 235 and 236 program. The failure of these subsidy programs

[5] A detailed analysis of the Detroit experience is provided in Brian Boyer, *Cities Destroyed for Cash.* (Chicago: Follett Publishing Co.), 1973. Details regarding the 235 and 236 programs can be found in the 1968 Housing Act.

[6] U. S. Department of Housing and Urban Development, *Housing in the Seventies.* (Washington, D.C.), 1972.

led to a burst of critical thinking regarding the dynamics and role of public intervention and subsidies, culminating in the 1974 Housing and Community Development Act.[7] Another outgrowth of the scandals was the incorporation of FHA as part of the management section of HUD.

The question of how best to solve America's housing needs while providing the most equitable means of guiding urban growth was the focus of the years 1973 and 1974. Critics of American housing policy argued that most federal housing policies were designed to aid citizens whose incomes as well as housing conditions were adequate by almost any standard. The theme of direct subsidies for the cost of construction instead of direct payments to the low-income or poorly housed family was the heritage of the 1930's. The realizations that direct subsidies to households might be the proper role of the federal government was gaining momentum in academic circles as well as in political circles.[8] By 1974, the nation began to explore the viability of block grants modeled after revenue sharing and direct subsidies to low-income households. In effect the 1974 housing act was to be the turning point in the nation's thinking about housing.

The 1974 Housing and Community Development Act

By 1974, housing starts had dropped 45 percent from their peak in the early 1970's. The nation was recovering from the jolts of the Watergate–Vietnam crisis as well as formulating a response to the prolonged effects of recession, inflation, and the energy shortage. The 1974 Act called for the spending of $7.9 billion in block grants for community development. Localities were encouraged to be flexible and creative with the provision that they must focus on low- and moderate-income housing.[9] It was believed that the act would bring about a sophisticated level of community development planning with a special emphasis on planning for housing need at a regional level.

The key to the 1974 Act, and possibly for housing policy in the 1970's, is the Housing Assistance Plan. Under the provisions of this section of the Act, local officials are required to survey low- and moderate-income housing needs and establish a program for meeting these needs. No community development funds may be received unless the Housing Assistant Plan (HAP) is included in the application for fund-

[7] A brilliant work on subsidies can be found in Henry Aaron, *Shelter and Subsidies: Who Benefits from Federal Housing Policies?* (Washington, D.C.: The Brookings Institution), 1973.

[8] An attack against building-oriented subsidies is presented in Arthur P. Solomon, *Housing the Urban Poor*. (Cambridge, Mass.: M.I.T. Press), 1974.

[9] Edward McCahill, "Housing in the Seventies," *Planning*, Vol. 40, no. 10, November 1974, pp. 19–21.

ing.[10] Complementing the HAP is the provision known as Section 8, a subsidy program designed to provide low-income households with flexibility in the housing market. Based on early experiments with rent allowances, Section 8 is a program under which lower-income families receive a subsidy to make up the difference between the market rent of a housing unit and the amount that residents could otherwise afford to pay. Eligibility is based on income with rent ratios varying between 15 and 25 percent of income.

At a time when the construction of public housing looked unlikely, the use of direct subsidies in the form of the Section 8 program offered a means of formulating a major breakthrough in the nation's housing policies. The changing political climate which held centralized or "big" government in low esteem was forcing housing professionals to reconsider the early visions of the 1930's. The idea of the government being the best landlord for the poor was drawing to a close. The unpopularity of publicly owned and managed housing, especially in the form of high-rise central city housing projects, was growing in all sectors of the society. Even the poor were rejecting public housing in many cities, citing the fact that many low-income projects had turned into dormitories of social pathology. This dissatisfaction led to a rekindling of the belief that the normal workings of the housing market might offer the best hope for achieving quality housing.

It is too early to evaluate the full ramifications of the 1974 Act. Whether or not local officials will meet the housing needs of low- and moderate-income families remains to be determined. It appears that the 1974 Act tried to integrate planning for housing into broader processes of comprehensive development planning. Whether or not lower-income families will benefit from Section 8 subsidies will become evident as housing policy is developed for the latter part of the 1970's. It is too early to determine the effects of consumer subsidies on local housing markets or whether they will significantly improve housing quality. One thing is certain: by 1974, housing policy was in the midst of a transformation which would begin to reshape our thinking regarding the role of the federal government in the provision of shelter.

Aid to Secondary Markets

New moves to stimulate the flow of funds into housing were made at the end of the 1960's.[11] The expansion of mortgage-backed securities was a major innovation of the 1970's. Facilitated by mortgage bankers,

[10] An excellent guidebook is available for those interested in how to prepare this plan: National Association of Housing and Redevelopment Officials (NAHRO), *A Local Housing Assistance Plan.* (Washington, D.C.), 1974.

[11] *House and Home*, "Next for Fannie Mae—A Move Into Conventional Mortgages," Vol. 35, No. 2, p. 12.

commercial banks, and savings and loan associations these securities are sold directly to investors or placed with underwriters who are active in the mortgage market. Special emphasis in the early years of the 1970's was placed on tax shelters as a means of encouraging the flow of capital into the mortgage money market. This aspect of housing policy is likely to receive increasing attention over the coming decade as explorations are encouraged by the federal government to establish a variety of methods for stimulating investment in housing.

The Hunt Commission

Officially known as the President's Commission on Financial Structure and Regulations, this body evaluated the use and effects of the Federal Reserve's Regulation "Q," which restricts interest paid on savings by savings and loans and mutual savings banks. The Hunt Commission attempted to examine whether the elimination of rate controls on financial institutions would have the effect of encouraging savings deposits. The Commission proposed a nationwide charter for mutual savings banks which at that time were restricted to 18 states. The recommended changes were presumed to have a major impact on the flow of funds to housing. The most important aspect of this 1972 Commission was the encouragement of discussion on the subject of variable rate mortgages. Statutory rate ceilings on mortgages, particularly those administered through FHA or VA programs, were the focus of sharpened criticism.[12] The Hunt Commission made public the need for ongoing evaluation of the effects of interest rate regulation on the flow of capital into the housing sector of the economy. Its major accomplishment was to foster an understanding that the secondary mortgage market should receive top level attention as the nation became more sophisticated in its housing policy.

Growth of Consumerism in Housing

The influence of the home-building industry and banking sector on American housing policy received some mild blows from consumer advocates during the 1970's. Through the work of Ralph Nader, Americans were made aware of the lack of direct consumer input in the development of almost all aspects of national housing policy. By 1971, Nader was publicly challenging the Federal National Mortgage Association and the Federal Home Loan Mortgage Corporation for their exclusion of the housing consumer in establishing housing policy.[13] Nader contended that the major fault of the conventional mortgage

[12] "President's Panel Urges Free FHA Rate and Direct Federal Subsidies for Home Buyers," *House and Home*, Vol. 41, No. 2, February 1972, p. 18.

[13] "Consumers on the March: Their Objections Force Changes in Mortgage Documents," *House and Home*, Vol. 39, No. 4, April 1971, p. 22.

was that they gave the lender complete control over one's home with certain provisions allowing for random "inspections" as well as the exercise of discretionary power over such processes as settlement awards. Little action resulted from this criticism, however, although the attention stimulated public awareness.

The growth of the consumer movement had other effects on housing. Questions of racial and sexual discrimination in mortgage lending practices began to receive growing attention. Ralph Nader drew attention to shoddy construction standards in mobile homes, which brought about quality improvements in design as well as in building materials. Consumer group efforts helped to change the prepayment penalties mandated by lenders as well as draw attention to the practices of banks in mortgage financing. One of the most exciting developments that grew out of the consumer movement was the Home Owners Warranty Program of the National Association of Home Builders. By 1974, the home-building industry was willing to accept a voluntary program of supervision over its builders, whereby the builder would be responsible for faulty workmanship and material for the first year of occupancy.[14] Through the use of an insurance program, the builder was able to "guarantee" the quality of his work. As a result, the consumer of housing was given some degree of protection.

Further efforts on the part of consumers led to the Real Estate Settlement Procedures Act (RESPA) of 1975, which was written to simplify the closing procedures at the selling of property. Unfortunately by July 1, 1976 it was repealed and basically rendered obsolete. Its original purpose was to cut down the cost of property transfers which had risen to unacceptable levels by 1975. Other reforms initiated by the consumer movement focused on obtaining interest on escrow accounts required by mortgage lenders. The combined efforts of the consumer movement was to remind the construction and banking industries, along with the federal housing agencies, that the consumer was no longer willing to remain outside the housing policy arena.

Housing Trends: Predicting 1980

Halfway through the 1970's one finds no clear direction from which to predict future trends. Attempts at localism evolve as does the consumer movement. Increasing disillusionment with public housing had brought governmental construction of housing to a virtual standstill. The most spectacular evidence of the failure was the dynamiting of the 43-building complex in St. Louis known as the Pruitt-Igoe project.

14 "Builder's Warranty: The Guaranty Program goes Public At NAHB Convention," *House and Home*, Vol. 45, No. 3, March 1974, p. 12.

Battered by the complex sociopsychological pathologies of the 1970's poor, the project failed under the weight of crime, vandalism, and unstable households.[15] Throughout the nation public housing became synonymous with compounds for the problem families of society. Communities avoided the construction of low-income housing with whatever strategies they could develop.[16]

The 1970's will also be known as a period of increasing abandonment of housing as well as a period of population exclusion and no-growth policy. Throughout the nation the abandonment of hundreds of thousands of housing units was taking place at ever increasing rates. At a time when parts of some American cities began to resemble European cities devastated by the bombs of World War II, the suburbs fought to enact stringent limits on their growth in the face of court-ordered challenges to promote racial and class integration. The State of New York established a statewide Urban Development Corporation (UDC) in the late 1960's to develop low- and moderate-income housing. Granted the power to issue its own bonds as well as to override local zoning, many believed that a working model for achieving racial and class integration was available. However, when the UDC attempted to introduce low-income housing in the wealthy Westchester County suburbs of New York City, the state legislature prevented them from realizing its social goals. The power of local residents in opposing low-income housing was so strong that the State was unable to interfere with the traditions of local control over land use.

No Growth Movement

The "no growth" movement emerged as the key issue in land use planning during the 1970's. The ecology movement argued that the resources of the planet are limited, and localities had to begin planning for the delivery of services to an ever expanding population.

The classic example of the no-growth movement translated into law was the Ramapo, New York development plan. In 1972 the town adopted an 18-year phased development program which was upheld by the courts of New York. It was a program which allowed new housing and urban development only in those areas which had existing sewer and water connections as well as recreational facilities. Its effect was to limit both new housing and people.

Other parts of the country began to explore alternative strategies for

[15] William Moore, Jr., *The Vertical Ghetto: Everyday Life in an Urban Project*. (New York: Random House), 1969.

[16] Refer to Joseph P. Fried, *Housing Crisis U.S.A.* (New York: Praeger Publishers), 1971, for a detailed examination of the problems evolving during this decade.

limiting growth. The city of Boulder, Colorado refused to provide water and sewer connections to developments whose land was outside the city limits, reversing earlier policies of encouraging speculative growth. Boulder also levied a city sales tax increase to be used to acquire open space and flood plains at the periphery of the city. By 1975 more and more cities, states, and counties throughout the nation were exploring approaches to growth control. Petaluma, California was given court approval in 1975 to impose a yearly quota of building permits for 5 years in order to plan the rational use of land.[17] Issues to be faced in the latter part of the 1970's will be the resolution of no-growth policy with growing demands for class and racial integration in the suburbs. It is expected that court suits challenging local housing policy will increase, particularly with the 1976 Supreme Court case of *Gautreux* v. *Chicago Housing Authority*. This case ordered Chicago's Housing Authority to stop concentrating the poor in black ghettos.

Summary

Uncertainty regarding the proper role of the government in meeting the housing needs of its citizens remains as the legacy of the first half of the 1970's. At a time when decent housing was beginning to be viewed as a right rather than a reward, housing policymakers found themselves confused as to the proper response to the confusion of the nation. It was clear that earlier dreams would not disappear and that housing policy would have to reflect a new society as well as a new awareness of sharing, scarcity, and freedom.

Many problems remained unsolved. The unmet housing needs of lower-income families might very well have to await a resurgence of belief in the public sector. The continued abandonment of older neighborhoods in the central cities will require a corrective policy similar to earlier urban renewal efforts. Vast amounts of land could be acquired by localities, if federal money were made available. Efforts to bank the land in anticipation of future needs in housing, economic development, and recreation could give cities the means to provide opportunities to their citizens. Equally important will be continued support for efforts made in neighborhood preservation. Cooperative and condominium ownership will most likely become available to lower-income households as a way of maintaining the ownership of housing. The work of the National Center for Housing Management, begun in the late 1960's, provides a centralized source of information on the operation of apart-

[17] For an analysis of court cases on planned integration in suburbia as well as population control policy, see Sylvia Lewis, "The Jury's Out on Growth Control," *Planning*, Vol, 41, No. 1, January 1975, p. 8.

ment buildings. It is likely that continued research in the areas of management and social services will broaden the dimensions of low-income housing policy.

Planning for a more orderly suburban development is gaining increasing support throughout the country. It would appear that the construction of housing according to community as well as metropolitan plans will eventually be accepted. Growing court pressure for opening the suburbs to people of all incomes and races will probably result in greater choice in the type of housing available. Ideally, new construction will be designed to accommodate the diversity of our population. For example, the elderly in our society are projected to reach almost 20 percent of the population by the 1980's. Their needs, along with those of single people, will have to be accommodated in the suburbs as well as the central cities. It is certain that efforts will be made to provide living environments that do not isolate this segment of the population from the society.

Summarizing the early years of the decade as a way of anticipating the future is risky. It is hard to gauge the future policies of the federal government and their effect on state and local efforts. It does appear that we will experience a decentralization of housing policy with the courts providing national leadership in areas such as integration. Future evaluation of the 1970's will be to view this era as a period of major thinking about the role of the public sector in the provision of shelter. With increased awareness for the quality of our living environment one hopes that housing policy will reflect the creativity necessary to realize communities of quality and opportunity.

Bibliography

ANDREWS, RICHARD, *Urban Land Economics and Public Policy*. New York: Free Press, 1971.

BRUCE-BRIGGS, B., "The Cost of Housing," *The Public Interest*, Summer, 1973.

The Costs of Sprawl: Environmental and Economic Costs of Alternative Residential Development Patterns, Real Estate Research Corporation, 1974.

CUOMO, MARIO, *Forest Hills Diary: The Crisis of Low Income Housing*. New York: Random House, 1974.

DE BOER, JOHN C., *Are New Towns For Lower Income Too?* New York: Praeger Publishers, 1974.

DRURY, MARGARET, *Mobile Homes*. New York: Praeger Publishers, 1972.

FRIED, JOSEPH P., *Housing Crisis U.S.A.* New York: Praeger Publishers, 1971.

GOETZ, CHARLES, *What is Revenue Sharing?* Washington, D.C.: The Urban Institute, 1972.

HEROUX, RICHARD, *Financial Analysis and the New Community Development Process.* New York: Praeger, 1973.

Housing in the Seventies, Report of the Department of Housing and Urban Development, Washington, D.C., 1973.

ISLER, MILTON L., *Thinking About Housing.* Washington D.C.: The Urban Institute, 1970.

MACY, JOHN, *Publicly Provided and Assisted Housing In The U.S.A.* Washington, D.C.: The Urban Institute, 1972.

MANDELKER, DANIEL and ROGER MONTGOMERY, *Housing in America: Problems and Perspectives.* Cincinnati, Ohio: Bobbs-Merrill, 1973.

MIELDS, HUGH, JR., *Federally Assisted New Communities, The Urban Land Institute.* Washington, D.C., 1973.

The National Survey of Housing Abandonment. The Center for Community Change, The National Urban League, September 1971.

A Nice Place To Live: Report of the Twentieth Century Fund, Task Force On Prospects and Priorities of New York City. New York, 1973.

PAWLEY, MARTIN, *Architecture Versus Housing.* New York: Praeger, 1971.

People Before Property: A Real Estate Primer and Research Guide, The Community Research and Publications Group. Urban Planning Aid, Inc., Massachusetts, 1972.

SCHUSSHEIM, MORTON, *The Modest Commitment to Cities.* Lexington, Mass.: D. C. Heath, 1974.

STERNLIEB, GEORGE and LYNNE SAGALYN, *Housing: 1970–1971.* New York: AMS Press, 1972.

SOLOMON, ARTHUR P., *Housing the Urban Poor: A Critical Evaluation of Federal Housing Policy.* Cambridge, Mass.: M.I.T. Press, 1974.

TAGER, J., *The Urban Vision.* Homewood, Ill.: Dorsey Press, 1970.

TAGGART, ROBERT, III, *Low-Income Housing: A Critique of Federal Aid.* Baltimore, Md.: John Hopkins Press, 1970.

Task Force Report, *The Use of Land: A Citizen Policy Guide to Urban Growth,* 1973.

WELFELD, IRVING H., *European Housing Subsidy Systems,* Washington, D.C.: U. S. Government Printing Office, 1972.

WILBURN, MICHAEL. *Optimizing Profits In Large Scale Real Estate Projects.* Washington, D.C.: The Urban Land Institute, 1972.

CHAPTER 11

THE SECONDARY MORTGAGE MARKET

CURTIS W. TUCK[*]

The Secondary Mortgage Market Defined

THE SECONDARY mortgage market can be defined as the aggregate of the sales of mortgages[1] during a given period of time.

To many, it is surprising that mortgages can even be sold by the original lender. Some homeowners have expressed disbelief when they learn, usually in a form letter from their mortgagee, that henceforth they should forward monthly payment to a firm unknown to them in a distant city. But they learn upon inquiry, as this writer did in 1963, mortgages can be and are bought and sold regularly in large dollar volumes, as are stocks and bonds and accounts receivable and other such evidences of assets and obligations. The market, at first, may be difficult to visualize, but it is active and has a great impact on housing.

---

[1] Oakley Hunter, "The Federal National Mortgage Association: Its Response to Critical Financing Requirements of Housing," *The George Washington Law Review*, Vol. 39, No. 4, May 1971, pp. 819–820.

---

[*] CURTIS W. TUCK is a former Director of Public Affairs of the Federal National Mortgage Association. Currently he is Publisher and Editor of the *Lahontan Valley News*, Fallon, Nevada.

Overview of Mortgage Market

Any detailed discussion of the secondary mortgage market and its participants presumes knowledge of the primary mortgage market, which has been touched on in preceding chapters.

By way of review, you will recall that the significant participants in the primary mortgage market are borrowers and those institutions and individuals who lend money so consumers can buy houses. Primary lenders in the United States are mainly the deposit institutions—the state and federally chartered savings and loan (and building and loan) associations, the mutual savings banks, and state and federally chartered commercial banks. Life insurance companies were a more significant factor until 1965, when their mortgage holding began to decline. Federal agencies, federally chartered but privately owned corporations, individuals, and miscellaneous others complete the list of participants in the primary market.

Table 11–1 gives a recent history of the growth of residential mortgage lending by the various entities, including both primary and secondary market entities. Table 11–2 translates these holdings into percentages. Note the dollar growth by savings and loan associations, commercial banks, federally related institutions and individuals, and others and the percentage declines experienced by life insurance companies and others. As indicated by Table 11–1, the overall investment in mortgages in the United States has grown rapidly in the last 18 years, despite four periods of so-called "tight" money.

One commonly accepted yardstick by which to measure mortgage market performance is the amount of "new" money going into mortgages annually. This figure is variously referred to as "net new mortgage credit," "net mortgage investment," or "new money." The terms refer to the difference between all mortgage loans made and the amount paid off against existing mortgages through monthly payments, foreclosures, refinancing, payments in full, and so forth.

In 1965, for example, mortgages of all kinds absorbed $25.8 billion in *net new* mortgage credit, with the residential market accounting for $18.9 billion of this total. Table 11–3 shows that in 1973 net new mortgage credit totaled just over $70 billion, with the residential market accounting for $48.0 billion (see Table 11–4). The comparable figures for 1976 and estimates for 1977 are also shown in Tables 11–3 and 11–4.

We commented earlier on the level of participation in the total mortgage market by various lenders and the growing dominance of the market by the savings and loan associations. By 1975 their share of the market had expanded to 67 percent.

Another important feature of the residential mortgage market is the

TABLE 11–1. Mortgage Loans Outstanding on One-to-Four Family Homes by Type of Lender
(In millions of dollars)

Year End	Savings Associations	Mutual Savings Banks	Commercial Banks	Life Insurance Companies	Federal Agencies	Individuals and Others	Total
1950	$ 13,116	$ 4,312	$ 9,481	$ 8,478	$ 1,468	$ 8,315	$ 45,170
1955	30,001	11,100	15,075	17,661	3,015	11,398	88,250
1960	55,386	18,369	19,242	24,879	7,136	16,275	141,287
1965	94,225	30,064	30,401	25,589	6,396	22,262	212,937
1970	124,970	37,342	42,329	26,676	22,093	26,765	280,175
1971	142,275	38,641	48,020	26,604	26,553	27,741	307,834
1972	167,049	41,650	57,004	22,466	30,250	30,139	348,558
1973	187,750	44,427	67,998	22,000	35,454	32,349	390,298
1974*	201,986	45,001	73,665	22,380	45,817	31,277	420,136

* Preliminary
SOURCE: The *Washington Star*, September 26, 1975.

TABLE 11–2. Figures in Percentages

Year End	Savings Associations	Mutual Savings Banks	Commercial Banks	Life Insurance Companies	Federal Agencies	Individual and Others
1950	29	10	21	19	3	18
1955	34	13	17	20	3	13
1960	39	13	14	18	5	12
1965	44.3	14	14	14	3	10
1970	44.6	13	15	10	8	10
1974	48.1	11	18	5	11	7

SOURCE: The *Washington Star*, September 26, 1975.

TABLE 11–3. Net Mortgage Investment
(Billions of dollars)
(Seasonally Adjusted Annual Rates)

	Home	Multifamily	Commercial	Farm	Total
1965	22.9	3.6	4.5	2.3	33.3
1970	15.0	6.9	7.2	.8	29.9
1971	30.6	9.7	9.9	2.4	52.6
1972	43.8	12.8	16.8	3.6	77.0
1973	44.9	10.4	19.1	5.5	79.9
1974	33.3	6.9	15.3	5.0	60.5
1975	41.4	N/A	11.2	4.6	57.2
1976	65.3	1.6	13.7	6.1	86.8
1977	93.1	6.9	20.9	8.7	129.7

SOURCE: Board of Governors of the Federal Reserve System.

TABLE 11–4. Net Residential* Mortgage Investment: Selected Lenders
(Billions of dollars)
(Seasonally Adjusted Annual Rates)

	Savings and Loan	Mutual Savings Banks	Life Insurance Companies	Commercial Banks	FNMA	Other	Total
1965	8.0	3.6	2.7	3.7	0.5	8.0	26.5
1970	9.1	1.2	0.9	(1.0)	4.5	7.2	21.9
1971	20.8	3.1	(1.4)	6.4	2.3	9.1	40.3
1972	28.2	4.1	(1.7)	10.8	2.0	13.2	56.6
1973	23.3	4.0	(0.8)	12.2	4.4	12.2	55.3
1974	14.9	1.4	(0.2)	7.2	5.4	11.5	40.2
1975	24.9	1.7	(1.4)	0.8	2.2	13.2	41.4
1976	40.3	3.3	(2.0)	8.4	1.1	15.8	66.9
1977	52.4	5.6	(1.7)	15.8	1.5	26.4	100.0

* Home and residential multifamily.
SOURCE: Board of Governors of the Federal Reserve System.

TABLE 11–5. FHA–VA Mortgages as a Percent of Net
Residential Mortgage Investment
(Billions of dollars)

	Government Underwritten	Total Net Residential* Investment	Percent
1965	4.0	26.5	15.1
1970	9.0	21.9	40.7
1971	11.5	40.3	28.5
1972	10.4	56.6	18.4
1973	3.9	55.3	7.1
1974	5.2	40.2	12.9
1975	6.8	41.4	16.4
1976	7.1	66.9	10.6
1977	N/A	100.0	N/A

* Home and residential multifamily.
SOURCE: Board of Governors of the Federal Reserve System.

fluctuating role of the mortgages insured by the Federal Housing Administration (FHA) and those guaranteed by the Veterans Administration (VA), frequently referred to as FHA/VA mortgages. As can be seen in Table 11–5, FHA/VA mortgages in 1965 accounted for a little more than 20 percent of net new mortgage credit. In 1970, the FHA/VA share of the market exceeded 45 percent, a high point since the post-World War II housing boom. This increase was partly due to an increase in the volume of federally subsidized housing, which is FHA-insured, and to a shortage of mortgage funds in the hands of lenders who concentrate on "conventional" loans (those not backed by the FHA or VA), primarily the savings and loan associations.

By 1975, the FHA/VA share of the market had dropped to 19 percent (see Table 11–5) after federally subsidized housing programs were cut back, thus reducing FHA volume of loans insured. The FHA/VA share has continued low, while the supply of funds for conventional mortgages has increased.

Secondary Market

If the primary market involves the home buyer and a lender, then who is involved in the "secondary" market (which should not be confused with second mortgages given to *homeowners* for home improvements and other purposes)?

Perhaps a crude analogy will help to clarify the distinction between the primary and the secondary mortgage markets, which merge conceptually to form the total mortgage market.

College students are painfully familiar with the costs and process of buying college textbooks each semester or quarter. The procedure of purchasing texts in the university bookstore can be compared with the primary market. The bookstore has the goods; the student the money or credit card. The transaction is a "primary" act—the giving of a book for a price paid. In the mortgage market, the comparable transaction is the lender loaning his customers money to buy a house. The lender takes back a written promise to pay by the borrower, a mortgage or deed of trust, and a "primary" transaction has been accomplished.

When the student decides for whatever reason to "liquidate" his investment in the textbook at the end of a particular college course, he can offer the book for sale, by advertising its availability in personal contacts with fellow students and by pinning advertisements on nearby bulletin boards. Or, if he wants to participate in the more formal, institutional used-book market, he can sell at prevailing prices at the end of the term to bookstores or traveling used-book buyers. The sale of the book by the student can be seen as the secondary, or resale, market.

While the principal actors are not the same, something similar happens in the secondary mortgage market. The "primary" lender or institution that put up the money to allow the home buyer to get into a home ends the transaction holding a negotiable instrument called a mortgage (or deed of trust). The institution collects monthly payments from the homeowner, who has pledged the home as security for the loan made by the lender.

Let's say the lender—in this case a savings and loan association—decides, as did the student, it wants to convert this piece of paper called a mortgage into ready cash. How does it enter its own "secondary" market? As was the case with the student, the lender must let it be known that it wants to sell its wares, its loans. It can advertise by word of mouth (telephone perhaps) or participate in a more institutionalized process which will be discussed below. But the sale is completed eventually, be it to another institution or individual.

By way of review, then, the primary market involves those who want money, home buyers or builders, approaching those who loan money, predominantly institutional lenders such as savings and loan associations, savings banks, and mortgage bankers. The making of the mortgage is a "primary" transaction. The "secondary" market transaction occurs when the lender sells that mortgage to another investor. Thus, the secondary market can be defined as the aggregate of the sales of mortgages during a given period; for example, one year.

Lending institutions work both sides of the street. They can be acting as primary lenders in the morning by closing three mortgage loans with eager couples buying homes. In the afternoon, the same institutions can be secondary market participants through the sale of mortgages from their portfolios or the purchase of mortgages offered by another institution. One way to distinguish primary from secondary mortgage transactions is to determine whether there is a consumer (homeowner) directly involved. If there is, it is likely a primary transaction. If institutions are buying or selling already created or soon-to-be created mortgages, they are dealing in the secondary market. Primary lenders, such as savings and loan associations and savings banks, buying and selling mortgages to each other may be said to be operating in the secondary mortgage market. There are some institutions, however, that deal exclusively in the secondary mortgage market, never originating loans to home buyers but only buying and selling the debt obligations (mortgages) resulting from real estate transactions.

Some of the more important secondary mortgage market institutions are the Federal National Mortgage Association (Fannie Mae or FNMA) formed in 1938; the Government National Mortgage Association (Ginnie Mae or GNMA), formed in 1968 as a constituent agency of the U. S. Department of Housing and Urban Development (HUD); and the Federal Home Loan Mortgage Corporation (known as Freddie Mac, FHLMC, and the Mortgage Corporation), formed in 1970 as a wholly owned subsidiary of the Federal Home Loan Bank Board.

The Federal National Mortgage Association

As you may recall from Chapter 4 on the 1930's by Fish (this volume), Fannie Mae was chartered in 1938 pursuant to Title III of the National Housing Act of 1934. It was a child of the Depression and an offspring of the Reconstruction Finance Corporation (RFC), a key tool of FDR's New Deal effort to get the country's economy back on its feet.

The key function of Fannie Mae in its early days was to buy the then fledgling FHA-insured mortgages, which had been authorized by the 1934 Act, and which were a new and unproven financing instrument in the mortgage market. The theory was that if the government provided an institution to buy the FHA loans, lenders would have more confidence in them. They also would be more willing to make more FHA loans.

FNMA's success in its early years was not dramatic, but it did purchase loans and offered assurance to lenders. As the economy picked up steam and the country slowly came out of the Depression and moved through the war years, the FHA loan—and later the VA-guaranteed loan—gained in acceptance by lenders and popularity with borrowers. FNMA also sold loans to investors who could not easily obtain them in sufficient quantity elsewhere. FNMA was on its way to establishing a degree of liquidity for mortgages. By the end of 1956 FNMA's portfolio of mortgages had reached $648 million. (See Table 11–6.)

FNMA was rechartered in 1954 to spell out its three basic functions:

1. To conduct a secondary market operation—buying and selling FHA-insured and VA-guaranteed home mortgages. The goal here was to "provide supplementary assistance to the secondary market for home mortgage investments, thereby improving the distribution of investment capital available for home mortgage financing."
2. To operate Special Assistance Functions (SAF); in other words, provide financing for certain *subsidized* housing programs that the federal government originated from time to time.
3. To manage and liquidate the portfolio of subsidized and other mortgages that had been acquired over the years.

From the time of its origin, there had been much discussion of the possibility of having the secondary market operation of Fannie Mae financed by private funds. The separation of the secondary market activities from the subsidized operations came about as a result of the Housing Act of 1968. Fannie Mae was converted to a federally chartered, but privately owned, tax-paying corporation.

After the 1968 Act, the corporation passed through transitional stages, achieving its present private-control status in May 1970. For example, the President of FNMA was an appointee of the Secretary of Housing and Urban Development during most of 1968, a appointee of the President of the United States during most of 1969, and has been an appointee of the Board of Directors since May 1970.

FNMA's operations as a private corporation were intended, from their inception, to be both profitable and subject to full federal corporate income taxes. Its obligations are not backed by the full faith and credit of the United States and it has received no federal subsidy. It nevertheless retains important links with the federal government.

Relationships with Federal Government

FNMA is subject to federal supervision which may take several forms. The Secretary of Housing and Urban Development (HUD) has regulatory powers over FNMA to assure that the Charter Act provisions are carried out. The Act also provides for specific controls. The aggregate amount of cash dividends paid in one year cannot exceed an amount that the Secretary of HUD may establish, taking into consideration the current earnings and capital condition of the corporation. The Secretary may require that a reasonable portion of FNMA's mortgage purchases be related to the provision of housing for low- and moderate-income families, but with reasonable economic return to the corporation. Offerings of stock and of debt securities by FNMA must have the

TABLE 11-6. FNMA Secondary Mortgage Market Activity by Calendar Year*
(Dollars in thousands)

Year	Purchases	Sales	Repayments	Other Credits	Year-end Portfolio	
					Number of Mortgages	Amount
Total*	$55,073,836	$3,157,222	$11,982,401	$5,557,686	$1,531,948	$34,376,527
1954	24	—	—	—	2	24
1955	86,049	—	393	—	9,483	85,680
1956	574,538	5,014	6,154	335	62,114	648,715
1957	1,021,044	2,887	28,721	2,310	146,860	1,635,841
1958	259,535	465,568	39,156	9,962	128,337	1,380,690
1959	784,569	3,474	47,472	14,525	187,144	2,049,788
1960	980,495	42,093	64,116	21,083	259,138	2,902,991
1961	624,390	521,999	79,016	54,433	254,976	2,871,933
1962	547,427	390,667	104,029	78,085	253,151	2,846,579
1963	181,290	779,824	109,723	76,531	191,712	2,061,791
1964	197,548	78,091	120,044	64,295	190,787	1,996,909
1965	756,933	46,562	125,612	62,193	239,978	2,519,475
1966	2,080,617	73	133,047	70,690	388,409	4,396,282
1967	1,399,602	11,744	169,912	92,224	469,930	5,522,004
1968	1,944,379	358	217,743	77,969	586,634	7,170,313
1969	4,242,974	—	266,279	67,425	833,142	11,079,583
1970	5,531,892	20,293	342,732	190,794	1,086,303	16,057,656
1971	4,039,794	335,523	613,764	633,421	1,166,276	18,514,742
1972	3,864,134	208,299	1,014,265	830,713	1,221,306	20,325,599
1973	6,252,239	70,773	1,241,724	806,713	1,344,600	24,458,628
1974	7,018,565	4,292	1,036,127	728,218	1,473,552	29,708,556
1975	4,319,992	1,984	1,322,841	787,870	1,533,440	31,915,853
1976	3,632,051	86,075	1,997,294	527,405	1,533,756	32,937,130
1977	4,783,755	81,629	2,902,237	360,492	1,531,948	34,376,527

* Also the corporation's fiscal year.

407

approval of the Secretary, as must FNMA's requirements that those who service mortgages for the corporation shall hold stock in the corporation. The approval of the Secretary of HUD is also required for increases above a certain level in the ratio of the corporation's debt to its capital. Issuance by the corporation of various forms of debt securities and their maturities and rates of interest are subject to approval by the Secretary of the Treasury.

There are several privileges that FNMA has that are not normally accorded to other private corporations. Its obligations have "agency" status in the credit market. They are legal investments for federally supervised banks, savings and loan associations, and other financial institutions. This enlarges the corporation's access to credit. Also, the Secretary of the Treasury is authorized in his discretion to purchase obligations of FNMA up to the amount of $2.25 billion outstanding at any one time. This authority has come to be known as the "Treasury backstop authority." It has not been used since FNMA achieved its present private status in 1970, and the corporation intends to conduct its affairs in such a way that there will be no need to use the authority. Its existence, however, apparently reinforces the advantages of the corporation's "agency" status.

The Government National Mortgage Association

When FNMA was spun out of the federal government by an Act of Congress, it retained its role as a secondary market for home mortgages. The remaining functions—special assistance and management and liquidation of the old portfolio of government-assisted mortgages—were retained in government, in the new U. S. Department of Housing and Urban Development, known as HUD. A new corporation, an official federal agency, was created to carry out those functions. That corporation was named the Government National Mortgage Association, better known by its nickname Ginnie Mae.

Today, we have the two corporations—Ginnie Mae, a constituent agency in HUD, and Fannie Mae, a private company but with certain attachments to government.

Ginnie Mae Securities

One of the features of the 1968 Housing Act was provision for the Government National Mortgage Association to guarantee the timely payment of interest and principal on a new type of security instrument designed to attract non-mortgage investors.

These securities would be issued by private firms which held FHA or VA mortgages. The mortgages would be placed in a trust to back the securities. In addition to the safety afforded by the pools of mortgages held in trust by the issuer, the securities are also guaranteed by GNMA and are backed by the full faith and credit of the United States Government.

Although the volume of securities issued initially was not great, an active market for them has developed, and during 1976 $13.8 billion were issued, and by the end of 1976 $30.6 billion were outstanding.

There is some public confusion over the GNMA securities. They are *not* issued by Ginnie Mae; they are issued by private firms; GNMA acts as the guarantor.

Generally speaking, the interest rate on the security is ½ of 1 percent lower than the interest rate on the mortgages in the mortgage pool. The issuer, therefore, is receiving more interest on the mortgages than he is paying on the securities. He must pay GNMA $6/100$ of 1 percent as a guarantee fee, however, and he also has the expense of servicing the mortgages. In addition, he has some risk in that he must make the monthly payments to the buyers of the securities whether or not he receives the money from the homeowners whose mortgages are in the pool—and this can mean borrowing money to do so. This represents an expense.

The record of the GNMA securities program has been good, and the instances where GNMA has had to pay off a security under its guarantee have been few.

GNMA has in recent years used the GNMA securities as a method of selling mortgages from its portfolio. GNMA would pool large volumes of mortgages and in one more or less simultaneous transaction sell the mortgages to private investors, who would then put them in trust and issue GNMA securities. By "packaging" the mortgages, larger security issues could be created and investment bankers could be induced to bid against each other for them, thereby increasing the return to GNMA and reducing the government's loss on the sales of the mortgages.

Points and Discounts

Although it was suggested earlier that mortgages are bought and sold like stocks and bonds, there are some important differences. For one thing, the secondary market for mortgages is not centrally located (as, for instance, the New York Stock Exchange). For another thing, the outstanding principal balance of a mortgage decreases month by month, and a mortgage that has a balance of $10,000 at the time of origination may have a balance less than that when it is sold.

In addition, the coupon rate of a mortgage may not reflect the current market conditions (a buyer will not accept 8 percent on an FHA mortgage if he could get 9 percent on a good conventional mortgage).

To adjust the yields on mortgages to market conditions at the time of sale, mortgages are "discounted," and the buyer pays less than the unpaid principal balance at the time of the sale. This has the effect of giving the buyer a higher yield than that stated in the mortgage itself.

Discounts are stated in "points" and one point is equal to 1 percent of the unpaid principal balance of the mortgage. By way of example, a 9 percent mortgage discounted four points (that is to say, sold for 96 percent of the unpaid principal balance of the mortgage) will yield the buyer 9.59 percent.

Since government-imposed ceilings limit the interest rate on FHA and VA mortgages, "points" are more often a problem with FHA and VA mortgages than with conventional mortgages, since interest rates on conventional mortgages can be adjusted readily to reflect changing market conditions.

Tandem Plan

Fannie Mae and Ginnie Mae have in recent years worked together to assist in carrying out federal housing programs, notably subsidized housing programs that private industry would not finance because of high-risk factors.

During the 1960's, the country was undergoing social ferment and change. While the country was financing an expanding war in Vietnam, the Congress was also enacting "Great Society" legislation designed in part to make more and better housing available to low- and moderate-income families.

Faced with the need to provide some housing quickly and to minimize the costs to the taxpayers, a financing method that blended into the existing housing finance structure was selected over one that called for massive, direct lending from the U. S. Treasury and the carrying of tremendous amounts of mortgages on the federal books as part of the federal debt. The plan that was devised is what has become known as the Tandem Plans.

The Tandem Plans, created in 1969, had as their goal to buy mortgages with federal funds and to sell mortgages to private, permanent investors to the maximum extent possible, returning to the U. S. Treasury most of the money used in buying the mortgages.

In brief, the Tandem Plans were designed to maximize production of certain types of housing while minimizing the cost to the federal government—or to get the most "punch" for each tax dollar spent. They also provided a mechanism for government injection of mortgage funds into the credit system—mortgage funds which could be targeted to benefit specific groups of people or to stabilize the mortgage market in periods of financial extremes. As a mechanism for these purposes,

Tandem Plan operations were a quick and effective means of carrying out political decisions.

The concept behind the Tandem Plans, while little understood, is relatively simple. Under the plan, GNMA enters into contracts with mortgage lenders—mortgage banking companies, savings and loan associations, commercial banks, and others—to purchase certain types of mortgages at higher prices (i.e., lower yields) than those offered in the open market. Purchases are made by GNMA on expectation that the mortgages can later be sold at or near market prices, the prices at which other investors will buy mortgages. Any difference between the purchase and sale prices would be absorbed by GNMA as a form of government subsidy. The subsidy, in essence, is one cost to taxpayers of performing a social good—creating housing for those families unable to pay the cost of housing or to obtain the necessary financing.

This plan as originally developed was a "tandem" operation because GNMA and FNMA contracted to work together. The agreement called for FNMA to purchase, under certain circumstances, those mortgages that GNMA asked it to purchase. Thus, with FNMA acting as a buyer of last resort in the process, GNMA had some assurance of a market for the mortgages it purchased. GNMA also paid fees to FNMA for the latter's acceptance of responsibility to buy the mortgages if GNMA chose not to do so. This was called a warehousing fee. GNMA also paid FNMA a fee for issuing mortgage purchase commitments on its behalf, keeping records of the transactions, and handling other administrative chores that are involved in the business of mortgage finance.

Tandem Plan Process

Let us walk through the steps of the Tandem process just to clarify how it typically works. For an overview of the steps involved, see Figure 11–1.

First (Step 1), the builder proposes to build housing, either single or multifamily—homes or apartments. To obtain financing, he must approach a mortgage lender or mortgage originator. The mortgage lender, a mortgage banker, savings and loan, etc., applies to FHA for a commitment for mortgage insurance and obtains the commitment that FHA will insure the mortgage if the builder constructs it as agreed.

The lender then obtains a commitment (Step 2) from GNMA to purchase the mortgage, at a predetermined price, for example at 98 percent of the amount of the mortgage or $98.00 per $100.00 of value. GNMA issues the commitment (Step 3).

The builder can then go ahead with construction and ultimately sell the house to a purchaser. The purchaser pays for the housing with a

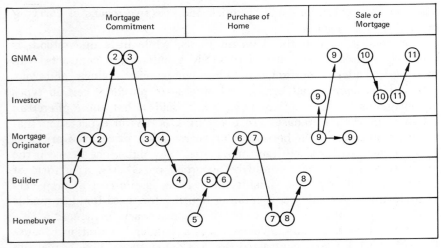

FIGURE 11–1. GNMA Tandem Plan.

1. Builder requests mortgage commitment.
2. Mortgage originator requests GNMA commitment.
3. GNMA issues commitment to mortgage originator.
4. Mortgage originator issues mortgage commitment to builder.

---

5. Home buyer agrees to purchase home and requests mortgage financing.
6. Builder arranges financing under mortgage commitment.
7. Mortgage originator makes mortgage loan to home buyer.
8. Home buyer pays builder for home.

---

9. Mortgage originator keeps mortgage or
    (A) Sells to GNMA at commitment price.
    (B) Sells to investor at negotiated price.
10. GNMA sells mortgage to investor at auction (Pension fund, S&L, FNMA, etc.).
11. GNMA takes cash from investor to repay Treasury borrowings and absorbs any loss on sale as subsidy.

loan from the mortgage lender (Steps 4, 5, 6, and 7). The mortgage lender can keep the mortgage or immediately turn around and sell the mortgage to GNMA under GNMA's purchase commitment (Step 9A), or sell it to another investor at a negotiated price. This means the lender recovers most or all the money he loaned to the purchaser without great delay. The mortgage lender's incentive for going through this process is the 1 percent loan origination fee charged at the time of loan closing, plus the promise of mortgage servicing fees. Mortgage servicing fees are paid for collecting monthly payments from the home buyer, and other chores.

The process can be illustrated in capsule form in the following hypothetical example.

Assume GNMA has $2 billion with which to begin its operation of purchasing mortgages at above-market prices to stimulate home building and the general economy. GNMA issues commitments to purchase mortgages totaling $2 billion at 98 cents on the dollar, or for a price of 98 percent of par. However, the market price for these mortgages, when they are purchased, is 96 percent of par.

GNMA then wants to sell the mortgages to permanent mortgage investors but must complete the transaction at market prices. It can either auction the mortgages to the highest bidders or call upon FNMA to purchase them at market prices, with GNMA paying a price differential to increase the yield to FNMA, if needed (Steps 10 and 11). This is, in effect, a subsidy that the home purchaser benefits from, although he never sees it and may know nothing about it.

Assume that GNMA elects to sell the mortgages through an auction and that the average price for the $2 billion worth of mortgages is 96 percent of par. In such an auction GNMA would absorb a 2 percent loss, or the difference between the price of 98 that it paid for the mortgages and the price of 96 at the auction.

GNMA would have paid out $2 billion for the mortgages and would receive from the auction proceeds $2 billion minus $40 million, or $1,960,000,000. Using this $1.96 billion, GNMA could repeat the same process of buying mortgages at above-market prices, selling them at market prices, and taking any loss on the difference between the purchase and sale prices. But the net effect would be to stimulate construction of thousands of housing units—approximately 40,000 per billion dollars.

There have been seven major Tandem Plans in all, the last two being for the purpose of buying up *un*subsidized FHA and VA mortgages (Programs 21 and 22). One of the most recent plans was launched in 1971—housing was in a slump and a national election was coming up in 1972. President Nixon approved the Super Tandem Plan, which authorized $2 billion for buying up unsubsidized mortgages on new housing in an effort to stimulate the construction industry and stimulate the economy.

Who pays for the subsidy? When the banker tells the builder that he will give him a mortgage at 98 percent of the face value, the builder might add the amount of the discount to the selling price of the house, so the home buyer pays that part of the subsidy (he pays part of his own subsidy in other words). But it is paid back relatively painlessly over a long period of time at, say, 8 percent interest in his monthly mortgage payments. The 1 percent commitment fee is also included in the selling price of the house, along with the discount points. When Ginnie Mae sells the mortgage to Fannie Mae at a market rate, say 96 percent of the face value of the mortgage, the immediate 2 percent loss there is made up by the United States Treasury, so the taxpayers are paying that part of the subsidy. Now that GNMA is also buying conventional mortgages, taxpayers are subsidizing housing for more middle-income families.

But even the subsidy by the taxpayers is less than might be first imagined. In some periods, through foresight and good fortune, GNMA has retained mortgages bought at above-market prices and sold them later in more advantageous times—some at a profit. Some mortgages accumulated in 1971 under the "Super" Tandem Plans were sold in 1972 at prices that cut the government's loss on billions of dollars in purchases to $50 million.

These plans benefit builders and bankers by removing most of the risk involved in lending to low-income families. Tandem Plans are subject to political decisions and political pressures—and putting money in the mortgage market by their use stimulates economic activity.

Recent Changes

In recent years, the Tandem Plans have been all but dormant. The federal government has continued to utilize FNMA secondary market and administrative facilities in what some erroneously label a newer tandem plan. However, the procedure has important differences that are overlooked by many observers.

Under the new plan, GNMA issues commitments to purchase, and purchases certain types of conventionally financed and FHA/VA mortgages. The work is performed by FNMA personnel in five regional FNMA offices under an agreement with GNMA. However—and these are key points of difference—FNMA does not receive a warehousing fee for holding the mortgages or commitments, nor does it have an expressed contingent liability to purchase the mortgages from GNMA at a previously established price, as it did under the Tandem Plans.

GNMA now accumulates the mortgages on its books, selling them periodically, both through auctions of whole mortgages and through negotiated private sales, to a variety of permanent mortgage investors, including FNMA.

The more common method of disposing of the FHA and VA mortgages since 1975 has been the auction of securities that are secured by pools of FHA and VA mortgages.

The Federal Home Loan Mortgage Corporation

The Emergency Home Finance Act of 1970 authorized the establishment of a secondary mortgage market agency within the Federal Home Loan Bank System. Titled the Federal Home Loan Mortgage Corporation (FHLMC), it was nicknamed Freddie Mac. Its capital comes from the System Banks. It is a federally chartered corporation exempt from income tax.

Over the preceding years, FNMA's constituent base had grown largely out of the mortgage banking industry, which was active in the production of FHA home mortgages. The savings and loan associations, on the other hand, were largely involved in conventional mortgages. This being the case, and given their general reluctance to become involved with government agencies, which FNMA had been, few savings and loan associations sold mortgages to FNMA.

The legislative move to provide a secondary market outlet for savings and loan associations began with proposals to permit FNMA to buy conventional mortgages as well as FHA and VA mortgages. Had these early proposals been enacted, many savings and loan associations would, in effect, have been forced to do business with FNMA if they wanted to sell mortgages in the secondary market on a large scale.

Although it would have been possible for the savings and loan associations to establish a relationship with FNMA, they were by tradition more oriented to the mechanism of the Federal Home Loan Bank system, so a new secondary market, the FHLMC, was set up to take care of them. At the same time, though, FNMA also received authority to buy conventional mortgages.

As set up by the 1970 legislation, the new corporation's parent is the Federal Home Loan Bank Board, whose members are also the directors of FHLMC. (The Bank Board supervises federally chartered savings and loan associations and mutual savings banks.) FHLMC's goal is similar to that of Fannie Mae and Ginnie Mae: to increase the secondary market volume of sales and purchases of residential mortgages, and, in the words of the corporation's 1972 Annual Report, "to increase the effective supply of mortgage financing, the flexibility of mortgage investors and the attractiveness of mortgage investments."

FHLMC and other mortgage investors make a profit or a loss, depending on the difference (called "spread") between the average of interest they are receiving on the mortgages they hold and the average of interest they must pay on the bonds and mortgage-backed securities that they borrow money on. When interest rates are high and they borrow, their profits shrink because the spread narrows. Maisel and Roulac say:

The rate the FHLMC pays to borrow is less than that paid by borrowers on mortgages because the securities it issues are more marketable. Its borrowing rates are also lower because the FHLMC is a government-sponsored agency. In addition, it sells its securities to small lenders, pension funds, and others who do not have the staff to check, analyze, and account for individual mortgages. Such lenders accept a lower rate than they would on mortgages because they are saved time, risk, and effort.[2]

The volume of purchases and sales of mortgages in each year of FHLMC's operation is illustrated by Table 11–7.

The larger volume in 1974 and 1975 is noted as including mortgages purchased under a Treasury program. The Mortgage Corporation, along with FNMA, was asked to participate as agent for GNMA in a mortgage assistance program announced by President Ford in October 1974. The program allotted $3½ billion to each for the purpose of buying qualifying conventional mortgages bearing lower than market rate interest costs. The Mortgage Corporation acted as GNMA's agent for underwriting and servicing the mortgages and later sold most of them to investors.

Conclusion

Using the broadest definition of the secondary market, it can be said that this market has been with us for a long time. Persons and institutions bought and sold mortgages long before a modicum of organization was introduced into the mortgage market in the 1930's. There was even a small mortgage insurance industry before the Depression of the 1930's. However, due to differences between local political jurisdictions and lack of uniformity of real estate laws, documents, and practices, that secondary market was largely localized.

Because of a lack of mobility of the product, real estate and early day housing finance had—and to a degree still has—a bias toward localism. That is one of the reasons why both real estate and lending interests have, over the years, looked a bit suspiciously on the more organized national secondary market, which some see as an encroachment on taken turf.

For one thing, while for the most part an unseen and unappreciated participant, except when few other funds are available, a secondary market investor can be viewed as an outside party in the buying, selling, and lending transaction. He or she is an importer of money, usually to capital deficit areas, but is not welcomed with open arms by all.

The secondary lender's assurance of funding stimulates the primary lending in some cases, but real estate and lending persons find this is

[2] Maisel and Roulac, p. 250.

TABLE 11–7. Residential* Mortgage Activity by Lender Group: Residential Mortgage Debt Held
(Billions of dollars)

Year	Total	Savings and Loan Associations	Mutual Savings Banks	Commercial Banks	Life Insurance Companies	FNMA	Other	FHLMC	GNMA	Mortgage Backed Securities
1955	102.5	30.6	15.6	15.7	21.6	—	19.0			
1956	113.9	34.8	17.7	16.9	24.2	0.6	19.7			
1957	122.9	38.9	19.0	17.0	25.0	1.6	21.4			
1958	134.5	44.1	20.9	18.4	25.9	1.4	33.8			
1959	147.6	51.2	22.5	20.2	27.3	2.1	24.3			
1960	161.6	57.6	24.3	20.3	28.7	2.9	27.8			
1961	176.0	65.5	26.3	21.2	29.9	2.9	30.2			
1962	192.3	74.1	29.1	23.4	31.1	2.8	31.8			
1963	211.2	84.9	33.8	26.3	32.6	2.1	31.5			
1964	231.2	94.3	36.5	28.7	35.7	2.0	34.0			
1965	257.7	102.3	40.1	32.4	38.4	2.5	42.0			
1966	273.3	106.0	42.3	34.9	40.5	4.4	45.2			
1967	291.2	112.8	44.7	37.6	41.5	5.5	49.1			
1968	312.1	120.8	46.7	41.4	41.8	7.2	48.9	0	4.3	1.0
1969	335.1	129.7	48.7	44.6	41.9	11.0	52.9	0	4.9	1.4
1970	358.3	138.8	49.9	45.6	42.8	15.5	57.5	0.4	5.2	2.6
1971	398.8	159.6	53.0	52.0	41.4	17.8	61.9	1.0	5.3	6.8
1972	455.4	187.8	57.1	62.8	39.7	19.8	70.1	1.9	5.1	11.1
1973	509.3	209.9	61.1	74.9	38.9	24.2	75.1	2.6	4.0	18.0
1974	549.3	224.8	62.1	82.4	38.7	29.6	77.6	4.6	4.8	23.8
1975	591.4	249.5	63.8	82.9	37.2	31.8	78.4	5.0	7.4	34.1
1976	661.1	289.3	67.3	94.3	35.3	32.9	83.1	4.3	4.2	49.8
1977	761.8	341.7	72.8	110.1	33.6	34.4	91.9	3.3	3.6	70.2

Note: Sum of components may not equal totals due to rounding. Also this data is based on the Federal Reserve series of Outstanding Mortgage Debt. This series is not fully comparable to their "Flow of Funds" data because "Flow of Funds" includes data from REITS and other sources not counted in the "Outstanding Mortgage Debt" series.

* Home and residential multifamily.

SOURCE: Board of Governors of the Federal Reserve System.

417

often a difficult process to explain to buyers and sellers. It is particularly painful to explain to home sellers who receive purchase contracts from FHA and VA buyers and must, many times, pay points. Paying a lender to make a loan to the person who wants to buy your house can be both financially and emotionally traumatic, especially if you are selling your house below the appraisal price to start with. Builders view "points" as a cost of doing business and attempt to add the anticipated cost of points into the selling price of the house. Most lay sellers don't think in such terms, at least not in their first sale.

Some lenders and real estate persons also don't like to deal in the secondary market financing because it forces them to think in broader contexts and involve themselves with "outsiders," who may have too many forms to fill out and don't really know or appreciate local market practices or conditions. While this group is declining in number, some appraisers, real estate brokers, and lenders of various types often work in close, personal relationships in which they feel comfortable in transacting hundreds of thousands of dollars worth of business on each other's words. Persons with such associations and practices sometimes look upon a request for documentation of their appraisals and opinions from an "outsider"—such as a secondary market lender—as a personal affront.

However, when the tables are turned, and they are on the purchasing end, whether it be mortgages or stock in a company, they question everything and want assurances similar to those of a secondary mortgage market investor.

Another objection often heard in the mortgage market is that the U. S. Government is crowding out the private investors by buying up mortgages or pumping too much money into the mortgage market when little or none is needed. This can be termed the "pocketbook" objection to nontraditional mortgage investors. When deposit institutions are flush with savers' funds, the cry of "federalization of the mortgage market" is heard most frequently. Lenders want all government and government-sponsored agencies out of the field so they can charge what the traffic will bear and also avoid all the federal red tape, including the more than 50 feet of papers that must be filled out for the most common type of FHA loan.

But, when the tables are turned on the institutions and they are suffering from the strange institutional lending ailment known as "disintermediation," lenders of various types "reform." They enthusiastically pat the staff members and officers of Fannie Mae, Ginnie Mae, and Federal Home Loan Mortgage Corporation on the back and praise their "support" of the mortgage market. They do this—and they did it with vigor in 1969–1970 and parts of 1974 and 1975—because at some points this mixture of private and public permanent investors—

FNMA, GNMA, and FHLMC—are virtually "the only games in town." And those gambling words are chosen carefully, both in this text and by lenders, particularly those in the mortgage banking industry. In many ways, Fannie Mae, which borrows short-term funds and lends long-term and bets on making money on the spread between the cost of money and the yield on the mortgage portfolio, is truly, as FNMA Chairman Oakley Hunter has often claimed, "the world's largest floating crap game."

CHAPTER 12

LEGISLATIVE PROCESS FOR HOUSING

CARL A. S. COAN*

Introduction

THE WRITERS of the United States Constitution wisely divided the responsibilities of our government among three bodies. Article I, Section 1 decrees that "All legislative Powers be vested in a Congress of the United States, which shall consist of a Senate and a House of Representatives." Article II, Section 1 decrees that "The Executive Power shall be vested in a President of the United States of America." Article III, Section 1 decrees that "The judicial Power of the United States shall be vested in one Supreme Court, and in such inferior courts as the Congress may from time to time ordain and establish."

The subject of this chapter is the "Legislative Process for Housing." This has basic reference to the Congress and how it functions, but this process cannot be explained fully without proper reference to the functions of each of the other two bodies of the government and the part they play in the writing and implementation of federal housing laws.

---

* CARL A. S. COAN (1911–1976) graduated from the University of Pennsylvania in 1932 and did masters degree work both there and at American University. He was in the U. S. Bureau of the Census from 1941 to 1956, in the U. S. Public Housing Administration from 1956 to 1957, was Director of Research for the Senate Subcommittee on Housing from 1957 to 1961, and was Staff Director of the Subcommittee from 1961 to 1976. In recent years he was consultant to the Agency for International Development on international housing matters.

This chapter was written just prior to Mr. Coan's death and reflects circumstances at that time.

In elementary civics courses we all learned that the Congress writes the laws, the Executive branch carries out the laws, and the Judicial branch assures equity and justice in the administration of the laws. This seems like a clear-cut delineation of responsibility. But, in actual practice, there is much interaction and overlapping of responsibility among all three bodies of government. For example, the passage of legislation by the Congress is invariably influenced by the policies of the Executive, which can often effectively defeat or control the final outcome of legislation.

Every department and office in the Executive branch has an immense budget to hire staff for legislative liaison and public relations work. Many of these resources are used to lobby Congress to influence the outcome of legislative proposals. The U. S. Department of Housing and Urban Development (HUD) alone has a staff of 17 people in its Congressional Relations Office. Furthermore, no bill approved by the Congress can become law until it is presented to the President for his signature or his veto, and in the latter case it can become law only by a two-thirds affirmative vote of each House of Congress.

Except for the President himself, the most powerful executive office in influencing the actions of Congress is the Office of Management and Budget (OMB). Every government department and government official in the Executive branch must first obtain clearance from the OMB before submitting a formal opinion or statement to the Congress. Furthermore, once legislation becomes law, it is the OMB which decides whether or not to implement the law as passed, particularly if federal funds are involved. Many times, legislation merely authorizes the President or the Secretary of HUD to implement programs but does not mandate that he do so. The President has delegated to the OMB the responsibility for releasing or withholding the release of funds necessary for the implementation of new programs. In recent years, we have seen extensive use of this OMB veto over the implementation of housing programs.

Another device used by the Executive in influencing the outcome of legislation is the placing of severe restrictions on the use of the authority granted by the statute. This is of marginal legality, depending on the wording of the statute, but unless the action is challenged in court, the President can get by with such restrictions, even though they may be contrary to the intent of Congress. A case in point involves the severe restrictions placed on the Section 235 homeownership program when it was reinstated by then Secretary Carla Hills in October 1975. By increasing the home purchase down-payment requirement nearly ten-fold over the statutory minimum, and by reducing the subsidy by about one half, the program became practically unworkable. As of July 1976, a full six months after the implementation date, only 307 Section

235 units were completed under the new restrictions. It is believed that many more units could have been completed under the more liberal statutory requirements.

The courts also play an important part in the actions and final results of legislation passed by the Congress. For the most part, court action is negative. An example is a court ruling that certain provisions of law or regulation infringe on the constitutional rights of individuals or other entities. However, the courts have played a leading role in recent years acting in a positive sense to require the Executive branch to implement laws or to release funds properly authorized by law but which have been arbitrarily withheld by the President or his agency heads.

In one such case, the court ruled that Secretary Carla Hills was in violation of the law in withholding the use of surplus Section 236 subsidy funds to help meet deficits in operational costs for certain 236 projects. There have been 10 such decisions forcing HUD to release the funds in individual cases.

The legislative branch is considered by many as the most powerful government branch because it has the authority to write laws and to appropriate funds to carry out the laws. However, passing a law is of no value unless the funds are actually disbursed. It is often said that the real power of the Congress is its so-called "power of the purse." It derives this power directly from the Constitution (Article I, Section 9), which states in part that "No money shall be drawn from the Treasury, but in consequence of appropriations made by law."

Actions in conflict with this power, and ones which threatened the continued viability of the Congress, were the impoundments of appropriated monies by the President in recent years. This threat was largely removed in 1974 by passage of the Congressional Budget and Impoundment Control Act, which established a procedure to be used by the Congress to overrule the President and, if necessary, by court action to force the release of impounded funds. This Act is one of the most significant legislative acts ever written to keep in balance the respective roles of the Executive and Legislative bodies of the government with respect to budget controls and spending authority.[1]

The first test of the new law to force the release of funds duly appropriated by the Congress but impounded by the President was made in behalf of the Section 235 homeownership assistance program. About $264 million of Section 235 contract authority was impounded by the President in January 1973. After passage of the Budget Control Act of 1974, the President was required to request authority to rescind Congressional authority to spend appropriated funds. Congress

[1] *Editor's Note:* These programs have been updated as of November 1978.

turned him down and triggered a court suit to compel the release of funds and reinstatement of the program. Finally, after an adverse court ruling, the Administration agreed to reinstate the program. The reinstatement announcement was made in October 1975 to be effective January 1, 1976, almost three years after the Presidential impoundment.

It is ironic to note that one of the principal objections to the Section 235 program announced by the Administration was the low downpayment requirement under the law. The statement was made by HUD that low down payments often lead to early defaults and abandonment of the property because, with such small equity in the property, it is easy for a homeowner just to walk away from the house whenever he gets in arrears on his monthly payments. This theme, however, was placed in a different perspective when President Ford, during his campaign, announced he would support a new law cutting down payments by up to 50 percent to encourage homeownership among middle-income home buyers under the regular FHA mortgage insurance program, Section 203(b).

These illustrations of the interaction between the Executive and the Legislative bodies are mentioned to demonstrate that simply writing a bill and passing it into law does not necessarily ensure its implementation as intended. The illustrations given also reflect the problems of administration when differing political parties share the White House and the Congressional responsibilities. Regardless of what party is in control of the Presidency or the Congress, there is always a degree of friction between the two bodies, but it is accentuated to a serious degree at times when the two bodies are of different political parties, particularly at times prior to the presidential election. Differences can also arise depending on the personalities involved. The eight years of the Eisenhower presidency were relatively peaceful years in Executive–Congressional relations when compared with the years since Nixon was elected to his second term and Mr. Ford picked up the reins with a Presidential race in the offing.

My general conclusion is that the real power of government is in the Presidency with all of its resources of access to the press, thousands of talented, top-notch professionals on staffs, its discretionary authority of disbursing many billions of dollars in contracts, grants or loans to business groups, universities, public interest groups, and state and local political subdivisions. The Congressional "power of the purse" is far less potent than that of the Executive disbursement power.

The goal of maintaining the balance of power and avoiding excessive power residing in one place, or even in one man, was an objective of the framers of the U. S. Constitution. It has remained the goal of the leaders of Congress and the courts since the nation was established.

The recent Watergate incident demonstrated the strength of this system when this balance of power was threatened.

The Legislative Process

Let us go back and examine in more detail how the Congress operates, particularly with respect to the passage of housing legislation. There is no mystery to the legislative process. It is basically the offering, consideration, and approval (or disapproval) of proposed Federal laws. Because we have a bicameral legislature—each legislative proposal must be approved by both bodies.

A number of steps are involved in the process. They may seem tedious and time-consuming, but they are essential to the democratic process and to the perfection of proposals before they are finally approved into law. One of the most practical safeguards of the American democratic system is that process which recognizes the rights of minorities and gives ample opportunity for all sides to be heard, regardless of their views. The time required for full and open discussion of an issue, first at the Committee level, then before the full Senate or the full House, is well justified in the improvement of a good proposal, or many times by the defeat of a bad one.

Organization of the Congress

Reference to the Congress is to both houses—the U. S. Senate, composed of 100 members, two from each state, and the House of Representatives, consisting of 435 members apportioned by population among the respective states. Senators have six-year terms, and members of the House have two-year terms. The short term of office for members of the House is intended to keep them more attentive to the current views of their constituency. The longer term for senators is designed to provide them an opportunity to take a long-range view of legislative actions, to be more statesman-like, and to lead their constituencies in policy matters rather than being just a follower of current thought and possible faddish political views. A six-year term gives the electorate an opportunity to appraise the overall record of a senator between terms and thus provides the senator with more independence in voting. A House member is always running. He is much closer to the people of his district in many respects and often casts his votes based on the narrow concerns of his own district, whereas a U. S. Senator, with his broader constituency of a whole state, can cast votes in a broader perspective.

Nevertheless, all members of Congress know that their continuation in office depends on their performance in serving their constituents and voting consistently with the majority views of their constituents. Members may be admired for taking views independent of those held by their constituents, but they may not stay long in Congress if they stray too far from home base.

The Committee System

The basic work of the Congress is done in and through committees. Considering the volume of legislative proposals offered each year, the Congress could not function otherwise. In the 94th Congress, there were nearly 16,000 bills introduced in the House and more than 3,000 bills introduced in the Senate. Each bill is referred to the committee which is responsible for the subject matter of the proposal.

There are 22 standing committees and 8 special committees in the House of Representatives. The corresponding makeup of the Senate is 16 to 6.[2] Each committee is assigned an area of responsibility, and all bills involving such responsibility must go through that committee. Sometimes a proposal contains subjects overlapping the jurisdiction of two or more committees. These bills can be referred to each committee either concurrently or in succession.

Committees are organized under rules of the Senate or the House with a chairman and ranking member of the majority and minority parties. Each committee has specific dates for meeting, but generally they meet at the call of the chairman.

Housing and Urban Affairs are under the jurisdiction of the Committee on Banking, Finance and Urban Affairs of the Senate and the Committee on Banking, Currency and Housing of the House of Representatives. Originally, each was called the Committee on Banking and Currency, with responsibility over all banking, coinage, and financial matters involving money and credit and economic stability. Housing is a relatively new congressional subject. It was first introduced as a federal responsibility in the early 1930's. It was placed under the jurisdiction of the Banking and Currency Committee because the very core of an effective housing program is the financing of housing. Urban affairs was added later as a natural offshoot of housing in its broadest sense of shelter and environs. The responsibility of the Committee now covers all matters related to shelter, the condition of neighborhoods, urban mass transit, water and sewer lines, the redevelopment of cities, and the development of new towns.

Each of these major committees has subcommittees—the Subcommittee on Housing and Urban Affairs in the Senate and the Subcom-

[2] One special committee on Nutrition and Human Needs has been abolished by a reorganization plan.

mittee on Housing and Community Development in the House. The
Senate Subcommittee has 10 members, and the House Subcommittee
has 26 members. The Subcommittee members have the basic responsibility for housing and community development legislation proposals
and to make recommendations to the full committee, which, in turn,
reports to the full House for final action.

Housing is a popular subject, and members often jockey for position
to ensure a place on the Housing Subcommittee. The positions are filled
usually by seniority with exceptions made for "trade-offs" for other
attractive committee assignments. The chairman of the committee has
the initial responsibility for making the appointments. These are finally
approved by majority vote of the committee.

A few years ago Senator John Sparkman of Alabama, who was then
chairman of the Banking, Housing and Urban Affairs Committee, was
pressured by so many members to be placed on the Housing Subcommittee that he placed them all on the Subcommittee. In 1975, when
Senator Sparkman resigned his committee chairmanship to become
chairman of the Senate Foreign Relations Committee, he was succeeded
by Senator William Proxmire of Wisconsin. Senator Proxmire set up
the current Subcommittee arrangement of only 10 members.

Legislative proposals originate in a variety of ways. Any member of
Congress may introduce a legislative proposal in the form of a bill or
a resolution. The initiative for major shifts in policy or in programs
usually originate with the Executive branch of the government. Major
policy shifts are more apt to occur when both the Legislative and
Executive branches are controlled by the same political party. This
has not been so since the Administration of President Lyndon B. Johnson. With split control between the two parties, the Republican Administration proposed several new programs which ran into difficulty
with the Democratic-controlled Congress, and it has been very difficult
working out agreements satisfactory to both. The same was true with
several proposals originated by the Congress, which met resistance from
the Administration. The impasse between the two bodies became particularly severe at the start of the second Nixon Administration in
January 1973.

Other initiatives in legislation are made by members themselves who
often are representing constituencies interested in special programs or
in a new twist to existing programs. The Congressional committee
staffs naturally are the recipient of many constituent proposals, which
they prepare for introduction by the chairman or a member of a subcommittee. When a member introduces a bill for a constituent about
which he has some reservations, he introduces it with the notation "by
request" appearing on the bill.

Some bills introduced are so-called omnibus bills; that is, they cover a number of subjects. Others are single-purpose bills limited to one specific item. During the 94th Congress, 38 bills were introduced in the Senate and referred to the Housing Subcommittee. These bills covered a broad range of subjects, including rural housing, housing for the elderly, public housing, FHA housing, flood insurance, crime insurance, water and sewer loans, urban planning, mass transit, and secondary mortgage market facilities.

Legislative Hearings

Bills are introduced into the Senate, where they are read twice, and unless there is objection, they are then referred to the committee having jurisdiction over the subject matter of the bill. Sometimes, bills are referred to several committees. For example, a recent energy conservation bill was referred to three committees in the Senate, all of which had some claim to the subject.

Once a bill is referred to a committee and there is sufficient support for the proposal, hearings are held. Testimony is received from the public, as well as from the Administration, on the merits of the bill and recommendations are made as to its disposition. The Housing Subcommittee in the Senate prefers to have extensive hearings covering many bills at one time, because in many respects, the subject matter is overlapping and time can be saved by use of this method. In 1975, two weeks of hearings were held on all 14 bills before the Committee at that time. Special hearings were also held on individual bills subsequent to the "omnibus" hearings.

The hearing process in the Congress has many critics. One criticism is that there are too many hearings going on at one time, resulting in only one or two Senators showing up for a routine hearing. This is disappointing to the witnesses, some of whom may have traveled long distances to give the U. S. Congress their views on matters which to them are of the highest significance. Many times oral testimony is limited to 10 minutes. Even though a full statement of testimony is printed in the hearing record for committee members to read later, witnesses may think they are cheated by a 10-minute presentation to a single member of the Senate. Many times, of course, extremely interesting exchanges take place between the witness and members which are effective in bringing out the issues and in building a record on which final decisions are made on the passage of legislation.

Another criticism is the dominant presence of industry witnesses on subjects vital to the general public. This reflects the nature of the Washington scene which has a high concentration of diverse lobby groups paid to monitor legislation. These groups have the resources to present professional and well-documented testimony favorable to their

causes. Public-interest groups, on the other hand, cannot afford to do
the staff work needed to keep on top of legislation and present expert
testimony. Because of this, many students of government claim that
the process is favorable to industry.

Members of congressional committees are aware of this shortcoming
in the hearing process and have attempted to correct it. Public-interest
witnesses who, it is believed, have no axe to grind but who will speak
in the general interest of the public are often solicited to testify. Many
times the chairman of a hearing will question at length such witnesses
to ensure a fair representation in the hearing record.

Improvements are still called for, however, to make this system more
democratic and to ensure optimum coverage of the issues involved.
One suggestion that seems to have merit is to have a committee's staff
conduct preliminary exploratory hearings to boil down the issues to
matters which could be further explored at formal hearings before the
members.

Committee Markup of Legislation

Following the public hearings, the Committee sits in sessions open to
the public to "markup" the bills pending before it. Generally, an agenda
of the basic issues pending before the committee is drawn up by a
committee's staff. Agenda items are voted up or down or amended, and
a final bill is prepared to be reported to the Senate or House.

The voting during markup sessions is not always sweetness and light.
Strong feelings are often expressed on specific issues, many times along
partisan lines. More often, however, the committee divides along conservative–liberal lines, with a majority of the Republicans and a few
Democrats forming the conservative block.

The members of the Congress are, for the most part, gentlemen and
professionals in the art of politics. They fight hard to win their points
but rely on the democratic process and accept their wins and losses with
grace and understanding. If a member or group of members lose an
issue in the committee, opportunity is given to express minority or
additional views in the official report made to the Senate.

The chairman of a committee exercises a great deal of power in
hearings and can often guide legislation to meet his viewpoint. Chairmen control the referral of bills to subcommittees, schedule hearings
and markups, and are often given proxies by members who are necessarily absent from a markup session. Proxy voting is permitted during
the markup, but may not be used toward the count necessary to make
up a committee quorum. No bill may be reported to the Senate or
House unless a quorum is present at an official committee meeting. If

a quorum is not present, there must be unanimous consent to report a bill.

Proxy voting in committees has been under fire for several years. There are two perspectives. On the one hand, proxy voting is seen as an expeditious way of moving legislation through a committee by avoiding the delays caused by absent members. On the other hand, premature action may be taken on important provisions through the initiative of one or two Senators voting proxies of absent members.

One method credited with saving the committee system and proxy voting from serious abuse is the current practice of committee staff meeting prior to the committee markup session to discuss the issues and learn in advance what amendments are likely to be offered and what positions the various members are likely to take. Such meetings enable a Senator's staff member to advise the Senator of current developments. The members are thus alerted in advance of the subject matter and issues to be debated and voted on at committee markup sessions. There are a number of ways they can affect the outcome even though they must be absent from the markup session.

The committee system has its weaknesses, but for the most part, it has enough checks and balances built into it to make it an effective process for moving legislation from introduction onto the floor of either the Senate or the House.

Senate Floor Action

Once a bill is reported, it is placed on the Senate calendar and must wait its turn to be taken off the calendar and considered by the Senate. Approximately 1,200 bills and resolutions were placed on the Senate calendar in the 94th Congress.

A bill is usually taken off the calendar by a unanimous consent request. If there is objection to a bill being considered, it is necessary for a Senator to offer a motion, which motion is subject to a majority vote of the Senate. If there is objection to considering a bill, filibuster tactics can be used to talk against the bill and prevent the matter coming to a vote. There is a crucial distinction in such matters between the Senate and the House. The rules of the Senate, unlike those of the House, permit extensive debate and permit unlimited time to the expression of minority views.

Upon obtaining the floor, a Senator may speak for as long as he likes. However, debate can be limited if 16 Senators sign a cloture petition and a three-fifths majority of those present and voting approve the cloture. Amendments to a bill are in order and can be approved by a simple majority of those present. No proxy voting is permitted.

Once all amendments to a bill are considered, a third reading is made, and the bill is subject to either a voice vote or a yea and nay recorded vote. A simple majority is necessary for passage. The bill is then enrolled and forwarded to the House of Representatives.

Conference

A similar process on the bill takes place in the House of Representatives. Once a bill has passed both Houses, if it has no differences, it is sent to the President for his signature. If there are differences, which is the usual case, a Conference Committee is appointed by both Houses and a conference is held to work out the differences. Conference meetings are extremely interesting. There is often a wide range of views among the participants. In the conference on the Housing Authorization Act of 1976, the Senate had 8 conferees—5 Democrats and 3 Republicans. The House had 16 conferees—11 Democrats and 5 Republicans.

Generally, there are four forces at work in a Conference Committee meeting—the majority and minority in the Senate and the majority and minority in the House. There is also a hidden fifth force—the Administration. On the surface it would appear utterly impossible to reach a consensus among the often wide differences between the two bills before the Conference Committee. At one time the meetings were closed to the public and agreements were often reached by a few strong and clever leaders horse-trading back and forth to come through with a balanced bill to report back to their respective houses. Since 1975, the Conference Committee meetings have been open to the public, and, from personal observation, it appears members are compelled to consider the agenda items in a more orderly way, with justification expressed for each final decision.

The presence of the public in Conference Committee meetings is permitted, but not mandatory. In the last two years, most Conference Committees have opened their doors, except for matters involving national security or highly sensitive personnel matters.

A full assessment of the success of this new "sunshine" procedure is not yet possible. Some claim that the only outsiders present at tedious markup sessions are the industry lobbyists who are paid to be there. Private citizens may venture in out of curiosity, but rarely does "John Q. Public" sit it out and follow or understand what is going on at the Conference. With only special-interest groups present, there is some doubt about the advantage of the open-door policy. Many times, a member seems compelled to vote a certain way because of political pressure on him accentuated by the presence of a special-interest lobbyist during the markup session.

This presence, of course, can work both ways. The glaring eye of a constituent working for the public interest can be a positive force. Some members claim they are so busy working on issues that they are not aware of the public presence during markup sessions. But, on the other hand, some of the veterans in the Congress will recall instances of outright demagoguery by a member, who spoke out on issues for the benefit of the public or the press during the public markup sessions, whereas in former closed sessions, he would have been silent.

Vote on the Conference Report

Once the Conference Committee has completed its work, a report on the agreed-upon bill is filed with each House, along with a Statement of Managers (Conferees) to explain the report. Each House must then vote on the Conference Report and approve it before it goes to the President. Many a Conference Report is turned down and returned to the same or different Conference Committee to reconsider and report back to the two Houses. There have been instances of long tie-ups of Conference Committees, but sooner or later they usually work out a compromise and get the bill through.

The President's Signature

A bill passed by both Houses of Congress can become law only if
1. It is approved by the President.
2. It is held by the President for 10 days without his signature while Congress is in session.
3. It is vetoed by the President, but the veto is overriden by a two-thirds vote of both Houses.

The President has 10 days (not including Sundays) to act on a bill. If by that time he has failed to approve it and the Congress, by adjourning, is no longer in session, the bill does not become law. This is called a pocket veto.

If the President vetoes a bill, it is returned with his objections to the House from which it originated. (If it carries an "H.R." number, it would be returned to the House of Representatives; if it carries an "S." number, it would be returned to the Senate.)

Usually, the vetoed bill is submitted promptly to the Congress and voted on once more. The question put before the House is, "Will the House on reconsideration agree to pass the bill, the objections of the President to the contrary notwithstanding?" If fewer than two thirds of the members present vote in the affirmative, the bill is killed. If two thirds or more of the members vote in the affirmative, the bill is sent along with the President's objections to the other House, where a similar procedure takes place. Both Houses approving an override makes the bill become law, regardless of the President's objections.

It is evident that a bill introduced into the Congress has a long, tedious, and rough road ahead before it can become law. Many proposed laws never make it, and many of them make it only after drastic revisions and sometimes emasculating amendments. As noted earlier, this may not be the perfect system, but it is well designed to maximize the democratic principles under which our nation operates.

Every citizen has a right to make his views known, and elected representatives have the opportunity to comment on proposed legislation and support the measure or oppose it. Minority views are freely accepted as part of the written record. If the measure is critically offensive to the minority, the Senate permits unlimited debate to hear the objections, and an individual Senator can actually kill a bill by extended debate, unless debate is cut off by a cloture petition filed and approved by three fifths of the Senators present and voting.

Both Houses, both major parties, and the President participate in the final outcome of each bill. But the major responsibility for its content and for the general performance of Congress rests with the majority party in control of the Congress. Despite the many safeguards to protect minority views, the concept of majority rule still prevails. All in all, with its many checks and balances, the system is a fair and effective one. Considering the many human frailties incumbent in any system of government, it would be difficult to conceive of a better procedure for the enactment of laws.

The weakness in the performance of the Legislative branch of government is not in the system under which it operates but in the failure of American citizens to participate in its procedures. This means participating in electing the most qualified, responsive, and conscientious persons as members of Congress, in supporting the passage of effective legislation in the interest of the general public, in insistence on performance by the Executive in administering the laws as intended by Congress, and in becoming well-informed citizens on how it is all put together.

The Content of Housing Legislation

Most federal housing laws provide authorizations for the federal government, through its various agencies, to provide assistance or support to improve the living conditions and standards of the American people.

Although individual efforts were made in the passage of Federal Laws to help provide support for housing as early as 1918, little of consequence was done until the Depression of the early 1930's stimulated federal action.

The first major bill to provide direct federal assistance for housing was the National Housing Act of 1934, which authorized the establishment of the Federal Housing Administration mortgage insurance system. The bill also authorized a system of government insurance of deposits in savings and loan associations, which inured to the benefit of housing by assuring the availability of mortgage credit for home financing. The FHA mortgage insurance system revolutionized mortgage lending for home purchases and, along with federal support for savings and loan associations, provided the major impetus for a shift from a nation of renters to a nation of homeowners. It was essentially a program for middle-income Americans who, prior to that time, could not afford to purchase and own their homes. Later, after World War II, the federal government added the Veterans' Administration loan guaranty program, which complements the FHA system, and credit must be shared between the two for shifting the ratio of homeownership in the United States from 43.6 percent in 1940 to 64.4 percent in 1973.

The next major effort of the federal government was the enactment of laws to help clear slums and provide decent housing for the poor. The United States Housing Act of 1937 authorized the establishment of local public housing authorities with financial support from the federal government to help these authorities eliminate unsafe and unsanitary housing conditions in the nation's cities and towns by tearing down existing slum housing and building housing for occupancy by low-income families. The federal government provided financial support for the capital costs needed to clear the land and build the housing. The local government supported the project by providing local tax relief, and rents paid by the tenants took care of operating costs. (The rent schedules were determined locally and varied from 16 percent to 25 percent of family income, with a set minimum rent.)

In the early years, this rental and finance formula worked well. In fact, most projects returned money to the federal government from receipts over and above operating costs. In recent years, two things occurred. Costs rose sharply, and tenant occupancy shifted from a cross section of the low-income families to a predominance of the poorest welfare families which could not afford more than a token rent. In 1969 federal law placed a limit on rents. Low-income families could pay no more than 25 percent of net income for rent. To make up the resulting loss of income to the local housing authorities, the federal government now provides an additional subsidy (operating subsidy) to make up for the deficit. In fiscal year 1977, this amounted to $575.6 million for the 1.2 million public housing units receiving subsidies.

The next big effort in federal assistance to housing came in the Housing Act of 1949, when the federal government committed itself to help fund the cost of eliminating slums and blight in the nation's cities. The first program was called the Slum Clearance Program but was later changed, in 1954, to the Urban Renewal Program.

Unlike the public housing program, the land cleared of slums and blight was to be disposed of at its fair value for uses in accordance with an urban renewal plan which each participating city was required to prepare. The renewal plans called for community improvements and the orderly elimination of slums and blight. Under this program, more than $13 billion in grants were approved for 3,284 projects in 1,258 cities by June 30, 1974, when the program began to be phased out.

A modification of the Urban Renewal Program was the Model Cities Program. It was authorized in 1966 as a demonstration to speed up the renewal of the cities by undertaking a comprehensive plan involving not only physical renewal but also economic and social renewal, including improved health care, educational facilities, crime elimination, and generally improved living conditions. A total of 151 cities participated in the program, and approximately $2.4 billion in grants were made available to these cities. As was the case in all other programs, the plan was to be developed and carried out by an agency of the participating city, with concurrence of the mayor or of the official governing authority.

Also as part of the urban renewal effort, considerable attention was paid to the rehabilitation of housing within rundown or deteriorating neighborhoods. The most successful program was the Federally Assisted Code Enforcement Program (FACE) under which federal funds in the nature of low-interest-bearing rehabilitation loans (3 percent loans under Section 312, Housing Act of 1964) and direct grants (Section 115, Housing Act of 1949) were made to families and others to finance property improvements in areas subject to intensive local code enforcement. Other than this, the rehabilitation of deteriorating housing has turned out to be a very difficult program to get rolling in a large enough volume to make much of an impact.

Other urban development programs assisted with federal funds have included planning grants, public facility loans and grants, grants for acquisition of open space, urban beautification and historic preservation, and grants to assist in the financing of urban mass transit systems. In 1974, all of these programs were consolidated into one big Community Development Program under which federal funds were distributed among the nation's cities, towns, and large counties to help them eliminate slums and blight and to upgrade and renew the community's physical structures. Primary emphasis was on efforts to improve the living conditions of low- and moderate-income families. As of September, 1976, about 5,000 local governmental units were receiving federal assistance under this program at a yearly level of approximately $3 billion.

In the years that the federal programs have moved from a simple public housing slum-clearance program to the current complex more sophisticated community development program, a series of steps were also taken to improve the federal delivery of financial assistance to help finance housing for low- and moderate-income families. Today (1976) we have the following active programs:

1. FHA and VA mortgage insurance programs. (See Chapters 4 by Fish and 5 by Nenno.)
2. Public housing subsidy program for low-income families.
3. The Urban Initiatives Program to concentrate assistance to severely troubled public housing projects.
4. Title 8 (U. S. Housing Act of 1937) rental assistance program for low- and moderate-income families.
5. Section 235 (National Housing Act) interest reduction home-ownership housing program for lower-income families.
6. Section 312 (Housing Act of 1964) rehabilitation loan program.
7. Comprehensive planning program (Section 701, Housing Act of 1954).
8. Section 202 (Housing Act of 1959) housing for the elderly and handicapped, under which federal government direct loans at below-market interest rates are made available to finance the construction of housing.
9. Government National Mortgage Association to provide special assistance to housing by purchasing mortgages at below-market-interest rate from those institutions that lend mortgage money to homeowners and owners of rental projects.
10. Rural Housing Program (Title V, Housing Act of 1949), under which the Farmers Home Administration (FmHA) guarantees mortgages and makes direct mortgage loans to finance the construction of housing for families in rural and small-town areas. Interest subsidies are also available for lower-income families to purchase or to rent at prices they can afford.

See the Appendix at the end of this chapter for further information on programs 2 through 10.

Housing Issues

In recent years, serious differences between the Administration and the Congress have developed on the form and level of federal housing and community development programs. The sharp break occurred in January 1973, when the Administration arbitrarily shut down all federal subsidy programs. It was announced as a moratorium at the time, with promises that after a study, the programs would be continued, provided they were found to meet the objectives for which they were created.

In September 1973, the Administration completed its study and prepared a report called "Housing in the Seventies." For the most part, the study was extremely critical of the housing subsidy programs—Section 235, 236 and public housing—and recommended they be discontinued. The Congress reacted with a counterstudy prepared by the Congressional Research Service of the Library of Congress. Secretary of HUD James T. Lynn and members of the Senate Committee on Banking, Housing, and Urban Affairs, clashed during an oversight hearing on the findings of the two reports, drawing opposite conclusions. Despite highly critical statements and charges of violation of Congressional intent, the Administration failed to change its position that the housing subsidy programs be discontinued.

Hearings were conducted on October 2, 3, and 4, 1973 to consider the Administration's alternative proposals, which turned out to be the Section 8 (U. S. Housing Act of 1937)[3] rental assistance program. The Administration replied to criticism of it that it would be the only "show in town." If the builders or housing sponsors wanted federal aid, Section 8 would be the only program available.

During the markup session, a number of changes were made by the Senate Committee to make the program a feasible one, but generally the Committee went along with the Administration's request. However, in order to assure no further break in the provision of federal assistance to needy families for housing, the Committee amended the Section 235, 236, and public housing programs to meet some of the objections raised by the Administration in its study. Meanwhile, the Administration would not budge from its adamant position that these programs were not to be reinstated.

The next clash occurred when the Senate and House met in Conference on the 1974 housing bill. The more vocal House members on the Conference Committee dominated the House Conferees and many of the Senate provisions were compromised. The most serious loss was a failure of the Conference Committee to write statutory language into the bill which mandated the continuance of the Section 235 home-ownership program and also public housing. The language was permissive, which, under ordinary circumstances, would be adhered to.

[3] *Editor's Note:* The Housing and Community Development Act of 1974 revised the U. S. Housing Act of 1937. Among the changes was the addition of a new program authorized by Section 8 of the 1937 Act as amended. Section 5 of the amended Act is the provision that authorized annual contributions to local public bodies for the traditional public housing program. When Section 8 was added it got its funding from the same pot.

However, it was soon evident that the Administration had no intention of reinstating these programs. The Section 8 rental assistance program had enough discretionary language to permit the Administration to place maximum emphasis on Section 8 rental assistance for existing housing rather than on new housing. This decision was justified by Secretary of HUD Carla Hills during an oversight hearing before the Senate Committee, saying that she believed assistance should go to families rather than to houses. Senator Proxmire, Chairman of the Committee conducting the oversight hearing, countered that all agreed that the beneficiary should be lower-income families, but a program of subsidies directed only to support rents with little or no support for new construction would not solve the housing shortage, but would merely cause rent increases.

This issue of subsidies for new versus existing housing carried over into the writing of final statutory authority for the Housing and Community Development Act of 1976, as well as the HUD appropriations bill for fiscal year 1977. A wiser Senate committee wrote in mandatory language which removed a large part of the discretion from the Secretary in order to ensure that the major part of the fiscal year 1977 funds would be earmarked for new construction. The Committee also earmarked funds for conventional public housing construction, which the Administration had practically eliminated since 1973. This strong antagonism by the Administration to public housing was a carry-over from years of Republican opposition to the program. President Nixon as a Congressman and as a Senator was one of the leaders fighting the continuation of public housing as socialistic and un-American. His followers in the White House and the Office of Management and Budget probably had inherited his strong feelings on this.

It is interesting to note the response made by the Administration in its opposition to public housing. It proposed a Housing Allowance Program. This is almost identical to the old Rent Certificate Program promoted by the Republicans in their long years of opposition to public housing. This would be like a housing welfare program with all families below a certain income eligible for rental assistance to help pay their rent. In 1973, when the Administration proposed this on an experimental basis for the elderly alone, the cost was estimated at $12 billion. It is safe to say the Congress would never go for a program of this magnitude. The 1974 housing act authorized the Administration to conduct experiments with such a plan and authorized $40 million of contract authority to carry on the experiments.

Space does not allow a full elaboration on all the elements involved in the selection of a program of housing subsidies to reach the maximum number of needy persons at a cost that the Congress can be expected to approve. Obviously, such a program needs to maximize

assistance toward rehabilitation of existing housing and support subsidies for new housing only as necessary to increase the housing inventory.

There are many pieces that need to be assembled to develop a national housing program to meet our nation's commitment to a decent
home and suitable living environment for every American family. Some
recommendations on future action are as follows:

The biggest problem today in fulfilling the national housing goal is
the high cost of housing. This is the result of inflation accentuated by
a three-year-old housing construction depression which, as long as it
continues, will further aggravate the price situation.

A study made in 1975 by the Subcommittee on Housing and Urban
Affairs and published as "Estimates of Housing Needs 1975–1980"
shows a basic need for new housing inventory of 2.4 million units a
year. The level of construction in 1975 was as low as 1.2 million
regular units plus 200,000 mobile homes. In late 1976, despite the
so-called economic recovery, regular housing starts were at an annual
rate of a little more than 1.4 million units. With mobile home production at an annual rate of 250,000, new inventory is being added at
a rate of 1,650,000 units, which is far short of the 2,400,000 units
needed just to stand still.

As starts drop, shortages occur, and prices rise, and this is what
has happened. The median sale price of a new single-family home in
May 1976 was $43,200 which is up from $39,500 in May 1975, and
$23,400 in 1970. It is estimated that 80 percent of the country's popu-
lation is priced out of the new housing market.

Purchases of new homes are almost exclusively by families upgrading
their standards by leveraging the equity from the sale of an inflated
existing house to purchase an inflated higher-priced new house. The
ones getting hurt are the young home seekers who cannot come forth
with the equity requirements. The couple with both man and wife
working can make the grade in some cases, but the couple with the
wife forced to stay home with children is completely left out.

To carry out our national housing policy under today's conditions
of shortages and high prices presents a serious challenge. The entire
situation has been made doubly serious by the depressed state of the
housing industry since Nixon's 1973 moratorium on federal housing
programs. The Administration response to the moratorium was an unworkable program of conventionally financed new housing with rents
subsidized under a new Section 8 provision of the Housing Act of
1937. Even with many changes, it still has not caught on. Even if it
does the subsidy cost is so high, there is serious doubt the Congress
will continue to appropriate funds at a level to meet the nation's needs.

The 1968 estimate of need for subsidies was an average of 600,000 units a year. That estimate has been recently reduced to about 400,000 units a year, which would be enough to replace the estimated 4 million occupied substandard units over a 10-year period.

The question is: Can the country afford such a goal, or, more appropriately, will the Congress appropriate the money at such a high cost? The Administration is relying almost exclusively on subsidies authorized by Section 8 of the Housing Act of 1937 to meet the low-income housing needs.

It is my belief that Section 8 is the most costly program the nation has ever conceived, and I believe Congress will not continue to fund it. The average Section 8 subsidy cost for fiscal year 1977 is estimated at $4,290 for newly constructed or substantially rehabilitated units and $2,520 per unit per year for existing housing. The President's 1977 budget called for about $1 billion contract authority or more than $15 billion in budget authority for 125,000 newly constructed units and 165,000 existing units.

To meet a goal of 400,000 new or rehabilitated subsidized units, the cost would be more than $1.7 billion of contract authority and as much as $50 billion of budget authority. The same costs would be required in fiscal year 1978 and each year thereafter for 10 years if we were to meet the goal of 4 million subsidized units within 10 years. This cost is enormous and it would be impossible in my opinion to expect Congress to appropriate the required amount of money.

We must come up with a better answer. In the first place, we must rely more heavily on private enterprise to build housing in greater numbers at a cost that middle-income America can afford. Over the years, American families have been housed not by government, but by the private construction of housing financed by private lenders. Furthermore, most middle-income Americans have been brought up in existing housing, and we must continue to rely on that stock to provide the shelter needs of our people in the future, particularly those who need subsidies.

Our program must be directed to the full utilization of government resources (federal, state, and local) in combination with private enterprise to:

1. Preserve existing housing stock. Part and parcel to this effort is the preservation and renewal of neighborhoods, consisting not just of brick-and-mortar shelter, but with attractive surroundings that are physically safe and secure and provide minimum amenities for quality living.

2. Encourage new construction and rehabilitation at moderate cost and upkeep and at levels needed to meet our growing demands.

On the first of the above items, I would rely on community development funds with heavy emphasis on neighborhood preservation tech-

niques such as those recently worked out by Neighborhood Housing
Services. This is an organization sponsored by the Federal Home Loan
Bank Board and HUD. It has demonstrated the potential success of a
neighborhood preservation program by mobilizing local pride and leadership with support from local financial lending institutions and from
local and state government, as well as the federal government. The
program is only in its infancy, but, with broader support, can be expanded sharply. Code enforcement, rehabilitation loans, and liberal
financing terms would accompany local spending for neighborhood
improvements to accomplish the purposes of this endeavor.

To encourage new construction and rehabilitation, we may need
some or all of the following:

1. Deep subsidies for public housing for the lowest-income families,
   which housing would be located to the maximum extent feasible
   on scattered sites and nonimpacted areas. The decision whether
   the housing be new or rehabilitated would be made at the local
   level, partially dictated by the limitation (contract authority and
   budget authority) of funds allocated to that community by HUD.

2. An actively supported homeownership assistance program for
   new or rehabilitated housing with an interest rate subsidy subject
   to family income. Provided proper controls are made on income,
   there should be no necessity for an income eligibility ceiling for
   occupancy of such units. The latest estimate on Section 235 homeownership units first authorized in the 1968 Housing Act is that
   the average subsidy cost is about $550 a unit per year, with the
   subsidy running out in about 10 years, making a total subsidy of
   $5,500 a unit. This amount can be even less if the income
   eligibility ceiling is removed and families can be encouraged to
   purchase a home with a very thin federal subsidy.

3. A GNMA-supported mortgage purchase program providing a
   thin interest subsidy to be implemented by a triggering index
   similar to the proposal made by the Senate in its Emergency
   Housing Act of 1975. Mortgage purchases would be made by
   GNMA whenever the level of housing starts dropped below a
   preestablished number. The GNMA purchase price for mortgages
   would be set to establish a below-market rate of interest to the
   purchaser. The rate would be low enough to encourage home
   purchases and yet not so low as to be a heavy burden on the U. S.
   Treasury. By GNMA's rolling over such mortgages—selling them
   to other investors in the mortgage market—the budget impact
   would be minimal. Ceilings on the mortgage amount and on the
   price of homes financed under this program would be set to encourage construction of modest cost housing to be occupied by
   moderate-income families.

4. Section 202 of the Housing Act of 1959 is one of the most popular programs for the elderly and the handicapped. As amended by the 1976 Housing Authorization Act, the interest rate chargeable to the borrower would be the average interest rate on all interest-bearing obligations of the United States computed at the end of the fiscal year next preceding the date on which the loan is made. That rate is expected to be around 6½ percent.

   Early in 1976, applications were filed with HUD by more than 1,500 nonprofit sponsors, of which only 136 were accepted because of the limitations on funds. The 1976 Act added an additional authorization of $2.5 billion, making a total of $3.3 billion available for direct loans to finance those projects. At $30,000 a unit, this would provide about 100,000 units to be financed through fiscal year 1979.

5. Other programs requiring federal assistance for housing include the Section 312 rehabilitation loan program, the Farmers Home program under Title V of the Housing Act of 1949, and the Veterans Administration loan guaranty program. Each of these should be continued at the maximum level feasible within budget limitations.

In addition to the above programs, the federal government should take all possible measures to ease the way for residential construction. Mortgage credit, low interest rates, moderation in the cost of building materials, and favorable labor laws are the most important ingredients to productive home building.

Other problems which cause slowdowns in construction are generally locally controlled, such as zoning regulations and restrictive building codes. It is hoped that the National Institute of Building Sciences, authorized by Congress in the 1974 Act, will be drawing up some code proposals for adoption at state levels to remove some of the existing roadblocks to a more efficient construction program.

A new entry into cheaper housing is the modular home and what some have been calling the compact house. Mobile homes are still being produced at a level of 200,000 to 300,000 units. It is believed that this industry will develop a manufactured small home that can be transported and located on its lot and be financed as realty under Title II of the National Housing Act. Under this title, financing can be spread over 30 years, and the monthly payments would be more suitable to a lower-income family purchasing a mobile home with financing for 5 to 10 years.

Other innovative, cost-saving designs are being drawn up which will offer more modest-priced homes to meet the need for the "affordable" home to beat today's high prices of land and material.

APPENDIX

Low-Income Public Housing

Federal aid to local public housing agencies to provide decent shelter for low-income residents at rents they can afford.

NATURE OF PROGRAM: Local public housing agencies develop, own, and operate low-income public housing projects, financing them through the sale of tax-exempt obligations. HUD furnishes technical and professional assistance in planning, developing, and managing the projects and gives two kinds of financial assistance: preliminary loans for planning; and annual contributions to pay the debt service of PHA obligations, assure low rents and maintain adequate services and reserve funds. Rents that are based on the residents' ability to pay contribute to the costs of managing and operating the housing.

Several different methods are used to provide housing. Under the "Turnkey" program, the PHA invites private developers to submit proposals, selects the best proposal, and agrees to purchase the project on completion. Under conventional-bid construction, the PHA acts as its own developer, acquiring the site(s), preparing its own architectural plans, and advertising for competitive bids for construction. The PHA may also acquire existing housing, with or without rehabilitation, from the private market under the acquisition program.

APPLICANT ELIGIBILITY: Public housing agencies established by local governments in accord with State law.

LEGAL AUTHORITY: U. S. Housing Act of 1937, as amended (P.L. 75–412); Title 11, Housing and Community Development Act of 1974 (P.L. 93–383).

ADMINISTERING OFFICE: Assistant Secretary for Housing—Federal Housing Commissioner, Department of Housing and Urban Development, Washington, D.C. 20410.

INFORMATION SOURCE: HUD Area Offices.

CURRENT STATUS: Active.

SCOPE OF PROGRAM: Approximately $101.6 million of contract authority was approved for 49,400 units during fiscal year 1977; about $137.5 million has been budgeted for 50,000 units during fiscal 1978.

As of June 30, 1977, 34,200 units were under construction, and 39,500 were in the preconstruction processing stage. A total of 1.2 million units are under assistance, sheltering about 3.4 million people, almost half of whom are elderly.

Urban Initiatives Program

A new program that concentrates assistance to severely troubled public housing projects.

NATURE OF PROGRAM: An interagency effort that includes the Departments of Labor, Justice, and Interior under HUD's leadership. There are five areas of help: (1) management assistance; (2) revitalizing neighborhoods near projects; (3) providing crime insurance; (4) interagency assistance of both physical and social anticrime efforts; and (5) involvement of public and private sectors and neighborhood groups in social and economic help for the neighborhood.

LEGAL AUTHORITY: U. S. Housing Act of 1937 (P.L. 75–412), as amended by Section 7(d), Department of Housing and Urban Development Act of 1965 (P.L. 89–174), as further amended by Title II of the Housing and Community Development Act of 1974 (P.L. 93–383), further amended by the Housing and Community Development Act of 1977 (P.L. 95–128).

ADMINISTERING OFFICE: Assistant Secretary for Housing—Federal Housing Commissioner, Department of Housing and Urban Development, Washington, D.C. 20410.

INFORMATION SOURCE: Project Management Division, Office of Assisted Housing, Room 6248, HUD.

CURRENT STATUS: Active.

SCOPE OF PROGRAM: HUD has earmarked $267 million for 67 PHAs for fiscal year 1979.

Lower-Income Rental Assistance (Section 8)

A rent subsidy for lower income families to help them afford decent housing in the private market.

NATURE OF PROGRAM: HUD makes up the difference between what a lower-income household can afford and the fair market rent for an adequate housing unit. No eligible tenant need pay more than 25 percent of adjusted income toward rent. Housing thus subsidized by HUD must meet certain standards of safety and sanitation, and rents for these units must fall within the range of fair market rents as determined by HUD. This rental assistance may be used in existing housing or in new construction or substantially rehabilitated units. Different procedures apply in each case.

Local public housing agencies administer the existing housing program, certifying eligible tenants, inspecting the units proposed for subsidy, and contracting with approved landlords for payment. (Tenants execute separate leases with landlords to pay their share of rent.)

Nonprofit and profit-motivated developers, alone or together with public housing agencies, submit proposals for substantial rehabilitation or new construction in response to invitations from HUD; or they may apply to their State housing finance agency. On approval of the proposals, HUD contracts to subsidize the units to be occupied by eligible families.

APPLICANT ELIGIBILITY: Tenants must be lower-income households with incomes amounting to 80 percent of the area median income or less. Project sponsors may be private owners, profit-motivated and nonprofit or co-operative organizers, public housing agencies, and State housing finance agencies.

LEGAL AUTHORITY: Section 8, U. S. Housing Act of 1937 (P.L. 73–479), as added by Housing and Community Development Act of 1974 (P.L. 93–383).

ADMINISTERING OFFICE: Assistant Secretary for Housing—Federal Housing Commissioner, Department of Housing and Urban Development, Washington, D.C. 20410.

INFORMATION SOURCE: HUD Area Offices.

CURRENT STATUS: Active.

SCOPE OF PROGRAM: 169,396 units of new construction or rehabilitation and 161,581 units of existing housing were reserved and slated for Federal subsidy in fiscal year 1977. Since the start of the Section 8 program in early summer of 1975, 946,218 units have been reserved and 295,000 of these were occupied as of September 30, 1977.

Homeownership Assistance for Low- and Moderate-Income Families (Revised Section 235)

Mortgage insurance and interest subsidy for low- and moderate-income home buyers.

NATURE OF PROGRAM: To enable eligible families to afford new homes that meet HUD standards, HUD insures mortgages and makes monthly payments to lenders to reduce interest to as low as 4 percent. The mortgage payment cannot exceed 20 percent of adjusted income, and the homeowner must make a down payment of 3 percent of the cost of acquisition. There are dollar limits on loans and sales prices. Mortgage limits are $32,000 ($38,000 for homes for 5 or more persons), and in high cost areas $38,000 ($44,000 for homes for 5 or more persons). The income limit for initial occupancy is 95 percent of the area median income.

Prior to 1976, this program provided larger subsidies to lower-income households and required a substantially smaller investment from them.

APPLICANT ELIGIBILITY: A home buyer's adjusted income may not exceed a certain percentage of local median income. There is no restriction on assets.

LEGAL AUTHORITY: Section 235, National Housing Act (1934), as added by Section 101, Housing and Urban Development Act of 1968 (P.L. 90–448).

ADMINISTERING OFFICE: Assistant Secretary for Housing—Federal Housing Commissioner, Department of Housing and Urban Development, Washington, D.C. 20410.

INFORMATION SOURCE: HUD Area Offices.

CURRENT STATUS: Active in its revised form.

SCOPE OF PROGRAM: Cumulative activity through September 1977: 478,553 units have been insured with a value of about $8.6 billion.

Rehabilitation Loans

Loans to assist rehabilitation in federally aided Community Development Block Grant, Urban Homesteading (Section 810), Urban Renewal and Code Enforcement areas.

NATURE OF PROGRAM: Direct Federal loans finance rehabilitation of residential, mixed use, and nonresidential properties in the above areas certified by the local government. By financing rehabilitation to bring the property up to applicable code, project or plan standards, the loans prevent unnecessary demolition of basically sound structures. A loan may provide for insulation and installing of weatherization items. Loans may not exceed $27,000 per dwelling unit or $100,000 for nonresidential properties.

APPLICANT ELIGIBILITY: Property owners in the aforementioned federally aided areas and business tenants of such property whose leases have at least as long to run as the terms of the loan. The applicant must evidence the capacity to repay the loan and be unable to secure necessary financing from other sources on comparable terms and conditions. Preference is given to low- and moderate-income applicants.

LEGAL AUTHORITY: Section 312, Housing Act of 1964 (P.L. 88–560), as amended.

ADMINISTERING OFFICE: Assistant Secretary for Community Planning and Development, Department of Housing and Urban Development, Washington, D.C. 20410.

INFORMATION SOURCE: HUD Regional Offices and Area Offices, and housing and community development agencies of local government.

CURRENT STATUS: Active. Congress has authorized continuation of the program through September 30, 1979.

SCOPE OF PROGRAM: From 1964 through September 30, 1977, rehabilitation loan reservations aggregated about $471 million with $85 million in reservations in fiscal year 1977. The new law, the Housing and Community Development Amendments of 1978, authorizes $245 million for fiscal 1979, but no more than $60 million may be used for multifamily projects.

Comprehensive Planning Assistance

Grants to help State and local governments finance comprehensive planning activities.

NATURE OF PROGRAM: A broad range of planning and management activities is supported by grants of up to two thirds of the cost of a project. The comprehensive planning defined by this program is an ongoing process by which needs are determined and long-term goals set for land use, housing, and community facilities, and proper weight given to human and natural resources, and the improvement of the living environment.

APPLICANT ELIGIBILITY: States, for both intra- and interstate planning; metropolitan clearinghouses; councils of governments; Indian Tribal groups or other governmental units having special needs.

LEGAL AUTHORITY: Section 701, Housing Act of 1954 (P.L. 83–560), as amended; Title IV, Housing and Community Development Act of 1974 (P.L. 93–383).

ADMINISTERING OFFICE: Assistant Secretary for Community Planning and Development, Department of Housing and Urban Development, Washington, D.C. 20410.

INFORMATION SOURCE: HUD Regional Offices and Area Offices.

CURRENT STATUS: Active.

SCOPE OF PROGRAM: As of September 30, 1977, $822,949,408 had been reserved for projects, and $21,331,318 allocated to studies, research and demonstrations.

Direct Loans for Housing for the Elderly or Handicapped (Section 202)

To provide housing and related facilities for the elderly or handicapped.

NATURE OF PROGRAM: Long-term direct loans to eligible, private, nonprofit sponsors finance rental or cooperative housing facilities for elderly or handicapped persons. The current interest rate is based on the average rate paid on Federal obligations during the preceding fiscal year. (Until the program was revised in 1974, the statutory rate was 3 percent.) Section 8 rental housing assistance is available for elderly housing.

APPLICANT ELIGIBILITY: Private, nonprofit sponsors may qualify for loans. Households of one or more persons, the head of which is at least 62 years old or is handicapped, are eligible to live in the structures.

LEGAL AUTHORITY: Section 202, Housing Act of 1959 (P.L. 86–372).

ADMINISTERING OFFICE: Assistant Secretary for Housing—Federal Housing Commissioner, Department of Housing and Urban Development, Washington, D.C. 20410.

INFORMATION SOURCE: HUD Area Offices.

CURRENT STATUS: Active.

SCOPE OF PROGRAM: From the date of enactment through 1972, loans for 45,275 units have been approved with a value of $579,444,000. After a brief suspension, the program was revised and reactivated by the Housing and Community Development Act of 1974. From resumption to September 30, 1976, loans were approved for 26,400 units; 21,000 units were approved for fiscal year 1977 and approximately 25,000 units are anticipated for fiscal year 1978. In fiscal 1979, $800 million has been authorized for the program; $50 million of the total has been earmarked for loans for development of rental housing and related facilities for the handicapped, primarily nonelderly.

GNMA Special Assistance Mortgage Purchases ("Tandem")

A secondary mortgage market created by Government National Mortgage Association purchases of mortgages from private lenders to expand and facilitate investment in housing.

NATURE OF PROGRAM: The Government National Mortgage Association (GNMA) was originally established as a secondary market for federally-insured residential mortgages not readily saleable in the private market. These mortgages generally financed housing for groups or in areas with special needs.

More recently GNMA was authorized to purchase both federally-insured and conventional mortgages at below-market interest rates to stimulate lagging housing production. These mortgages are then resold at current market prices with the government absorbing the loss as a subsidy.

APPLICANT ELIGIBILITY: FHA-approved mortgagees may apply to sell federally underwritten mortgages to GNMA. Lenders approved by the Federal National Mortgage Association or the Federal Home Loan Mortgage Corporation to participate in their conventional mortgage purchase programs may apply to sell conventional loans to GNMA.

LEGAL AUTHORITY: Housing and Urban Development Acts of 1968 and 1969 (P.L. 90–448 and 91–152), Housing and Community Development Act of 1974 (P.L. 93–383), Emergency Home Purchase Assistance Act of 1974 (P.L. 93–449), Emergency Housing Act of 1975 (P.L. 94–50), Housing Authorization Act of 1976 (P.L. 94–375), and the Housing and Community Development Act of 1977 (P.L. 95–128).

ADMINISTERING OFFICE: Government National Mortgage Association, Department of Housing and Urban Development, Washington, D.C. 20410.

INFORMATION SOURCE: Regional offices of the Federal National Mortgage Association in Atlanta, Chicago, Dallas, Los Angeles, and Philadelphia. Also see administering office.

GNMA Guaranteed
Mortgage-Backed Securities

Privately issued securities based on pools of federally underwritten mortgages. The securities are guaranteed by the Government National Mortgage Association to attract capital into the residential mortgage market.

NATURE OF PROGRAM: The Government National Mortgage Association (GNMA) guarantees the timely payment of principal and interest to holders of securities issued by private lenders and backed by pools of HUD-insured and VA-guaranteed mortgages. The guarantee is backed by the full faith and credit of the United States Government.

The modified "pass through" security guarantees monthly payments of principal and interest due on mortgages in the pool regardless of whether they are collected from the mortgagors. All prepayments and claims settlements also are passed through to the security holders.

Potential issuers of securities pool federally underwritten mortgages of homogeneous type (single-family, multifamily project, or mobile home) and interest rate. Once the pool has been approved and the certificates prepared by GNMA, issuers can market securities directly to investors or through securities dealers.

APPLICANT ELIGIBILITY: Applicants must be FHA-approved mortgagees in good standing and generally have a net worth of not less than $100,000.

LEGAL AUTHORITY: Housing and Urban Development Act of 1968 (P.L. 90–448).

ADMINISTERING OFFICE: Government National Mortgage Association, Department of Housing and Urban Development, Washington, D.C. 20410.

INFORMATION SOURCE: See administering office.

CURRENT STATUS: Active.

SCOPE OF PROGRAM: GNMA has guaranteed over $49 billion in mortgage-backed, pass-through securities from the inception of the program in early 1970 through November 1977.

CHAPTER 13

TWENTIETH CENTURY HOUSING DESIGN FROM AN ECOLOGICAL PERSPECTIVE

K. KAY STEWART*

Introduction

SHELTER is a basic human need. Families are dependent upon their environments for the resources with which to fulfill this need satisfactorily. The traditional definition of housing as "shelter," a "commodity," or "product" is not adequate because housing includes far more than just shelter. Housing is better defined as a process involving the

* K. KAY STEWART is Associate Professor of Housing, Design, and Consumer Resources at Oklahoma State University. Prior to receiving a Ph.D. degree in housing at Cornell University in 1973, she taught housing and interior design at the University of Maryland and Kansas State University.

interaction between an organism and its environment. The organism may be a single individual, a family, or other communal group. The environment includes the natural environment along with the political, economical, social, and cultural environments surrounding the organism. Defined in this way, housing can be studied as a part of the ecological process—the relationships between organisms and their dynamic environments—whereby individuals seek to meet their shelter need within their environmental resources. Rapoport[1] points out that the dwelling forms result from a complex phenomenon which defies any single explanation but involves the responses to the environment of people holding different attitudes and ideals. The differences in the interplay of social, cultural, physical, economic, and religious factors create different responses in house form from one culture to another or from one area to another.

As human needs change in their societal context, so must the design of shelter change. Housing design is a consequence of a whole range of sociocultural factors which occur in a broad ecological context. The analysis of housing as a process occurring within an ecological system illuminates the interrelatedness between the individual or family unit and the natural and/or man-made environment in which the housing process occurs. The purpose of this chapter is to examine factors which have influenced the design of family shelter since the beginning of the twentieth century. The human ecology framework of Amos Hawley,[2] which focuses on the interrelationships among population, organization, environment, and technology, is particularly appropriate for understanding why changes have occurred in the design of the American dwelling.

One of the basic human ecology principles states that the relationship between two ecological variables is not unidirectional. Just as changes in population influence changes in technology, technological changes influence population growth and distribution. There is, however, a noticeable time lag between changes in living conditions and the expression of these changes in the design of dwelling units. Changes in technology and family life style have occurred rapidly during the 20th century, while changes in housing design have not. The methods of planning and building houses have changed, but the basic forms of most houses today are not too dissimilar to those popular at the turn of the century. Since changes in the design of housing are the result of a whole range of social, cultural, and environmental factors, it is helpful to examine the ecological framework in which these interactions occur.

1 Amos Rapoport, *House Form and Culture*. (Englewood Cliffs, N.J.: Prentice Hall), 1969, p. 46.

2 Amos H. Hawley, *Human Ecology*. (New York: Ronald Press), 1950.

Housing From an Ecological Viewpoint

The word ecology comes from the Greek word meaning "a house" or a "place to live" but is now commonly defined as the study of the relationships between organisms and their environment. Ecology views the world as a system of dynamic interdependencies so great that the life of an organism is bound up with the conditions of the environment and groups of organisms within that environment.[3] The interdependence or "web of life" is illustrated by plants being eaten by insects and small animals, which are, in turn, eaten by birds and larger animals. Insects are also involved in pollination of plants and serve a supportive role for plant growth and reproduction. Man, like all other living things, is bound up in this web of life. In all our years of development, "nothing has altered the fact of man's dependence on the organic as well as the inorganic elements of the environment."[4]

Man, however, is not forced to stay in one niche because of his adaptability and his versatility in relating himself to other organisms. In times when technology was simple and crude, man's relations with other organisms were close as he competed for food and shelter. Each acquisition of new technique or a new use for an old technique alters man's relations with the other organisms. Each advance in technology enhances the human organism's control over the habitat and raises its position higher on the scale of dominance.[5]

Human ecology includes the study of both the form and the development of organization in populations of living things. It includes the conception of life as a continuous struggle for adjustment of aggregates of organisms to their environment. A population adjusts to its physical world through the coordination and organization of individual actions to form a functional unit. As the number of individuals in the community increases, there is increasing pressure on the existing resources. This produces a complex interaction of organism with organism and organism with environment through which individuals adjust to each other so as to utilize more effectively the resources in the environment.[6]

As man is inescapably dependent on his fellows, it appears that communities or combinations of individuals sharing responsibilities and opportunities are a natural ecological unit. These communities develop spatial forms that relate to the natural environment in the beginning, but as man becomes more in control of the environment, the community forms are only loosely related to the natural environment.

Population growth and migration were strong influences on change

3 Hawley, *op. cit.*, p. 3.
4 *Ibid.*, p. 55.
5 *Ibid.*, p. 65.
6 *Ibid.*, p. 67.

within the community structure in America as urban concentrations began to replace the former rural way of life. This city growth produced unusually dense concentrations of people, creating a more complex set of interrelationships. It was interregional expansion that gave rise to large compact cities. Then, when efficient, highly flexible means of movement and communication over short distances appeared, the local community began to expand as well—moving out from the center. The topography along with the transportation routes influence the shape and content of various zones which surround the center of population concentrations.

Amos Hawley illustrates interrelatedness within an ecological system as he discusses the effects of redistribution on the functions of the community.

Redistribution affects all functions of the community. Administrative offices of industrial enterprises congregate in the metropolis but without loss of contact with their scattered producing activities. Manufacturing, originally concentrated at the center to benefit from close access to labor supplies, markets, sources of power and shipping facilities, finds its range of choice of site greatly enlarged and therefore tends to move centrifugally. Despite the local scatter of manufacturing function, their interrelations become more numerous and more sensitive. Agriculture is faced with a new competition arising from the invasion of rural lands by urban functions, including not only manufacturing but recreational, commercial and residential activities as well.

Service centers likewise are brought into competition with one another. The more specialized services gravitate to the large cities, leaving only the most routine services in the small places. On the other hand, new services initiated first in the metropolis, when they become generally accepted, diffuse outward to smaller subcenters. In the shifting and realignment of relations many old villages and towns disappear, while new ones take form at more strategic locations. Each service center or subcenter tends to assume a more or less specialized role in the service structure of the expanded community. Traditional categoric units also yield to the change. Kinship and neighborhood units lose many of their functions and are replaced by specialized units the members of which are often widely scattered.

These changes are accompanied by population redistribution . . . there is movement outward from the center and there is accretion in the peripheral areas from intercommunity movement. Population scatter is explainable largely in terms of increased speed of commutation travel and of communication afforded by the new forms of overcoming distance.[7]

Technological innovations influence population distribution and the spatial arrangement of physical structures designed to meet the needs

7 *Ibid.*, pp. 430–431.

of the organisms within communities. The acceptance and utilization of technological innovations however, are influenced by the social and cultural values of the group. Housing design, then, is influenced not only by the natural environment, the size and characteristics of the population, and the available technology, but also by the social organizations within the society, economic and political activities, and cultural values. In order to more fully understand housing, it is necessary to have some definition of the image and meaning of housing for a given culture. Within each society there is some set of beliefs about who should share the same roof and some normative definition of "adequate" housing. Rapoport suggests that housing design changes as the social image of "right" or "adequate" housing changes. Changes in design are more likely the reactions to symbol and fashion that occur within the limits of available materials and technology.[8] The Industrial Revolution in the 19th century greatly increased the available technology and materials, which influenced the design and location of housing. However, even today Americans still hold to the image of "right" housing as a private house with a fence, trees, and even open space—an image retained from Colonial living patterns.

The Influences of the Industrial Revolution

Throughout history the family has been the major social institution, although this was true prior to the Industrial Revolution more than in present-day society. Changes in family life style have directly influenced the design of dwellings over the years. Colonial society centered around a family which was closely knit, largely self-sufficient, and played an important role in social control. Agriculture was the main industry and farming operations were performed manually. Families were large, since each child was an additional helper for the work that had to be done. The home was the center for industry and the family was a relatively independent economic unit. Comforts were largely limited to what the family could produce in and around the home. The family occupying the house consisted not only of parents and their children but grandparents, unmarried relatives, and orphaned children from other families.

Colonial homes were designed with large kitchens and work areas with smaller sleeping rooms which were frequently in the form of lofts. Homes were built by the occupants, usually with the assistance of neighbors. These "house raisings" frequently became community affairs. As building materials were limited to those available in the surrounding natural environment, housing design reflected both the climate and the

[8] Rapoport, *op. cit.*, pp. 130–135.

heritage which the colonists had brought with them from their home-lands.

In 1850, housing was needed for approximately 23 million people, 85 percent of whom lived in rural areas while only 5 percent lived in cities larger than 100,000. At this point, the house had not yet been divorced from the farmland and the farming operation, except in the cities, so the farmhouse was probably the most representative dwelling of that time. Farmhouses varied in design from the log cabins and sod houses that were built along the western frontiers, to the plantation houses in the South, which were built in the Federal or Georgian style.

Housing in urban areas varied according to the topography of the city, available transportation, the timing of construction, and local custom. As early as 1800 some four-story dwellings appeared, and by 1820 the row house was well established in downtown areas. These houses were two to four stories in height and, according to their location, were composed of brick, stone, or clapboard. The strong tradition of homeownership in Philadelphia and Baltimore made the row house the favored style. The four-story "three decker" was popular in Boston and Newark after about 1850. This structure acquired its name from the three wooden galleries or decks that were built one above the other on the three upper floors. The street level was used for business.[9]

Growth in Population and the Demand for Housing

The Industrial Revolution reached America by the early 1800's. Every aspect of the revolution had its own attendant influence on the form and quality of human environment—population, city growth, social organization, family patterns, and housing. Even though there were "local variations in detail," the remarkable factor was the international and intercontinental scope of the growth which occurred. "What is true of Philadelphia and Sydney is almost equally true of Berlin and Lyons and Manchester. The same forces were at work, impelled by the same credos and purposes."[10]

The population of the United States increased by leaps and bounds from a total of just over five million in 1800 to over 23 million by 1850 and nearly 63 million by 1890. This growth occurred despite the gradually increasing use of birth control, high rates of infant mortality, and widespread disease in congested areas.

Such facts alone might well account for a certain amount of overcrowding along the way, even if the increase were evenly distributed geographically,

9 Charles N. Glaab and A. Theodore Brown, *A History of Urban America*. (New York: Macmillan), 1967, p. 160.

10 Catherine Bauer, *Modern Housing*. (New York: Houghton Mifflin), 1934, p. 10.

real wages high enough to pay an "economic" rent, and the building industry geared to supply the average demand.[11]

But the population was by no means evenly distributed, because the centers of industry developed near accessible sources of power and drew people from rural areas into urban concentrations. The growth of factories created a demand for labor and immigrants from other countries poured into the cities in search of jobs.

The mechanization which had given birth to the factories also changed the farming operation and reduced the need for manpower in rural areas. A gradual migration of the population from rural to urban areas began in the early 1800's but did not reach a sizable quantity until around 1890. The shift was evidenced by the increase in population in urban areas: 6 percent in 1800, 15 percent in 1850, and 35 percent by 1890—a trend that was to continue into the 20th century.[12]

Rapid population growth in urban areas created a sudden and sizable demand for housing in the cities, where land was in limited supply. The effects of the vast centralizing movement on the human environment were described by Bauer.

Overcrowding, of course. Overcrowding in every department of the housing operation. Congestion of people in rooms; "extra" families in dwellings; contraction of room areas and of the number of rooms per dwelling; overstuffing of both rooms and dwellings into tall honeycomb rookeries and tenements; overcoverage of land by building; and the endless multiplication of packed residential blocks, without benefit of even the slenderest intervening slice of open area—whether country, park, playground, grass-plot, or mere breathing-space. Overcrowding, moreover, of every family's budget with a newly exorbitant rent item.

But how could this be? According to the most respectable nineteenth-century economic theories . . . the increased demand should have fostered tremendous competition; and the competition should have resulted in large-scale production and greater efficiency; and that should have produced in turn a better and cheaper product, profits for the most efficient, and general satisfaction all around. But alas, if there is any commodity to which that little equation applies less than to any other commodity, it is land—land and buildings. Large-scale production of a kind there was, and even, in a sense, there was greater "efficiency": less land and less building per person. And profits there certainly were. But the satisfaction, however intense, was limited to a few, and the dwellings themselves got steadily worse and more expensive.[13]

The growth of population in cities came so fast that there was no time to develop or reformulate ideas as to the aesthetic, economic, or

11 *Ibid.*, pp. 10–11.
12 See Table 2–1, Chapter 2.
13 Bauer, *op. cit.*, pp. 11–12.

social nature of the city or to create a new organic form in which to house the deluge of people. There was little control over the influx of new residents either from the city authorities or from the convictions of the people. The overwhelming rush of prosperity was met with a chaotic response in housing.

New York Tenement House Acts in 1867, 1879, and 1887 set regulations on the amount of land that could be covered, the amount of window opening for each room, and the number of families who could occupy a dwelling unit. These Acts, however, were not enforced to a degree sufficient to provide sanitary and healthful housing for urban immigrant families.[14] This initial reaction to the Industrial Revolution was to be part of city design for a long time. Bauer pointed out that during a comparatively short period "the basic standard for a whole era of construction was established."[15] A new housing "norm" had developed and "for generations thereafter any movement away from it was merely a matter of degree, of slow and expensive and frustrated reform."[16]

At the same time that the tenement slums were growing, "palaces" were being built by the very wealthy. The Vanderbilt Mansion was built in 1881 on Fifth Avenue in New York City at a cost of approximately $3 million. Palace after palace was built along the avenue by rising businessmen. Limestone, marble, and travertine were the favored materials, and ornament was carefully applied both inside and out.[17] By 1860 apartments had begun to appear and by 1880 they were being built by the hundreds to house the growing numbers of wealthy city residents. The first apartments were relatively simple—frequently converted brownstones. Improvements in the hydraulic elevator made apartments more convenient and thus more popular. The single-family home was still desired by most and those who could afford to live in that fashion did so. As rail transportation developed in the 1880's and 1890's, city residents began to escape the crowded conditions and move outward along the transportation lines into the developing suburbs. After 1887, the electrically powered trolley and the elevated railroads permitted even greater residential dispersion.

Mechanization of Work Processes

The factory and the household had one crucial goal in common—the improvement of organization and reduction of waste labor. This was the

[14] Glenn H. Beyer, *Housing and Society.* (New York: Macmillan), 1965, p. 451.

[15] Bauer, *op. cit.*, p. 17.

[16] *Ibid.*

[17] Christopher Tunnard and Henry H. Reed, *American Skyline.* (Boston: Houghton Mifflin), 1955.

goal toward which mechanization moved. The reduction of household labor was achieved through the mechanization of work processes that had previously been performed by hand: ironing, laundering, dishwashing, carpet sweeping, along with heating and refrigeration. Organization of the work process actually began before the invention of mechanized tools. The organization of the kitchen into working zones that were located in planned relation to each other and to kitchen tasks of storage, food preparation, serving, and cleaning up was being carefully considered by the mid-1800's.[18]

Along with industrialization came new inventions, new machinery, new techniques, and new forms of production and distribution that influenced the design and arrangement of housing. Wood- or coal-burning cast iron stoves began to replace the fireplace for heating or cooking about 1820, and steam heating systems came into use soon afterward. Gas and electric stoves were available by the late 1800's but did not become popular until the early 1900's. Commercial ice-freezing machines and iceboxes for the homes were in use by 1880. Oil and gas lamps were in use during the 19th century, and by 1874 Edison had patented the electric light. Water supply, plumbing, and sanitation developed slowly during the 19th century. Water closets began to be installed inside homes after the mid-1800's and bathtubs increased in popularity toward the end of the century in the homes of the well-to-do urban families. The impact of these new inventions came much more slowly to rural areas of the country.

Changes in Family Life

The Industrial Revolution also represented a real revolution for the American family. It not only displaced agriculture as the main economic base, but for the first time the place of work and the home were physically separated. Advances in farming methods reduced the necessity for large numbers of family laborers. Continued industrial development made it possible for families to purchase goods rather than producing all the items needed for living. As a result, the family's economic independence decreased, and additional children were no longer an economic advantage.

Migration broke up extended families and created new marriage patterns and family life styles. As men were drawn into the cities to work, there were some profound changes in the role of women. First the woman's family was moved to the city and with this move came smaller family quarters—often tenements or apartments. Several of the

[18] Siegfried Giedion, *Mechanization Takes Command.* (New York: Oxford University Press), 1948, p. 513.

home occupations were taken over by the factory, and women began to seek employment outside the home.

By 1850 one fourth of all factory workers were women. As children joined the women in the factories there was a reduction in family-centeredness and a weakening of the authoritarian role of the father. Immigration and the resultant mixing that occurred in urban areas created the opportunity for the mixing of ideas and ideals, thereby increasing the heterogeneity of family patterns. Burgess and Locke suggest that out of this mixing came a concept of family that was quite different from the traditional patriarchal family of earlier periods.[19] The "companionship family" which emerged was based on affectional bonds rather than on economic bonds.

With industrialization there was an accompanying strong movement toward the conjugal type of family where the focus is on the husband–wife relationship, and the nuclear family became relatively independent of other relatives. The extended or joint family was found less often, and the equality of the sexes began slowly to emerge. Independent couples in conjugal families could move freely in response to employment opportunities.

The impact of the swiftly changing social and economic forces that influenced American family structure was reflected in the changing needs and wants of families with respect to shelter. In earlier days a family could plant itself on the soil and remain there for generations. Early small-village dwellers prided themselves on their possession of land with ownership of homes as a badge of independence. Slowly the land was cut away, and all that remained of this once proud acreage was a narrow city lot where strangers built their houses closely on both sides. The tie to the soil lessened for urban families who had begun to see the need for remaining flexible and mobile in order to respond to employment opportunities.

The typical "turn-of-the-century" house was important in its reflection of an era. Although a home of that type is not necessarily desired today, it still represents to many people what "home" was, in a quieter and more leisurely period. Houses were large, custom built by local labor under the direction of the prospective owner. Local materials were used, frequently in a lavish manner. Many homes were paid for at the time of construction, since mortgaging was considered to be a dangerous financial risk.

The typical house had a large kitchen and pantry, a separate dining room, often two parlors, a number of bedrooms, a spacious attic, a large cellar, a veranda, and a back stoop. While the two-story house was

---

19 Ernest W. Burgess and Harvey J. Locke, *The Family, From Institution to Companionship.* (New York: American Book Co.) 1945, p. 27.

typical, wealthy families might have had a third floor for servants' sleeping quarters. Although there were few mechanical conveniences, central heating was not uncommon—though comparatively inefficient. Gas and oil lamps were common, but a few homes had electric lights. Running water and inside bathrooms were included in urban homes but did not appear in rural areas until later.

The Industrial Revolution as a Change Factor

Ecology—the study of the development of organizations or communities—assumes interaction among the components of the ecological system and infers that change is occurring. Change in this context refers to "nonrepetitive alterations of existing patterns of relationships."[20] These changes seem to occur in a cyclical fashion where pressures build up against the existing situation until changes must occur—then the whole community readjusts to another point of equilibrium.

The Industrial Revolution, with the population growth and redistribution which accompanied it, was a strong change agent in community structure in America and in the way these communities were housed. The Industrial Revolution directly influenced the design of housing through production techniques, materials, and the mechanization of household equipment. However, its indirect impact through urbanization, changes in family life style and social organization, and improvements in transportation was an even greater influence on the design of housing. The interrelatedness of variables in an ecological system was amply illustrated during the time of adaptation to the Industrial Revolution.

Turn of the Century to the Depression

Social Reform Movement—A Change in Organization

As the nineteenth century drew to a close the agitation for tenement reform reached its height in reports, legislative commissions, and attempts at laws and codes to make the sordid living conditions in the slums illegal.

The only product of the agitation, however, was gradual and ultimately ineffectual restrictions on types of houses to be erected in the future. Those already existing and the patterns already established remained unimpaired.[21]

There was some legal encouragement for gradually increasing provision of services and utilities such as water, sanitary plumbing, sewers,

[20] Hawley, *op. cit.*, p. 319.
[21] Charles Abrams, *The Future of Housing.* (New York: Harper and Row), 1946, p. 8.

refuse collection, paved streets, and transportation. Bauer observed that, had these efforts been used creatively to establish a new and better form of environment, there would have been some real progress in standards of living.

But, there was very little either creative or progressive about either the purpose or the immediate results of the early sanitary regulations. They arose out of stark necessity, and in that spirit they were administered.[22]

In 1901, New York City passed a Tenement House Act that proved to be a significant regulatory influence on the design of tenements in the ensuing years. This was a comprehensive act that contained clear-cut definitions for interior spaces, protection from fire, adequate light and ventilation, and minimum sizes of rooms. It also contained provisions for planning individual apartments to insure privacy and a requirement of running water and water closets in each apartment. This act served as a pattern for regulatory legislation in many other cities. Tenements built after 1901 were called "new law" tenements which indicated noticeable changes in design.

By 1910 over one fourth of the states had laws similar to the New York Tenement Act of 1901, but the degree of enforcement varied considerably. Laws with wider application, called housing laws, were being passed about the same time to cover the design of one- and two-family houses, hotels, and other types of dwellings. All of these laws were designed primarily to limit the construction of bad housing but did little to encourage the development of new, good housing.

Certainly slum dwellings did not cover the entirety of the urban areas. The interest in expansion and unbridled individualism had created an urban disorder that began to concern the American businessman—resulting in the "City Beautiful Movement." The cleaning up and beautifying of the city was their way of trying to make amends for past errors. It was through this movement that the palaces of the wealthy really flourished, and significant contributions were made in public building, such as libraries, museums, terminals and civic centers.[23]

By 1916, attitudes had changed somewhat from an emphasis on city beautiful and civic design to the control of land use through zoning, with legal restrictions on the height and use of buildings, in an attempt to build better cities. Zoning appeared in the early 1900's as a complement to the housing codes. Housing codes had been framed in terms of what the advocates of the legislation hoped would be possible to impose at the center of the city, but they did not allow for more severe restric-

22 Bauer, *op. cit.*, p. 19.
23 Tunnard and Reed, *op. cit.*, p. 179.

tions to be used further out. Zoning, as an exercise of police power in the interest of public health, safety and welfare, permits a differentiation of requirements in different parts of the city. Zoning regulates the way in which land is to be used, population density, setback requirements from the streets, height of buildings, and the percent of the lot that can be covered by the structure. Although challenged in the courts, the constitutionality of the local government's right to use police power to regulate private property was well established by the 1920's. Where the early zoning laws had placed emphasis on considerations of light and air in overcrowded urban areas, the emphasis by the late 1920's was on separation of the actual uses of property.

The process of adaptation to factors in the environment is illustrated in Figure 13–1. Increasing population and the urbanization which resulted from changes in technology built up pressure against the existing situation and set off a chain of influences and adaptations leading to a new point of equilibrium.

The time period from the Industrial Revolution through the 1920's illustrates the process of adaptation within an ecological system, as diagrammed in Figure 13–1. Changes in technology created a demand for more concentrated population, thus urbanization increased rapidly. Extremely crowded conditions were accompanied by an increasing death rate because the environment, which had comfortably supported the population in previous years, was no longer adequate. Economic losses caused social concern, resulting in political action to change the social organization. Zoning and housing laws were used to bring the ecological system back to a new point of equilibrium. The diagram illustrates only one of the many examples where a change in one component of the ecological system produced interactions with other components to build

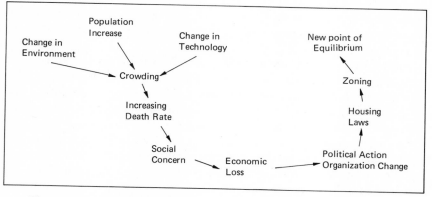

FIGURE 13–1. The process of adaptation in an ecological system.

up pressure against an existing condition and set off a chain of adaptations leading to a new equilibrium.

Mechanization and Technology

Population growth, urbanization, and industrialization continued impacting cities in the early years of the twentieth century. The rise in mass production that occurred during this period is perhaps best symbolized by the initiative of Henry Ford, who in 1909 set up the first mass production plant for the automobile. He was able to couple mass production with mass distribution and from that point on freedom of movement made possible by the automobile was to drastically influence the spatial form of cities and residential development.

The housing problem that had been in existence since the days of the early New England textile factories finally came into national focus with World War I. There had been an increasing body of professionals, municipal authorities, social workers, and architects, who saw the urgency of the housing problem but were not effective with their message until the war effort began to call workers into defense centers. It was the influx of these workers which revealed the inability of private enterprise to provide decent housing at affordable rates. The federal government had to provide homes for defense workers and in the process a few notable planned towns sprang up—like Yorkship Village near Camden, New Jersey.[24]

The inspiration for the planned communities came from the Garden City Movement in England where the solution to urban congestion was seen to be planned towns, combining the best features of city and country. In America, this was the first time that residential towns had been designed by trained planners and architects. It was in these planned communities that curvilinear street patterns began to replace the former gridiron approach in residential areas. Not all the "new towns" were based on the Garden City idea, since many industrial towns were created by corporations which were forced to provide homes for employees.

Mechanization increased rapidly after World War I and reached new heights between the two World Wars. When it became possible to fabricate standardized concrete blocks, the construction industry had an economical, fireproof material to use in the construction of apartment houses. In many areas, the town house was abandoned in favor of the apartment. During the 1920's, huge blocks of luxury flats were built in the cities across the country to "accommodate the newly rich and the well-to-do unwilling to struggle with the 'servant problem' in a society so affluent that a servant class, no longer renewed by immi-

---

[24] Tunnard and Reed, *op. cit.*, p. 221.

gration, was rapidly disappearing."[25] The controls placed on immigration in 1924 had substantially reduced the servant class in the cities.

American home architecture during the 1920's appeared generally simpler in form and more obviously related to the natural environment. The allusions to historic styles became much less specific than had been true during the nineteenth century. The typical house of the 1920's had fewer but larger rooms and was looser and more sprawling in plan. The porches and verandas became smaller or were completely removed in favor of terraces. The addition of carports and garages meant that larger lots were needed. The cleaner lines and reduced ornamentation may have resulted as much from the disappearance of craftsmen and the consequent increased expense of labor as from an intentional change in design. The changes that occurred were not just a conscious expression of changing and developing technology.[26]

The prosperity of the 1920's coupled with the continuously increasing urban population set off a building boom that reached a peak of 937,000 units in 1925, greatly increasing the housing stock both in the city proper and in the suburbs. Undoubtedly the greatest impetus to suburban development was the mass production of the automobile and the development of highways. Automobile production had reached 2.5 million by 1915 and in 1927 the first cross-country highway was completed. As rural families were moving into the cities, city families were moving out to the suburbs. By 1920, more of the population lived in urban than in rural areas. This movement of the population created a demand for housing of different types. Rural families moving into the cities were searching for multifamily rental units near places of employment, while suburban families were looking for single-family detached homes. Small suburban villages quickly mushroomed into sizeable towns, and land speculators opened up developments of raw land, selling lots for single-family homes.[27] By the late 1920's, the apartment had moved to the suburbs in the form of the "garden apartment." These buildings faced an interior court and were separated from the street in front by a small green area.[28]

In ecological literature, the term "succession" is used to "describe the series of events or stages involved in the replacement in an area of one type of occupant or land use by another"[29] The concept of succes-

[25] Constance M. Green, *The Rise of Urban America*. (New York: Harper and Row), 1965, p. 142.

[26] Alan Gowans, *Images of American Living*. (Philadelphia: Lippincott), 1964, pp. 422–423.

[27] Nelson N. Foote, et al., *Housing Choices and Housing Constraints*. (New York: McGraw-Hill), 1960, pp. 84–85.

[28] Tunnard and Reed, *op. cit.*, p. 223.

[29] Hawley, *op. cit.*, p. 321.

sion was illustrated by the growth of cities. Lindeman and Anderson observed that American cities appeared to be composed of concentric rings around the central core. A ring of slum dwellings, marginal industry, and cheap stores surrounded the central business core. The next ring was composed of some industry along with apartments and modest homes of the working class who had to live near industry. The fourth ring was primarily single-family homes of the middle class, and the fifth ring was residential suburbs. There was a gradual transition from one ring to the next, and the innermost rings gradually widened and moved outward. In response, the suburban ring moved even further out.[30]

Around 1920 mechanization entered the domestic sphere, and the entire house became susceptible to mechanization. Specialized work places in offices or factories had replaced the home workshop and, in turn, the scientifically conceived workplaces influenced efficiency in home design. By the early 1900's compact bathrooms were appearing frequently in American homes. The built-in recessed tub appeared in 1915 and was standardized to a length of five feet by 1920 when it began to rapidly replace the clawfooted bathtub which preceded it.[31] The more forceful impact of mechanization did not occur until after the Depression of the 1930's.

The Depression Years

Adaptation or adjustment to the Industrial Revolution involved increasing specialization and thus greater interdependence among people in America. No longer did families grow their own food, build their own homes, and make their own clothes. Mass production had illustrated that concentrating on the production of one product in one location and another product in another location resulted in greater overall production for the country as a whole. Individuals became more dependent on the production/distribution network in meeting their needs for goods and services, using money as the medium of exchange.

The stock market crash of 1929 greatly altered organization within American society, producing an environment which could no longer adequately provide for the people who inhabited it. Unemployment increased drastically, money supplies were rapidly exhausted, goods and services were difficult if not impossible to acquire, and individuals were forced to revert to the more independent actions of earlier times in order to survive. Other adaptive behavior included returning to relatives on the farm or doubling up with relatives in the city. In response to the

30 Tunnard and Reed, *op. cit.*, p. 232.
31 Giedion, *op. cit.*, p. 608.

TABLE 13–1. Total Birth Rate, Total Death Rate, and Expectation of Life (in Years) at Birth: 1900–1970

Year	Total Birth Rate	Total Death Rate	Life Expectation in Years	
			Male	Female
1970	18.4	9.5	67.1	74.8
1965	19.4	9.4	66.8	73.7
1960	23.7	9.5	66.6	73.1
1955	25.0	9.3	66.7	72.8
1950	24.1	9.6	65.6	71.1
1945	20.4	10.6	63.6	67.9
1940	19.4	10.8	60.8	65.2
1935	18.7	10.9	59.9	63.9
1930	21.3	11.3	58.1	61.6
1925	25.1	11.7	57.6	60.6
1920	27.7	13.0	53.6	54.6
1915	29.5	13.2	52.5	56.8
1910	30.1	14.7	48.4	51.8
1900	32.3	17.2	46.3	48.3

SOURCE: U. S. Bureau of the Census, *Historical Statistics of the United States, Colonial Times to 1970*, Bicentennial Edition, Part 2. Washington, D.C.: U.S. Government Printing Office, 1975, pp. 49, 55, 59.

apparent hopeless conditions in the environment, the birth rate declined rapidly. (See Table 13–1.)

The housing industry suffered a severe blow. Construction had begun to fall off after 1925 and the Depression slowed private building activity almost to a standstill. Not only were fewer and fewer buildings constructed, but each year the size of new dwellings diminished. In response to the lower incomes and lower birth rates, the speculative-builder house changed from the 2-story norm to the 1½-story cottage, and 1-room efficiency apartments became common.[32] Old homes and the larger existing apartments were converted into smaller units as an alternative to new construction.

There were some special urban aspects of the Depression.

Housing in cities had always been inadequate, and for a century housing reformers had been demanding changes. Now conditions suddenly worsened. Building nearly came to a halt. Repairs were not made. Slums expanded. Between 1928 and 1933 construction of residential property fell ninety-five percent; the amount spent annually on housing repairs dropped from fifty million to half a million dollars. In 1932, 273,000 people lost their homes, and during the next year a thousand homes a day were being foreclosed.[33]

[32] Foote, et al., *op. cit.*, p. 87.
[33] Glaab and Brown, *op. cit.*, p. 299.

The interrelatedness of the components in the ecological system are amply illustrated by the impact of the Industrial Revolution. This drastic change in technology influenced the growth and distribution of the population. Urban communities formed and demanded housing and services. In response, social, economic, and political organizations developed to perform certain specialized functions necessary for the ongoing of the total community. As long as all the organizations were functioning well, growth and development could continue. However, when the economic organization failed, all components of the system felt the impact. People were dissatisfied and desperate, so the threat of revolution grew. The imbalance of poor, starving people had to be corrected in order to restore "equilibrium" in the society. Thus, the federal government, another community organization, was forced to take action in an attempt to find ways of coping with the problem.

Post-Depression Through World War II

When business came to a standstill in the spring of 1933, the finance capitalism that had prevailed for 75 years began to change into a system of cooperative capitalism where government, agriculture, and labor joined with business to find ways to successfully restore the economy. The government began to take responsibility for welfare and service. For the first time, the federal government entered the housing field in a significant way. The Federal Housing Administration was created in 1934 and given the power to "insure loans for renovation and modernization and to insure mortgages on owned homes or rental apartment buildings."[34] With the guarantee by the federal government, lending agencies were willing to lend money at 4 percent on a fixed payment loan for 25 years. This cheaper and easier financing stimulated the demand for new housing and the construction industry began to make a slow recovery.

In an effort to reduce unemployment, public works projects were begun, with highway construction as one of the biggest efforts. Limited access highways were built around some major cities, making it easier to commute from city to suburbs. Suburbs had previously been located close to streetcar and rail lines, but, with the improvements in highways and increased production and use of automobiles, suburbs began to grow further from the city and the established transportation routes.

The growth in suburban development would probably not have occurred had it not been for the changes in home financing, which occurred at about the same time as improvements in transportation to and from the city. The easier credit terms also had an impact on the

34 Foote, et al., *op. cit.*, p. 87.

construction industry. Builders were able to construct numbers of dwellings at one time rather than selling off plots of land for the construction of single-family houses to individual specifications.

FHA is thus largely responsible for the growth of operative builder organizations in the late thirties and for the beginnings of standardization: the small home repeated in its essential characteristics throughout the entire development.[35]

Large tracts of open land at the outer edge of the city were acquired by developers who wanted to take advantage of FHA financing.

The advent of the 40-hour week also had an impact on suburban development. Before 1933, the suburbs had been the rich man's paradise. Working classes who put in 60 hours at the factories were not interested in commuting long distances. With the standardization of the 40-hour week in the 1930's, the average American could commute daily and have free weekends to spend around home.[36] The opportunity for suburban living and the availability of mortgage financing greatly increased the preference for the single-family-owned homes.

The preference for the single-family-owned home had been developing for many years. In fact, the essential qualities which distinguish American housing were established by about the time of the Civil War when "home" became primarily a place of residence rather than a place of domestic manufacturing. There was a feeling that the home should be organized in ways that would be conducive to both physical health and spiritual well-being of the family.[37] Rooms were designed for specific activities—living room, dining room, etc.—with the arrangement of furnishings reenforcing the intended use of the space.

This characterization of the home was widely accepted. There was general agreement that the best way to handle all the functions of home was in a single-family detached house. Thus, changes in the economic conditions joined with technological advancements to make it possible for more American families to attain the housing goal toward which they were striving—a single-family-owned home in a suburban location.

Public Housing

While suburban development was increasing at the outer edges of cities, the inner city slum problems continued to cause concern. Slums were occupied not only by poor immigrants and rural migrants but by middle-class working classes who suffered from unemployment during

[35] *Ibid.*

[36] Tunnard and Reed, *op. cit.*

[37] David P. Handlin, "The Detached House in the Age of the Object and Beyond." In: C. Wedin and L. Nygren (eds.), *Housing Perspectives: Individuals and Families.* (Minneapolis, Minn.: Burgess Publishing Co.), 1976, pp. 28–37.

the Depression and had been forced to seek housing in urban slums. Concern about slum conditions had been expressed off and on from the 1800's, but by 1930 sufficient social concern had been aroused to create a demand for public action. The earlier tenement house legislation, which resulted from a demand for public action, was an effort to limit bad housing. The public housing program, also a result of a demand for public action in the 1930's, began as a positive step to do something to provide better housing for the poor in the society.

The idea of housing built by the government and offered to poor families at minimal costs was not readily received. However, a number of vociferous and influential advocates fought long and hard for the idea, and public housing finally became law in the Housing Act of 1937. Compromises were necessary to get the bill through Congress. Rather severe cost restrictions were placed on public housing units and minimum standards of space and amenities applied. A second compromise required that an equal number of slum units be removed for each public housing unit constructed, since the purpose of the program was to eliminate slums—as well as to increase employment and aid the poor. This restriction meant that public housing projects were most frequently built in or near blighted areas—a condition which was to continue for a number of years. Some projects, prior to World War II, were reasonably well designed and integrated with the surrounding neighborhoods, but this was rarely the case following the war.

Part of the support for public housing in the early years came from those who wanted to improve the slums to make better and more responsible citizens of the slum dwellers. There was a poorly founded belief that the environment was the secret of human behavior and putting people into new and clean surroundings would result in cleansed human beings. This was not the case. Public housing in its planning was tied to human sentiments regarding what ought to happen, rather than on probabilities for achieving the desired goals. Public housing was saddled with a burden of social reform that it could not hope to carry out.

Public housing encouraged further standardization by introducing the "project" concept of mass housing. "Although public housing has never accounted for more than a small portion of new construction in any given year, its mass housing concept [was] adopted elsewhere."[38] Special tax exemptions and federal mortgage provisions to build large-scale urban rental developments for the middle-income group were available just before World War II. Some large insurance companies took advantage of these incentives and constructed large rental communities which were similar in character to public housing in their

[38] Foote, et al., *op. cit.*, p. 88.

concentration of units into one project. "Thus the institutional character of mid-twentieth century housing was extended beyond public housing into the private rental market."[39]

The all but complete elimination of private building during World War II was an even further impetus toward mass housing. The representative building type during those years was emergency housing— usually in mass developments designed to serve defense industries and military establishments.

New mass building methods were developed to speed construction and further reduce expense . . . for the first time residential building began to take advantage of industrial techniques and to change from its status as a localized craft product. The five years of World War II thus created almost a revolution in building practices. But to great numbers of consumers, the house became, during this period, a temporary expedient and a minimum accommodation.[40]

The application of available technology to the housing industry and a growing trend toward standardization contributed to the start of one of the most noticeable changes in housing design in recent years—the mobile home.

Mobile Homes

As early as 1937, predictions were being made that "trailers" would become a popular form of housing in America. During the same period, others in the housing and design professions were predicting that the trailer would never amount to anything because of its cramped space and the public's aversion to such a mobile form of housing.

By 1936, it was estimated that 250,000 "trailers" were in use by nearly one million people. The demand for mobile housing increased during the decade from 1930–1940 as a result of economic and social changes. For some elderly, the mobile home was a reasonable solution to their housing needs as it was for seasonal laborers and for those forced into a nomadic way of life in search of employment during the Depression of the 1930's.[41]

As new factories were built and idle plants were put into production during the early 1940's, there was a sudden need for housing in specific locations across the nation. Temporary housing was needed for construction workers and permanent housing was needed for the factory employees and military personnel. By this time technology was available to permit the construction of mobile homes in considerable quan-

---

[39] *Ibid.*

[40] *Ibid.*, pp. 88–89.

[41] Harold A. Davidson, *Housing Demand: Mobile, Modular, or Conventional?* (New York: Van Nostrand-Reinhold), 1973, p. 9.

tity, so mobile homes were seen as a type of housing that would meet the immediate need without risking overbuilding. Mobile homes became a part of the defense housing program. Production figures went from 1,300 units a year in 1930 to 16,000 units a year in 1940. This sudden increase in demand was accompanied by lowered construction standards, which resulted in housing of substandard quality—but housing which met the immediate need.[42]

The Break from Traditional Architectural Styles

The crash of 1929 and the Great Depression really shook American confidence in its old Victorian systems. The Victorian traditions were pushed aside to signal the end of an old order and the beginning of a new one. This was the time to develop an American art that was not built on an allusion to past styles but was a product of American needs, materials, and technology.

It was in the residential area that much of the pioneering work in architecture was begun. Adventurous clients enabled architects in the 1930's to experiment with some rather radical changes in residential design. Frank Lloyd Wright designed houses that were stripped of useless ornament and gingerbread. Standardized windows were used in large horizontal strips. The inside surface detail was replaced with natural textures and warm earth colors of birds, sand plaster, natural oak, and raw linen. Entire walls disappeared as smaller separate purpose rooms were blended into outdoor spaces.

Europe had led the way in the development of the International Style which broke so completely with restraints of traditional architecture. The contemporary movement in architecture was greatly intensified in America when a number of the leading architects from Europe came to the United States and brought their ideas with them.[43]

The International Style taught that good architecture had to be "functional." Included in this concept of "functional" was the idea that architectural designs are conditioned by economic forces and available technology, so good architecture should grow out of the community's needs and resources. This cast the architects in the role of scientists who were helping to lead in the march toward the brave new world of the 20th century.[44]

The devotion to science and the machine came out strongly in the 1930's and 1940's. The Internationalists spoke of the house as a "machine for living." To be a user of a machine was to be in the spirit of

[42] *Ibid.*, p. 11.

[43] Leonardo Benevolo, *History of Modern Architecture.* Vol. 2: *The Modern Movement.* (Cambridge, Mass.: M.I.T. Press), 1971.

[44] Gowans, *op. cit.*, pp. 440–441.

the century. These ideas were embodied in the stark exposures of the structure and the simplicity and mechanical insistence on efficient planning. There was a decided rejection of ornament as such. Buildings were composed of flat roofs, large expanses of plain walls with much exposed steel and glass and an emphasis on horizontal line. This was indeed the age of confident command over nature by the utilization of science.

The International Style architects worked in opposition to the idea that a dwelling was a series of boxlike rooms. They rejected the idea that a window was a hole punched into a solid wall. Glass walls permitted the lawn to be an extension of the living area and provided considerable improvements in lighting and ventilation. Spaces within the interior were less confined as well: parlors, sitting rooms, halls, dining rooms, and even dens disappeared as such and were merged into a large living space that was designed so that many functions could be carried on at the same time.[45]

As the economy permitted, Americans focused attention on redesigning objects of mass production. Household mechanical equipment along with trains and automobiles were redesigned with streamlined forms. Under the emphasis on scientific household engineering, the home kitchen underwent drastic design changes, beginning just before and continuing after the Depression. Industrial designers were a primary force in the shaping of public taste in the 1930's as they enclosed mechanized home equipment in streamlined casings, built in appliances, and integrated them with working surfaces and storage spaces.[46]

Prior to the Depression, kitchens had been simply conglomerations of equipment and storage with no thought given by one manufacturer as to how its product might relate to products of other manufacturers. Around 1935, the organized work process kitchen, known as the streamlined kitchen, became available. Components were standardized so that items could be arranged in a variety of ways and were easily interchangeable. The appearance of electrified appliances encouraged the "building in" of refrigerators, sinks, table top ranges, and even electric dishwashers and garbage disposers. Industry sponsored time-and-motion studies to develop principles of scientific housekeeping that could be incorporated into the streamlined kitchen design. Scientific management became the design force of the day.[47] The isolated kitchen was abandoned, and there was a movement toward a concentrated mechanical core and a kitchen that was integrated into the rest of the house while being open to the eating area. By 1945, the mechanized kitchen

[45] Bauer, *op. cit.*, p. 200.
[46] Giedion, *op. cit.*, p. 608.
[47] *Ibid.*, p. 616.

had become a dominant feature of the house plan and an active center of household life.[48]

The mechanization of the kitchen was closely connected with the development of processed or commercially prepared foods, the reduction in the supply of household servants, the increasing involvement of women outside the home, and an increasing demand for leisure time. As is characteristic of any ecological system, these factors were interacting with each other, and all were influenced by the values of the social organization, the available technology, environmental conditions, and population changes.

Post–World War II Through 1959

The dwellings that had been constructed during the 1930's and early 1940's showed a long-range shrinkage in size of units. In the 1920's, the average dwelling unit was 4.8 rooms but had dropped to 4.26 rooms for the decade 1940–1950. Private building had been minimal from about 1925 through the Depression and World War II, so the units which were constructed during that time were largely a product of public effort through public housing and defense housing, along with the operative builder cottages and the efficiency apartments of the 1930's. Existing housing had been divided into smaller units during the Depression and the war. All of these factors contributed to the smaller size of units.

The veterans returned to America after the war with home and family on their minds. Many couples had been forced to postpone marriage and childbearing until the war ended, so there was a high rate of family formation for several years after 1945. The birth rate increased from 20.4 in 1945 to 24.1 in 1950 (see Table 14–1). By 1950 the population had increased to over 170 million, and nearly 100 million of these were urban dwellers.

This flood of returning veterans who sought housing for their rapidly expanding families was met by a housing shortage of critical dimensions. "Once more the Federal government stepped in, this time with the no-down-payment, VA-insured mortgage for veterans who wanted to buy houses."[49] This new mortgage assistance, along with the existing FHA-mortgage insurance for the nonveterans, made possible a substantial housing boom during the postwar period, but for the most part these were minimal size units that could be constructed rapidly by using mass methods of construction that had been developed during the war. Consumers who had grown used to Depression and wartime

48 *Ibid.*, pp. 624–625.
49 Foote, et al., *op. cit.*, p. 89.

stringencies accepted minimal housing because of the limitations of supply in the face of excessive demand for housing. The new house of the late 1940's was much smaller than those that preceded it. It had only one story, and was without basement, attic, or separate dining room. It probably had a kitchen, living room with dining room alcove, two bedrooms, and a bath. All of the rooms were much smaller than they had been fifty years earlier. "Between 1945 and 1950, the representative dwelling became the minimum two bedroom VA or FHA development house bought with little or no equity."[50] Although small, these new houses had efficient automatic furnaces, water heaters, electric lights, modern baths, and a kitchen equipped with cupboards, range, refrigerator, and sink. Housing had begun to change from "a concept of shelter and living space to a minimum wrapping for a complicated array of mechanical equipment and appliances."[51]

World War II was the beginning of some significant changes in residential architecture. There was a demand in America for the construction of entire communities for the concentrations of industrial workers. Where other countries experienced a paralysis of architecture during the war, America experienced a new challenge that led to experimentation in factory design or prefabrication of parts of a house.[52]

The first large-scale attempts at prefabricated building began after the Depression, but some small-scale attempts had begun as early as 1907 and continued through the period of rapid suburban growth prior to 1929. Stick-building, by which dwellings are prepared piece by piece with most of the work done on the site, was the most common method for residential construction until the 1940's. Precut and component fabrication was the next level of standardization that permitted some components—such as roof trusses, doors, windows, etc.—to be prepared off the site and then transported to the site for installation. The walls and partitions could be surfaced with whatever material was desired. These techniques helped to make the postwar development house different from its predecessors. The new development house was standardized in design, and mass produced, using presite cutting of materials, prefabricated parts, and assembly-line erection. Sometimes entire dwellings were prefabricated and simply put together on the site. Approximately 37,000 units of this type were constructed in 1946, and by 1950 the annual number had risen to 55,000 units.

Newer materials, such as plywood, concrete or cinder block, and asphalt tile, were substituted for more expensive materials, such as wood, brick, stone, or ceramic tile. However, in spite of these econo-

[50] *Ibid.*

[51] *Ibid.*, p. 90.

[52] Talcott Parsons, *Architecture Through the Ages*. (New York: Putnam), 1953, p. 649.

mies, houses were far more expensive per square foot than had been the custom-built houses at the turn of the century.

Attitudes toward housing in the postwar period changed as well. Because houses were so small, they were regarded as a tentative expedient rather than a permanent abode as was characteristic of earlier years.

Thus, the various changes in technology, urban density, construction costs, mortgage credit, family patterns, and general attitude toward the home have transformed the dwelling (over the first fifty years of the twentieth century) from manually operated spacious permanence to mechanical small uniform expediency in design.[53]

The rising cost of conventional construction and the time involved in building the units enhanced the market for more rapidly produced mobile units. The trailer that had served as temporary housing developed into mobile units that were sufficiently large and well equipped to serve as permanent housing by 1950. Units contained completely furnished kitchens and bathrooms. These units averaged 8 feet wide and 25 feet long. Prior to the war mobile units were used primarily for travel, during and immediately following the war as temporary housing. By 1954 the market had increased substantially and included migratory workers, military personnel, and numbers of retired people.[54]

Apartment buildings sprang up after the war in response to the immediate demand for housing. Before the war, the buildings were constructed with large unbroken facades and uniform rooflines. There were mechanical punctuations of windows that did not permit much light to enter. However, after World War II the apartment buildings were constructed with recessed balconies or jutting bays to add the third dimension to structures. Much more glass was used to admit light into the interior spaces. Although incentives were offered to builders of postwar rental apartments, the construction industry as well as the young families with children were much more interested in the single-family home. Mortgage insurance programs (VA and FHA) made homeownership available to many families who could never have considered it otherwise. Concentric rings of houses mushroomed up beyond the existing suburbs as suburban sprawl really got rolling.

Suburban Tract House

Although the availability of mortgage funds was a very important impetus for suburban development, it was not the only factor. A favorable economic condition developed after the war as income levels rose and the general level of prosperity increased. By 1957 new households

[53] Foote, et al., *op. cit.*, p. 91.
[54] Davidson, *op. cit.*, pp. 11–12.

were being formed more rapidly than the population increased, as children married at an earlier age or left home to establish another household. There had been a gradual but continuous redistribution of the labor force from extractive and basic manufacturing industry into service or white-collar jobs. This brought a shift toward middle-class goals in housing—a desire for the suburban single-family home. Since real income for the population was increasing, in spite of rising prices, there was not only a desire for suburban living but a real market demand. The expanding middle class wanted to "proclaim its new-found status" and express its concern for bringing up children in the "wholesome, clean-air" environment of the suburbs.[55]

The 1950's were the years of vast suburban development—primarily in the form of "tract houses." These moderate-income houses were built by the hundreds or even thousands on large areas of land that had been stripped of trees so that construction could be accomplished quickly and economically. The monotonous repetition of the "look-alike" houses was also done in the name of economy. There was still a symbolism in the single-family-owned suburban home—in spite of its minimum characteristic—that met the psychological needs of families. Row after row of almost identical houses, each with a picture window in the living room, lined suburban streets, which were the playgrounds for the numerous small children of the young families which made up the suburban population.

The increased use of the automobile had been a significant factor in the growth of the suburbs, but its influence on housing design did not stop there. Automobiles affected the interior plan of houses as well as the plans of cities.

The front porch, that social center for friendliness and relaxation, was discarded and a garage was built on the back of the lot instead. The once quiet, pleasant street became filled with cars, fumes, and noise. Friends and neighbors rode rather than walked past and the porch on the front of the house became, more and more, an unpleasant place to relax. Additionally, the automobile influenced changes in the orientation of the house plan as well. The major entrance to the house moved from the street side to a door nearest the driveway or garage and the need to further escape the noise of the street frequently caused the living room to be moved to the rear of the house, shifting the service areas, kitchen, and baths to the street side. Houses have also moved toward the front of the lot with larger space behind rather than in front. The backyard is now filled with living spaces, terraces, patios, barbeques and the like, instead of gardens, clotheslines, and a chicken or two.[56]

55 Foote, et al., *op. cit.*, p. 76.

56 Harold H. Alexander, *Design: Criteria for Decisions.* (New York: Macmillan), 1976, pp. 125–126.

The increase in the availability of the automobile along with the new methods of production illustrate very well the impact of technological change on the design of family residences.

Organizational Change—The Family Structure and Function

The increasing specialization and high level of technology during World War II caused some changes in social values, family values, and family structure, which in turn influenced the design of houses. Prior to modern times, families had served a variety of functions including education, protection, recreation, economic support, and affection.[57] In the early years, the entire family had to cooperate in order to survive, but slowly the American family lost many of these functions or transferred them to other organizations. The economic function moved from the home to the factory, store, office, or restaurant, leaving little economic activity as a part of the city apartment or suburban home. The education function was transferred to the schools, and teachers served in the role of substitute parents. The recreation function was sometimes provided by motion pictures, social groups, radio, and television. The protection function was transferred to the police and fire service, but the affection function tended to remain with the family. These functions have not disappeared entirely from the family —they are just being shared with other institutions within the society rather than being performed only by the family. Along with these changes in function, the rule in the home became more democratic, instead of authoritarian, so that all family members became involved in decisionmaking and parents showed more concern for the social development and intellectual achievement of their children.

Since the family was no longer the basic economic as well as social unit, those persons who did not want to marry could chose some alternative style of living. Individuals could exist outside the nuclear family and even maintain single-person households if they desired. Such choices were available first to the wealthy but became available to the larger group as affluence continued to increase after the war.[58]

The transfer of family functions influenced a number of changes in house design. The change in the economic function was accompanied by a reduction in the size of families. Table 13–2 shows that the average number of persons in the household had decreased from 5.0 in

[57] William F. Ogburn, "The Changing Functions of the Family." In: Robert F. Winch and Louis Goodman (eds.), *Selected Studies in Marriage and the Family.* (New York: Holt, Rinehart, and Winston), 1968, p. 27.

[58] William J. Goode, "The Role of the Family in Industrialization." In: Robert F. Winch and Louis W. Goodman (eds.), *Selected Studies in Marriage and the Family.* (New York: Holt, Rinehart and Winston), 1968, p. 64.

TABLE 13–2. Average Size of Household: 1890–1970

Year	Average Number of Persons
1970	3.1
1960	3.4
1950	3.5
1940	3.8
1930	4.1
1920	4.3
1910	4.5
1900	4.8
1890	5.0

SOURCE: U. S. Bureau of Census, *Census of Housing: 1970.* Vol. I: *Housing Characteristics for States, Cities, and Counties.* Part I: *United States Summary.* (Washington, D.C.: U. S. Government Printing Office), 1972, p. S6.

1890 to 3.5 by 1950. This reduction in family size meant that less space was required in terms of interior house space or space surrounding the home. As families increased their utilization of mass-produced goods and services, there was no longer so great a need for attics, sheds, storage cellars, work rooms, sewing rooms, etc. Easy access to processed food supplies and shops reduced the size of storage space needed in closets and pantries. Hotels and clubs provided space for entertaining large groups, and much of the family recreation was done outside the home. Homes were more likely to be designed for a maximum of comfort and convenience rather than as show places for grand formal entertaining. The drawing rooms and grand staircases of former years had been exchanged for open plans with flexible spaces that could be adapted to the family's more informal life style and adjusted to meet the family's changing needs.

The "companionship family," based on affectional bonds rather than economic bonds, had replaced the more traditional patriarchal family of earlier years.[59] Space and facilities for nurturing, within the "companionship family," were needed to replace the space for workshops that had been used when the economic function was so important. The "family room" or general-purpose room, designed for family interaction, was an outgrowth of the companionship life style and replaced the farm kitchen that was so frequently the place of family interaction in earlier

[59] Burgess and Locke, *op. cit.*, p. 27.

times. The more typical plans of the 1950's and later were more likely to be open arrangements that allow the major living units to flow into each other—utilizing suggestions of spatial divisions instead of stationary or permanent wall divisions. Families began to shift from a formal to a fluid and informal living pattern. The more open plan and the multipurpose family room developed in response to this need for informality in the home.

Families not only differ from each other in terms of where they live and how much they can afford to pay for housing, but an individual family is constantly changing in ways that influence its housing design requirements. Family size and stage in the life cycle have direct impact on the type of housing that is needed at any point in time. The young newly married couple may want to live in or near an urban area close to work and recreation facilities. Thus the couple may choose to rent an apartment which demands less in terms of time and maintenance. Growth of the family increases space needs within the home and the demand for ownership of a single-family home increases. Single-family ownership rises to a peak at about age 35–54 and then declines slightly as families in the contracting stage of the life cycle begin to reduce the size of their homes in response to the decreasing family size.

Families also differ in terms of the values that they hold, and these values influence a family's decision about the design of its home. Values do not change readily and thus have a prevailing influence on housing choice. Beyer and Montgomery studied the relationship between family values and housing design and identified four basic value groups: economy, family-centered, personal, and prestige. The families which valued economy were the most conservative and conventional and placed highest value on price and durability of the home. The family-centered family wanted the house design to enhance the well-being of the family and provide for interactions among family members. The family which emphasized personal values stressed the personal enjoyment and privacy of individual family members. The fourth group valued prestige and regarded their house as a symbol of their success, so they stressed impressiveness over convenience or efficiency.[60] These differences in value orientation emphasize the need for variety in housing alternatives within any market so that families can select the type of housing that relates to their value orientation.

As affluence increased in the 1950's, families had more resources with which to acquire housing consistent with family values. By about 1950, the demand for minimum housing had been met, and an era of unprecedented prosperity was beginning. In response to such prosperity,

[60] Glenn H. Beyer and James E. Montgomery, *Houses Are for People.* (Ithaca, N.Y.: Cornell University Press), 1955.

the average size of the dwelling began to increase and the suburban "split-level" home became the modern substitute for the pre-Depression two- and three-story houses.[61]

The Influence of Standards, Codes, and Zoning

It is not the leading architects and designers who determine residential design in America. In practice, what is built is less and less determined by architects and more and more determined by forces of circumstances operating at any given time. Builders are inclined to interpret the rapid sale of a house as evidence that the design standards are good ones. However, the sale of the homes may only be a reflection of a housing shortage or locational preference that offset the design deficiencies. In practice, builders are restricted by cost factors, consumer acceptance, attitudes of the lenders, building codes, Federal Housing Administration standards, and zoning ordinances.

At the national level, the minimum property standards of the government housing and health agencies influence design and construction—"from the kinds of materials and products that go into a house to structural design, to mechanical equipment, and water supply and sewage disposal requirements."[62] In 1950 the American Public Health Association (APHA) defined activities generally performed in a dwelling and calculated the space which was needed to perform these activities. APHA saw the home as primarily an instrument of health and felt that it had a duty to establish fundamental health objectives to govern the design of the dwelling. The major concern was space in terms of total living space for families of various sizes. This concern came in response to the minimum space provided in the "economy houses" built immediately after the war.

The most serious problem which confronts us is the trend toward reduction of the total space available (for a family of a given size as indicated by its bedrooms) to lower and lower levels. As one drives through the suburban areas where active building has taken place, it is often difficult to determine which is the house and which is the garage.[63]

The resulting recommendations were 750 square feet for a two-person household, 1,000 square feet for a three-person household—up to 1,550 square feet for a six-person household. These standards were about 25 percent greater than space provided in the better public housing projects and about double the space of the "economy houses" which

[61] Foote, et al., *op. cit.*, p. 91.
[62] Beyer, *op. cit.*, p. 497.
[63] American Public Health Association, Committee on the Hygiene of Housing, *Planning the Home for Occupancy.* (Washington, D.C.: Public Administration Service), 1950, p. vi.

met the Federal Housing Administration minimum standards at that time. The minimum standards tended to become the maximum and resulted in enormous developments composed of almost identical dwellings that varied little from one coast of the country to the other. The FHA and APHA minimum standards as a condition of financing promoted uniformity in new home construction where developers found it easier to conform than risk delay in awaiting approval for financing and occupancy. Standards were very important because, through their influence on the building industry, they virtually dictated the size of millions of dwelling units.

Building codes were established to regulate new construction and major remodeling. This was society's attempt to ensure quality of products to be rented or purchased. Although building codes served the housing consumer, they have also been used to "serve the self-interest of some parts of the housing industry by protecting certain traditional materials and work methods and by impeding technological innovations."[64] Thus, building codes have served as a constraint to the innovation in building techniques that would naturally have occurred given the technological changes within the environmental system.

The early zoning laws placed emphasis on considerations of light and air in overcrowded urban areas. By the late 1920's the emphasis had changed to the separation of the actual uses of property. Since World War II, zoning has increasingly been used to control development and design so that it occurs in an orderly fashion. Pressures of increasing population concentrations resulted in more housing being built each year in subdivisions at the edges of urban centers. Counter-pressures began to build up as environmentalists and concerned citizens expressed concern over the way in which land was being subdivided and developed. Added to this was the objection by the longtime suburban residents of the influx of apartments and new subdivisions of even greater density. Zoning was selected as the tool for prohibiting apartments and low-income housing from entering suburban developments—by increasing minimum lot requirements to unrealistic sizes or increasing minimum square footage for dwelling units. These requirements influenced the size and thus the price of the house that would be built, since many developers build according to the size and the price of the lot. Minimum floor space requirements were said to be in the interest of public health and safety, but they effectively discriminated against owners of less expensive homes.

The prewar public housing had been built under really minimum standards in terms of size and amenities. By 1940 some minimum standards had been developed for space, light, and ventilation, which enlarged the units somewhat. However, in order to utilize the land as well as possible and keep the initial costs down, public housing projects were most often high-density developments with minimal-sized rooms. Architects were required to design under rigid formulas that restricted design of projects to an obsolete and congested mold which gave little or no consideration to tenants' needs. Mumford referred to these projects as standardized dormitories that did not achieve economies sufficient to justify their design.[65] In order to try to increase economies, the housing authorities often omitted doors from closets and cupboards—which created even greater burdens for the low-income tenants. Such units could hardly be considered ideal housing for families with small children. Economy coupled with lack of imagination "produced boxlike rows which left tenants feeling like occupants of loosely packed, aseptic sardine tins on grocery shelves."[66] Unhappily, the belief that prevailed in the 1940's—that better housing would make better neighborhoods and thus better citizens—proved fallacious in the 1950's.

Efforts to build public housing outside the slum areas met with such resistance that projects were built primarily within the slum boundaries. Funds were limited, sites were expensive to prepare and demand for units was so great that high-rise seemed to be the best design solution. But high-rise was the wrong kind of housing for the children and youth of poor families. Parental supervision was more difficult when children were playing many stories below. Teenagers were brought together in more intense concentrations, and gang problems were abundant. Concentrating the poor in such projects increased the visibility of their social disorganization.

Design restriction intensified the problems, and two particular factors inhibited a concern for the design of public housing units.

First, a grudging attitude accompanied aid to the poor. . . . The basic legislation makes it clear that every project shall be undertaken in such a manner that it will not be of elaborate or extravagent design or construction . . . in practice this has generally been taken to mean that public housing style should be Spartan and unadorned.[67]

The second factor was limited appropriations. The 1949 Housing Act specified that economy should be promoted both in construction and

[65] Lewis Mumford, *From the Ground Up.* (New York: Harcourt Brace Jovanovich), 1956, p. 127.

[66] Constance McLaughlin Green, *The Rise of Urban America.* (New York: Harper and Row), 1965, p. 164.

[67] Leonard Freedman, *Public Housing.* (New York: Holt, Rinehart and Winston), 1969, p. 116.

administration. In practice, there was little opportunity for a relaxed approach to expenditures, since appropriations in the early 1950's were so small as to permit few opportunities for extravagance. Low-cost public housing in most cities was a collection of monolithic institutional apartment structures, pared down in amenities and aesthetics. The sheer size of such units heightened the antipathy to them by middle-class neighborhoods of predominantly single-family homes. By the end of the 1950's, even the public housing advocates were admitting the program's failures. "It was the restrictions built into the program from the outset and the environment of hostility which enveloped it as it struggled to grow that had contributed so largely to its failures."[68]

Standards, zoning, codes, and regulations are all responses by the social organization to conditions in the environment. Each of these regulations was an attempt by the social organization to influence conditions. Public housing was the organization's response to a social problem. Society had realized that not all families had the kind of housing that was desirable for maintaining decent living conditions. However, there was considerable resistence from within the organization to providing the quantity of housing assistance that was needed, so the offerings were minimal at best. The numbers of families needing housing and the social organization limiting the funds available resulted in the massive and unattractive public housing projects of the 1950's.

1960 to the Present

Sociodemographic Changes

The housing needed by a family at any given point in time is closely related to the stage of the family life cycle. It is readily recognized that space needs change quickly with the addition of children to the family, but the type of housing needed or desired changes as well. The young couple may be content with renting a small apartment, but with the addition of the second child—or when the first child reaches school age—the couple will probably begin looking for a single-family home, preferably one that can be purchased. Single-family homeownership continues to be the dominant pattern through the expanding and launching stages of the family life cycle and is probably preferred by retired couples as long as they can maintain such a residence.

Some important demographic changes occurred in the nation's population during the 1960's, and these changes were reflected in the type of housing which was produced. Postwar babies, born in the late 1940's and early 1950's, became the young adults of the 1960's and

[68] *Ibid.*, p. 122.

1970's. The population grew by 26 million between 1960 and 1970 and almost 50 percent of this growth occurred within the 15- to 24-year age group.[69] This is the age group where marriage frequently occurs, and as was expected the rate of marriages began increasing in the mid-1960's and reached a peak in 1973 before a gradual decline began. Young people today are marrying later and deferring child-bearing or in some cases preferring to remain childless. Those who do choose to rear children are, on the average, having smaller families (see Table 13-2).

Some striking changes have taken place in the mix of dwelling types constructed during the 20th century. From 1900 to 1937 the ratio of new single-family housing units to all new units declined, reaching a low in 1927 of 57 percent. There was a reversal of this trend during the suburban exodus, and by 1950 over 90 percent of all new housing units were single-family.[70] In the 1960's, this trend again reversed itself as the percent of the population in the 20- to 29-year age group increased. The percent of housing starts which were multifamily units increased rapidly from 1959 to 1963 and reached a high of nearly 34 percent in 1972. This occurred at about the same time that the rate of marriage reached a peak—approximately 20 years after the height of the post-war "baby booms."

One of the most remarkable population changes to occur during the 20th century is the proportionate increase in the number of persons over the age of 65 years. This change has been brought about by a decrease in the birth rate—resulting in fewer people in the very young age groups—and a decrease in the death rate among the older age groups in the population. The number of older people in the United States has increased over fivefold in the 20th century, while the number in the middle-age sector has increased only three and a half times.[71]

There has also been a dramatic increase in the percent of one-person households in the United States and a slight increase in the number of two-person households (see Table 13-3). A single-person household may be a young single, a divorced person, or an elderly person. In 1960, 13 percent of the households contained one person and over half of these were 60 years of age or older. An additional 47 percent of the two-person households contained one or more persons over the age of 60. As physical abilities decline, elderly persons need housing

[69] George Cristie, "We Can't Afford Another 1960's Housing Decade," *The Commercial and Financial Chronical*, Thursday, February 26, 1970.

[70] Thomas C. Marlin, *Projections of Demand for Housing by Type of Unit and Region*, Agriculture Handbook No. 428. U. S. Department of Agriculture, Forest Service, May 1972.

[71] Tessie Agan and Elaine Luchsinger, *The House*. (Philadelphia: Lippincott), 1965, p. 14.

TABLE 13–3. Percent of Population in Various Sizes of Households:
1940–1970

Household Size	1970	1960	1950	1940
1 person	17.6	13.3	9.3	7.7
2 persons	29.6	28.0	28.0	24.8
3 and 4 persons	32.6	36.2	41.1	40.5
5 and 6 persons	15.1	17.0	15.9	18.3
7 or more persons	5.1	5.5	5.7	8.7

SOURCE: U. S. Bureau of the Census, *U. S. Census of Housing, 1960.* Vol. I, *States and Small Areas.* Part I: *United States Summary.* (Washington, D.C.: U. S. Government Printing Office), 1963, p. XXIX; and *U. S. Census of Housing, 1970,* Vol. I, *Housing Characteristics for States, Cities and Counties.* Part I: *United States Summary.* (Washington, D.C.: U. S. Government Printing Office), 1972, p. S8.

designed for safety and easy care. The housing problems of the elderly gained increasing attention in the 1960's, with Americans becoming more aware of the growing proportion of elderly in the population and the uniqueness of their needs. In 1961 special provisions were written into the Housing Act to increase housing subsidies to elderly public housing tenants and allow more funds for specially equipping low-rent projects to be occupied by the elderly. These special provisions in the legislation greatly increased the number of housing projects for the elderly across the country.

The increased mobility of the American family means that homes may be lived in for a shorter period of time than was characteristic of the earlier part of the 20th century. Mobility has produced a new motive for home building—homes are less likely to be designed for specific families. Instead, designs are done in more general terms with the emphasis on new gadgets, appliances, and materials. In today's mobile society, homes are more apt to be selected on the basis of resalability than on livability, and the resale value may well hinge on the number of mechanical conveniences contained in the home.

Rural to urban migration has been the dominant trend in the 20th century, but Calvin Beale points out that the migration trend may be reversing.[72] Beginning about 1940, the population increased in urban areas in the 1950's. The reversal in the migration trend came during per year left the farms. A net of 5 million people left nonmetropolitan areas in the 1950's. The reversal of the migration trend came during 1970–1973 when metropolitan areas gained only 2.9 percent, while nonmetropolitan areas gained 4.2 percent. A continuation of this re-

[72] Calvin Beale, "Population and Employment Patterns Affecting Rural Housing," Conference Proceedings, *Quality Housing Environment for Rural Low-Income Families,* September 11–13, 1975, Atlanta, Georgia, pp. 15–20.

verse migration would have a very important impact on the location of housing demand in the future.

Family Values

Not only is housing influenced by the social conditions but also by family values. Family preferences for formality or casual approaches to living can have an impact on decisions to create homes with formal dining areas or large family living spaces where cooking, eating, and lounging occur together. The preferences for outdoor cooking have produced design of housing which integrates the backyard area with the interior areas of the home.

According to the value placed on homemaking as opposed to professional involvement of the mother outside the home, the design for the home differs. One family may view the home as primarily a place for family interaction and the nurturing of children, while another emphasizes individual development and looks with distaste upon many or all the traditional housekeeping functions.[73]

The style of the exterior and the interior of a home reflects—within resalable limits—the personality of the residents and may be selected on the basis of the residents' concept of who they are. Many people will even admit to buying a house that bolsters the image of self, since the house in the American culture is a symbolic statement of the status of the family in the society.[74]

Few families build their own homes today as they did in colonial America, so they lack the control over design that the earlier families had. Most housing today is constructed by builders who interpret the demand for housing and utilize designs which they feel will appeal to the market. Housing design is geared toward the normative American family—a white middle-class family with mother, father, and not more than two children. However, the "standard family" is not the only housing consumer. Today a "family" may be a group of unrelated people who live together in a communal arrangement and thus have quite different housing needs than the normative family. Unmarried couples and other communal groups tend to avoid purchases that must be paid for over a period of time, so they are not likely to purchase a home. Builders responded to the increasing singles market by building singles apartment complexes, but not much response has been made toward the needs of "communal families." These families are fre-

---

[73] John P. Dean, "Housing Design and Family Values." In: William Wheaton, et al. (eds.), *Urban Housing.* (New York: Free Press), 1966, pp. 127–138.

[74] Clare Cooper, "The House as a Symbol of Self." In: Jon Lang, et al. (eds.), *Designing for Human Behavior.* (Stroudsburg, Pa.: Hutchingson and Ross), 1974, p. 132.

quently forced to compromise their values and adapt to the "standard home."

Danziger and Greenwald[75] predict that communes will, in the future, be an alternative within marriage as well as an alternative to marriage. As a growing number of married couples, with or without children, combine in communes there will be a demand for housing that is designed to provide privacy for the individual couples as well as community rooms for sharing.

Values of the Society

As a society we value those things that are symbols of security and prestige and attach increasing importance to privacy. These attitudes and values are defined by our culture and influence individual and family preferences for housing designs. The open plan that was advocated by the International Style architects beginning in the 1920's was not readily accepted by many of the American public who desire more privacy than the plan affords.[76]

Unlike some cultures, Americans seem to place rather significant value on the concept of privacy, and thus families or households desire separate housing. The form in which this privacy is to be obtained and the degree of privacy will vary according to the individuals and families making the housing choices. The desire for privacy from those outside the household is very important and has a direct impact on the design of subdivisions, apartment developments, condominiums, etc.

Privacy from outsiders can be achieved in two major ways: (a) separating dwellings by means of open space surrounding each unit, and (b) walls or fences for visual separation.[77] Of course there are many combinations of these methods as well as various means of applying each one. It may not be necessary to build a privacy wall if the designer arranges multifamily units such that the windows of one dwelling do not face directly into the windows of another. Well-planned siting of housing units can provide effective privacy even where density is high.

The home is a reflection of the family who lives there. However, attitudes about acceptable housing are influenced by advertising, salesmanship, and the communication media. People in our culture are conditioned to want a house form that enables family units to be

[75] Carl Danziger and Matthew Greenwald, *Alternatives: A Look at Unmarried Couples and Communes.* (New York: Institute of Life Insurance), 1975, p. 29.

[76] Rapoport, *op. cit.*, pp. 130–135.

[77] Wallace Smith, *Housing: The Social and Economic Elements.* (Berkeley, Calif.: University of California Press), 1971.

separate and unique entities with privacy and protection, but not so unique as to preclude resale.

The high-rise apartment does not include ownership of land—a value that permeates the American people. This lack of separate territorial identity impedes the acceptance of high-rise as the preferred home design.[78] Mobile homes are also viewed as failing to meet the true image of an acceptable home design, but they are a reasonable compromise for many lower-income families.

Homeownership has long been an important value in the American society and will no doubt remain important for a long time to come. It may be, however, that it is beginning to be replaced by some other symbols of status. Ownership of boats and trailers for leisure activities is rapidly gaining status. Vacation travel is also increasing as a symbol of status as families make the decision to invest their income in things other than homeownership. Sternlieb[79] points out that, although these other symbols are increasing in importance, the privately owned home is still the focal point of the myth or reality of the good life for the middle class and other classes that are desirous of moving upward.

As a society we have clung to the familiar forms of traditional architecture. Even the "new" housing design frequently turns out to be only a revival of earlier ideas. It is somewhat difficult to understand how, in an age of very rapid change in so many areas of life, housing can remain so traditional. Americans are inclined to consider the familiar styles to be the beautiful ones—an attitude which results in our living in a "sea of architectural imitation" as new materials are forced into old molds of the familiar house designs.

Changes in Environment and Technology

Obtaining control over the thermal environment has had measurable effects on the design of housing. In the early homes, rooms were planned around fireplaces which created drafts. In order to control these drafts, rooms were placed in cell-like compartments with tightly fitting doors. Hallways, located near the center of the house, provided access from room to room, but these were dark and drafty areas. The development of radiant and panel heating and other central heating systems eliminated the draft problem and increased the flexibility of room design along with the arrangement of furniture. By 1970, 43 percent of the homes were heated with warm-air furnaces and nearly 36 percent of the homes had air-conditioning.

[78] Cooper, *loc. cit.*, p. 134.

[79] George Sternlieb, "What Housing for Blue-Collar Workers?" In: Grant S. McClellan, *Crisis in Urban Housing*, The Reference Shelf, Vol. 45, No. 6. (New York: H. W. Wilson Co.), 1974, pp. 61–68.

Technological improvements in heating and cooling meant that climate could be all but disregarded. Stationary windows and walls of glass appeared more frequently. The housing which was indigenous to specific regions—such as the stone houses of Philadelphia or the adobe houses of New Mexico were found less often. Improvements in transportation made it possible to move materials easily from one area of the country to another, so builders were not limited to local materials. Respect for materials declined as synthetic materials were used for imitation of design from any part of the world. Today there are vast and meaningless imitations of past styles that show no sensitivity to how or why the style originally developed. Events such as these led Mumford[80] to conclude that the effect of technology has been to narrow the scope of individual taste and personality in home design to the point that many houses seem almost to oppose their natural habitat.

In spite of the technological skills that would make possible a variety of innovative forms, the sentimental attitude toward home, the preference for the familiar, and the resistance to change combined to encourage traditional design and construction methods. Changes in building technology, unlike changes in some other industries, have come so slowly that builders could assimilate them and yet not disturb the appearance of homes to a significant degree. Although the methods of planning and constructing houses have changed, the basic form and appearance of most houses today is not too dissimilar to those constructed at the beginning of the century.

There has long been a hope for some technological breakthrough that would greatly reduce the cost of housing construction and maintenance. Some new materials and methods have been developed, but no substantial cost reductions have occurred. Architects and builders have utilized a variety of approaches in their efforts to improve housing and reduce costs. These include: replacing single-family housing with high-rise or high-density cluster housing, developing total communities rather than just housing developments, stressing function rather than space, using prefabricated components, and constructing modular units, including the mobile home. The technology for modular construction (where room or sectional modules are completed at the factory, shipped to the site, placed on the foundation or framework for holding the units and connected to the utilities) is available, but only about 6 percent of all residential construction is of this type today.[81]

Operation Breakthrough, initiated by the Department of Housing and Urban Development in 1969, was an attempt to stimulate mass-

---

[80] Lewis Mumford, *Sticks and Stones*. (New York: Dover), 1955, p. 183.

[81] William Angell, "Housing Alternatives." In: Carol S. Wedin and L. Gertrude Nygren (eds.), *op. cit.*, p. 269.

produced housing technology. Federal funds supported the expenses of design and development of experimental projects and the construction of prototypes for mass-produced housing. Problems confronting the success of the program included the reluctance of manufacturers to produce housing for which there was no ready market (consumers are slow to accept the unusual in design), resistance from the construction labor unions, bureaucratic delay, and problems with obtaining financing. It was expected that plastics would be a promising building material for mass-produced housing, but the energy shortage has made plastics too expensive to be considered as a basic material. Although Operation Breakthrough was less than a complete success in terms of reducing the cost of housing through innovative construction techniques, it was successful in getting fragmented local building codes combined into uniform state housing codes in several locations. The former specification codes were changed to performance codes and factory-built housing was approved.

There was a rapid increase in the number of mobile home units produced from 1960 to 1970 (see Table 13–3). As a percentage of annual housing starts, mobile homes increased from 7.3 percent in 1960 to a high of 21.6 percent in 1973 before the decline began. This was the same time period in which multifamily housing production increased, and both of these housing construction activities were in response to the same demographic changes, increase in the number of persons in the 20- to 29-year age group and those over 65. The 1970 census revealed that mobile home dwellers were more likely to be in households which were smaller than the national average, had lower incomes, were under 37 years of age or over 55 years of age and were married. These families preferred mobile home living because of the low cost, ease of maintenance, and the financing package which includes house, furnishings, and appliances.

Designs of mobile homes have improved greatly during the last 15 years. They have increased in length and width, developed clearly distinguishable separate rooms in the interior with one or more bathrooms, and incorporated new materials and fabrication techniques to create a home that arrives fully equipped with furnishings, interior finishing, and appliances. Double-wide and expansible units were available in 1962, and by 1967 the length of the units had increased up to 64 feet. The 14-foot wide mobiles were in production by 1969 and increased in popularity into the 1970's as highway restrictions lessened to permit movement of these wider units. The plywood and canvas structures of the early years have been replaced by units with aluminum skins, drywall construction on interior walls and ceiling, increased fireproofing and soundproofing, and increased weight to resist windgusts. The units still have wheels but Bair describes the wheels as "increasingly vestigial remnants"[82] since 85 percent of the units in use today are permanent homes and 60 percent have never been moved.[83] The double-wide units, some containing over 2,000 square feet of living space, are being placed on prepared foundations which make them all but indistinguishable from many one-story prefabricated or even conventionally built structures.

Mobile home parks, which were formerly seas of mud with no drainage facilities or rubbish disposal sites, have undergone changes too. Parks were, and in many areas still are, zoned out of urban areas and forced to remain at the periphery of the city. Politically, changes in local zoning and building codes are encouraging attractive mobile home park development on choice locations within the confines of the city.[84] This process will be further enhanced by the 1975 Housing and Urban Development regulations for the construction of parks. Newer parks resemble planned-unit developments, and in some cases it is difficult to distinguish one from the other.

Family income in relation to the cost of conventional housing construction in comparison with the selling price of mobile homes has direct influence on the mobile home demand. Rapidly rising construction wages, land cost, and raw material prices have put conventional housing costs beyond the reach of lower-income families. The median sales price for new homes was around $20,000 in 1960 and had risen to $32,000 in 1973 and to over $44,000 by 1976. Mobile homes are one of the few new home alternatives available under $20,000, and by 1974 over 90 percent of the homes sold under $20,000 were mobile homes. Many American families have been forced to redirect their desire for a single-family conventional home to ownership of a mobile home. Ownership of an independent single-family home is an important social value in America, and our consumption orientation keeps us interested in the newest products available. The idea of being able to purchase a somewhat less expensive single-family mobile home and trade it in for a newer one at a later date has contributed to the growing demand for mobiles. Until recently, control over production standards for mobile homes has been weak or nonexistent, and design quality has been minimal. The recent regulations for controlling the quality of construction of mobile units and the design of parks should reduce some of the earlier problems with mobile homes.

The cost of new homes has been skyrocketing during recent years, but new houses have increased in size considerably. Probably half the

[82] Frederick H. Bair, Jr. "Mobile Homes—A New Challenge." In: Robinson Everett and John Johnston (eds.), *Housing*. (Dobbs Ferry, N.Y.: Oceana Publications), 1968, p. 100.

[83] Davidson, *op. cit.*, p. 14.

[84] *Ibid.*, p. 139.

increase in price of new homes stems from the fact that the homeowners are getting bigger and better equipped homes; homes are now about 50 percent larger than they were in 1950 and they include many built-in appliances. However, this trend toward larger and more mechanically equipped homes may change drastically as a result of the energy crisis. Limited energy supply has caused the cost of utilities to rise by about 200 percent since 1967. Such a drastic increase in cost to homeowners and renters has encouraged builders to work toward the production of "energy-efficient" homes that are fully insulated, smaller in size, and equipped with less mechanical equipment. Considerable work is being done with alternate sources of energy for home heating and cooling— solar seems to be the most likely substitute energy source at the present time.

The attitudes of the lending agencies who provide money for home mortgages greatly influence the design of homes in the United States even though the lenders have no training in design nor experience in building. Lenders encourage uniformity and mediocrity in design because they are more inclined to lend money on a house that is known to be a good risk—one that is considered a "safe investment." Both Federal Housing Administration and Veterans Administration inspection and appraisal practices are known for their aversion to any design innovation and have been strong influences on the design of suburban development homes in particular. Builders have found it easier to repeat an approved formula which they know will be approved by lenders. FHA codes have been partially responsible for creating the balcony disease in apartment buildings. A balcony counts as a room for FHA loan purposes. Since the builder can get a loan allowance of twice the cost of constructing the balcony, it is no wonder that balconies have appeared on apartments in Alaska.[85]

Public Housing Design in Recent Years

Marie McGuire, as Public Housing Commissioner, began to push for better design in public housing. In her 1961 annual report she discussed the lack of imagination and institutional appearance of public housing. She then hired "imaginative architects" and made them available to local housing authorities. Although some better-designed projects resulted from this effort, there is still a long way to go. The improved designs won plaudits and architectural awards, but this backfired because they drew criticism by those who felt that the poor did not deserve well-designed housing. Public housing should be designed only to the level of minimum social acceptability.

[85] John B. Halper, "The Influence of Mortgage Lenders on Building Design." In: Everett and Johnson (eds.), *op. cit.*

The housing acts of 1961, 1965, and 1968 did try some new approaches to remedying the deficiencies experienced in public housing of the 1950's. The 1961 Housing Act sought to upgrade quality in existing large projects by providing neighborhood facilities, stores, and commercial centers. Various devices were employed to break away from the old patterns of large, high-rise projects. "Vest pocket projects" were built on small scattered sites along established streets or on scattered vacant lots. Some of these were even designed to blend into existing neighborhoods. Other programs completely bypassed the construction of special public housing projects by leasing apartments in private housing with the local authority paying the difference between market rent and what the tenant could afford to pay. The 1968 Act even specifically prohibited high-rise elevator projects for families with children unless there was no other practical alternative.

The only changes that were readily accepted by the general public have been extension of public housing opportunities to the elderly and handicapped. There are now federal regulations which require that public housing and other public buildings be accessible to the handicapped.

The desire for safe and secure neighborhoods is probably the single biggest cause of families leaving central cities. It would take major institutional changes to reduce the causes of crime—poverty, unemployment, urban decay—or to improve police and justice systems for deterring crime. Oscar Newman's[86] research suggests that opportunity to commit crime can be reduced by housing design that does not require any major institutional changes. The single family house provides buffers or boundaries for a strong sense of ownership and involvement with the dwelling. Many public housing tenants have similar desires to show the same proprietary concern for the environments as do middle-class homeowners. However, the design of most public housing prohibits or at least discourages tenants from exhibiting this proprietary behavior. New advocates of public housing encourage design that would foster territoriality, a sense of community, and surveillance of intruders. This can be accomplished by design which clearly specifies areas as belonging to a dwelling unit, as private space, while other areas are designed to be semiprivate or public. Entrances should serve a limited number of apartments and stairways or elevators should be attached to short hallways on each floor. In this way the entrance to a cluster of apartments becomes the territory of the residents. Newman's basic premise is that housing projects should be designed so that paths of movement into and out of the various territorial zones of activity

[86] Oscar Newman, *Defensible Space*. (New York: Macmillan), 1973.

are under constant surveillance of the residents as they perform their day-to-day activities.

As human needs change in their societal context, so must the design of shelter change. Housing design is a consequence of a whole range of sociocultural factors which occur in a broad ecological context. The evaluation of housing as a process occurring within an ecological system illuminates the interrelatedness between the individual or family unit, the natural and man-made environment, the social organization, and the level of technology available at any point in time.

Bibliography

ABRAMS, CHARLES, *Man's Struggle for Shelter in an Urbanizing World.* Cambridge, Mass.: M.I.T. Press, 1966.

———, *The Future of Housing.* New York: Harper and Row, 1946.

AGAN, TESSIE and ELAINE LUCHSINGER, *The House.* Philadelphia: Lippincott, 1965.

ALEXANDER, HAROLD H., *Design: Criteria for Decisions.* New York: Macmillan, 1976.

ALLEN, EDWARD (ed.), *The Responsive House.* Cambridge, Mass.: M.I.T. Press, 1972.

ALPAUGH, DAVID (ed.), *Design and Community.* (Student Publication of the School of Design.) Raleigh: University of North Carolina, 1970.

American Public Health Association, Committee on the Hygiene of Housing, *Planning the Home for Occupancy,* Public Administration Service, Washington, D.C., 1950.

BAUER, CATHERINE, *Modern Housing.* Boston: Houghton Mifflin, 1934.

BEALE, CALVIN L., "Population and Employment Patterns Affecting Rural Housing." From proceedings of conference on "Quality Housing Environment for Rural Low-Income Families." Atlanta, September 1975.

BECKER, FRANKLIN D., *Design for Living.* Ithaca, N.Y.: Cornell University Press, 1975.

BENEVOLO, LEONARDO, *History of Modern Architecture.* Vol. 2: *The Modern Movement.* Cambridge, Mass.: M.I.T. Press, 1971.

BEYER, GLENN H., *Housing and Society.* New York: Macmillan, 1970.

———, *Housing: A Factual Analysis.* New York: Macmillan, 1958.

———, T. W. MACKESEY, and J. E. MONTGOMERY, *Houses Are for People.* Ithaca, N.Y.: Cornell University Press, 1955.

BIRCH, DAVID (Principal Investigator), *America's Housing Needs: 1970 to 1980.* Cambridge, Mass.: Joint Center for Urban Studies of the Massachusetts Institute of Technology and Harvard University, 1973.

BOTT, ELIZABETH, *Family and Social Network.* London: Tavistock, 1971.

BURGESS, ERNEST W. and HARVEY J. LOCKE, *The Family, From Institution to Companionship.* New York: American, 1945.

DANZIGER, CARL and MATHEW GREENWALD, *Alternatives: A Look at Un-*

married Couples and Communes. New York: Institute of Life Insurance, 1975.

DAVIDSON, HAROLD A., *Housing Demand: Mobile, Modular or Conventional?* New York: Van Nostrand-Reinhold, 1973.

DIXON, JOHN M., "Housing Choices." *Progressive Architecture*, March 1976, p. 39.

EVERETT, R. O. and J. D. JOHNSTON (eds.). *Housing.* Dobbs Ferry, N.Y.: Oceana Publications, 1968.

EWALD, WILLIAM R., JR. (ed.), *Environment for Man.* Bloomington, Ind.: Indiana University Press, 1967.

FITCH, JAMES MARSTON, JR., *American Building 1: The Historical Forces That Shaped It.* Boston: Houghton Mifflin, 1966.

FOOTE, N. N., J. ABU-LUGHOD, M. M. FOLEY, and L. WINNICH, *Housing Choices and Housing Constraints.* New York: McGraw-Hill, 1960.

FREEDMAN, LEONARD, *Public Housing: The Politics of Poverty.* New York: Holt, Rinehart and Winston, 1969.

FRIED, JOSEPH P., *Housing Crisis U.T.A.* New York: Praeger, 1971.

GANS, HERBERT J., *People and Plans.* New York: Basic Books, 1968.

GIEDION, SIEGFRIED (ed.), *A Decade of Architecture.* Zurich: Editions Girsberger, 1951.

GIEDION, SIEGFRIED, *Mechanization Takes Command.* New York: Oxford University Press, 1948.

GLAAB, CHARLES N. and A. THEODORE BROWN, *A History of Urban America.* New York: Macmillan, 1967.

GOTTLIEB, L. D., *Environment and Design in Housing.* New York: Macmillan, 1965.

GOWANS, ALAN, *Images of American Living.* New York: Lippincott, 1964.

GREEN, CONSTANCE M., *The Rise of Urban America.* New York: Harper and Row, 1965.

HAMLIN, TALBOT, *Architecture Through the Ages.* New York: Putnam, 1953.

HARRISON, HENRY S., *Houses.* National Institute of Real Estate Brokers of the National Association of Realtors, 1973.

HARTMAN, CHESTER W., *Housing and Social Policy.* Englewood Cliffs, N.J.: Prentice-Hall, 1975.

HATJE, GERD and URSULA HATJE, *Design for Modern Living.* New York: Harry N. Abrams, 1962.

HAWLEY, AMOS H., *Human Ecology.* New York: Ronald Press, 1950.

HODGELL, MURLIN, "Today's House." *Journal of Home Economics*, Vol. 44, No. 2, February 1952, pp. 94–96.

HOLLAND, LAURENCE B. (ed.), *Who Designs America?* Garden City, N.Y.: Doubleday, 1966.

HONIKMAN, BASIL (ed.), *Responding to Social Change.* Stroudsburg, Pennsylvania: Dowden, Hutchinson and Ross, 1975.

JOEDICKE, JURGEN, *A History of Modern Architecture.* New York: Praeger, 1959.

JOHNSTON, R. J., *Urban Residential Patterns.* New York: Praeger, 1971.

JONES, CRANSTON, *Architecture Today and Tomorrow*. New York: McGraw-Hill, 1961.

KELLY, BURNHAM AND ASSOCIATES, *Design and the Production of Houses*. New York: McGraw-Hill, 1959.

KEYSERLING, LEON H., *The Coming Crisis in Housing*. Washington, D.C.: Conference on Economic Progress, 1972.

KOUSKOULAS, VASILY (ed.), *Urban Housing*. Detroit: Wayne State University, 1973.

LANG, JON (ed.), *Designing for Human Behavior*. Stroudsburg, Pennsylvania: Dowden, Hutchinson, and Ross, 1974.

LAWTON, M. POWELL, *Planning and Managing Housing for the Elderly*. New York: Wiley, 1975.

LEDBETTER, WILLIAM H., JR., "Public Housing—A Social Experiment Seeks Acceptance." In: Robinson O. Everett and John D. Johnson, Jr. (eds.), *Housing*. Dobbs Ferry, N.Y.: Oceana Publications, 1968.

McCLELLAN, GRANT S. (ed.), *Crisis in Urban Housing*. New York: Wilson, 1974.

MARSTON, JAMES, JR., *American Building 2: The Environment Forces That Shape It*. Boston: Houghton Mifflin, 1972.

MICHELSON, WILLIAM, *Man and His Urban Environment*. Reading, Mass.: Addison-Wesley, 1970.

———, "Potential Candidates for the Designer's Paradise, A Social Analysis from a Nationwide Survey." *Social Forces*, Vol. 46, 1967, pp. 190–196.

MUMFORD, LEWIS, *From the Ground Up*. New York: Harcourt Brace Jovanovich, 1965.

———, *Roots of Contemporary American Architecture*. New York: Grove Press, 1959.

———, *Sticks and Stones*. New York: Dover, 1955.

MYERSON, M., B. TERRETT, and W. L. C. WHEATON, *Housing, People, and Cities*. New York: McGraw-Hill, 1962.

The National Housing Conference, *The Housing Yearbook*. Washington, D.C., 1963.

NATTRASS, K. and B. M. MORRISON (eds.). *Human Needs in Housing: An Ecological Approach*. Millburn, N.J.: R. F. Publishing, 1975.

NELSON, G. and H. WRIGHT, *Tomorrow's House*. New York: Simon and Schuster, 1946.

NEUTZE, MAX, *The Suburban Apartment Boom*. Baltimore, Md.: Johns Hopkins Press, 1968.

NEWMAN, OSCAR, *Defensible Space*. New York: Macmillan, 1973.

PAWLEY, MARTIN, *Architecture Versus Housing*. New York: Praeger, 1971.

PERIN, CONSTANCE, *With Man in Mind*. Cambridge, Mass.: M.I.T. Press, 1972.

PICKERING, ERNEST, *The Homes of America*. New York: Bramhall, 1951.

PYNOOS, J., R. SCHAFER, and C. W. HARTMAN (eds.). *Housing in Urban America*. Chicago: Aldine, 1973.

RABENECK, ANDREW, DAVID SHEPPARD, and PETER TOWN, "The Structuring of Space in Family Housing: An Alternative to Present Design

Practice." In: K. Nattrass, *Human Needs in Housing: An Ecological Approach*. R. F. Publishing Co., Inc., Millburn, N.J., 1975, pp. 195–202.

RAPOPORT, AMOS, *House Form and Culture*. Englewood Cliffs, N.J.: Prentice-Hall, 1969.

RICHARDS, J. M., *An Introduction to Modern Architecture*. Baltimore, Md.: Penguin, 1965.

ROGERS, KATE ELLEN, *The Modern House, U.S.A.* New York: Harper and Row, 1962.

RYDER, SHARON LEE, "Upstairs Downstairs." *Progressive Architecture*, March 1976, pp. 40–41.

SAFDIE, MOSHE, *Beyond Habitat*. Cambridge, Mass.: M.I.T. Press, 1973.

SCULLY, VINCENT, *American Architecture and Urbanism*. New York: Praeger, 1969.

SMITH, WALLACE F., *Housing*. Berkeley, Calif.: University of California Press, 1971.

SOMMER, ROBERT, *Personal Space*. Englewood Cliffs, N.J.: Prentice-Hall, 1969.

STEPHENS, SUZANNE, "Unheavenly Cities?" *Progressive Architecture*, March 1976, pp. 58–60.

TUNNARD, CHRISTOPHER and HENRY H. REED, *American Skyline*. Boston: Houghton Mifflin, 1955.

U. S. Bureau of the Census. *Census of Housing: 1970. Volume I, Housing Characteristics for States, Cities, and Counties. Part I United States Summary*. Washington, D.C.: U. S. Government Printing Office, 1972.

————, *Census of Population: 1970. Volume I, Characteristics of the Population. Part A, Number of Inhabitants. Section 1—United States, Alabama—Mississippi*. Washington, D.C.: U. S. Government Printing Office, 1972).

————, *We, The Americans: Our Homes*. No. 3 Report, 1970 Census. Social and Economic Statistics Administration, Washington, D.C.: Government Printing Office, October, 1972.

————, *US Census of Housing: 1960. Volume I, States and Small Areas. Part I: United States Summary*. Washington, D.C.: U. S. Government Printing Office, 1963.

Urban Housing and Residence in the 1970's. *American Institute of Planners Journal*. September 1974, Vol. 40, p. 306.

WEDIN, C. S. and L. G. NYGREN, *Housing Perspectives*. Minneapolis, Minn.: Burgess, 1976.

WEIMER, A. M., "Future Factors in Housing Demand: Some Comments." In: *Essays in Urban Land Economics*. Los Angeles: University of California, 1966.

WHEATON, W. L. C., G. MILGRA, and M. E. MEYERSON (eds.), *Urban Housing*. New York: Free Press, 1966.

WINCH, R. F. and L. W. GOODMAN, *Selected Studies in Marriage and the Family*. New York: Holt, Rinehart and Winston, 1968.

WINNICK, LOUIS, *American Housing and Its Use*. New York: Wiley, 1957.

YORKE, F. R. S., *The Modern House*. London: Architecture Press, 1957.

CHAPTER 14

WORLD HOUSING TODAY

THOMAS R. CALLAWAY*

* THOMAS R. CALLAWAY is Director of the Technology and Documentation
Division of the Office of International Affairs, Department of Housing and Urban
Development (HUD). He was trained as an architect, interior designer, and

(*Continued*)

Introduction

WITH today's rapid communications, we live in an age of awareness of global problems. When we speak seriously of food, population or shelter, it is no longer in the context of our community, nation, or even of our continent. As never before, we are aware of the interrelationship of nations and people, who, in spite of differences in history, religion, economic means, or political beliefs, find themselves facing common problems and the need to share solutions. While many aspects of life have improved considerably with the passage of time, some of those most basic to existence and well-being leave large questions to be answered. Among the latter is shelter. Since the United Nations began to record the extent and quality of development in worldwide family shelter two decades ago, the picture has worsened considerably—particularly in the less developed countries, which make up a large part of the world's geography.

Looking at probable changes between now and the year 2000, urban population in presently rural developing countries will triple, so that some 65 percent of their citizens will be living in urban centers by the end of this century. Urban infrastructure, which was designed to handle a 2 to 4 percent increase in annual shelter needs, now faces as much as a 12 percent annual increase. To meet this need, some 8 to 10 units per year per 1,000 population would have to be built in much of the developing world. (Some 8 units per 1,000 population are built each year in Europe.) The fact, however, is quite different for most of the world's 4 billion people: only 2 to 5 units per 1,000 population are actually being built. This means that, in urban areas alone, the worldwide housing deficit is growing at the rate of some 4 to 5 million units per year.

Where do these people go? Squatter settlements, which may be known as barrios or bidonvilles, are home for many millions. Others are absorbed into existing dwellings, often with densities allowing only a floor space for sleeping, and little or nothing in the way of sanitary and other facilities. According to United Nations studies, such overcrowding in urban centers has reached 63 percent in El Salvador, 48 percent in Sri Lanka, and 47 percent in Zambia.[1] While not having a significant squatter problem, Europe is not free of overcrowding,

---

1 World Housing Survey, United Nations, 1974.

---

cartographer. He has traveled and worked in some 55 countries in Europe, Africa, Latin America, and the Near and Far East, and has published monographs, articles, and technical references on subjects ranging from codes and standards to rural/urban migration.

which reportedly reaches 17 percent in Poland and 15 percent in Yugoslavia. To keep these figures in perspective, it must be remembered that the United Nations measure of overcrowding is based on an occupancy of more than three persons per habitable room. Only North America and much of Europe escape this manifestation of rapid urban growth, which, while less obvious than squatter settlement, leaves everything to be desired.

Another problem of overcrowding not necessarily based on massive numbers per dwelling relates to new family formations. In much of the world, a newly married couple may have to look forward to 3 to 10 years of living with the family of one of the parents before there is real hope of acquiring an apartment, much less a detached dwelling, of their own.

A fact not addressed by the "more than three per room" measure is the size of the room itself. In Eastern Europe and elsewhere where production of units rather than quality of shelter has been the guideline, room size and services have been minimal. Those who think in terms of a United States "standard FHA dwelling" are dealing with a third to 50 percent more space and utilities than many other industrialized nations, and three to five times the space and amenities provided under the best public programs of most developing countries.[2]

Because most new urban dwellers cannot achieve even these more modest standards, it is useful to look at squatter settlements, where 25 square feet per person would be considered a luxury. United Nations studies indicate that 90 percent of Addis Ababa, 61 percent of Accra, 31 percent of Pusan, 61 percent of Calcutta, 60 percent of Ankara, 30 percent of Rio de Janiero, 60 percent of Bogota, and 72 percent of Santo Domingo are squatters.

To provide perspective, this means that 612,000 of Addis Ababas' 900,000 inhabitants live in mud and wattle dwellings, and 5.3 million persons in Calcutta live in slums with "one room or less per family."

It is in such squatter settlements that the majority of urban growth will continue to take place. As a result, it is not difficult to see that the poor—people with few material resources and no salable urban skills— can account for as much as 50 percent of urban population.

The rate of urban growth is revealing if we consider that, worldwide, urban dwellers accounted for 19 percent of the population in the 1920's, and 37 percent in the mid-1970's. It is estimated that this will be 50 percent before the year 2000. For the less developed areas, the urban population was only 8 percent in the 1920's.[3] Thus, no matter how disturbing today's figures may be, plans for realistic solutions

[2] United Nations estimate.
[3] World Housing Survey, United Nations, 1974.

must take into account the fact that meeting today's housing needs is only a beginning—that, in fact, due to rural-to-urban migration and general population growth, housing needs in much of the world will not have leveled off much before the end of the century.

Factors in Housing Production

"What is it going to cost me for shelter?" This question is asked by millions every day, and the answers that come back are in many forms. In many instances, the answer is "More than you can afford," but it may also be "There is not adequate housing production even if you can afford it." To oversimplify, the problems of finance for persons or governments generally fall into three categories. First, of course, is having too few resources. This may stem from an absolute absence of resources or a lack of institutional framework in which to generate savings, form policy, create an "industry," and produce shelter.

Second, there is the question of priority. Economists have only recently recognized the fact that housing is an integral part of development. A recent United Nations survey confirms what has long been known in the international construction community. Construction accounts for at least half of domestic fixed capital formation, essentially independently of the level of development. Of this figure, 20 to 50 percent is in housing, with the higher percentages in less-developed areas. Some 50 to 55 percent of industrial production is related to the building industry, and 6 to 15 percent of the labor force is in construction, with the higher labor figure in industrialized countries.[4] The low figure of construction employment in less-developed areas is deceiving, in that it refers to an industry sector, and does not include the millions of human-years invested in self-help construction, largely in the family housing category.

The third factor relates to the balance of resources and standards. Stemming from national pride, social concern or political considerations, most governments find it difficult or impossible to admit that anything less than a "standard house" should be built for the less advantaged when using government funds. While commendable in intent, the result is the provision of a fairly high standard of shelter for a few and frustrated hopes for many. A more realistic approach, benefiting much greater numbers of families, is seen in the sites-and-services programs sponsored by the World Bank, United States Agency for International Development, and increasing numbers of local governments. While not providing shelter in its first stage, this approach results in all-important land tenure which is an incentive to maximum self-help efforts and

4 United Nations International Labor Organization estimate.

provides the basis for more formalized housing finance as resources of the individual, or the government, increase.

Institutional Arrangements

The institutional question is of prime importance. Realistically, housing finance must depend chiefly on national resources, both because of the volume of funds required, and the highly local nature of labor and material needs. While external loans and grants are useful as "seed capital" or "pump priming" during the initial institution building phase, the scale supported by external assistance is at the project, rather than the program level. External grants are of necessity small, and loans of sufficient magnitude for program operations place a long-term drain on the national economy, and may, in fact, deplete local resources necessary to meet future needs.

The most successful institution to date for generating local savings for housing of middle-income families is the savings and loan association. American technical assistance from the National and U. S. savings and loan leagues and HUD, through the Agency for International Development (AID), as well as seed loans from AID, resulted in the creation of a broadly based savings and loan system in Latin America.

More than 200 savings and loan associations are active in Latin America, ranging from one in Panama with 27,500 savers and 1,000 units[5] financed to 80 associations in Brazil, with 5,700,000 savers and 345,000 units financed. Other countries utilizing savings and loan associations include Argentina, Bolivia, Chile, Colombia, Costa Rica, the Dominican Republic, El Salvador, Paraguay, Peru, and Venezuela. They represent 8.5 million savers with $4.2 billion in current savings, and have financed some 783,900 units with a loan value of $6 billion. United States technical assistance has also been used to provide the basis for savings and loan systems in Ethiopia, Ivory Coast, Nigeria, and Zaire.

Because savings and loan associations are essentially "high overhead" institutions, and because they must normally answer to a board of directors for the state of their investment portfolio, the system has not provided housing for truly low-income families. However, in providing private sector financing for large numbers of middle-income homes, it has dramatically reduced the need for government support in this area. In addition, these associations provide a major reservoir of experience in handling large numbers of mortgages in a number of countries.

Commercial banks have been involved in limited housing financing in most areas of the world. By definition, a commercial bank is best

[5] Units include both single-family detached dwellings and apartments.

geared to individual, short-term, relatively high interest rate, sound risk transactions. As a result, the fact that such banks have not entered the low-income housing field on a large scale is not surprising. This is particularly the case in developing countries, which have few sources of funding for commercial and industrial activity, and which lack experience with large-scale mortgage portfolios.

To qualify for housing loans, borrowers from commercial banks in Africa and Latin America must often make down payments of up to 50 percent and repay their loans in a period of three to five years. In such countries as Botswana, Gambia, and Liberia, which lack alternative funding institutions, commercial banks have been a major source for middle-income housing.

Cooperatives as focal points for savings as well as management have proven useful to middle- to lower-middle-income families. Chile, Colombia, Egypt, Ghana, Tunisia, Uganda, and Tanzania are among the countries using cooperatives for this purpose. In Egypt, for example, one report indicates that the Egyptian Cooperative Organization for Building and Housing provides 80 percent loans at 4.5 percent interest. Cooperatives have tended to be most appealing where government funding is provided. This form of group ownership, while offering overhead and management advantages (such as a single mortgage per project), does not have the appeal of individual ownership.

Insurance companies have entered the housing field in developing countries with market economies. They are popular sources for middle- and upper-income families in the Asian region, particularly in India, and in African countries, such as Kenya, have been found to be a useful support to the housing industry. Public and semipublic institutions are also being used extensively in Latin America, Asia, and to a lesser extent in Africa. Costa Rica established its National Institute of Housing and Urban Affairs (INVU) in 1954 to provide direct construction loans. El Salvador's system utilizes its savings and loan institutions to facilitate loans to low-income families. By broadening their loan base, the number of savers rose by 7,000, and loans increased by 670 in a nine-month period. The Singapore Housing and Development Board built 220,000 new subsidized housing units during the period 1960–1975 for its city of 2.1 million people. Singapore places very heavy stress on housing, with almost one fifth of its total development expenditure being in this field.

For lower-income families, the incentive to save in an institutional framework depends largely on their ability to identify with the institutions in a personal way. As a result, credit unions, which can accept small deposits, provide small loans, and have officers elected from their membership, are finding wide use and have even greater potential.

"Friendly" or burial societies, originally formed to assure the necessary ceremonial at death, and depending for success on the good will of members, have used the lottery system to allocate limited resources for construction loans.

While these and other known systems will continue to provide resources for shelter, imagination and need will undoubtedly combine to create new institutions better suited to the needs of low-income families in developing areas. An essential element in such institutional development is the recognition of the fact that people can and do accomplish more for themselves than we generally recognize.

Role of the International Community

In light of the current and increasing magnitude of the world's shelter problem, what is the appropriate role of the international community, whether through bilateral or multilateral channels? In answer, we must acknowledge both the limitations to and opportunities for meaningful activity. In the long run, housing needs will be met through the use of local resources—utilizing largely local materials and technicians and implementing local policy—or they will not be met at all. Basically then, all we in the international community can do is help create or strengthen the capability of nations to deal with their own problems in what must ultimately be their own way.

Training and Institutional Development

Training of large numbers of professionals and subprofessionals is essential in all areas of the housing field, which ranges from policy formulation, design, industrial development, logistics, and construction supervision to finance and management. Selectivity both in types of training and location of training is essential. While certain types of professional training demand teaching skills and facilities available only in the United States and other industrialized nations, whenever possible, training should take place in the country concerned. The "brain drain," on one hand, and the degree of relevance of training to local problems, on the other, are two important factors. Where highly specialized facilities are not necessary, in-country training, with reduced cost of travel and maintenance, allows for participation by large numbers of students and reduces the time away from work involving those essential to continuing programs.

Institutional development is an important element of external assistance for most developing countries. Industrialized as well as less-developed countries look to the experience of other nations in creating new institutions or changing the direction of existing activities. Four elements are basic to such institutional transfer:

1. It must be done at an appropriate stage in development.

2. The basic potential or nature of the institution must reflect what is expected in the way of accomplishment in its new setting.
3. The institution transferred should be *adapted* to local conditions, and not adopted "whole cloth" without consideration of social, economic, and technological differences in the new setting.
4. New institutions should be complementary to other elements of local development. Duplication or imposition of activities locally unacceptable are counterproductive in any society.

Technology Transfer

Closely related to institutional development is the question of technology transfer. Given the desire to speed up development, a lack of understanding of economic and other implications of such transfer, and a tendency to adopt "prestige" technologies, "suitability" becomes the key factor.

What is suitable? That which is affordable by both nation and *end user*. That which is reproducible using a maximum of local human and material resources. That which will not only meet a need, but, often more important, a long-term *effective demand*, in terms of ability to produce, economically acquire, and maintain in sufficient volume to justify production relative to other needs of the society. A current example is industrialized building, which, in spite of its reputation, is frequently *not* less costly than conventional systems. Also, factory production, using a few relatively high-skilled persons, must be weighed against local levels of unemployment and underemployment. In addition, industrialized systems require continuing availability of long-term financing, good ancillary facilities, such as transportation and power, and consumer acceptability. Moreover, they often require costly importation of equipment, material, and personnel. On the other hand, adequate financial resources and scarce local labor may make such systems the ideal solution.

Very often, we tend to think only in terms of new or "advanced" technologies. Frequently, existing "intermediate" or less complex technologies offer the most satisfactory, as well as the most economic solution. Even "obsolete" or discarded technologies, resurrected in light of declining energy resources, due to a better understanding of the materials and processes involved, or due to our natural tendency to "reinvent the wheel," offer workable alternatives to societies at all levels of development. For example, at least two African countries are redeveloping their clay tile industry, which has been allowed to lie dormant in favor of imported materials. Such efforts will reduce the drain on hard currency, supply local jobs, and produce material with improved insulating and aesthetic qualities.

Technical Assistance and Information Exchange

Technical assistance is an essential factor in development. Among industrialized countries it is an accepted element in international trade, related to both goods and services. Among industrialized and less developed nations or institutions, it is the basic element in *gaining time* in "counterpart training," in adapting external technologies, processes, and management systems, and in developing local technologies and systems. To be effective, the "foreign" technician must be understanding of, and adaptive to, local mores, needs and desires, skills and materials. The effective technician does not impose, but determines what is most appropriate, in light of available human and material resources and acceptability. The effective technician must have the goal of literally "working himself or herself out of a job." At the end of the tour the technician must, if at all possible, leave behind the local ability to carry on the process or program which he or she came to initiate. To accomplish this end, the local government or institution has the responsibility of providing sufficient and appropriate counterparts and resources. While poor or inappropriate technical assistance can often be blamed for failure of programs, it is frequently a lack of local cooperation, policy support, or allocation of resources for long-term programs that lead to the real or apparent failure of technical assistance.

Information exchange is the least costly, and at the same time the most essential element of international cooperation. In fact, technical assistance and technology transfer are simply the more complex form of information exchange. The problem a few decades ago was the lack of information. Today, for those actively involved in the process, the problem is apparently an overabundance of information. Even within industrialized countries, problems of selectivity and evaluation of available data have become critical. For less-developed countries and institutions, indiscriminate information exchange can easily be more confusing than helpful. As a result, those providing data must be selective in what they provide, both in general content and suitability to the intended use. For industrialized nations, a large percentage of foreign data is acquired initially for analysis and research, with application to programs in light of comparable data a second phase of use. For developing countries, most data are acquired with the intention of more or less direct, and often immediate, application to a real problem for which no adequate local data are available.

Based on the foregoing, training must be considered with technology transfer and technical assistance as an element of information exchange, since local ability to evaluate and utilize acquired data provides its only value. Information which cannot be applied to real situations becomes part of an academic exercise which countries of the developing world can ill afford.

Research

Research is a tempting element in the information process. However, I have left research to last, because, relatively speaking, it is the least important, the most costly, and the most abused. The greatest problem with research is that it often becomes an end in itself, with no hope, or intent, for immediate application to real problems. As a result, much research can be justified and rejustified as successful when, in fact, only application at some future date can prove or disprove its real value.

The fact is that our "how to" knowledge has far outpaced our ability to apply this knowledge productively. For the most part, the technology of how to build our needed housing already exists. The fact that a particular technique is not known where it is needed does not necessarily justify expenditure of scarce local resources for reinvention—it does call for a more effective means of information exchange, based on a general knowledge of "who has done what."

What is generally lacking is policy, an institutional base, trained and experienced professionals, knowledge of the means for better use of available material resources, or the means of generating adequate capital resources. The research needed in most of these instances is a determination of the most appropriate existing means of supplying the deficient elements.

The foregoing does *not* mean that research as such is redundant or undesirable. It does mean that research should be used to fill *gaps* in knowledge after every reasonable attempt has been made to determine, in light of *international* experience, that a gap actually exists. Research is also justifiable out of sheer curiosity, where resources permit, in that there is always potential for a better way of doing almost anything. Nevertheless, while research is, in fact, an essential part of *long-term* development, it must not be allowed to become an end in itself, nor to actually retard development. More important, it must be recognized that very few items that we need in solving the *technical* or *institutional* aspects of world housing problems have not evolved and been tested somewhere at some time. This is true if we make the essential admission that the answer to housing needs for much of the world must be very basic, and must be measured in terms of improvement in quality of life, rather than attainment of some preconceived idea of what should constitute a "standard" dwelling.

The Matter of Financing

Lack of financial resources plagues all governments to some degree, and becomes a focal point of concern in providing for shelter in developing countries. However, while no one can argue away a very real capital resource problem, three facts must be faced.

First, the world's housing needs cannot and will not be met through *international* resources.

Second, the availability of money alone does not resolve the housing problem, which includes policy, institutional, industrial people, and time components.

Third, in light of the foregoing, even if unlimited economic resources were available, the solution to housing needs would be slow and of mixed quality. While this is stating the obvious, it bears restating that individuals and nations should not see a quick and easy solution to their needs in international funding.

Aside from sheer volume, which again is painfully obvious, shelter demands a high degree of local participation in materials and manpower, with large-scale investment over a long period of time. Because of increasing population, shifting of population location, and the inevitable (and desirable) increase in standards, the advisability of mortgaging a country's future access to the world money market to meet today's housing needs is questionable.

This does not mean that grants, loans, and guarantees presently available, or likely to be made available, should not play a role in international housing. On the contrary, "seed capital," or "pump priming," as it has been known, is a useful and legitimate means of producing and strengthening a nation's capacity to build an industry, accelerate the acquisition of essential experience, and, of great importance, facilitate the building of an institutional base essential to the generation of local capital.

The savings and loan industry, the credit union movement, housing cooperatives, and mortgage guaranty institutions, are all examples of successful local institution building through the use of external seed loans and technical assistance. With a few notable exceptions, external grants, loans, and guarantees should be complemented with appropriate technical assistance to assure the best use of these resources in building *long-term* capacity. This is the stated purpose of the recently created International Habitat and Human Settlement Foundation (IHHSF) and has been, historically, the basis of the more successful operation of the several regional development banks, the World Bank, the United Nations Development Programme (UNDP), and bilateral programs such as those of the Agency for International Development (AID).

In each of the successful international funding "experiments," whether based on the savings and loan, credit union, or cooperative approach, there was grave doubt as to availability of individual resources for savings. In each case it has been found that there are considerable local resources for saving *if* people are convinced that something can be gained by using the "new" institutions. Such examples of private enterprise have been successful where suspicion of government and traditional banks has kept resources "under the mattress," and has netted local moneylenders 20 percent and more in interest for improvements to squatter dwellings by those who "could not afford to borrow money." Whether expressed in savings or in self-help construction, proof is often provided that we were wrong to lack faith in people's own abilities and resources.

For those without an income of any sort—and for those of very small means—some level of subsidy is necessary. For those with very modest means, savings institutions with which they can identify, coupled with some level of self-help as part of what FHA once called "sweat equity" within an institutional framework tailored to a country's needs and abilities, *can* help to close the gap on the frightening statistics presented by the World Housing Surveys. In short, we must go back to the fact that, in the long run, housing needs will and can be met through the use of local resources, utilizing local materials and technicians, implementing local policy—or they will not be met at all.

Dozens of "world" institutions, scores of regional bodies, hundreds of bilateral arrangements, and many thousands of national and local agencies attempt to address some facet of housing need. No single list exists of the policy, professional, administrative, financial, research, industry, construction, sociological, legal, and management bodies that deal with this most complex and universal need. I will not pretend to provide such a list in this limited space. However, for those interested in additional data and other points of view, or who wish to study in depth this fascinating, frustrating, and yet rewarding field of international housing, I provide below a brief summary of some of the names, activities, addresses, and major publications of a few international institutions. Some are a part of the United Nations system, while others were created as a result of United Nations action or lack thereof. Others are nationally based, but serve a truly international audience, either as a part of our own or other nations' official aid programs, or because concerned professions or professionals determined that an international forum was essential to their own national growth. Not all are related directly to very low-income housing, but all have served, or could serve, as institutional models to meet some significant segment of housing need.

United States Involvement in International Housing

United States involvement in international housing has been extremely diverse and of relatively long standing. It has involved several federal government agencies, and numerous elements of the private sector, supported by AID contracts, foundation grants, or through the provision of professional services in the open market. In fact, the United States has provided the longest, most diversified and largest scale support to international housing of any nation in the world, particularly as related to aid to developing countries. While the volume of aid from United States (and all other) sources has provided only a fraction of the needed technical assistance, information, training and financial resources, the existing institutional capability of many developing nations to deal with their housing problems is due directly, or indirectly, to United States assistance or models. In addition, the resources of the United Nations system, the development banks, and voluntary organizations have, in large measure, come from United States aid allocations or voluntary contributions of United States citizens.

The following items on United States involvement do not cover the field. However, the examples chosen represent the most significant level of continuing activity. They also represent officially supported activities of the United States government in this critical field. The account begins with a partially historical note on HUD's international operations, since the Office of International Affairs was the pioneer, has provided continuity, and still represents considerable expertise in this field.

The Department of Housing and Urban Development

Involvement in international housing dates from the 1930's, when the then newly formed Federal Housing Administration (FHA) looked to European experience while formulating its own policies and administrative procedures. It was not until 1944, however, that a full-time international office was formed in the National Housing Agency (NHA) to supervise the export of technology, prefabricated units, and critical materials to Europe under what was to become the Marshall Plan. That same year, technical assistance was provided to less developed countries in South America, the Caribbean, Africa, and the Far East. In 1945, housing attaches were posted to London, Paris, and Rome. By 1946, the office was working with the United Nations and the Pan American Union, had instituted a program which arranged training for persons from 35 countries, and had stepped up its information and documentation program to less developed nations.

With establishment of the Housing and Home Finance Agency (HHFA) in 1947, work had already begun with the UN Economic Commission for Europe (ECE), and a reporting system was established in the U. S. Embassies abroad to provide a broad exchange. A 1949 directive from the Department of State reaffirmed the HHFA role in technical assistance and training under what was known as the Point Four Program. This began a more intensive era of activity, including the dispatch of a reconstruction team to Germany, and assistance in establishment of the Inter-American Housing Research and Training Center (CINVA) in Bogota, Colombia, as well as technical assistance to countries of the Near East and Latin America.

While HHFA was continuing technical assistance, documentation, and training, in 1954 the Foreign Operation Administration (FOA) assumed administrative responsibility for the housing component of United States foreign assistance. The following year, the first formal operating agreement with FOA was signed in the form of a Participating Agency Service Agreement (PASA).

In 1956, the HHFA international staff was known as International Housing Services (IHS). The International Cooperation Administration (ICA) was then a year old, having replaced FOA. Professionals from IHS represented the United States in a number of international organizations, assisted in establishment of both government and private organizations in the international field, and, in 1959, became, for a few years, the U. S. secretariat for the International Council for Building, Research Studies and Documentation (CIB).

Following the renaming of the staff as the Office of International Housing (OIH), continuity in staff and programs was maintained to service the Agency for International Development which succeeded ICA. During this period, the emphasis was on self-help, improved use of indigenous materials, training of local professionals, and the establishment of basic housing finance and administrative institutions.

Beginning in 1964, an international operation was undertaken within FHA for the sole purpose of providing feasibility review and other services in support of AID's Housing Investment Guaranty Program (HIG). More than a hundred projects were processed before AID's own staff and private sector contract institutions absorbed this duty in 1969.

Role of the Office of International Affairs

In 1965, the Department of Housing and Urban Development was established as an Executive branch agency, and the designation of the Office of International Affairs was changed to the Division of International Affairs. (It was later to become the present Office of International Affairs.) This change recognized a broadened interest in the international program which had been growing for some time. It resulted from the need to deal with urban development as a whole, rather than housing as a separate process. Programs continued to deal with self-help and basic construction technologies, but now included planning, secondary housing finance, and concern for community development in the broader sense. The Office continued to provide United States positions on international urban matters, participated in and led delegations to international organizations, and began selectively entering into more formal agreements for the exchange of technical information and expert teams in areas of mutual interest.

In 1972 a basic change took place in international operations due to government-wide reductions in personnel. With staff reduced by almost half, positions providing technical assistance and training, as well as in-house research and analysis units were eliminated. As a result, the program balance shifted to "import" of technology rather than "export" as had been the case, while the major emphasis was on aid to developing countries.

To facilitate the change in emphasis and compensate for reduced staff, the international information system was systematized and converted to a computer base for bibliographic and research purposes. The publications program was then broadened to concentrate on providing American users with information on foreign programs, research, calendars of international events, trade opportunities, in-depth studies on subjects of priority interest, detailed "country profiles," and accessions lists.

In five years, the circulation of basic documents increased from less than 1,000 to some 16,000. Some quarter of a million items are supplied on demand annually, with additional large numbers being supplied through the U. S. Government Printing Office and the National Technical Information Service. A basic technology series is maintained for developing country users, with many hundreds of requests being honored each year. The responses provided to such requests range from a single document or letter answering a technical question to, in one recent instance, several thousand documents for use in a regional United Nations program in the Far East.

Incoming foreign data are reviewed to glean possible innovative concepts, to meet program needs of specific HUD and private sector priorities, to service current research projects undertaken or funded by the Department, and for possible translation into the most used languages—French, Spanish, Russian, and German. Also sought is material of sufficient general interest to be published. Program and research professionals from other federal agencies, Congress, state and local governments, the design professions, professional and trade associations, and numerous other nongovernmental groups, as well as international organizations and foreign professionals, draw on the system.

Reflecting the dual role of the Office in serving United States needs and supporting foreign policy, the more formal bilateral agreements have been initiated from two points of view. At the request of the Department of State, HUD has entered into agreements with West Germany, France, Iran, Spain, and the USSR. The arrangements with the USSR include separate agreements covering environmental considerations and "Housing and Other Construction." In the cases of Sweden,

Japan, and the United Kingdom, HUD initiated agreements based solely on the mutual exchange of technical and program data. In all instances, every attempt is made to assure mutual benefit from such exchanges.

Participation in the United Nations Environmental Program (UNEP) and the International Referral Service (IRS), for which the Office of International Affairs is the U. S. subfocal point for Human Settlements data, are recent developments. Cooperation with the UN Center for Housing, Building and Planning, the Economic Commission for Europe (ECE), the Organization for Economic Cooperation and Development (OECD), Committee on the Challenges to Modern Society (CCMS), CIB, and others, date from the early days of these programs.

As the pioneer in international housing, HUD and its predecessor agencies have assisted in creating or strengthening a large portion of the institutions, both national and international, involved in the international housing process. While its own role with the developing world has changed, the Office has provided continuity, direction, and a valuable base of information and experience to the international housing process.

Agency for International Development (AID)

Beginning in the early 1950's, three entities—the Foreign Operations Administration (FOA), the International Cooperation Administration (ICA), and more recently the Agency for International Development (AID)—provided the administrative framework, loans, grants, guarantees, and much of the technical assistance in support of housing in developing countries. In the earliest days, earth construction, aided self-help, and basic institutional concerns constituted the focus of the program inherited in part from the Housing and Home Finance Agency.

While the program was worldwide, the greatest volume and variety of activity was in Latin America. Because the region was relatively advanced, it was possible to go into a "second generation" of institutional development fairly quickly. As a result, the savings and loan, mortgage insurance, and secondary market concepts took hold during the 1960's. The AID Housing Investment Guaranty (HIG) came into being during the same period, again with most of the activity in Latin America.

Through the 1950's and early 1960's, the emphasis was on technical assistance. With the emergence of the Alliance for Progress, regionalization of all AID activities by sector, and a shift to loans and guarantees as focal elements of the program, technical assistance in the housing sector began to decline. In the Far East, in such areas as Korea and the Philippines, an emphasis on planning and policy developed. In Africa, the early self-help programs gave way to the HIG program and limited institutional development related to savings and administrative institutions. However, recent developments, such as accelerated industrialization in the mideast oil countries in the 1970's, have caused a resurgence of concern for institutional development.

With the expansion and centralization of the HIG program, regional bureau activities in the housing field declined or disappeared during the late 1960's. A parallel development was a centralized Technical Assistance Bureau (TA), which, in spite of its name, was mainly concerned with research and policy. An office of Urban Development and an Office of Science and Technology within the Technical Assistance Bureau have addressed a number of issues related to housing from the broader perspective of urban development, and the special problem of material development and reconstruction following disaster. In the latter field, earthquakes and wind damage in such areas as Peru, Nicaragua, the Philippines, and Bangladesh led to contract research in structural systems, better use of earth in construction, and basic roofing materials. Over the years, AID and its predecessors provided hundreds of millions of dollars for housing low-income families through the agency's own efforts and through funding of the Inter-American Bank, the Social Progress Trust Fund, and others.

Because housing cannot stand on its own without basic utilities, communications, and some level of industrial development, AID Engineering, Community Development, and other AID components have made significant contributions to these areas of the housing field. One of the greatest problems related to the AID program, as well as other international efforts, has been the emphasis on sector rather than coordinated development. AID policy is currently being addressed toward rectifying this problem. Recent AID recognition of the urban poor as an area of emphasis, combined with coordinated development efforts, opens new possibilities in the shelter field.[6]

AID Housing Investment Guaranty Program (HIG)

In 1961 Congress authorized $10 million in guaranty authority for private investment in Latin American housing, to be administered by AID under the Foreign Assistance Act. As initially conceived, the Housing Investment Guaranty Program (HIG) was to provide pilot demonstration projects to illustrate means of producing dwellings on a large scale, provide pools of experience in dealing with large numbers of mortgages, promote the use of advanced technologies and involve United States builders in overseas activity. HIG effectively illustrated large-scale production and generated a pool of valuable experience with

[6] AID Handbook, *Urbanization and the Urban Poor*, May 1976.

mortgage lending, particularly through the newly created savings and loan institutions. The program soon lost its pilot demonstration image, and additional projects often were planned in a given country before initial projects were completed. American developers were involved in putting together all early projects.

Early in the 1960's authority was given for limited HIG activity in Africa and the Far East. This eventually resulted in programs in such places as Taiwan, Bangkok, Tunis, and Abidjan.

In 1965, Congress broadened the guaranty authority to promote projects involving local housing finance institutions, trade unions, co-operatives, lower-income housing, and local long-term investment.

By the mid-1960's, legislation was passed allowing investment of up to 1 percent of assets by the savings and loan industry in HIG projects, under the regulations of the Federal Home Loan Bank Board, and with a guaranty by AID. At this stage, the major banks began to play a lesser role, and the savings and loans entered the program on a scale which continued to meet demand under a billion dollar guaranty authority.

Current AID guaranty charges are normally near ½ of 1 percent, with a host country guaranty reducing the risk to AID. The competitive program has been phased out, and current loans are made to local institutions without the involvement of a United States developer.

In recent years, attempts have been made to reduce the cost of houses under the program, and to include basic land development, or "sites-and-services," for self-help builders. Institution-building aspects of the program have also been emphasized to promote long-term benefit.

The HIG program is currently administered on a worldwide basis by the AID Office of Housing, which was created for this purpose. The administrative and technical staff of the Office of Housing is supplemented by contracts with such organizations as the National Savings and Loan League and the Foundation for Cooperative Housing. These organizations provide services in Washington, D.C., function as members of feasibility teams to borrowing nations, and assist the regional operation of the Office of Housing. The program has a 1.2 billion dollar guaranty authority, $840 million of which has been committed to actual construction, in some 37 countries.

Overseas Private Investment Corporation (OPIC)

Originally an integral part of the Agency for International Development (AID), the Overseas Private Investment Corporation (OPIC) is currently a semiautonomous corporation utilizing guaranty authority under the Foreign Assistance Act. Authorized in 1969 to operate outside AID, the Corporation has, since 1974, participated with private insurers in the Overseas Investment Insurance Group. This group is comprised of 12 United States insurance companies and the Lloyds of London system.

The Board of Directors of OPIC is chaired by the Administrator of AID, and has its own President and Chief Executive Officer for Operations. The Under Secretary of State for Economic Affairs and the Under Secretary of Commerce represent U. S. government interests, but the majority of directors come from the private sector.

OPIC is a mechanism to use private United States capital for development in less industrialized nations. To date, some 80 developing countries have received services under the program, with the majority of activity in countries with per capita incomes of less than $450 per year. The program provides for development of local expertise, and incorporates a high level of local ownership and management of industrial projects of mutual interest to U. S. investors and the host country. Feasibility studies and monitoring services as a means of assuring that any project is, in fact, of interest and benefit to the host country.

OPIC guarantees are "specific risk" in nature, and cover expropriation, inconvertibility, war, revolution, or insurrection. This program has allowed a wide variety of United States private participation in industrial and social development programs.[7] While a major portion of activity has been in such areas as goods production, health care and general industry, road construction, water supply and other service areas, it has also facilitated housing development. There has been a limited involvement in construction financing, and the program has potential in the area of industrialized building and components manufacture. HIG and OPIC programs currently provide the only significant means of channeling United States private capital into housing and related programs in less developed countries.

Peace Corps

Since its inception in 1960, the Peace Corps has been involved in housing, basic utility, and related services programs in many parts of the developing world. Self-help housing, rural housing, housing for teachers, water supply, waste disposal, and the building materials industry have all played a role in the basic community development, and person-to-person programs typical of the agency. Attempts have been made over the years to increase the ratio of qualified professionals to volunteers in such fields as architecture, engineering, planning, and construction supervision. While such specialized recruitment has met with varying degrees of success, self-help and other shelter programs have continued as part of the community development effort—often carried out by enthusiastic and frequently successful amateurs.

[7] OPIC Annual Report, 1975.

The Peace Corps is known for its deliberate attempt to avoid bureaucracy—carried to the point of limiting involvement of individuals to
five years within the system. While this has led to a certain lack of
continuity and "recycling" of approaches to such matters as training,
technical support, and record keeping, the program maintains a great
deal of vitality and stays surprisingly close to its original concept.

Disaster relief is one of the many areas in which shelter programs
have involved fairly large numbers of volunteers. Earthquake, flood,
drought, hurricane, and aftermath of war have seen volunteers working
with both temporary shelters and permanent rehousing through organized self-help. These projects have ranged from very local efforts
involving one or a few volunteers and the inhabitants of a village or
neighborhood to large cooperative efforts with U. S. agencies, such as
AID, and international organizations, such as CARE, and various agencies of the United Nations. Housing of earthquake refugees in El
Salvador, housing for teachers in Gabon, and domestic water supply
in the Dominican Republic were among numerous projects in the
emergency field.

Organization of credit unions and cooperatives, housing management, home repair, home economics for newly settled rural/urban
migrants, rural housing in new settlements, and design of earthquake
and wind-resistant shelter are among the projects undertaken by volunteers as primary assignments, or as spare time efforts in "their" communities. Peace Corps volunteers are currently involved in more than
70 projects in the category of "Urban Development and Public Works"
in almost 40 countries, illustrating the potential of such "person-to-
person" activity.[8]

Federal National Mortgage Association (FNMA)

Popularly known as "Fannie Mae," the Federal National Mortgage
Association provides the essential service of buying and reselling a
large volume of mortgages in the open market in the United States,
thus allowing lending institutions to continue lending when their assets
might otherwise be tied up in existing portfolio and required reserves.
This has allowed excess lending power in one area of the country or
from other industries to bolster lending potential in an area of high
housing demand through a "secondary market" mechanism. This concept is an extremely important one for developing countries, whose
initial efforts in the mortgage lending field are, of necessity, small and
require imaginative means to sustain consistent, long-term potential.

FNMA has provided information, advisory services, and technical
assistance to developing countries, particularly in Latin America. Examples of activity include evaluation of mortgage lending institutions

8 *Peace Corps Annual Operating Report*, Fiscal Year 1975.

and practices in Guatemala, work with the Ministry of Planning in Colombia in establishing a savings and loan system, and regional and national seminars in a number of countries on the operations of a secondary mortgage system.[9] Many of FNMA's international operations are carried out under programs of AID. However, FNMA also participates in activities of international organizations and cooperates with private agencies overseas on its own behalf.

National Savings and Loan League (NSLL)

The National Savings and Loan League was one of the pioneer institutions which facilitated the establishment of the vigorous savings and loan (S&L) movement in Latin America, and, more recently, provided basic elements for a similar program in several African countries. The National League began its international operations in 1956 under the International Cooperation Administration, and has continued and broadened its program with AID.

Based on its experience in support of a significant part of the U. S. savings and loan industry, the first and most significant of the National League's overseas activities was the development of savings and loan systems in such countries as Costa Rica, the Dominican Republic, El Salvador, Guatemala, Honduras, Nicaragua, Panama, Argentina, Bolivia, Brazil, Chile, Colombia, Ecuador, Paraguay, Peru, and Venezuela, as well as Ethiopia, the Ivory Coast, Nigeria, and Zaire, and most recently Iran. National home finance systems have been assisted in some 21 countries. In addition, the National League has, under contract to AID, provided housing development feasibility studies in 27 countries and inspection of housing projects in 26 countries.

For example, consultation and technical assistance beginning in 1964 contributed to the formation of Brazil's savings and loan system, now the largest in South America. From 1971 to 1974, the National League maintained a regional office in Guatemala to provide construction inspection, project planning, and technical support to low- and middle-income housing projects financed by AID in Central America. The office is now located in Tegucigalpa, Honduras. A similar office was maintained in Tunisia until 1969. Washington-based staff have carried out housing surveys in such areas as Swaziland, Indonesia, and Kuwait.[10]

Foundation for Cooperative Housing (FCH)

The Foundation for Cooperative Housing (FCH) was created in 1950 as a research and educational organization to facilitate the de-

[9] FNMA Operating Report.
[10] National Savings and Loan League, Community Development Division, *Who We Are and What We Do.*

velopment of cooperatives in the United States. Working with low- and middle-income groups, FCH domestic programs dealt mainly with FHA-insured projects, but also worked with the Ford and other foundations on nonprofit housing and with such agencies as the Bureau of Indian Affairs on cooperative homeownership programs.

In 1962, the Agency for International Development (AID) contracted with FCH to carry out surveys in Latin America. Since then, FCH has worked with AID in many parts of the world on cooperatives, and in support of such programs as the Housing Investment Guaranty (HIG) Program. Aided self-help, housing finance, management, feasibility studies and general technical assistance have been carried out for AID and in cooperation with other agencies and AID contractors.[11]

Washington based, FCH has had staff on long-term assignments in various countries of Latin America and Africa, and numerous short-term assignments in both the Near and Far East.

The United Nations System

Many parts of the United Nations system address themselves to some elements of the world's housing problem. In addition to those described, specialized agencies and regional programs provide services basic to development of this sector. Because many of these services are not necessarily considered in the context of housing development, the "program" is not only extremely diverse, but is, for the most part, uncoordinated.

The UN Food and Agricultural Organization (FAO) has had minor activity in the rural housing field, and has provided food as incentive and subsistence for families involved in organizing self-help construction. The World Health Organization (WHO) and such regional bodies as the Pan American Health Organization (PAHO) provide essential research, technical assistance, and program funding in water supply and waste systems development and installation. The UN Conference on Trade and Development (UNCTAD) has potential for technology bodies that lack some expertise, or which do not have current activity complementary to housing development.

World Bank (International Bank for Reconstruction and Development—IBRD)

The World Bank (IBRD) provides the largest single multinational channel for development loans to less industrialized nations. It was established in 1945 as a part of the United Nations system. Powers of the Bank are vested in the Board of Governors, with one Governor

[11] *Two Decades of Cooperative Development*, Foundation for Cooperative Housing, Washington, D.C.

and one alternative from each member country. For operations, there are 20 Executive Directors, five of whom are elected by members having the largest number of shares, and the remaining 15 by the remaining members. The President is selected by the Executive Directors.

In providing infrastructure loans and related technical assistance, the IBRD concentrated on agricultural development, transportation, electrification, education, water supply, and similar programs. Because of the sheer magnitude of the problem and the traditional attitude of economists toward housing as a "social or consumer" area rather than as a development tool, the World Bank avoided investment in or serious consideration of the shelter field. In recent years, however, basic land development for self-help housing has become part of the IBRD program as "sites-and-services." Long-term plans of the Bank call for substantial expansion of sites-and-services, for which more than $100 million has already been loaned to such countries as Senegal, Korea, Jamaica, El Salvador, Nicaragua, Tanzania, Zambia, Botswana, and Indonesia.[12] With recent Housing Sector Policy statements, the Bank has opened the way for possible loans for conventional housing under certain circumstances.

The sites-and-services concept of the Bank is flexible enough to allow for varying kinds of self-help labor, for minimal services or sanitary "cores," and, in some cases for the first element of a basic dwelling. In all cases, it is recognized that the administration of such projects is extremely complex, and that technical assistance is required. In some instances, such technical assistance is included in the loan. While the sites-and-services approach has tremendous potential in view of the impossibility of providing all families with "standard shelter," much needs to be learned about the administration of such programs on a truly large scale. Undoubtedly, experience with the projects already committed and planned will affect the Bank's policy toward further ventures in the shelter field.

International Development Association (IDA)

The International Development Association is part of the "Bank Group," authorized in 1960. IDA can provide loans on somewhat more flexible terms than IBRD.

Some sites and services loans have been joint IBRD/IDA. IDA is governed by Officers of the World Bank.

International Finance Corporation (IFC)

The International Finance Corporation (IFC) is closely associated with the World Bank, but is a separate legal entity with its own funds. Its objective is to promote the growth of private enterprise. IFC brings

[12] *World Bank Annual Report* of June 30, 1976.

together private investors, investment opportunities, and experienced management where there is no government guaranty of repayment. Such investment may come from within the country concerned or may be external. Such private sector projects have been initiated in more than 40 less developed countries.

IFC is governed by Executive Directors of the IBRD whose countries are also members of IFC. These form a Board of Directors who support the President.

United Nations Housing Activities

United Nations Centre for Housing, Building and Planning

In the late 1940's, a small branch for Housing, Building and Planning was formed within the U. N. Secretariat's Department of Economic and Social Affairs. Its duties included research, formulation of policy, organization of seminars, and preparation of publications. With growing recognition of the immensity of the problems in the broad field, a 27-nation Committee on Housing, Building and Planning was established through the Economic and Social Council in 1962 to provide leadership. In order to have a more effective working body to carry out the policies and programs defined by the Committee, the Centre for Housing, Building and Planning was constituted in 1965.

Reporting to the Under Secretary for Economic and Social Affairs, the Centre drew on the staff and work of the earlier Branch, but with a greatly expanded scope of work. With its Housing, Building, Planning and Information and Documentation Branches, the Centre was responsible for implementing the U. N. Technical Cooperation program in its field, in cooperation with the Office of Technical Cooperation (OTC) of the Economic and Social Affairs Department. Funding came from the regular budget of the United Nations, and both the technical assistance and Special Fund elements of the United Nations Development Program (UNDP).

The Centre has carried out feasibility studies, provided training, advisory services, technical assistance, and specialized documentation in support of its objectives. Planning projects have been carried out in the areas of national physical planning, regional and urban planning, rural physical planning, settlement and redevelopment, disaster reconstruction, land use, legislation and management, infrastructure and services, and transportation. Housing activities have included sites and services, policy formulation, land development, squatter resettlement, low-cost and rural housing, cooperative housing, and institutional support. In the building field, materials and methods, prefabrication, architectural design, and materials substitution have been areas of concern. A relatively recent emphasis on tourism led to development planning and projects in the organization, promotion, and operation of that field. Some 65 countries received assistance in one or more of the above fields in 1976.

Experts in the many professional areas required for this program are recruited from all nations within the U.N. system. Notices of vacancies and new project personnel needs are sent to Ministers of Foreign Affairs worldwide and to major urban development institutions. Qualified professionals for assignments ranging from a few weeks to one or two years are nominated by these national institutions, or make direct contact with UNDP officers. Rosters of applicants are ranked according to experience, training, language ability, etc., and are forwarded to the appropriate Department or Ministry in the country seeking assistance. The final selection is by the host country.

Numerous professionals have contributed to the Centre/UNDP program and, in turn, have broadened their own experience and understanding of world human settlements problems. While very appealing to many, the U.N. recruitment process is slow, and it is often many months before an applicant knows whether he has been approved. Young professionals, particularly those fresh from university, must seek their initial experience elsewhere. For various reasons, including assurance of professional proficiency, the United States requires approximately ten years of experience in a given field for all applicants.[13]

The Centre was incorporated into the Habitat: Centre for Human Settlements by Resolution of the General Assembly in December of 1977.

United Nations Habitat and Human Settlements Foundation (IHHSF)

One of the recommendations of the 1972 Stockholm Conference on the Environment called for an institution to address the housing finance needs of developing countries. Submitted to the General Assembly for consideration, this recommendation led to approval for the initiation of an International Habitat and Human Settlements Foundation (IHHSF), whose operational plan was to be formulated by the Executive Director of the newly formed U.N. Environmental Program (UNDP).

The 58-nation Governing Council of UNEP called for the early implementation of IHHSF operations. As a result, staffing of the Foundation and feasibility studies were started in 1975, and detailed administrative arrangements and general operational procedures were approved by the UNEP Governing Council at its fourth session in the Spring of 1976.

Initial funding of the foundation was $4 million from the UNEP

[13] Activities Report of the U.N. Centre for Housing, Building and Planning, 1975.

budget for a four year period beginning in January of 1975. The Foundation is authorized to seek and accept voluntary contributions from nations, other U.N. bodies, and private sources. It may also administer any funds allocated to it by the United Nations Development Program (UNDP). The Executive Director of UNEP was required to submit an activities report with estimates of resources and expenditures every two years to the Governing Council of that body.

Objectives of the IHHSF involve provision of seed capital, identification of innovative approaches to investment and financial strategies, and mobilization of local resources. To accomplish these objectives, Foundation professionals draw upon world experience of both public and private sectors. Technical assistance is provided in establishing or strengthening local savings and administrative institutions, training of staff, and providing operational plans. In addition, effort is made to identify appropriate technologies for the local building industry, and transfer or adaptation of technology is facilitated.

The Foundation is located in Nairobi.

The Foundation was incorporated in the Habitat: Centre for Human Settlements by General Assembly Resolution in December of 1977.

Habitat: Centre for Human Settlements

The proposal to create a single coordinating body for all human settlement activities grew out of preparation for the 1976 Habitat Conference, held in Vancouver, British Colombia. While the Conference did not resolve all issues related to the creation of such a coordinating body, it did forward a recommendation for consideration by the General Assembly at its Fall 1976 session. The recommendation called for the coordinating body to carry out activity in the six priority areas identified by the Habitat Conference—namely, settlements policies and strategies; settlement planning; shelter, infrastructure and services; land; public participation; and institutions and management.

Like the Conference, the 31st Session of the General Assembly did not come to agreement on such issues as location of the new Centre. As a result, it was the 1977 General Assembly which passed Resolution 32/162 creating Habitat: Centre for Human Settlements to be physically located in Nairobi, Kenya. The Centre has a 58-nation Commission for Human Settlements as its governing body, and is headed by an Executive Director. The Commission, replacing the Committee on Housing, Building and Planning of the Economic and Social Council held its first organizational meeting in New York in April of 1978.[14]

The Centre essentially combines the activities, staffs, and resources of the former Centre for Housing, Building and Planning and the U.N.

14 Commission on Human Settlements E/C.11/2, March 16, 1978.

Habitat and Human Settlements Foundation. The Centre's activities will be heavily oriented to the regions, where staffs will work directly with U. S. Regional Economic Commissions, research and training organizations.

In addition to its own resources, the Centre will draw on and contribute to the substantial human settlements activities of other U.N. agencies such as UNIDO, UNICEF, UNDP, ILO, FAO, UNESCO, WHO, etc. With the assistance of the U.N. Administrative Committee on Coordination (ACC) the Centre will attempt to coordinate all U.N. activities related to its mandate to assure best use of available resources. The Centre itself is to address those priority concerns which are not covered by activities of other agencies. For example, projects directed to environmental aspects of human settlements are to remain in the UNEP. As the two organizations will share certain facilities in Nairobi, it is assumed that cooperation between the Centre and UNEP will be particularly significant.

United Nations Environment Programme (UNEP)

Formed in 1973 as a result of the 1972 Stockholm Conference on the Environment, the United Nations Environment Programme (UNEP) has a Governing Council of 58 nations and is headed by an Executive Director. Reflecting the recommendations of the 1972 Conference, Human Settlements were defined as a top priority. This was reflected in the formation of the United Nations Habitat and Human Settlements Foundation (IHHSF), which was, until the formation of Habitat: Centre for Human Settlements, a part of UNEP. Also, the UNEP provided much of the early impetus for the Habitat Conference in Vancouver, held from May 31–June 11, 1976, and provided funds for the audiovisual presentations of many less developed countries for that Conference.

Because one of the basic purposes of UNEP is to address important environmental issues not currently handled by other elements of the UN system, some elements of human settlements activity have been included in the Programme activities. When defined as appropriate for UNEP action, the Programme has three alternatives—direct action by its own staff; the provision of funds to another U.N. agency related to the subject of concern; or contracting with government or private institutions outside the U.N. system. Because the field of human settlements is so broad, all three methods have been used. Those related to the housing field include a program for integrated approach to upgrading of slums and marginal settlements in the Philippines and Indonesia (with the former Centre for Housing, Building and Planning), and a study of the architecture and environment of the Arab region (under contract).

For the near future, UNEP will concentrate on support of environmentally sound technologies, promote global dissemination of research, convene regional meetings to address human settlements technology for Africa and West Asia, possibly train documentation personnel to support technology programs, encourage citizen participation, support courses for architects and town planners, and support regional research in low-cost housing, water supply, and waste disposal.[15]

International Referral Service (UNEP/IRS)

One of the concerns that led to the establishment of the United Nations Environment Programme is the problem of access to adequate relevant information on various aspects of the environment, including human settlement. As a result, from its formulative session in 1973, UNEP has worked toward the formation of a worldwide referral system. This System became operational in 1975. As it was recognized that a single repository for data on any single facet of the environment, much less the wide range of subjects of concern, is out of the question, it was determined that a catalog of existing sources of such data be compiled, to be drawn upon as needed through a central referral center.

To implement the IRS system, a secretariat was established in the Nairobi headquarters of UNEP. At the same time, a number of national focal points were established as primary contact points with the Nairobi complex. These focal points in turn designated national subfocal points in each of the major areas of concern to the 58 nations of UNEP. The subfocal points act as sources of data and as referral centers to other sources in their own subject areas. As a continuing process, data on the types of information and services provided by the various sources are fed into the Nairobi computer center. Addition of new sources, and updating of existing material are to continue indefinitely.

To use the system, a person or institution needing data will present a request to his national focal point or subject subfocal point, where it will be coded according to the key word system used in the Nairobi complex. The focal point will forward the request to central IRS, which will run a computer search for a listing of appropriate sources worldwide. On receipt of the worldwide list of sources, the user is then free to contact directly any or all institutions listed. Needless to say, the more precisely a request is phrased, the more concise will be the list of sources received.

In the United States, the Environmental Protection Agency (EPA) has been designated as the national focal point for IRS. The American subfocal point in the area of Human Settlements is the Office of Inter-

[15] *The Environment Program* (UNEP), *Report of the Executive Director*, UNEP/GC/90, 1977.

national Affairs of the Department of Housing and Urban Development (HUD/OIA). OIA draws on its existing international information system, searches out additional sources, and coordinates its work with EPA.[16]

IRS has tremendous potential for facilitating exchange in the human settlement/housing field, particularly for less developed areas where data on new techniques as well as general reference material is limited or lacking. However, IRS is not meant to be a one-way program. The system is available to "data donors" and general industrialized country users on the same basis as those in greatest need.

International Labor Organization (ILO)

Basically concerned for the quality and provision of worker's housing, the ILO carries out a broad range of programs related to the industry. A General Conditions of Work Branch is concerned with policy, while the Management and Development unit deals with the questions of productivity in the construction field.

The Vocational Training Branch provides regional programs for training of building and construction workers, and is active in many parts of the developing world. Other specialized activities include work with cooperatives and rural housing, and coordination with civil engineering and public works activities.[17]

In its Geneva Headquarters in the Palais des Nations, the ILO works through the various UN Regional Commissions, has subregional training centers, and sponsors local and "traveling" seminars.

Regional Economic Commissions

Regional operations of the UN system generally reflect all program areas of concern to the Secretariat, but with the nature and scale of operation reflecting the desires, resources, and available alternatives of the nations within the region.

Economic Commission for Europe (ECE)

Established initially as a Panel of Experts on Housing Policy in the late 1940's, a Subcommittee on Housing was later set up under the Industry and Materials Committee. Because the potential scope of operation was much broader than originally recognized, a separate Committee on Housing, Building and Planning was set up in 1963. Duties included exploration of means to improve housing and related

[16] *UNEP, International Referral Systems, General Information,* U. S. Environmental Protection Agency, 1975.

[17] *The United Nations and the International Labor Organization,* U. S. Government Printing Office.

social and community facilities, development of building materials industries, and development of policy on planning and renewal.

To carry out its duties, the Committee establishes working parties dealing with socioeconomic aspects of housing, building materials and construction, and urban renewal and planning. These in turn have working groups as needed to study problems of particular concern. Groups of experts report directly to the Committee on a regular basis in the areas of Building and Planning Statistics, and Problems and Policies.

Providing a forum for intergovernmental exchange of experience and information, the Committee sponsors studies, research, and study tours, and promotes direct contact between its members. Because the ECE represents the more advanced technological areas, and its members have a long-established institutional base, the ECE has the broadest range of activities, and attempts to provide services to other regional operations where possible. This being the case, the programs of the ECE are more policy- and less production-oriented than are the programs of the other regional commissions.

Program areas have included planning, housing finance, housing industry, various facets of industrialized building, and, in more recent years, such areas as energy and the environment. Due to its deep involvement in the reconstruction of Europe during the early days of the Commission, and its obvious need for association with this largest group of industrialized nations, the United States is a member of the ECE.[18]

Economic Commission for Africa (ECA)

The Economic Commission for Africa (ECA) maintains a small housing staff, and has carried out a number of housing related functions over the past two decades. Continentwide building materials and industry surveys have provided basic data for development, as well as highlighting critical voids in the system. Information is disseminated from the Ethiopian headquarters of ECA as well as from and through national research and training centers. Meetings of the ECA governing bodies and its various committees address housing problems, plan regional activities, and fund research and field operations. Regional seminars are held in such fields as aided self-help, housing finance, and industry development.[19]

[18] *Economic Commission for Europe—Membership, Structure and Activities*, information paper, ECE, Geneva, 1976.
[19] *The Role of ECA in Economic Expansion and Social Growth in Africa*, UNECA, Addis Ababa.

Economic and Social Commission for Asia and the Pacific (*ESCAP*)

Known for many years as the Economic Commission for Asia and the Far East (ECAFE), ESCAP has addressed human settlements issues through a Subcommittee on Housing, Building and Planning. Efforts have centered on such problems as improving the efficiency of the building industry, undertaking studies on building standards, and assisting member governments in the establishment of standards institutions. Urban and regional planning, new towns, land policy, design for seismic and windstorm conditions, slum and squatter problems are among the issues addressed. Expert teams, seminars, training programs and research are all part of the program. The operation has headquarters in Bangkok, with ties to research and training centers in such countries as India, Indonesia, and Japan.[20]

The many of other internationally oriented organizations tend to have one factor in common. For the most part, they each represent a single profession or a set of activities related to the individual and his work, with less emphasis on national membership. Certain regional organizations are the major exceptions. While in some cases a professional society or other institution may be the member, in many cases individual participation rather than delegation participation provides the basis for major meetings and work programs.

Summary

The world housing situation is grave, with worldwide shelter need growing at the rate of 4 to 5 million units per year. Slums, overcrowding, rural to urban migration, and a rate of population increase which can easily double today's world population of over 4 billion by the year 2000 all lend to the gravity of the problem. While 37 percent of the world's population is now urban, the end of the century will see 50 percent of all people living in urban centers. Housing production now meets only one third of the need for replacement, new family formation, and shift of population. As this situation will continue through the end of the century, the whole process of urban development, particularly in less developed areas where population shifts will be felt the most, demands new assessment and activity without precedent in history.

Essential factors for adequate activity include:
- Policy direction and national priority.
- Recognition that, while important, money alone does not solve

---

[20] *Economic and Social Commission for Asia and the Pacific*, ESCAP, Bangkok, Thailand.

housing needs, and that there is no single, simple, or quick solution to housing problems.

- Policy, economic, social, and technical institutions, coordinated and suited to local needs.
- Trained and experienced professionals and subprofessionals who relate to local conditions and capabilities.
- Technology transfer, nationally and internationally, with stress on *appropriateness* and based on adaptation rather than adoption.
- Information exchange, nationally and internationally, to create awareness of existing alternatives.
- Research, program oriented, directed to fill gaps in knowledge and improve processes, but *not* as an end in itself.
- Technical assistance, directed to national and local institutional development, and inducement and support of maximum self-help at all levels.

The institutions and activities described in this chapter represent a range of concerns and experience which closely reflect problem areas faced by all nations in the development of housing programs. Whether the basic problem is one of quality, as in the industrialized nations, or of quantity, as in most developing nations, all elements described are essential to the urbanization process. There is a natural sequence in which institutions can be developed most appropriately. Whether combined or individually administered, all must be present if the total process is to succeed.

Even with means of producing housing, shelter alone has little value without places of work, means of communication and facilities for educational, commercial, religious, and recreational activities. Just as the elements described in this chapter are interdependent, so is the role of shelter a factor which must be weighed in light of the full range of priorities and capabilities of the society.

Appendix: Listing of Housing Related Organizations and Publications

ORGANIZATIONS AND ADDRESSES	TYPE OF PUBLICATIONS
Office of Housing Agency for International Development Washington, D.C. 20523	Annual Report
Overseas Private Investment Corporation 1129 20th Street, N.W. Washington, D.C. 20548	TOPICS (monthly publication)
Peace Corps 806 Connecticut Avenue, N.W. Washington, D.C. 20525	Peace Corps Annual Operations Report

ORGANIZATIONS AND ADDRESSES	TYPE OF PUBLICATIONS
Federal National Mortgage Association 1133 15th Street, N.W. Washington, D.C. 20005	Quarterly Report Annual Report
National Savings and Loan League 1101 15th Street, N.W. Washington, D.C. 20005	National Savings and Loan League Journal
Foundation for Cooperative Housing 2101 L Street, N.W., Suite 409 Washington, D.C. 20037	Annual Report Technical Manuals
World Bank (International Bank for Reconstruction and Development) 1818 H Street, N.W. Washington, D.C. 20433	Annual Report
UN Centre for Housing, Building and Planning United Nations New York, N.Y. 10017	Human Settlements
United Nations Environment Programme P.O. Box 30552 Nairobi, Kenya	United Nations Environment Programme News

United Nations Habitat and Human
  Settlements Foundation
P.O. Box 30552
Nairobi, Kenya
	UN Habitat and Human
	  Settlements Foundation
	  News
	Annual Reports

International Referral Service (IRS) U.S. International Environmental Referral Center, PM-213 c/o U.S. Environmental Protection Agency 401 M Street, S.W. (Room 2902 WSM) Washington, D.C. 20460 (Focal Point)	Information Bulletin Catalog

Office of International Affairs
U.S. Department of Housing and Urban
  Development
451 7th Street, S.W.
Washington, D.C. 20410   (IRS Subfocal
  point)
	HUD International Bulletin
	HUD International Special
	  Reports
	HUD International Review
	HUD International Informa-
	  tion Source Series
	Ideas and Methods Exchange
	  Series

International Labor Organization Palais des Nations Geneva, Switzerland	International Labor Review Information News

ORGANIZATIONS AND ADDRESSES	TYPE OF PUBLICATIONS
Economic Commission for Europe Palais des Nations Geneva, Switzerland	Quarterly Bulletin on Statistics for Europe Economic Bulletin for Europe
Economic Commission for Africa Addis Ababa, Ethiopia	New Acquisitions in the UNECA Library Economic Bulletin for Africa
Economic and Social Commission for Asia and the Pacific Bangkok, Thailand	Economic Bulletin for Asia and the Pacific
International Council for Building Research Studies and Documentation (CIB) Weena 704, P.O. Box 20704 Rotterdam, The Netherlands (International)	Building Research and Practices
National Academy of Sciences 2101 Constitution Avenue, NW Washington, D.C. 20027 (US Secretariat CIB)	Proceedings News Reports
International Association for Housing Science P.O. Box 340254 Coral Gables Miami, Fla. 33134	Newsletter
Bouwcentrum P.O. Box 229 Rotterdam, The Netherlands	
International Cooperative Housing Development Association 5159 Kerpen Burgstrasse 47, Germany	Newsletter (Bimonthly)
Union International des Architects 4, Impasse d'Antin Paris VIII, France	UIA Bulletin
International Union of Local Authorities 5 Paleisstraat The Hague, The Netherlands	Local Government Through- out the World (Journal) Planning and Administration Bibliographia Course Manuals
International Union of Testing and Research Laboratories for Materials and Structures (RILEM) 12 rue Rancion 75 Paris-15, France	Materials and Structures Review

Bibliography

Bibliographies on international housing are many and diverse in content, and I will not pretend to present a comprehensive listing here. However, the student of international housing should find the following few items and collections of value in his studies. Specialized data can be secured by contacting the organizations described in the text.

American Council of Voluntary Agencies for Foreign Services, Inc. Technical Assistance Information Clearing House, *Housing Assistance for Developing Countries.* New York, 1975, pp. 48.

Cornell University, Program on Policies for Science and Technology in Developing Nations, *Low-Cost Housing for Developing Countries—An Annotated Bibliography 1950–1972.* New York, 1974, pp. 214.

Council of Planning Librarians, *A Selective Bibliography on International Housing, 1960–1975.* Illinois, 1975, pp. 20.

Department of Housing and Urban Development, Office of International Affairs, *Foreign Accessions Lists.* Washington, D.C., 1975, 1976, 1977, 1978.

International Council of Building Research, Studies and Documentation—CIB, *List of CIB Publications.* Rotterdam, 1975, pp. 6.

Ministry of State, Urban Affairs, *Directory of Canadian Urban Information Sources.* Ottawa, 1974, pp. 160.

Organization of American States, *OAS 75–76 Catalog of Publications.* Washington, D.C., 1974, pp. 95.

United Nations, Centre for Housing, Building and Planning, *Cumulative List of United Nations Documents and Publications in the Field of Housing, Building and Planning.* New York, 1975, pp. 164.

United Nations, Department of Economic and Social Affairs, *Community Programmes for Low-Income Populations in Urban Settlements of Developing Countries.* New York, 1976, pp. 43.

United Nations, Department of Economic and Social Affairs, *World Housing Survey 1974.* New York, 1976, pp. 192.

United Nations, *Habitat: United Nations Conference on Human Settlements Vancouver, 31 May to 11 June 1976.* New York, 1976, pp. 127.

PROJECTIONS

Gertrude S. Fish

The Past

Kenneth Boulding wrote recently that

We stand in the present moment like a weaver at a loom; the pattern of the cloth stretches back into the past, and though the future is misty, we hope some of the pattern will persist into it. It is only by better knowledge of the past, however, that we can hope to increase the certainty of our image of the future.[1]

The patterns of the past have been chronicled in this book. In the preceding chapters we have seen several patterns of activity that relate to housing.

Some of the patterns repeat over long stretches of the fabric; some repeat in a shorter span. The difficulties of enforcing laws in relation to housing when the supply is always short was brought out in the chapters by Margaret Woods, and those difficulties have continued in force. The Industrial Revolution, with its attendant waves of immigration and rural-to-urban migration, probably has been the strongest single influence on housing in all its aspects over the last 100 years. The national attitude toward rewards only for those who work (in relation to the provision of housing for the poor) has been modified slowly and in minor degrees. The chapter on the 1930's pointed out that it took about 100 years from the time that a housing inspector defined bad housing conditions as a social problem (1834) to the time when society voted to provide some units for those unable to attain them for themselves (the Public Housing Law, 1937). It also took 100 years for the freed slaves (1862) to gain full citizenship and civil rights (Civil Rights Act, 1964).

The relation of real estate cycles to business cycles is shown in Figure 4–2 in Chapter 4, and the time involved in one cycle seems to be around 15 years. Swings in the amount of subsidized housing coincide with changes in the political parties in power, with the Democrats encouraging more redistribution of the national income than the Republicans. Wars seem to create shortages of housing by preempting

[1] Kenneth Boulding, "The Evolution of Energy." In: *The Cornell Alumni News*, December, 1977, Cornell Alumni Association, 626 Thurston Ave., Ithaca, N.Y. 14853, p. 27.

INDEX